global cities and immigrants

Critical Studies of LATINOS/AS in the Americas

Yolanda Medina and Ángeles Donoso Macaya
General Editors

Vol. 6

The Critical Studies of Latino/as in the Americas series
is part of the Peter Lang Trade Academic and Textbook list.
Every volume is peer reviewed and meets
the highest quality standards for content and production.

PETER LANG
New York • Bern • Frankfurt • Berlin
Brussels • Vienna • Oxford • Warsaw

global cities and immigrants

a comparative study of chicago and madrid

EDITED BY FRANCISCO VELASCO CABALLERO
AND MARÍA DE LOS ANGELES TORRES

PETER LANG
New York • Bern • Frankfurt • Berlin
Brussels • Vienna • Oxford • Warsaw

Library of Congress Cataloging-in-Publication Data

Ciudades globales e inmigrantes. English
Global cities and immigrants: a comparative study of Chicago and Madrid /
edited by Francisco Velasco Caballero, María de los Angeles Torres.
pages cm. — (Critical studies of Latino/as in the Americas; Vol. 6)
Translation of: Ciudades globales e inmigrantes. Madrid: Universidad Autónoma de Madrid, 2013.
Includes bibliographical references.
1. United States—Emigration and immigration—Government policy.
2. Spain—Emigration and immigration—Government policy. 3. Emigration and immigration law—
United States. 4. Emigration and immigration law—Spain. 5. Immigrants—Illinois—
Chicago—Social conditions. 6. Immigrants—Spain—Madrid—Social conditions.
7. Chicago (Ill.)—Emigration and immigration. 8. Madrid (Spain)—
Emigration and immigration. I. Velasco Caballero, Francisco, editor of compilation.
II. Torres, María de los Angeles, editor of compilation. III. Title.
JV6483.C4913 305.9'06912094641—dc23 2014024886
ISBN 978-1-4331-2618-5 (hardcover)
ISBN 978-1-4331-2617-8 (paperback)
ISBN 978-1-4539-1396-3 (e-book)
ISSN 2372-6822

Bibliographic information published by **Die Deutsche Nationalbibliothek.**
Die Deutsche Nationalbibliothek lists this publication in the "Deutsche
Nationalbibliografie"; detailed bibliographic data are available
on the Internet at http://dnb.d-nb.de/.

The paper in this book meets the guidelines for permanence and durability
of the Committee on Production Guidelines for Book Longevity
of the Council of Library Resources.

29 Broadway, 18th floor, New York, NY 10006
www.peterlang.com

Printed in the United States of America

Table of Contents

Introduction

Globalization has accelerated the movement of people across political borders, as economic restructuring has made cities and their metro areas into depositories of the majority of these global migrant groups. In many cities, including ours, immigrants are the motor of economic development and civic rejuvenation—even as they are politically shunned and denied legal citizenship and its protections across the globe and the nation. Indeed, immigration has provoked heated debates across the world as nations are also facing economic decline and political crises. Intellectually, many of the ideas that frame the debate around immigration predate globalization to a time when nation-states defined economies, politics, and, in many cases, culture.

One articulation of this debate—contested by the case studies in this book—is that federal governments should control immigration matters. The claim is that enforcement policies are the right of federal governments and a consequence of dividing humanity along nation-states. Deportation law and policy are performances of sovereign authority, meaning that they are vast spectacles through which authority establishes its reign (De Genova & Peutz, 2010). In the United States alone, over 1.3 million undocumented immigrants have been deported in the last two years. Certainly, these large numbers of transnational migrants bring into sharp conflict questions of national border security, as well as the rights of people on the move. In many cases, national policies have responded more to security concerns than the rights of immigrants—even when their policies have run contrary to the economic interests of regional and local governments—raising questions about the nature of democracy itself (Honig, 2001).

At the heart of this book are several theoretical questions. One is about the increased importance of municipal and local governments in a globalized world, particularly regarding immigrants. As the world globalizes and national governments attempt to tighten their grips, the failure of national policies to address the needs of new global situations encourages local governments to develop policies that resolve these new conditions. Is the place of municipal governments—especially concerning what has traditionally been in the realm of national governments—changing? What are the social forces that have influenced this (Ramakrishnan & Wong, 2007)? And what does this suggest about the limits of national governments in regard to new global change?

Immigrants, particularly the undocumented, live in contradictory spaces defined by hostile national governments and more friendly local governments—at least in large global cities. For democratic countries in which notions of citizenship are deeply embedded in the nation-state, this creates a new conflict in which political and social rights are guaranteed locally but not nationally. This also raises the question about rights and what these look like in local settings. Can we envision a form of local citizenship (Guarnizo, 2012; Villazor, 2010)? Are local and regional governments the places for democratic action?

In the United States and Spain—while immigration is a federal policy on paper—city and state governments have increasingly played a role in shaping both the enforcement and integration experiences of immigrants. This creates a local politics of immigration that is strongly shaped by local views of economic, political, and security interests, as well as differing perceptions of immigrants' rights and place in the polity (Wells, 2004). These policies are not explicitly about immigration, but rather an array of issues ranging from issuance of driver's licenses or permits to the provision of educational benefits. They are also instances in which local governments refuse to enforce federal laws (Newton & Adams, 2009), even as national governments increasingly rely on them to do so (Booth, 2006). There may be a host of factors that influence the outcome of local immigration policies, from the location of fiscal policies (Boushey & Luedtke, 2006) to the presence of immigrants and the ideologies of particular regions (Chavez & Provine, 2009). Likewise, it is important to note that it is usually in large urban areas where local governments have developed policies and practices that run contrary to the national impulse to exercise sovereignty through a hard line against immigrants. Local governments have felt compelled to protect and create safe zones and policies that encourage positive incorporation of immigrants (Bilke, 2009). In contrast, restrictionist policies have been more prevalent in smaller towns (Gilbert, 2009) and in areas without the presence of large global cities, where, in fact, the state and local policies have become more punitive than the federal government.

All of this suggests that the process of globalization and urbanization may be at play in influencing this debate and what, in effect, is the blurring of foreign and domestic policy roles for different levels of government (Herbert, 2009).

Those positive, localized strategic policy moves and their consequences on the lives of people are what we wish to analyze here in order to begin developing and understanding the dynamics of how these policies came to be and what they tell us about spatial changes of political units and notions of citizenship in a global world. This autonomy from federal policy, however, should not be viewed as something easily achievable or unproblematic. It has involved years of organizing and advocacy work, and has led to conflicts and struggle—some of which remain as yet unresolved—among the federal and local governments and local public officials. Moreover, in contrast to some European countries that do provide resources for undocumented immigrants, there are no federal public funds in the United States that are specifically earmarked for undocumented immigrants. This means that debates over local enforcement and integration policies—even in cases inclusive of all immigrants—cannot escape broad international debates about undocumented immigrants' rights to access resources and remain in this country. This leaves local governments to be mediators and, at times, even determinants of incorporation and enforcement policies that affect undocumented immigrants (Vanderkooy & Nawyn, 2011).

In the face of national inaction on this pressing issue, research on the role and place of local governments pertaining to immigration policies can shed light on alternatives (Varsanyi, 2010). While the debate is at a standstill at the national level, parallel efforts of incorporation and enforcement, or restriction, at the local level point to different models, visions, and opportunities. Many of these have already been set in motion and can provide a basis for novel ways of thinking about immigration policy, personhood, citizenship, and belonging in a comparative context. To the best of our knowledge, this sort of comparative mapping of the multi-national and local deportation/incorporation landscape has not been previously attempted.

NOTES ON THE COMPARATIVE CONTEXT

In this comparative project, we have brought together an interdisciplinary group of scholars to examine the ways in which two global regions confront the dilemmas faced by local governments as they try to incorporate new residents—while their respective national governments demand increased vigilance against immigrants. In the early 1990s, scholars comparing national immigration policies of industrialized, immigrant-receiving countries seemed to converge in the notion that there was a need for stricter immigration policies (Cornelius, Tsuda, Martin, & Hollifield, 2004). Today, we still find this to be the case and, furthermore, there may be similar responses at the local level. Our study focuses on two global cities with similar national contexts. Chicago and Madrid represent cities that have received a large influx of immigrants in the last two decades—Chicago mainly from Mexico and other Latin American countries, and Madrid from African and, increasingly, Asian countries. In both cities, not all immigrants maintain legal statuses. Both are cities that have a tradition of incorporating immigrants, and as such, we think that studying their practices sheds light on the larger comparative perspectives about each nation-state and contributes to an understanding of good practices in global cities. They are also dissimilar, providing room to understand how historical and cultural contexts may influence the ways immigrants are thought of in differing spaces.

National and Local Governments

Both the United States and Spain have a centralized authority in charge of enforcing immigration laws, including deportations. However, there are important differences—as there are in other countries (Ellermann, 2009)—which should be noted from the start. In most countries, the amount of leeway that local governments have in regard to immigration is a matter of law. Because of federalist tradition in the United States, local governments have more autonomy. In contrast, the centralized government of Spain has more defined authority. Additionally, there are marked differences between the two countries in the structure and distribution of legal authority over immigration matters. Indeed, part of the comparative process of this collection was coming to an understanding of what local governments were in each country. In the United States, we decided on all governments outside the federal government—given the diversity and different levels of power that municipal, county, and state governments have—whereas, in Spain, the main emphasis is on municipal government.

Despite its strong centralized authority, Spain has an interesting politico-cultural phenomenon at play in terms of limiting that central authority, which effectively creates a certain degree of leeway for local governments. That is, there is an explicit appreciation that central government needs to be kept in check. The new democracy demands that each level of government remain within its boundaries—especially the national government—as centralization of power can threaten the young democracy. Local autonomy in the United States is deeply embedded in the structure of its political apparatus, which may have also, historically, come from national suspicion of central authority during its own democratic origination centuries ago.

Who Belongs

There are also very different notions of who belongs in society, and how belonging is culturally and legally defined (Kristeva, 1991). The United States has a long historical narrative of being an immigrant nation, even as newcomers have historically faced marginalization and racialization. Fear-driven, public debates have concluded in programs that reject newcomers. But parallel to these actions, there has been social mobilization on behalf of newcomers that has engendered a politics of identity. A movement that demands equality and fairness, and has—in the last thirty years—resulted in periodic legalization projects. Spain, however, does not have a long history of immigration, though there are historical moments of rejecting groups of people based on religion and nationality. Contrary to the United States, fear-driven debate about immigrants in Spain has, in fact, resulted in programs to bring them into the national cultural landscape and out from the shadows.

Identity politics is not necessarily a language deployed in Spain to the same extent that it is in the United States. Related to notions of belonging are legal processes though which newcomers can become citizens. Terms used to describe, for instance, undocumented immigrants suggest different approaches. In the United States, "illegal alien" is the technical term for an immigrant without papers, suggesting a transgression. In Spain, they are called "irregulars," perhaps suggesting bureaucratic adjustments.

Another significant difference is that Spain has a long tradition of granting local membership to newcomers. Rooted in feudal times, municipalities require that residents register. Known as the "apadronamiento," this process grants certain rights to, demands certain responsibilities of, and, most importantly, "documents" the individual.

There are also important differences in how long it takes someone to be "arraigado," or rooted. In the United States, longevity is not a means to belonging, rather it is a legal process. (Cubans are an exception which is codified in the Cuban Adjustment Act.) In Spain, if someone has been in the country for at least three years—whether they are "regular" or not—they have a shot at remaining.

There are also important considerations in terms of family units. Although the United States did incorporate family unity as an important factor in granting residency to individuals in 1965, this principle has eroded. While family unity remains a major pathway for immigrants to come to the United States and gain lawful status, the federal government has also deported record numbers of immigrants, including parents of thousands of U.S.-citizen children, effectively ignoring family unity in immigration policy.

Place of the States in Society's Well-Being

An important difference between Spain and the United States that affects the outcome of immigrant incorporation is the appreciation of the place of the state in the welfare of people. Unlike European countries, the United States has a much leaner welfare state. While equality for all is a social narrative, it is not the role of the state to guarantee the outcome, but instead to only guarantee a fair process. Non-profit organizations and religious institutions fill this role, though government agencies fund many of their programs. Spain has a more generous notion of the responsibility of the state towards the most vulnerable populations, and immigrants have generally fallen into this category. As such, immigration debates in Spain tend to revolve around where to cut spending, whereas the United States argues about denying benefits altogether.

One exception to this is education, which has been guaranteed in both countries, although, in the United States, education is only guaranteed through high school—except when an individual state passes legislation specifically expanding higher education benefits to undocumented students.

OUTLINE OF THE BOOK

How these different legal, political, and social traditions regarding immigrants play out in two global cities is the main concentration of this book. The book will provide a U.S. and Spanish comparative national perspective on the relationship between local and national governments where immigration policies are concerned, as well as provide the legal context of the rights of immigrants in both countries. Within this framework, several case studies will look specifically at how local governments have dealt with incorporation and enforcement policies, education, and political and civic participation in each region. The first two parts of the book describe the legal framework which outlines the autonomy local governments may have in regard to immigration policy and looks at the rights of immigrants. Subsequent parts will include a case study from each city and culminate with a comparative discussion of the case studies.

In Part One, the question addressed is: can local governments have immigration policies? Laurie Reynolds and Francisco Velasco Caballero trace the legalities of local governments and the legal histories that have allowed these government levels to have immigration policies. In Part Two, Matthew Kuenning and Tomás de la Quadra-Salcedo Janini focus on the legal rights of undocumented immigrants. Part Three analyzes local governments' role in enforcement of federal policies and in incorporation of new immigrants. Amalia Pallares and Maria de los Angeles Torres look at instances where municipal, county, and state governments have refused to enforce federal policies, and where they have enacted programmatic and legislative initiatives that incorporate immigrants. Silvia Díez Sastre presents similar instances in Madrid. In Part Four, Nilda Flores-Gonzalez and José María Rodríguez de Santiago detail educational opportunities afforded to immigrant children. Lastly, in Part Five, Xóchitl Bada, Carmen Navarro, and Susana Sánchez Ferro look at immigrant civic and political participation and mobilization, taking into account the legalities that draw the contours therein. The comparative sections contain comparative notes on the chapters. These will be discussed in their entirety in the final reflections.

REFERENCES

Bilke, C. (2009). Divided we stand, united we fall: A public policy analysis of sanctuary cities' role in the "illegal immigration" debate. *Indiana Law Review, 42*(1), 165–194.

Booth, D. (2006). Federalism on ICE: State and local enforcement of federal immigration law. *Harvard Journal of Law & Public Policy, 29*(3), 1063–1084.

Boushey, G., & Luedtke, A. (2006). Fiscal federalism and the politics of immigration: Centralized and decentralized immigration policies in Canada and the United States. *Journal of Comparative Policy Analysis: Research and Practice, 8*(3), 207–224.

Chavez, J., & Provine, D. (2009). Race and the response of state legislatures to unauthorized immigrants. *The Annals of the American Academy of Political and Social Science, 623*(1), 78–92.

Cornelius, W. A., Tsuda, T., Martin, P. L., & Hollifield, J. F. (Eds.). (2004). *Controlling immigration: A global perspective* (2nd ed.). Stanford: Stanford University Press.

De Genova, N. & Peutz, N. (2010). *The deportation regime: Sovereignty, space and the freedom of movement*. Durham: Duke University Press.

Ellermann, A. (2009). *States against migrants: Deportation in Germany and the United States*. Cambridge: Cambridge University Press.

Gilbert, L. (2009). Immigration as local politics: Re-bordering immigration and multiculturalism through deterrence and incapacitation. *International Journal of Urban and Regional Research, 33*(1), 26–42.

Guarnizo, L. E. (2012). The fluid, multi-scalar, and contradictory construction of citizenship. *Comparative Urban and Community Research, 10*, 11–37.

Herbert, S. (2009). Contemporary geographies of exclusion II: Lessons from Iowa. *Progress in Human Geography, 33*(6), 825–832.

Honig, B. (2001). *Democracy and the foreigner*. Princeton: Princeton University Press.

Kristeva, J. (1991). *Strangers to ourselves*. (L. S. Roudiez, Trans.). New York: Columbia University Press. (Original work published 1991)

Newton, L., & Adams, B. E. (2009). State immigration policies: Innovation, cooperation or conflict? *Publius: The Journal of Federalism, 39*(3), 408–431.

Ramakrishnan, S. K., & Wong. T. (2007, November). *Immigration policies go local: The varying responses of local governments to undocumented immigration*. Retrieved March 6, 2013, from http://www.law.berkeley.edu/files/RamakrishnanWongpaperfinal.pdf

Vanderkooy, P., & Nawyn, S. (2011). Identifying the battle lines: Local–national tensions in organizing for comprehensive immigration reform. *American Behavioral Scientist, 55*(9), 1267–1286.

Varsanyi, M. (Ed.). (2010). *Taking local control: Immigration policy activism in U.S. cities and states*. Stanford: Stanford University Press.

Villazor, R. C. (2010). "Sanctuary cities" and local citizenship. *The Fordham Urban Law Journal, 37*(2), 573–598.

Wells, M. J. (2004). The grassroots reconfiguration of U.S. immigration policy. *International Migration Review, 38*(4), 1308–1347.

PART ONE

CHAPTER ONE

Immigration Federalism and Local Regulation in the United States

LAURIE REYNOLDS, UNIVERSITY OF ILLINOIS
AT URBANA-CHAMPAIGN

INTRODUCTION

Over the past decade, local governments have increasingly become a place where policy debates about immigrants and immigration occur. For some cities, the newly arrived have brought vitality, diversity, and economic activity. When the immigrants' arrivals are seen as a positive force in the community's development, the local government is likely to find ways to facilitate the integration of the newcomers, unconcerned about whether or not they arrived lawfully in the U.S.[1] For other municipalities, in contrast, immigration poses a perceived threat to stability, prosperity, and safety. In those places, regulation is likely to have a decidedly anti-immigrant tone, as local governments seek to use their licensing and general regulatory powers to restrict the presence of immigrants to those who are here lawfully, and to find ways to exclude or to make life difficult for those who are not.[2]

In addition to these decidedly grassroots, "bottom-up" forces for immigration regulation and control, the impetus for local action has come from the "top down" as well. Because of its pervasive and unchallenged authority to regulate immigration, the federal government, unsurprisingly, has taken some explicit steps to permit, prohibit, encourage, or perhaps even require local involvement with immigration law. In addition, the fifty states, though not possessing broad powers over immigration regulation, do have inherent police power over their constituents' health, safety, and welfare, as well as broad sovereign authority over their political subdivisions. Pursuant to those powers, a state may impose mandates or limit local freedom to respond to the aliens in their midst. Thus, any evaluation of local powers to regulate immigrants or their effects on a particular community must include a careful review, not only of the current federal attitude towards immigration, but also of the legal regulatory framework adopted by the local government's creator state. As federal, state, and local attitudes about the proper approach to local immigration regulation diverge, the potential for political and legal conflict increases commensurately.

This chapter describes the interaction between and among federal, state, and local governments, focusing on how that tripartite relationship affects the scope of local powers to deal with immigrants.[3] There is a certain, almost palpable tension, for instance, between the black letter legal doctrinal principle that federal law can easily preempt state and local regulation of immigration, on the one hand, and the equally well-established principle of federal constitutional law that the federal government cannot directly order a state or local governmental unit to act. As principles of federal constitutional and statutory primacy in immigration intersect with federal constitutional protections of state sovereignty, as well as with a wide panoply of state and local regulations of immigration, the legal landscape becomes clouded with uncertainty and ever-changing with the political winds.

Proposals for legislative reform of federal immigration laws have repeatedly failed to advance through Congress. And as some communities feel overwhelmed with an influx of immigrants, subnational regulatory actions have increased dramatically. It would be a mistake, however, to believe that these efforts stem exclusively from impatience with national immigration reform or to speculate that local activity would cease if only Congress could find the political will to adopt comprehensive immigration law reform. Because U.S. cities, towns, villages, counties, and special districts are the units of government most immediately and directly affected by the population increases and heightened service demands brought about by immigration, and because the impact of immigration on those communities will continue to be felt irrespective of federal legislative reform, subnational legislative efforts to respond to local realities and problems that stem from or are affected by the presence of immigrants are likely to continue.

LOCALISM AND IMMIGRATION

A Tradition of Localism

Somewhat surprisingly perhaps, the federal Constitution makes no mention of local governments. As a matter of legal doctrine, then, municipalities and other political subdivisions of the states can point to no federal positive law or principle that establishes their parameters, defines their powers, or regulates their status. Local governments, therefore, are exclusively an emanation of the states' plenary power. The United States Supreme Court described this situation most famously when it stated in *Hunter v. Pittsburgh* that:

> Municipal corporations are political subdivisions of the State, created as convenient agencies for exercising such of the governmental powers of the State as may be entrusted to them.... The number, nature and duration of the powers conferred upon these corporations and the territory over which they shall be exercised rests in the absolute discretion of the State.[4]

Notwithstanding the federal constitutional silence and the official "creature of the state" model of local government law, the Supreme Court has on different occasions strayed from the *Hunter v. Pittsburgh* rhetoric and has deferred to the firmly ensconced tradition of localism and broad local government powers in the U.S. federal system.[5] Over the years, the Court has decided a number of highly charged cases in which plaintiffs sought federal court intervention to remedy the inequalities that local government autonomy and independence had produced. Notwithstanding arguments that the local governments involved in these cases should be brought under the clear umbrella of state control, in several important cases the Court declined to intervene. As a result—and in response to different plaintiffs' claims that local action produced racial segregation in metropolitan area school districts,[6] that the local property tax system was responsible for financial inequality in the financing of local education,[7] or that local land-use regulation excluded the poor and minorities from local communities[8]—the Court upheld the local governments' actions and highlighted the importance of localism and the independence and flexibility it gives to local policy development. The majority opinion in *Milliken v. Bradley* illustrates the extent of the Court's deference to local control:

> No single tradition in public education is more deeply rooted than local control over the operation of schools; local autonomy has long been thought essential both to the maintenance of community concern and support for public schools and to the quality of the educational process.[9]

In federal law, then, though local governments can point to no explicit constitutional protection or status, the vitality, independence, and broad initiative powers of local government action are recognized and respected by the Supreme Court. As a result, an extraconstitutional value of localism permeates the Court's jurisprudence and has imbued its decisions with deference, respect, and praise for the lowest level of representative government in the U.S. federalist system.

The Localism Component of Immigration Regulation

Whatever the disputed boundaries among and between federal, state, and local powers over immigration and immigrants, the reality is that the impact of immigration in the United States is felt first and foremost at the local level. Cities, counties, and some special districts (such as school districts and public health districts) constitute the front line in managing the effects of immigration on the larger society. They are the first places to which immigrants turn when personal networks cannot satisfy their needs. Given the longstanding tradition of localism and local legislative initiative, it is not at all surprising that any review of local involvement reveals a multitude of regulatory approaches and a wide political divergence. Local regulation of immigration is a natural corollary to, and emanation of, several well-established local policy concerns, each of which will be discussed in the following paragraphs.[10]

For one thing, local governments typically have the legislative discretion to draw the lines that will determine the constituents of their community. The statutory procedures that determine the community's borders through annexation, incorporation, and de-annexation, for instance, require the community to decide whether to bring in or cut off land and the people who occupy it. Though the legal issues tend to revolve around compliance with technical procedures involving petitions, hearings, elections, and votes, the disputes are frequently based on stated or unstated arguments about "us" vs. "them."[11] This is the same dynamic that pervades local regulation of immigrants and immigration, with the community's elected officials being called upon to make fundamental decisions about how to incorporate the newly arrived into the community or, in the alternative, whether to try to exclude a group that may be seen as different, threatening, and cost-imposing.

Second, and particularly in these times of economic distress, some of local governments' major and prolonged policy disputes revolve around how to pay for services. Outside the context of immigration, local governments frequently look for ways to impose costs on outsiders, such as non-residents, who may use local services without paying for them. In these cases, cities may establish fees or other non-tax revenue raising devices to ease the financial burden of providing services to those who are not subject to the local government's powers of taxation. Similarly, many local governments confronted with large increases in immigrant population find themselves overwhelmed with high service demands and low revenues to fund those services. According to one Congressional Budget Office paper, tax revenues contributed by immigrants generally exceed the cost of the services they receive. The revenue surplus, however, occurs at the federal level, where many immigrants pay income taxes and contribute to Social Security and Medicare, benefits they are unlikely to receive. At the local level, where immediate service demands are the greatest (particularly in terms of education and health care), the best estimate is that local governments are asked to provide services that far exceed the recipients' contributions to local tax revenues.[12] Because local government taxation powers are generally narrow and subject to voter- or legislature-imposed tax caps, and because many of the newly arrived are poor, the fiscal squeeze is a real one. Purely as a financial matter, then, immigrants present many of the same challenges as other groups (such as non-residents), whose members impose a financial cost on the rest of the established local community.

Finally, defining the character of the local community is perhaps the quintessential and most fundamental local government policy concern. Through regulatory devices such as zoning, subdivision regulation, and other land-use techniques, local governments adopt a wide range of ordinances and policies to establish and preserve the character of their community. As a result, local government units range from densely populated, diverse, multinational communities to exclusive and homogeneous suburban enclaves. Each one of them has at its disposal the land-use planning devices that set the tone for the overall community. At its core, local regulation of its character is essentially dependent on the power of local government to exclude uses, and consequently people, through decisions about what kinds of development the community will allow. State courts are generally, though not universally, approving of these exclusionary efforts. The Supreme Court, in fact, described this local power in somewhat glowing terms in one case in which the challenger had alleged that local zoning laws impermissibly interfered with personal autonomy, mobility, and association. The Court defended the community's desire to determine the character of its community, and thus implicitly defended the community's right to exclude, with expansive praise:

> A quiet place where yards are wide, people few, and motor vehicles restricted are legitimate guidelines in a land use project addressed to family needs. This goal is a permissible one.... The police power is not confined to elimination of filth, stench, and unhealthy places. It is ample to lay out zones where family values, youth values, and the blessings of quiet seclusion and clean air make the area a sanctuary for people.[13]

As a preeminent land-use planning law scholar once said: "Zoning, thy name is exclusion."[14] And in fact, the use of land-use devices to exclude those whom the community designates as unwanted strangers dates to the earliest days of zoning and land-use planning in the United States. The impetus for the adoption of New York City's first zoning ordinance in the early 1900s, for example, was in no small measure the prevalence of anti-immigrant sentiment. Consider the following description of the reasons why New York City was eager to adopt its first zoning ordinance and to exclude non-residential uses from the area near Fifth Avenue:

> [New York City Commissioners] wanted the garment industry to get out of Fifth Avenue... because the things which were the essences of the garment industry—the strange tongues,

> the outlandish appearance and the very smell of its immigrant laborers...—violated the ambience in which luxury retailing thrives.[15]

In sum, much of what local government does involves, broadly defined, a resolution of disputes over those who are "in" and those who are "out," over those who should receive services and those who should not, and over those who fit within the community's self-image and those who are seen as interfering with its character. Local initiatives to establish or enlarge territorial boundaries, to find ways to recoup the cost of services provided, and to define permissible land uses, all involve fundamental decisions about the makeup of the community. The point here is not to applaud the exclusionary impact of much local regulatory action, but merely to highlight that local efforts to regulate the effect of immigration on their communities fit comfortably within the scope of other long-established local legislative initiatives. Understood from the vantage point of state and local government law, local regulation of immigrants is an unexceptional example of local governments' longstanding and unquestioned interest in protecting and promoting community values.

THE ALLOCATION OF POWER OVER IMMIGRATION IN THE U.S. FEDERAL SYSTEM

Federal Powers

Though in fact subnational regulation has coexisted with federal immigration law since the early days of federal involvement,[16] the predominant and generally unquestioned legal maxim had been that immigration is the exclusive domain of the national government. That broad pronouncement stems from both Supreme Court case law,[17] as well as from the explicit language of the U.S. Constitution.[18] It has, however, been the subject of renewed interest and scholarly debate, with some arguing for recognition of the important state and local role in immigration regulation.[19] To say that federal regulation of immigration is exclusive may be, in the words of Cristina Rodriguez, a "lie."[20] Or perhaps the current reality of shared powers, widely known as the phenomenon of immigration federalism,[21] is better understood as a reflection of the fact that most subnational regulation actually fails to meet the definition of "immigration regulation" and is thus not subject to the brush of federal exclusivity. In any event, whether the better view is that federal exclusivity has been rejected, or that the scope of exclusivity itself has never been so broad as to rule out all subnational regulation, local government powers are typically sufficiently wide-ranging to include the adoption of legislation and implementation of some regulatory controls that focus on the immigration status of people within the local government's borders.

The Supreme Court's opinion in *DeCanas v. Bica*[22] is crucial to understanding the scope of federal plenary power in immigration. Although the Court, in that case, did describe federal immigration powers as "unquestionably exclusive,"[23] it added the important qualification that "the Court has never held that every state enactment which in any way deals with aliens is a regulation of immigration and thus per se preempted by this constitutional power."[24] More precisely, the Court offered the following definition of immigration regulation: "a determination of who should or should not be admitted into the country, and the conditions under which a legal entrant may remain."[25] Applying that definition to subnational regulation, if a state or local law is found to fit within the *DeCanas* Court's definition of "immigration regulation," the subnational law is invalid and the judicial inquiry need go no further. Unlike the preemption analysis that is described in the next section, the presence or absence of federal legislation is irrelevant to the *DeCanas* inquiry. Quite simply, any state or local regulation or law that constitutes "immigration regulation" exceeds the scope of the government's power because it has impermissibly intruded into an exclusive federal sphere.

So long as local laws steer clear of the *DeCanas* prohibition, they will not be invalidated as an impermissible intrusion into the federal government's exclusive powers. In this vein, it bears noting that the California law at issue in *DeCanas*, which prohibited the knowing employment of an unlawful immigrant, was upheld against the challenge that it intruded on federal exclusivity in immigration regulation.[26] Thus, both the language of the opinion and the state law to which it applied clearly refute the claim that federal law establishes an expansive area of regulatory prerogatives that is beyond the scope of state and local government initiatives.

Although the core of federal *exclusivity* in immigration law may be limited, the national government has virtually unlimited powers, not only to legislate directly, but also to shape the permissible contours of state and local power in this area. The power to direct, prohibit, or encourage state and local law stems from the interaction between the Constitution's specific, enumerated grant of power over immigration to the federal government and the thrust of the Constitution's Supremacy Clause,[27] under which federal actions will displace, invalidate, or preempt inconsistent state and local efforts, so long as the federal government acts within the scope of an enumerated power. And when it comes to immigration, that enumerated federal power is extremely broad. In fact, the Supreme Court has never invalidated a federal immigration law as beyond the scope of Congressional power. Aside from Supreme Court opinions guaranteeing procedural rights to immigrants facing criminal charges or deportation,

Congress and the Executive branch have received "a virtual carte blanche on immigration matters."[28]

Federal preemption of state and local laws pursuant to the Supremacy Clause does not require a judicial conclusion of federal exclusivity, but rather a showing of federal legislative intent (either express or implied) to disallow regulatory efforts at the state and local level. The starting point of the preemption analysis, then, is the unstated assumption that the subnational law would be valid but for conflicting federal legislation. That means that as federal laws and the underlying congressional intent change, the permissible scope of state and local regulation changes as well. At any point in time, the scope of un-preempted local powers in immigration will crucially depend on the existing federal statutory and regulatory frameworks. Thus, as federal attitudes about immigration regulation change, the scope of state and local powers changes as well. As a result, the permissible range of local powers in immigration is crucially dependent on the current expression of that congressional intent.

The doctrine of preemption is highly nuanced, the result of a long history of Supreme Court jurisprudence, but its basics are quite straightforward. Federal law may preempt subnational law either expressly (as articulated in a federal statute by Congress), or impliedly, through judicial interpretation and analysis of the competing federal and non-federal laws. When it comes to federal laws involving areas in which the states have traditionally regulated, the Supreme Court has adopted a "presumption of non-preemption,"[29] reflecting the seriousness with which the Court takes state sovereignty. Though Congress's power to invalidate subnational laws dealing with immigration appears to be nearly unchecked, the Court articulated similar anti-preemption attitudes in its 2011 immigration law opinion.[30]

As its name suggests, express preemption involves an explicit statement by Congress that denies state or local power to act in a particular context. In immigration law, the most recent relevant example of express preemption is Section 1324a(h)(2) of the Immigration Reform and Control Act, which prohibits state imposition of "civil or criminal sanctions" on those who employ undocumented immigrants, with an exception for "licensing and similar laws."[31] Though the scope of the licensing exception is not immediately apparent on its face and was the basis of the Supreme Court's opinion in *Chamber of Commerce of the U.S. v. Whiting*,[32] what is clear is that Congress desired to remove general civil and criminal sanctioning power from the states. In the case of an expressly preemptive federal provision, there is no room for legal argument or debate. The national government's expansive constitutional authority over immigration authorizes a virtually unchecked power of express preemption.

Though express preemption is the clearest and most straightforward type of preemption, the preemption doctrine also includes two judicially created tests to imply preemption even when the federal law has not expressly articulated a preemptive intent. The tests are similar in that they both strive to determine the unstated will of Congress in relationship to a particular state or local regulation, yet they employ slightly different legal inquiries.[33]

Under the "occupation of the field" branch of implied preemption, a court will invalidate a state or local law if it concludes that Congress's actions are so extensive that they leave no room for legislative involvement by any other level of government. In its analysis, the court will focus on the breadth of the regulatory enforcement scheme and the comprehensiveness of the legislation to reach a determination whether Congress intended to allow complementary or supplemental state or local regulation. In *Chamber of Commerce of the U.S. v. Whiting*,[34] for instance, the Supreme Court refused to find that the federal Immigration Reform and Control Act intended to occupy the field of regulating employee immigration status. Key to the Court's conclusion on field preemption were its findings that: (1) the federal law explicitly preserved some state licensing authority (thus making it hard to argue that there is impliedly no room for concurrent state regulation); (2) the state law did not upset the federal balance between burdening employers and preserving employee privacy because the state law explicitly tracked federal standards; and (3) employment is a traditional area of state concern. This three-pronged inquiry suggests a legal template with which to evaluate local immigration regulation. The Court's subsequent opinion in *Arizona v. United States*,[35] however, applied the same occupation of the field preemption doctrine to invalidate an Arizona statute that made violation of a federal immigration law (requiring registration by immigrants) a violation of state law. Though state and federal crimes frequently penalize the same conduct, the Court found that the state law impermissibly entered into "an area the Federal Government has reserved for itself,"[36] that is, the registration of aliens. Going forward, what seems clear is that field preemption remains a viable challenge for those subnational laws that deal with aspects of immigration that have been dealt with by Congress.

The doctrine of "conflict preemption" also opens the door to wide-ranging judicial flexibility and discretion to invalidate state and local laws. At its core, conflict preemption is a judicial tool that invalidates a subnational law whose implementation would substantially interfere with the effectuation of a federal statute.[37] Once again, the *Whiting* opinion provides a good example of how this type of preemption will play out in immigration law. In that case, a plurality of the Supreme Court refused to find a conflict between federal immigration law and a state law requiring employers to verify the immigration status of their employees, even though the state law arguably subjected Arizona employers to greater restrictions and responsibilities vis-à-vis immigrants than were required under federal law. Key to the finding of "no conflict" was the Court's conclusion that the state law's procedures and consequences were substantially identical to federal law requirements.[38] As a result, Arizona's law was deemed to be complementary and in harmony with the federal law, escaping invalidation under the doctrine of conflict preemption. The *Arizona v. United States* Court took the conflict doctrine a little further, finding a conflict between Congress's *failure* to penalize employees for employment in violation of immigration laws and Arizona's imposition of a penalty on that same conduct.[39]

Although the two most recent Supreme Court opinions dealing with implied preemption in the context of immigration are certainly doctrinally consistent, they reveal slightly different judicial emphases on the importance of state sovereignty and the presumption of non-preemption of state law. In fact, while the *Chamber of Commerce of the U.S. v. Whiting* Court stressed that implied preemption imposes a "high threshold" on the judicial analysis, and that a "freewheeling judicial inquiry" is inappropriate,[40] the *Arizona v. U.S.* made no mention of these principles, focusing instead on the primacy of federal power in immigration. As these two cases show, the subjective determinations involved in judicial application of the doctrines of field preemption and conflict preemption create a wide space for judicial reliance on personal political predilections. Whether or not a local landlord-tenant law conflicts with federal immigration law or intrudes into an area intended to be occupied by federal immigration law, for example, will inevitably depend in part on a court's sympathy for the local efforts and its assessment of the federal law offered as the preempting statute. The inevitability of judicial subjectivity does not, however, mean that implied preemption is either standardless or unprincipled. Underlying the judicial tests are other doctrines that should inform any court's foray into implied preemption. Specifically, the importance of inherent state sovereignty and the corollary fact that the federal government is a government of enumerated, rather than inherent, powers, should temper a judicial rush to preemption. This is not to say that all state or local regulation of matters pertaining to immigrants or immigration should be immune to legal challenge, of course, but only that the courts should approach implied preemption questions with caution.

State Sovereignty

Although many of the current legal disputes over local immigration regulation do not involve the local government's creator, that is, the state in which the local government sits, the states' status as autonomous sovereigns with inherent police power may be relevant to two types of legal challenges to local government powers in immigration. Specifically, state sovereignty may be relevant to a dispute over the scope of local authority under state, and not federal, law, because states have plenary discretion to determine what local governments can and cannot do in virtually any area of law or policy. Second, state law and state sovereignty may be relevant if there is a debate about federal power to require local participation in federal immigration endeavors, in particular those instances in which the state objects to the federal-local cooperation. That means that state sovereignty may act both as a sword vis-à-vis its local government (in which case the state may forbid, require, or enable local action), and as a shield vis-à-vis the federal government (in which case state sovereignty may prevent federal empowerment of local government against the state's wishes). This section considers each aspect of state sovereignty separately.

Any time the federal government tries to require subnational governments to participate in a national program or to implement any part of a federal regulatory scheme, questions and arguments about state sovereignty become relevant. In several important Supreme Court cases examining the state-federal relationship, the Court has invalidated explicit federal legislative directives that purported to require state or local action. In one case, Congress had ordered states to take title to radioactive waste generated within their borders;[41] in another, Congress had required local government police officers to conduct background checks on potential gun purchasers.[42] Invalidating both federal laws as an impermissible violation of state autonomy and of the Constitution's reservation of undelegated power to the states,[43] the Court's rhetoric harkened back to the dual sovereignty view of federalism: "States are not mere political subdivisions of the United States. State governments are neither regional offices nor administrative agencies of the Federal Government.... The Constitution instead 'leaves to the several States a residuary and inviolable sovereignty.'"[44] And its categorical prohibition of federal mandates was clear: "The Federal Government may not compel the States to enact or administer a federal regulatory program."[45]

Parallels between these cases and federal immigration policies are stark. If, for instance, Congress cannot require local police officers to conduct background checks pursuant to federal gun control regulation, it is hard to articulate legal arguments that would allow the federal government to force those same officials to implement federal immigration law.[46] Congress can, of course, preempt state and local laws that it deems to interfere with the federal immigration regulatory scheme. Similarly, it has a wide latitude to condition its disbursement of federal revenues to state and local governments on their participation in federal programs.[47] What appears equally well-established, though, is that Congress cannot explicitly mandate state or local enforcement of a federal law or regulatory scheme.

Applying these basic principles of federalism to the debate over the federal government's current efforts to mandate local involvement with implementation of its immigration policies program yields interesting legal questions. It is not at all evident that Congress or the federal executive branch can in fact require local governments to submit fingerprints to determine the immigration status of the individuals booked and detained locally. Nor do those same legal principles support the claim that local authorities must respect the federal government's request that they detain, in local jails and at local expense, the individuals whose fingerprints have been transmitted and whose immigration status appears unlawful, thus triggering a federal interest in detaining the same individual.[48]

As a matter of state legal doctrine, state statutes, and state constitutional provisions, the fifty states have expansive preemptive power over the local governments they have created. Much as the federal government can freely preempt state and local involvement with immigration, state preemption of almost any local law can be achieved through the same express and implied preemption doctrines described earlier.[49] A state could, for instance, easily preempt a local landlord-tenant or employer licensing ordinance that required federal immigration status checks, even though those local laws may well be upheld for purposes of federal law. As a matter of state law, then, there are few, if any, legal barriers[50] to state legislative decisions either to prohibit local immigration regulation or to require local governments to participate in state or federal immigration regulatory schemes. In fact, the courts in several cases disputing the validity of local laws making immigration status a part of local business regulation and landlord-tenant controls made a point of asking whether the challenged local laws had been preempted by the state.[51]

Potential Federal-State-Local Conflict

In light of the tripartite relationship between and among the federal, state, and local governments, it is easy to imagine how conflicting political attitudes about immigration could create a legal conflict. Stated somewhat simplistically, if the state finds itself in opposition to a specific federal policy, while one of its local governments aligns with and attempts to implement that federal policy, the divide is cast between, on the one hand, the federal and local governments, and on the other hand, the state. Although this type of federal-state-local conflict is relatively rare in federal court jurisprudence, immigration regulation presents a perfect storm for its emergence.[52]

Take, for example, the federal government's Secure Communities or E-Verify programs, both of which encourage local governments to cooperate with federal regulations and databases.[53] If a state objects to that federal policy and seeks to prohibit its political subdivisions from participating, what emerges is a clear and sharp federal-state dispute over the scope of local power. The legal doctrinal quandary to which there appears to be no definitive answer is whether principles of state sovereignty will allow the state government to exercise its power as the creator of the local government to prevent the local action or, conversely, whether the federal government's plenary powers in immigration matters will be sufficient, not only to preempt contrary state law, but also to enable local governments to act without state authorization and in defiance of state wishes.

Though there are few reported examples of this type of legal dispute, when one occurs it raises unresolved, centuries-old debates about the allocation of governmental power, the merits of centralization, and the importance of state sovereignty interests to the federalism debate generally. The cases that have made their way to the Supreme Court have been resolved in two inconsistent ways. On the one hand, the Court may recite the state sovereignty rhetoric of its 1907 opinion in *Hunter v. City of Pittsburgh*,[54] with its famous statement that "the number, nature, and duration of [local] powers…rests in the absolute discretion of the state."[55] When it takes that approach, the Court allows the state law restriction to take priority, thus leaving the local government incapable of exercising its powers to further the federal goal.[56] In the alternative, the Court may ignore or dismiss state sovereignty concerns and rule on behalf of the local-federal partnership, rejecting arguments based on clear state opposition to the local government's action and focusing instead on the importance of the federal interest at stake.[57]

Unfortunately, the Supreme Court's opinions give no clear guidance on when lower courts should prefer one of the two doctrinal analyses over the other. Moreover, the uncharted waters are rendered even murkier by the fact that local governments have no explicit federal constitutional status.[58] But the potential for a federal-state-local conflict to erupt in the immigration law arena is very real, given the wide divergences between state and local governments about the federal government's immigration policies.[59] Its judicial resolution will depend on, among other things, the perceived strength of the federal interest, the importance given to the Court's rhetoric defending and praising state sovereignty, and an assessment of the local government's preexisting relationship with its state in terms of the state-local allocation of power.

THE SPACE FOR LOCAL IMMIGRATION REGULATION

Having established the general legal frameworks from which local regulation of immigration will be evaluated, this section focuses on how the principles should apply in legal challenges to local ordinances and policies. Though the outcome in any particular case is by no means clear and will involve sorting through a maze of, at times, seemingly conflicting legal principles, some general guidelines can be established. In this endeavor, I adopt a categorization of local immigration regulation developed by Professor Rick Su,[60] which categorizes local laws as either direct, indirect, or facially neutral.

Direct Local Regulation

Direct regulation occurs when local governments assume the power to implement federal law directly. In application of the program commonly referred to as §287(g),[61] for instance, federal and local officials sign a Memorandum of Understanding, whereby the federal government authorizes local government officials to enforce federal immigration law directly. In this situation, local officials are essentially deputized as agents of the federal government and can detain immigrants. Because of its cooperative nature, participation is limited to willing local governments that share the federal government's attitude about illegal immigration.

A slightly more passive form of direct local regulation occurs when local governments simply act as a conduit for federal agencies. Pursuant to the more recent Secure Communities program (often referred to as S-Comm), when local police officers book an individual in jail, the fingerprints are transmitted not only to the FBI and other law enforcement agencies of the United States, but to immigration officials as well. At that point, federal immigration agents may issue a detainer to request that the local government notify the federal government forty-eight hours previous to releasing the individual from local custody, thus allowing immigration authorities time to assume custody and execute their own arrest.[62]

The end results of these two programs, §287(g) and S-Comm, are nearly identical;[63] both culminate in custody with federal immigration officials. But the two programs entail very different levels of local involvement. While the §287(g) program requires independent local assessment and application of federal standards, under S-Comm local discretion is removed, or at least pushed up to an earlier point in the process,[64] because the local official's involvement is limited to the transmission of data to the federal government.

Because the federal government automatically transmits all fingerprints submitted by local authorities to the FBI to Homeland Security and immigration authorities,[65] the range for local opposition to the program may seem limited. No local government has stopped sending fingerprints to the FBI; such a decision would immediately be reversed by the state. But in actuality, local governments have found creative, and apparently legal, ways to avoid participation. Most direct, perhaps, are the ordinances that refuse to honor detainer requests unless and until the federal government reimburses the county for the cost of the 48 hours of additional detention.[66] Another slightly less categorical approach agrees to honor some, but not all, detainer requests, specifically only those issued for certain convicted felons.[67] Taking a slightly different tack, but reflecting the same anti-S-Comm attitude, the mayor of Washington, D.C. promulgated an executive order telling police to stop fingerprinting individuals arrested for some minor offenses, such as D.C.'s open container law. In the absence of fingerprints, there is no information to transmit to the federal government.[68]

When federal policies filter down to the local level, then, the local government retains its authority to refuse to participate, at least so long as its state does not require local involvement. The local government also has discretion to adopt creative work-arounds, much as several local governments have done to limit their participation in S-Comm, again assuming the absence of state interference and limitation. By refusing to honor federal detainer requests, or by changing local fingerprinting practices, the local government is able to avoid blending its local law enforcement powers with federal immigration controls.

Indirect Regulations

Indirect regulation of immigration refers to those local laws that condition permission to engage in locally regulated activities on an individual's lawful immigration status. Most commonly these laws regulate the rental of housing or the hiring of employees within the local government's territory. The ordinances typically incorporate federal standards of lawful presence in the United States, and require employers or landlords to verify the immigration status of the individuals they hire or to whom they rent. This type of local regulation got a huge boost in the 2011 Supreme Court opinion of *Chamber of Commerce v. Whiting*,[69] which upheld an Arizona law that revokes the business license of any employer who "knowingly or intentionally employs an unauthorized alien."[70] That provision, in turn, incorporates the federal E-Verify system, pursuant to which an employer can verify the employee's immigration status with the federal database, and thus be deemed presumptively compliant with state law.

Rejecting the challengers' claim in *Whiting* that the Arizona law was an impermissible regulation of immigration, or that it had been preempted by federal law, the Supreme Court read the Immigration Reform and Control Act's exemption for state licensing powers[71] as allowing the state to require employers to verify the federal immigration status of their employees as a condition precedent to authorization to conduct business in the state. Although the case involved a state and not a local employer licensing system, the Supreme Court has ordered the lower federal courts to further consider the legality of a similar local ordinance in light of the Court's decision.[72] It seems likely that local regulation of the employer-employee relationship, so long as it follows the contours of the Arizona statute, will fall comfortably within the same federal statutory licensing exemption.

While the legality of local regulation of the employer-employee relationship seems well-established and subject to fairly clear limits, the same cannot be said of local landlord-tenant laws that include lawful immigration status as a condition to leasing property within the jurisdiction. Even in the aftermath of the Supreme Court's second opinion in two years[73] dealing with subnational regulation of immigration, the landscape remains extremely cloudy. The uncertainty stems from several facts: the lack of specific federal statutory authorization for landlord-tenant regulations;[74] the absence of direct Supreme Court guidance; the wide range of approaches taken by landlord-tenant laws; and the divergent opinion of lower federal courts that have dealt with this type of local regulation.

Most, but not all, lower federal courts have invalidated local landlord-tenant laws.[75] A survey of those cases, when combined with the hints found in the Supreme Court's *Whiting* and *Arizona* opinions, suggest that their legality is likely to depend on a number of factors.[76] First and foremost, local laws that most closely track the licensing provisions upheld by the Court in the employment context are easiest to defend against preemption challenges. Making the landlord, rather than the tenant, the target of the regulation also removes some of the more obvious preemption objections. Incorporating federal immigration standards, rather than creating a new local definition of a lawful immigrant is also crucial. And finally, those laws that avoid the addition of penalties, or the establishment of separate judicial review procedures to enforce violations, also stand on stronger legal doctrinal ground. In short, though there is no definitive legal answer, the local landlord-tenant ordinance that is limited to conditioning the landlord's continued ability to engage in the local rental business on his or her compliance with a local requirement to verify the federal immigration status of all tenants is more likely to survive legal challenges than those that contain any of the other features described earlier. What remains to be seen is whether the Court will provide a comfortable margin for local regulations of different types or, in contrast, whether local powers will be narrowly construed as limited to employer-employee licensing laws.

Neutral Laws

The facial neutrality of a local ordinance does not immunize it from attack under federal law. If a law is adopted with discriminatory intent against aliens,[77] or if it is enforced in a discriminatory way against individuals on the basis of their origin or race, it will be invalidated under federal constitutional law. This point was made most famously in the 1886 case of *Yick Wo v. Hopkins*,[78] in which the Supreme

Court invalidated a San Francisco ordinance regulating the construction and operation of laundromats because it was enforced only against non-citizen Chinese in the city. The crucial point to be made here is that a facially neutral regulation is likely to be invalidated in court only if the opponents can show discriminatory intent or discriminatory application. In most cases, things are not that clear cut. One recent analysis of zoning in some California communities, for instance, suggests that local laws prohibiting garage sales, and prohibiting the fresh-air drying of laundry, were actually directed at Latino neighborhoods.[79] Another article reports a sweep for housing code occupancy violations in Long Island, New York, which resulted in the eviction of more than 100 Latino immigrants, most of whom were thought to be unlawfully present in the United States.[80]

The adoption and implementation of facially neutral laws whose validity can be defended with legitimate local policy concerns, such as preserving the community's character and aesthetics or preventing overcrowding, are likely to be on solid legal ground, at least in the absence of specific evidence of discriminatory intent. Of course, a facially neutral regulation may run afoul of other, independent constitutional guarantees, such as the First Amendment's protection of freedom of speech. On that basis, then, in Redondo Beach, California's anti-day-laborer law was invalidated without judicial resort to questions about whether the legislation embodied a prohibited anti-immigrant intent.[81]

Local governments' wide-ranging powers to regulate their built environment and to protect their constituents' health, safety, and welfare undoubtedly include the power to regulate in many ways that, depending on the context, may effectuate either a sympathetic or a hostile attitude about the immigrants in the community. In these cases, it is the political and legislative arena, rather than a legal forum, where the battles are likely to be won or lost.

CONCLUSION

Local governments are likely to continue to take a position on how to best respond to the presence of immigrants in their communities. Just as the country is badly divided over the proper course for reform of federal immigration law, so too does the range of local opinion plot out along the entire political spectrum. Since local government attitudes about immigration range from one of embracing welcome to one of outright hostility, it is to be expected that legislative efforts will display the same variety. The legal space for local regulation is wide enough to include a substantial amount of local flexibility and innovation, encompassing a number of techniques to reflect and implement the community's relationship with its immigrant population. Regardless of the politics underlying the regulation of immigration, the legality of any local ordinance or policy will be strengthened if it adheres to several general guidelines, which are based on the legal principles reviewed in the previous pages.

For one thing, local officials should refrain from an act of open defiance of federal law, and steer clear of regulation that might be seen as invading the exclusive purview of federal power, that is, "a determination of who should or should not be admitted into the country, and the conditions under which a legal entrant may remain."[82] Second, if the local endeavor is intended to restrict the ability of unlawful immigrants to participate in the local marketplace, by regulating, for example the housing market or the workforce, the criteria used by the local government should track federal standards as closely as possible. Any substantial deviation from the federal standards, or any attempt on behalf of the local government itself to make its own determination of the legality of an individual's presence in this country, is likely to be challenged. Third, the most defensible local ordinance is one that stays close to the licensing law upheld in *Whiting*, and resists efforts to impose penalties or to establish new judicial procedures. Finally, the local ordinance should restrict its scope to the types of issues traditionally deemed to be within the scope of the local government's police power. Ordinances whose impact may extend beyond the local government's territory, or whose subject is not closely tied to traditional local concerns and targets of regulation, are prime targets for preemption challenges.

Because local ordinances vary tremendously in terms of the details of their scope, their regulatory framework, and the consequences that flow from their implementation, broad generalizations are difficult. The legal viability of any particular local law will depend on how it actually applies in a particular case, both as a matter of how it affects the local community, as well as how it interacts with state and federal regulatory schemes. And as state and federal attitudes and legislation about immigration change, so too will the parameters of permissible local regulation.

In some ways, affording flexibility and discretion to state and local governments may remove pressure for national action. Federal representatives of those states that have adopted strict state laws are now perhaps less likely to pressure for similarly punitive legislation at the national level. In the final analysis, the legal evaluation of subnational regulation is likely to push towards a delicate balance between, on the one hand, recognition of the legitimate local interest in responding to the varied circumstances in which immigrant communities develop across the country, and, on the other hand, the overriding federal interest in ensuring that immigration policy is a cohesive regulatory system, one which treats individuals fairly and respects civil liberties. Even in a system that is built on a foundation of expansive federal regulatory and enforcement powers, local actions are an important component of that overall cohesion and will continue to form the basis from which immigrants are integrated into the federal system—recognizing that there is a space for federal, state, and local regulation to coexist.

NOTES

1. Local efforts to help the undocumented get along despite their precarious legal status could, for example, establish local identification cards that police and local businesses will accept, such as the City of New Haven, Connecticut has done. More dramatically, a local government might refuse to participate with the efforts of higher levels of government to apprehend and deport unauthorized aliens, much as the Cook County Board of Supervisors refuses to honor federal requests, known as detainers, to hold unauthorized immigrants who have been booked in Cook County Jail.
2. Most common are local laws prohibiting landlords from entering leases with individuals who cannot confirm their lawful immigration status, or laws denying business licenses to local employers who have not confirmed the immigration status of their employees.
3. A number of states, including Arizona, Alabama, Utah, Oklahoma, Georgia, South Carolina, and Indiana, have passed statutes of their own. Those state laws are beyond the scope of this chapter, except to the extent that a provision of one of those laws may affect the powers of local governments to enact and enforce regulations dealing with immigration and immigrants.
4. *Hunter v. City of Pittsburgh*, 207 U.S. 161, 178 (1907). This statement has been qualified by the important subsequent Supreme Court case of *Gomillion v. Lightfoot*, 364 U.S. 339 (1960), in which the Court stressed that plenary state control over local governments does not immunize the state legislature from federal constitutional scrutiny as it exercises that plenary power. In *Gomillion*, the Court invalidated the Alabama legislature's decision to reconfigure the borders of the city of Tuskegee to remove nearly all African American voters from the city's territory as a violation of the federal Constitution.
5. For the preeminent legal analysis of the difference between formal legal doctrinal local powerlessness and real local power, see Richard Briffault, *Our Localism: Part I—The Structure of Local Government Law*, 90 Colum. L. Rev. 1 (1990) and Richard Briffault, *Our Localism: Part II—Localism and Legal Theory*, 90 Colum. L. Rev. 346 (1990).
6. *Milliken v. Bradley*, 418 U.S. 717 (1974).
7. *San Antonio Independent School District v. Rodriguez*, 411 U.S. 1 (1973).
8. *Village of Arlington Heights v. Metropolitan Development Corporation*, 429 U.S. 252 (1977).
9. *Milliken v. Bradley*, 418 U.S. 717, 741–42 (1974).
10. For an excellent analysis of this phenomenon, see Rick Su, *A Localist Reading of Immigration Regulation*, 86 N. Car. L. Rev. 1619 (2008).
11. For example, consider how racial issues may surface in municipal incorporation, see *In re Incorporation of the Borough of Bridgewater*, 488 A. 2d 374 (Pa. Commw. 1985); and how socio-economic inequalities may underlie annexation, see *In the Matter of the Enlargement and Extension of the Municipal Boundaries of the City of Jackson, Mississippi*, 691 So. 2d 978 (Miss. 1997) or de-annexation, see *Ryan v. Mayor & Council of Demarest*, 319 A. 2d 442 (N.J. 1974).
12. Congressional Budget Office, *The Impact of Unauthorized Immigrants on the Budgets of State and Local Governments* (2007).
13. *Village of Belle Terre v. Boraas*, 416 U.S. 1, 9 (1974).
14. Donald Hagman, *Taking Care of One's Own through Inclusionary Zoning: Bootstrapping Low and Moderate Income Housing by Local Government*, 5 Urban Law and Policy 169 (1982).
15. Seymour L. Toll, *Zoned American* 158 (1969).
16. See, e.g., *Mayor of the City of New York v. Miln*, 36 U.S. 102 (1837) (upholding New York law that regulated immigrants arriving in New York harbor); *Patsone v. Pennsylvania*, 232 U.S. 138 (1914; upholding state law prohibiting hunting by aliens).

17. Admittedly, the Supreme Court has endorsed federal exclusivity in immigration; see, e.g., *Galvan v. Press*, 347 U.S. 522, 531 (1954); *Takahashi v. Fish and Game Commission*, 344 U.S. 410, 419 (1948); *Hines v. Davidowitz*, 312 U.S. 52, 66 (1941).
18. See U.S. Const. Article I, §8, Cl. 4, which empowers Congress "To establish a uniform rule of naturalization."
19. For particularly persuasive arguments, *see* Rick Su, *A Localist Reading of Local Immigration Regulations*, 86 N.C. L. Rev. 1619 (2008); Cristina M. Rodriguez, *The Significance of the Local in Immigration Regulation*, 106 Mich. L. Rev. 567 (2008).
20. See id. at 574.
21. That term was coined in Peter J. Spiro, *Learning to Live with Immigration Federalism*, 29 Conn. L. Rev. 1627 (1997).
22. 424 U.S. 351 (1976).
23. Id. at 354.
24. Id. at 355.
25. Id.
26. Subsequent to the *DeCanas* opinion, Congress explicitly preempted the state powers upheld by the Court in a federal law. See 8 U.S.C. § 1324(a)(h)(2) (prohibiting "any State or local law imposing civil or criminal sanctions…upon those who employ…unauthorized aliens").
27. U.S. Const. Article 6, Cl. 2 provides that "[the] Constitution, and the Laws of the United States…shall be the supreme Law of the Land."
28. See Spiro, supra note 21, at 1630.
29. See *Medtronic, Inc. v. Lohr*, 518 U.S. 470, 485 (1996) ("[W]e start with the assumption that the historic police powers of the States were not to be superseded by the Federal Act unless that was the clear and manifest purpose of Congress.") That presumption against preemption was most recently reaffirmed in *Wyeth v. Levine*, 129 S. Ct. 1187, 1194–95 (2009).
30. Although no Supreme Court case has explicitly applied the presumption of non-preemption in the immigration context, which admittedly is unlikely to fall within the purview of areas traditionally regulated by the states, the Court has urged the lower courts to be slow to imply preemption of subnational immigration law where Congress has not spoken. See *Chamber of Commerce v. Whiting*, 131 S.Ct. 1968, 1985 (2011). One lower federal court, however, explicitly applied the presumption of non-preemption in a challenge to the state of Arizona's law regulating immigrants. See *U.S. v. Arizona*, 641 F.3d 339, 345 (9th Cir. 2011). That decision was reversed in *Arizona v. U.S.*, 132 S.Ct. 2492 (2012), and the Court's opinion made no reference of the presumption of non-preemption.
31. 8 U.S.C. § 1324a(h)(2).
32. 131 S.Ct. 1968 (2011). In that case, the Court upheld an Arizona law that conditioned state licences to do business in the state on the employer's verification of the lawful immigration status of all employees.
33. For a comprehensive Spanish language survey and analysis of the U.S. preemption doctrine in immigration law, *see* Francisco Velasco Caballero, *Un Ejemplo de Funcionamiento de la "Preemption" Norteamericana: La Regulación de la Inmigración*, REAF num 13, abril 2011, pp. 11–50.
34. 131 S. Ct. 1968 (2011).
35. 132 S.Ct. 2492 (2012).
36. Id. at 2502.
37. Some courts define two slightly versions of conflict preemption—impossibility (parties cannot comply with both laws) and obstacle (effectuation of the subnational law would create an obstacle

to the full implementation of federal law). See *U.S. v. Arizona*, 641 F.3d 339 (9th Cir. 2011) (court applies both obstacle and impossibility preemption doctrines to state immigration law).

38. Both the state and federal laws in this case relied on the federal E-Verify system. In brief, E-Verify is an internet-based system, which allows employers to confirm the immigration status of their employees for purposes of complying with federal law (it is a federal crime for an employer to knowingly hire any unauthorized immigrants; compliance with E-Verify guarantees that the employer will be in compliance with that restriction). The main difference between the federal and state statutes, at least for purposes of conflict preemption, was the way in which E-Verify was used. The Arizona law made use of E-Verify mandatory by employers; federal law left it optional. See *Whiting*, 131 S.Ct. at 1976. The Court found that difference inconsequential to the preemption analysis, even though Justice Breyer in dissent argued that the Arizona law should be invalidated because it imposed additional burdens on employers, beyond those imposed by the carefully balanced federal law. See id. at 1992 (Breyer, J., dissenting).
39. The Court found that: "Congress made a deliberate choice not to impose criminal penalties on aliens who seek, or engage in, unauthorized employment." *Arizona v. United States*, 132 S.Ct. at 2504. See also id. at 2496.
40. *Chamber of Commerce v. Whiting*, 131 S.Ct. 1968, 1985.
41. See *New York v. United States*, 505 U.S. 144 (1992).
42. See *Printz v. United States*, 521 U.S. 898 (1997).
43. "The powers not delegated to the United States by the Constitution, nor prohibited by it to the States, are reserved to the States respectively, or to the people." U.S. Const. amend. X.
44. *New York v. United States*, 505 U.S. at 188.
45. Id.
46. Although a case can be made that the federal government can require state or local authorities to transmit information, see *Printz v. United States*, 521 U.S. 898, 918 (1997), the Court explicitly reserved judgment on that question. Moreover, current state and local government opposition to federal immigration enforcement programs does not involve a refusal to transmit the relevant data. Rather, the objections are implemented through a refusal to enforce the federal government's request that the local officials hold local detainees until federal immigration officials can decide whether to take custody. Any suggestion that the federal government could require local respect of detainers would extend well beyond the scope of whatever state sovereignty exception there may be for federal requests for information.
47. By conditioning the receipt of federal funds on state or local compliance with federal regulatory standards, the federal government can shape subnational policy without directly entering the debate over state sovereignty's shield from federal mandates. See *South Dakota v. Dole*, 483 U.S. 203 (1987), in which the Supreme Court upheld Congress' use of the spending power to condition dispersal of federal highway funds to those states that raised the drinking age to twenty-one. Should the federal government choose to use the power of the purse to encourage state and local compliance with federal requests to respect detainers issued by immigration officials, the constitutional questions involving state sovereignty would be removed from the equation.
48. These facts describe, in general terms, the federal government's Secure Communities program, which is discussed in more detail at text accompanying notes 61–68, infra.
49. See discussion at text accompanying notes 31–40, supra. See also Paul Diller, *Intrastate Preemption*, 87 B.U. L. Rev. 1113 (2007), for an excellent analysis of state preemption of local laws.
50. In a few narrow circumstances, involving a particular type of home rule system, a local government may have limited immunity from state prohibitions. See generally Richard Briffault & Laurie

Reynolds, *Cases and Materials on State and Local Government Law* 331–332; 371–406 (7th ed. 2009). It is hard to imagine a dispute involving immigration regulation, however, in which a conflicting local law would take precedence over a state legislative prohibition, at least in the absence of federal government involvement and directives.

51. Though they reached different conclusions, the lower court judicial opinions in *Lozano v. City of Hazleton*, 496 F. Supp. 2d 477, 521–29 (M.D. Pa. 2007; invalidating local law under state law) and *Gray v. City of Valley Park*, 2008 WL 294294 at *18–19 (E.D. Mo. 2008; upholding validity of city ordinance under state law), both undertook a specific analysis of the possible preemptive power of state law.
52. For elaboration of the contexts in which federal-state-local conflicts arise and are resolved, see Laurie Reynolds, *A Role for Local Government Law in Federal-State-Local Disputes*, 43 Urb. Lawyer 977 (2011).
53. For brief descriptions of these programs, *see* note 38 *supra* and text accompanying notes 61–68, infra.
54. 207 U.S. 161 (1907).
55. Id. at 178.
56. See, e.g., *Nixon v. Missouri Municipal League*, 541 U.S. 125 (2004).
57. See, e.g., *Lawrence County v. Lead-Deadwood School District No. 40-1*, 469 U.S. 256, 261–64 (1985; identifying federal interests in giving local governments the "freedom and flexibility," id. at 263, to use federal revenues to deal with the increased service needs imposed on their jurisdictions by the presence of tax-exempt federal lands); *City of Tacoma v. Taxpayers of Tacoma*, 357 U.S. 320, 327 nn. 8–9 (1958; stressing the federal interests in national defense, navigable waters, and interstate commerce).
58. See generally Briffault & Reynolds, supra note 50, at 68–173 for analysis of how the lack of textual reference has affected the Supreme Court's treatment of local governments. Professor Joan Williams's important article was one of the first to highlight the inconsistent theories that underlie the Court's opinions. See Joan C. Williams, *The Constitutional Vulnerability of American Local Government: The Politics of City Status in American Law*, 1986 Wis. L. Rev. 83.
59. Hints about the kinds of issues these disputes would raise can be seen in *City of New York v. United States*, 179 F.3d 29 (2d Cir. 1999) and *United States v. Illinois*, 2009 WL 662703 (C.D. Ill. 2009). In the former case, the City of New York unsuccessfully challenged the legitimacy of a federal statute that preempted a municipal executive order that prohibited City officials from providing information about the immigration status of aliens to the federal government. Though the federal court noted that Congress could not command New York to provide that information, it found no legal barrier to the federal government's preemption of the city's prohibition. The distinction between a federal law compelling local governments to act (unconstitutional) and one prohibiting local governments from prohibiting voluntary transmittal of data (constitutional) is not immediately obvious.

    In a somewhat different federal-state-local context, the state of Illinois passed a statute intending to prevent the private sector's use of the federal government's E-Verify system. See 820 ILCS § 55/12. Although the law was deemed preempted by federal law in *United States v. Illinois*, 2009 WL 662703 (C.D. Ill.), the Court did not discuss the state statute's explicit preemption of local government ability to require local employers to participate in the E-Verify system. See 820 ILCS § 55/12(d). California has passed a similar statute, preempting local government power to require individuals to participate in E-Verify. See Cal. Assembly Bill No. 1236, October 10, 2011 (dubbed the "Employment Acceleration Bill"). It is not at all clear how federalism principles would play out against the backdrop of this very straightforward state law preemption provision.

60. See Rick Su, supra note 19.
61. This program originated in the Illegal Immigration Reform and Immigrant Responsibility Act of 1996, see 8 U.S.C. § 1357. It has essentially been replaced by the subsequent Secure Communities initiative.
62. Compliance with a detainer request is voluntary. See 8 C.F.R. §287.7.
63. S-Comm has been described by opponents as "Version 2.0" of the 287(g) program.
64. Though local officials have no discretion involving application of federal immigration law under S-Comm, they certainly retain substantial control over its trigger, that is, the initial decision whether to book an individual or not. Anecdotal evidence suggests that some police officers are quicker to arrest certain individuals than they were before S-Comm.
65. See Kirk Semple and Julia Preston, *Deal to Share Fingerprints is Dropped, Not Program, The New York Times*, August 6, 2011.
66. See Cook County Ordinance No. 11-O-73, adopted September 7, 2011, available at https://agenda.cookctyclerk.com/Upload/Ordinance_pdf_090711_88.pdf (p. 8).
67. For a copy of this policy, adopted by Santa Clara County, California, see http://www.sccgov.org/SCC/docs%2FSCC%20Public%20Portal%2Fattachments%2FBOS%20Summary%2F2011%2FSummary101811.pdf (p. 4; authorizing detainers for those who were convicted of a felony within the last ten years or released from prison within the last five years).
68. For the details of this program, see Tim Craig, *D.C. Won't Cooperate with Federal Immigration Enforcement, The Washington Post*, Oct. 19, 2011, available at http://www.washingtonpost.com/local/dc-politics/dc-wont-cooperate-with-federal-immigration-enforcement-may-or-says/2011/10/19/gIQAznSpyL_story.htm
69. 131 S.Ct. 1968 (2011).
70. Az. Rev. Stat. §§ 23–211, 212.
71. The federal law expressly prohibits "any State or local law imposing civil or criminal sanctions" upon employers, but contains an express exemption from that prohibition for "licensing and similar laws." 8 U.S.C. § 1324(a)(h)(2).
72. See *Lozano v. City of Hazleton*, 131 S.Ct. 2958 (2011; vacating the decision below and remanding for consideration in light of *Whiting*. The case involves both an employer licensing provision virtually identical to the one in *Whiting*, as well as a landlord-tenant regulation that injects an E-Verify submission into the rental housing transaction.)
73. In *Arizona v. United States*, 132 S.Ct. 2492 (2012), the Court invalidated a number of state law provisions as impliedly preempted by federal law.
74. This fact crucially distinguishes the landlord-tenant ordinances from the employer-employee ordinances, which come to the judicial analysis with a specific federal statutory authorization of "licensing and similar laws." 8 U.S.C. § 1324a(h)(2).
75. See, e.g., *Lozano v. City of Hazleton*, 620 F.3d 170 (3rd Cir. 2010); *Keller v. Freemont*,—F. Supp. 2d –, 2012 WL 537527 (D. Neb. 2012; invalidating some, but not all provisions of a local landlord-tenant law); *Villas at Parkside Partners v. City of Farmers Branch*, 675 F. 3d 802 (5th Cir. 2012); *Garrett v. City of Escondido*, 465 F.Supp. 2d 1043 (S.D. Cal. 2006).
76. See, e.g., *Gray v. City of Valley Park*, Mo., 2008 WL 294294 (E.D. Mo. 2008), aff'd in part, 567 F.3d 976 (8th Cir. 2009). Note, also, that the district court opinion *Keller* upheld the section of the ordinance requiring prospective tenants to provide information on their immigration status. The ordinance went too far, in the court's opinion, because of the way in which it imposed penalties on both the landlord and the tenant if the tenant could not establish lawful immigration status.

77. See, e.g., *Village of Arlington Heights v. Metropolitan Housing Development Corp.*, 429 U.S. 252 (1977).
78. 118 U.S. 356, 374 (1886).
79. See Stacy Ann Harwood, *Planning in the Face of Anti-Immigrant Sentiment*, Forthcoming in Michael Rios and Leonardo Vazquez, Eds., Dialogos Chapter 2 (2012).
80. See Rick Su, *Local Fragmentation as Immigration Regulation*, 47 Hous. L. Rev. 367, 368 (2010).
81. See *Comité de Jornaleros de Redondo Beach v. City of Redondo Beach*, 657 F.3d 936 (9th Cir. 2011).
82. That language is the clearest definition available of the scope of the exclusive federal sphere. See *DeCanas v. Bica*, 424 U.S. 351, 355 (1976).

CHAPTER TWO

Can There Be a Local Immigration Policy?

FRANCISCO VELASCO CABALLERO,
AUTONOMOUS UNIVERSITY OF MADRID

OVERVIEW

Are local immigration policies possible in Spain? Answering this question from a legal perspective requires a determination as to whether Spanish local governments (primarily municipal and regional) have constitutional or statutory powers to undertake immigration regulation. In Spain, this question is particularly significant, because of the formal relevance of the concept of competencies within the multi-level system of governmental power established by the 1978 Constitution. In principle, in Spain, every political subdivision receives a specific sphere of power (i.e. competency) that must be respected by all other government entities. This principle appears to be particularly strict when it comes to the distribution of competencies between the central state and regional levels of government (Comunidades Autónomas, or autonomous communities). With regard to municipal government competencies, however, the delineation is more flexible and fluid. This appears to be the case, although Article 137 of the Constitution (CE) provides a vague guarantee of "local autonomy," because the specific local competencies (i.e. their spheres of power) are established by the laws of the national government and of the different autonomous communities.

In any case, once a local competency has been established, either by national or regional laws, its exercise must be strictly respected by all other government units. In my view, this basic description of local competencies in Spain does not coincide with the U.S. allocation of power to local government units. In my opinion, although U.S. public law is based upon the concept of jurisdiction (similar to the Spanish concept of competency), it shows more flexibility with regard to the scope of governmental power at all levels. The legal doctrinal principle is known in the United States as preemption, and it is the ultimate arbiter in disputes over the territorial distribution of governmental power. As applied, the principle relies less on the formal relevance of the competencies of each governmental unit and, rather, favors the action of the highest level of government acting pursuant to a legitimate sovereign power (usually federal over state; and federal, as well as state, over local governments).

If we draw our attention to the legislation adopted in some U.S. municipalities, which seeks to prevent the housing or employment of undocumented immigrants, it becomes immediately apparent that the main legal issue is not so much whether localities do or do not have the power (competency) to adopt these ordinances, but rather whether the local action infringes on a higher state or federal law (Velasco, 2011, p. 22). It is, therefore, a question of superiority of power rather than one of competency. In Spain, this dispute would be a matter of competency, that is, whether local governments do or do not have the competency to regulate the living conditions of immigrants. As a result of this legal difference, it is easier to understand why in Spain, and not in the United States perhaps, the primary question is whether local governments have competencies on immigration, and, if so, to what extent.

Let us start with a basic empirical observation: whatever the legal basis of local competency may be, as a matter of fact, Spanish localities adopt and implement immigration policies. In fact, Spanish local governments often openly promote the integration of immigrants, irrespective of whether the immigrants can establish their legal presence in the country. In only a few cases are there city policies that, directly or indirectly, impede the local integration of immigrants, and these are generally targeted at immigrants from a particular part of the world or religion.

As far as integration is concerned, almost all Spanish municipalities implement some policies to promote the integration of immigrants. This general assessment can be held even if public resources to these local policies have fallen significantly since 2012. The situation in Spain differs from that of highly centralized countries, like France, where specific policies dealing with the integration of immigrants (different from general social policies) are reserved to the national government (Kadouci & Neraudau, 2008, p. 141). Consider these common examples of Spanish local government actions: prevention of xenophobic or racist behaviors; prevention of social exclusion; language instruction; cultural activities; local mediation between landlord and immigrant for open access to housing; lodging for temporary workers; programs targeted at immigrant women; job training (technical and social guidance); educational integration of women and young people;

technological training for young immigrants and women; integration of young immigrants through the fine arts; encouragement of empathy among the different sectors of the population; encouragement of public participation by immigrants; and promotion of social and economic development within the immigrants' countries of origin.

Examples of restrictive local actions, though far less frequent and explicit, also exist: restricting or prohibiting registration in the local census for undocumented (irregular) immigrants; repeated police stops of people with racial features indicating foreign ancestry; lack of accommodation for construction of religious buildings likely to be favored by immigrants; and prohibition of the Islamic burka (complete covering of the female body) within municipal buildings.

LEVELS OF GOVERNMENT AND IMMIGRATION POLICIES

We have just seen that, in fact, municipalities develop policies dealing with immigrants. In this regard, they are not unique: every political subdivision in Spain, exercising public power, carries out activities in relation to immigration. As a result, it is correct to say that there is not one singular immigration policy; rather, there are European, Spanish, autonomous (regional), and local immigration policies. At times, such policies are formally implemented (through the promulgation of directives and European regulations, laws, and state regulations) and at other times, implemented through political actions (appropriation of funds for the integration of immigrants, socializing plans, programs of acceptance, etc.). Public policies of immigration make a clear distinction between the control of migratory flows, on the one hand, and integration of immigrants on the other. The control of migratory flows is both a labor issue and one of policing. Integration comprises many different types of actions, both with regard to immigrants as well as with regard to the native population (which must adapt to the reality of immigration).

Generally, there is no substantial inconsistency between and among the public policies of immigration adopted at different levels of government. This conclusion can be drawn from a comparison of the migratory policies of the different Member States of the European Union (Michalowski, 2008, p. 67). However, the fact that the different levels of government adopt consistent policies does not mean that all of those governmental units should become involved with the two components of immigration regulation (control and integration) to the same degree. The European Union focuses, above everything else, on policies of immigrant control (border crossings, permission to enter, or residency permits), and is only in a very limited way (financially) concerned with integration (López, 2010, p. 36). The Spanish State also acts primarily in the area of immigration control, and promotes integration only secondarily. Autonomous communities rarely participate in the control of migratory flows, but are very active when it comes to social integration. Finally, local governments also carry out very limited control functions, with their main activity being the encouragement of integration and socialization. All these activities of the different government authorities are intimately related to each other. Each one conditions the others. The activity of every unit of government is connected in a network with those activities carried out by the others. It is important to note, however, that municipal policies regarding the integration of immigrants will crucially depend on an external reality over which they have no power—that is, the control or lack of control of migratory flows as they are regulated by the European Union and the Spanish government (Klopp, 2002, p. 12; Aguado, 2002, p. 9).

Of all of the units of local government, it is the municipality that normally undertakes the task of developing a local policy of immigration. Although these actions are usually undertaken independently, there are some relevant examples of joint local actions, either by intermunicipal agreement or at the subregional (county) level (Barreta, 2007, p. 79). Provinces (local governments consisting of municipal governments) and the islands (Canaries and Ballearic) undertake very little in the way of immigration policies (Moya, 2006, p. 165). Two facts may explain this outcome. First of all, the concentration of immigrant populations tends to occur, with some notable exceptions, in large or medium-sized cities. This explains the limited intervention of the provinces which—according to Article 36 of Law 7/1985, of November 26 (establishing the Local Government Legal Framework [LBRL])—are endowed with competencies that are basically functional or secondary (i.e. in order to supplement any perceived inadequacy of measures adopted by small localities).

The second explanation is financial. Although provinces and the islands theoretically have the power to develop their own immigration policies, those that would seem to require a supramunicipal level for effective implementation, the financial programs of the state (Settlement Funds) and autonomous communities either ignore them or explicitly prohibit their involvement. Without funds, the development of policies, such as those dealing with the integration of immigrants, becomes prohibitively expensive.

LOCAL COMPETENCIES ON IMMIGRATION

At present, there is not a specific and express local competency on immigration. This means that no law directly considers immigration regulation to be a specific local power. Only with regard to the integration of immigrants can an argument be made that Article 2 ter of Organic Law 4/2000, of January 11, on Rights and Liberties of Foreigners in Spain and their Social Integration (LODLEIS), specifically establishes a local competency. This point will be discussed further at a later point. In any case, the lack of an express and specific local competency on immigration does not mean that local governments cannot develop immigration policies. Some local actions may be justified as emanating from the generic or open clauses of Spanish law. Other actions can be indirectly justified as derivative of other express local competencies (in social services, education, housing, or urban development).

Universal Competency Clause

Some scholars have argued that local power to adopt immigration policy (at least with respect to the integration of immigrants) is derived from a sort of general local government competency allegedly existing in Spanish Law (Aguado & Cerrillo, 2005, p. 42). In my opinion, such a general clause of local competency does not really exist. It is true that a distinguished sector of the legal academy has argued that a universal competency clause for municipal governments can be inferred from Article 137 CE as generally granting "local self-government." But, to my mind, this argument is not defensible. Article 137 of the Constitution (CE), in its guarantee of local autonomy, does not contain a universal clause of competency similar to that of Article 28 II of the German Constitution (Barnes, 1998, p. 54; Fanlo, 2006, p. 1432). In my opinion, Articles 137 and 140 CE only guarantee directly the minimums of functional autonomy to local governments, and implicitly authorize laws to raise these minimums. As a result, the laws do not serve the function of restricting an extensive local autonomy ex Constitutione (the alleged general clause of local power). Rather, they apply to shape and raise the constitutional minimal standards of local autonomy as derived from the Constitution (Velasco, 2010, p. 45).

Local Complementary Competency

Although I do not believe that the universal competency clause can be interpreted as authorizing local action regarding the living conditions of immigrants, the complementary municipal competencies (Article 7.4 LBRL), in contrast, can provide the necessary legal basis. The principle of complementarity refers to the fact that municipalities can "complement" the activity of other governments. It also suggests that local implementation of the principles of the social state regarding the social conditions of their residents can go beyond the parameters of programs adopted by either central government or the autonomous communities. In essence, we are dealing with a complementary competency similar to the one that applies, in some instances, to the Treaty on the Functioning of the European Union (in some matters, the European Union is empowered to complete or reinforce the measures or policies of the Member States). In any case, it is important to highlight that the effective exercise of that complementary municipal power must respect the state or regional policies that are being complemented (STC 214/1989, FJ 12 a). As we can see, this principle of "complementary" competency is limited because it only serves to allow a government to complement the action of other entities, not to act de novo and unrestrictedly. But the principle has great explanatory value when applied to the integration of immigrants, because the state as well as the autonomous communities can develop policies allowing important additional, complementary actions in specific municipalities.

Sectoral Competencies

Beyond the complementary competency of Article 7.4 of LBRL—which establishes a limited competency precisely because it is stated to be complementary—the legal basis for local government development and adoption of immigration policies is to be found in the sectoral laws (on housing, social services, or even immigration) of the state and of the autonomous community. These are the laws that, pursuant to the mandate of Article 25.2 LBRL, must allocate specific competencies to municipal governments. Therefore, these sectoral rules are the ones that most directly establish the legitimacy of local actions that are directly or indirectly related to immigration.

From a sectoral point of view, we can now ask whether the new Article 2 ter LODLEIS did confer a local competency with regard to matters on the integration of immigrants. According to the first paragraph of Article 2 ter LODLEIS: "Public authorities shall promote the full integration of foreigners into Spanish society within a framework of harmony among different cultures without any limit other than those imposed by the Constitution and the Law." The second paragraph of the same Article 2 ter LODLEIS adds:

> Public authorities shall incorporate the goal of integration between immigrants and the receiving society, across all policies and public services, encouraging economic, social, cultural and political participation by immigrants, according to the Constitution, Charters or Statutes of Autonomy, and all laws, and according to principles of equal treatment.

Strictly speaking, neither of these paragraphs of the new Article 2 ter LODLEIS follows the technical requirements of a state grant of competency. The first paragraph of Article 2 ter LODLEIS contains a general mandate to act, and this mandate applies to all units of government. But precisely because of its general character (addressed to all government units), it is difficult to interpret this language as an affirmative attribution of concrete power to any particular political subdivision. Similarly, the second paragraph of Article 2 ter LODLEIS imposes a duty on government to act with a general and cross-cutting concern for the integration of immigrants. The most compelling interpretation of this language is that the mandate is based upon the assumption that the different public authorities to which it is addressed already possess the governmental competency to act with regard to immigration. In spite of these technical, text-based arguments, the constitutional principle of local autonomy allows the interpretation that Article 2 ter LODLEIS establishes local competency—at least a residual one—to promote the integration of immigrants. This local competency is of course not an exclusive one—and is limited by state and regional plans on immigration—nor does it substitute for other local competencies. In other words, the substantial implied limitations on this residual local competency would not be relevant to determine the scope of local power in cases where a more specific and explicit grant of local autonomy can be applied.

LIMITS AND DETERMINING FACTORS IN THE EXERCISE OF LOCAL COMPETENCIES

To this point, it has been shown how localities can develop policies of immigration, either under the protection of some broad and general clauses of competency, or under express sectoral attributions. If we accept this defense of local government power to operate in the area of immigration, the next question has to do with the limits on the exercise of that power.

European, State, and Regional Regulation

Let us begin with the obvious: all local actions and policies are subject to European Law (pursuant to the principle of prevalence), to the Constitution, and to the laws of the state and autonomous communities. Consider how those laws condition and limit municipal discretion. First, European rules (directives, regulations, and judicial opinions) have little impact on the scope of local action. This is precisely because European-level regulation concerns itself primarily with the control of migratory flows, and in this area local action is minimal. Second, the Constitution, and particularly the fundamental rights that it recognizes, is directly and strictly applicable to local governments. Basic rights, like religious freedom (Article 16.1 CE) or the right to education (Article 27 CE), are essential to the living conditions of immigrants, and these provisions directly shape and limit the scope of local discretion. In this regard, consider the conflict created by local ordinances forbidding the use of the veil (burka) worn by many Muslim women, primarily immigrants, in local government offices. Finally, local governments are limited, not only by laws of the national government, but also by those of their autonomous community (the regional government). In a subsequent part of this article, we will focus on some of the many other laws (dealing with social services, housing, education, etc.) that condition government initiatives.

Of all the laws, Organic Law 4/2000, of January 11, on the Rights and Liberties of Foreigners in Spain and their Social Integration (LODLEIS) is the most directly binding on local government activity. Consistent with European migratory policy, LODLEIS establishes two principal focal points of regulation: control of migratory flows (both with regards to cross-border and internal movement) and the integration of immigrants (Aguado & Cerrillo, 2005, p. 40). Control of migratory flows is accomplished primarily in the system of visas, work permits, residency permits, and border control (denial of entry and deportation) regulated by the provisions of LODLEIS and its implementing administrative regulations. Integration is anticipated and defined in basic terms in LODLEIS, but the true reach of this power depends on the State's adoption of plans and budgets. Regarding integration, the LODLEIS distinguishes, though not always clearly, between legalized immigrants and those who do not possess legal authority to remain in the country. Legalized immigrants are entitled to most of the same legal protections as Spanish citizens.

Those in an irregular situation are treated with tolerance by the legal regime, whose objective is to guarantee dignified treatment, but not authorization to remain in the country. This basic distinction can be seen in the way in which LODLEIS, in Articles 3 to 15, establishes different rights for immigrants based on their legal status. So, for instance, foreign residents (i.e., regular ones) are entitled to receive all public health services on an equal basis with the Spanish people. In contrast, unauthorized immigrants are only entitled to receive some of these services: adults can receive only emergency health services to treat serious illnesses or accidents; those under the age of eighteen are entitled to all health services; and pregnant women are entitled to pre-natal, delivery, and post-natal care (Article 12 LODLEIS). This structural legal distinction between regular and irregular immigrants necessarily conditions local policies of immigration. Although local governments can improve the living conditions of immigrants (in regard to the minimum standards established by LODLEIS), such improvement cannot go so far as to remove the distinction between the two classes of immigrants (authorized and irregular) to whom the law refers.

Autonomous communities also influence the scope of local immigration policies. Only in very few instances, however, have their policies been implemented through the adoption of legislation. The Valencian Community's Law 15/2008, of December 5, on the integration of immigrants in the Valencian Community, as well as the Catalonian Law 10/2010, of May 7, on the reception of immigrants and those returned to Catalonia, are both exceptions to this generalization. Most frequently, the autonomous communities' policies regarding the integration of immigrants are found in the regional plans of harmonious living-together of immigration. Frequently identical from one autonomous community to another, these plans adopt similar strategies, programs, and actions: focusing on welcoming services, training, employment assistance, intercultural mediation, protection of youth, and language instruction.

Financial Conditionings

The most common local immigration and integration policies are essentially spending programs. These efforts include welcome centers, providing mediation services, orientation, education, and job training; or encouraging the social activities of immigrant associations. All of these efforts are costly. Given the unquestioned structural weakness of local public finances, it can be easily inferred that local competencies on immigration are directed by the state and, increasingly, in the hands of the autonomous communities. Local programs promoting the integration of immigrants depend on subsidies from the state or the autonomous communities, either within the framework of the Fund for Settlement and Integration (state or regional), or from other earmarked expenditures.

In the last decade, the state has been involved with local initiatives regarding integration in two ways: through the Fund of Support for the Settlement and Integration of Immigrants and Educational Support and by means of direct subsidies to different municipalities. The Fund of Support was created in 2009 and was renewed annually until 2012. It is uncertain whether it will be reinstated as soon as the budget deficit is under control. The Fund of Support was part of a normal budgetary transfer from the state to the autonomous communities. Although the resources of this fund were distributed to the autonomous communities, giving them the power to select the local projects to be financed, a large part of the revenues transferred were earmarked for local plans of integration. These funds came with some conditions attached: specific amounts were targeted for three different types of programs: acceptance and immigration; educational reinforcement; and care for unaccompanied minors from the Canary Islands. In addition to the economic resources of the Settlement Fund, the state (chiefly through the Department of Employment and Immigration) also provides—even under the current financial crisis—direct and specific grants to individual municipalities. These latter grants are awarded on a competitive basis, and local governments may be in direct competition with private non-profit agencies for these limited funds.

At the same time, every autonomous community provides funding for specific local projects of integration. Until 2012, a part of the regional funding derived from the revenues transferred to them by means of the State Fund of Support.

Nowadays, the regional funding for local projects consists of self-generated revenues of the autonomous communities. The distribution of these resources means that every autonomous community selectively finances—through calls for proposals—specific local plans of integration. Though the details may vary, the basic process is the same: localities submit proposals for funding through a competitive process, organized by the autonomous community, seeking revenues to finance projects to enhance the integration of immigrants and harmonious coexistence within its borders. To receive funding, the local proposals must meet the requirements established by the autonomous communities. In this way, local competencies on immigration are, in the final analysis, not an emanation of any independent local power, but rather derivative of and shaped by the state and regional governments.

Cooperation as a Limit

Immigration policy is frequently implemented through intergovernmental cooperation, and Spanish law explicitly recognizes that aspect, specifically in Article 2 ter LODLEIS (introduced by Organic Law 2/2009). In this context, government competencies operate like a network of powers, with each entity respecting the decisions and actions of the other government units involved (Catalá, 2009, p. 57). Local governments form an important part of this network. For example, the Second Strategic Plan of Citizenship and Integration of the State (2011–2014) expressly anticipates voluntary local government participation in schemes established by the national government. It is true that the state plan labels the participation of local entities as optional, which suggests that the type of cooperation envisioned is a truly horizontal one, guided by the precepts of a national plan. But it is also true that local government's discretion is narrowly limited to the decision whether or not to join in the actions proposed by the state plan (or by the autonomous plans). In fact, in its assessment of the 1st State Plan of Citizenship and Immigration (2007–2011), the state considered the fact that regional and local plans simply adopted the national strategy as evidence of their success. Something similar happens with autonomous (regional) plans on integration. These plans, identical in their structure and content to the state plan, formally envision cooperative relationships with local governments. This veneer of cooperation, however, masks a strict control of local action by the autonomous community (primarily through financial subsidies to municipal governments for the implementation of the goals established in the regional plan). In short, it is clear that local governments do not find themselves in a true position of cooperation in regard to the state and its autonomous communities. They lack real power to have influence on supralocal plans on immigration. Their political discretion is limited to the decision whether or not they should act as indirect agents of a higher government to implement that unit's articulated immigration policy. This method of inter-governmental cooperation, combined with the reality of financing through conditional grants, tarnishes the ideal of true horizontal cooperation among political subdivisions endowed with competencies in immigration.

LOCAL ACTIONS AND COMPETENCIES IN IMMIGRATION

We already have seen that Spanish local governments develop policies affecting the living conditions of immigrants. We also have seen how the competency to undertake these actions can be understood as emanating from a variety of national or regional (autonomous) laws. What follows is a consideration of typical local policies (in the areas of housing, education, etc.), an analysis of their specific basis in local competencies, and some suggestions about the limits of these local competencies. As we will see, most municipal policies are related to the concept of integration, even though some local efforts to control migratory flows can be identified.

Administrative Policies of Migratory Flows

Public policies on immigration must always deal with how to control the migratory population flows. These policies may be focused on border control, as provided in the European regulation no. 562/2006 of the European Parliament and Council, of March 15, 2006 (Schengen Border Code), or focused on the movement of immigrants within the country. There is no doubt that border control of migratory flows is an exclusive national state power (Articles 149.1.2 and 29 CE). Migratory controls inside the country are also reserved, generally, to the state. In some instances, however, the autonomous communities may exercise some control over issues involving work permits for foreigners, according to the new Statutes of Autonomy (STC 175/2011). As a basic corollary of this exclusive state power, local governments lack competencies of administrative and police control in the field of immigration. Even though it is true that local governments may have police forces of their own (Article 173 of the Royal Legislative Decree 781/1986, April 18: TRRL), the permissible functions of local police forces are strictly and precisely limited in Article 51 of Organic Law 2/1986, of March 13, on Security Forces (LOFCS). The statutory listing of local police functions does not mention immigration, leading to the conclusion that police involvement with immigration affairs is reserved to the National Police (Articles 12.1[a] 1 and 2 LOFCS). Within these strict limits, however, local police forces and administrative offices may cooperate with the state in the implementation of its immigration policy in at least three different ways: preparing reports (informes de arraigo) that evaluate the socialization and integration of an immigrant and are used by the national government in the legalization process (Article 124.2 of the Royal Decree 557/2011, of April 20: Regulations of Status of Foreigners); preparing reports on the adequacy of housing for immigrants who seek family reunification (Article 18.2 LODLEIS); and by reporting administrative irregularities noticed by chance in the exercise of other local competencies (Article 3 of Organic Law 1/1992, of February 21, on Civic Security Protection). In all of these cases, the local government assumes a role of assistance and collaboration with the State's administration (Moya, 2006, p. 133), always acting under the umbrella of strong national control.

Promotion of Coexistence

Many local initiatives in immigration have to do with societal coexistence: for example, actions against racism and xenophobia; increased use of public spaces (especially those places frequented by immigrants); facilitating language immersion, as an important factor in the immigrants' integration; training aides skilled in intercultural socialization; providing mediation assistance with familial and group conflicts; and afterschool activities.

Catalan Law 10/2010, of May 7, dealing with the integration of immigrants, is the only autonomous community law to explicitly establish municipal competency to promote the "social cohesion of the population and the acceptance and integration of immigrants." In other instances, however, local competency to enact initiatives and integration programs is not as easily defended. For one thing, many of these local initiatives go beyond the narrow field of social assistance, as that term is strictly defined in the laws of the autonomous communities. That is because these local measures do not seek primarily to help those in need, but rather to foster a high level of social coexistence and cohesion between immigrants and citizens. Nor do local competencies in the area of education support all of these local actions. Though language instruction seems to fit comfortably within the local competency in education, other immigration initiatives, such as cultural mediation, do not, and they must rely on the complementary competency articulated in Article 7.4 LBRL. In fact, that provision would seem to support all local initiatives in this area, so long as they are designed to complement the plans and regulations adopted by the state and the autonomous communities from the vantage point of the social state.

Involvement in Politics

Local governments frequently attempt to involve immigrants in the local political community. In Spain, some immigrants are entitled to participate in politics on an equal footing with Spanish citizens. Citizens of the European Union, for instance, have full electoral rights in local elections. In addition, international agreements may grant local voting rights to citizens of other countries, such as Norway or Chile. Based primarily on an analysis of Romanian voting in Spanish local elections, it seems that immigrant electoral patterns are similar to those of Spanish nationals (with at most a slight political tilt to the left), and that significant national-ethnic political groups have not emerged (Cebolla & González, 2008, p. 208). More sophisticated analysis of the impact of this formal political power is needed. Studies have not analyzed the effect of the immigrant vote on public policy (although, in principle, it is predictable that a significant concentration of immigrants would have an influence upon local public policies).

Most immigrants, excluding Europeans and the citizens of a few other countries, do not have the right to vote in local elections. For these individuals, political participation is channeled in two ways. First, all immigrants have the right of ordinary administrative participation, recognized in Article 6.2 LODLEIS (for example, in public informational meetings, in budgetary participatory processes, in general hearings conducted by the local governments). Second, some local laws and ordinances have created different councils or administrative organizations specifically for immigrants. From the point of view of integration, some may question the wisdom of this separate administrative machinery (Mir, 2002, p. 156). Recent assessment of the results suggests scarce outcomes. In any case, the relevant point to be made here is that all of these modes of participation are justified as an expression of local powers of self-organization (Article 4.1[a] LBRL) and, as specified in Article 69 LBRL, they cannot impair or restrict the powers of the local authorities (Moya, 2006, p. 150).

There is, finally, some question whether a local government entity can, pursuant to its power of self-organization, authorize the political or administrative participation of irregular immigrants. Although the question is still unresolved, in my opinion, this action falls beyond the scope of that local power. In this case, and in contrast to our later discussion of social assistance, the local authorization of political participation for undocumented immigrants cannot be interpreted as a complementary action of the locality (addressed in Article 7.4 LBRL), which expands to irregular immigrants the minimum social benefits granted in Article 14 LODLEIS to regular immigrants (those without legal residency). In the case of participation—above all, in the case of the representative forms of participation—local governments would be violating the terms of Article 6.2 LODLEIS, which limits participation of immigrants solely to residents. And, to my mind, this term can only be understood as including those foreigners holding a legal title of residency in Spain (Velasco, 2010, p. 93). Some scholars dispute my argument (Mir, 2002, p. 170; Aguado, 2004, p. 209; Villaverde, 2010, p. 32), but I find their rebuttal unconvincing. In my view, local action to allow political and administrative participation for irregular or undocumented immigrants cannot be justified as an enlargement of the rights recognized by LODLEIS, but rather constitutes a prohibited alternative regulation in conflict with the law's specific distinction between regular and irregular immigrants in terms of the rights it provides. In this case, then, local power of self-organization (Articles 4.1[a] and 69 LBRL) would be exercised in violation of the state law on foreigners.

Prevention and Remediation of Social Exclusion

Municipal governments have a well-established tradition of providing social assistance to immigrants. Their goal is to avoid the social exclusion that frequently results from situations of vulnerability or dependency. Social services seek to prevent immigrant alienation, which is often accompanied by a sense of rejection and/or delinquency. In spite of the importance of local action in this area, the truth is that local plans of integration or coexistence rarely focus extensively on what, in the strict sense, could be called social assistance. So, for example, the II Plan Madrid of Social and Inter-cultural Coexistence (2009–2012) includes in its section on social integration and coexistence only a few programs directly related to a policy of social assistance. These include programs of orientation; after-school activities for children; specific programs of protection and support for abused foreign women; and, depending on country of origin, temporary housing in homes owned by the municipality.

The scarcity of local social assistance programs organized specifically for immigrants may be the result of two facts. First, most local policies of social assistance focus more objectively on the situations of vulnerability, dependence, or exclusion (Moya, 2006, p. 158), in addition to the specific and individual needs of groups (by age: minors, adults, elderly), rather than focus on the national origin of the people being served. As a result, even though many immigrants benefit from local social assistance programs, their receipt of services stems not from their condition as immigrants, but rather from the fact of their need. For the same reason, these programs of social assistance are not developed or described in local plans of immigration. In addition, local social services are highly controlled, planned and programmed by the autonomous communities, and so they easily fall outside the scope of local political strategies (and therefore do not appear in local plans of immigration and coexistence). In this regard, local entities act more as indirect agents of the autonomous communities than as autonomous units of government with their own policies of social assistance.

Local social assistance is carried out according to the local competencies' scheme established by Articles 25.2 (k) and 26.1 (c) LBRL. That is, the laws on social assistance of the autonomous communities must ascribe specific competencies or tasks to their local governments. Let us remember that autonomous communities are—exclusively—competent when it comes to "helping social groups in need of special care" (see Articles 26.1.23 and 24 of the Statute of Autonomy of Madrid). As a result, it falls to the laws of the autonomous communities to establish municipal competencies in the area of social services. This means that local governments, bound by the rules of their autonomous community, are usually left with nothing more than minimal competency of management, with no initiative power to shape the programs or to articulate their own local political option (Tolivar, 2009, p. 20).

One unresolved question is whether local government entities, especially municipalities, can provide additional social services to immigrants, that is, services that are not part of the network of social services established by every autonomous community. A city, for instance, might decide to provide specific financial support for the purpose of providing housing, rent subsidies, or lodging in municipally owned housing. These services are normally not identified in the plans of the autonomous communities, which tend to authorize local governments to provide basic services or primary health care. These supplemental local programs, then, would be outside the scope of the autonomous system of social services. The consequences of this situation would be two-fold: first, these specialized municipal service programs would be ineligible to receive funds transferred from higher levels; and second, the local competency to provide these services could no longer be based on the corresponding autonomous rule of social services. Nevertheless, that basis of competency might be found in Article 7.4 LBRL, which empowers localities "to engage in activities that are complementary to those ascribed to other units of government." The complementary local competency makes complete sense in terms of the basic premises of the welfare state, where the social services provided by one public entity do not prevent another from improving or supplementing the basic level of service, at least in the absence of a legislative prohibition. And that is exactly the situation that arises when a local government provides additional and specialized social services to immigrants. These local initiatives, outside the system of social services adopted by the autonomous community, are a local complement to the autonomic system, and fully covered by Article 7.4 LBRL.

Whether a local government can choose to provide certain social services to irregular immigrants is a question that merits special consideration. Remember that Article 14 LODLEIS limits the availability of some social services to legalized resident immigrants. In addition, some autonomous communities have adopted legislation that mirrors national laws to determine which immigrants may participate in programs funded by the federal revenues that are transferred to the autonomous communities for distribution (see, for example, Article 10.2 of the Law of Madrid 11/2003). In my opinion, legal doctrine supports the argument that a municipality has the authority, derived from Article 7.4 LBRL, to provide specialized social services to irregular or undocumented immigrants. In all instances, this decision will be left to the total discretion of the local government and is not a legal duty established by higher levels of government. In fact, the most persuasive interpretation of the relationship between Article 14 LODLEIS and the autonomous (regional) rules on social services is that undocumented immigrants have a legal right only to basic social services or primary health care managed by local governments within the autonomous system of social services. The irregular immigrants themselves are powerless to claim these supplemental or additional services. Nevertheless, the municipal government itself has the power, in the exercise of its autonomy and under the protection of Article 7.4 LBRL, to provide undocumented immigrants some or all of the social services enjoyed by legal foreign residents. That discretion would extend to the provision of all services that are seen as protecting the immigrants' dignity and preventing their social exclusion. These social services would not be based directly on Article 14 LODLEIS or on the autonomous communities' laws on social services, but on the general power of local governments (according to Article 7.4 LBRL) to supplement benefits provided by the state and the autonomous communities.

Education

Education is essential to the integration of immigrants and immigrant communities. All studies and public immigration policies concur on this point. For instance, Article 9.3 LODLEIS explicitly states: "public authorities shall insure that foreigners receive the educational services necessary for better social integration." For the most part, the competency on education belongs to the autonomous communities, and is executed within the framework of national laws. As a result, local government officials have little discretion to adopt their own education policies for immigrants. For the most part, local decisions will have to do with educational infrastructure and assistance to schoolchildren. With regard to infrastructure, local governments have the power to establish preschools for children under the age of three (Article 12.2 of Organic Law 2/2006, of May 3, of Education: LOE). These schools are essential, not only for the social integration of young immigrant children, but also to facilitate their parents' employment. In this way, local governments can advance the integration of immigrants by establishing schools in those neighborhoods with a higher concentration of immigrants. In addition, they may also provide assistance to low-income students, at all levels of schooling, by providing tuition scholarships, free transportation, or subsidized meals. Although this type of local assistance is not covered by the competency established in the Organic Law of Education, it is included in Article 7.4 LBRL, which authorizes complementary municipal activities in, among others sectors, education. Apart from that, municipal governments can have a voice, as established in Article 86.2 LOE, in those decisions that establish the territorial boundaries of every educational center (that is, the designation of each school's attendance zone) and the establishment of attendance priorities (which favor those children who live in closest proximity to a particular school). In general, though, the autonomous communities impose severe limits on the scope of local participation, authorizing nothing more than municipal procedural participation in the decision making process.

Local Land-Use Control

Common wisdom posits that if immigrant communities are not integrated into the urban landscape, the formation of urban immigrant ghettos is inevitable. In some Spanish cities, the segregation of space is already a reality, especially with regard to Moroccan immigrants. Therefore, municipal plans of integration stress the need to distribute the immigrant community across city neighborhoods. This effort seeks to use planning to reverse the "natural human desire to neither work nor live in heterogeneous communities" (Ponce, 2002, p. 201). In this way, municipal governments rely on their local zoning code, which designates permitted uses on all parcels within the local government's jurisdiction, to accomplish the political goal of integration. Through the application of these local ordinances, the law can combine residential, industrial, or commercial uses in each neighborhood, producing the desired concentration of similar residential or commercial uses. By assigning an office use to parts of the urban center, for instance, some of the immigration population can be shifted to other parts of the city. Zoning regulations and classifications can also segregate people. For instance, zoning requirements that establish large minimum lot sizes and low-density development inevitably result in residential segregation on the basis of income. Extensive stratification of types of residential uses through zoning also leads to socioeconomic segregation (Ponce, 2002, p. 173).

In Spain the competency of urban planning belongs to each municipality, so long as it operates within the framework of the urban planning legislation adopted by the autonomous communities. As a result, the autonomous community laws of urbanism must be the source of authority for the adoption of local planning tools sufficient to achieve the integration of the immigrant community. These laws must also specify which zoning techniques can be used by the municipalities. In general, every municipality has wide discretion to determine the uses to be permitted within its border, and with that comes the power to establish residential zones. As a result, municipal competencies in urban planning and land use are sufficiently broad to allow the adoption of local policies to integrate the immigrant community.

The success of local urban policies to integrate the immigrant community depends on the combination of, on the one hand, zoning regulations for the development of government-owned housing and, on the other hand, the availability of certain types of financial assistance for housing. These two components are found in the laws and housing plans of the autonomous communities (which will be discussed in the next section). Currently, local urban plans may designate specific parcels (undeveloped or developable) with a zoning classification that specifies residential public housing. Furthermore, the laws of the autonomous communities usually establish minimum standards for parcels designated with this classification. Municipal urban planning could in fact establish new categories of residential uses created specifically for the integration of immigrants. Using this approach, for example, a municipality could adopt a specific residential land use category of "welcoming housing" or "homes for immigrants with special needs." Even though municipal competencies to promote integration policies are extensive, local governments have not yet used their zoning laws in the extent described here.

Housing

In any enumeration of municipal policies to promote the integration of immigrants, access to housing is normally a priority. There are many possible options, namely: access to publicly owned or subsidized housing; renting, with or without option to buy; individual rent subsidies; municipal action to facilitate the use and rental of unoccupied residences; and temporary stays in public or private homes. All of the options described above follow, to a greater or lesser extent, two separate goals: distribution of immigrants within an urban environment (urban policy) and aid to people in need (social assistance policy).

Currently, in Spain, the general scope of government powers in housing is defined in the national State's housing plans. Although the Spanish government does not have an express competency in the area of housing, its involvement is based on a general competency in matters regarding the "bases and coordination of the economy" (Article 149.1.13 of the Spanish Constitution). In addition, the housing legislation and plans adopted by the autonomous communities, which have exclusive competency in this matter, also form an important part of the overall legal framework within which municipal housing policies must operate. As far as foreigners are concerned, access to public protection houses (VPP) remains guaranteed, according to LODLEIS Article 13, only to resident immigrants, that is, only for those whose residency is legal in Spain. This means that any legalized immigrant who meets the objective requirements of the different plans (essentially, family income) is eligible for housing assistance on the same basis as Spanish citizens (Aguado & Cerrillo, 2005, p. 135). Moreover, local housing plans can, within the powers left to them by the laws and regulations of the autonomous communities, promote housing opportunities for immigrants. These programs may consist of building housing for protected groups, endorsing the construction of "insertion homes" or "welcome homes," or providing assistance with rent mediation. Similarly, local policies to select residents for publicly owned or subsidized housing could—within the framework of the state or regional legislation—favor immigrant access (just as in the case of, for example, young people or mistreated women). Another issue, different from that of local competency, is the political feasibility of specific political programs favoring immigrants, or adopting criteria that award them preferential treatment in public housing. The resolution of this issue will crucially depend on the political and electoral visibility or invisibility of a large portion of the immigrants in Spain.

Another matter, which deserves at least some attention, is whether a municipality may establish specific housing assistance for irregular immigrants. We have already mentioned that resident foreigners qualify for public housing assistance on an equal footing with Spanish citizens (Article 13 LODLEIS). Undocumented immigrants clearly fall outside of that provision. In regard to the specific assistance programs of the autonomous communities, it has been asserted that foreigners' social rights regulated in LODLEIS by national legislation, including the right of housing, constitute a minimum standard that legislators in the autonomous communities, in the exercise of their competencies, can supplement in the area of social assistance (Aguado & Cerrillo, 2005, p. 136). This opinion is doctrinally sound in general terms. In fact, it might even be applied to local governments. If that were the case, and given the limited scope of municipal competency in social services, the specific legal source of municipal power would lie in the complementary competency of Article 7.4 LBRL, which expressly refers to housing.

CONCLUSIONS

Most medium-sized and large Spanish cities develop immigration policies. The deep economic crisis in Spain since 2008, though it has dramatically reduced the funds appropriated to local governments, has not eliminated the local policies on immigrants. They are usually policies of integration, although some localities have adopted measures to control or restrict immigration. In general, these municipal activities are based on local competencies. It is true that neither the Constitution nor laws ascribe to local governments a specific competency in immigration. But other legal competencies are broad enough to include local activity in this area of public policy. In the first place, Article 7.4 of the Law Establishing Local Governments' Legal Framework (State Law 7/1985) attributes to local governments the general competency to complement the activity of other government units. In addition, the different sectoral laws (from the state or from the autonomous communities) establish local government competencies in the areas of urban planning, housing, education, or social services. All of these powers can easily be used to promote the municipality's policies to integrate immigrants.

Although local governments have sufficient legal competency to implement policies dealing with immigrants' living conditions, their political options are limited. First, most local activities are subject to conditional financing (through subsidies) by the state or the autonomous communities; and, of course, the government that provides the financing is also the one that establishes the goals of the program. Second, both the state and the autonomous communities thoroughly control local activity on immigration, usually through the provisions of their integration plans, in which the scope of local action is predetermined.

REFERENCES

Aguado i Cudolá, V. (2002). La aplicación del marco jurídico de la inmigración en las administraciones locales: un primer balance (I). Cuadernos de Derecho Local, 0, 7–43.

Aguado i Cudolá, V. (2004). Hacia una nueva población local: El padrón como instrumento para la realización de políticas públicas y para el ejercicio de derechos de españoles y extranjeros. Anuario del Gobierno Local 2002. Barcelona: Institut de Dret Públic.

Aguado i Cudolá, V., & Cerrillo Martínez, A. (2005). *Las condiciones de vida de los inmigrantes.* Madrid: INAP.

Barnes Vázquez, J. (1998). Subsidiariedad y autonomía local en la Constitución. Anuario del Gobierno Local 1997. Barcelona: Institut de Dret Públic.

Barreta Bochaca, J. (2007). Continuidad y cambios en la gestión de la inmigración. Papers, 85, 71 ff.

Catalá i Bas, A. H. (2009). Inmigración y gobierno multinivel. In R. Tur Ausina (Ed.). *La integración de la población inmigrante en el marco europeo, estatal y autonómico español* (p. 35 ff). Madrid: Iustel.

Cebolla Boado, H., & González Ferrer, A. (2008). *La inmigración en España 2000–2007: De la gestión de flujos a la integración de inmigrantes.* Madrid: CEPC.

Fanlo Loras, A. (2006). La atribución de competencias a las entidades locales en la Ley estatal de régimen local. *El Consultor*, 7, 1429 ff.

Kadouci, N., & Neraudau, E. (2008). L'intégration des étrangers en France. In J. Blázquez Navarro (Ed.). *Regiones, Unión Europea e integración de inmigrantes* (p. 139 ff). Barcelona: Atelier.

Klopp, B. (2002). *German multiculturalism: Immigrant integration and the transformation of citizenship.* Westport, CT: Praeger.

López Cárcamo, Z. (2010). El programa común de integración de inmigrantes en el marco de la política común de inmigración legal. In S. Díez Sastre (Ed.). *Inmigración y gobiernos locales* (p. 17 ff). Madrid: Marcial Pons.

Michalowski, I. (2008). Modelos de acogida en Alemania, Francia y los Países Bajos: diseño y efectividad de los programas de acogida e integración. Documentos CIDOB. *Migraciones*, 12, 67 ff.

Mir i Bagó, J. (2002). Municipios e inmigración: Los ayuntamientos ante la nueva Ley de extranjería. Anuario del Gobierno Local 2001, Barcelona: Institut de Dret Públic.

Moya Malapeira, D. (2006). Immigració. In A. Galán Galán (Ed.). *La descentralització de competències de la Generalitat als ens locals de Catalunya* (Vol. 2). Barcelona: Fundació Carles Pi i Sunyer.

Ponce i Solé, J. (2002). *Poder local y guetos urbanos.* Madrid: INAP.

Tolivar Alas, L. (2009). Servicios sociales locales: competencias propias e impropias. *Revista de Estudios Locales*, 123, 16–33.

Velasco Caballero, F. (2010). Políticas y competencias locales sobre inmigración. In S. Díez Sastre (Ed.). *Inmigración y gobiernos locales* (p. 65 ff). Madrid: Marcial Pons.

Velasco Caballero, F. (2011). Un ejemplo de funcionamiento de la preemption norteamericana: la regulación de la inmigración. *Revista de Estudios Autonómicos y Federales*, 13, 11 ff.
Villaverde Menéndez, I. (2010). La inscripción de extranjeros en el padrón local: a propósito de la polémica decisión del Ayuntamiento de Vic. *El Cronista del Estado Social y Democrático de Derecho*, 12, 32 ff.

Comparative Notes on Local Government Involvement in Immigration

LAURIE REYNOLDS, UNIVERSITY OF ILLINOIS
AT URBANA-CHAMPAIGN FRANCISCO VELASCO CABALLERO,
AUTONOMOUS UNIVERSITY OF MADRID

In reality, local governments in both Spain and the United States are involved, more or less directly, in immigration affairs. Or perhaps it is more precise to say that local governments are becoming more involved in the lives of their immigrants. In both countries, local initiatives are usually undertaken at the city level, although counties in the U.S. also exercise certain authority, particularly with regards to police control of undocumented immigrants. While both countries show examples of local regulation of immigration, the concrete implementation of these policies contrasts sharply in terms of scope and substance.

In the U.S., direct local government involvement tends to focus only on undocumented immigrants, although a few large cities (such as New York, Seattle, or San Francisco) staff departments dealing with immigration affairs generally. When it comes to the initiatives adopted with respect to these undocumented immigrants, municipal policies in the U.S. vary greatly along the political spectrum. There are, for instance, the so-called Sanctuary cities, such as San Francisco or New Haven, Connecticut, that seek to protect the undocumented from federal arrest or removal actions. Other cities, in contrast, assume an anti-immigrant posture by restricting participation in the local housing or employment market to those immigrants who can document their legal presence in the country. This means that, in the U.S., local government involvement is limited in terms of its substance (in that it focuses almost exclusively on the regulation of undocumented immigrants), but broad in its politics, because a survey of these local ordinances reveals both anti-immigrant and pro-immigrant measures.

In contrast, Spanish local government involvement in immigration affairs covers a different spectrum. Local Spanish immigration policies are almost uniformly focused on the integration of immigrants. These policies entail substantial expenditures of public revenue and seek to promote the full inclusion of foreigners in the local community. Moreover, these pro-immigrant policies rarely distinguish between documented and undocumented immigrants. There are, of course, some local governments that seek to impose barriers to the integration of undocumented immigrants, but in Spain they are extremely rare. As a result, and in contrast to the U.S., Spanish local government activity involving immigration tends to be broad in scope of coverage (in that it extends to and applies to all immigrants regardless of their legal status in the country), but politically narrow, because the goal—almost always—is integration.

The differences between Spanish and U.S. local government regulation of immigrants result from the confluence of a number of factors: social, cultural, political, and legal. In terms of the legal constraints that apply, the scope of local power in the two countries is crucially different. The following paragraphs compare the ambit of local power in the two legal systems.

Local government power in immigration depends crucially on the constitutional distribution of powers. The following two observations explain the structural constitutional differences that are relevant to the shape of local power in Spain and in the U.S.

On the one hand, the Spanish and U.S. Constitutions display an extremely important difference in terms of the treatment and status of local governments. The U.S. federal Constitution only mentions two political entities—the federal government and the state governments; there is no explicit reference to local governments. As a result, local governments are deemed to be "creatures" of the state in which they are located (*Hunter v. Pittsburgh*, 1907), which means that their territorial jurisdiction and the scope of their powers are left to the legislative discretion of the state that created them. In Spain, in contrast, the Constitution directly recognizes the existence of local governments (which include municipalities, provinces, and islands) and specifically guarantees their existence and their autonomy (Article 137 of the Constitution and STC 32/1981). Moreover, according to a solid thread of constitutional jurisprudence, Spanish local government units are regulated directly both by the national government (which determines the basis of the local regulatory regime) and by the regional governments (which complement the national regulation). An obvious corollary of this initial distinction is the fact that Spanish local governments have a natural relationship with the federal government, while they enjoy a fair amount of autonomy from their regional governments (the Comunidades Autónomas, or autonomous communities).

In contrast, in the U.S., the relationship between the national government and local governments is less intense and less direct, and the city or county's autonomy from its creator state is, at least formally, extremely limited. This formal municipal dependence on the total power and control of the state, however, is softened by political reality. A strong national tradition of home rule, which transfers broad governing powers to municipal governments, provides a de facto political protection of local autonomy vis-à-vis state legislatures. These different local-subnational and local-national relationships in the two countries may partially explain why, in Spain, local immigration policies are subject to national control (and, to a lesser extent, the regional control of the Comunidades Autónomas), while in the U.S., local collaboration with federal immigration officials may be problematic if the state's attitude about immigration conflicts with federal policy.

In addition to the formal textual distinctions, the two legal systems apply different background legal principles and doctrinal concepts to define and shape the contours of local government powers. In Spain, local government power is defined by the concept of "strict competencies," which envisions an allocation of non-overlapping and distinct spheres of powers. In the Spanish system, therefore, the doctrine of preemption, which applies to resolve conflicting assertions of power, is of only minimal importance. In the U.S., however, the constitutional system envisions a more flexible and fluid allocation of powers among the federal, state, and local levels. In cases of conflict between and among regulations and laws promulgated at different levels, the higher sovereign's authority can displace or preempt the lower governments' legislative initiatives (U.S. Const., Article 6, Cl.2). This different articulation of the territorial substantive limits of government power in the two countries may have explanatory power for the differences in local government regulation of immigration, notwithstanding the fact that in both countries power over foreign affairs is explicitly conferred to the national or federal government (Spanish Constitution, Article 149.1.2. CE; U. S. Constitution, Article 1, §8, Cl.4).

In the U.S., local governments adopt a wide range of laws to regulate the living conditions of undocumented immigrants, well aware that a properly adopted state or federal law can displace or preempt the local initiative. In Spain, in contrast, cities do not directly or specifically regulate the living conditions of undocumented immigrants, because of the clear understanding that this subject matter falls exclusively within the national government's sphere of powers.

With these caveats, we can now analyze in detail the legal basis of local action dealing with immigration, both in Spain and the U.S. In neither of the two countries is any specific power over immigration transferred directly to the local level. In fact, in both countries, the subjects of foreign affairs and immigration are areas expressly reserved to the national government. Moreover, it is important to distinguish two different types of policies: those that control the migratory flows of immigrants, and those that deal with the integration of immigrants into local society.

The control of migratory flows, as such, is not a local power in either country. Nevertheless, local regulations that indirectly affect the movement of immigrants are frequently adopted in the U.S., where cities participate indirectly in the control of migratory flows in two different ways: by conditioning local permission or licenses on the legal immigration status of an individual; and second, by collaborating, or refusing to collaborate, with the federal government in its efforts to apprehend undocumented immigrants. This local activity reflects some of local governments' traditional powers and concerns—specifically, longstanding local interest in the character of the community, the ability to define the community it governs, and general police power to protect the health, safety, and welfare of the government's constituency.

In Spain, in contrast, municipalities do not engage in any activities that deal with migratory flows of people, either directly or indirectly. Spain's general Law of Foreign Affairs (Organic Law 4/2000, of January 11, dealing with the Rights and Liberties of Foreigners in Spain and their Social Integration) prohibits local government regulation that distinguishes between documented and undocumented immigrants. What Spanish local governments may do is to collaborate with the national government by filing individual reports that result in the granting of residency permits. These reports assist the national government's process by analyzing the immigrant's degree of connection and immersion in the community and the availability of living quarters for the individual. These actions are explicitly provided for in the Law of Foreign Affairs (Article 18.2 of Organic Law 4/2000).

In Spain, local integration of immigrants is an important—indeed pressing—policy; in the U.S., in contrast, it appears to be less well-developed. In Spain, local policies to promote the integration of immigrants are developed by numerous municipal departments (social services, housing, planning, education, etc.). Their legitimacy stems from general Spanish law, which authorizes municipalities to develop "complementary" policies consistent with other government laws and regulations, primarily at the national and regional level (Article 28 of Law 7/1985, April 2, which establishes the Bases of Local Regimes). Some large U.S. cities, similarly, have recently begun to develop policies and departments focused on integrating immigrants, both documented and undocumented; this innovation is not widespread and limited to a few particularly immigrant-friendly cities. As a matter of legality, these efforts appear to fit comfortably within the U.S. cities' home-rule powers and appear to stand on solid legal ground.

The legitimacy of at least some local government action dealing with immigration, both direct and indirect, appears well-established in both countries. As these policies are implemented, the local governments' relationships with central powers (the national governments) and subnational powers (U.S. state governments and Spanish regional governments, or the Comunidades Autónomas) vary in terms of their intensity.

The relationship between the national government and local governments in the area of immigration is clearly more intense in Spain than in the U.S. Keep in mind that in Spain, the local governments have direct relationships with both the national government and the regional governments. They are not simple "creatures" of a higher government unit, as they are in the U.S. In Spain, the national government imposes limits on municipal immigration policies in two ways: via the nationally promulgated "strategic plans of citizenship and integration"; and through the financial incentives offered for municipal projects that focus on the integration of immigrants. These multi-year strategic plans of citizenship and integration (currently 2011–2014) establish general objectives and preferred policies for the integration of immigrants. They are not plans connected with specific legislation, but the local governments that adapt their initiatives to these national plans find special and direct national funding available in the "Fund for Assistance for the Integration of Immigrants."

In addition, the municipal actions of collaboration with the national government in the area of migratory control are strictly controlled at the national level by the Spanish central state itself. There are obligatory steps to be adopted, and there is no room for municipal political autonomy. In contrast to the Spanish situation, the relationship between the national government and local governments in the U.S. is less intense. Municipal collaboration in the regulation of migratory flows (such as the federal program "E-Verify") is not required by federal law, but comes only as the result of voluntary municipal collaboration. Because the local governments are subordinate to the states in which they are located, it is not difficult to imagine an intrastate conflict between a state that objects to local participation in the federal program and a local government eager to collaborate with the national government. The legal issues raised by this scenario involve the very core of the U.S. federalist system, and it is unclear how they would be resolved.

The relationship between local governments and subnational governments (regional communities in Spain and states in the U.S.) is at first glance more intense in the U.S. than in Spain. In the U.S., the connection between states and their political subdivisions (local governments) is a hierarchical one, with local governments inferior to and dependent on their states for their every power. As a result, states have the formal power to impose a certain immigration policy (favorable or antagonistic to immigrants) on their cities and counties, so long as that state policy does not conflict with federal law. This currently occurs in some states, principally in the southern U.S., which purport to allow their local governments to assume indirect control over undocumented immigrants. Still unresolved by the Supreme Court's case law is the extent to which a municipal government can collaborate with federal immigration policies and regulatory schemes in the face of explicit state opposition.

In Spain, in contrast, the relationship between local governments and their regional autonomous communities is more relaxed and indirect. This follows logically from the earlier observations that Spanish local governments were not created by the regional governments, but rather exist as a partially autonomous subnational government unit (even with regard to those regional governments). At the same time, the strong direct ties between Spanish municipalities and the national government—not just in matters of immigration, but in general—has the indirect effect of weakening the local governments' relationship with the regional entities (Comunidades Autónomas). Formally, each Comunidad Autónoma has the power to supervise and direct local government activity through the adoption of laws and "plans for the integration of immigrants." But, to date, only two of a total of Spain's Comunidades Autónomas have adopted laws that explicitly regulate local government activity regarding the integration of immigrants. Moreover, the regional "plans for integration" are in reality an implementation of the "plans of citizenship and integration" adopted at the national level. Finally, the Comunidades Autónomas have not provided financial incentives for local implementation of these integration plans, which of course means that the plans are rarely adopted by the local governments.

PART TWO

CHAPTER THREE

Overview of the Rights of Unauthorized Immigrants in the United States

MATTHEW KUENNING, UNIVERSITY OF ILLINOIS AT URBANA-CHAMPAIGN

INTRODUCTION

My questions are very general: what rights do unauthorized immigrants have in the United States? What are the prospects for expanding or decreasing those rights in the future? Most of what follows addresses the first question. I conclude with some brief speculation about the second. Before beginning, I try to clarify the questions by defining my terms.

First, by "rights" I mean any sort of claim, entitlement, or the like, which may be recognized and enforced by courts in the U.S. Thus, I limit the discussion to the law. I won't be discussing any of the important questions about what is due to unauthorized immigrants as a matter of justice, morality, or principles of human rights that have not been written into law in the U.S. On the other hand, I do not limit the discussion to the constitutional rights of unauthorized immigrants. Any sort of law is good enough to make a right.

Of course having a right is not the same thing as having the power to enforce it. This chapter does not discuss important questions about the degree to which unauthorized immigrants lack the power to enforce what rights they do have. I only assume that unauthorized immigrants are not so powerless as to make idle discussion of their rights.

Second, by "unauthorized immigrant" I mean a person who resides in the U.S. who is (1) not a citizen or national of the U.S., and who is (2) present in the U.S.

in violation of the immigration laws, but (3) lacks any sort of official permission to remain. Some resident non-citizens are present in violation of the immigration laws but have official permission to remain. For example, aliens who entered illegally, but have bona fide asylum applications pending, or whose removal orders have been stayed, or who have been granted parole in place, are not unauthorized immigrants according to my usage. The question of what rights attach to the many forms of quasi-legal status possible under U.S. immigration law such as the ones just mentioned is beyond the scope of this chapter.

There are two main ways to be an unauthorized immigrant in the U.S. The first is to somehow enter the country without being inspected and admitted by an immigration officer, such as by crossing the border clandestinely. In the jargon of U.S. immigration law, these people are called EWIs, which stands for "Entered Without Inspection." The second way is to be inspected and admitted by an immigration officer, but then violate the terms of one's admission by, for example, being admitted as a B-2 "tourist" for six months but staying past that time, or by being admitted as an F-1 student to pursue a full-time course of study but then dropping out of school. People who become unauthorized immigrants by violating the terms of admission are usually called "overstays," though not all violations involve staying beyond a specified date of departure.

Finally, I use the word "unauthorized" to avoid the words favored by the opposing sides in the polemics about unauthorized immigration, namely "illegal" and "undocumented." By avoiding both words, I do not mean to say both sides are equally in the wrong. However, I do think using the polemical terms tend to impede reasonable discussion of the issues. For example, whatever the virtues of using the word "undocumented" may be, it is potentially misleading because it is possible to be an unauthorized immigrant but have valid immigration documents.

RIGHTS WITH RESPECT TO IMMIGRATION

It is tempting to say unauthorized immigrants have no rights with respect to immigration. After all, unauthorized immigrants by definition are present in the U.S. in violation of the immigration laws and lack any sort of official permission to remain. They are therefore subject to being forcibly removed because they are either "inadmissible" or "deportable."[1] However, it does not follow that whenever the agents of ICE[2] or the Border Patrol find someone they know to be an unauthorized immigrant, they may take him to the border or the airport and summarily expel him. Contrary to an analogy one often finds in the polemics, the law does not treat unauthorized immigrants like trespassers on private property. A landowner may summarily expel a trespasser provided he uses reasonable force to do it.[3] It is not so with unauthorized immigrants.

Depending on the circumstances, an unauthorized immigrant may be subject to "expedited" or summary removal.[4] In other cases, he may be entitled to full removal proceedings before an Immigration Judge.[5] In either event, the federal Constitution, as well as statutes and regulations, give him various rights. In general, all aliens in removal proceedings have a right to procedures that are fair and provide a reasonable opportunity for the alien to be heard.[6] However, what is fair and reasonable depends on the context, and as the name suggests, those aliens subject to "expedited" removal get much fewer procedural protections than those in full removal proceedings.

In addition to procedural rights, in many circumstances, unauthorized immigrants also have substantive rights with regard to immigration. Again, a full survey is not possible here, and a couple of examples will have to suffice. U.S. law provides for asylum, which includes relief from being removed from the U.S. and a pathway to lawful permanent resident status. Asylum is available to any alien, regardless of status, who is present in the U.S. or who arrives in the U.S., provided he alleges and proves the requisite facts.[7] Moreover, there are procedures designed to ensure aliens with bona fide asylum claims have an opportunity to present them. Thus, an unauthorized immigrant who would otherwise be subject to expedited removal is entitled to certain procedures if he expresses fear he will be persecuted or tortured in his country.[8] Nor are the rights available in removal proceedings limited to asylum and similar claims. Thus, for example, an unauthorized immigrant who has been continuously present in the U.S. for at least ten years, and who meets certain demanding criteria, may request that the Attorney General exercise his discretion to grant him lawful permanent resident status.[9]

Unauthorized immigrants also have immigration rights outside the context of removal proceedings. For example, an alien who overstays, but then enters into a bona fide marriage with a U.S. citizen, thereby becomes an "immediate relative" who is eligible for status as a lawful permanent resident.[10] As an immediate relative, the law permits him to "adjust status" to become a lawful permanent resident and thus legalize his presence without returning to his home country or suffering any other penalty or adverse consequence.[11] An EWI who marries a citizen acquires a different and less advantageous set of rights, but under certain circumstances she still might acquire lawful status based on the marriage.[12]

One last example: on June 15, 2012, President Obama's Secretary of Homeland Security, Janet Napolitano, declared that a large class of unauthorized immigrants who arrived in the U.S. as children would be granted "deferred action."[13] A grant of deferred action includes a limited assurance the alien will not be removed from the U.S. and, what is of overriding practical importance, permission to work. Strictly speaking, there is no right to deferred action because it is founded in the discretion of those who enforce the law to choose which lawbreakers to pursue and which to let go. No one has a right to be let go; no court will recognize and enforce such a claim. But the deferred action program resembles a right because it routinely and predictably provides benefits based on defined criteria that carve out a large class of eligible beneficiaries.

To attempt to explore all of the rights unauthorized immigrants have with respect to immigration would mean discussing a substantial part of immigration law itself. Suffice it to say that there are many such rights and the important task of identifying them and asserting them forms a large part of the practice of immigration lawyers in the U.S.

BASIC RIGHTS

Unauthorized Immigrants Have the Right to Go Into Court to Seek Redress of Wrongs

According to the definition I am using here, a right is something that may be recognized and enforced by a court. It follows that the right of access to the courts is the precondition for having other rights. Aliens generally enjoy access to the courts of the U.S. on an equal footing with other persons.

In *Yick Wo v. Hopkins*, the Supreme Court held that the Equal Protection clause of the Fourteenth Amendment applies to all "persons," notwithstanding their status as aliens:

> The rights of the petitioners...are not less because they are aliens and subjects of the emperor of China....The fourteenth amendment to the constitution is not confined to the protection of citizens. It says: "Nor shall any state deprive any person of life, liberty, or property without due process of law; nor deny to any person within its jurisdiction the equal protection of the laws." These provisions are universal in their application, to all persons within the territorial jurisdiction, without regard to any differences of race, of color, or of nationality; and the equal protection of the laws is a pledge of the protection of equal laws.[14]

Yick Wo involved a San Francisco city ordinance requiring laundries to be in buildings of brick or stone. The ordinance also permitted the City Council to waive the requirement. The waivers were always granted to whites, but always denied to Chinese. The Court held such discriminatory application of the law to be unconstitutional. The opinion makes no mention of the immigration status of Yick Wo or the other petitioner, but the language quoted above makes clear that all persons enjoy the protection of the Due Process and Equal Protection clauses.

One might then conclude that unauthorized immigrants, because they are "persons" entitled to the protection of the Constitution, would necessarily enjoy access to the courts.[15] However, the question is not so simple. Since *Yick Wo*, courts have in fact held, almost without exception, that unauthorized immigrants enjoy the same right of access to the courts to seek redress of wrongs as other persons. However, although the Equal Protection clause is sometimes cited in this context, the cases do not make clear whether the right of unauthorized immigrants to access the courts is rooted in the Constitution or in less fundamental law.

In the earlier cases, courts relied on statutes and the common law rather than expressly relying on constitutional guarantees to arrive at the result that unauthorized immigrants have access to the courts. For example, in *Janusis v. Long*, a tort case arising from an automobile accident, the Supreme Judicial Court of Massachusetts reasoned that presence in the U.S. in violation of the immigration statutes is not akin to the common law status of outlawry.[16] That is, to be present in violation of the immigration laws does not make one an outlaw in the literal sense of a person who stands outside the protection of the law.

In *Martinez v. Fox Valley Bus Lines*, the defendant argued that an unauthorized immigrant who is present in violation of federal immigration laws is barred from access to federal courts. A federal judge sitting in Chicago also framed the question (partially) in terms of outlawry:

> The position of the defendant is that if an alien citizen of a friendly country is unlawfully in the United States he may be despoiled of his property, contracts with him may be breached, that he may be unlawfully assaulted and injured, and that he is without redress, except as the authorities may choose to prosecute criminally anyone who, in his dealing with the alien, has violated some criminal law. I cannot agree with this contention.[17]

In sum, an unauthorized immigrant does enjoy the protection of the law. He is not an outlaw. Therefore he may come into court to invoke that protection.

However, neither *Janusis* nor *Martinez* holds that the reason why unauthorized immigrants are not outlaws is that they are "persons" as that term is used in the Fifth or Fourteenth Amendments. On the contrary, *Martinez* opines Congress could have made outlaws of unauthorized immigrants.

> Congress, had it seen fit so to do, might have provided that an alien making an illegal entry into the country should be denied all civil rights, and the protection of the Fourteenth and Fifth Amendments. Congress has not so acted.[18]

Instead of relying on the Constitution, both *Janusis* and *Martinez* merely reject the arguments offered by the respective defendants that the plaintiff's status as an unauthorized immigrant did make him an outlaw in some relevant sense. For example, *Martinez* reasoned that the plaintiff was not relevantly like an unregistered foreign corporation illegally doing business in Illinois, in that such a corporation will not be heard in Illinois courts because a statute says so, but no statute bars unauthorized immigrants from the courts of the U.S.[19]

Unusual among the earlier cases was *Coules v. Pharris*, in which the Supreme Court of Wisconsin held that the federal public policy, embodied in federal immigration law, of protecting citizens from competition in the labor market required denying unauthorized immigrants access to the courts of Wisconsin to recover unpaid wages.[20] The Wisconsin Court, in a tort case decided forty-five years later, overruled *Coules*.[21] The court in the latter case cited the Bible and the state constitution:

> There is no public policy that is served by refusing access to our courts to illegal aliens who are injured through the negligence of another. The source of our basic concepts of justice between people is that there should be even handed justice meted out to all. "Ye shall have one manner of law, as well for the stranger as for one of your own country." Leviticus 24:22.
>
> Our Wisconsin Constitution, Article I, Section 9 provides: "Remedy For Wrongs. Every person is entitled to a certain remedy in the laws for all injuries, or wrongs which he may receive in his person, property, or character; he ought to obtain justice freely, and without being obliged to purchase it, completely and without denial, promptly and without delay, conformably to the laws."
>
> Our law permits recovery for injuries negligently inflicted on one's person. The [Wisconsin] Constitution says every person, it does not limit its protection to citizens or aliens lawfully admitted. We hold that illegal aliens have the right to sue in the courts of the State of Wisconsin for personal injuries negligently inflicted upon them.[22]

This answers the question in Wisconsin. But the question remains whether the point extends to the use of the word "person" in the U.S. Constitution.

In *Moreau v. Oppenheim*—a business dispute between the French owners of Arabian horses and the owners of a Texas horse farm—the federal Fifth Circuit Court of Appeals went only so far as doubting, without deciding, whether the plaintiff's alleged status as illegal aliens would take them outside the protection of the Fourteenth Amendment and prevent them from coming into federal court.[23] The *Moreau* court then cited *Martinez* and other cases for the proposition that unauthorized immigrants are not outlaws.[24] On that basis the court rejected the argument that the plaintiffs could not claim damages based on the defendants' unjustified interference with the plaintiffs' business if the plaintiffs' ability to conduct that business depended on violating the immigration laws.[25] Unauthorized immigrants are not outlaws, but it remains to be seen whether and to what degree it lies within the power of Congress and the state legislatures to treat them as such if they so choose.

In this regard, the ultimate fate of one provision in recent legislation enacted in Alabama, known as H.B. 56, may prove very important. Section 27 of H.B. 56 purports to prohibit Alabama courts from enforcing contracts when one party to the contract is an unauthorized immigrant and the other party knew or had "constructive knowledge" of that fact.[26] The Eleventh Circuit Court of Appeals has invalidated Section 27, on the ground that it conflicts with federal immigration law.[27] The court reasoned that Section 27's clear purpose and effect is to make life so difficult for unauthorized aliens in Alabama that they will leave the state, so Section 27 intrudes on the exclusive authority of the federal government to expel aliens. But Section 27 has not been struck down on the ground that unauthorized aliens have a right to contract that is guaranteed by the Equal Protection clause of the Fourteenth Amendment or by the statute designed to enforce the Fourteenth Amendment.[28]

In sum, it has been clearly established for decades that unauthorized immigrants enjoy access to the courts and therefore have rights in the general sense that they have the ability to assert claims and have them enforced. It is not clear whether this is the case because the Constitution provides this right, or whether it is merely because unauthorized immigrants are not "outlaws." Unauthorized immigrants are not outlaws only because Congress and the legislatures of the states have not yet seen fit to declare that they are. This contrasts with the situation in the context of the criminal law, where it is clear that the rights of unauthorized immigrants are the same as other persons' rights because the Constitution guarantees it.

Unauthorized Immigrants Have the Same Rights as Others When Accused of a Crime

Since the case of *Wong Wing v. U.S.* in 1896, it has been clearly established that unauthorized immigrants who are accused of a crime enjoy the same procedural rights as all other criminal defendants.[29] *Wong Wing* involved Chinese laborers who became unauthorized immigrants by the operation of new legislation. The legislation had previously been challenged and upheld by a bitterly divided Court in *Fong Yue Ting v. U.S.*[30] *Wong Wing* was a challenge to a section of the same law, not at issue in *Fong Yue Ting*, which provided that Chinese laborers found to be present unlawfully could, prior to deportation, be imprisoned at hard labor for up to a year.

The Court held in *Wong Wing* that although Congress could provide for the detention of aliens to affect their removal from the U.S., and Congress could make it a crime to be unlawfully present, the Constitutional guarantee of due process prohibited that aliens be punished as criminals for unlawful presence unless the fact of guilt were established by a judicial trial.[31] The Court cited *Yick Wo* for the proposition that an alien is a "person" protected by the Due Process and Equal Protection clauses of the Fourteenth Amendment. The court reasoned that:

> Applying [*Yick Wo*'s] reasoning to the fifth and sixth amendments, it must be concluded that all persons within the territory of the United States are entitled to the protection guaranteed by those amendments, and that even aliens shall not be held to answer for a capital or other infamous crime, unless on a presentment or indictment of a grand jury, nor be deprived of life, liberty, or property without due process of law.[32]

Wong Wing has definitively settled that all the Constitutional rights of criminal defendants attach equally to unauthorized immigrants. Thus, for example, the right to Miranda warnings, which is rooted in the Fifth Amendment, applies even to an alien who was apprehended at the border in the act of trying to be admitted to the U.S. by fraud.[33]

In criminal cases, there is no distinction between unauthorized immigrants and other defendants. In civil cases, unauthorized immigrants are entitled to go into court on the same terms as others. What substantive rights they have when they get there will depend on the applicable laws and not on any broad principle that excludes them as a group or mandates that they must be treated the same as others. In the next two sections, I sample some of the more important of the particular rights the law allows or denies to unauthorized immigrants in the areas of public benefits, education, and the workplace.

PUBLIC BENEFITS

When dispensing public benefits, state and local governments generally may not discriminate against lawfully resident aliens.[34] However, where Congress authorizes or mandates denial of public benefits to a class of aliens, then it is permissible for the states to deny benefits. With certain exceptions, Congress has mandated that state and local governments deny public benefits to unauthorized immigrants.[35] The most important exceptions are for emergency medical care and other aid necessary for the protection of life and safety,[36] and for benefits provided under state laws that affirmatively make unauthorized immigrants eligible for benefits.[37] Thus, unauthorized immigrants generally have no right to publicly funded benefits.

Unauthorized Immigrants Have Access to Publicly Funded Emergency Medical Care

Federal law requires that "any individual" who appears at the emergency room of a hospital that participates in Medicaid must be examined and, if the individual has an emergency medical condition, must be treated until his condition is stabilized or he is appropriately transferred.[38] The law further provides that care provided to unauthorized immigrants may not be reimbursed through Medicaid benefits, except that Medicaid benefits may be paid for emergency medical care.[39] Thus, unauthorized immigrants have a right to emergency medical care at public expense. Unauthorized immigrants have no claim to non-emergency care unless, of course, they have insurance or can otherwise pay for it.

Case law has defined the scope of an emergency medical condition. Thus, for example, serious head injuries suffered in an automobile accident are emergency medical conditions, so that treatment is reimbursable under Medicaid, while chronic conditions resulting from the same accident are not.[40] On the other hand, long-term treatment for leukemia that had become acute by the time the patient went to the emergency room was a covered emergency condition.[41]

Unauthorized Immigrants are Generally not Eligible to Obtain Driver's Licenses

Driver's licenses are issued at the state level. If a state chooses to do so, it may refuse to issue a driver's license to unauthorized immigrants. Thus, for example, Georgia passed such a law in 2001, which withstood a challenge on Equal Protection and other grounds in *John Doe-2 v. Georgia Department of Public Safety.* The court reasoned that, while, in general, alienage classifications in state law may be suspect and therefore difficult to sustain if challenged, states need only a rational basis for discriminating against unauthorized immigrants.[42] The *Doe-2* court held Georgia could rationally deny driver's licenses to unauthorized immigrants because of the perceived risk that unauthorized immigrants were less likely to be financially responsible for accidents.[43] Thus states may, if they choose, deny driver's licenses to unauthorized immigrants.

As part of the REAL ID Act of 2005, Congress encouraged states to deny driver's licenses to unauthorized immigrants.[44] To date, thirty states have taken Congress's cue and denied driver's licenses to those who cannot demonstrate lawful presence. Consequently unauthorized immigrants generally have no right to drive in the U.S. and are subject to criminal prosecution if they do drive.

EDUCATION

The Equal Protection Clause Affords Unauthorized Immigrant Children the Right to Attend Public Primary and Secondary Schools

In *Plyler v. Doe* the Supreme Court invalidated a Texas statute requiring immigrant children who could not prove legal status to pay tuition, as it violated the Equal Protection Clause of the Fourteenth Amendment.[45] This case establishes some important principles, and the practical importance of its result—that basic education at public expense is open to all regardless of immigration status—is obvious. However, the reasoning of this case has little application outside the context of free basic education.

The Court first held that unauthorized immigrants are protected by the Equal Protection Clause in spite of the fact that, by its terms, it only applies to persons "within [the state's] jurisdiction."[46] Texas argued that unlawful immigration status put children outside the state's jurisdiction. Relying on *Yick Wo* and other cases, the Court held that phrase could not be read to exclude unauthorized immigrants without undermining the fundamental purpose of the Equal Protection Clause to abolish all invidious class and caste-based legislation.[47]

The Court next held that unlawful immigration status is not a suspect classification and that public education is not a fundamental right for purposes of the Equal Protection Clause.[48] Nevertheless, the Court held the law's discrimination against unauthorized immigrant children could not count as rational, and could not be upheld, unless it furthered a "substantial goal of the State."[49] The requirement of furthering a "substantial" goal is more stringent than the minimum test that applies to equal protection challenges, which is that the law in question be rationally related to a legitimate state interest.[50] *Plyler* reasoned that a law discriminating against unauthorized immigrant children should pass a stronger test because children are not responsible for their immigration status, and denial of access to basic education has particularly severe consequences.[51]

After concluding the Texas law must pass a more stringent test, the Court held that it could not meet that test. First, the fact that the children's presence in the U.S. is unlawful under federal law does not license state discrimination against the plaintiff children. Congress has not established a policy of denying education to those present unlawfully.[52] Second, Texas's rationale for the law is insufficient. Conserving public resources does not constitute a sufficient state interest to justify discrimination against illegal alien children, and the goals of warding off illegal immigration, reducing the burdens imposed by illegal immigrant children, and reserving education for those likely to remain in the state, were all examined and held to be insubstantial.[53]

As Chief Justice Burger predicted in his dissent, the nature of the Court's reasoning limits the importance of this case to the particular issue of public elementary and secondary education.[54] The points that the plaintiffs were children and that denial of basic education has severe consequences were crucial to the Court's reasoning, which means the case provides limited support for challenges to laws outside the area of education that impact unauthorized adults. On the other hand, *Plyler*'s holding that unlawful immigration status is not a suspect classification supports such laws.[55]

Unauthorized Immigrants in Most Instances Have Access to Public Higher Education, but on Generally Less Favorable Terms Than Others

Unauthorized immigrants are not eligible for federal financial aid to attend a post-secondary school, and in most states are not eligible for state financial aid. There is an ongoing dispute regarding the degree to which states may facilitate the access of unauthorized immigrants to their systems of higher education.

Federal law prohibits states from providing subsidized or "in-state" tuition on the basis of residence in the state to unauthorized immigrants, unless the same benefit is available to all U.S. citizens regardless of residence.[56] California grants in-state tuition to everyone who graduated from a high school in California, regardless of immigration status, provided the student attended high school in California for three years. California's law was challenged on the ground that it violates the federal law. The California Supreme Court upheld the California law, holding there is no conflict with the federal law because granting in-state tuition on the basis of high school attendance and graduation is not equivalent to granting that status "on the basis of residence."[57] The U.S. Supreme Court declined to accept the plaintiffs' appeal. Twelve other states—including other states with high immigrant populations such as Texas, New York, and Illinois—have laws similar to California's. In the remaining states, unauthorized immigrants are not eligible for in-state tuition.

A handful of states further restrict the access of unauthorized immigrants to public higher education, beyond the denial of in-state tuition. For example, in Virginia, as the result of an advisory opinion of the state's Attorney General, each institution is permitted to decide whether to enroll unauthorized immigrants. Virginia's policy to allow institutions to bar unauthorized immigrants has been upheld against various constitutional challenges at the level of the district court.[58]

The majority of states fall in the middle; they do not offer in-state tuition, but have no other bars to unauthorized immigrants.

WORKPLACE RIGHTS

Since 1986, it has been a violation of federal immigration law to knowingly hire or employ an unauthorized immigrant.[59] The law requires that, for each newly hired employee, the employer must attest on Form I-9 to have examined certain prescribed documents verifying that the employee is authorized to work, and employees must attest that they are so authorized.[60] Thus federal law prohibits unauthorized immigrants from being employed in the sense that, as a practical matter, it is impossible for an unauthorized immigrant to be employed unless either he or his employer violates the law.[61] However, from that fact it does not follow that unauthorized immigrants have no important workplace rights. With some exceptions, the rights that apply generally in the workplace also apply to unauthorized immigrants.

Numerous state and federal statutes prohibit employers from engaging in or permitting various kinds of discrimination and retaliation in the workplace. Unauthorized immigrants fall under the terms of these statutes; they are employees, too. However, often the most important remedy available to workers is back pay, which is pay the worker would have earned had his rights not been violated. It is logical to ask whether a worker who is not legally entitled to work qualifies for a remedy that looks to work he would have done. The leading case in this area is the Supreme Court's decision in *Hoffman Plastic Compounds v. NLRB*.[62]

Hoffman Plastic Held Unauthorized Immigrant May Not be Awarded Back Pay Under the NLRA

In *Hoffman Plastic*, the Supreme Court held that an employee's status as an unauthorized immigrant precluded an award of back pay as a discretionary remedy awarded by the National Labor Relations Board (NLRB) for the employee's discharge in violation of the National Labor Relations Act (NLRA). The Court had previously held in *Sure-Tan, Inc. v. NLRB* that unauthorized immigrants were "employees" protected by the NLRA, so an employer violated the NLRA when it reported unauthorized immigrant employees to the immigration authorities to retaliate for the workers' union activities.[63] *Sure-Tan* also held, however, that aliens are deemed "unavailable" to work, and are therefore not entitled to back pay, as to any period during which they were not in the U.S. and could not lawfully return.[64] In so holding, the Court reversed an award of six months back pay the lower court had fashioned as a compromise between the competing goals of, on the one hand, not rewarding violations of the immigration laws and, on the other, providing a remedy that would deter employers from violating the rights of unauthorized immigrants under the NLRA.[65]

Sure-Tan involved employees who had voluntarily departed to Mexico to avoid being deported after their employer turned them in to the Immigration and Naturalization Service. In *Hoffman Plastic*, the NLRB took the position that *Sure-Tan* should be limited to the situation in which the unauthorized worker is outside the U.S.[66] The Court rejected that view and instead reasoned that to award back pay to an alien who could not lawfully work in the U.S. would "unduly trench upon explicit statutory prohibitions critical to federal immigration policy," namely the prohibitions designed to discourage employment of unauthorized immigrants.[67] The Court reasoned that remedies other than back pay, such as an injunction ordering the employer to cease unfair labor practices, had also been applied and they would be enough to promote the purposes of the NLRA without conflicting with federal immigration policy.[68]

Hoffman Plastic expressly declined to revisit the holding of *Sure-Tan* that unauthorized immigrants are employees under the NLRA.[69] The only court to consider the question since has held that neither the rationale of *Hoffman Plastic* nor the fact that subsequent to *Sure-Tan* Congress made it unlawful to employ unauthorized immigrants is sufficient reason to alter the rule that unauthorized immigrants are employees under the NLRA.[70] Thus unauthorized immigrants continue to enjoy the right to form a union without suffering retaliation by their employers. But they must exercise that right without the threat of an award of back pay to enforce it.

Since *Hoffman Plastic*, a number of courts have addressed, in various contexts outside the NLRA, whether *Hoffman Plastic*'s rationale precludes awarding unauthorized immigrants remedies that are based in one way or another upon the immigrants' unlawful employment in the U.S. In almost every case, courts have held that the rule announced in *Hoffman Plastic* is limited to denying back pay under the NLRA. Therefore, in spite of *Hoffman Plastic*, unauthorized immigrants enjoy most, but not all, of the workplace rights other workers do.

Worker's Compensation Laws That Provide Disability Payments and Other Benefits to Workers Who are Injured on the Job Also Protect Unauthorized Immigrants

Courts both before and after *Hoffman Plastic* have generally held unauthorized workers are entitled to the benefit of both state and federal worker's compensation laws. For example, in a recent case, *Bollinger Shipyards, Inc. v. Director, Office of Workers Compensation Programs*, the Fifth Circuit upheld an award under a federal worker's compensation statute.[71] The court articulated three reasons why *Hoffman Plastic* did not mean unauthorized workers must be denied benefits if they are injured in the course of employment.

The court reasoned, first, that the worker's compensation statute in question made an award of benefits mandatory if the factual predicate were proved, while an award of back pay under the NLRA is discretionary.[72] Therefore, the purpose of the worker's compensation statute could only be fulfilled by awarding benefits; unlike *Hoffman Plastic*, there was no question of alternative remedies that would serve the purpose of the employment law without conflicting with immigration policy of discouraging unauthorized work.[73]

Second, the court reasoned that, because unauthorized immigrants have the right to sue in tort for negligence, they must have the right to recover under worker's compensation statutes. Worker's compensation laws provide workers benefits on a no-fault basis, and workers get these in exchange for the loss of the right to sue an employer for on-the-job injuries that were the employer's fault.[74] In other words, the court reasoned that if unauthorized workers are to lose the right to sue employers on a fault basis, as other workers have, then they must also have the same right to receive no-fault benefits that other workers have.

Third, worker's compensation benefits, unlike back pay, do not compensate for work that would have been performed unlawfully, but instead compensate for an injury.[75] In other words, worker's compensation is unlike the back pay at issue in *Hoffman Plastic* because it pays people for getting hurt, not for being fired.

In *Madeira v. Affordable Housing Foundation, Inc.*, the federal Second Circuit Court of Appeals reached a similar result in a case involving a New York worker's compensation statute.[76] In addition to arguments similar to those in *Bollinger*, *Madeira* reasoned that the wrong to be remedied by the back pay award in *Hoffman Plastic* was the unlawful discharge of the employee, and discharging an unauthorized immigrant is required under the immigration laws once the employer knows the employee's immigration status.[77] By contrast, the wrong to be remedied in a worker's compensation case is a personal injury, and of course the immigration laws do not in any way require or authorize employers to physically injure unauthorized workers.[78]

It is worth noting that the defendant in *Bollinger* made arguments similar to those made in earlier cases that unauthorized immigrants are a species of outlaw who cannot claim the protection of the courts. The defendant compared an unauthorized immigrant who claims compensation for a workplace injury suffered while working in violation of the immigration laws to a drug dealer or a pirate claiming compensation for loss of the ability to carry on his trade.[79] The court does not bother to answer this argument, except to dismiss it as "histrionic" and "melodramatic."[80]

Courts have carved out one exception to the general rule that unauthorized workers are entitled to worker's compensation, namely that unauthorized workers are not entitled to benefits designed to prepare them for alternative employment in the U.S. where such employment would violate federal immigration law.[81]

Unauthorized Immigrants Have the Right to be Paid the Legally Mandated Wages for Work Done

The federal Fair Labor Standards Act (FLSA) and similar state statutes mandate a minimum wage and require extra wages for overtime work.[82] Courts have uniformly held that unauthorized immigrants are entitled to back pay under the FLSA.[83]

A recent opinion in this line of cases, *Lin v. Chinatown Restaurant Corp.*, is especially interesting because it collects and examines what the court took to be the five reasons that have been offered in previous cases for the rule that unauthorized immigrants may be awarded back wages under the FLSA, as well as other workplace rights, and found all five wanting.[84] For example, *Lin* rejects the argument that denying workplace rights to unauthorized immigrants will make them more attractive to employers and therefore encourage illegal employment. After pointing out that the same argument had been raised by the dissent and rejected by the majority in *Hoffman Plastic*, *Lin* suggests that the argument cuts both ways: if a smaller bundle of workplace rights makes unauthorized workers more attractive to employers, it makes unauthorized work less attractive to employees.[85] *Lin* may be wrong on this point, but the argument at least shows there is an unanswered empirical question about the effect of workplace rights on unauthorized employment. Instead of the arguments the court found in the cases, *Lin* relied on the plain language of the statute, which makes an award of unpaid wages mandatory when a violation of the FLSA has been proved.[86]

On the closely related issue of whether unauthorized immigrants are entitled to recover under state wage payment laws, courts have also generally held that they are.[87] In *Coma Corp. v. Kansas Dept. of Labor*, the Kansas Supreme Court upheld an award of unpaid wages and a penalty against the employer by holding, first, that unauthorized workers are "employees" entitled to relief under the Kansas statute, and second that the Kansas statute as so construed is not preempted by federal immigration law.[88] The Kansas court followed *Madeira* and other cases to hold that the rationale of *Hoffman Plastic* does not mean that states are generally precluded from providing benefits to all employees, including unauthorized immigrants.[89]

The Kansas court went on to discuss whether the employment contract between the parties was void and unenforceable because it was illegal under federal immigration law. The particular wording of the Kansas statute made important the question of whether the employment contract was lawful. The court reasoned, *inter alia*, that to make such employment contracts void for illegality would contravene a strong public policy of the state that wages should be paid for work performed.[90] With the notable exception of the early, and subsequently overruled, case of *Coules v. Pharris*, courts have rejected the contention that unauthorized immigrants cannot enter into valid contracts of employment and are not entitled to their wages.[91]

Unauthorized Immigrants Have no Right to Unemployment Insurance

Federal law prohibits payment of unemployment insurance to unauthorized immigrants.[92] Unemployment insurance is administered at the state level. Every state, by law or regulation, prohibits payment of benefits to unauthorized immigrants. For example, in Illinois an alien worker must either be a lawful permanent resident or be permanently residing in the U.S. under color of law.[93]

The phrase "permanently residing under color of law" generally includes those aliens excluded from my definition of "unauthorized" because, although they lack lawful status under the immigration laws, they nevertheless have some form of official permission to remain in the U.S. Thus, for example, an EWI (someone who entered without inspection), but who has pending a bona fide application for asylum may be eligible to work in the U.S. and may be eligible to collect unemployment if he becomes unemployed.

In sum, unauthorized immigrants enjoy many rights in the workplace, albeit not all of the rights enjoyed by others. There is no general rule against workplace rights for unauthorized immigrants, in spite of the fact that federal law prohibits employing them. They are not "outlaws" in this area.

CONCLUSION: IN THE FORESEEABLE FUTURE, THE RIGHTS OF UNAUTHORIZED IMMIGRANTS WILL EXPAND OR CONTRACT BY SMALL STEPS

As shown earlier, the rights of unauthorized immigrants are to be found in the details of the law. Only a general reform could establish principles governing the treatment of unauthorized immigrants. It is, in general, true that unauthorized immigrants have access to the courts and therefore they may seek to recover damages for torts and sue to enforce contracts on the same terms as other people. But the opinions in most of these cases make clear that the unauthorized immigrant's rights depend on the specific language of the applicable statutes and regulations.

It appears unlikely Congress will act in the foreseeable future to expand the rights of unauthorized immigrants in any way. The prospects are especially dim now for any "amnesty" that will permit any significant subset of unauthorized immigrants to attain legal status. At the time of this writing, President Obama and his supporters in Congress appear unable to enact comprehensive immigration reform that would include an amnesty. Thus, for the foreseeable future, any expansion of rights for unauthorized immigrants will only be achieved by small steps.

On the other hand, it is possible some states may continue to try to reduce the rights of unauthorized immigrants. Because courts have not yet raised the legal principle that unauthorized immigrants are not outlaws to the status of a Constitutional rule, it is both legally and politically possible under current conditions for some state and local legislatures to take away large bundles of rights from unauthorized immigrants all at once. The contracts provision of Alabama's immigration law, discussed earlier, is an example.[94] If the U.S. Supreme Court were to uphold it or uphold a similar law, that would effectively strip the right to make contracts with unauthorized immigrants in any state that chose to enact such a law. Unauthorized immigrants would become outlaws, if only with respect to the law of contracts.

Of course, if the Supreme Court were to strike down such a contracts provision by holding that the Constitution forbids treating unauthorized immigrants as outlaws precisely because they are persons entitled by the Constitution to the equal protection of the laws, then legislation like the Alabama contract provision will be permanently blocked. The rights of unauthorized immigrants would then be significantly expanded through judicial decision.

NOTES

1. See 8 U.S.C. §§ 1182(a) and 1227(a).
2. ICE stands for Immigration and Customs Enforcement, the internal immigration police.
3. See, e.g., the Illinois statute on this point, 720 ILCS 5/7-3.
4. See 8 U.S.C. § 1225(b)–(c).
5. See 8 U.S.C. § 1229a.
6. *Jacinto v. INS*, 208 F.3d 725, 727 (9th Cir. 2000).
7. 8 U.S.C. § 1158(a)(1).
8. See 8 C.F.R. § 235.3(b).
9. 8 U.S.C. § 1229b(b). Similar to deferred action, discussed infra, there is no right to the relief provided by this statute, which is known as "cancellation of removal" or COR. The decision whether to grant or deny the relief to an eligible unauthorized immigrant is entrusted by statute to the discretion of the Attorney General (which means to the Immigration Judge and the members of the Board of Immigration Appeals appointed by the Attorney General) and there is no right, in the sense of a claim enforceable in court, to a favorable exercise of that discretion. However, if an unauthorized immigrant is eligible, he does have a right to have the Attorney General's discretion exercised in his case, whether favorably or unfavorably. COR is not the only form of discretionary relief available to unauthorized immigrants.
10. 8 U.S.C. § 1151(b)(2)(A)(i).
11. 8 U.S.C. § 1255(a) and (c).
12. See 8 U.S.C. §n1255(a), which requires an alien be inspected and admitted or paroled into the United States to be eligible to "adjust status." Aliens who are eligible to become lawful permanent residents but who are not eligible to adjust status may obtain their permanent residency only by applying abroad at a U.S. consulate for an immigrant visa.
13. See www.uscis.gov/childhoodarrivals
14. *Yick Wo v. Hopkins*, 118 U.S. 356, 368–369 (1886).
15. 42 U.S.C. § 1981 was enacted to implement the Equal Protection Clause of the Fourteenth Amendment. Section 1981(a) provides that, "All persons within the jurisdiction of the United States shall have the same right in every State and Territory to make and enforce contracts, to sue, be parties, give evidence, and to the full and equal benefit of all laws and proceedings for the security of persons and property as is enjoyed by white citizens, and shall be subject to like punishment, pains, penalties, taxes, licenses, and exactions of every kind, and to no other."
16. *Janusis v. Long*, 284 Mass. 403, 188 N.E. 228 (1933).
17. *Martinez v. Fox Valley Bus Lines*, 17 F. Supp. 576, 577 (N.D. Ill. 1936). I have to say "partially" because the common law concept of outlawry also put the subject outside the protection of the criminal law. The defendant in *Martinez* apparently was not willing to go that far.
18. 17 F. Supp. at 577.
19. 17 F. Supp. at 578.
20. *Coules v. Pharris*, 212 Wis. 558, 250 N.W. 404 (1933).

21. *Arteaga v. Literski*, 83 Wis.2d 128, 265 N.W.2d 148 (1978).
22. *Arteaga*, 83 Wis.2d at 132–133.
23. *Moreau v. Oppenheim*, 663 F.2d 1300, 1307–1308 (5th Cir. 1981).
24. 663 F.2d at 1308.
25. Id.
26. Alabama H.B. 56 § 27(a) is codified at Ala. Code § 31-13-26(a). It provides in pertinent part that, "No court of this state shall enforce the terms of, or otherwise regard as valid, any contract between a party and an alien unlawfully present in the United States, if the party had direct or constructive knowledge that the alien was unlawfully present in the United States at the time the contract was entered into, and the performance of the contract required the alien to remain unlawfully present in the United States for more than 24 hours after the time the contract was entered into or performance could not reasonably be expected to occur without such remaining." The rest of Section 27 provides certain exceptions and qualifications.
27. *United States v. Alabama*, 691 F.3d 1269, 1292 ff. (11th Cir. 2012).
28. See 42 U.S.C. § 1981(a). The federal district court for the Northern District of Alabama rejected this claim in No.11-cv-02484, in its Memorandum Opinion and Order of September 28, 2011 at 90–93.
29. *Wong Wing v. U.S.*, 163 U.S. 228 (1896).
30. *Fong Yue Ting v. U.S.*, 149 U.S. 698 (1893).
31. 163 U.S. at 235–237.
32. 163. U.S. at 238.
33. *U.S. v. Henry*, 604 F.2d 908, 914 (5th Cir. 1979).
34. *Graham v. Richardson*, 403 U.S. 365 (1971).
35. 8 U.S.C. § 1621.
36. 8 U.S.C. 1621(b).
37. 8 U.S.C. § 1621(d).
38. 8 U.S.C. § 1395dd.
39. 42 U.S.C. 1396b(v).
40. *Greenery Rehabilitation Group, Inc. v. Hammon*, 150 F.3d 226, 232–33 (2d Cir.1998).
41. *Szewczyk v. Department of Social Services*, 275 Conn. 464, 881 A.2d 259, 273–274 (2005).
42. *John Doe-2 v. Georgia Dept. of Public Safety*, 147 F. Supp. 2d 1369 (N.D. Ga. 2001).
43. *Doe-2*, 147 F. Supp. 2d at 1376.
44. P.L. 109–13 § 202 et seq.
45. *Plyler v. Doe*, 457 U.S. 202 (1982).
46. 457 U.S. at 213.
47. 457 U.S. at 211–213.
48. 457 U.S. at 224.
49. Id.
50. See, e.g., 457 U.S. at 216.
51. 457 U.S. at 218–223.
52. 457 U.S. at 226.
53. 457 U.S. at 228–230.
54. 457 U.S. at 243.
55. See note 46 *supra*.
56. 8 U.S.C. § 1623.
57. *Martinez v. Regents of the University of California*, 50 Cal. 4th 177, 241 P.3d 855 (2010).

58. *Equal Access Educ. v. Merten*, 305 F. Supp. 2d 585 (E. D. Va. 2004).
59. 8 U.S.C. § 1324a(a)(1).
60. 8 U.S.C. § 1324a(b).
61. Congress did not, however, directly prohibit work by unauthorized immigrants. Many courts have given this fact some weight in holding that unauthorized immigrants have workplace rights.
62. *Hoffman Plastic Compounds, Inc. v. NLRB*, 535 U.S. 137 (2002).
63. *Sure-Tan, Inc. v. NLRB*, 467 U.S. 883, 891–892 (1984).
64. *Sure-Tan*, 467 U.S. at 903.
65. *Sure-Tan*, 467 U.S. at 904.
66. *Hoffman Plastic*, 535 U.S. at 147.
67. *Hoffman Plastic*, 535 U.S. at 151.
68. 535 U.S. at 152.
69. 535 U.S. at 149, n. 4.
70. *Agri Processors Co. v. NLRB*, 514 F.3d 1, 8 (D.C. Cir. 2008).
71. *Bollinger Shipyards, Inc. v. Director, Office of Workers Compensation Programs*, 604 F.3d 864 (5th Cir. 2010).
72. *Bollinger*, 604 F.3d at 877.
73. Id.
74. *Bollinger*, 604 F.3d at 878.
75. *Bollinger*, 604 F.3d at 879.
76. *Madeira v. Affordable Housing Foundation, Inc.*, 469 F.3d 219 (2d Cir. 2006).
77. *Madeira*, 469 F.3d at 247.
78. Id.
79. *Bollinger*, 604 F.3d at 871.
80. Id.
81. E.g. *Ortiz v. Cement Products, Inc.*, 708 N.W.2d 610 (Neb. 2005); *Tarango v. State Industrial Ins. System*, 25 P.3d 175 (Nev. 2001).
82. 29 U.S.C § 201 et seq.
83. See, e.g., *Lin v. Chinatown Restaurant Corp.*, 771 F. Supp. 2d 185 (D. Mass. 2011), cases cited therein.
84. *Lin*, 771 F. Supp. 2d at 186–189.
85. *Lin*, 771 F. Supp. 2d at 189, citing *Singh v. Jutla & C.D. & R's Oil, Inc.*, 214 F. Supp. 2d 1056, 1062 (N.D. Cal. 2002).
86. *Lin*, 771 F.Supp.2d at 189–190.
87. See, e.g., *Coma Corp. v. Kansas Dept. of Labor*, 154 P.3d 1080 (Kan. 2007).
88. *Coma Corp.*, 154 P.3d at 1083–1087.
89. Id.
90. *Coma Corp.*, 154 P.3d 1088–1093.
91. See, e.g., *Gates v Rivers Constr. Co., Inc.*, 515 P.2d 1020, 1023 (Alaska 1973). In this case the employer knew the alien was working in violation of his immigration status, and that fact played a role in the court's reasoning. However, the court reasoned also that to allow employers to exploit unauthorized immigrants by refusing to pay wages would encourage the employment of unauthorized immigrants.
92. 26 U.S.C. § 3304(a)(14)(A).
93. 56 Ill. Admin. Code 2905.
94. See note 26 supra and related text.

CHAPTER FOUR

Legal Status of Immigrants

Rights for Illegal Immigrants?

TOMÁS DE LA QUADRA-SALCEDO JANINI,
AUTONOMOUS UNIVERSITY OF MADRID

INTRODUCTION

This work aims to analyze the rights of a particular group of aliens as recognized by Spanish law: those that currently live in the country and are unauthorized to do so. To this end we will study the rights that are granted to aliens without legal residency in Spain, both according to the Constitution and to the rest of Spanish law. Firstly, however, we must examine the conditions that must be met for an alien to be able to live in Spain legally, since it is the non-fulfillment of these conditions that determines whether residency is unauthorized or illegal.

With regard to aliens from outside the European Union and the European Economic Area,[1] on whom our study is centered, the conditions necessary for obtaining legal residency are governed by Organic Law 4/2000 of January 11, on the rights and freedoms of aliens in Spain and their social integration (henceforth referred to as "Immigration Law"), which was modified by Organic Law 8/2000 of December 22, Organic Law 14/2003 of November 20, Organic Law 2/2009 of December 11, and Organic Law 10/2011 of July 27, among others.

In the Immigration Law mentioned above, which lists the requirements for legally entering national territory, three general situations in which an alien can legally reside in Spain are also given: temporary stay, temporary residency, and permanent residency[2]. Temporary stay refers to the act of remaining in Spanish territory for a period of no more than ninety days. Once this period has lapsed, an extension of the stay or an authorization of residency must be obtained in order to remain in Spain. Temporary residency refers to the situation in which an individual is authorized to remain in Spain for more than ninety days and less than five years. Permanent residency refers to the authorization to live in Spain indefinitely and work with the same conditions as Spanish nationals. Following the amendments of Law 2/2009 of December 11, permanent residency is now referred to as long-term residency.

In order to be included in each one of these three categories, a series of requirements must be met. To obtain authorization for temporary stay, the alien should be in possession of a valid visa, except in cases in which this is not deemed necessary in international agreements signed with Spain. The alien must also present the documents deemed necessary by law that justify the aims and conditions of her stay, and provide proof that she is in possession of sufficient means of living for the period to be spent in Spain. To obtain temporary residency, the alien either should provide proof that she has sufficient means to meet any living and accommodation expenses, including, if necessary, those of her family, throughout the period for which residency is requested without needing to undertake any professional activity during her stay, or declare intention to work as self-employed or employed if she has obtained authorization to work.[3] The law therefore states that, in order to reside temporarily in Spain, the applicant must either have the sufficient economic means to do so or undertake gainful activity on the condition that the corresponding work permit is obtained. To obtain permanent residency (now referred to as long-term residency), the applicant must have temporarily resided in the country for a continued period for five years.

If the requirements detailed above are not met, the residency of an alien in Spanish territory is not considered legal. The recognition by legislation of the legal residency of aliens has an important consequence: the legal affirmation of aliens with legal residency to access, in addition to civil rights, many social rights in equal measure as Spanish nationals.[4] Nonetheless, it is important that we ask ourselves what rights aliens without legal residency are entitled to under Spanish legislation. We will now look at what the Constitution and the rest of the law say, implicitly and explicitly, about the rights of unauthorized immigration.

THE CONSTITUTION AND THE RIGHTS OF UNAUTHORIZED IMMIGRANTS

Let us firstly examine what the Constitution states with regards to the rights of unauthorized immigrants. In accordance with Article 13.1 of the Constitution "aliens shall enjoy the public freedoms guaranteed by the present Title [Title 1], under the terms to be laid down by treaties and the law."

In its early judgment 107/84 of November 23, the Constitutional Court established a three-fold classification regarding the rights of aliens, upon stating "there are rights that apply equally to Spaniards and to aliens and whose regulation must be the same for both—all those rights directly linked to human dignity would form part of this group[5]. Certain rights, however, do not apply in any way to aliens, such as those recognized in Article 23 of the Constitution[6] (with the exception of the contents of Article 13.2[7] SC). Other rights will or will not apply to immigrants depending on the terms of the international treaties and laws, and in such cases it is acceptable for the treatment of aliens to differ from that of Spanish nationals"[8].

In 2007, the Constitutional Court had the opportunity to make itself heard regarding the constitutional rights of unauthorized immigrants in eight judgments gathered under the heading Judgment 236/2007 of November 7. The Court declared in this judgment that "even though the Constitution does not distinguish between aliens depending on the regularity of their stay or residence in Spain, it may however be constitutional for the law to address this difference in order to configure the legal status of aliens, provided that in doing so no constitutional precepts or rights are violated" (LC 2). The Court states that Article 13.1 SC (of the Spanish Constitution) "refers to all aliens, as opposed to persons of Spanish nationality, despite the fact that they may find themselves in Spain in a variety of different legal situations."

The Court deems that "the entitlement and exercise of the fundamental rights of aliens in Spain should be assumed from the precepts contained in Title 1, interpreted systematically. In order to determine these, firstly it is necessary to address every precept recognising rights included in this Title, given that the problem of their entitlement and exercise depends on the affected right.... And secondly, the regulation contained in Article 13 CE" (LC 3).

According to the Constitutional Court "the non-compliance with the requirements of aliens remaining or residing in Spain does not permit the legislature to deprive them of the rights that correspond to them constitutionally in their capacity as persons, irrespective of their administrative situation." However, "failure to comply with those legal requirements prevents aliens from exercising specific rights or contents thereof which, by their very nature, are incompatible with an unauthorized situation" (LC 4). When it comes to unauthorized immigrants, then, the Court seems to differentiate between the rights that correspond to them as persons and other kinds of rights.

With regard to these first rights, those which are essential in order to guarantee human dignity, the Court states that the legislature cannot modulate or adjust their content, nor in any way deny their exercise by aliens, whatever their situation may be, since these are rights that "belong to the person as such and not as a citizen." The Court reminds us that when it comes to these rights, it is not possible to treat immigrants differently from Spaniards since they are entitled to exercise such rights "in conditions fully comparable [to those of Spaniards]" (LC 3).[9] According to the Court "the degree of connection of a specific right with dignity should be determined on the basis of its content and nature, which will, in turn, permit specification of the extent to which it is essential for the dignity of a person, following in this case the Universal Declaration of Human Rights and the treaties and international agreements referred to in Article 10.2 CE" (LC 3).

With regards to the remaining rights, those which are apparently not as essential in order to guarantee the dignity of a person, the Constitutional Court distinguishes between those which the Constitution attributes directly to aliens and those which the Court Constitution does not directly attribute to aliens. Only the latter can be denied to unauthorized immigrants.

For the identification of the first kind of rights, that is, those accorded to aliens *ex constitutione*, the Constitutional Court states that "the terms of the precepts of Title 1 recognizing the rights referred to in Article 13.1 SC should be particularly taken into account, amongst other criteria, since these refer normally to their holders using different expressions ('all,' 'all persons,' 'Spaniards,' 'no one,' 'citizens') or by employing impersonal formulas ('it is recognized,' 'it is guaranteed')" (LC 4). When it comes to these rights, "the law cannot deny such rights to aliens, although it can establish 'additional conditioning factors' with respect to their exercise by aliens" as long as the essential content of the right is respected.[10] Judgment 236/2007 states that the law can establish specific conditions for unauthorized aliens with regards to these rights, as long as the aforementioned limits are adhered to.

In terms of those rights that are not attributed directly to aliens by the Constitution—such as the right to work,[11] the right to receive unemployment benefits,[12] or the right to freedom of movement and residence[13]—but which are only granted constitutionally to Spaniards, the law is not obliged to recognize these as rights for aliens. However, it may extend them to non-nationals, although it may not do so in the same terms as those described for Spaniards. The court states, precisely regarding this group of rights, that "the legislature may take into account the facts of their legal and administrative status in Spain, and demand that aliens obtain authorization for their stay or residence as a requisite for the exercise of constitutional rights which, by their very nature, make it impossible to fulfill the requirements that the same law has established for entering and remaining in Spanish territory. This option is not constitutionally illegitimate" (JCC 107/1984). This was previously established by the Constitutional Court itself, for example, with regards to the requirement for administrative authorization for residence in order to recognize the capacity to enter a valid work contract.

With respect to this group of rights, the freedom of the law would, however, be restricted by the international agreements signed by Spain, and also by the principle of proportionality.[14] In accordance with Judgment 236/2007, "the conditions for the exercise of the rights established by the law shall be designed to preserve other rights, property or interests which are constitutionally protected, and to preserve adequate proportionality with the intended purpose," without this limitation for the law specifically referring, in this case, to any of the groups of rights studied.

However, once this classification was established, academic criticism has argued that when it was applied practically by the Constitutional Court to the different legal precepts contested in Judgment 236/2007, it lost relevance, because the Court ended up linking human dignity with all the constitutional rights generally granted to aliens. As a result, the argument regarding dignity lost its power to make distinctions.[15] For each right the legislature was granted a different amount of freedom in its configuration, as a function of a criterion that the Court had not sufficiently explained and that some authors attributed to the flexible criterion of having a greater or lesser connection to the right to human dignity.[16]

Academic criticism has argued that the Constitutional Court does not explain why in some cases, for example, when it comes to the regulation of rights to assembly,[17] association,[18] and unionization,[19] the legislature's freedom to differentiate between Spaniards and aliens is greater than in other cases, such as those that regulate rights to education,[20] effective judicial protection,[21] and personal freedom.[22]

In this way, the Constitutional Court deems that the legislature can set specific conditions for the exercise of rights to assembly and freedom of association for unauthorized immigrants in Spain, as long as the content of those rights is respected, to the degree the Constitution guarantees those rights to all persons, whatever situation they may find themselves in. In the case of such rights, unauthorized immigrants in Spain are not constitutionally granted equal treatment.

On the other hand, the Constitutional Court believes that the right to non-compulsory education for children under eighteen should be recognized for unauthorized immigrants under the same terms as for Spaniards, since this a right that "all" are entitled to, whether they are nationals or aliens, and whatever their legal situation in Spain.[23]

Lastly, without examining Judgment 236/2007, in these pages it is possible to raise the question regarding the entitlement of constitutional social rights, recognized fundamentally in Chapter 3 of Title 1 under the section on "the governing principles of social and economic policy." Some authors have posed the question as to whether aliens should be entitled *ex constitutione* to this entitlement. Let us remember that "the governing principles" have a different legal regime from that of the fundamental rights, since they are not directly enforceable by the courts, despite the fact that they are binding mandates for public powers exercising their competences.[24]

Academic criticism disagrees as to whether aliens should be entitled to the social rights detailed in Chapter 3 of Title 1 of the Constitution as those rights have been developed by the legislature. In this way, Vidal would exclude the application of Article 13 of the Constitution from the rights of Chapter 3 and would, therefore, maintain that the law is free to extend or withhold these rights to aliens or, depending on the circumstances, to a determined group of aliens. From this point of view, aliens would not possess any rights when it comes to social rights. In addition, should their entitlement to these rights be recognized, the legislature would be free to establish requirements as it sees fit, and to distinguish between different groups of aliens.[25]

Goig, however, is of the opinion that in Article 13.1 the Constitution recognizes that aliens are entitled to the rights and freedoms listed in Title 1 of the Constitution, including "the governing principles of social and economic policy," although these would need to be developed by legislation.[26] Likewise, Roig believes that the principle of equality of Article 14 would suppose extending the entitlement to social rights to aliens, making the constitutional protection of aliens equal to that of nationals with no differences other than those that are strictly necessary and proportionate to the intended purpose, for example, the aims of immigration policy.[27]

In the absence of a clear jurisprudential procedure regarding the entitlement of "the governing principles of social and economic policy" once they have been implemented, an analysis of the infraconstitutional legal system is required. As a result of recent cutbacks and the new obstacles in the access to social rights for unauthorized immigrants, the question as to whether the Constitution prohibits the reduction of the protection already agreed upon has arisen. This prohibition would be based on the so-called principle of non-regression.

STATUTES OF AUTONOMY AND THE RIGHTS OF UNAUTHORIZED IMMIGRANTS

Firstly, we must analyze the Statutes of Autonomy and what they state regarding entitlement of the different rights that they recognize. We should remember that the Spanish Constitution entrusts the Statutes of Autonomy with shaping territorial distribution of power by assigning them the role of fixing the responsibilities of respective autonomous regions within the framework of the Constitution.[28]

The majority of the Statutes of Autonomy modified in the 8th legislature (2004–2008) include a table of rights in their provisions. Together with these tables of rights in the Statutes, the two main innovations of these statutory reforms are:

1) The attempt to convert many of the social rights gathered in these tables into true legal rights directly enforceable by the ordinary judicial courts.
2) The attempt to guarantee access to the rights and social benefits to all people equally.

However, both innovations were deemed to be unconstitutional by the Constitutional Court in Judgments 247/2007 and 31/2010. Let us put aside our discussion of the first innovation[29] for the time being and focus our attention on the second (in the following section) and how it has been stripped of its authority by the Constitutional Court in its judgment 31/2010 (in the next section).

The Failed Statutory Attempt to Guarantee Equal Access to Social Rights for all People

The right for aliens, whether or not their residence in Spain is authorized, to receive the same treatment as Spaniards in their access to social rights and benefits would have been recognized, in the case of certain autonomous regions, by establishing this right in the new Statutes of Autonomy.[30] Some of the new Statutes of Autonomy did indeed recognize certain social rights for all people in equal measure. The recognition in the Statutes of Autonomy of the right to access social services and benefits for all people equally—compared with the recognition of that same right in the Immigration Law, the General Law of Health, or the different regional laws on social services, for example—would bring about a greater guarantee of this right. This is due to its inclusion in the Statute of Autonomy, a law that carries particular weight due to the fact its reform would require the renewal of the "political agreement between the autonomous region and the Spanish State,"[31] which grants to the statutory content special protection against regional laws and the laws of the central state.

This "protective armor" for social rights for all people is seen in the new Statute of Autonomy of Andalusia, which sets out in its Article 12 that public policy is aimed to "all persons within the administrative residency/neighbourhood in Andalusia" and that all will be holders of the rights and obligations mentioned in Title 1,[32] which include many social rights. It therefore seems that the Statute of Autonomy aims to stop legal residency from being the gateway to many rights and promotes making administrative residency (*vecindad administrativa*) as the requisite for the access to rights. Spanish law stipulates that in order to hold administrative residency, an individual is not required to possess legal residency.[33]

Of course, linking access to rights to mere administrative residency would not mean that an alien, whether he is a member of the European Union or not, becomes a legal resident just because he is included in the municipal register of inhabitants. Conditions of legal residence are determined by the laws of the Central Spanish State, which has power over matters regarding immigration and alien registration (149.1.2 SC).[34] However, it seems that the Statute of Autonomy provides for an alien with administrative residency in Andalusia to become entitled to the rights recognized by the Statute (and the rules of the autonomous region) by virtue of having administrative residency, even though the alien is not a legal resident in Spain, since the Spanish State's exclusive responsibility over immigration and alien registration matters does not mean that the regional competences could not affect the living conditions of illegal residents in Spain who live in the regional territory.[35]

This impact that autonomous regions have on the situation of aliens in Spain has been confirmed by the Constitutional Court's recent Judgment 31/2010 on the Statute of Autonomy of Catalonia, which states that "the evolution of immigration in Spain limits the construction of the governmental powers provided in article 149.1.2 [of the Spanish Constitution[36]] as a broad provision of unlimited scope that weakens the sector specific powers of the Autonomous Communities that have a clear impact on the migrant population, with regards to which the delivery of certain social services and their corresponding public policies (education, social and health care, housing, culture, etc.) have acquired significant importance" (LC 83).[37]

However, the new Statute of Autonomy of Andalusia did not only purport to give aliens with administrative residency in Andalusia the social rights listed in Title 1 of the new law. The Statute of Autonomy also aimed to confer on these aliens rights in conditions equal to Spanish nationals.

The precepts of some of the new Statutes of Autonomy (not just the Andalusian Statute) that establish rights of a social nature do now indeed recognize the entitlement of all persons equally to those rights. The new Statute of Autonomy of Andalusia, for example, states that it "guarantees *everyone the right to equal access* [emphasis added] to the benefits of a public social services system." In the same way, in the new Statute of Catalonia, it is stated that "*all persons have the right to equal access* [emphasis added] to the benefits provided by the social services of public responsibility" or that "*all persons have the right to equal access* [emphasis added] to health services of public responsibility free of charge, in accordance with the terms established by law." At the same time, the new Statute of Aragon establishes "the entitlement of all persons to access public health services in conditions of equality, universality and quality." The literal wording of the precepts that recognize social rights ("everyone" or "all people") would imply that the aim is for all people to be able to access these rights, whatever their nationality and whether they are legally residents in Spain or not.[38]

This recognition was not affected in any way by the fact that the Constitutional Court's opinion 247/2007 of December 12 has put an end to the distinct legal regime of rights and principles explicitly intended by the legislature, redirecting the rights under the legal regime of the principles. Even though these were treated as guiding principles and not true legal rights, they were precepts that link regional powers when exercising their responsibilities.[39] The rights enshrined in the Statutes of Autonomy do indeed have to do only with the respective regional institutions and not the Spanish State. Despite this limitation, however, they have to do with important social authorities, including not only the autonomous regions,[40] but also local powers (provincial and municipal), since they are also authorities within their respective autonomous region.[41] Had the aforementioned construction prospered, it would be impossible for regional and local entities to establish legal differences depending on whether someone is an alien or a Spaniard and, for that matter, whether someone is a legal or illegal resident, since those targeted by public policies and the owners of the rights dealt with in the Statutes are *all persons* to whom the Statutes would have recognized *equal access* to such rights.

It was the Constitutional Court itself that highlighted the importance of a literal reading of the rules when recognizing the entitlement "all persons" to a particular right. When referring to the right to effective judicial protection established in Article 24 of the Constitution, for example, the Constitutional Court stated that this is one of the fundamental rights "that belongs to a human being as such, not as a citizen," a conclusion which is drawn from the "literal reading of the cited article ('all persons'), as well as other reasons."[42] Of equal importance to constitutional jurisprudence is the reference to "all persons" made in international documents on rights ratified by Spain when interpreting, in accordance with the terms of Article 10.2 SC,[43] the scope of the entitlement to constitutional rights. Thus, in relation to the right to education guaranteed in Article 27.1 of the Spanish Constitution, the Constitutional Court stated "it refers to 'all persons,' whether they are nationals or aliens, *and whatever their legal situation in Spain may be* [emphasis added]." This conclusion is reached by interpreting the expression from Article 27.1 in accordance with the international texts mentioned, where the expressions "all people have" or "nobody can be denied" (the right to an education) are used. The use of the reference to "all persons," therefore, in a rule relating to rights (in our case the Statute of Autonomy which recognizes rights that, although not constitutional, they are included within the framework of constitutionality as limiting rules with respect to the exercise of the public powers of the autonomous regions and localities[44]) involves the recognition that these rights belong to both Spaniards and aliens alike.

The recognition granted to the social rights of all persons in the new Statutes of Autonomy, therefore, indicate the recognition of aliens' entitlement to these rights, whatever their legal or administrative situation may be. These social rights are recognized for all people in equal conditions, meaning that the fact that an individual is foreign cannot be taken into account when regulating the scope of social rights. In some autonomous regions with a reformed Statute, the idea was that the simple fact that an individual was an actual resident in the territory would grant her access to the social benefits and rights offered.

This consequence constitutes an important guarantee of access to social rights, a guarantee that is also strongly safeguarded because a Statute of Autonomy is a rule of particular weight, since its reform would require an agreement between the regional parliament and the central parliament, as well as the approval via referendum of that region's citizens in the case of autonomous regions such as Andalusia or Catalonia. Another factor contributing to its weight is the fact that it constitutes a limiting rule with controlling authority to judge the constitutionality of the other rules. But, was it the real intention of the framers of these Statutes to recognize social rights for everyone on an equal footing? Were the framers aware of the implications that the new rules would have with regard to immigrants?

If we focus our attention on the processes of drawing up the Catalan and Andalusian Statutes, we can only reply to this question with an affirmative answer, at least in those two cases.

Thus, at the stage when the parliamentary groups were stating their positions in the debate about the reform of the Statute of Autonomy of Andalusia in the Spanish Congress of Deputies (the lower house of the Spanish legislature), the spokesman for the Socialist Group (Grupo Parlamentario Socialista), Deputy López Garrido, stated that:

> Some things are negative for the Popular Party (PP), such as the rights and duties of citizens that in this Statute now belong to all those who live in Andalusia, Spaniards or aliens.[45]

In light of this justification of the recognition of everyone's entitlement to rights in the new Statute, the autonomous M.P. from the Popular Party Sanz Cabello went on to express his disagreement with the terms of the statutory text in the final debate on the proposed reform of the Statute of Autonomy of Andalusia, held in the Andalusian Parliament, stating that "the Statute of Autonomy should establish, also out of respect for the constitutional framework, that those entitled to the new rights and those to whom public policies are directed are we Andalusians, without prejudice to E.U. or Spanish legislation regarding aliens." Likewise, in the process of drawing up the new Statute of Catalonia, those involved were fully aware that the recognition of the social rights was referring to all people.

Amongst the documents that the *Institut d'estudis autonómics* (the true author of the draft copy of the new Statute of Autonomy) handed to the parliament of Catalonia, of particular interest is that it contains a reference to the entitlement of the rights recognized in the Statute of Autonomy. The document includes a detailed report and a draft of the text of the First Title on rights and duties. In accordance with the detailed report of the document from the Institute, "in the draft copy of the regulatory text no general precept was finally included on the entitlement of rights due to the difficult nature of establishing a general clause capable of foreseeing with accuracy all situations relating to all the rights and duties recognized in the Statute. It has been decided that the matter of entitlement will be dealt with case by case, depending on the nature and character of each right, thus indicating who is entitled to each right, one at a time. Three categories are referred to in particular: 1) *all persons*, 2) *citizens in general, on the understanding that these are Spanish nationals* (for example, when it comes to access to the civil service) and 3) *citizens of Catalonia*, on the understanding that these are those who have the political status of Catalans, for example, in their right to vote."

In the draft copy of the text, in each of the precepts that covers rights, we find that those entitled to each right are specified in accordance with the three categories referred to in the aforementioned report. We discover that many of the social rights are granted to all persons, even including the concept of "in conditions of equality." The draft copy of the regulatory text from the Institute, for example, states that all persons are entitled to equal access to quality publicly funded health care[46] and access to a publicly funded social services system, both primary and specialized.[47] We can assert that those involved in drawing up the new Statutes of Autonomy of Catalonia and Andalusia were fully aware that the recognition of rights was to all persons. It is another matter whether (in a moment of economic growth) those involved were aware of the potential economic consequences that the recognition of social rights for all people may have in the future.

The literal reading of the statutory precepts that recognize the social rights, and their systematic interpretation, should be done taking into consideration, on the one hand, constitutional jurisprudence on the entitlement to rights (without forgetting that the rights recognized in the Statute of Autonomy are not constitutional rights but are indeed rights, or principles included in the constitutional framework [*bloque de constitucionalidad*] according to JCC 247/2007, that are standardly used to judge the action of the public powers) and, on the other hand, the parliamentary background, which would imply that access to these rights is granted equally to all people living in these regions, whether they are legal or illegal residents. Regardless of the consequences (economic or social) of recognizing the equal access to all social rights for all aliens, it is clear that this was established in the respective Statutes of Autonomy.

Establishing a connection between the access to rights and merely living in a particular area does not mean that an alien automatically becomes a legal resident due to his or her inclusion in the municipal register of inhabitants or due to the fact that he or she lives in that area. The conditions of legal residence are determined by the law of the Spanish State, which has sole power over matters of immigration and alien registration (149.1.2 SC). It was, however, intended that an alien who lives in Catalonia, for example, should become entitled to the rights recognized by the Statute of Autonomy of Catalonia for this reason, even though he was not legally residing in Spain and should in fact be deported. The terms welcomed in the new Statutes of Autonomy were based on the idea that if unauthorized immigrants are not deported upon the enforcement of immigration law, then they cannot be kept in an indefinite situation in which they are deprived of rights, since this would mean that two kinds of people were living, in practice, in the same territory.

However in Judgment 31/2010, the Constitutional Court "overthrew" the intention of the new Statutes of Autonomy to guarantee access to rights and social benefits to all persons equally.

JCC 31/2010: The Impossibility That Statutes Extend the Entitlement to Rights to Aliens

Judgment 31/2010 of the Constitutional Court resolved the constitutional challenge that the Popular Party posed to the Statute of Autonomy of Catalonia (the SAC). In its LC 18, the Popular Party challenged sections 1 and 3 of Article 15, which refer to Catalan citizens' entitlement to statutory rights.[48]

The Constitutional Court declared that "the rights recognized in the Statute can only be linked to Catalan public powers and are only granted to citizens of Catalonia."[49] Nevertheless, it states, in accordance with Article 15.3 of the Statute of Autonomy, that entitlement can be extended "to other Spaniards or, where necessary, to aliens, always 'in the terms established by law,' which will obviously be, in each case, the pertinent law; that is to say, also the law of the Spanish State." Despite this, according to the Constitutional Court "in so far as none of the sections of Article 15 [of the Statute of Autonomy] even questions the reality of the above, we can only conclude they are not unconstitutional as charged."

Given the facts presented in this chapter, the Constitutional Court argues on the one hand that the Statute of Autonomy of Catalonia never aimed to recognize the rights of aliens and, on the other hand, in any case this intention would not be in line with the Constitution.

As to the first point, the court bases its rejection of the claim that the Statute wished to recognize the entitlement of aliens to social rights on the terms of sections 1 and 3 of Article 15 of the new Statute of Autonomy. It also bases its argument on its interpretation of the terms of Article 37.4 of the Statute itself. In order to deny the statutory intention to guarantee access to rights and social assistance to all persons in conditions of equality, the Constitutional Court proposes that Article 37.4 of the SAC notes that the fundamental rights recognized in the Constitution and in the treaties and international agreements ratified by Spain cannot be affected by the rights and principles recognized in the Statute. The Court deduces that the Statute of Autonomy has not created different fundamental rights than those that figure in the Constitution or contradicted them, neither has it affected the application of these rights with regards to their ownership, regulation, and conditions of exercise. However, Article 37.4 SAC does not seem to state this exactly. It provides:

> None of the provisions of this Title [I of the Statute] can be developed, applied or interpreted in any way that may reduce or limit the fundamental rights recognized by the Constitution or by the international treaties and agreements ratified by Spain.

The precept forbids the reduction or limitation of the scope of constitutional rights and of those figuring in international texts, but does not lay down a general ban on their impact through, for example, an extension of those entitled to them. For the Constitutional Court, the Popular Party's challenge to Sections 1 and 3 of Article 15 SAC had to do with the possible contradiction between the statutory provisions regarding who is entitled to the rights recognized in the Statute and the fact that "the Constitution determines the scope of those possibly entitled to rights on its own, with reference to nationality."

Let us recall that Article 15.1 of the SAC states that citizens of Catalonia are the holders of the rights and obligations recognized by the Statute itself, and by the Constitution, and the international treaties and agreements having to do with fundamental rights and liberties that have been signed by Spain. Article 15.3 SAC states that the rights of citizens of Catalonia, as recognized in the Statute, "may be extended to other persons, in the terms established by law." The Constitutional Court denies that the Statute aimed to grant rights to aliens, declaring that Article 15.1 states that the rights recognized in the Statute can *only* be enjoyed by citizens of Catalonia. This interpretation, the Court said, is confirmed by the terms of Article 15.3, which states that the rights of citizens of Catalonia recognized in the Statute can be extended to other persons, on the terms established by law.

It is impossible to share this point of view, despite the declarations of the Constitutional Court, because it is simply not the case that Article 15.1 states that the rights recognized by the Statute can *only* be enjoyed by the citizens of Catalonia.[50] This provision, in fact, states that the citizens of Catalonia are entitled to the rights recognized in the Statute of Autonomy, as well as those recognized in the Constitution and in international treaties, without meaning that the citizens of Catalonia are the only persons entitled to these rights. These citizens are without doubt entitled to these rights, but in order to determine who is entitled to the rights recognized in the Statute of Autonomy, the wording of each of the rights should be consulted. Article 15.1 does not state, in any way, that the rights recognized in the Statute can only be enjoyed by the citizens of Catalonia. What it does state, in fact, is that they are entitled to these rights, but this does not mean that other Spaniards or aliens cannot be entitled to them, too. This entitlement should be deduced from each of the particular provisions that recognize rights,[51] which are now principles as per the doctrine agreed in JCC 247/2007. This determination banned the Statutes from including individual rights, requiring the law to give content to the mandate established in the Statute of Autonomy. It is important to note, however, that the law is bound to the Statute's provisions regarding entitlement to rights.

Article 15.3 foresees that those rights recognized by the Statute for the citizens of Catalonia only (for example, political rights) may be extended to other persons by the law. In these scenarios, these rights are granted by the Statute of Autonomy to the citizens of Catalonia only.

The Constitutional Court's interpretation of the terms and aims of the Statute of Autonomy regarding the entitlement to rights ignores the literal wording of the statutory provisions and the intentions of their authors.

The Constitutional Court bases its second argument (the impossibility that the Statute grants rights to aliens) on the correspondence that must exist between rights recognized by the Statute and principles, on the one hand, and the powers of the region (and their fulfillment), on the other. This leads the Court to the conclusion that the rights recognized by the Statute can *only* be enjoyed by citizens of Catalonia. Nonetheless, that entitlement can be extended to other Spaniards or, when applicable, to aliens, as long as this is "on the terms established by law," which will obviously be, in each case, those laws enforceable; that is to say, also the laws of the central state.

It seems that the Constitutional Court wishes to avoid risking that the entitlement of aliens to social rights be recognized when state powers are exercised. Indeed, the extension of entitlements to aliens supposes the Statute of Autonomy itself regulates certain substantive spheres, apparently shackling the exercise of state powers in the substantive areas in which rights are recognized. The question that seems to underlie the Court's categorical statement in Judgment 31/2010 is to what extent the recognition of a wide entitlement to rights (for example, when it comes to health care) may limit the Spanish State's future exercise of power over the basic and general coordination of health matters (Article 149.1.16 SC).[52] It may be thought that the decision over who should benefit from health services should be the responsibility of the Spanish State through its authority over the basic rules.[53]

However, this eventual alteration of the Spanish State authority is already restricted by the Statutes of Autonomy themselves, making it certainly unnecessary to limit the extension of entitlement to statutory rights in a general manner, as has been done by Judgment 31/2010.

The extension of the entitlement to rights brought into effect by the Statutes of Autonomy is not unconditional. In fact, it is conditioned by the Statutes of Autonomy themselves, since the regional insitutions must have a material competence that it is possible to link with a specific right that has been outlined in the Statute. This is apparent in those statutory provisions that state that the rights mentioned in the Statutes of Autonomy would not mean any changes in the distribution of authority, nor the creation of new powers or changes to those currently in place.[54] This means that the eventual obligations that can be derived for regional insititutions regarding the recognition of rights in the Statute of Autonomy would only be such should the region be in charge of a power related to that particular right. The scope of the regional powers depends largely on how the Spanish State defines the scope of its own authority. The extension of the entitlement to the rights would therefore depend on how the central state exercises its own powers.

The Statute of Autonomy would have made an extension of the entitlement to the rights that was in itself conditioned.

Certainly, the margin the Spanish State has to influence the extension of entitlement to statutory rights will not be the same in all cases. The State's capacity to influence the statutory recognition of everyone's right to work through the exercise of its authority over employment legislation would not be the same in other areas, where the autonomous communities have exclusive authority, such as in the area of social assistance. In the latter area, that of social assistance, the fact that the autonomous communities have exclusive authority in this field should allow them to freely determine who should benefit from these services and this could even be done in the Statute of Autonomy. However, in order to avoid the extension of entitlement to rights from affecting the Spanish State's capacity to exercise its own powers, the Constitutional Court decided to veto this extension in general, instead of conditioning the distribution of powers in each area and instead of analyzing in each case the eventual influence that it may have on the powers of the state.

Following Judgment 31/2010, the extension of rights to aliens is only allowed "on the terms established by law," which will obviously be, in each case, valid laws; that is to say, the laws of the Central State. In this way, the regions will be able to extend social rights to aliens, legal or illegal, on the grounds of their own authority, for example when it comes to social care, through regional law, although they cannot do this in the Statute of Autonomy. Before it was proposed that some of the Statutes of Autonomy extended rights to all, it was the laws themselves, both Spanish and regional, that recognized rights for aliens, including unauthorized immigrants.

LEGISLATION AND THE RIGHTS OF UNAUTHORIZED IMMIGRANTS

Until the recent legal reform of 2012, which the conservative government justified as a necessity of the economic crisis, aliens without legal residence were entitled to a considerable number of social rights under the infraconstitutional legal system. This was the case with the right to health care, for example. Before the reform implemented in April 2012, Article 12 of the Immigration Law stated that aliens in Spain that were included on the municipal register of inhabitants were entitled to health care on the same terms as Spaniards.

In terms of emergency health care, it was not even necessary to fulfill the requirement of being registered in the municipality. The previous Section 2 of Article 12 of the Immigration Law stated that aliens in Spain were entitled to emergency public health care due to serious illness or accident, whatever their cause may be, and were entitled to receive such treatment until they were discharged. The rules covered all aliens, including those that were not registered in their municipality (because they did not live, for example, in Spain and were in the country on a temporary basis as tourists or travellers). This meant that until 2012, aliens that lived in Spain were entitled to health care on the same terms as Spaniards, whether they were legal residents or not. The only requirement for this was that they were included on the municipal register of inhabitants, which did not, in turn, require them to be legal residents. Since September 1, 2012,[55] however, and as a result of the government's reform through Royal Decree-Law[56] 16/2012 of April 20,[57] aliens without legal residence in Spain are no longer entitled to health care services.[58]

The withdrawal of the right to health care for unauthorized immigrants by basic state legislation has led to fierce political and legal debate. Some autonomous communities have continued to provide health care to unauthorized immigrants in spite of Spanish law. We believe that the decision to continue to provide these services has its legal founding in the fact that the decision to grant entitlement to services is not fully reserved to the Spanish State since the autonomous communities are also entitled to establish their own portfolios of services, that should naturally include, at the very least, the national health system's list of common services. The autonomous communities should also, therefore, be deemed capable of extending the rights to health services within the framework of basic Spanish legislation on the matter. The Spanish State's power to establish the basic elements of health care should not mean that it is exclusively in charge of deciding who is entitled to health care, since an autonomous community can decide to increase the entitlement to rights by charging it to its own budget.

When it comes to other social rights, such as the right to social services and social benefits, the Immigration Law distinguishes in Article 14 between aliens with legal residence and other immigrants. The first group is entitled to access social services and benefits (not only the general and basic, but also special services and benefits) on the same terms as Spaniards, while the second group, including aliens who are not legal residents, is only entitled to basic social services and benefits.[59]

With regard to employment rights, in 2009, Article 36.3 of the Immigration Law established that the absence of a residence and work permit would not make a work contract invalid with respect to the rights of the alien worker, nor would it be an obstacle to benefits in cases covered by international agreements or other applicable law on the protection of workers. However, one exception is laid out in the article, which states that under no circumstances may a worker without a residence or work permit be entitled to unemployment benefits. The recognition of the rights and benefits relating to employment does not, of course, change the administrative situation of the alien, who will continue to be an unauthorized immigrant and, as such, can be deported.

With regard to the right to housing,[60] until 2009, certain local regulations recognized that all persons were entitled to this right. The only requirement for this was having previously resided for a certain amount of time in the municipality, which could be demonstrated using the register of inhabitants. Legal residency was not necessary.

As can be seen, the Spanish legal system recognized, up until the economic crisis, that unauthorized immigrants were entitled to access a significant amount of social rights, with the only requirement in some instances being that the individual figured on the municipal register.[61]

CONCLUSION

The recognition of the social rights to aliens in Spanish law can no longer be based on the exclusive powers of the Spanish State over immigration, since, in accordance with the doctrine established in the recent Judgment 31/2010 on the Statute of Autonomy of Catalonia,

> the evolution of immigration in Spain limits the construction of the governmental powers provided in 149.1.2 [of the Spanish Constitution] as a broad provision with unlimited scope that weakens those sector specific powers of the Autonomous Communities that have a clear impact on the migrant population, with regard to which the delivery of certain social services and their corresponding public policies (education, social and health care, housing, culture, etc.) have acquired significant importance.[62]

It is therefore necessary for the Spanish State to justify its intervention in these areas in enabling provisions other than those recognized in Article 149.1.2 SC on immigration and alien registration matters. According to these enabling provisions, only the Spanish State can shape the legal regime that makes an alien an immigrant and deals with the circumstances that are initially inherent to this status, but this cannot be a broad provision with unlimited scope. The central state has sole responsibility over the entrance and shelter of aliens, but this does not mean that the regions cannot exercise their own powers when it comes to social policies.

Despite this, the autonomous communities' use of their own powers affecting the foreign population (health care, social services, etc.) cannot hinder the Spanish State from exercising its own powers with regards to this group. Nor can the autonomous communities limit the state's powers to legislate generally on policy related to social services, the health care system, or employment. In this way, in its JCC 31/2010, the Constitutional Court stated that the allocation of responsibilities to regions in the Statute of Autonomy should not hinder the Spanish State from exercising its own exclusive powers recognized in Article 149.1 SC (on matters such as health, social security, the general management of the economy, etc.), whether these coincide with the autonomous powers on the same physical space or legal object, or they are regarding matters of shared interest.

It is precisely the broad interpretation that the Spanish State has been making of its own powers that has brought about the restriction, in practice, of the regions' capacity to adopt their own social policies with regards to the immigrant population. The economic crisis has led the Spanish State to decide to withdraw the right to access to a series of social rights to unauthorized immigrants, rights which it had recognized until now. It is yet to be seen whether this is compatible with the principle of non-regression or whether it is compatible with the allocation of powers between the Spanish State and the autonomous regions. The Constitutional Court has the last word.

NOTES

1. With regard to aliens from within the European Union, and those to whom their own law is applicable as in the case of nationals of states included in the agreement on the European Economic Area, European Union law and national laws on transposition should be consulted.
2. Certain specific conditions are also provided for in the legislation, for example, the authorization of a temporary stay to study that allows the alien to remain in Spain for more than ninety days (for the duration of study) to undertake studies or futher education at an authorized educational institution in Spain on a full-time basis, from which the student obtains a certificate or qualification.
3. Or be entitled to family reunification.
4. Quadra-Salcedo Janini, T., "Los derechos sociales de los extranjeros: nuevas y viejas garantías" in *Inmigración y Gobiernos Locales*, dir. Diez Sastre, S., Marcial Pons (2010).
5. The Constitutional Court has reiterated that some rights under Title 1 "correspond to aliens due to constitutional mandate and any treatment other than that which is equal to that accorded to Spaniards is not possible" (JCC 107/1984, LC 3) since they are entitled to exercise such rights "in conditions fully comparable [to those of Spaniards]" (JCC 95/2000 of April 10, LC 3). These rights are those that "belong to the person as such and not as citizens; in other words, these rights are essential to ensure human dignity which, pursuant to 10.1 of our Constitution is fundamental to Spanish political order" (JCC 107/1984 of November 23, LC 3; 99/1985 of September 30, LC 2; and 130/1995 of September 11, LC 2). We have also referred to these as rights that are "inherent to the dignity of human beings" (JCC 91/2000 of March 30, LC 7).
6. "Article 23
   1. Citizens have the right to participate in public affairs, directly or through representatives freely elected in periodic elections by universal suffrage.
   2. They likewise have the right to access on equal terms to public office, in accordance with the requirements determined by law. Citizens have the right to participate in public affairs, directly or through representatives freely elected in periodic elections by universal suffrage."
7. "Article 13
   2. Only Spaniards shall be entitled to the rights recognised in Article 23, except in cases which may be established by treaty or by law concerning the right to vote and the rigth to be elected in municipal elections, in accordance with the principle of reciprocity."

8. JCC 107/84 of November 23, LC 4.
9. This would be case of freedoms such as "the right to life, to physical and moral integrity, to intimacy and to ideological freedom (JCC 107/1984, LC 3), the right to freedom and security (JCC 144/1990 of September 26, LC 5), and the right not to be discriminated on account of birth, race, sex, religion or any other personal or social condition or circumstance (JCC 137/2000 of May 29, LC 1). All have been expressly recognized by the Constitutional Court as belonging to individuals as such. This list should not, however, be considered a closed and exhaustive one" (JCC 36/2007 of November 11).
10. According to the Court, the law "must, in all cases, respect constitutional prescriptions, as that precept cannot be accepted (Article 13.1 SC) allowing the law to freely configure the content of the right when this has been directly recognized by the Constitution to be a right of aliens."
11. "Article 35
    1. All Spaniards have the duty to work and the right to employment, to free choice of profession or trade, to advancement through their work, and to sufficient remuneration for the satisfaction of their needs and those of their families; moreover, under no circumstances may they be discriminated against on account of their gender."
12. "Article 41
    The public authorities shall maintain a public Social Security system for all citizens which will guarantee adequate social assistance and benefits in situations of hardship, especially in cases of unemployment. Supplementary assistance and benefits shall be optional."
13. "Article 19
    Spaniards have the right to choose their place of residence freely, residency and and to move about freely within the national territory.
    Likewise, they have the right to freely enter and leave Spain subject to the conditions to be laid down by the law. This right may not be restricted for political or ideological reasons."
14. Gutiérrez Gutiérrez, I., "Volver a las fuentes. Los derechos fundamentales de los extranjeros en la Constitución y en la jurisprudencia constitucional." *Revista General de Derecho Constitucional* 12. Iustel. (2011).
15. Gutiérrez Gutiérrez, I., "Volver a las fuentes…" op. cit., pp. 33 & ss.
16. Vidal Fueyo, C., "La jurisprudencia del Tribunal Constitucional en materia de derecho fundamentales de los extranjeros a la luz de la STC 236/2007" in Revista Española de Derecho Constitucional 85 (2009), p. 378.
17. "Article 21
    1. The right to peaceful unarmed assembly is recognised. The exercise of this right shall not require prior authorisation.
    2. In the event of meetings in public places and of demonstrations, prior notification shall be given to the authorities, who may ban them only when there are well founded grounds to expect a breach of public order, involving danger to persons or property."
18. "Article 22
    1. The right of association is recognised.
    2. Associations which pursue ends or use means classified as criminal offences are illegal.
    3. Associations set up on the basis of this article must be recorded in a register for the sole purpose of public knowledge.
    4. Associations may only be dissolved or have their activities suspended by virtue of a justified court order.
    5. Secret and paramilitary associations are prohibited."

19. "Article 28
    1. Everyone has the right to freely join a trade union. The law may limit the exercise of this right or make an exception to it in the case of the Armed Forces or Institutes or other bodies subject to military discipline, and shall regulate the special conditions of its exercise by civil servants. Trade union freedom includes the right to set up trade unions and to join the union of one's choice, as well as the right of the trade unions to form confederations and to found international trade union organisations, or to become members thereof. No one may be compelled to join a trade union.
    2. The right of workers to strike in defence of their interests is recognised. The law regulating the exercise of this right shall establish the guarantees neccessary to ensure the maintenance of essential community services."
20. "Article 27
    1. Everyone has the right to education. Freedom of teaching is recognised.
    2. Education shall aim at the full development of the human character with due respect for the democratic principles of coexistence and for the basic rights and freedoms."
21. "Article 24
    1. Every person has the right to obtain the effective protection of the Judges and the Courts in the exercise of his or her legitimate rights and interests, and in no case may he go undefended.
    2. Likewise, all persons have the right of access to the ordinary judge predetermined by law; to the defence and assistance of a lawyer; to be informed of the charges brought against them; to a public trial without undue delays and with full guarantees; to the use of evidence appropriate to their defence; to not make selfincriminating statements; to not declare themselves guilty; and to be presumed innocent.

    The law shall determine the cases in which, for reasons of family relationship or professional secrecy, it shall not be compulsory to make statements regarding alleged criminal offences."
22. "Article 17
    1. Every person has a right to freedom and security. No one may be deprived of his or her freedom except in accordance with the provisions of this article and in the cases and in the manner provided by the law.
    2. Preventive detention may last no longer than the time strictly required in order to carry out the necessary investigations aimed at establishing the facts; in any case the person arrested must be set free or handed over to the judicial authorities within a maximum period of seventy-two hours.
    3. Any person arrested must be informed immediately, and in a manner understandable to him or her, of his or her rights and of the grounds for his or her arrest, and may not be compelled to make a statement. The arrested person shall be guaranteed the assistance of a lawyer during police and judicial proceedings, under the terms established by the law.
    4. A habeas corpus procedure shall be regulated by law in order to ensure the immediate handing over to the judicial authorities of any person arrested illegally.

    Likewise, the maximum period of provisional imprisonment shall be stipulated by law."
23. JCC 236/2007 of November 7, LC 8. "In accordance with constitutional jurisprudence, the right to non-compulsory education for alien minors is included within the right to an education. Therefore, constitutional jurisprudence deduced from the constitutional rulings relating to the right to an education, interpreted in accordance with the international agreements ratified by Spain, that the constitutionally guaranteed content of that right, in its application, is not limited to basic education, but rather in the case of minors is also extended to higher levels of education,

although these are not constitutionally compulsory or obliged to be free of charge. Pursuant to Article 9 of the Immigration Law, following the amendments of Organic Law 2/2009 of December 11, aliens under the age of sixteen are entitled and obliged to receive an education, including access to a basic education that is free and compulsory. Aliens younger than eighteen are also entitled to post-compulsory education.... Should they reach the age of eighteen during the school year, they remain entitled to this right until the school year should end".

24. According to Article 53.3:
"The substantive legislation, judicial practice and actions of the public authorities shall be based on the recognition, respect and protection of the principles recognised in Chapter Three. The latter may only be invoked in the ordinary courts in the context of the legal provisions by which they are developed."
25. Vidal Fueyo, C., *Constitución*...op. cit., p. 136 & ss.
26. Goig Martínez, J., "Inmigración y derechos fundamentales. Jurisprudencia" In *Legislación y Políticas Migratorias en España*, Universitas Internacional (2008), p. 55.
27. Roig Molés, E., "Los derechos de los extranjeros: titularidad y limitación" in *Problemas constitucionales de la inmigración: una visión desde Italia y España. II Jornadas Italo-españolas de Justicia constitucional*, coord. Miguel Revenga. Tirant Lo Blanch (2004), pp. 618 & ss.
28. Fossas Espadaler, E., *El principio dispositivo en el Estado Autonómico*, Marcial Pons-IVAP, Madrid-Barcelona-Buenos Aires, 2007.
29. In its Judgment 247/2007 of December 12, the Constitutional Court banned the different legal regime that was explicitly wanted by some of the new Statutes of Autonomy, between the rights and the principles, and redirected the legal regime of the rights to the legal regime of the principles. Therefore, aside from the specific areas in which the Constitution itself allows the Statute of Autonomy to create legal rights and that the judgment relates to the Statute's role to establish "the name, organization and seat of its own autonomous institutions," that is the rights in the area of the rights to political participation, the Statutes of Autonomy cannot, pursuant to the judgment of the Court, establish on their own rights strictu sensu, but rather guidelines, aims, or mandates for the autonomous public powers. This leads the Constitutional Court to interpret that even if literally the Statutes refers to rights, these statutory prescriptions should be clearly understood as mandates of the autonomous public powers that do not generate true legal public rights that are enforceable before an ordinary court.
30. Quadra-Salcedo Janini, T., "El derecho de residencia como derecho a tener derechos en los sistemas políticos compuestos." Presentation given at the 8th Conference of the Spanish Association of Constitutional Law Specialists, Madrid, January 2009.
31. Amendment of the Statutes of Autonomy shall conform to the procedure established therein (the agreement of the regional parliament is required) and shall in any case require also the approval of the central Parliament through an organic law.
32. Without prejudice to legislation on the right to participate in public matters.
33. The administrative residency is met with the requirement of being registered in the municipality. Administrative residency/neighborhood, as opposed to regional citizenship which demands continued residence in an area for a certain period of time, is established by the main address of an individual, whether or not their residence be legal, at a specific time. Pursuant to Article 15 of the law regulating the lsis of local government "*all persons living in Spain* are obliged include themselves in the municipal register of inhabitants of the area in which they usually live." The registration certificate is relatively easy to obtain, even for an alien without legal residence, since all that is needed is a document identifying the person requesting to be included in the municipal

register. If the address given as the main home is not owned by the applicant (and they cannot provide proof that they live there, such as a rental contract or the most recent water, gas, or electricity, etc., statement figuring the name and address of the applicant) and they wish for the address to be put down as their main home, all that is needed is signed authorization by the owner of the home and a photocopy of their national ID document, passport, or any other ID document.

34. In this sense, we should remember that Article 18.2 of the Law regulating the Basis of Local Government states that "the registration of aliens on the municipal register of inhabitants will not be considered proof of their legal residence in Spain. Neither will it grant them access to any rights they may be entitled to under current law."

35. Quadra-Salcedo Janini, T., "Los derechos sociales de los extranjeros: nuevas y viejas garantías" in *Inmigración y Gobiernos Locales*, dir. Diez Sastre, S., Marcial Pons (2010).

36. According to Article 149.1.2 SC "the [Spanish] State holds exclusive power over nationality, immigration, emigration, status of aliens, and right to asylum."

37. Before the Catalan judgment, Montilla noted that Article 149.1.2 cannot be set out as a horizontal title of unlimited scope that allows any public state intervention regarding immigrants, since it would involve storming the regional rules of the autonomous regions. Cf. Montilla Martos, J. A., "Las funciones y competencias de las Comunidades Autónomas en inmigración," AA.VV., coord. Eliseo Aja, *Las Comunidades Autónomas y la inmigración*, Tirant lo Blanch e Institut de Dret Public de Barcelona, Valencia (2006), pp. 26 & ss. Roig Molés, E., "Autonomía e inmigración…" op. cit., p. 360 & ss. Vidal reminds us that "the State would maintain sole power over the administrative and legal situation of the immigrant, taking charge of those aspects directly related to the entrance and exit of immigrants and the administrative authorizations regulated under title 2 of the Immigration Law under the title 'Legal status of aliens', as well as the infractions and sanctions of Title 3 of the Immigration Law. However, the granting of public services such as education, health, housing, social services, culture, etc. to immigrants would not be linked to Article 149.1.2 SC but rather to the various different regional rules of the autonomous regions, although the State's power to determine the bases of certain matters would still be respected." Vidal Fueyo, C., "Nuevas variables a tener en cuenta en el diseño del estatuto jurídico de los inmigrantes." *Revista General de Derecho Constitucional* 3 (2007), p. 4 & ss.

38. The new Statute of Castilla y León, for example, has been more restrictive than those of Catalonia or Andalusia since it has limited equal access to the regional Social Action Program only to citizens of the region. In accordance with the Statute of Autonomy, these citizens are those Spaniards with administrative residency in any of the municipalities of the region. When it comes to aliens, the new Statute of Autonomy has established that the rights it grants to citizens of Castilla y León will be extended to aliens with administrative residency in the region pursuant to the terms established in the legal provisions that develop those rights.

39. We should remember that the Constitutional Court stated in its JCC 247/2007 that both rights (with the exception of those regarding political and institutional participation that the judgment links with the role of the Statute to establish the "name, organization and seat of its own autonomous institutions") and principles referred to in the Statutes of Autonomy "would, in order to be fully effective, need to be developed by the regional legislator, so that the principle or right outlined would lack direct justiciability until its legal regime was specified by the regional legislation, since only then would the associated legal rights of citizens take shape." Despite this, the Constitutional Court also stated "nothing is stopping the Statute of Autonomy, as a basic institutional rule of the autonomous region, from imposing criteria or guidelines directly on the

autonomous public powers when allocating them their competences." Therefore, aside from the particular areas in which the Constitution itself allows the Statute to create legal rights and the judgment links with the Statute's role of establishing the "name, organization and seat of its own autonomous institutions," that is to say rights regarding political participation, the Statutes of Autonomy cannot establish legal rights strictu sensu on their own, but rather provide guidelines, aims or mandates to the regional institutions. On this subject, see Quadra-Salcedo Janini, T., "El régimen jurídico…" op. cit..

40. The regions are granted authority in their respective Statutes of Autonomy that gives them a significant amount of power to intervene when it comes to developing the Social State. Key responsibilities include those involving social assistance, education, health, housing, or town planning. In this way, as Suárez Corujo notes, "the regions' competence over social assistance indicates the recognition of their ability to impose social interventions other than those within the realm of Social Security system that are destined to attend to needs that are not (satisfactorily) met by the mentioned state system of Social Security." Suarez Corujo, B., *La protección social en el Estado de las autonomías. Un examen de los artículos 149.1.17. & 148.1.20.ª ante los procesos de reforma estatutaria*. Iustel (2006), p. 280. On this matter, see Sáenz Royo, E., "Derechos de protección social y Estado autonómico: los márgenes constitucionales de actuación del Estado y de las CCAA" in *Derechos económicos y sociales*, dir. Embid Irujo, A., Iustel (2009).
41. Thus, the Advisory Counsel of Catalonia stated, referring to the statute as a basic institutional rule, that "it is fundamentally a rule established to direct and, at the same time, limit the public powers of Catalonia and, as part of its power, the local entities of the region" Opinion no 269, of 1 September 2005 at the request of the parliament of Catalonia, p. 42. This does not mean that the interiorization of the local regime aimed for by some Statutes of Autonomy should necessarily be accepted.
42. In accordance with JCC 236/2007, this conclusion is drawn "not only from of the literal wording of the article ('all persons') but also because this same conclusion is reached by interpreting it, as is required by Article 10.2 SC, in accordance with Article 10 of the universal declaration of human rights, with Article 6.1 of the Rome Convention of 4 November 1950, and with Article 14.1 of the International Covenant on Civil and Political rights of New York (19 December 1966). In these texts, the equivalent right to that which the Spanish Constitution calls effective judicial protection is granted to 'all persons' or 'everyone,' whatever their nationality." In the same way, regarding the right to a non-compulsory education for minors, the Constitutional Court declares that "on the other hand, from the provisions examined and their correct interpretation it is concluded that the right to an education guaranteed in Article 27.1 SC refers to 'everyone' whether they are a Spaniard or an alien, and whatever their legal situation in Spain may be. This conclusion is reached by interpreting the expression in Article 27.1 SC in accordance with the aforementioned international texts, where the expressions 'all people have' or 'nobody can be denied' (the right to an education) are used. As has been seen, the access to scholarly establishment and the right to use, in principle, the means of instruction that exist at a given moment, should be guaranteed, pursuant to Article 1 CEDH (State Human Rights Comission), 'to all persons depending on the jurisdiction of a contracting State.' The expression included in Article 1 CEDH, interpreted along with Article 14 CEDH (JECHR (Judgment of the European Court of Human Rights) in the case of Ireland against the United Kingdom) of 18 January 1978 § 238; the case of Prince Hans-Adams II of Lichtenstein of 12 July 2001, § 46), should be understood to also include those people who are not nationals and who have an authorized or illegal status."

43. According to Artícle 10.2 SC "the principles relating to the fundamental rights and liberties recognised by the Constitution shall be interpreted in conformity with the Universal Declaration of Human Rights and the international treaties and agreements thereon ratified by Spain."
44. See Quadra-Salcedo Janini, T., "El régimen jurídico…" op. cit., p. 39 & ss. As we will see in the following section, this will determine that the central state can influence the extension of the entitlement aimed for by the Statutes of Autonomy when exercising their responsibilities. Read the following sections.
45. Plenary Session number 168, held on Tuesday, May 23, 2006. No reference is made as to whether it refers to illegal or legal immigrants, as it only mentioned the aliens who live in Andalusia.
46. Article 20 of the draft copy handed in by the Institut that would then become Article 23 of the new statute was approved with the following wording: "All persons have the right to access health services of public responsibility in equal conditions and free of charge, in the terms established by law."
47. Article 22 of the draft copy handed in by the Institut that would then become Article 23 of the new Statute was approved with the following wording: "all persons have the right to access the benefits of the network of social services of public responsibility in equal conditions" with the significant addition of the reference to everybody's right to access "in equal conditions."
48. Pursuant to Article 15: "1. Citizens of Catalonia are owners of the rights and obligations recognized by the rules referred to in Article 4.1.…3. The rights recognized in the present Statute to be the entitlement of citizens of Catalonia can be extended to other persons, in the terms established by the law." Article 4.1, which mentions Article 15.1, refers to "the rights recognized in the present Statute, the Constitution, the European Union, the Universal Declaration of Human Rights, the European Convention for the Protection of Human Rights and other treaties and international agreements signed by Spain that recognize and guarantee fundamental rights and freedoms."
49. The judgment adds "as is fully stated in Article 15.1 SAC", although whether this is indeed what is stated in this article is certainly questionable, since Article 15.1 does not establish that the statutory rights can *only* be enjoyed by the citizens of Catalonia, but that the citizen of Catalonia are entitled to the rights recognized in a series of rules, including the statute.
50. Defined in Article 7.1 of the statute, which states that "Spanish citizens that have administrative residency in Catalonia possess the political status of Catalans or citizens of Catalonia. Their political rights are exercised in accordance with the present Statute of Autonomy and with the law."
51. This was the intention of the statutory legislation. Let us not forget that, in accordance with the *Institut d'estudis autonomics*' detailed report, "It has been decided that the matter of entitlement of rights will be dealt with case by case, depending on the nature and character of each right, indicating who is entitled to each right, one at a time."
52. According to Artícle 149.1.16 SC "the State holds exclusive competence over external health measures; bases and general coordination of health matters; legislation on pharmaceutical products."
53. However, the decision regarding the entitlement to health care is questionable if it is a matter reserved to the central state, which holds the competence over the bases and the general coordination of health matters. The autonomous regions have been granted power to establish their own portfolio of services that should naturally include, at the very least, the national health system's list of common services. It could be thought that the autonomous regions are able to widen the entitlement to the health services within the framework of the basic legislation of the central state on this matter.

54. Thus, Article 37.4 of the Catalan Statute states that "the rights and principles of the present Title do not reflect any alterations in the assignation of responsibilities, nor the creation of any new titles of responsibility or modifications to those currently existing."
55. Pursuant to the First Temporary Provision of Royal Decree-Law 16/2012 of April 20 "those persons who, before the present Royal Decree-Law should come into force, have access to healthcare services in Spain and are not insured on the basis of any of the scenarios of Section 2 of Article 3 of Law 16/2003 of 28 May, may continue to enjoy this right until 31 August 2012 without having to provide proof of their status as an insured party."
56. According to Article 86,
    "1. In cases of extraordinary and urgent need, the Government may issue temporary legislative provisions which shall take the form of decree-laws and which may not affect the regulation of the basic State institutions, the rights, duties and liberties contained in Title 1, the system of the Autonomous Communities, or the General Electoral Law.
    2. The decree-laws must be submitted forthwith to the Congress of Deputies, which must be summoned for this purpose if not already in session. They must be debated and voted upon in their entirety within thirty days after their promulgation. Congress must expressly declare itself in favour of ratification or repeal within said period of time, for which purpose the Standing Orders shall establish a special summary procedure."
57. Royal Decree-Law 16/2012 modifies Article 12 of the Immigration Law, which now states that "aliens are entitled to health care in the terms provided for in the legislation in force regarding healthcare." The legislation in force is no other than Law 16/2003 of May 28, on the cohesion and quality of the national health system modified by Decree-Law 16/2012 itself. In accordance with point 1 of the new Article 3 of Law 16/2003 of May 28, on the cohesion and quality of the national health system, "healthcare in Spain, charged to public funds, will be guaranteed through the national health system, to those persons who possess the status of insured person." Section 2 of the new Article 3 defines those who have the status of insured persons and aliens with no legal residence are not included in this category according to the new precept. The requirements for obtaining the status of insured person or person entitled to health care are:

    To be an employed or self-employed worker, registered for social security purposes or with like status.

    To be a pensioner in the social security system.

    To be a recipient of any other periodic social security benefit (including unemployment benefits and subsidies).

    To have used up all entitlement to unemployment benefit and be registered as a jobseeker.

    To be a national of Spain or another EU member state, of the European Economic Area or Switzerland resident in Spain.

    To be an alien with a valid residence permit (NIE—Alien Identification Number), provided that you do not go above certain income thresholds determined in the legislation.

    Be the spouse or spousal equivalent of the insured person.

    Be the former spouse with entitlement to receive a compensatory pension, or the offspring or other such dependent of less than twenty-six years of age or older than twenty-six and suffering from a disability equal to or exceeding 65%, as long as the individual resides in Spain and is the responsibility of the insured person.
58. Nonetheless, the new regulations maintain that aliens that are not registered or authorized as residents in Spain are still entitled to health care in certain circumstances. Thus, the new Article 3 of the amended Law 16/2003 of May 28 states that aliens are entitled to emergency health care

due to serious illness or an accident, whatever its cause may be, until they are discharged. The right to health care during pregnancy is also recognized, as is health care during birth and after birth, as well as health care for children under the age of eighteen.

59. According to Section 3 of Article 14, "aliens are entitled to basic social services and benefits *whatever their administrative status may be.*" In any case, in accordance with Section 2 (and having stated that "aliens who are legal residents are entitled to general, basic and specific social services and benefits, in the same conditions as Spaniards") aliens with disabilities who are less than eighteen years old and whose permanent address is in Spain, are entitled to the treatment, services and special care required to treat their physical or psychological condition.
60. Let us not forget that, in its wording in the year 2000, Article 13 established that resident aliens and those registered in the municipality in which they have their permanent address, were entitled to access the public system for housing assistance in the same conditions as Spaniards.
61. On this subject see Zarauz, J., *Incidencia del padrón municipal en el ejercicio de los derechos de las personas extranjeras en situación irregular.* Ararteko (2007); Ezquerra Huerva, A., "Extranjería y régimen local: la inscripción de los extranjeros en el Padrón Municipal de Habitantes," Reda 140 (2008); Aguado I Cudolá, V., "Hacia una nueva Población municipal: el Padrón como instrumento para la realización de políticas públicas y para el ejercicio de derechos de españoles y extranjeros," Anuario de Gobierno Local (2003); and Velasco Caballero, F., "Políticas y competencias locales sobre inmigración," in *Inmigración y gobiernos locales, dir.* S. Díez Sastre, *Inmigración y gobiernos locales*, Madrid-Barcelona-Buenos Aires (2010).
62. LC 83. Despite this, the totality of authorities over benefits and social care (for example in Article 138.1 Statute of Autonomy of Catalonia) attributed to the Government of Catalonia in the areas of the social and economic integration of immigrants "must under no circumstances be understood to have pushed aside the sole power of the State over immigration matters." In this sense, the exclusive powers regarding the initial shelter of immigrants [Article 138.1 a) SAC] that appellants brand as particularly unconstitutional, should be considered to be ascribed to the area of initial social and health interventions and guidance, as is revealed by its literal tone.

Comparative Notes on the Rights of Unauthorized Aliens

MATTHEW KUENNING, UNIVERSITY OF ILLINOIS AT URBANA-CHAMPAIGN, TOMÁS DE LA QUADRA-SALCEDO JANINI, AUTONOMOUS UNIVERSITY OF MADRID

The fundamental difference between the two legal systems seems to be rooted in the fact that United States' courts still have not ruled clearly with respect to whether it is the U.S. Constitution that provides for the rights of unauthorized aliens, or if that is instead the domain of state and local laws. By contrast, the Spanish Constitutional Court has held that unauthorized aliens, by virtue of being persons, are accorded a series of rights under the Spanish Constitution on an equal basis with Spanish nationals.

As a consequence of the fact that in the U.S. certain rights of unauthorized aliens have not been judicially declared to be Constitutional rights, it would seem to be both legally and politically possible that federal, state, or local legislatures may limit their rights in the future. On the other hand, it is also possible that courts will hold broadly that unauthorized aliens cannot be treated as if they are "outlaws," excluded from the protection of the law, because they are covered under the aegis of the Equal Protection Clause, which refers to "persons." A ruling of this type would foreclose much of the potential freedom of legislatures to impose limits on the rights of unauthorized aliens.

An important example of the kind of question that remains open in the U.S. system is whether a state legislature is permitted to declare that the contracts of unauthorized aliens are not enforceable, as the legislature of Alabama has recently purported to do. The Constitution guarantees equal protection of the laws to all "persons," and certainly unauthorized immigrants are persons. The question is whether their status as persons who are present in violation of the immigration laws limits the extent to which they may claim the protection of other laws. In the Spanish case, the Constitution and the rulings of the Constitutional Court have made clear that such measures against unauthorized aliens are not permitted.

The fact that the Spanish Constitutional Court has affirmed that the Spanish Constitution affords certain rights to unauthorized aliens allows one to distinguish, in the analysis of the Spanish system, between constitutional rights and rights recognized elsewhere in the legal system. In the case of non-constitutional rights, it is possible to analyze rights recognized in the Autonomy Laws as a unique and recently reformed element of the Spanish legal system.

Both of the preceding chapters briefly analyze the conditions that must be fulfilled for an alien to reside legally in each country, since it is the failure to fulfill those conditions that will determine whether a given alien is residing in the country without authorization. Next, the authors provide an analysis of the recognition, whether constitutionally based or not, of a series of rights conferred upon unauthorized aliens in each of the legal systems.

Beginning the comparison with respect to particular rights, one may conclude that the right of unauthorized immigrants to judicial protection in the form of access to the courts has been fully accepted in both legal systems. In the Spanish system, it would be recognized directly under the Constitution according to the doctrine developed by the Constitutional Court. In the U.S., it is still a matter of debate among jurists whether access to the courts, outside the context of criminal law, is provided for by the use of the term "person" in the Fifth and Fourteenth Amendments; or whether, on the contrary, such access is founded on sources outside the U.S. Constitution and therefore subject to being changed by Congress or by state legislatures. In the area of the criminal law, the U.S. Supreme Court has clearly affirmed that unauthorized immigrants also have all the rights provided to defendants by the Constitution.

With regard to the right of access to public benefits by unauthorized aliens, there are also certain similarities between the two systems, while at the same time one may remark on the existence of differences between their normative bases. Both systems have recognized the right of access to emergency health care. In the Spanish case, that recognition is based on the Constitution through the connection between life and physical integrity and human dignity. In the case of the U.S., it is tied to a mandate of Congress. Since 1986, Congress has mandated that hospitals with emergency departments must treat all persons requiring emergency care, and that the government will reimburse hospitals for emergency care provided to any indigent person. It is unclear whether Congress has the authority to remove this right to emergency medical care from unauthorized immigrants, or whether the U.S. Constitution would prohibit doing so.

On the other hand, in both systems there is no legal right to access health benefits for non-emergency care. In the Spanish case, this is so following the effective date of the recent Decree 16/2012, of April 20, regarding urgent measures to guarantee the sustainability of the National Health System and improve the quality and security of its benefits. Previously the right of access to non-emergency care was afforded to unauthorized aliens who were registered residents in Spain. It remains to be seen whether this change in the law will be upheld by the Constitutional Court if it is challenged.

There are also similarities between the U.S. and Spain in the recognition of the right to education for minors. However there are, again, discrepancies in what is cited as the foundation for that right. In the Spanish case, the foundation for the right is the Spanish Constitution, since the Constitutional Court has held that the right to education for minors (which is supposed to extend to non-obligatory education of minors) ought to be afforded to unauthorized aliens on the same terms as to Spaniards, since they are covered under the Constitutional grant of this right to "all," regardless of their legal status in Spain. On the contrary, in the U.S., limitations on the access to primary and secondary education for minors would be theoretically possible. There is precedent, however, that any such attempt at limiting education to minors must pass a level of scrutiny more stringent than mere reasonableness, since minors are not responsible for their unauthorized status and to leave them outside the educational system would have serious consequences for them. The U.S. Supreme Court has not accepted that the need either to conserve public resources or to prevent illegal immigration is an adequate purpose to justify limitations on access to education for minors. Congress, however, has prohibited using public funds for higher education of undocumented immigrants unless specifically enabled by state legislatures.

With regard to the workplace rights of unauthorized immigrants, in both systems it is understood that the illegal status of the worker will not, in general, be an obstacle to the recognition of workplace rights. Nor will it be an obstacle to obtaining the benefits to which they may be entitled. However, again, the basis for recognizing these rights is different. In the U.S., the availability of workplace protections depends on the definition of the word "employee" in the relevant statutes. Unauthorized aliens have been held to be employees even though their employment is unlawful. Of course, the legislatures could change these definitions.

The analysis of the rights afforded to unauthorized aliens in each of the legal systems allows one to observe the important similarities and differences between them. The fundamental difference has to do with the rule that they rely on. That is, while in Spain the Constitutional Court has had the opportunity to affirm that the failure to comply with the requirements for being legally present or residing in Spain does not permit the legislature to deny unauthorized aliens the rights that they have constitutionally as persons. In the U.S. system, a doctrinal discussion continues regarding the extent to which unauthorized aliens are included under the equal protection clause. To the extent they are not included, the space for the federal and state legislatures to extend or limit rights would be that much greater.

PART THREE

CHAPTER FIVE

Local Autonomy From the Burdens of National Sovereignty

A Case Study of Local Immigration Policies in the City of Chicago, Cook County, and the State of Illinois

AMALIA PALLARES, UNIVERSITY OF ILLINOIS AT CHICAGO
MARIA DE LOS ANGELES TORRES,
UNIVERSITY OF ILLINOIS AT CHICAGO

The authors want to thank Rigo Padilla for his research assistance and Fred Tsao for his incisive comments.

INTRODUCTION

Chicago's development is closely tied to incoming groups of immigrants from almost every part of the world. Mayor Rahm Emanuel, elected in 2011, has declared that Chicago will become the most immigrant-friendly city in the U.S. Unlike smaller, rural towns and regions in other parts of the U.S., there is a stated recognition of the importance of immigrants' contributions to the city's economy and identity.

Immigration has continued to define the essence of Chicago. Since the late 1970s, there has been an increase of immigrants—mainly from Latin America—who have settled in Chicago and its surrounding blue-collar counties. While the federal government has hardened its stance against undocumented immigrants, state policies, as well as municipal and county ordinances, have challenged federal practices that are harmful to the incoming population. Immigrant communities have a long history of mobilizing for city services and, more recently, have been leaders of national immigrant rights movements, including the DREAM Act movement. Chicago's local governments, as well as the state of Illinois, have been at the forefront in the refusal to collaborate with federal enforcement policies.

They have also taken an innovative lead in incorporating immigrants, including those who are undocumented.

Politically, Chicago is a Democratic city whose demographic and political power gives Cook County and Illinois governments a Democratic majority. Some of the main constituencies of Democratic politicians include labor, social service, community-based, and non-profit organizations and health providers. African American and Latino voters are also part of this base, which leads to strong advocacy for liberal labor, health, and social policies that are broad and inclusive of immigrants. For example, even before the creation of the All Kids health program described later, Illinois already had one of the most generous state health policies. This was in large part a consequence of the advocacy efforts of health and social service agencies. Additionally, immigrant rights organizations and social movements advocate to state and city governments directly and also use their influence with supportive politicians—namely Latino officials and coalitions.

Additionally, as Latinos have increased their electoral power—with a rising number of Latino electors, aldermen, and state representatives, as well as wards and districts with Latino majorities or hyper-majorities—there has been a growing commitment to resolutions and proposals that protect and promote immigrant rights. After all, new Latin American immigrants do settle into established Latino communities and become part of the economic, social, and political fiber. At the city level, Latino aldermen usually propose these resolutions. At the state level, Latino elected officials may propose legislation or work with non-Latino politicians whose districts have a significant Latino voting bloc as proposers. These non-Latino politicians' motives are often strategic but, generally, garner strong support from Latinos.

This economic and political context helps explain why the City of Chicago, Cook County, and, ultimately, the state of Illinois can generally be characterized as supportive of the rights of undocumented immigrants and invested in immigrant integration. Moreover, many Chicago and state politicians publicly endorse this position at public events and appearances. For example, former Mayor Richard Daley—a descendant of Irish immigrants—attended and spoke in the massive immigration marches of 2006, 2007, and 2008. One caveat to note is that suburban counties and communities in downstate Illinois are more likely to be Republican and less supportive, making the experience of immigrants in those areas quite a different one.[1]

While the federal government has the authority over immigration laws—particularly regarding enforcement—it relies on local governments to help implement policies. Local governments, however, are charged with the task of dealing with large numbers of immigrants—many who have settled in global metropolitan areas and are oftentimes undocumented. Some local governments, particularly states, have opted for enforcing federal laws when they determined that the federal government was being lax in its duties. Others, however, have decided not to collaborate with the federal government. This has consequently been a contested arrangement.

Specifically, at the heart of this chapter is an inquiry into the multiple concepts and practices underlying the deportation (or enforcement of federal immigration law) and incorporation of immigrants in Chicago and Illinois. We will explore various instances in which the City of Chicago, the Cook County government, and the state of Illinois—entities distinct from the federal government—have opted not to collaborate with federal government enforcement programs, as well as instances in which they have initiated innovative programs to incorporate immigrants. For each instance, the political context is provided as an analysis of the arguments used. In conclusion, we are interested in understanding how these practices at the local level suggest new ways of interpreting citizenship in a global world and, thereby, create alternative sites for democratic practices.

CHICAGO BECOMES A SANCTUARY CITY

Chicago is a large Democratic city that has been a site of mature and intense immigrant rights political activism, and fits the model of the "sanctuary" or more permissive city, as studied by Ramakrishnan and Wong (2007). According to these authors, partisanship is the most important factor in determining whether a city is restrictionist (Republican majority) or permissive (Democrat majority). Additionally, while not a perfect correlation, permissive cities tend to be large while restrictionist cities are medium-sized. Finally, the presence of political activism is another key variable, as permissive policies are six times more likely to exist in areas with protests than in areas without them (Hedrick, 2011).

These factors were at play in the early 1980s, when Harold Washington was elected the first African American mayor of the city of Chicago. An extraordinary coalition of African Americans, Latinos, and progressive white voters made his victory possible (Cordova, 1998), though Latino voters were critical to his general election (Gills & Alkalimat, 1989). Washington reciprocated in the early months of his administration by naming a Commission on Latino Affairs, which he charged with conducting research and developing policies to better provide opportunities and services to the city's growing Latino communities (Torres, 1991).

At this point, immigration per se was not central to the overall Latino agenda. Although the majority of Latinos in Chicago were Mexicans, at the time many were legal residents. Activist groups—some that had been central to Harold Washington's victory and had members who were named to the Latino Commission—were involved in grassroots movements working with the most vulnerable populations, including undocumented immigrants (Torres, 2004). For them, the defense of the undocumented took the form of labor protection and concerns over federal deportations, which were on an uptick as the flow of immigrants was increasing. Local police, including the Chicago Police Department, were beginning to ask individuals they had stopped to show proof of legality. These practices did not affect only Latinos, since Chicago was a city with significant numbers of undocumented immigrants from western and eastern Europe as well. The immigration issue in Chicago was not as racialized as it was in the Southwest U.S. As such, members of the Latino Commission—many representing a series of sectors and nationalities—advocated for a local municipal strategy on immigration that could address questions of employment and services, as well as the cooperation of local police with federal immigration officers.

An executive order was necessary since the city council was in a battle with the mayor and obstructed most of his legislative initiatives. Through his office, Mayor Washington had the executive power to instruct the departments in his administration, including the police, on how to conduct city business (Mousin, 2005). Executive orders stand as legal mandates in lieu of legislation, and so the order essentially prohibited city departments from asking any person receiving services from the city, stopped by the police, or applying for employment about their immigration status. The issuance of this executive order was possible for a variety of reasons. Principally, Latinos were perceived to be a critical part of the mayor's coalition. His closest allies were Mexican advocates such as Jesus "Chuy" Garcia, who had been a leader in the movement to defend undocumented workers. In addition, this issue provided the mayor with an opportunity to draw in white ethnic aldermen who had formed an opposition bloc against him. Indeed, Alderman Roman Pucinski—a leader of the Polish-American community—attended the press conference in which the mayor announced this order. This was the first time since the mayor had won his election that someone from the opposition appeared in public with him.

There was also the contentious relationship between municipal government and the Republican Reagan administration. Deep cuts in federal funding to typically Democrat-controlled municipal governments made it easier for the mayor to also ask why municipal governments should be forced to pay for federal government activities that were not mandated by law. Furthermore, there was a national movement to have municipal governments declare their cities "sanctuaries." As a result of the war in Central America, many undocumented refugees were finding their way to U.S. cities. Churches of various denominations were involved in creating "sanctuaries," and the number of sanctuary cities was increasing throughout the country. Then, in 1986, Congress passed the Immigration Reform and Control Act, which among other things, obligated employers to require proof of legal residency or citizenship from all job applicants, making the prohibition of collaboration between police and federal agents an imperative aspect of Mayor

Washington's order. After the mayor's death in 1987, his successor Eugene Sawyer extended the order. After his 1989 election, Mayor Richard M. Daley did the same, though he received some criticism from a national anti-immigrant group.

In 2006, the city council codified the executive order and passed a law that was signed by Mayor Daley and, basically, reiterated the policy of non-cooperation with the federal government unless otherwise required by federal or state laws. During the debate on this proposal, Alderman Ed Burke reminded his fellow council members that, in 1850, Mayor James Curtis had issued an executive order forbidding Chicago police from cooperating with the federal government in the enforcement of the federal Fugitive Slave Act. This act had required authorities in northern states where slavery had been abolished to capture and return to their "owners" any escaped slaves found in their territories. And so it was not the first time that the city had opted for a human rights agenda in contrast to the federal government (Mousin, 2005).

It is important to note that Chicago's sanctuary policy is also a policy of integration. According to Ridgley (2008), sanctuary rulings have significance beyond the prevention of increased enforcement, as they are the first site of protection or defense. She analyzes how San Francisco's sanctuary resolution eventually evolved into long-term legislation, political discourse, and institutional practices that aimed to protect rights of all immigrants in the city. By offering some provisions for the confidentiality of immigration status, the city sanctuary movement challenged the exclusion of non-citizens from substantive rights such as housing, health care, education, police services, employment, and social assistance.

In addition to the sanctuary resolutions, Chicago has adopted several resolutions supporting immigration reform and validating the rights of undocumented immigrants. Like the cities of Boston, San Francisco, Sonoma, Seattle, and Cleveland, the Chicago City Council assumes a role of protector and advocate, regularly passing declarations urging state and federal officials to implement policy that is more inclusive of immigrants. Examples include several resolutions imploring the U.S. government to pass a moratorium that would prevent the massive deportation of undocumented immigrants, support the DREAM Act, and revise immigration law to allow the legalization of most undocumented immigrants. Some resolutions are addressed to the state, such as the 2007 request to the Illinois Senate to allow undocumented immigrants to obtain driver's licenses. Others are addressed to the federal government in specific cases against individual deportations.

Since most of these resolutions have no power to change policy, they are primarily symbolic and may raise questions. For example, why do advocacy groups go through the efforts of lobbying for these resolutions? And why do aldermen go to the trouble of introducing them? The resolutions do serve a purpose for politicians and advocacy organizations. Since immigration is such an important issue for most of the Latino population, and city government cannot change federal law, these resolutions allow aldermen to become immigrant rights advocates in the eyes of their constituents. They can publicly denounce the injustices of federal law and articulate a vision of justice for immigrants based on a concept of equality of all the cities' residents. For immigrant rights advocates, the city council frequently provides the initial platform as the first level of government that publicly supports or sponsors their claims and position.

La Familia Latina Unida (LFLU)—a group of thirty-five families seeking relief from deportation for one or more of its family members—organized a number of trips to Washington, D.C., to lobby for a private bill and advocate for legalization of undocumented parents who have at least one child who is a citizen. In their initial phase of organizing (2006–2007), they lobbied the Chicago City Council for resolutions in support of legalization and those advocating for the rights of undocumented parents, as well as a moratorium on deportations (Pallares, 2010). The process involved lengthy hearings, press conferences in which advocates and aldermen participated, and the speeches by several aldermen advocating for reform. These efforts provided significant local publicity for the cause, an opportunity for the aldermen to show their support, and a resolution that LFLU members could take to D.C. to show congressional representatives that the city of Chicago supported them.

As mentioned earlier, while political and economic interests favor this immigrant incorporation, there are also local ideologies of belonging that support city advocacy. Some of the key ideas mentioned in the city council discourse are notions of security, historical presence, and economic contribution, as well as human, family, and civil rights. Notions of security are associated with the sanctuary resolution, as Chicago and other city's enforcement officials have repeatedly expressed concerns with immigration laws that would stop victims and witnesses from revealing needed information—hence interfering with crime solution and prevention.[2] Historically, Chicago's relationship with immigration has formed a basic part of its identity, with immigrants as the city's builders. The city council's Moratorium Resolution—confirmed on April 26, 2006—states, "For the past one hundred fifty years, the City of Chicago has been hope and home to immigrants from throughout the globe." The mayor observed, "We are reminded that the history of Chicago is the history of immigrants, their sacrifices and achievement." He then exhorted all legislators to demonstrate compassion for the families and communities who would be impacted by their decision.

In addition to the historical dimension, this same resolution also highlighted the economic and social contribution of immigrants—another recurrent theme—indicating that, "Immigrants are 26% of the workforce and an unquantifiable part of the city's history, character and functions." In a March 1, 2006, resolution opposing the federal Sensenbrenner Bill (H.R. 4437), the city council stated,

"Undocumented immigrants contribute to the vitality of the city by filling key roles in its economy, paying taxes and contributing to its schools, neighborhoods, churches and communities." The recognition of the role of labor immigrants in the city is also clearly maintained in a May 26, 2004, resolution urging the U.S. Congress to adopt a comprehensive immigration bill in which it is noted, "Our society and economy have many sectors whose stability is dependent upon the labor of immigrants, and in particular on those who have no legal status, undocumented immigrants who are eager to come out of the shadows and become full members of this nation and this city to which now they contribute so much."

Concerns about the rights of immigrant families are expressed in declarations such as the April 9, 2007, "Family Unity Day," which urges all residents to "participate in a day of prayer, peaceful gathering and petitioning of representatives for an end to the tragedy and suffering of the separation of immigrant families, urging Illinois Congressional delegation to support reform." Additionally, the October 2008 Moratorium Resolution exhorted all elected officials and congressional candidates to provide their support in the name of families and to denounce raids.[3] In terms of civil rights of a population that includes and extends beyond the immigrant population, this declaration expressed a concern with the issue of racial profiling—something that becomes necessary to enforce federal immigration policy and therefore violates municipal code—noting that, "These anti-immigration actions have created a climate of division and a destruction of communities as well as a proliferation of the perpetration of hate crimes and the continuation of racial profiling." The same document claims that it is impossible to crack down on the undocumented without inflicting great suffering on many people who are not violating the law and without throwing segments of communities into disarray.

A review of the political processes that led to these declarations reveals that the Chicago City Council is a site for social movements, community organizations, and local politicians to come together—particularly as many of these organizations are resources for those politicians who have close ties to community activists and depend on them for campaign support. The hearings, usually initiated by Latino aldermen, are opportunities for said leaders to reinforce their position as strong immigrant advocates, who are working directly with activists. For activists, city council resolutions are no longer simply a first step in a long struggle for federal change, but a platform, a safe space from which to demand state and federal officials to heed the call. It is important to understand these hearings not necessarily as an end in and of themselves, but as a means to the political construction of an immigrant-friendly regime. They are part of a system in which different social and political actors seek to reinforce their power and further their causes by advocating on behalf of the city, pressuring other levels of government and encouraging these government levels to actually come together.

In 2011, Rahm Emanuel, who had been a congressman and the chief of staff to President Barack Obama, won the mayoral race in Chicago. However, he won a very small percentage of the Latino vote. As advisor to the Democratic Party, Rahm Emanuel had advocated that Democrats take a hard stance against immigrants. Indeed many immigrant advocates blamed him for Obama's abysmal record on immigration reform and voted against him. Immediately after taking office, his stance changed, and he began appearing in press conferences with immigrant advocates. Within the first months of his administration, he created a New Americans Office. In December 2012, he unveiled his plan that outlined 27 initiatives

> to build a thriving, diverse and welcoming city over the next three years. The plan, which is the first of its kind in the nation, highlights the potential economic impact when the City supports the creation and expansion of immigrant-owned businesses; develops, attracts, and retains talent and expertise from other countries; and aims to bolster the City's status as a vibrant and welcoming international city. (City of Chicago, 2012)

COOK COUNTY

In Illinois, one of the latest contestations between local government levels and the federal government comes from Cook County. County governments encompass a larger geographic area than cities (Duncombe, 1977); in fact, Cook County encompasses several cities, including Chicago. The county has an elected Board of Commissioners, ten from Chicago and seven from surrounding municipalities. These individuals oversee a series of entities, most importantly the public hospital system and Cook County public safety—which includes the Sheriff's Office, jail system, and local court system. As such, in terms of law enforcement, this group represents an important cornerstone between federal and local governments.

In the wake of a national movement to deny services to non-citizens, including legal residents, a group of county commissioners spearheaded by Roberto Maldonado—who had been on the staff of Harold Washington's Commission on Latino Affairs—introduced a resolution similar to the city's that reiterated every person's entitlement to services regardless of legal status. This statement was particularly important since it provided undocumented immigrants with health services from Cook County hospitals and clinics.

However, as deportation numbers increased, the boundaries between local and immigration officials began to blur. A group of commissioners—this time headed by Jesus "Chuy" Garcia, who had also been part of Harold Washington's group, and Board President Toni Preckwinkle—began to explore ways to curtail the collaboration between county government and the federal government. Specifically, they were concerned with the federal government's requests to hold individuals who may be wanted by the U.S. Immigration and Customs Enforcement (ICE) longer than what is required by criminal procedures. When an individual is arrested and charged with a crime, they are sent to the county jails where they eventually appear before a judge who formalizes charges and sets a bond—if it is determined that the accused is not a flight risk or an imminent threat to society. When bond is posted, the individual is set free until the trial. However, the county had been asked to hold individuals on the ICE detainers list for an extra 48 hours, giving ICE the opportunity to detain and deport the accused.

Detainers presented an occasion for the county to exert some independence from the federal government. Commissioner Garcia introduced a proposed ordinance stating that—in the name of fairness and equality—every detainee would be treated the same, and no extra jail time would be imposed on someone who had an ICE detainer. The central argument included in the ordinance has to do with inconsistencies in the manner that ICE requests for detainers; it is not clear what procedures they use, or whether or not a person is indeed deportable. As such, the ordinance essentially asserts that these requests would not be honored unless ICE had a warrant for the specific individual. In addition, the ordinance contends that the county is being forced to pay for the extra days that a person is being held beyond the bond period (Cook County Board of Commissioners, 2011).

The legislation passed after the county had spent roughly $15 million per year, or $143 per detainee per day (Olivo, 2011). Commissioner Jesus "Chuy" Garcia was quoted as saying,

> It is about ensuring the fair treatment of all people. In America, we don't detain people without probable cause. That would violate constitutional guarantees like due process and equal protection. But these detainers are not based on probable cause, and they have been imposed on U.S. citizens, including veterans, by mistake. (Lu, 2011)

Creating a two-tracked system for people who were identified by ICE as needing extra holding days was a violation of due process procedure and had serious constitutional implications (Cunningham, 2012).

The passage of this ordinance was particularly significant since it occurred during a period of heated immigration debate in the U.S., and it touched on public safety issues. Nonetheless, it is justified with the language of equal access and fits within the county's own strategic visions of streamlining procedures to make justice accessible to all (Cook County Board of Commissioners, STAR, 2011). It also suggests the critical place of Latinos within local politics. Though Jesus "Chuy" Garcia had been an early proponent of the defense of undocumented immigrants, he had for a long time been out of the public eye. His 2011 election to the Cook County Board marked a comeback. The landscape in the community had changed, and what was once a marginal issue for Latinos had become central to the Latino agenda. For him, it was a way of reentering and resituating himself in what was now one of the most critical issues for the community.

Toni Preckwinkle, who had been a close ally and alderman to the Obamas, retained a long record of progressive politics and coalition building. She had also been an advocate for a more humane public safety policy and, consequently, this issue resonated with her perspectives of social justice and equality for all accused criminals.

Although Chicago and its local governments are leaders in many of these ordinances, there are other places in which they are being discussed and litigated. The Cook County ordinance was based on a recent federal ruling in Indiana that determined ICE detainers are voluntary requests and not criminal warrants. Similar ordinances exist in San Francisco and two counties in New Mexico (Olivo, 2011), and have been enacted in Santa Clara County, California; New York City; New Orleans; Newark, New Jersey; King County, Washington; and elsewhere in Connecticut and California.

STATE OF ILLINOIS

While the Chicago and county policies have been mostly symbolic, with some exceptions, state policies have had more teeth and proved to be integral steps in the incorporation of Illinois immigrants by detaining federal policies of enforcement. Additionally, in terms of incorporation, the state has instituted the following: New Americas Initiative, Day Labor Act, All Kids, Illinois DREAM Act, the In-State Tuition Bill, and—most recently—the granting of temporary driver's licenses to undocumented immigrants. Governors and other state politicians have partnered with immigrant, community, educational, and health associations to create policies that protect immigrants from fast-track deportations and provide all immigrants access to certain services and opportunities. However, Illinois's most important non-enforcement statement has been the attempt to withdraw from a national program called Secure Communities.

In the wake of the September 11, 2001, terrorist attacks, the U.S. Congress enacted a series of legislative initiatives, including the creation of a Homeland Security Department that would house the former Immigration and Naturalization Services—which had previously been under the Justice Department. The intent was to tighten borders and identify potential terrorists. It further centralized immigration powers under the executive branch, and at the same time it outlined ways in which states and local law enforcement would participate in the detaining and deporting of criminal undocumented immigrants. As part of these efforts, a national program called Secure Communities was launched to enlist counties in national efforts to identify undocumented immigrants. Essentially, this program asks counties to use a clearance procedure that is already in place—in which fingerprints of detainees are checked against an FBI data bank—and also need to clear through an ICE data bank. If ICE determines that the suspect lacks immigration status, it issues a detainer, requesting that the individual be held for 48 hours beyond when that person would otherwise be released so that ICE can apprehend that individual for deportation proceedings. The Illinois State Police signed an agreement of cooperation with ICE in 2009.

Secure Communities was successful in terms of the record number of individuals deported. Since Obama took office, more than 400,000 individuals a year have been detained and deported, due in part to Secure Communities. Coupled with the fact that an immigration offense—which had historically been considered a civil crime—was now elevated to a criminal offense, with a felony charge after a person is caught a second time, there have been an unprecedented number of deportees and incarceration of individuals on felony charges related to immigration. A series of administrative initiatives have contributed to this, including the creation of a quota system by the Obama administration in order to spend all the money Congress appropriated for deportations. The mechanism that accelerated the process was the Secure Communities program.

While Secure Communities hit record numbers, it failed in its mission to identify only criminals—and, more specifically, violent criminals. Instead, it was non-criminal undocumented immigrants who made up the majority of those caught in the enforcement net. As immigration research institutes began to document the backgrounds of those who had been deported, local activists throughout the country began mobilization to change these procedures.

The Illinois Coalition for Immigrant and Refugee Rights (ICIRR) took the lead to advocate that the state sever its agreement with the federal government's program, arguing that 46% of people whom ICE had arrested under Secure Communities had no convictions and another 31% had convictions for only minor offenses. As a first step, the State Assembly passed the "Smart Enforcement Act" (HB 1598), which:

- Enabled counties that do not want to participate to opt out;
- Required counties that do participate to report certain information regarding immigrants flagged by the program;
- Barred use of state funds for deportation of immigrants not convicted of any crimes (ICIRR, 2011).

By arguing that Secure Communities caught the wrong people, created mistrust between police and immigrant communities, and cost taxpayers money, advocates succeeded in convincing Governor Pat Quinn to issue a letter of termination to the Illinois Memorandum of Agreement with Homeland Security. In his letter, the governor states, "Secure Communities was supposed to help detect those convicted of serious criminal offenses. According to its own statistics only about 30% of those detained in the state of Illinois fit this description" (Quinn, 2011).

There are a variety of factors that contributed to the governor's willingness to break an agreement with the federal government. He has had a history of progressive politics and, as such, he was compelled by the argument that this program was deporting hard working, decent people in greater numbers than criminals. In addition, while the immigration issue may not have been central to the Latino political agenda in the early 1980s, clearly it had become central in the new millennium. Latinos, mainly Mexicans, make up about 25% of the city of Chicago. New communities have emerged throughout Illinois, making it easier for statewide elected officials to address issues pertinent to this community from the state level. Governor Quinn had a strong base of support in the Latino community and, accordingly, was willing to take on this political issue. As noted earlier, questions of immigration were not racialized in the Midwest as they were in the Southwest.

Still, the federal government overrode the governor's decision to withdraw from to reinstate Secure Communities. Homeland Security even issued a letter claiming that states do not have the right to opt out of the program. ICE has since fully deployed Secure Communities throughout Illinois and the rest of the United States as of January 2013. Even though, according to the Constitution, the federal government cannot dictate police practices to state and local governments, the federal government still had authority to order the state to comply.

INCORPORATION/EMPOWERMENT

The state of Illinois partnered with the ICIRR to create the New Americas Initiative in 2004, a program aimed at naturalizing immigrants. ICIRR administers the $3 million per year program—involving workshops and naturalization campaigns organized by ICIRR's umbrella organizations—which has led to important increases in naturalization rates. Additionally, in the same year—2004—the initiative was signed, then-Governor Rod Blagojevich signed the New Americans Executive Order, creating an office that helps newcomers fully assimilate to the state by providing better improved and more coordinated immigrant services. Moreover, the state partners with ICIRR and the Illinois Department of Human Services (IDHS) to run the Immigrant Family Resource Program (IFRP), which facilitates immigrant access to public benefits. IFRP funds organizations that provide immigrant families with information and screening to determine their eligibility for public benefits and services, as well as case management services, and access to interpretation and/or translation services for immigrants who have difficulty communicating with IDHS.

Most recently, the state of Illinois has—in partnership with ICIRR, AmeriCorps, and the Robert R. McCormick Foundation—launched "Uniting America," an initiative designed to encourage volunteerism and community dialogue between immigrants and non-immigrants. Uniting America recruits long-time residents and new Americans to work together in the areas of U.S. citizenship, ESL classes, and after-school tutoring. Immigrant and long-term residents also work together to organize community service events.[4]

HEALTH

In July 2006, Illinois launched the nation's first universal coverage program for children—the All Kids program—which provides affordable, state-subsidized health insurance at an affordable price for all children in Illinois. Approved by both legislative chambers (32–23 vote in the Illinois Senate and 79–28 in the Illinois House) and signed into law in November 2005, it made Illinois the first state to provide universal care for all children regardless of immigration status, health status, or income. It was broadly supported by several non-governmental agencies (NGOs), including Citizen Action/Illinois, the Illinois Hospital Association, the Chicago Teachers Union, and ICIRR. While support for this program was very strong, one of the concerns was that it would make Illinois a magnet for the undocumented population (Coughlin & Cohen, 2007). The governor, a son of Serbian immigrants, argued that it benefited all to have undocumented children immunized and healthy, as—particularly for those able to become citizens in the future—their healthiness would also benefit their communities. Further, Illinois Public Act 094-0693 states that leaving children without insurance hurts the insured because the cost of paying for the care of the uninsured is ultimately shifted to higher premiums for the insured.

This program is one of the strongest expressions of the state's commitment to undocumented children. An annual audit released in April 2010 found that the program, after accounting for member contributions, cost the state a net of $70.2 million (of a total of $84.2 million in claims) since the state cannot seek any federal reimbursement for undocumented children (State of Illinois, Office of the Auditor General, 2010). While the program's record-keeping has been questioned—the audit claims some documented children were identified as undocumented, preventing Illinois from getting federal matching funds—a significant number of children added to the program are undocumented (Yount, 2011). According to Yount, in June 2011, 69% or 51,669 of the 74,975 children covered were reported as undocumented.[5] The release of the 2010 audit did generate controversy, as some media outlets and anti-immigrant groups questioned the use of millions of dollars in state funds for the health of undocumented children during a time of severe state financial crisis. One publication complained about the program's beneficiaries: "But the vast majority are illegal immigrants, who aren't doing at least one thing they're supposed to do—obey the law" (Yount, 2011). However, the program remains in place and has gained considerable national notoriety for being one of the most inclusive, accessible, and streamlined programs of its kind in the country (Kovach & Bouman, 2013).

The only health program available for undocumented adults is Illinois Cares Rx, which provides prescription drug assistance to low-income seniors and disabled people, regardless of immigration status.

LABOR

The Day Laborer and Temporary Service Act (HB 3471), which became effective in January 2006, requires agencies that place workers on a daily or temporary basis to register with the Illinois Department of Labor (IDOL) and comply with specified employment standards. Designed to protect the rights of 300,000 day laborers in Illinois—working in construction, landscaping, food processing, agriculture, and factory and domestic settings—the law creates penalties and enforcement procedures in cases when employment standards are violated and mandates that agencies have workers' compensation insurance. Though businesses that directly hired workers were obliged to follow basic labor laws, many third parties such as temporary agencies—some of which were unlicensed—had not been similarly regulated. The short-term nature of day labor and subcontracting pose significant barriers to the enforcement of laws, and these workers usually do not receive the same benefits or wages as full-time permanent employees who perform the same job (State of Illinois, Office of the Governor, 2005b)[6] Some of the most common targeted abuses are cheating workers of their wages by illegally deducting transportation and meal charges from their paychecks, as well as failing to protect their health and safety in the workplace.

While the Day Labor and Temporary Labor Service Act of 2000 already existed, the 2006 law ratcheted up the penalties for labor law violations and tightened the registration requirements for day and temporary labor agencies. Like other policies, several NGOs—including the Chicago Workers' Collaborative and Day Laborer Collaboration, the Chicago Interfaith Committee on Workers' Issues, the Chicago Federation of Labor, the Latino Union of Chicago, St. Pius Church, and the San Lucas Workers Center—advocated strongly for this legislation.

EDUCATION

The two most important education policies, affecting approximately 95,000 Illinois undocumented youth seeking higher education, are the In-State Tuition Bill and the Illinois DREAM Act. In 2003, the Illinois General Assembly In-State Tuition Bill

(HB 60) allowed undocumented students to attend college while paying in-state tuition, which is much more affordable than paying out of state or international tuition. Given the fact that undocumented students are ineligible for federal grants and loans, as well as many scholarships, paying the lowest tuition possible allows many more undocumented students to attend college. In order to be eligible, students must have attended an Illinois school for at least three years prior to high school graduation and graduated from an Illinois high school. Illinois was one of the first states to pass such a bill, and today there are thirteen other states with similar laws.[7]

A second key policy is the Illinois DREAM Act, passed on Memorial Day 2011, which establishes the Illinois DREAM Fund Scholarship that is accessible to undocumented immigrant youth. Additionally, the DREAM Act stipulates that all high school counselors be trained on the proper assistance for undocumented students seeking guidance counseling for college. Finally, the act establishes the creation of the Illinois DREAM Commission to administer the DREAM Fund, oversee implementation of the act, and research issues regarding undocumented student access to higher education.

Unlike the recently passed California DREAM ACT, however, this fund prohibits the use of moneys from the state and only allows receiving private donations that the commission is responsible for raising. The non-use of public funds and the elimination of a provision that would have allowed undocumented university students to drive were the two conditions that enabled the bill to gather sufficient support to come to a vote. These constraints reveal the limits of what was possible at the state-level at the time. While Chicago is mostly Democrat, downstate and some suburban communities tend to be Republican and were unlikely to vote for a bill that would have utilized public funds or created a provision to obtain a driver's license.[8] Even with these conditions, the Assembly vote was very close (61–53) in contrast to the State Senate vote a few weeks earlier (45–11). The final passage of the bill most likely relied not only on a massive advocacy campaign (including the support of dozens of organizations, educational institutions, Chicago Mayor Rahm Emanuel, Cardinal Frances George, and on some last minute negotiations and concessions between parties about other issues, including the redistricting map.

DRIVER'S LICENSES

One of the major obstacles for undocumented workers is the lack of documentation to drive. Many jobs require driving and many are located in places where there is little public transportation. The selling of fake driver's licenses was a thriving business in many immigrant communities. Creating this extra-legal process of documentation created multiple safety problems, including that many who paid for them were not properly trained to drive. Importantly, the lack of a license facilitated the arrest and deportation of undocumented immigrants initially charged with driving without a license and then at risk of facing deportation proceedings if ICE identified them in Cook County jails.

A coalition of public safety advocates, religious leaders, and pro-immigrant rights activists successfully advocated for the state to issue permits to all people regardless of immigration status. In January 2013, the state assembly voted to allow undocumented immigrants to obtain a temporary driver's license, finally granting a right that advocacy groups had struggled over for more than fourteen years. No state had passed a bill to grant licenses to undocumented immigrants since 2003—the only three other states to do so are Washington, Utah, and New Mexico. While the documents can only be used for the purposes of driving and not for identification, Illinois once again showed its willingness to create opportunities for undocumented immigrants. As in other pro-immigrant state legislation, the sponsors of the bill were members of the Latino legislative caucus. As a consequence of these efforts, the coalition achieved the passing of a bill that was broader than any previous legislative effort and included Mayor Emanuel, Secretary of State Jesse White, former Governor Jim Edgar, Governor James Pat Quinn, and in the last week before the vote, Illinois Speaker of the House Michael Madigan. The fact that eleven Republicans voted for the bill also attests to the growing power of the Latino vote and the bipartisan competition to obtain it.

In sum, a review of state policies that incorporate undocumented immigrants reveals a combination of increased access to basic protections and rights in the fields of education, labor, and health, as well as a pattern of partnering with community and immigrant rights organizations to provide resources that will allow immigrants to become more integrated and politically empowered. All of these policies have been executive and/or legislative responses to strong pressure and advocacy from labor, community, civil rights, and immigrant rights organizations.

However, we have also pointed out that weaker support for these policies outside the Chicago area, as well as an extended period of state fiscal crisis, has set important limits on state policies. Further, in order to advance an immigrant incorporation agenda and maintain the state's financial commitment to it, advocates for immigrant rights must simultaneously push for all opportunities possible while relying on delicate and complex negotiation processes. What remains clear is that the strength of the Latino vote in the 2012 presidential election did create more room to maneuver immigration reform issues, even at the local level.

CONCLUSIONS

There is a broader discussion at play about how effective any one of these local instances of independence from federal immigration policy can be (Keefe, 2010).

Still, the fact that local governments are making bold moves that pit them against a federal policy creates interesting windows into the complexities of empowerment politics, federalism, and ongoing debates about rights and equality in a global world.

U.S. state governments tend to play a stronger role in shaping local policy as they fall on different ends of a spectrum—from very restrictionist ones, such as Alabama and Arizona, to more immigrant-friendly or immigrant-accessible ones, such as Illinois and New York. Through legislation they are able to curtail immigrants' access to resources and services in the restrictive cases, or create policies and distribute funds for immigrant integration in more accessible states. In terms of enforcement, restrictionist states tend to implement more intense local information gathering and enforcement, while accessible states are more likely to question and even reject policies designed to have local authorities play a larger role in information gathering and deportation enforcement. By contrast, city and county governments have less of a distributive role, but can shape policy by entering into enforcement agreements that deputize local police and encourage the policing of immigrants' actions very closely—placing them at greater risk of deportation in restrictionist cases. More accessible areas, such as the city of Chicago and Cook County, tend to limit the amount of information they gather and share with the federal governments about an individual's identity and/or legal status in an effort to create a safe place in which migrants do not fear or avoid local authorities.

Both restrictionists and immigrant-accessible local governments are carving out a certain autonomy from a federal government, whose immigration policy they question as limited, broken, insufficient, or unfair. However, a key difference between the two is that while the former claim they are upholding national sovereignty (sometimes better than the federal state itself), the latter are pointing to the potential limits of sovereignty when it is pitted against personhood as well as local economic and political interests and conditions. While national sovereignty is not necessarily questioned in principle, it is weighed against other pressing interests, identities, and ideas that shape the willingness of public officials to implement existing federal policies and also lead to the generation of new ones. In this context, it could be stated that while the state and city government does not constitute national enforcement policy, its enforcement is mediated by it. Similarly, while there is no federal immigrant integration policy, nor clear national guidelines on how to do so, the state of Illinois is one of a few that has implemented policies to facilitate immigrant integration.

In developing alternative policies towards newcomers, Chicago and the state of Illinois have promoted a grounded form of local citizenship that encompasses local standards of justice as well as local government interests. This is evident in the number of resolutions the city has passed that go beyond designating itself as a sanctuary city to become an advocate for immigrant rights and immigration reform. It also includes the state of Illinois's recent policies in health, labor, highway safety, integration, and education, creating a state framework that leads to the recognition of the personhood of undocumented immigrants and their incorporation into state programs. While all of the significant incorporation policies are state policies, it is important to point out that the city of Chicago has the sufficient demographic and political weight and influence to significantly shape each of the state policies described in this chapter.

In recent years, geographers have come to understand the city as a significant space in which the substance and meaning of citizenship is given form.[9] They have explored the ways in which a substantive and meaningful citizenship is constituted by political agents in local places. Staeheli (2008) argues that substantive citizenship is shaped in localities as nation-states are removed from things that matter most to individuals and communities. This is not to say that citizenship within the nation-state is irrelevant, but rather that the nation-state is not the only scale at which citizenship is constructed or given meaning. Mark Purcell (2003) points to a new politics in which Lefebvre's concept of inhabitance forms the foundation of political membership. According to Lefebvre, the right to the city is earned by living in the city. Everyday life is the central pivot of the right to the city and those who go about their daily routines in the city, both living in and creating urban space, are those who possess a legitimate right to the city. In this view, inhabitance replaces national citizenship as the basis for membership, unhinging people's claim to belonging from the sovereignty of the nation-state and from the nation as the primary political community (Purcell, 2003, p. 578).

Varsanyi (2006) studies a broad range of local immigration policies in different states, arguing that they are forms of recognition of undocumented immigrants at the local level.[10] She proposes an ideal of grounded citizenship that does not depend on explicit consent to enter and remain in a bounded community, but on the mere reality of presence and residence in a place. She argues that these local policies are de facto form and consent and that, while they do not bestow citizenship, they do stretch the legal boundaries of who is considered a valid member of the public. Further, and most importantly for this chapter, she claims that these policies do not invoke international human rights or cosmopolitan ideals as their foundation, but instead are motivated by local and national conceptions of justice as well as local or state practicalities.

Both local conceptions of justice and economic and political practicalities have shaped Chicago and Illinois policies. As a gateway city, Chicago has a long history of immigrant presence and incorporation. Immigrant communities are a vital part of the dynamic local economy, and immigrants are business entrepreneurs as well as sources of flexible labor for potential investors. This economic infrastructure requires its preservation as an immigrant-friendly city. In a post-Fordist society, Chicago's metropolitan area has recreated itself as a global service economy and tourist destination that relies heavily on a service sector, which has key niches for immigrant labor. As such, its pro-immigrant policies respond to a global phenomenon and suggest new ways of thinking about inclusion and membership in global cities.

NOTES

1. Discrimination against Latino immigrants in housing led the U.S. Department of Justice to sue the city of Waukegan in 1996 over an ordinance that "allowed only a husband and a wife, their children and a maximum of two additional relatives to live in one house or apartment, regardless of size." For more on this issue, see Kuczka and Flink (1997). Additionally, in 2002, Waukegan had an ordinance put into effect that towed the cars of anyone caught driving without a license, though it was later found to be unconstitutional. See Rodriguez (2008) for more information on this instance. In 2006, the village of Carpentersville attempted to pass an ordinance which would have denied business permits and government contracts to employers who hired undocumented workers and also fined landlords $1,000 for knowingly renting to undocumented immigrants. Many immigrants moved to other communities as a consequence. After much controversy, the village board delayed implementing the measure indefinitely. While it is unlikely to resurface again, Carpentersville also has a towing ordinance that fines people $500 for returning their cars when they are stopped and do not have a license (Keilman, 2010).
2. In a March 29, 2006, amendment to the municipal code, it was said that "[the local enforcement of immigration laws] would cause a chilling effect on crime prevention and solving if both witnesses and victims are called upon to weigh a need to cooperate with local authorities against a fear of deportation, thereby undermining long-standing efforts to engender trust and cooperation between law enforcement officials and immigrant communities" (City of Chicago Joint Committee on Finance and Human Relations, 2006). Additionally, the International Association of Chiefs of Police, the Major Cities Chiefs Association and the California Police Chiefs Association all issued statements against the involvement of local police in the enforcement of immigration law (p. 72). There is a position paper released by the Major Cities Chiefs Police Association—representing police executives from the country's 63 largest jurisdictions—which states that if undocumented immigrants fear deportation from local police they'll never talk, even if witness to or victims of a crime. The first point—collaborating with the federal government—takes police resources and impairs capacity to ensure safety of communities.
3. It begins, "We, the Mayor and members of the City of Chicago City Council, assembled here this eighth day of October, 2008 A.D., do hereby renew our call for an immediate cessation of all wholesale raids, deportations and separation of the families of undocumented immigrants and urge all candidates for the United States Congress and United States Senate as well as all candidates for President of the United States to commit themselves publicly to a moratorium on all raids, deportations and separation of families until comprehensive immigration reform is passed and, furthermore, commit themselves publicly to pressing for the enactment of comprehensive immigration reform in the first one hundred days of the next Congress."
4. For more information, visit: http://icirr.org/content/uniting-america-1
5. However, according to the same audit in the sample of 48 children the audit found that 19% were in fact documented, meaning the 69% is most likely an overstatement.

6. "Governor Blagojevich signs Legislation to help protect 300,00 workers" Office of the Governor, State of Illinos Press Release. August 9, 2005. http://www.state.il.us/agency/idol/News/DLSPress.htm
7. Other states that permit undocumented immigrants to obtain in-state tuition are California, Connecticut Kansas, Maryland, Massachusetts, Nebraska, New Mexico, New York, Oklahoma, Texas, Utah, Washington, and Wisconsin. Another 12 states have explicitly refused to grant in-state tuition to illegal immigrants. In June 2011, the U.S. Supreme Court rejected a challenge to California's policy of granting reduced, in-state tuition at its colleges and universities to graduates of its high schools, regardless of immigration status.
8. Attempts to pass a drivers' certificate for undocumented immigrants had passed the House, but failed to pass the Senate in 2007.
9. (Secor, 2004; Staeheli, 2003, 2008, 2012)
10. Admitting *matriculas consulares* as a form of identification or providing in-state college tuition for undocumented students are examples of this type of recognition.

REFERENCES

Cook County Board of Commissioners. (2011). Policy for responding to ICE detainers [Proposed ordinance]. Retrieved from http://www.national immigrationproject.org/community/Cook%20County%20ordinance%20against%20detainers.pdf

Cordova, T. (1998). Harold Washington and the rise of Latino electoral politics in Chicago: 1982–1987. In D. Montejano (Ed.), *Chicano politics and society in the late twentieth century* (pp. 31–57). Austin: University of Texas Press.

Cunningham, A. (2012). Letter to President Toni Preckwinkle in http://www.huffingtonpost.com/2012/04/11/toni-preckwinkle-cook-cou_n_1417864.html

Duncombe, H. S. (1977). *Modern county government.* Washington, D.C.: National Association of Counties.

Gills, D. C., & Alkalimat, A. (1989). *Harold Washington and the crisis of black power in Chicago: Mass protest.* Chicago, IL: Twenty-first Century Books and Publications.

Hedrick, J. (2011). *Welcoming the huddled masses: Sanctuary policies in American cities.* Retrieved from http://hedrick.blogs.rice.edu/files/2011/03/SWPSA2011_Hedrick_Sanctuary.pdf

Kovach, A., & Bouman, J. (2013). *The Affordable Care Act's tools for attacking racial health disparities.* Retrieved from http://povertylaw.org/clearinghouse/article/affordable-care-act%E2%80%99s-tools-attacking-racial-health-disparities

Lutton, W. (1995). Chicago provides 'sanctuary' for illegal aliens. *Social Contract Journal, 5*(3),.

Mousin, C. B. (2005). A CLEAR view from the prairie: Harold Washington and the people of Illinois respond to federal encroachment of human rights. *Southern Illinois University Law Journal, 29*, 285, 295.

Pallares, A. (2010). Representing la familia: Family separation and immigrant activism. In A. Pallares & N. Flores-Gonzalez (Ed.), *Marcha: Latino Chicago and the immigrant rights movement* (pp. 215–236). Champaign, IL: University of Illinois Press.

Purcell, M. (2003). Citizenship and the right to the global city: Reimagining the capitalist world order. *International Journal of Urban and Regional Research, 27*(3), 564–590.

Quinn, P. (2011, May 4). Letter to Mark Rapp, Acting Commission of Immigration Enforcement, re: Secure Communities Program. Retrieved from http://epic.org/privacy/secure_communities/sc_ill.pdf

Ramakrishnan, S. K., & Wong. T. (2007, November). *Immigration policies go local: The varying responses of local governments to undocumented immigration.* Retrieved from http://www.law.berkeley.edu/files/RamakrishnanWongpaperfinal.pdf

Ridgley, J. (2008). Cities of refuge: Immigration enforcement, police and the insurgent genealogies of citizenship in U.S. sanctuary cities. *Urban Geography, 29*(1), 53–77.

Staeheli, L.A. (2008). Citizenship and the problem of community. *Political Geography 27*(1): 5–21.

Torres, M. A. (1991). The commission on Latino affairs: A case study of community empowerment. In P. Clavel & W. Wiewel (Eds.), *Harold Washington and the neighborhoods: Progressive city government in Chicago, 1983–1987* (pp. 165–187). New Brunswick, NJ: Rutgers University Press.

Torres, M. A. (2004). A search for meaningful voice and place: The IPO and Latino community empowerment in Chicago. In G. Cardenas (Ed.), *La causa: Civil rights, social justice, and the struggle for equality in the Midwest.* Houston, TX: Arte Público Press.

Varsanyi, M. (2006). Interrogating urban citizenship vis-à-vis undocumented migration. *Citizenship Studies, 10*(2), 229–249.

News Reports

Cable, J. (2005, June 9). Illinois law aims to protect temporary laborers. *EHS Today.* Retrieved from http://ehstoday.com/news/ehs_imp_37631

Keefe, A. (2010, February 16). Local sanctuary laws not as protective as they seem. *Medill Reports.* Retrieved, from http://news.medill.northwestern.edu

Keilman, J. (2010, May 25). Carpentersville tries to move on after '06 immigration battle. *Chicago Tribune.* Retrieved from http://articles.chicagotribune.com

Kuczka, S., & Flink, J. (1997, May 16). Waukegan rationalizes payoff of suit. *Chicago Tribune.* Retrieved from http://articles.chicagotribune.com

Olivo, A. (2011, September 8). Cook County bucks immigration officials: Board votes to reject federal requests to hold suspected illegal immigrants jailed in minor cases. *Chicago Tribune.* Retrieved from http://articles.chicagotribune.com

Rodriguez, L. (2008, December 23). *Federal judge finds city of Waukegan violated the First Amendment rights of city protestors.* Retrieved from http://www.maldef.org/news/releases/waukegan_12232008/index.html

Savage, D. (2011, June 6). Supreme Court allows California to grant in-state tuition to illegal immigrants. *Los Angeles Times.* Retrieved from http://articles.latimes.com

Yount, B. (2011, April) *New audit, old problems with All Kids expanded program.* Retrieved from http://watchdog.org/39584/ilshn-new-audit-old-problems-with-all-kids-expanded-program/

Press Releases

City of Chicago, Office of the Mayor. (2012). Mayor Emanuel unveils first-ever Chicago New Americans plan [Press release]. Retrieved from http://www.cityofchicago.org/content/dam/city/depts/mayor/Press%20Room/Press%20Releases/2012/December/12.4.12NewAmericans.pdf

State of Illinois, Office of the Governor. (2005a). Governor Blagojevich announces landmark immigrant policy: New Executive Order is first of its kind in the nation [Press release]. Retrieved from http://www.illinois.gov/PressReleases/ShowPressRelease.cfm?SubjectID=65&RecNum=5598

State of Illinois, Office of the Governor. (2005b). Governor Blagojevich signs legislation to help protect 300,000 workers [Press release]. Retrieved fromhttp://www3.illinois.gov/pressreleases/ShowPressRelease.cfm?SubjectID=2&RecNum=5074

Reports and Audits

City of Chicago Joint Committee on Finance and Human Relations. (2006, March 29). *Amendment of Title 2 of municipal code of Chicago by creation of new chapter 173 to disallow disclosure of and conditioning benefits and services on individual's citizenship and residency status.* Retrieved from http://docs.chicityclerk.com/journal/2006/march29_2006/march29_2006_part3optimize.pdf

Cook County Board of Commissioners, STAR. (2011). *Public safety.* Retrieved from http://blog.cookcountygov.com/performancemanagement/public-safety/

Coughlin, T., & Cohen, M. (2007, August). A race to the top: Illinois' All Kids initiative. *Kaiser Commission on Medicaid and the Uninsured.* Retrieved from http://www.kff.org/uninsured/upload/7677.pdf

Illinois Coalition for Immigrant and Refugee Rights. (2011, January 14). *Immigration enforcement: The dangerous reality behind "secure communities."* Retrieved from http://icirr.org/sites/default/files/ImmigrationEnforcementTheDangerousRealityBehindSecure%20Communities.pdf

State of Illinois, Office of the Auditor General. (2010, May). *Program audit of the covering All Kids health insurance program.* Retrieved from http://www.auditor.illinois.gov/Audit-Reports/Performance-Special-Multi/Performance-Audits/10-All-Kids-Hlth-Ins-Pgm-Full.pdf

State of Illinois., Office of the Auditor General. (2012, October). Covering All Kids Health Insurance Program (Summary report digest). Retrieved from http://www.auditor.illinois.gov/Audit-Reports/Performance-Special-Multi/Performance-Audits/2012%20Releases/12-All-Kids-Prgm-Digest.pdf

Tramonte, L., (2011, April 26). *Debunking the myth of "sanctuary cities."* Retrieved from http://immigrationpolicy.org/sites/default/files/docs/Community_Policing_Policies_Protect_American_042611_update.pdf

CHAPTER SIX

Immigration Control and Policies of Integration of Immigrants at a Local Level

SILVIA DÍEZ SASTRE, AUTONOMOUS UNIVERSITY OF MADRID

The distribution of powers in migration matters in the current European legal landscape follows this scheme: the General State Administration is responsible for control of the migration flows and regional and local authorities are in charge of the tasks of the integration of immigrants (Catalá i Bas, 2009, pp. 35–37). With regard to the Spanish legal system, the General State Administration is concerned with the regulation in matters of nationality, control of the migration flows, and the right of asylum. The entry, exit, work permit, stay, and residence of immigrants fall within the competence of the General State Administration according to the Constitution (Article 149[1][2] CE). With the adoption of the new Statutes of Autonomy, some autonomous regions may participate in fixing the quotas and, within their powers, in defining the rights and obligations of immigrants in their territories (de la Quadra-Salcedo Janini, 2012). Previously, autonomous regions were already allowed to participate to a certain extent in the determination of foreign workers' annual quota (Díez Bueso, 2003, p. 186).

Based on Article 149(1) and (2) CE—and from within the framework of European Union Law—the General State Administration has passed Organic Law 4/2000 of January 11 on the rights and freedoms of foreign nationals in Spain and their social integration (LODLEIS), substantially amended in 2009. The provisions of this law are completed by its Development Regulation, adopted by Royal Decree 557/2011 of April 20 (RLODLEIS), which introduced certain developments in the legal regime of immigration control. Hence, the General State Administration defines the rights and obligations of foreign nationals according to their status as EU citizens, third-country nationals in a legal situation, asylum seekers, beneficiaries of the status of refugee, and non-EU nationals in an irregular situation (Pérez Sola, 2008, p. 20; Pérez Caramés, 2012, pp. 161 et seq.). The progress accomplished by each person in the integration process has only recently begun to be taken into account in order to determine the migratory status of a foreign national, as will be discussed later (Díez Bueso, 2003, p. 179; Tryjanowski, 2010, pp. 169–186).

Considering this distribution of powers regarding immigration control in Spain, the role of local authorities and, specifically, that of municipalities, is rather limited. Traditionally, municipalities participated only indirectly in the control of migration flows; their main role on migration matters was focused on the policies of integration of immigrants. The participation in the control of immigration consists in the elaboration of reports regarding two administrative procedures carried out by the General State Administration: those aimed at the regularization of immigrants, and those aimed at family reunification of foreign nationals. Currently, after the adoption of the RLODLEIS, the extent of the participation of municipalities in the elaboration of those reports is subject to the decision of the corresponding autonomous region. It is possible that municipalities directly issue the report or that the autonomous region reserves that power to itself, leaving a secondary role to municipalities, that of collecting the necessary data for the report.

Alongside that participation in the exercise of regional powers, municipalities have the chance to intervene in the implementation of immigration control policies through the exercise of their own powers. In fact, Article 2 bis (g) LODLEIS requires all public authorities to fight irregular immigration as a corollary to migration powers. Municipalities, more specifically, can lighten the effect of state controls through registering foreign nationals in irregular situations in the municipal census. The lack of registration in the municipal census fosters, to the contrary, the application of the regulations on immigration control. On the other hand, local police—where such exist—can contribute to the task of identifying immigrants, aiding the application of migration control policies. In such cases, a classic problem in the protection of the fundamental right to equality and the prohibition of discrimination results when identification controls consider solely the physical appearance of the persons whose identification is required. Doubts also arise regarding police access to the municipal census data in order to control the migratory status of specific individuals.

The main goal of this chapter is to analyze the means by which municipalities participate in the execution of state policies of immigration control. With this aim in mind, we will describe municipal powers regarding the issuing of the reports required for the regularization or family reunification of immigrants. Secondly, we will analyze the role of municipalities as managers of the municipal census. Following, we will set out the problems derived from the exercise of identification controls of foreign nationals by local police. As a counterpoint, a brief mention will be finally made to the role of municipalities in the policies of immigrant integration, which is their particular domain in the management of migration issues.

PARTICIPATION OF MUNICIPALITIES IN ADMINISTRATIVE PROCEDURES OF IMMIGRATION CONTROL

Traditionally, state regulation on migration matters provided the cooperation of municipalities in immigration control through the participation in certain administrative procedures. However, the adoption of the new LODLEIS Development Regulation in 2011 restricted the participation of municipalities in such procedures. The competence to issue certain reports in the framework of regularization or family reunification procedures is attributed to autonomous regions. It is they who will decide, in this case, whether they deem it appropriate to attribute such power to local entities within their territory. Hence, municipalities may indirectly cooperate with the General State Administration through the issuing of three kinds of reports: the report on social rooting in order to obtain a temporary residence permit for reasons of social roots, the report on the efforts of integration for the renewal of temporary residence permits, and the report on the adequacy of housing in order to exercise the right to family reunification. The legal regime in effect of each of these reports is analyzed next.

REPORTS ON SOCIAL ROOTING IN ORDER TO OBTAIN A TEMPORARY RESIDENCE PERMIT

The Spanish legal system provides for the possibility of obtaining a temporary residence permit for reasons of social roots. Although the legal regulations consider this case as an extraordinary mechanism of regularization of the administrative status of immigrants, it is actually the most common means of obtaining a residence permit. The highest number of foreign nationals regularized through this mechanism was reached in 2009. However, in the following years, the economic crisis has caused a decrease in the number of temporary residence permits granted through these means (*El País*, November 24, 2011).

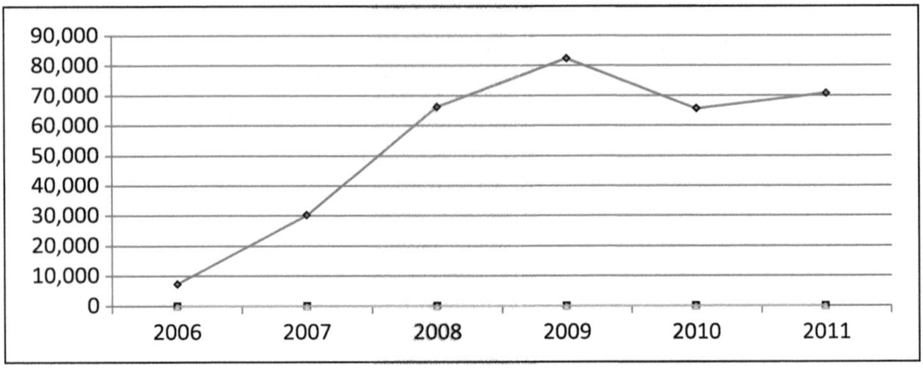

Figure 6.1
Source: Adapted From *El País*, November 24, 2011.[1]

[1] Available online: http://politica.elpais.com/politica/2011/11/24/actualidad/1322125831_984714.html

According to Article 31(3) LODLEIS, the Administration may grant a temporary residence permit for reasons of social rooting. In such cases, Article 68(3) LODLEIS provides that, prior to the granting of social rooting, autonomous regions or, in some cases, municipalities, shall issue a report on the social integration of the foreign national whose habitual residence is in their territory. Before 2011, the competence to issue the reports on social rooting belonged to municipalities (Article 46[2] RD 2392/2004 of December 30). This situation resulted in divergent interpretations of the criteria for obtaining the report on social rooting. For instance, the three-year stay was proven in some cases by the entry stamp on the passport and, in other municipalities, by a three-year registration in the municipal census. Some municipalities, such as Azpeitia, in the Basque Country, required the completion of courses on Basque language and culture in order to grant the report on social rooting. Others, such as those of Tarragona, L'Hospitalet de Llobregat, and Salt, requested of the state, at the beginning of 2011, that municipalities could consider the possible breaches of Coexistence Ordinances in order to grant the reports on social rooting. There was, therefore, an important divergence in the criteria applied to determine the social rooting of a foreign national (Aja, 2012, p. 208).

The reform introduced by Royal Decree 557/2011 of April 11 (Article 124)—in the context of the reform of the LODLEIS in 2009—implied that the competence to grant the report on social rooting was expressly attributed to autonomous regions. The autonomous region empowered to issue the report may, of course, consult the municipality of the applicant's place of residence in order to gather the necessary information for the elaboration of the report. If it deems it adequate, it can even transfer the competence to issue the report to the municipality. In such cases, the autonomous region shall inform the Secretariat of State for Immigration and Emigration, so that the report can have legal effect.

In both cases—whether it is the autonomous region or the municipality that issues the report—there is a thirty-day deadline for the issuance of the report from the date of its request. If this deadline is not met, the applicant may prove his or her social rooting by any means recognized by the law. The minimum content of the report is set by Article 124(2) RLODLEIS. This indicates the social rooting factors that can be provided by the administration, which are, among others, the following: the applicant's duration of residence in his or her habitual residence (where he or she must be registered); financial support; links with relatives residing in Spain; and efforts of integration through the programs of social, labor, and cultural integration.

This regulation is detailed in an Instruction of the Directorate General of Immigration (Instruction DGI/SGRJ/3/2011, on the implementation of the Regulation of Organic Law 4/2000, on Rights and Freedoms of Foreign Nationals in Spain and their Social Integration, regarding the reports on social rooting). This instruction is addressed, in principle, to the peripheral bodies of the General State Administration. However, it actually governs the completion of reports on social rooting by the competent autonomous region or municipality. For instance, the instruction provides that the autonomous region "in whose territory the foreign national has his or her habitual residence, that is, the place where he or she is registered," will be the one entitled to grant the report. On the other hand, according to the regulation, the instruction allows the autonomous region to delegate the power for the elaboration of the report to the municipality where the foreign national is registered. In such case, the autonomous region shall inform the Secretariat of State for Immigration and Emigration; failure to do so will imply that the report does not meet the legal requirements. Currently, only four autonomous regions have retained the power to issue the report on social rooting, as shown in the following table:

Table 6.1

Autonomous Region	Competent Authority for the Issuance of the Report	Competent Department for the Issuance of the Report
Andalucía	Municipality	—
Aragón	Municipality	—
Asturias	Municipality	—
Cantabria	Municipality	—
Castilla y León	Municipality	—
Castilla-La Mancha	Municipality	—
Cataluña	Generalitat	Department of Welfare and Family
Ceuta	Autonomous City	Regional Government's Department of Social Affairs
Comunidad Valenciana	Municipality	—

(*Continued*)

Autonomous Region	Competent Authority for the Issuance of the Report	Competent Department for the Issuance of the Report
Extremadura	Municipality	—
Galicia	Municipality	—
Islas Baleares	Municipality	—
Islas Canarias	Autonomous Region	Regional Government's Department of Welfare, Youth and Housing
La Rioja	Municipality	—
Madrid	Autonomous Region	General Directorate of Immigration (Regional Government's Department of Social Affairs)
Melilla	Autonomous City	Regional Government's Department of Social Affairs
Murcia	Municipality	—
Navarra	Municipality	—
País Vasco	Basque Autonomous Government	Directorate of Immigration and Diversity Management (Department of Employment and Social Affairs)

Source: Ministry of Labour and Social Security, General Secretariat of Immigration and Emigration*

* http://extranjeros.empleo.gob.es/es/InformacionInteres/Informes_CCAA_Entidades_locales/Informe_arraigo/index.html

Furthermore, the instruction provides that once the power has been delegated to municipalities, the reports issued by the autonomous region shall no longer be accepted. However, it should be noted that even in the cases where autonomous regions keep the competence for the elaboration of the reports, municipalities cooperate in the fulfillment of the required procedures for their issuance, such as conducting an interview with the applicant. Therefore, in such cases, municipalities act as indirect administration of the autonomous region. In any case, the reports issued by local bodies before June 30, 2011 are valid.

The instruction reiterates the thirty-day deadline from the date of the applicant's request. If this is not met, the applicant may pursue any means of evidence stipulated by law that may provide the minimum content required for the reports on social rooting. The instruction offers some examples: documents attesting his or her stay in Spain; census registration or public documents showing a relation with public institutions as a consequence of his or her presence in the Spanish territory; documents regarding the holding of a title of occupancy of a home; documents relating to the financial means of the foreign national; documents showing the existence of a family link with relatives residing in Spain; and certificates attesting the pursuit of social, employment, and cultural programs of integration. If the report is issued after the deadline and once the applicant has provided other documentation to demonstrate his or her situation of social rooting, he or she may be able to choose whether to submit the report for the Aliens Office to take it into consideration.

Regarding the content of the report on social rooting, the previously-mentioned instruction provides that it has to include, at least, the following points: time of stay of the foreign national in his or her habitual residence; financial means; family links with residents in Spain; and efforts of integration through the pursuit of social, employment, and cultural programs of integration. In addition, the Directorate General of Immigration has established a template for the completion of the report on social rooting, which shows the narrow scope of discretion autonomous regions and municipalities have when performing this task. However, these can include some conditions for the granting of the report on social rooting, always in compliance with the criteria established by the General State Administration. Along that line, the autonomous region of Madrid—which is one of the regions that has not delegated power to municipalities for the elaboration of the report, although the latter cooperate in this task—since February 1, 2012, has established that the completion of a course and a language exam are conditions in order to obtain the report on social rooting. More specifically, it is necessary to take the training modules on integration of the program "Know Your Laws" in order to acquire knowledge of the Constitution and immigration laws. In addition, foreigners who are non-Spanish speakers must pass a language test called PECOLE (Prueba de Eficacia Comunicativa Oral en Lengua Española, or Effective Oral Communication in the Spanish Language). The Integration and Participation Centres (CEPI) are the ones in charge of the organization and management of such courses in the autonomous region of Madrid. Hence, the integration of immigrants becomes a requirement in order to obtain the report on social rooting. This option means a higher formalization and a toughening of the requirements for a temporary residence permit. It seems to comply with the legal framework established by the General State Administration, which provides that all public authorities must promote the integration of immigrants (Article 2 LODLEIS).

REPORTS ON THE EFFORTS OF INTEGRATION FOR THE RENEWAL OF TEMPORARY RESIDENCE PERMITS

According to Article 31 LODLEIS, the renewal of temporary residence permits shall be linked to the efforts of integration carried out by the foreign national when some of the legal requirements are not met. Such effort must be proven by a positive report from the autonomous region of the place of residence attesting the foreign national's training activities aimed at integration (Article 31[7], last paragraph LODLEIS). This legal provision is currently developed by the new LODLEIS Regulation of 2011. RLODLEIS requires autonomous regions to issue a report on the efforts of integration in the following cases: renewal of the temporary non-lucrative residence permit; renewal of the temporary residence permit for family reunification; renewal of the temporary residence and self-employed or employed by others work permit. The effort of integration accredited by this report may be alleged by the foreign national as information to be taken into account when some of the necessary requirements for the renewal of the permit are not met (Articles 51[6], 71[6], 109[6] RLODLEIS 2011).

The minimum content of the report is established by the regulation: certification, if relevant, of the active participation of the applicant in training activities aimed at the learning and respect of the Spanish constitutional values, the values of the Statute of Autonomy of the region of residence, the European Union values, human rights, public freedoms, democracy, tolerance, and equality between men and women, as well as learning the official languages of the place of residence. The certification shall, in its case, indicate the time of training dedicated to such matters. The regulation also provides that the report must only consider the training activities carried out by public entities or duly authorized private entities (Articles 51[6], 71[6], 109[6] RLODLEIS 2011).

This regulation was completed by an Instruction of the General Directorate of Immigration (Instruction DGI/SGRJ/8/2011 on the implementation of the Development Regulation of Organic Law 4/2000 on Rights and Freedoms of Foreign Nationals in Spain and their Social Integration, regarding the reports on the efforts of integration). According to this instruction, autonomous regions were entitled to add more requirements to the minimum content of the report, provided that they were directly connected with the efforts of integration of the foreign nationals. In that sense, like it happened with the report on social rooting, the autonomous region of Madrid requires the completion of certain integration and Spanish language courses. In addition, the instruction established in detail the requirements, as well as, in the case of non-compliance, how to substitute by the submission of a report on the efforts of integration. However, this instruction was repealed shortly after its adoption in July 2012, for "not having contributed to the goals of clarification and consistency in the application of the legal institution." This means that the report on the efforts of integration remains an important element to be considered in the renewals of temporary permits, and that the autonomous regions are competent to issue such reports based on the criteria they deem relevant.

REPORTS ON THE ADEQUACY OF HOUSING FOR THE EXERCISE OF THE RIGHT TO FAMILY REUNIFICATION

The right to family reunification is one of the most important rights granted by law to foreign nationals (Articles 16–19 LODLEIS). This right has been laid out by international bodies, mainly through the case law of the Court of Strasbourg in relation to Article 8 of the European Convention on Human Rights—which enshrines the right to respect for private and family life—and Directive 2003/86/CE of September 22, 2003, on the right to family reunification of the third-country nationals (Villaverde Menéndez, 2003, pp. 158 et seq.). The regulation of the exercise of such rights might be regarded as a way to control and restrict migration flows, since it prevents the free arrival of relatives of persons already in the country and, generally, their full integration (Díez Sastre, 2010, pp. 278 et seq.; Soriano Miras & Rico Becerra, 2012, pp. 231 et seq.).

Reunification regards the relatives of the sponsor who are among the following categories: a) spouse of the sponsor, provided that they are not legally or de facto separated and that the wedding was not celebrated in abuse of law—in that sense, the amendment of the LODLEIS by Organic Law 2/2009 has extended to unmarried couples the right to reunification (Article 17[4]; Aprell Lasagabaster, 2009, pp. 11–13); b) minor children—including adopted children of the sponsor or his or her spouse, or the adult children of the sponsor or his or her spouse—where they are objectively unable to provide for their own needs on account of their state of health; c) minors or adults who are unable to provide for their own needs when the alien resident is the legal representative; d) first-degree relatives—in the direct ascending line of the sponsor, or his or her spouse or partner—over sixty-five years of age and with enough reasons to justify residence in Spain (Article 17[1] LODLEIS; Arieta-Araunabeña, Gamboa, & Labaca, 2009, pp. 29 et seq.). In order to exercise the right to reunification regarding the listed relatives, the applicant must justify the compliance with certain legal requirements in an ad hoc procedure. The law provides that the person concerned must prove an adequate housing and sufficient financial means to meet his or her needs and those of his or her family (Article 18[2] LODLEIS). The control of the adequacy of the housing shall be done through the elaboration of a report by the autonomous region or the municipality (Article 18[2] third paragraph LODLEIS). The Development Regulation of the LODLEIS provides the details of such regulation.

The previous Royal Decree 2393/2004 of December 30, which enacts the LODLEIS Regulation, set a series of requirements in order to exercise the right to family reunification: a) legal stay in the country for at least one year and obtaining a permit to reside for at least another year; b) accredited possession of an adequate house; c) evidence of sufficient financial means, thus complying with requirements of the constitutional mandate to ensure family protection (Villaverde Menéndez, 2003, p. 171; Articles 38 and 42[2]). Article 42 of this regulation (now repealed) provided the procedure for the exercise of the right to family reunification. The person concerned could submit to the competent body a request of temporary residence for the relatives whose reunification was sought. The request, according to the official template, had to be accompanied by a number of documents justifying the compliance with the noted requirements. Among them, insofar as is relevant here, there was the "documentary evidence certifying the availability of adequate housing on the part of the applicant in order to meet his or her needs and those of the family." Although the law indicates that the report on the adequacy of housing could be a competence of the autonomous region or the municipality of residence of the applicant (Article 18[2] par. 3 LODLEIS), this task was conferred by regulations to local bodies (Article 42[2]e RLODLEIS 2004). Hence, the municipality of residence of the sponsor was competent to issue the report on housing, unless the autonomous region provided otherwise (Velasco Caballero, 2010, p. 80).

The adoption of the new Development Regulation of the LODLEIS amended the rules regarding the issuance of the report on the adequacy of housing for the exercise of the right to family reunification. According to Article 55 RLODLEIS 2011, the autonomous region (and not the municipality) is the competent administration for the elaboration of such report (Aja, 2012, p. 470). Nonetheless, it is foreseeable that the autonomous region may consult the municipality of residence of the foreign national in order to gather information on the adequacy of housing. Furthermore, nothing prevents the competent autonomous region to confer upon municipalities the power to issue the report. In these cases—as with the report on social rooting—the autonomous region shall inform the Secretariat of State for Immigration and Emigration. In any case, the deadline for the issuance of the report either by the autonomous region or the municipality is thirty days from the request. If such deadline is not met, the compliance with the requirement of adequate housing could be justified by the applicant through any means accepted by law.

The content of the report is delimited in RLODLEIS and the instruction DGI/SGRJ/4/2011, on the implementation of the Regulation of Organic Law 4/2000, on Rights and Freedoms of Foreign Nationals in Spain and their Social Integration, regarding proof of the availability of adequate housing in procedures of residency for family reunification. It shall address, at least, the following matters: legal basis for the occupancy of the house; number of rooms; intended use of each of the rooms of the house; number of people living there; and living conditions and equipment (Article 55[5] RLODLEIS 2011). The problem lies in how to evaluate these living, occupancy, and equipment conditions in order to issue a positive report. It is harder to objectively assess these matters than the requirement of sufficient financial means to support the relatives.

It seems reasonable that the municipality addresses the ordinary housing standard for the rest of the local population in terms of space and physical conditions, as specified by Article 7(1)a of the Directive 2003/86/CE, on the right to family reunification: evidence of the availability of an "accommodation regarded as normal for a comparable family in the same region and which meets the general health and safety standards in force in the Member State concerned." That said, identifying the ordinary housing standard is a different question. Therefore, municipalities must provide adequate reasons for their assessment of the housing conditions. Too strict an interpretation could conceal undesirable and prohibited practices such as the attempt to avoid the settlement of immigrants in general, or of certain immigrants, fostering their displacement to neighboring municipalities. The report on housing conditions does not seem a means for the municipality to exercise a right to establish the number or kind of immigrants in its territory. Its scope of discretion regards the control of the sponsor's adequate housing and reasonable living conditions in comparison with the local population. Municipalities cannot apply higher standards than those met by the neighbors' housing.

Along that line, it could be rather useful to clearly and objectively set the criteria according to which the adequacy of housing will be assessed, both in autonomous region legislation and local regulations (Aguado & Cerrillo, 2005, p. 41). Only then, an adequate degree of predictability for the exercise of the immigrants' right would be attained, providing at the same time the judiciary with rigorous control parameters. However, failing a written criteria catalogue, the criteria already applied to similar cases can always be invoked. Municipalities develop an administrative practice, which has to be consistent in the successive cases of elaboration of the report for reunification. A deviation could therefore be controlled by the judiciary on the grounds of the principle of equality or the principle of the protection of legitimate expectations, depending on the case. This way, it can be guaranteed the protection of the sponsor against a possible denial of the reunification on the basis of a housing report that disregards without justification the criteria previously applied in similar cases.

CONCLUSION

According to the legislation in force, the participation of municipalities in the described procedures—for the obtaining of a temporary residence permit for reasons of social rooting, and for the renewal of temporary residence permits and for the exercise of the right to family reunification—clearly depends on the will of autonomous regions. In some cases, the role of municipalities will be confined to a mere cooperation with the autonomous region by providing the necessary data for the issuance of the reports; in other cases, municipalities will be the competent authority for their issuance. All the same, it may be concluded that the municipalities' scope of discretion to perform those functions is very restricted. As it has been shown, regulation by the General State Administration—either through LODLEIS, its Development Regulation, or even the Instructions of the Directorate General of Immigration—directs to a high level of detail the procedure and content of the reports. Thus, the role of municipalities in these cases is limited to a simple indirect administration, either of the General State Administration or the autonomous region administration.

With regard to the new regulation, attention should be drawn to the initiative of the autonomous region of Madrid, which links the obtaining of reports on social rooting and efforts of integration to the completion of cultural and language integration courses. Those kinds of activities were, until now, positively considered by the administration, but they were not required as a condition to define the migratory status of foreign nationals. Progress is thus made along the lines laid down by other Member States in the European Union, which pose numerous problems around the dynamics of the integration process and the efforts the host society has to make in order to promote the integration of immigrants (Tryjanowski, 2010). The framework set up by these legal requirements should be studied and analyzed in depth in the future.

DELIMITATION OF THE LOCAL POPULATION THROUGH REGISTRATION IN THE MUNICIPAL CENSUS

One of the main functions attributed to municipalities consists of the compilation, maintenance, revision, and custody of the municipal census (Article 17[1] of the Law providing the Basis for Local Regulation 7/1985, LBRL). The municipal census is the administrative record containing the residents of a given municipality. The information contained in it constitutes proof that they reside in the municipality and have their habitual residence there (Article 16[1] Law providing the Basis for Local Regulation). However, despite the apparently fully local character of this municipal competence, the truth is that the census is an instrument of registration for the state. It is the General State Administration who determines, with a high level of detail, the regulation regarding the running and operation of the census. It is also the General State Administration who exercises executive powers over the municipal census through, for example, the approval of instructions directed to municipalities (Velasco Caballero, 2010, pp. 86 et seq.). This is an essential piece of information, since it determines the impossibility for the municipalities to decide who is entitled to register in the census and who is not. It is the General State Administration who will determine the status of who is a resident of the municipality. At the same time, the fundamental right of free movement (Article 19 CE) precludes municipalities from standing in the way of the registration of some persons over others. Particularly, it keeps a given municipality from rejecting the registration of foreign nationals in a regular situation who are entitled to the right established in Article 19 CE.

This information is relevant to determine the role of municipalities regarding the management of the census, and, this way, solve the issues that have arisen concerning the possible registration of irregular immigrants. In 2008, the Municipality of Torrejón de Ardoz (Region of Madrid) modified the conditions that permitted registration with the goal of avoiding overcrowding in housing. According to the new regulation, which aimed at evading conflict among neighbors, the number of persons that may live in a house was limited based on its square meters—specifically, a minimum of twenty functional square meters per person if an apartment is shared without a close degree of kinship. Afterwards, in 2010, the Mayor of Vic (Region of Catalonia) consulted the Ministry of Interior in order to settle on whether it was compulsory for the municipality to register foreign nationals that did not hold a passport with the mandatory visa (de la Quadra-Salcedo Janini, 2010, pp. 151 et seq.; Aja, 2012, pp. 307–308). These municipalities pretended to contribute to the control of irregular immigration by exercising their management powers of the municipal census, impeding the extension of social rights to persons in an illegal administrative condition. The heart of the matter, therefore, lies in the connection that may be established between the municipal census and the granting of rights to foreign nationals. Currently, the issue has been formally resolved. The State Legal Service has concluded that municipalities should register the irregular immigrants as well. However, an issue of interpretation concerning local regulation connected to immigration laws is now laid out. The way the legislation on local regulation is interpreted by the State Legal Service subverts the granting of rights to foreign nationals contained in the immigration laws.

Article 5 LODLEIS establishes that foreign nationals that are legally residing in Spain have the right to move freely within the Spanish territory, as well as to choose their residence. Once they have chosen their residence, municipalities will include in the census foreigners that have their habitual residence in the municipality (Article 6[3] LODLEIS). The registration in the municipal census implies the possibility of exercising the rights established for that reason in the legislation on local regulation with regard to public participation (Article 6[2] LODLEIS). The municipal census is, by virtue of this, an instrument that defines the rights granted to residents in the municipality, and, as a result, those rights granted to foreign nationals living in the municipality. Registration in the municipal census shall be considered, as well, a necessary legal condition to be entitled to health care in the same conditions as Spanish residents (Article 12[1] LODLEIS). Not being registered in the municipal census, this right is considerably limited, except for minors who will nevertheless be entitled to health care in the same conditions as Spanish residents (Article 12[3] LODLEIS): all foreign nationals are entitled to emergency public health care in the case of an accident or serious illness and continuous medical care until certified discharge (Article 12[2] LODLEIS); and pregnant women are entitled to public health care during their pregnancy, at childbirth, and post-partum (Article 12[4] LODLEIS). Regardless of the census, the law also differentiates between foreign residents—who reserve the right to access public aid regarding housing and social security services and benefits under equal conditions as Spanish residents (Articles 13 and 14[1] LODLEIS)—and the rest of foreign nationals, who will only have the right to basic social services (Article 14[3] LODLEIS). The same distinction is made to the effects of exercising the right to reunite family members as it is established in the law (Article 17 LODLEIS). In other cases, the law does not differentiate between foreign nationals in order to recognize their rights, as it happens with regard to the right to effective legal protection and the right to free legal assistance (Articles 20[1] and 22 LODLEIS).

Table 6.2 Rights of Foreign Nationals in Spain

	In any Administrative Situation	Residents (Administrative Title Holders)
Foreign Nationals in General	Documentation	Freedom of movement
	Emergency public health care	Right to vote and stand as a candidate in cases where there is reciprocity
	Effective legal protection	Right to carry out teaching assignments
	Freedom of assembly	Right to be part of the contract administrative staff
	Freedom of association	Right to access the public housing aid system
	Freedom of trade unionism	Right to basic and specialized welfare treatment
	Right to strike	Right to social security coverage
	Right to free legal assistance	Right to reunite family members
	Right to education	Right to work
	Right to basic welfare treatment	—
Minors	Right-duty to compulsory education	—
	Right to health care	—

(*Continued*)

Registered in the Municipal Census	— —	Municipal participatory rights Right to health care under equal conditions as Spanish nationals
Women	Right to health care during pregnancy, at childbirth and post-partum	—

Adapted from the model of the Integration Plan 2009–2012, Autonomous Region of Madrid*.

* Available online: http://www.madrid.org/cs/Satellite?blobcol=urldata&blobheader=application%2Fpdf&blobheadername1=Content-disposition&blobheadername2=cadena&blobheadervalue1=filename%3DPLAN+INT.09-12.pdf&blobheadervalue2=language%3Des%26site%3DPortalInmigrante&blobkey=id&blobtable=MungoBlobs&blobwhere=1220469199467&ssbinary=true

In accordance with immigration laws, the difference can be established between two main groups of foreign nationals to the effect of determining the rights to which they are entitled: resident foreign nationals (in a regular situation) and non-resident foreign nationals (in an irregular situation). Beyond this distinction, rights are attributed to minors and women under certain circumstances. Regarding this classification, registering in the municipal census only constitutes an additional requirement in order for foreign nationals to access the right to political participation. Likewise, the role of registration in the municipal census when defining individuals' health rights must be considered an inaccuracy on the legislator's side that nonetheless reveals equal consideration between residents and those registered in the municipal census. According to this catalogue of rights of foreign nationals in Spain, it cannot be stated that registration in the municipal census grants by itself rights beyond those regulated in the immigration laws. At the same time, it shows the incoherence that comes with differentiating the condition of local resident to foreign nationals in an irregular situation (Velasco Caballero, 2010, pp. 93 et seq.; on the contrary, Villaverde Menéndez, 2010, p. 205; and de la Quadra-Salcedo Janini, 2010, pp. 155 et seq.).

Where the possibility of registering irregular immigrants in the municipal census is concerned, we must take into account that in practice it is compulsory to register irregular immigrants. Therefore, municipalities cannot refuse to register in the municipal census an immigrant in an irregular administrative situation. In fact, the Integration Plan of the Region of Madrid for 2009–2012 states that any foreign national that is registered—regardless of his or her administrative situation—may eventually acquire municipal participatory rights and the right to health care under equal conditions as Spanish nationals. Therefore, municipalities have only a narrow scope of action in this realm since the lack of registration of a foreign national in an irregular situation could be considered illegal.

IRREGULAR IMMIGRATION CONTROL BY THE LOCAL POLICE

In order to complete the analysis of the role that municipalities play in controlling immigration, we must refer to the position of the local police in this field. Municipalities can create their own police bodies according to the regulation currently in effect (Article 51[1] Organic Law 2/1986 of March 13, on State security forces and bodies, LOFCS). This being said, the attribution of powers to these bodies is very limited. Moreover, the mentioned law does not make any provision for administrative or police control on the local level over the legal conditions of foreign nationals in Spain. This control is reserved to the National Police pursuant to Articles 12(1)a 1 and 2 LOFSC. The local police can only control possible infractions of immigration laws in the exercise of their duties. In these cases, the duty of mutual cooperation among the different state security forces and bodies implies that the local police can communicate this situation to the National Police (Article 3 LOFCS; Velasco Caballero, 2010, p. 80).

To the effects on which we are focused, it may be asserted that the local police can request the identification from people in the exercise of their duties (Article 20[1] Organic Law 1/1992 of February 21, on the Protection of Citizen's Security). In this regard, we must take into consideration that, according to Article 4(1) LODLEIS, "foreign nationals on Spanish territory have the right and the obligation to keep the documentation that proves their identity, issued by the competent authorities of the country of origin or of provenance, as well as the documentation that constitutes proof of their situation in Spain." This provision is expanded upon in Article 205(2) RLODLEIS, which obliges foreign nationals to show their documentation when required by agents or authorities in the exercise of their duties. With regard to this stipulation, it has been pointed out that a provision with regulatory status does not suffice to empower the police—at any territorial level—to carry out identity checks on foreign nationals on a general basis. The reason for that is the infringement of the principle of legal reservation established in Article 17(1) CE concerning personal freedom—to which all foreign nationals are entitled, regardless of their administrative situation (Pomed & Velasco, 2003, p. 149). The principle of legal reservation is strictly interpreted in these cases as a requirement for express legal authorization to enact specific limitations of individual rights. According to the above, the police would not have sufficient legal authorization to conduct random identity checks. In practice, however, this legal obstacle seems to be disregarded when it comes to carrying out these identity controls.

Hence, at a municipal level, local police can request documentation in the exercise of their duties. The problem lies in the way this identification can be conducted, that is, which indicators the local police may use to identify foreign nationals. This is the issue that is analyzed next.

IDENTIFICATION OF FOREIGN NATIONALS BASED ON RACIAL OR ETHNIC PROFILES

The identification of foreign nationals by the police—whether local, regional, or national—raises some concerns from a constitutional standpoint. It should be understood that an identification carried out based on indications linked to the individual—race, ethnicity, language, etc.—may constitute an act of discrimination banned by Article 14 of the Spanish Constitution, and by the actual LODLEIS. The legislator has defined what an act of discrimination consists of with regard to foreign nationals. It is an act that directly or indirectly leads to distinction, exclusion, restriction, or preference against a foreign national based on race, color, ascendency, national or ethnic origins, and religious beliefs and practices, and which has as an aim or effect destroying or limiting the recognition or exercise, in equal conditions, of human rights and basic freedoms in the political, economic, social, or cultural sphere (Article 23[1] LODLEIS). Moreover, the activity of the agents of the state could be discriminatory whenever they perform a prohibited act of discrimination against a foreign national for the sole reason of his or her condition of foreigner, or due to his or her race, religion, ethnicity, or nationality (Article 23[2]a LODLEIS). The question arises whether the use of an individual's race or ethnicity as the basis for police to request his or her identification can be considered an act of discrimination outlawed by the legal system.

THE CONSTITUTIONAL COURT'S DOCTRINE

The constitutional relevance of the issue concerning the identification of foreign nationals has warranted the judgment of the Constitutional Court on this matter. The leading case is the Constitutional Court ruling 13/2001 of January 29. This ruling decides on the application for *amparo* (constitutional protection) filed by three individual claimants: Ms. Rosalind Williams Lecraft, Mr. Federico Agustín Calabuig-París, and Mr. Iván Agustín Calabuig Williams, alleging violations of their fundamental right to effective legal protection (established in Article 24[1] CE) and to non-discrimination (recognized in Article 14 CE). The facts took place as follows: On December 6, 1992, a police agent requested Ms. Rosalind Williams to identify herself when she was getting off the train in the Valladolid railway station. Williams's husband, Mr. Federico Agustín, refused on her behalf, since he considered it discriminatory that the police only requested the identification of his wife, a black woman, and no one else wandering around the train station. Following this, the police agent requested the couple accompany him to the police offices in the railway station to proceed with identifying Ms. Rosalind Williams. After making sure that she was a Spanish national, they were both allowed to leave the offices. Afterwards, Ms. Rosalind Williams filed a liability claim against the Ministry of Interior aiming for a five-million-pesetas (€ 30,000) moral damage compensation because of the police action. The Ministry rejected the claim through Resolution of February 7, 1994, which was appealed before the Contentious-Administrative jurisdiction by Agustín and Williams. The National High Court issued a judgment dated November 29, 1996 rejecting the appeal.

In light of these established facts, the Constitutional Court gave a resolution on the application for *amparo* issued by the mentioned individuals. Regarding the contravention of the right to an effective legal protection (Article 24[1] CE), the Court points out that the ruling from the National High Court did not omit the constitutional level of the issue. It simply disregarded the compensating obligation of the administration because the damage caused to Ms. Rosalind Williams due to the police action was not anti-juridical. The Court also considered that the police request for identification was part of the burdens inherent to social living (Legal Ground 3). Thereupon, the Court focuses on the possible contravention of the prohibition of discrimination established in Article 14 CE. From the Court's standpoint, police requests for identification find legal foundation in the immigration laws and, in light of this legal foundation, it should be analyzed whether the prohibition of discrimination was contravened or not. We therefore should assume that "when police controls are performed to that end, some physical or ethnic features may be taken into consideration when it comes to foreign nationals as reasonable indications of their origins (not the national origins however)." The problem will always be the potential of racist motivation hidden within the exercise of legally established duties (Legal Ground 8).

So, in light of these general considerations, the Court examines the police performance that was carried out with respect to Ms. Rosalind Williams. The Court asserts that the request for identification addressed to Ms. Williams did not result from a blatant discrimination (Legal Ground 9). From its point of view, there would have only been a prohibited act of discrimination if the "racial features [...] had been taken into account when it came to requesting her documentation due to any reason other than its generic character indicatory of a higher probability of the condition of foreign national of Ms. Rosalind Williams." Subsequently, the mere use of ethnic references in a descriptive manner should not be considered—in the judgment of the Court—discriminatory itself.

According to this legal reasoning, the Constitutional Court states that in the established facts, there was no evidence of improper, ruthless, or humiliating treatment with respect to Ms. Williams, so that the racial criterion was only used as a mere indication of higher probability of the foreign status of the claimant, but not as a discriminatory support. The Court subsequently argues that "what would have been discriminatory is the application of a standard [a racial one in this case] irrelevant in order to individualize the persons for whom the legal system has provided the administrative measures; foreign nationals in the present case." Based on that line of argument, the Court rejects the *amparo* application. Nevertheless, one of the Magistrates of the Chamber took issue with the Court ruling. In his view, the immigration policy interpreted in such a generous way does not squarely fit the requirements that should be met in a social and democratic state governed by the rule of law. The non-discrimination clause demands, therefore, to interpret restrictively the controls on immigration.

The Court ruling did not satisfy Ms. Rosalind Williams, who, years later, brought the case before the United Nations Committee for Human Rights. The Committee issued a reasoned legal opinion in which the bottom line was that the treatment received by Ms. Rosalind Williams by the Spanish authorities had constituted an infringement of Articles 26 and 2(3) of the Covenant on Civil Rights. To the judgment of the committee, the States can legitimately check on the identity on a general basis in order to control illegal immigration. However, the physical or ethnic characteristics of a person are features that cannot serve as indications for a possible illegal situation in the country, since that would constitute a prohibited act of discrimination.

A CRITICAL VIEW ON THE CONSTITUTIONAL CASE LAW

The legal reasoning put forward by the Constitutional Court that contravening the prohibition of discrimination is appropriate in some instances, when it comes to police identification of foreign nationals, has been criticized by the majority of legal experts and by foreign national rights groups. The Court finds legal foundation in the reasonable logical inference made by the police stating that people from certain races or ethnicities are probably foreign and, on top of that, they are possibly in an irregular situation. In the judgment of the Court, it is admissible that the police use race as an identification factor to differentiate between Spanish nationals and foreign nationals, since it is a relevant standard to identify those addressed by the legal provision: immigrants.

Nonetheless, legal experts have pointed out that the prohibition of discrimination established in Article 14 CE prevents police from using standards such as race, ethnicity, or language as basis for requesting his or her identification and subsequently hold the person in detention in case he or she is in an irregular situation. There must be an objective reason—not based on these prohibited standards—to justify why identification or legal accreditation is requested from a foreign national (Sánchez Barrilao, 2002, p. 234). The problem does not lie in the existence of an illogical inference by the police agent who requests the identification from persons of a certain race; it could still be considered reasonable to think that a black person is a foreign national in Spain. The problem is that admitting the logical character of that inference invalidates the prohibition contained in Article 14 CE of taking into account somebody's inherent personal features, thereby inflicting burdens or prejudices on his or her legal sphere (Pomed & Velasco, 2003, p. 148). The Constitution prevents race, ethnicity, or language from being standards that limit individual rights. Rather, objective criteria not related to these prohibited attributes must be the basis for the limiting performance, in this case, the actions carried out by the police. Instances of this same police identification request that do not stem from profiling include border checkpoints, international transit areas, or even places where it is suspected that illegal activities connected to illegal immigration are taking place, such as drug smuggling.

If this critical view is applied to the Constitutional Court ruling that was discussed earlier, it could be concluded that the Court's solution to the case could have been framed according to the Constitution. The legal foundation would not find basis on the reasonableness of the police to use race as an indication to differentiate between persons, but on the fact that Ms. Rosalind Williams's identity check was conducted in a railway station, where it could objectively be asserted that there is a larger amount of foreign nationals, and, that being the case, of immigrants in an irregular administrative situation. There is no doubt that, once in the railway station, the differentiating criterion put in place by the police agent would probably be Ms. Williams's race, but it does not preclude that the police agent in the same railway station would request the documentation from a white person as well, in order to verify the person's identity.

POLICE ACCESS TO THE DATA OF THE MUNICIPAL CENSUS

Along with the identification of foreign nationals in the public space, the local police may contribute to control immigration by accessing the information contained in the municipal census in order to determine the migratory status of certain persons. The applicable rules to the concession of data contained in the municipal census are regulated by the Law providing the Basis for Local Regulation (LBRL) and in Organic Law 15/1999 of December 13, on Personal Data Protection (LOPD). According to Article 16(3) LBRL: "data contained in the municipal census will be ceded to other public Administrations at their request with no need for the previous consent of the data subject only when the data is necessary for the exercise of their respective duties, and exclusively in situations in which the residence and the domicile are relevant data." This provision thus regulates one of the exceptions to the need for the data subject's consent regarding the cession of his or her personal data. Only when data is ceded to other administrations for the exercise of their duties is it unnecessary to ask the data subject to obtain the consent. This provision states nothing regarding the use of data within the activity of the same administration. This is the reason why, in practice, the local police has less impediments to access municipal data from potential irregular immigrants (Aja, 2012, pp. 309–310). Being part of the same administration, it is understood that the police have no limitations when it comes to accessing this data.

Nevertheless, this is not the right interpretation. When the concession of data has a law enforcement purpose, the regulation of the LBRL must take into account what is established in Article 22(2) LOPD: "personal data gathering and processing for law enforcement purposes by the police force or corps without the consent of the data subjects shall be limited to the cases and data categories required to prevent objective risks to public safety or to repress offences, and such data must be stored in specific files established for this purpose and categorized by their degree of reliability." Thus, access to the municipal census by the police force—whether local, regional, or national—is conditional upon proof that the data subject poses a real hazard to public safety or of the commission of a criminal offense. This means that the local police cannot access the municipal census freely for the sole purpose of going against a possible illegal administrative act—e.g., an illegal stay on Spanish territory—whether or not the police in question are part of the local administration. In this sense, we must take into account the doctrine elaborated by the Spanish Data Protection Agency, which interprets the requirements to access the data of the municipal census for law enforcement purposes. In accordance with the criterion of the agency, the concession of personal data to the police must be done "only case by case and as a consequence of a particular investigating activity." This prevents the data contained in the municipal census from being incorporated as a whole to the police files, and demands proper justification in each case of the necessity and appropriateness of the requested data by police for the exercise of their duties.

IMMIGRANT INTEGRATION POLICIES AT A LOCAL LEVEL

Up to this point, the avenues for participation of municipalities in the enforcement of national immigration control policies have been discussed. What can be seen from what has been stated is that municipalities have little leeway with regard to the restrictive immigration policies. They normally play the role of a merely indirect administration, serving the interests of the either state or the regional administration. This makes sense within a power distribution framework in which the General State Administration dominates immigration powers and the autonomous regions and local bodies focus, essentially, on integrating immigrants. This is why municipalities have an apparently broader capacity to put in place their own public policies oriented to favor, to a greater or lesser extent, the integration of immigrants in the host society.

Nonetheless, it is truth that the local public policies of integration are very dependent upon their financing. This is why the lines of action of the municipalities in this field must converge with integration plans coming both from the General State Administration and the autonomous regions, which set the general orientation of the particular actions that could be financed at the local level (Velasco Caballero, 2010, p. 99). Currently, the Strategic Plan for Citizenship and Integration for 2011–2014 defines several areas of action regarding integration of immigrants. Some of these areas should be considered specific: hosting, employment, economic stimulus, education, health, social and integration services, mobility, and development; and others should be considered essentially cross cutting: peaceful coexistence, equal treatment and non-discrimination, childhood, youth and family life, genre, participation, and civic education. In each of the areas a diagnosis is made, priority lines of action are drawn, and a goal to achieve within them is established. The same approach is adopted in the Integration Plan from the Autonomous Region of Madrid 2009–2012. Several priority action areas are set out. Municipalities must accommodate their projects for integration to the lines drawn by the national and regional plans. Actually, relatively large municipalities may develop local plans that could help to coordinate policies of integration—this is the case, for example, of the Second Madrid Plan for Social and Cross Cultural Living Together 2009–2012 from the municipality of Madrid.

The capacity of municipalities to define their own public policies in each of the areas of action drawn by the Integration Plans may vary. We should pay attention to the legal foundation of their competence, which could lead to a broader or smaller scope of action for municipalities (Velasco Caballero, 2010, pp. 98 et seq.). In addition to this, we must take into consideration that there are mainly two types of municipal policies of integration: generic policies, which include the integration of immigrants as an indirect objective, considering immigrants within other under-served groups of people; or specific policies, that directly target the integration of immigrants, essentially addressing persons of foreign origin (Aja, 2012, pp. 444 et seq.). Within each area of action we might find both generic and specific policies of integration, or it is possible that priority is given to a certain kind of policy. For example, in terms of citizen co-existence, the actions for integration are normally addressed directly to immigrants through measures against racism and xenophobia, for public space revitalization, and via host country language and culture promotion programs. When it comes to political participation, integration tends to be promoted through specific policies that normally imply the creation of specific local organizations for the integration of immigrants.

Something different happens in the area of social services, where attention to immigrants in need—the most vulnerable sectors of society—is coordinated with generic measures (Velasco Caballero, 2010, pp. 100 ff.). With regard to housing, the integration of immigrants is fostered through generic social policies oriented to promote housing among the most disadvantaged people, combined with specific actions such as intercultural mediation favoring the rent of a house by immigrants (Díez Sastre, 2010, pp. 287 et seq.). Something similar happens concerning education where, the specific integration measures oriented to create extracurricular programs are combined with other generic actions, which address both foreign nationals and Spanish nationals—for example, the aid received by school cafeterias or the spaces for educational co-existence (Ponce i Solé, 2010, pp. 256 et seq.). This field should be analyzed on a case-by-case basis as it has been discussed here, but, at present, is strongly conditioned by the financial constraints of the actions for integration within the national and regional integration plans.

REFERENCES

Aguado i Cudolá, V., & Cerrillo Martínez, A. (2005). *Las condiciones de vivienda de los inmigrantes: La intervención de los entes locales.* Madrid: INAP.

Aja, E. (2012). *Inmigración y democracia.* Madrid: Alianza Editorial.

Aprell Lasagabaster, C. (2009, June). El anteproyecto de ley de reforma de la Ley Orgánica 4/2000, reguladora de los derechos y Libertades de los Extranjeros y su Integración Social (LOEXIS). *Revista General de Derecho Administrativo, 21*, 1–25.

Arieta-Araunabeña Alzaga, J., Gamboa Uribarren, B., & Labaca Zabala, M. L. (2009). El derecho al reagrupamiento familiar en la legislación, jurisprudencia y doctrina de España. *Cartapacio de Derecho, 16*, 1–55.

Catalá i Bas, A. H. (2009). Inmigración y gobierno multinivel. In R.T. Ausina (Ed.), *La integración de la población inmigrante en el marco europeo, estatal y autonómico español* (pp. 35–68). Granada: Iustel.

de la Quadra-Salcedo Janini, T. (2010). Los derechos sociales de los extranjeros: nuevas y viejas garantías. In Silvia Díez Sastre (Ed.), *Inmigración y gobiernos locales* (pp. 121–168). Madrid: Marcial Pons.

de la Quadra-Salcedo Janini, T. (2014). Legal status of immigrants: Rights for illegal immigrants? In M. los Ángeles Torres & F. Velasco Caballero (Eds.), *Global cities and immigrants. A comparative study of Chicago and Madrid.* New York: Peter Lang.

Díez Bueso, L. (2003). El marco competencial. In L. Pomed Sánchez & F. Velasco Caballero (Eds.), *Ciudadanía e inmigración* (pp. 177–202). Zaragoza: Monografía de la Revista Aragonesa de Administración Pública.

Díez Sastre, S. V. (2010). Inmigración y municipios. In S. Díez Sastre (Ed.), *Inmigración y gobiernos locales* (pp. 269–309). Madrid: Marcial Pons.

Izquierdo, A., & Cornelius, W. A. (Eds.). (2012). *Políticas de control migratorio: Estudio comparado de España y EEUU.* Barcelona: Edicions Bellaterra.

Pérez Caramés, A. (2012). La evolución reciente de las políticas de control migratorio en España. In A. Izquierdo & W. A. Cornelius (Eds.), *Políticas de control migratorio: Estudio comparado de España y EEUU* (pp. 142–211). Barcelona: Edicions Bellaterra.

Pérez Sola, N. (2008). Funciones y competencias de las Comunidades Autónomas en inmigración. In I. B. Rodríguez (Ed.), *Regiones, Unión Europea e integración de inmigrantes: Una perspectiva desde el Derecho comparado* (pp. 13–42). Barcelona: Atelier.

Pomed Sánchez, L., & Velasco Caballero, F. (2003). Inmigración y policía administrativa de seguridad. *Anuario de la Facultad de Derecho de la Universidad Autónoma de Madrid*, 7,135–184.

Ponce i Solé, J. (2010). Inmigración, escuela y segregación: el papel del Derecho público. In S. Díez Sastre (Ed.), *Inmigración y gobiernos locales* (pp. 209–267). Madrid: Marcial Pons.

Sánchez Barrilao, J. F. (2002, January). Identificación documental de nacionales y extranjeros. Comentario a la STC 13/2001, de 29 de enero. *Revista Española de Derecho Constitucional*, *64*, 217–238.

Soriano Miras, R. M., & Rico Becerra, J. I. (2012). Políticas de integración y asentamiento migratorio. In A. Izquierdo & W. A. Cornelius (Eds.), *Políticas de control migratorio: Estudio comparado de España y EEUU* (pp. 213–250). Barcelona: Edicions Bellaterra.

Tryjanowski, A. (2010). Integración de inmigrantes en Alemania: Reparto del riesgo en el procedimiento de integración. In Silvia Díez Sastre (Ed.), *Inmigración y gobiernos locales* (pp. 169–186). Madrid: Marcial Pons.

Velasco Caballero, F. (2010). Políticas y competencias locales sobre inmigración. In S. Díez Sastre (Ed.), *Inmigración y gobiernos locales* (pp. 65–120). Madrid: Marcial Pons.

Villaverde Menéndez, I. (2003). El reagrupamiento familiar y la política de contingentes. In L. Pomed Sánchez & F. Velasco Caballero (Eds.), *Ciudadanía e inmigración* (pp. 141–176). Zaragoza: Monografía de la Revista Aragonesa de Administración Pública.

Villaverde Menéndez, I. (2010). El padrón municipal, integración social y nueva ciudadanía social. Padrón *versus* nación. In S. Díez Sastre (Ed.), *Inmigración y gobiernos locales* (pp. 187–208). Madrid: Marcial Pons.

Comparative Notes on the Role of Local Government in the Enforcement of Migratory Law

AMALIA PALLARES, UNIVERSITY OF ILLINOIS AT CHICAGO
MARIA DE LOS ANGELES TORRES,
UNIVERSITY OF ILLINOIS AT CHICAGO
SILVIA DÍEZ SASTRE, AUTONOMOUS UNIVERSITY OF MADRID

The power to enforce migratory law is held formally, both in Spain as well as in the United States, by superior territorial jurisdictions—the central state and the federal government, respectively. This means that the approval of laws concerning the entrance, permanence, and departure of foreigners takes place at the federal and state levels—subject to the powers of the European Union in the case of Spain. It also means that the administrative and police measures aimed at enforcing compliance with these laws, and thus the control of illegal immigration, takes place at these levels as well. Inferior territorial entities—states, counties, and municipalities in the case of the United States and autonomous communities and municipalities in the case of Spain—assume an immigration management role limited by the implementation of public policies concerning the integration of immigrants. In practice, however, there are overlaps in the exercise of these powers that reveal a more complete map of power distribution. Thus, through funding, the state and federal governments respectively intervene in immigrant integration measures for their part, and the U.S. states and the autonomous communities, as well as municipalities, also intervene more or less directly and more or less decisively in the application of immigrant control measures.

In Spain, the state intervenes in the integration of immigrants by way of financing measures in concrete sectors (health, youth programs, social services, etc.) that are gathered, fundamentally, within the Strategic Plan on Citizenship and Integration 2011–2014, which includes the management of European funds linked with these objectives. The state, therefore, is connected directly with autonomous communities as well as with municipalities, which are responsible for implementing immigrant integration policies to the extent that their powers allow. These relationships can be explained by the territorial structure of the Spanish State, which grants autonomy to the autonomous communities, as well as—albeit on another level—to the municipalities. In the United States there is no official federal policy on immigration integration. In effect, the federal government finances social health and education policies for the general population, which, on occasion, may favor immigrants. But as a general rule, the immigrant population is not considered a primary beneficiary of these measures. Only in the case of primary and secondary education are there federal funds allocated for immigrant children regardless of their migratory status, given that the Supreme Court has found that such education is obligatory for all children. Thus, these public policies are not considered to be mechanisms that promote integration. The implementation of these social policies is managed between the federal and state governments, which, subsequently, will be in charge of ensuring that this funding reaches the municipalities. This dynamic, therefore, responds to the configuration of municipalities as "children of the states," whose autonomy is not recognized constitutionally at the federal level. For their part, the states are in charge of funding programs and policies visibly linked to integration—such as English language education—and which are managed by NGOs. In any case, it should be noted that in both countries, the state and federal funds for integration do not directly benefit illegal immigrants. Instead, it is at the regional and local levels that policies directed towards illegal immigration are designed.

The participation of municipalities, counties, States, and autonomous communities in the enforcement of immigration control measures is strongly conditioned by the distinct organizational models of territorial power relations in the United States and Spain. In the United States, the model grants significant freedom to the states and municipalities in the configuration of their own public policies concerning immigration, insofar as the federal government (in the case of the states) or the state (in the case of the municipalities) does not come to its own decision on the matter. In fact, it is common for states to clearly define, through concrete measures, favorable or restrictive immigration policies. Such measures include laws such as the New Americans Initiative, the Day Labor Act, or the Dream Act, and through programs like All Kids in the state of Illinois, which guarantee rights, resources, and services to illegal immigrants that are not recognized by the state government. The same happens with municipalities that demonstrate politically against or in favor of immigration control in their territory—for example, by means of political resolutions that establish compromises with their constituencies, given that municipalities are not able to legally contest federal regulations. "Sanctuaries" are one example, which normally arise as a result of a Democratic majority, and are generally found in large cities, whereas more restrictive areas are typically governed by the Republican party and are generally mid-sized cities—although the size of the city is not as important in this respect as its political orientation corresponding to the party in power.

However, this expanded freedom of the states in the United States is limited by the principal of preemption, whereby state laws that conflict with federal laws are deemed invalid. This translates, in practice, to the existence of multiple points of disagreement and possible conflict between these two levels of government. A good example is the differences that have arisen between the federal government and Arizona's law HB1070, which was recently brought before the Supreme Court by the federal government, alleging violation of the principal of preemption. A similar instance of conflict between state and federal levels is the state of Illinois's rejection of the federal Secure Communities program.

In Spain, on the contrary, the municipalities and the autonomous communities must respect the measures adopted by the state concerning the exercise of their powers, and must even collaborate with the state in exercising these powers on the terms that the state itself legally establishes. Autonomous communities and municipalities, therefore, find it very difficult to configure their own public policies towards immigration control. For this reason, it is not easy to establish a clear migratory policy framework according to political colors and types of population centers. However, it can be noted that, like in the United States, there is a more favorable tendency towards immigration in large urban centers than there is in mid-sized urban centers or rural areas; migratory control is more relaxed in progressive parties than in conservative or nationalist parties.

In Spain, the municipal, regional, and national governments collaborate in serveral different ways in order to enforce migratory controls. The migratory status control procedures for foreigners that have been implemented by the Spanish State rely on the participation of local entities and autonomous communities. The state, by way of Basic Law 4/2000, January 11, on the Rights, Freedoms, and Social Integration of Foreigners in Spain (Alien Act), establishes the participation of the autonomous communities and, where relevant, the municipalities, in temporary residence authorization procedures, temporary residence permit renewals, and family reunification. Traditionally, the municipalities have been the ones to collaborate on cases like this; however, since 2011—following a reform of the Alien Act—the state has given this responsibility to the autonomous community, which in turn must decide whether or not to delegate this power to the municipalities. However, practically all of the autonomous communities have delegated this power to the municipalities, with the exception of Madrid, Catalonia, Basque Country, and the Canary Islands, which have decided to enforce it directly.

The participation of the municipalities or of the autonomous community consists of issuing a report on the social stability of foreigners, their level of integration, and their living conditions (according to the type of procedure). This report is not binding, but it certainly has the ability to influence the final decision. In order to complete this task, the state establishes very detailed instructions that turn the municipalities and the autonomous communities into indirect administration for the state in this regard. The margin of configuration of a policy in the enforcement of these powers is very narrow. Despite this, certain restrictive tendencies in the application of this regulation should be noted in the case of the Community of Madrid, as well as in some U.S. states.

Since February of 2012, for the purposes of a report on social stability and integration efforts, Madrid has demanded the passing of a language test—for non-Spanish speakers—and a course on Spanish culture—the "Know Your Laws" program—that is intended to condition the migratory status of foreigners based on the demonstration of their integration efforts. In the United States, there is no similar collaboration between municipalities, counties, states, and the national government. The documentation necessary for the revision of an individual case is completed directly between the individual and the federal government, with the assistance of lawyers and/or NGOs. Therefore, any possible collaboration on the enforcement of migratory controls will not reach the level of formalization that has been determined by the territorial structure of Spain. Without a doubt, there exist restrictive municipalities that may establish procedures within the framework of their powers that are intended to limit the permanence of illegal immigrants in their territory—for example, modifying rental agreements—but neither municipalities nor states in the U.S. are integrated into federal immigration control procedures. Restrictive states have adopted certain measures to change this situation. The State of Alabama, for example, has adopted a law that assigns public school teachers the responsibility of documenting the legal status of their students and their students' parents. However, the application of this law has been suspended pending examination by the Supreme Court.

The national government's access to local information is another of the most important aspects in the enforcement of immigration control policies in both Spain and the U.S. Also on this point, the dynamics that govern the relations between the distinct territorial levels of power are very diverse. In the United States, municipalities enjoy the freedom to choose whether they will collaborate with the federal government in offering information regarding immigrants' legal status. For example, the E-Verify program offers voluntary collaboration agreements with municipalities in exchange for funding. This affords the municipalities a wide margin of decision, notwithstanding the possibility that the state may oblige or prohibit its local entities from collaborating with the federal government. Furthermore, in the United States there is no registration comparable to the Spanish system, and the municipalities do not grant the title of resident or neighbor to anyone. While county tax collection records exist, there is no systematic method of registering information on illegal immigrants as such. In the political context of the United States, not asking questions about one's migratory status is considered to be the best way to protect illegal immigrants.

In Spain, however, a fundamental task of the municipalities consists of elaborating on and maintaining the municipal census, which preserves residents' faith in the municipality and serves as a base for the development of the national electoral census. Through a discussion on the inclusion of illegal immigrants in this registry, it has been decided that these immigrants should be registered as a means of facilitating their access to a greater number of social benefits—in the case of health care, for instance, registration in the census allows them to receive health insurance cards and, therefore, access to all of the health services that would otherwise be much more restricted. At the same time, the transfer of local data—contained primarily in the municipal registry—is limited by the right to data protection. All of the municipalities, regardless of their political tendencies, are prohibited from sharing the information contained in the municipal registry with police authorities from the central atate, with the exception of individual instances in which the information being shared is necessary to counteract a real threat to the public safety or to prosecute criminal offenses (Article 22.2 of Basic Law 15/1999, December 13, on Data Protection). According to the interpretation given by the Spanish Data Protection Agency, only in cases where there exists a previous, well-founded suspicion may the information contained in the municipal registry be shared. Thus, a general rule has been established that operates the same in all cases, which does not allow the municipalities to use information on foreigners in an adverse manner for political gain.

Finally, an analysis must be made of the role of local police in the enforcement of migratory controls. In Spain, local police are not authorized to exercise the functions of immigration control agents. They may only exercise control over a person's migratory status if it becomes necessary while performing other duties, although in practice police are not entirely bounded by this limitation. Immigration control is the responsibility of the National Police (Articles 12.1a, 1 and 2 of Basic Law 2/1986, March 13, on Security Forces). In the United States, the situation was similar prior to 1997. Local police did not enforce immigration controls. But in 1997, Section 287(g) was added to the Immigration and Nationality Act via the enactment of the Illegal Immigration Reform and Responsibility Act of 1996. This precept allows state and local governments to come to an agreement that local police officers may be authorized to carry out the functions of immigration officials. The result of this measure has been a dramatic increase in the number of arrests and deportations, often initiated by minor traffic violations. This program has also caused controversy due to its discriminatory potential towards anyone who appears to be an immigrant, which has led to the interrogation and harassment of citizens. More recently, the Secure Communities program has made it easier for local police to cross-reference the fingerprints of a detained individual against those contained in the database of immigration control. As a result, thousands of arrests and deportations have been made of people who have not committed any crime whatsoever. The participation of local governments in these programs is voluntary, given that the federal government assumes that local governments will want to participate of their own accord. The voluntary nature of these programs has allowed, for example, the state of Illinois to not participate. Recently, however, in May 2012, the states of Connecticut and New York were forced to initiate the Secure Communities programs, despite having declared their opposition to them. This means that, unlike Spain, a duty to share information with the federal government is a real possibility. However, collaboration regarding the detention of immigrants will be more difficult to impose, given the presence of a consolidated opposition from local governments towards the detainment of people solely to review their migratory status when they have no pending court cases. This is the case, for example, in Cook County.

PART FOUR

CHAPTER SEVEN

Immigrant Education Policies in the Chicago Metropolitan Area

NILDA FLORES-GONZALEZ,
UNIVERSITY OF ILLINOIS AT CHICAGO
JULIO CAPELES, UNIVERSITY OF ILLINOIS AT CHICAGO
CAROLINA CALVILLO, UNIVERSITY OF ILLINOIS AT CHICAGO
RAJHAI WILSON, UNIVERSITY OF ILLINOIS AT CHICAGO
IRMA OLMEDO, UNIVERSITY OF ILLINOIS AT CHICAGO

In the United States, schools are the premier integrative public institution, as they are mandated to educate all children, including immigrant children. As such, they are also the gatekeepers to immigrant incorporation and play an important role in the integration or further marginalization of immigrants. Despite its central role in the integration of immigrants, schools across the U.S. vary greatly in their approach and implementation of educational policy. Because policies are not uniform, there is great disparity in the educational experiences of immigrant students across schools, districts, and states. In this chapter, we examine how Chicago and several of its suburbs approach the education of their growing immigrant student population. First, we provide background on federal and state policies that address the education of immigrant students. Second, we examine district policies that lead to unequal educational opportunities for immigrant students across school districts in the Chicago Metropolitan Area.

THE CHICAGO METROPOLITAN AREA AND ITS SCHOOL DISTRICTS

The Chicago Metropolitan Area (CMA) contains a major traditional gateway (Chicago) surrounded by satellite cities and suburban, exurban, and rural towns within an hour's driving distance from Chicago. Historically, Latinos have concentrated in Chicago and a few satellite cities, but this pattern has changed in the last two decades. In the 1990s, immigrants began to increasingly bypass Chicago to settle in cities and towns in the larger CMA (Suro & Singer, 2002). As a result, the seven counties comprising the CMA have experienced triple-digit percentage increases in Latino population, placing the CMA among the top metropolitan areas with the largest concentration of Latinos in the nation (Latino Policy Forum, 2011; Motel & Patten, 2012; Ready & Brown-Gort, 2005). In 2010, 90% of Latinos in Illinois lived in the CMA, and Latinos comprised 22% of the CMA population (Latino Policy Forum, 2011). Although Chicago continues to be the epicenter of Latino political, cultural, and economic activity, with the largest Latino population (38%) in the state, 52% of Latinos live in the suburban CMA (Latino Policy Forum, 2011). In fifteen of these suburbs, Latinos have become the majority of residents (Latino Policy Forum, 2011).

These demographic changes have had an impact in school districts across the CMA. By 2008, Latinos comprised 26% of the student population in the CMA 2008). Most Latino students are concentrated in the Chicago Public Schools (CPS), the third largest school district in the nation. With nearly 180,000 Latino students, CPS has the fourth largest concentration of Latino students in the nation. While 34% of Latino students attend school in Chicago (both public and private), 56% of Latino students in the state attend suburban CMA schools (Soltero, Soltero, & Robbins, 2010). There are twenty-one high school districts in the CMA that are at least 50% Latino (Bennet, Koval, & Spirou, 2010).

The Latino student population is very diverse, which makes meeting their needs more challenging. These differences include country of origin, native and foreign born, age at time of arrival, gender, English language skills, academic skills, legal status, and socioeconomic status. In addition, the Latino student population may include students of indigenous background, mostly from Mexico and Guatemala, and unaccompanied minors. It is not uncommon for Latino children to live in mixed status families in which some members are citizens (by birth or naturalization) or legal residents, and others are undocumented immigrants. Children in mixed status families live under the constant specter of deportation of self or a family member. Particular challenges are posed by immigrant students who arrive in the U.S. at high school age. In addition to poor English language skills, many have little previous formal schooling[1] and lack grade appropriate academic skills, and, sometimes, adequate native language skills necessary for academic tasks. Undocumented students also face additional challenges as they enter high school. Although undocumented children under the age of fourteen are ensured educational and health services[2] by the state, and are required by law to take driver's education and obtain a learner's permit, they are ineligible for driver's licenses.

Although 90% of CMA Latinos under age eighteen are U.S. born (Bennett, Koval, & Spirou, 2010), many grow up in Spanish-speaking households and require bilingual education. The CMA holds 90% of the state's English Language Learner (ELL) student population and fourteen of the fifteen school districts with the most ELL students (Illinois Advisory Council on Bilingual Education, 2011). CPS has the third largest ELL student population in the nation and the largest concentration of immigrant students in the state (Batalova & McHugh, 2010). In the 2011–2012 academic year, ELL comprised 16.6% of CPS students, most of them Mexican.[3] Yet, it is in suburban CMA where the immigrant student population has skyrocketed. Put together, suburban CMA has more ELL students than Chicago, and the numbers are expected to continue increasing (Illinois Advisory Council on Bilingual Education, 2011). From 2000 to 2006, there was a 20% increase in the number of Spanish-speaking children living in linguistically isolated households in the CMA, with the steepest increase (47%) happening in the suburban CMA (Institute for Latino Studies, 2008). Most ELL students are found in the lower elementary school years (K–3) with decreasing numbers in each consecutive school level, suggesting that by the third grade most ELL students have been reclassified as English fluent and supposedly able to receive instruction in English-only classrooms (Illinois Advisory Council on Bilingual Education, 2011). ELL students at the high school level are usually recent immigrants and face more challenges. Despite marked gains in English proficiency and academic achievement, ELL students lag behind their non-ELL peers. They have a lower graduation rate and lower scores on achievement tests stemming from their lower language skills (Illinois Advisory Council on Bilingual Education, 2011).

Gwynne, Pareja, Ehrlich, and Allensworth (2012) found that Latino ELL students in Chicago make up a diverse population with differences in school performance and graduation rates. Among students who are identified as ELL in elementary school, those who outgrow ELL programs before middle school outperform and have higher graduation rates than other ELL and non-ELL Latino peers. Students who are still ELL when they reach high school have the lowest performance and graduation rates. Somewhere in between are recent immigrants who are identified as ELL when they enroll in high school. These students tend to have good course performance but lower graduation rates, mostly due to their older age and lower educational expectations and/or pressure to become employed so as to help with family finances.

Lacking resources and the immigrant-oriented institutions that have historically helped integrate immigrants in traditional gateways like Chicago, suburban schools struggle to meet the needs of the growing immigrant student population. CPS, which serves 400,000 students in 681 schools and has had bilingual programs since 1969, faces challenges related to its massive size that do not afflict neighboring suburban school districts, which typically serve less than 5,000 students, manage eight to fifteen schools, and have little experience with bilingual education. Given these demographic changes and contextual differences in the region, it is imperative to expand the discussion of immigrant education in Chicago to the larger Chicago Metropolitan Area.

Here, we use publicly available data from federal, state, and districts sources to examine the education of immigrant students in D 299 Chicago Public Schools and six selected school districts in Lake County, just north of Chicago:[4] Waukegan CUSD 60, North Chicago SD 187, Round Lake CUSD 116, Wauconda CUSD 118, North Shore SD 112, and Township HSD 112.[5] Table 7.1 summarizes some of the general characteristics of these districts.[6]

Table 7.1. Characteristics of School Districts

District	Type of District	Total Enrollment	Latino Enrollment	Number of Schools	Communities Served
Chicago SD 299	Unified	404,151	44.1%	PK–8 (472); 9–12 (106); Charter (96); Contract (7)	Chicago
North Chicago SD 187	Unified	3,988	46.6%	PreK–K (1); K–5 (5); 6 (1); 7–8 (1) and 9–12 (1)	North Chicago
Waukegan CUSD 60	Unified	15,960	74.4%	PreK (3); K–5 (15); 6–8(5); 9–12 (3)	Waukegan
Round Lake CUSD 116	Unified	7,127	69.8%	K (1); PreK–5 (1); 1–5 (4); 6–8 (2); 9–12 (1)	Round Lake: Round Lake Beach
Wauconda CUSD 118	Unified	4,481	23.4%	PK–5 (2); K–5 (1); 6–8 (2); 9–12 (1)	Wauconda
North Shore SD 112	Independent	4,348	21.2%	K–5 (8); 6–8 (3)	Highland Park; Highwood
Township HSD 113	Independent	3,744	10.5%	9–12 (2)	Highland Park; Deerfield

Source: Illinois State Board of Education

Federal Policies Affecting Immigrant Students

The U.S. Constitution ensures free public education for all children regardless of legal or citizenship status. In 1982, *Plyler v. Doe*[7] ruled that states cannot deny free public education to undocumented students in grades K–12 because such denial violates the Equal Protection Clause of the Fourteenth Amendment of the U.S. Constitution. *Plyler v. Doe* found that denying a free public education to children who were brought by their parents to the U.S. without proper documentation discriminates against children because they are not at fault for their undocumented status.

In 1965, Title VII of the Elementary and Secondary Education Act[8] encouraged the development of bilingual education programs by providing school districts with funding for them. It also provided grants to universities for teacher training. Title VII stated that if children were to have access to the curriculum of the school, they would need to be able to understand what was being taught. For children with low English language skills, it called for the use of the child's native language until the child was fluent in English. This approach was reaffirmed under the Bilingual Education Act of 1974 and was further affirmed by the Supreme Court Case's *Lau v. Nichols*[9] that same year. Although *Lau v. Nichols* was initiated by Chinese Americans—who claimed that their children were not benefiting from the curriculum because they did not understand English—the case was applicable to all children whose home language was not English. According to federal regulations, as long as the curriculum is accessible and comprehensible to students with limited English proficiency, the type of program to implement is left to the discretion of state and local school districts.

Although there is a long history of teaching in languages other than English in U.S. schools and federal law supports bilingual education programs for students with limited English proficiency, the use of languages other than English for instruction has frequently been accompanied by controversy and opposition. In fact, federal support for bilingual education has diminished over the years. During the George W. Bush administration, Congress passed the No Child Left Behind Act of 2001 (NCLB).[10] The stated intent of this act was to improve the performance of disadvantaged children by holding states, districts, and schools accountable for student progress.[11] The basic tenet of NCLB is to narrow the gap in achievement between white middle class students and racial and ethnic minorities, low-income students, English-language learners (immigrants), and special education students. Opposition to NCLB centers on its reliance on high-stakes testing and accountability and the burden that it places on school districts, particularly cash-strapped districts, without the provision of adequate federal funds to implement programs that address NCLB goals. Under NCLB, all students are to meet certain Annual Yearly Progress (AYP) standards by 2014, including ELL students. Because AYP is measured by standardized testing, schools and teachers are under much pressure to improve test scores. This leads to "teaching to the test" by aligning the curriculum with standardized testing philosophy that does not include critical thinking skills (Hursh, 2007). The inclusion of ELL and special education in these measures deflates test scores. Federal mandate for free public education ends at the twelth grade. Although there are no federal laws barring undocumented students from attending college, costs are prohibitive for most of these students since they do not qualify for federal financial assistance. Grants and government-guaranteed student loans are limited to citizens and legal permanent residents. Every year, 65,000 undocumented students graduate from high school and, because of their legal status, are unable to secure legal employment or obtain government-based financial aid for postsecondary studies.[12] Those who manage to attend college cannot find legal employment upon graduation or advance their immigration status.

Seeking to provide a path to legalization and eventual citizenship for undocumented students, U.S. Senator Dick Durbin (D–Illinois) has proposed numerous times, without success, the Development, Relief and Education for Alien Minors Act[13] best known as the DREAM Act. First proposed in 2001, the DREAM Act seeks a path to legalization and eventual citizenship for undocumented youth who arrive in the U.S. as minors, complete several years of schooling in the U.S., graduate from high school, have good moral standing, and enroll in a two- or four-year college or join the armed forces. Lack of congressional action has propelled undocumented youth to take political action to push for the DREAM Act. Generally known as the Dreamers, these youth lobby, rally, protest, and engage in civil disobedience acts to call attention to their plight.

As a response to the Dreamers' actions, President Obama enacted the Deferred Action for Childhood Arrivals (DACA)[14] on June 15, 2012. This administrative action does not provide a path to legalization and citizenship, nor does it grant access to government-based financial aid for postsecondary education. DACA only grants temporary protection from deportation and work permits to undocumented youth under thirty-one years of age who entered into the U.S. by June 17, 2007 and before their sixteenth birthday, are currently in school or graduated from high school or obtained a high school certificate, are honorably discharged veterans, and do not have a criminal record.[15] DACA must be renewed every two years, and because it is an administrative action that allows for prosecutorial discretion, it can be revoked at any time. While the U.S. undocumented population is estimated at 11 million, only 1.8 million are potentially eligible for DACA. According to data released by the U.S. Customs and Immigration Services (USCIS), nearly 368,000 people applied for DACA in the four-month period after it took effect on August 15, 2012.[16] By mid-December, 103,000 applicants were approved for deferred action, 12,000 were rejected, and the rest are undergoing review. Government data shows that 70% of DACA applicants are Mexican nationals (USCIS, 2012).

State Policy Affecting Immigrant Students

Although there is a federal mandate for free public education (K–12) for all minors, including undocumented children, education is primarily a state responsibility. Since the late 1990s, states have been testing the boundaries of this federal mandate by passing laws that affect the educational rights of immigrant students. In 1994, California voters passed Proposition 187,[17] state legislation that sought to deny health care, public education, and other social services to undocumented immigrants. A federal court found the law unconstitutional. Other attempts seek to curtail the rights of immigrant students by focusing on bilingual instruction. Known as English-Only laws, these measures seek to restrict the use of languages other than English in the curriculum. English-Only laws have passed in three states: California, Arizona, and Massachusetts. A similar initiative was defeated in Colorado in 2001. More recently, Arizona's legislature passed HB 2281[18] prohibiting public schools from teaching courses deemed "un-American," effectively disbanding Mexican American studies from the public schools' curriculum. Another recent state law affecting undocumented students is Alabama's HB 56,[19] which requires public schools to determine the citizenship and immigration status of its students, and report these numbers to school districts who in turn are required to report them to the state Board of Education. Although Alabama HB 56 does not deny a free K–12 public education to undocumented students, it bars them from attending public colleges and universities.[20]

Illinois stands out as having some of the most inclusive educational policies for immigrant students. The Illinois State Board of Education's Students' Rights to Equal Education[21] establishes that the immigration status of the parent or child has no bearing on the rights of the student to enroll in public school and, in accordance with the U.S. Constitution, guarantees free public education through grade twelve and up to the age of twenty-one regardless of immigrant status. The state of Illinois requires every district to guarantee all immigrant students, including undocumented students and students with limited English proficiency, equal access to the full range of programs and resources. According to Title 23 Illinois Administrative Code 228,[22] schools with twenty or more limited English proficiency students who speak the same home language and are in the same grade level must offer transitional bilingual education (TBE), while schools with nineteen or less of these students per grade can elect to offer transitional bilingual education or transitional program of instruction (TBI). Under TBE, students are taught primarily in their home language while learning English as a second language (ESL) with the goal of transferring them to English-only classes after three years.[23] As students become more proficient in English, they transition into the TPI or ESL depending on their needs for language support.[24] The state of Illinois requires districts, at a minimum, to offer TBE and/or TPI, but also allows districts to design and implement—and use local funds for—other bilingual education programs beyond those required by law.

Illinois is leading the expansion of bilingual education beyond K–12 instruction nationwide. In 2010, Illinois extended Title 23 to include the requirement for public schools to offer bilingual educational services to students with limited English proficiency in preschool programs.[25] The mandate also requires that preschool bilingual teachers gain bilingual certification by 2014. In 2012, the state enacted HB 3819, which calls for the evaluation of bilingual programs. HB 3819[26] also calls for the consideration establishing "parent academies" as a means to promote school involvement among non-English speaking parents.

Although No Child Left Behind established minimum guidelines for teacher certification, it is the states that dictate and grant teacher certification. Universities provide teacher training, but students must meet the requirements for state certification to be licensed. In Illinois, bilingual/ESL teachers must pass the Basic Skills Test and have a bilingual and/or ESL certification, including specific types of courses.[27] Due to the growing immigrant population and the small number of teachers meeting bilingual/ESL certification, the state offers various programs to certify current teachers. The state also offers the Teacher Exchange Visitor Program,[28] which recruits highly qualified and English proficient teachers from Spain and Mexico to teach Spanish or in a bilingual education program for up to three years.

For most undocumented students, college tuition is prohibitive, particularly in those states where they are charged foreign student rates. Because of state subsidies, public universities charge reduced rates to in-state residents, higher rates to out-of-state students, and the highest rates to international students. Only twelve states, including Illinois, charge in-state tuition to undocumented students.[29] Under HB 60, undocumented students in Illinois qualify for in-state tuition if they have graduated from a high school in Illinois and attended high school in the state for at least three years.[30] Undocumented students do not qualify for state financial aid—either grants or loans—but they qualify for some private grants and scholarships that do not require legal status. Recognizing the financial difficulties faced by undocumented students, the state of Illinois recently passed SB 2185, better known as the Illinois DREAM Act.[31] Under the Illinois DREAM Act, undocumented students will have access to privately funded, state-administered scholarships, as well as college savings and prepaid tuition programs. Eligibility is restricted to students who have at least one immigrant parent and lived with a parent or guardian while going to high school in Illinois for at least three years before graduating or receiving a GED certificate.[32] The Illinois DREAM Act also calls for the establishment of training programs that will provide high school counselors, as well as admissions and financial aid staff at state universities, with information on college-funding opportunities for undocumented students.

The Illinois State Board of Education (ISBE) is the state governmental agency in charge of implementing and overseeing the educational mandate of the state in public and private K–12 education.[33] ISBE also proposes and advocates for educational policy to the Illinois General Assembly and governor. The board has nine members who are appointed by the governor and ratified by the state senate; its operations are directed by the state superintendent of schools. ISBE is further subdivided into fifty-six Regional Offices of Education and Intermediate Services,[34] headed by elected regional superintendents of schools. Cook County, where Chicago is located, is the exception, served by three regional sffices (north, west, and south) that each serve from one large county to up to nine small counties. In total, Illinois has 879 school districts and over 4,900 schools. Among their duties, regional offices serve as legal counsel, certifies teachers, trains bus drivers, disburses state and federal funds, reviews budgets and financial reports, and conducts facilities inspections.

District Policy Affecting Immigrant Students

As long as they follow federal and state regulations, school districts have much leeway in designing and implementing educational policies that impact immigrant students. As a result, districts vary greatly in their approach and implementation of immigrant-related educational policies. Because practice is not uniform, there is great disparity in the educational services for immigrant students across schools, districts, and states. In what follows, we will show how district-level factors complicate the implementation of educational policies addressing the needs of immigrant students.

School Budgets

In the U.S., education is financed by federal, state, and local funds, with the bulk of school funding coming from the local chest. The federal and state governments use a standard formula to fund districts based on a count of how many students are in the district, and provide some additional funds to schools that qualify due to their low-income, low English proficiency, and special education populations. Federal funds are intended to supplement state and local funds with allocations for high-poverty schools and special education programs. The federal government also offers funds through competitive grants for teacher, program, and school development. For instance, Race to the Top is a competitive grant that provides extra funding for states and local districts implementing school reform, and in 2011, Illinois was awarded $42.8 million.[35] Criticism of Race to the Top center on its top-down approach, the use of high-stakes testing as a measure of teacher performance, the promotion of charter schools over public schools, the imposition of common standards, and the disproportionate targeting of high-poverty and minority schools (Strauss, 2010; Wright, 2010).

States vary in the amount of funding they provide for education. Over the past two decades, Illinois has substantially decreased its educational budget to 35%, placing it at the bottom of educational spending among surrounding states (Mulhall, 2008). In a nationwide comparison, Illinois received a "C" in overall educational funding and the only "F" in the country on funding equity (Baker, Sciarra, & Farrie, 2010). Not surprisingly, Illinois's funding of bilingual education has steadily decreased, even while the ELL population continues to grow (Illinois Advisory Council on Bilingual Education, 2011). By spending less in schools, the state of Illinois (and the federal government) passes the burden of school funding to local governments. As a result, local districts provide 59% of the funds, while the state of Illinois and federal government contribute 35% and 5% respectively.

Not only is Illinois investing less in education, but it has one of the highest funding inequity rates in the nation. That is, some districts spend on their schools over three times what other districts spend (see Figure 7.1).

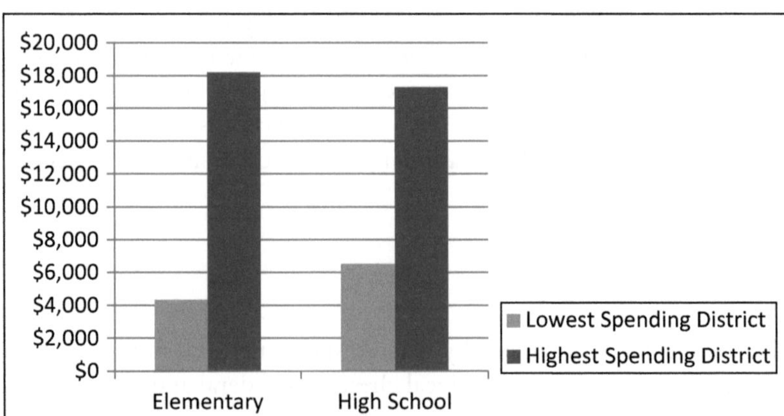

Figure 7.1. School Spending in Illinois

Indeed, we found great discrepancy in school funding across the school districts we studied (see Figure 7.2). While some districts' local funding hovered around 40%, in other districts local funding surpassed 80%.

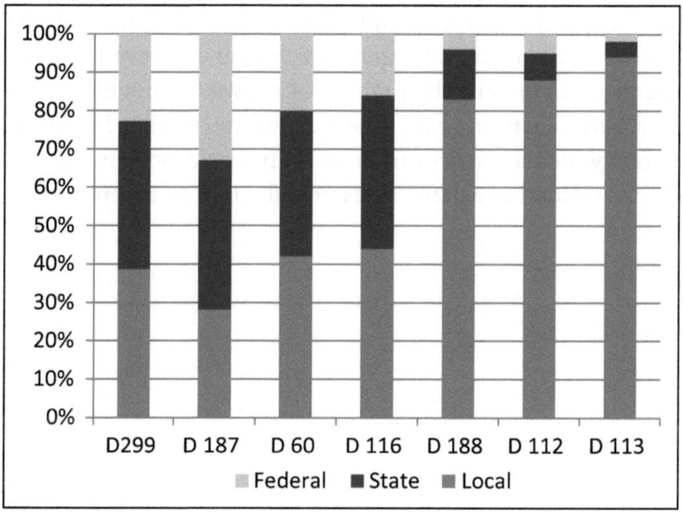

Figure 7.2. Sources of Funding for Each District

Those districts with higher local funding also spent much more on schools. For instance, the instructional expenditure per pupil in those districts was $2,000 to $5,000 more than in other districts (see Figure 7.3).

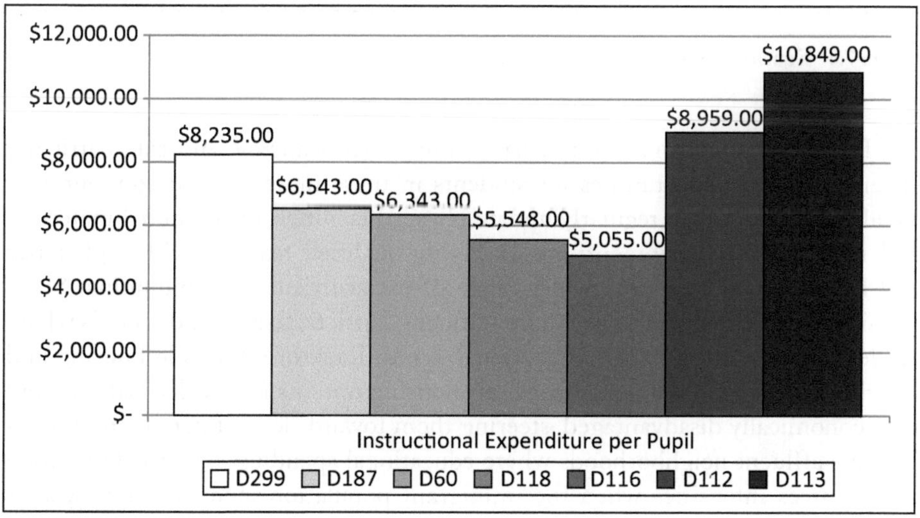

Figure 7.3. Instructional Expenditure Per Pupil by District

What lies at the source of funding inequity between districts is local wealth. Because local funding is based on local property taxes, wealthier communities with a higher property value can collect more revenue to fund their schools. Put simply, more affluent districts generate higher tax revenue and have more monies to spend on their schools. Figure 7.4 shows the huge discrepancy of the Equalized Assessed Valuation (EAV) for each of the districts in our study. EAV is the tax base upon which a district can draw for its basic local property tax revenue, reported in terms of total equalized assessed valuation of all properties within the school district.

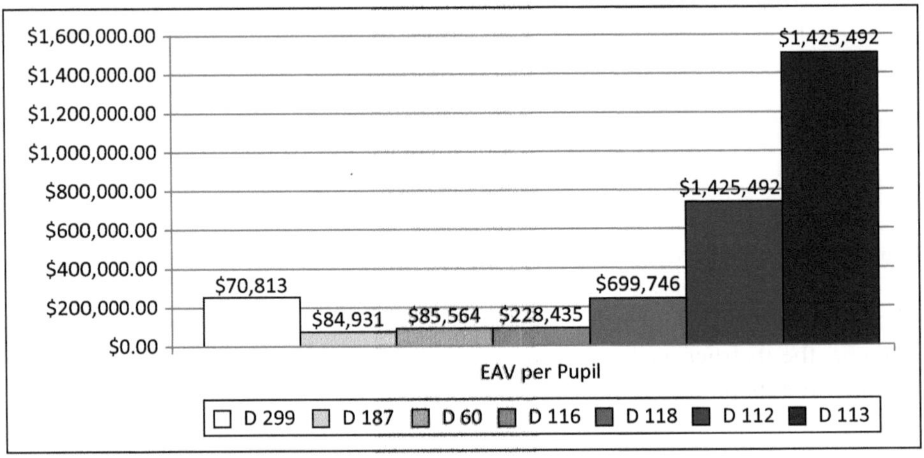

Figure 7.4. Equalized Assessed Valuation by District

Higher local expenditure translates into richer academic and extracurricular experiences and opportunities for students in these more affluent communities. Wealthier districts can regularly update physical facilities, instructional materials, and technological equipment; attract highly qualified teachers with higher pay and benefits; and provide a wider range of extracurricular programming. Since immigrant students tend to live in less affluent districts, they attend schools which are less able to address their educational needs. Lack of affordable housing and discriminatory real estate practices limit housing options for blacks, Latinos, and the economically disadvantaged, steering them towards less affluent communities and less affluent neighborhoods where educational spending is lower. This strain on resources intensifies when the immigrant population increases rapidly, as is happening in new destinations. Immigrants put an added strain on school budgets, as the growing immigrant population requires bilingual teachers, bilingual instructional materials, and often more classroom space to accommodate a larger and more diverse student population. More affluent districts often have the financial resources to accommodate immigrant students but, given current segregation patterns and the inflated cost of housing, the numbers of students they service is rather low when compared to less affluent districts.

School Segregation

Disparities are often replicated within districts, with some schools having more funding, better facilities, and more highly qualified teachers than others. Large school districts are notorious for school inequity that is reflective of racially and class-based residential segregation patterns in the district. Racial segregation has a long history in the U.S., where the *Plessy v. Ferguson*[36] ruling allowed racial segregation in public facilities, including public schools, under the precept of "separate but equal." As a result, black and Mexican students attended separate schools. In 1946, Mexican parents sued several California school districts for discriminating against Mexican students (who were legally defined as white) by forcing them to attend separate Mexican schools. Since Mexicans were legally defined as white, the plaintiffs claimed that Mexican students were being discriminated against based on ethnicity and language deficiency. *Mendez, et al. v. Westminster School District, et al.*[37] ruled that the segregation of Mexican students violated their constitutional right under the Equal Protection Clause. In 1954, *Brown v. Board of Education of Topeka*[38] ruled that separate educational facilities are inherently unequal, and, therefore, school segregation by race violates the Equal Protection Clause of the Fourteenth Amendment and is unconstitutional.

Despite a mandate to desegregate schools, many schools continue to be segregated. In the CMA, 22% of Latino students attend highly segregated public schools (Lutton & Vevea, 2012). Although suburban schools are becoming more diverse, 10% of Latino students attend racially isolated schools. Chicago, one of the most segregated cities in the nation, also has one of the most segregated school districts. In 1980, federal courts mandated CPS to desegregate and provide adequate educational services to ELL students (*U.S. v. Board of Education of the City of Chicago*, 80C5124 [N.C. Ill.]). Thirty years later, Chicago schools are still highly segregated, and ELL students continue to receive inadequate services. Although CPS was mandated to develop a plan to reduce segregation, it has failed to make progress; data shows that blacks and Latino students attend highly segregated schools (Lutton & Vevea, 2012). Half of black students attend extremely segregated schools (90% black). The number of racially isolated Latino schools has almost tripled, and 39% of Latino students in Chicago attend extremely racially isolated schools. In 2009, it was found that CPS continued to neglect ELL students, who languish in programs with inadequate facilities and instructional materials, are routinely denied or delayed special education services, have unqualified bilingual teachers, or simply are not provided with any ELL services.

Tracking

In addition to inequalities created by financial resources and racial segregation, students are provided with different educational experiences and opportunities through academic tracking.

The U.S. has a long history of sorting students into three programs of study: college preparatory, general or basic education, and vocational. Students in the college preparatory track take four years of the core courses (math, science, language arts, and social studies) and a foreign language. Basic education students are required three years of the core courses and one year of foreign language requirement. Vocational programs teach students a trade but, due to NCLB, standards require students to fulfill basic education requirements. Tracking may start in elementary school in the form of differentiation (accelerated math or language arts), but is more prevalent in high school.

Because suburban school districts tend to be small, tracking tends to happen within schools where minority students are overrepresented in the lower tracks. Many studies show that in integrated high schools, black and Latino students are concentrated in basic education and vocational tracks, while white students dominate the college preparatory track. In large school districts, tracking often occurs across schools. In CPS, there are nine different types of high schools from which students can choose. Masked in a rhetoric of "choices," many of these high schools are out of reach to most students. Attendance boundaries, lack of transportation, admission criteria, and lottery result in unequal access to schools of choice, and certainly to the highest-ranking schools in the district. In addition, the high volume of applications and the low number of slots stack the odds against gaining admission. For ELL students, the odds are particularly stacked against them because their language skills prevent them from performing competitively in entrance exams. For most black and Latino students, independent or privately operated contract and charter schools are often the only alternative to the neighborhood school.

Currently, CPS leads the nation in the number of charter schools it sponsors, and their numbers are increasing yearly. Charter schools are schools operated by non-profit as well as for-profit entities that are not subject to the state and district regulations, as other public schools are, but remain accountable for student achievement. Their popularity increased after the enactment of the NCLB in 2002. Parents seeking better schooling options for their children turn to charter schools. Yet, charter schools do not necessarily present a better option than the neighborhood school. A comprehensive study of charter schools found that only 17% of charter schools outperform public schools, while 37% fare far worse than public schools (Center for Research on Education Outcomes, 2009).

There is also variation on student achievement with ELL students in charter schools, showing gains in math and reading scores over similar students in public schools. Another concern deals with teacher quality: charter schools have more non-state-certified teachers, less-experienced teachers, and high teacher turnover (Stiut & Smith, 2010).

District and School Administration

Another factor affecting the education of immigrant students is the racial/ethnic composition of the school board. Research shows that Latino representation in school boards is directly connected to Latino representation in administration and teaching positions, as well as funding for bilingual programs, but indirectly related to student performance (Leal & Hess, 2011; Meier, Gonzalez Juenke, Leal, & Martinez-Ebers, 2011). District school board members are typically elected by popular vote or appointed by the mayor. In the suburban districts we studied, school board members were elected. Only Chicago has a school board appointed by the mayor. Because only U.S. citizens can vote, immigrants are greatly disadvantaged as they lack the political power to tip elections or influence mayors. Although immigrants tend to fare better when elections are ward-based rather than district-wide, they remain grossly misrepresented in school boards.

This pattern of underrepresentation of Latinos in district school boards was replicated in the districts we studied. Of the seven school districts, only three—D 299, D 187, and D 60—had Latino representation, and that was limited to only one Latino board member. Even in districts with large Latino student populations, it is rare to find Latino principals and/or assistant principals. Only D 299, D 60, D 166, and D 187 have at least one Latino principal. Despite the large proportion of Latino students in these districts, Latinos accounted only for 12–18% of principals.

Teachers

Current educational policies have deeply affected teacher demographics, teacher quality, and teachers' ability to address the needs of immigrant students. Most consequential for Latino students is the lack of Latino teachers. Research shows that students who are taught by teachers of their same social group will perform better academically. Yet, in the U.S., teachers are disproportionately white, even in predominantly non-white districts like some of the districts in our study. In fact, in none of the districts we studied is the proportion of Latino teacher to student equitable (see Figure 7.5).

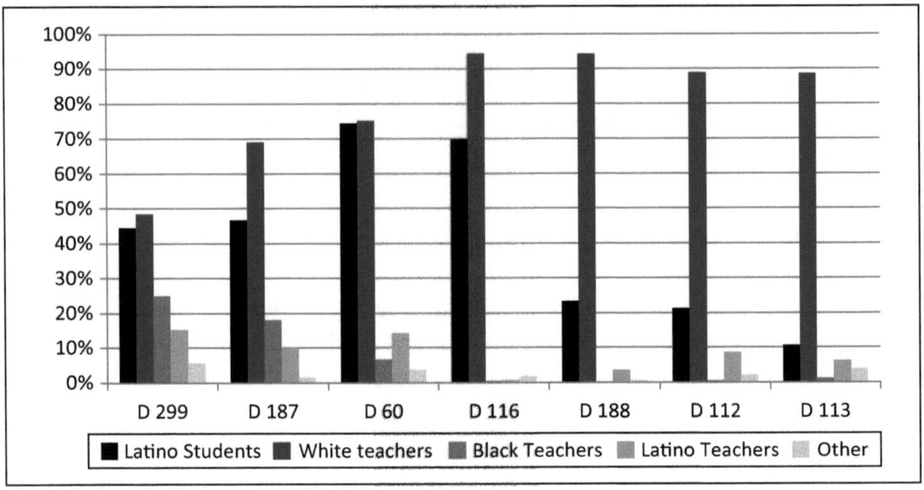

Figure 7.5. Teacher Race by District

With the exception of CPS, white teachers made up more than 70% of the teaching staff in the districts we studied. Most extreme is D 116, which has a student population that is 70% Latino, yet 94% of its teachers are white and only 0.8% are Latino. By contrast, the most equitable district is also the one with the lowest Latino population: D 113's Latino student population is 10% and Latinos constitute 6% of the teaching staff.

Racial disparity between teachers and students makes it difficult for teachers to meet students' needs. In the districts we studied, white teachers find themselves in a school where the student population has drastically changed. They have difficulty communicating with Spanish-speaking students and parents and must rely on bilingual school personnel for translations, which impedes spontaneous and/or natural conversations. Furthermore, their middle-class and racial background make white teachers unaware of the issues that affect immigrant students and their families.

Even the most well-intentioned teachers are seldom prepared to meet the pedagogical challenges of teaching immigrant students. Many teachers, bilingual certified or not, are unwilling or unable to engage in alternative teaching methods that could help their immigrant students. Some are reluctant to change their teaching methods to accommodate the needs of immigrant students. Others may be willing but not allowed to deviate from the curriculum, or required to "teach to the test," particularly in schools that are on academic probation. But most are simply not trained to meet the pedagogical challenges of teaching immigrant students.

Also consequential for immigrant students is the lack of certification and lack of training received by teachers working with immigrant students. Although the student population is changing across the country, colleges of education are not diversifying their training to reflect these demographic changes. Thus, many teachers lack the certification and training needed to work with immigrant students. More alarming is the failure of colleges of education to prepare bilingual teachers, which has resulted in a shortage across the U.S., particularly in new destinations, leading to immigrant students being taught by less credentialed teachers. Table 7.2 shows that districts with the highest immigrant student populations (D 299, D 187, D 60, and D 116) also have lower proportion of teachers with M.A. degrees, more teachers with emergency or provisional credentials, and more classes being taught by less qualified teachers.

Table 7.2. Teacher Characteristics by District

	Avg. Teacher Experience	Avg. Teacher Salary	Teachers with B.A.	Teachers with M.A.	Teachers with Emergency/ Provisional Credentials	Classes not Taught by Highly-Qualified Teachers
D 299	11.9 years	$74,990	35.4%	63.5%	1.3%	4.3%
D 187	15.2 years	$65,240	48.2%	51.3%	2.7%	11.7%
D 60	11.0 years	$56,253	46.9%	53%	1.9%	6.3%
D 116	12.4 years	$65,900	37.6%	62.4%	1.9%	0.9%
D 118	11.8 years	$73,097	27.2%	72.8%	0	0
D 112	11.5 years	$70,566	24.8%	75.2%	0	0
D 113	14.1 years	$106,030	6.4%	93.6%	0.3%	0

Bilingual Programs

Although the state requires districts to offer TBE and TPI programs for qualifying students, districts can replace them with, or offer them in addition to, other programs. Bilingual programs other than TBE and TPI are uncommon because they are left to the discretion and funding of the district. Most districts are uninterested and/or financially unable to broaden their bilingual programs beyond what is required by state law. This is partly due to the lack of Latinos on school boards, who are more likely to value bilingual education and push to fund it. Emphasis on high-stakes testing as a measure of school/teacher performance steers schools away from heritage language instruction, as ELL students are not exempt from testing.

Among the districts we studied, there were differences in their approaches to bilingual education. Being a traditional immigrant gateway, CPS has been offering bilingual education programs since 1969, and provides direct instruction in fourteen languages and language support and services for students from 109 different language backgrounds. By contrast, bilingual programs in suburban districts are recent and serve an overwhelming majority of Spanish-speaking ELL students.

As mandated by state law, all districts offer TBE and TPI with the exception of D 113—a high school district where all ELL students have reached proficiency or are classified as English proficient and only require TPI services (see Table 7.3).

Table 7.3. Types of Bilingual Programs by District

District	Types of Bilingual Programs	LEP Population
60	TBE; TPI	28.7%
112	TBE; TPI; Dual Immersion	13.5%
113	TPI	1.7%
116	TBE; TPI	25.2%
118	TBE; TPI	10.9%
187	TBE; TPI; Dual Immersion	20.5%
299	TBE; TPI; Dual Immersion	16%

TBE and Dual Immersion are more prevalent at the elementary and middle school level, while TPI is more characteristic of high schools. By the time they reach high school, most ELL students are reclassified as English fluent, and recent arrivals are few at this level. Dual-immersion programs were more prevalent in districts that had sizeable populations of English monolingual students—such as D 187 and D 112—as such programs require having English speakers and Spanish speakers in the same classroom learning both languages.

The scarcity of bilingual teachers seriously jeopardizes the quality of bilingual instruction and services in many districts. More affluent and desirable districts can "pick and choose" and often succeed in attracting highly qualified bilingual teachers. Less affluent districts often struggle to attract and retain them. Vacancies can be filled with foreign teachers from Mexico or Spain through the Visiting International Teacher Program. Most of the districts had, at one time or another, recruited teachers through this program, but only D 187 had recently recruited teachers from Spain. Importing teachers that speak Spanish may provide a short-term solution. It may also solve the language requirement, but not the cultural, class, and racial differences between visiting teachers and their students.

Parental Involvement

Federal and state legislation mandates districts and schools to engage parents in local decision making. To meet NCLB mandates, the ISBE sets standards for parental involvement.[39] It requires local districts (called local educational agencies or LEAs) that receive federal and state funds to develop a parental involvement plan that delineates district and school efforts to engage parents in decision making. Districts must hold an annual meeting with parents and review their policies each year. Although some funds are allocated for district efforts to engage parents, there are no strict guidelines as to how districts can use these funds. As a result, districts have discretion over the use of these funds. Because the requirements are lax, districts can easily meet them without having any meaningful participation from parents beyond having them attend a yearly meeting.

Illinois Administrative Code 228 requires that school districts that offer TBE must have a Bilingual Parent Committee (BPAC) that serves as a parent advisory committee. BPACs are made up mostly of parents, with representation from bilingual teachers, counselors, and community leaders. BPACS are involved in planning, operating, and evaluating bilingual programs. BPACs are required to meet at least four times a year and conduct training and meetings in a language understandable by parent members.

The state does not require districts to involve parents formally beyond BPACs. At the school level, the traditional structure for parental participation is the parent-teacher groups (PTA or PTOs). In suburban schools, these groups recruit parent volunteers, fundraise, and organize school events. Because of language barriers and cultural barriers, many immigrant parents do not participate in these groups. Unlike these suburbs, Chicago Public Schools have a more formalized and meaningful way for parental participation through the local school councils (LSC). A product of the 1986 School Reform to decentralize the school system, LSCs play a role in decision making at the school level. They are charged with selecting, hiring, and evaluating the school's principal, setting up and monitoring the school improvement plan, and approving the school.[40] In addition to the principal, the LSC is composed of eleven elected members: six parents, two community members, two teachers, and a student representative. Regardless of legal status, anyone over the age of eighteen who lives within the school designated boundary or has a child attending the school can vote on LSC elections for that school. Although whites are overrepresented in the LSC, Latino parents' rate of participation is significant (Designs for Change, 2002). For immigrant parents whose legal status as non-citizens usually keeps them from formal involvement, LSC has opened the doors to parental participation in decision making.

In the U.S., parents are seen as critical in the successful schooling of children. Many studies show that parental involvement is one of the most important factors for student success and the reduction of the achievement gap (Lee & Bowen, 2006, p. 194). Because immigrant parents are less involved in schools than other groups, teachers and staff often assume them to be uncaring and to value schooling less.

Immigrant parents place great value on their children's education, but they face serious challenges that make it difficult for them to take an active role in schools. They have little understanding of the U.S. educational system and its expectations for parental involvement. To them, parental involvement means something different than the traditional U.S. standards, thus they do not measure up to expectations (Marschall, Shan, & Donato, 2012). Immigrant parents also lack English-language proficiency, making it hard for them to engage in schools where meetings and events are run in English. In addition, they often lack the political power to successfully demand inclusion in decision making that affects their children's education. Parental involvement among immigrant parents increases when schools include them as equal partners and make an effort to understand their culture, language, and everyday hardships (Ramirez, 2003; Moll et al., 1992; Gonzalez et al., 2005).

CONCLUSION

Despite constitutional guarantees for equal educational opportunities for all children, the U.S. educational system has consistently failed to live up to its promise to non-white, physically and intellectually disabled, lower-income, and limited English proficient students. In this chapter, we reviewed federal, state, and district policy on educating Latino immigrant students with a keen eye on how these policies create educational disparities that adversely and disproportionately affect these students. Among Latino immigrant students, the ELL population stands out for being shortchanged and denied equal access to educational opportunities.

Establishing the rights of immigrant students to equal educational opportunities without creating the conditions that are conducive to their success is a hollow promise. Although there are policies that mandate bilingual education, there is a broad range in the way policies are implemented, especially given constraints that districts confront—such as availability of qualified bilingual teachers, adequate teaching materials or adequate funding for programs, and faculty development. Moreover, since policies are written in broad strokes, districts that are not really willing to make the commitment to these students will undertake procedures for minimal implementation. Ultimately, it is the lack of Latino and immigrant representation at the policy-making level that leads to these educational disparities. Stronger advocacy from board members, administrators, and parents is needed to truly transform our approach to immigrant education in this nation.

NOTES

1. It is not uncommon for residents of rural Mexico to attend elementary school only, as middle schools and high schools are located in larger towns that require daily commuting or living away from home. Few families can afford to pay for transportation and/or housing expenses.

2. The state of Illinois's All Kids Program offers comprehensive health insurance—including doctor visits and hospitalizations, dental care, vision care, eyeglasses, and prescription drugs—to low-income children, eighteen and under, who are residents of the state of Illinois regardless of legal status.
3. See: http://iirc.niu.edu/District.aspx?source=About_Students&source2=Educational_Environment&districtID=15016299025&level=D
4. We selected school districts within Lake County for comparison with Chicago for a number of reasons. First, it includes Waukegan, often considered a satellite city of Chicago (and the state's ninth largest city), with a small but continuous presence of immigrants, and notorious in the region for exclusionary immigration-related policies. Second, it is among the "collar counties" with the numerically largest number of Latinos, and it has experienced large and fast Latino population growth in the past thirty years. Third, focusing on Lake County allows us to compare localities with diverse ethnic/racial and socioeconomic profiles: from high to moderate to low immigrant population growth, from predominantly white to predominantly black to predominantly Latino, and from working and middle class to some of the wealthiest communities in the state of Illinois. Fourth, the communities selected vary in their reactions towards immigrants from exclusionary to neutral to inclusive. Finally, school districts in Lake County are under the jurisdiction of a single Regional Office (Lake County Regional Office) of the Illinois State Board of Education. Along with Chicago, these communities provide a microcosm of the CMA.
5. Here, "unified" type of district means that the district provides K–12 education (elementary, middle and high school) while an "independent" type of district has either K–8 or 9–12 education (elementary and middle school or high school). Also, there are diverse terms for school districts such as School District (SD), Community Unit School District (CUSD), and High School District (HSD).
6. Data presented here is part of a larger project funded by the National Science Foundation, the Russell Sage Foundation, UIC's Chicago Area Study, UIC's Institute for Policy and Community Engagement, UIC's Institute for Race and Public Policy, UIC's Great Cities, and UIC's Office of Social Science Research.
7. See 457 U.S. 202.
8. See Pub.L. 89–10, 79 Stat. 27, 20 U.S.C. ch.70.
9. See Title VII of the Elementary and Secondary Education Act of 1968.
10. See 107–110.
11. The NCLB Act requires states to (1) test students grades 3–8 annually in reading and math, and at least once in science; (2) set "adequate yearly progress" (AYP) goals for individual schools; (3) produce state annual report cards; and (4) ensure that teachers are highly qualified and have the pertinent credentials and certifications.
12. Immigration Policy Center. 2011. The Dream Act. http://www.immigrationpolicy.org/just-facts/dream-act Retrieved February 20, 1012.
13. See S 3827 (111th Congress).
14. See http://www.dhs.gov/deferred-action-childhood-arrivals
15. For more details see: http://www.uscis.gov/portal/site/uscis/menuitem.eb1d4c2a3e5b9ac89243c6a7543f6d1a/?vgnextoid=f2ef2f19470f7310VgnVCM100000082ca60aRCRD&vgnextchannel=f2ef2f19470f7310VgnVCM100000082ca60aRCRD#guidelines
16. For more information see: http://www.uscis.gov/portal/site/uscis/menuitem.eb1d4c2a3e5b9ac89243c6a7543f6d1a/?vgnextoid=1b52d725f5501310VgnVCM100000082ca60aRCRD&vgnextchannel=1b52d725f5501310VgnVCM100000082ca60aRCRD
17. Also known as the Save Our State Initiative.
18. See http://www.azleg.gov/legtext/49leg/2r/bills/hb2281s.pdf

19. See http://media.al.com/bn/other/Alabama%20Immigration%20Law%202011.pdf
20. See Alabama HB 56 Section 8.
21. See http://www.isbe.state.il.us/bilingual/htmls/imfaqs.html
22. See Title 23 Illinois Administrative Code 228 at www.isbe.net/rules/archive/pdfs/228ark.pdf
23. In Illinois, TBE requires that instruction in the core subjects, including language arts, must be in the home language of the ELL students, English instruction must align with English as a Second Language (ESL) programs, and instruction of history and culture of the students' home countries must be provided.
24. In Illinois, TPI requires instruction of core subjects in ESL, instruction of language arts in the students' home language, and instruction of history and culture of the students' home countries must be provided.
25. See http://www.isbe.net/rules/archive/pdfs/228ARK.pdf
26. See http://www.ilga.gov/legislation/fulltext.asp?DocName=&SessionId=84&GA=97&DocTypeId=HB&DocNum=3819&GAID=11&LegID=&SpecSess=&Session=
27. See IBSE's Bilingual Teacher Recruitment and Certification Resource Link at http://www.isbe.net/bilingual/htmls/biteacert.htm (Retrieved February 20, 2012).
28. See IBSE Teacher Exchange Visitor Program at http://www.isbe.net/bilingual/htmls/spanish_exchange.htm (Retrieved February 20, 2012).
29. See National Conference for State Legislators at http://www.ncsl.org/issues-research/educ/undocumented-student-tuition-state-action.aspx (Retrieved February 20, 2012).
30. See http://www.ilga.gov/legislation/BillStatus.asp?DocNum=60&GAID=3&DocTypeID=HB&LegId=195&SessionID=3&GA=93
31. See full text of SB 2185 at http://www.ilga.gov/legislation/fulltext.asp?DocName=09700SB-2185sam001&GA=97&SessionId=84&DocTypeId=SB&LegID=58384&DocNum=2185&GAID=11&Session=
32. GED is the general equivalency diploma and equivalent to a high school diploma.
33. For more on ISBE see http://www.isbe.state.il.us/default.htm
34. For more on regional offices see http://isbe.net/regionaloffices/pdf/roedirectory.pdf
35. See U.S. Department of Education's website: http://www2.ed.gov/programs/racetothetop/index.html
36. See 163 U.S. 537.
37. See 64 F.Supp. 544 (C.D. Cal. 1946).
38. See *United States v. Board of Educ. of the City of Chicago*, No. 80-5124 (N.D. Ill.), Amici's Response to Plaintiffs' Motion to Enforce English Language Learner Provisions of Amended Appendix C, at 9–10, filed March 13, 2003 (Docket No. 1521) *wn v. Board of Education of Topeka*, 347 U.S. 483, 74 S. Ct. 686, 98 L. Ed. 873 (1954).
39. See http://www.isbe.state.il.us/grants/html/parent.htm
40. http://www.cps.edu/pages/Localschoolcouncils.aspx

REFERENCES

Baker, B. D., Sciarra, D. G., & Farrie, D. (2010, September). *Is school funding fair? A national report card*. Retrieved from http://www.schoolfundingfairness.org/National_Report_Card.pdf

Batalova, J., & McHugh, M. (2010). *States and districts with the highest number and share of English language learners*. Retrieved from http://www.migrationinformation.org/ellinfo/FactSheet_ELL2.pdf

Bennet, L., Koval, J., & Spirou, C. (2010). Latinos and neo-regionalism in metropolitan Chicago. *Latinos in Chicago: Reflections of an American landscape* [White paper] (pp. 15–66). Notre Dame, IN: Institute of Latino Studies, University of Notre Dame.

Center for Research on Education Outcomes at Stanford University. (2009, October). *Multiple choice: Charter school performance in 16 states.* Retrieved from http://www.education.com/reference/article/multiple-choice-charter-school/

Designs for Change. (2002, January). *Chicago's Local School Councils: What the research says.* Retrieved from http://www.designsforchange.org/pdfs/LSC_rpt_final.pdf

González, N., Moll, L. C., & Amanti, C. (2005). *Funds of knowledge: Theorizing practices in households, communities, and classrooms.* Mahway, NJ: Erlbaum.

Gwynne, J., Stitziel Pareja, A., Ehrlich, S.B., & Allensworth, E. (2012, May). *What matters for staying on-track and graduating in Chicago Public Schools: A focus on English language learners.* Retrieved from https://ccsr.uchicago.edu/sites/default/files/publications/ELL%20Report_0.pdf

Illinois Advisory Council on Bilingual Education. (2011, December). *Report to the State Superintendent of Education, Governor, and Illinois General Assembly in response to Public Act 97–305.* Retrieved from http://www.isbe.state.il.us/bilingual/pdfs/IACBE_pa097-0305_report120111.pdf

Institute for Latino Studies. (2008, May). *Data for CMAP Latino Snapshot.* Retrieved from http://www.cmap.illinois.gov/documents/20583/a313538c-4b54-4fb1-8b24-c7545af427c3

Latino Policy Forum. (2011, October). *Latinos in the decade: The 2010 Census and Illinois.* Retrieved from http://www.latinopolicyforum.org/resources/document/sol_october2011_census.pdf

Leal, D. L., & Hess, F. M. (2011). The politics of bilingual education expenditures in urban school districts. In D. L. Leal & K. J. Meier (Eds.), *The politics of Latino education* (pp. 163–171). New York: Teachers College Press.

Lee, J., & Bowen, N. K. (2006, Summer). Parent involvement, cultural capital, and the achievement gap among elementary school children. *American Educational Research Journal, 43*(2), 193–218.

Lutton, L., & Vevea, B. (2012, June). *Greater segregation for region's black, Latino students: But white suburban schools see big increase in diversity.* Retrieved from http://www.wbez.org/print/100452

Marschall, M. J., Shan, P. R., & Donato, K. (2012, January). Parental involvement policy in established and new immigrant destinations. *Social Science Quarterly, 93*(1), 131–151.

Meier, K., Gonzalez Juenke, E., Leal, D. L., & Martinez-Ebers, V. (2011). How electoral structure affects Latino school board representation: Comparing 1986 and 2001. In D. L. Leal & K. J. Meier (Eds.). *The politics of Latino education* (pp. 122–136). New York: Teachers College Press.

Moll, L. C., Amanti, C., Neff, D., & González, N. (1992, Spring). Funds of knowledge for teaching: A qualitative approach to connect households and classrooms. *Theory Into Practice, 31*(2), 132–141.

Motel, S., & Patten, E. (2012, September). *Characteristics of the 60 largest metropolitan areas by Hispanic population.* Retrieved from http://www.pewhispanic.org/2012/09/19/characteristics-of-the-60-largest-metropolitan-areas-by-hispanic-population/

Mulhall, P. (2008). *The funding of K-12 education in Illinois: A marginal grade using any test.* Retrieved from http://igpa.uillinois.edu/system/files/09-ILRept08-FundK12Pg61-69.pdf

Ramirez, F. A. Y. (2003, June). Dismay and disappointment: Parental involvement of Latino immigrant parents. *The Urban Review, 35*(2), 93–110.

Ready, T., & Brown-Gort, A. (2005). *State of Latino Chicago: This is home now.* Notre Dame, IN: University of Notre Dame Institute for Latino Studies.

Soltero, J., Soltero, S., & Robbins, J. (2010). Latinos and education in the Chicago metropolitan area. *Latinos in Chicago: Reflections of an American landscape* [White paper] (pp. 67–124). Notre Dame, IN: Institute of Latino Studies, University of Notre Dame.

Strauss, V. (2010, July). New analysis blasts Obama's school turnaround policy—and tells how to fix it. *Washington Post.* Retrieved from http://voices.washingtonpost.com/answer-sheet/education-secretary-duncan/analysis-blasts-obamas-school-turnaround-policy.html

Stuit, D., & Smith, T. M. (2010, June). *Teacher turnover in charter schools.* Retrieved from http://www.vanderbilt.edu/schoolchoice/documents/briefs/brief_stuit_smith_ncspe.pdf

Suro, R., & Singer, A. (2002). *Latino growth in metropolitan America: Changing patterns, new locations.* Retrieved from http://pewhispanic.org/files/reports/10.pdf

Wright, W. E. (2010, November). *The great divide between federal education policy and our national need for bilingual citizens* [blog post]. Retrieved from http://speakingintonguesfilm.info/guest-blogs/the-great-divide-between-federal-education-policy-and-our-national-need-for-bilingual-citizens/

CHAPTER EIGHT

Immigrant Minors' Integration and Social Cohesion Policies Through the School

JOSÉ MARÍA RODRÍGUEZ DE SANTIAGO,
AUTONOMOUS
UNIVERSITY OF MADRID

PREFACE

It cannot be said that immigration is a new phenomenon in Spain, but compared to what is happening in other European countries, it can be said that it is in an early stage of development. In the last ten years, a report issued by the Office of the National Ombudsman—Immigrant Schooling in Spain: Descriptive and Empirical Analysis (2003)—has become widely read. The number of students with immigrant backgrounds was around 100,000 (data refers to the 2000–2001 school year), which accounts for 1.84% of the total number of students (p. 410 of the cited report). The increase, always moderate until 1997, doubled from 1997 up to 2001 (p. 411), which took place as the national student population in elementary, middle, and high school (up to eleventh grade) had supposedly remained stable. The percentage of immigrant students with respect to the total number of students varied notably among autonomous regions or autonomous cities. Whereas in Ceuta and Melilla immigrant students made up 12.3% of the total number of students, in Madrid the percentage was 4.4%, and in Galicia only 0.4% of students were immigrants (p. 76).

The report was based upon some papers that had already dealt with this issue by that time, trying to make it easier to analyze trends in order to make predictions. From the start, it made an important terminological choice regarding the use of the terms "alien" and "immigrant" in the report. Where it said "students of foreign origins," it obviously meant students schooled in Spain whose families came from other countries. The use of the term "immigrant" offered some difficulties, since this is not a condition derived from nationality, and it cannot undoubtedly be inferred from the information contained in the school records. To the effects of the report, we are to consider students with immigrant backgrounds those who are foreign except for the ones coming from the European Union or North America. We should take into account only the ones coming from countries that are considered to be the origin of an economic immigration, whose families come to Spain intending to improve their living conditions (vol. I, p. 8).

Figures have obviously changed since the report was published. In the 2009–2010 school year, 9.6% of students in Spain were foreign students (not taking into account the terminology distinction just made), and in the region of Madrid the rate was almost 14%.

The Spanish Constitution of 1978, a modern constitution in the European context, addressed immigration in one of its provisions (Article 42 CE), though it referred only to Spanish labor immigration abroad. In the last thirty-five years, socioeconomic conditions have changed and there is currently no provision in the Constitution addressing immigrants in Spain. The reason for this is that immigration was not a reality that deserved any regulation in a constitutional text clearly shaped by its "dense social spirit." During the recent years of economic downturn, notably, the number of immigrants arriving in Spain has remarkably decreased, and there are, again, Spanish immigrants in foreign countries.

In this chapter, we will take a look at surrounding countries where the immigration phenomenon is not that recent. From France and Great Britain, for different reasons, voices were heard pointing out that the educational system had partly failed as an immigrant integration factor. In Germany, also in the last fifteen years, what is on the table is not really how to get a minority of non-German-speaking children to learn the language, but what the state should do when, in some schools, the language spoken by the majority of students during lunch breaks is not German. "Deutsch im Schulhof" ("German in the school playground") is the expression around which the debate is centered. The case that has reached the German Federal Constitutional Court is not whether girl students are allowed to go to class with the Islamic veil, but whether a young Muslim woman (who has become a teacher in Germany) is allowed to teach her classes in a public school wearing the veil. These are cases that show us that immigration and its attendant issues in Spain is not a new phenomenon, but that it is, comparatively speaking, at an early stage.

Getting to the point, it is appropriate to assert a few things at the beginning, without delving into controversial issues: a) School is the best context for immigrant minors' integration, as well as the best instrument for social cohesion in the future—if school fails in its integration capacity, it is very difficult for any path after school to be successful; b) The existence of schools where, for example, the student body has more than 50% immigrants is a social issue that affects us all—if there is no integration today, there will be no social cohesion tomorrow; and c) immigrant minors' integration presently constitutes one of the biggest challenges to the capacities of our Social State when it comes to education (despite the fact that what really draws the attention of the Spanish public opinion are other matters).

Once every single Spanish student is entitled to education, it can be said that education becomes a responsibility of the state as a provider more than of the state in its social dimension if they are, in fact, different from each other. However, immigrant minors' integration is a priority typically considered a social duty for a state that guarantees the right to education. This is a good example of how the implementation of state social duties is a process: when the most blatant inequality disappears, we are free to see situations of inequality that did not before call our attention.

The starting point for the exposition that follows is the distribution of powers among the different government levels in Spain to face the immigration phenomenon in school, which will identify the role corresponding to each of the levels to implement policies fostering immigrant minors' integration in schools.

Without getting into fine distinctions and subtleties, we can start off with state legislative powers (above all, Article 149[1][2] [immigration and alien regulation] and Article 149[1][30] CE [basic regulation for the development of the right to education]), which make the state the corresponding entity for the guarantee of immigrant fundamental rights in school. In this regard, what is left unregulated will be taken care of by the Supreme and the Constitutional Courts. Autonomous regions will be a decisive factor in immigrant integration policies, by virtue of their powers on education. A role of cooperation and support belongs to municipalities, to create, exercising their powers in urban planning, the physical and material conditions to fight social segregation in schools.

SCHOOL AND FUNDAMENTAL RIGHTS OF IMMIGRANTS: STATE LEGISLATION AND HIGH COURTS' RULINGS

All Immigrant Minors Have the Right to Education (Article 27[1] CE in Relation to Article 27[4] CE) in Equal Conditions as Spanish Nationals

The fundamental right to basic compulsory and free education (Article 27[1] CE in relation to Article 27[4] CE) is granted to immigrant minors in identical terms as to Spanish minors. This is stated by Article 9(1) of Organic Act 4/2000 of January 11 on the rights and freedoms of aliens in Spain and their social integration (Ley Orgánica sobre derechos y libertades de los extranjeros en España y su integración social, LODLEIS). It establishes that all immigrant minors have the right and the duty of education in equal conditions as Spanish nationals (without imposing any other additional requirement regarding their legal situation in Spain). This right includes access to a compulsory basic and free education, the attainment of the corresponding academic qualification, and access to the public scholarship and financial aid system. Other Spanish regulation of this subject includes Articles 28 and 29 of the Convention on the Rights of the Child (1989), covering the child's right to education and the actual teaching aims, and Article 13 of the International Pact on Economic, Social and Cultural Rights (1966), which, nonetheless, only provides for elementary and middle school education as compulsory and free (Article 28[1]a of the Convention and 13[2]a of the Pact). However, this last provision is overcome by the free and compulsory character of Spanish high school.

In practice, this means that any parent, relative, tutor, de facto guardian or public administration in charge of the minor's guardianship that requests his or her free schooling in a compulsory educational level has the right to that schooling for the corresponding minor, regardless of the legal situation of the applicant. However, the minor may be affected in the future by that situation, since he or she might have to leave the country along with his or her legal guardian, in the event that the guardian is deported. Registering in the municipal census, in order to exercise the right to education by the minor, should not be made dependent on the legality of the parents' situation in Spain. This also means that schooling is de facto mandatory for every minor living in Spain who is compulsory schooling age. What has been said does not affect the legal situation of minors whose stay in Spain cannot be accounted for, which is addressed by specific regulations (among others, Article 35 LODLEIS: inquiring on his or her condition of minor, permanence in Spain or return to the country of origin).

OTHER RIGHTS WITHIN THE DUTIES OF THE STATE AS A PROVIDER AND FUNDAMENTAL RIGHTS IN THE SCHOOL CONTEXT

Both the Spanish and foreign doctrines have paid careful attention to other rights within the duties of the state as a provider (teaching religion in schools, for instance) and other issues, some controversial, regarding fundamental rights of immigrant minors. These issues naturally arise in school: religious symbols in class (crucifix and Islamic veil), class attendance by Muslim female students, compulsory girl schooling, etc. Generally speaking, it is reasonable to assert that these matters, when not regulated, will probably end up being resolved by the Supreme Court or the Constitutional Court's case law. They will directly assess constitutional principles when resolving these conflicts that the legislature has left unresolved.

AIMS OF EDUCATION (ARTICLE 27[2] CE) AND THE TWO CONCEPTS "SCHOOL AND IMMIGRATION"

In the context of the integration of immigrant minors is where we can locate the already existing debate on the "multicultural education" in an "open society." This chapter is not the place to precisely define these concepts, but we can clearly establish what should not be accepted as "multicultural education." On the one hand, it is not the simple model of uniform assimilation (as opposed to true integration) to the mainstream culture, which sacrifices the cultural identity of the minor. Nor, on the other hand, is it the ethical and cultural extreme relativism, which might challenge the effectiveness of our system's rights and constitutional principles. Instead, "Multicultural education is not built on ethical indifference, but on the assertion of universal principles that grant rights to all men and all cultures, also imposing responsibilities that make respect and mutual collaboration possible" (Siguan, 1998, p. 145).

This value system is put in place as it is brought into the educational system by Article 27(2) CE: full personal development respecting democratic principles of co-existence and fundamental rights and freedoms. The Constitutional Court has stated, with regard to ideological freedom and political pluralism, that in our constitutional legal system a "militant democracy" model does not belong. The reason for this is that there is not a heart of constitutional provisions inaccessible to reform that limit the room for political opinion (being, obviously, respectful of the Constitution). What applies to the ideological freedom and political opinions of those who are already educated does not apply to school. The school value system is necessarily defined by the Constitution, and in that framework, "multicultural education" should be carried out.

There is no doubt that day-to-day coexistence among students with different cultural backgrounds may contribute much more to students' education—as they learn to respect and positively consider other people's cultures—than hours of lectures. The dualism "school and immigration" signifies one of the most important challenges for schools to accomplish their goals and for an adequate integration of immigrants. Such ambitious goals are definitely not achieved without the appropriate policies.

SCHOOL AND IMMIGRANTS' INTEGRATION: THE REGIONAL ADMINISTRATION AS A DECISIVE FACTOR

When it comes to educational policies, municipalities play a secondary role. The narrow range of powers the local administration has when it comes to education (additional provision 15 of the Education Organic Act, Ley Orgánica de

Educación, LOE) prevents these entities from having a relevant role in the specifics of educational policy regarding immigrant minors' integration with the aim of social cohesion.

The administration that really plays a prominent role with regard to education is the regional administration. Legislating on education is in its hands, and it has the instruments to enforce this integration policy in various ways: defining school districts (Article 86 LOE), establishing the importance of admission criteria in public and state-funded private schools (Article 84[2] LOE), setting reserve quotas for immigrant students (Article 87[1]), and developing compensatory actions (Articles 80, 81 and 83 LOE). On this last method, for instance, in the Region of Madrid there are back-up classes for students in need of learning Spanish, support for the immigrant student population, and translation services to facilitate the relationship between schools and non-Spanish-speaking parents. Other compensatory actions are: translating official documents and providing scholarships for textbooks, school supplies, the school dining hall services, school transportation, etc.

An important charge is put, nevertheless, in the hands of the local administration: contributing to create an appropriate social and urban infrastructure to help the regional governments efficiently enact social integration policies. Success in social integration and the ultimate social cohesion ambitions depend, in the long term, on a fine coordination between the regional administration and the local administration use of its urban planning and housing powers.

DEFINING SCHOOL DISTRICTS (ARTICLE 86 LOE) AND THE IMPORTANCE OF THE DOMICILE AS A CRITERION FOR ADMISSION IN SCHOOLS (ARTICLE 84[2] LOE)

In conformity with Article 86(1) LOE, equality in the enforcement of school admission rules includes "the establishment of the same influence areas for public and state-funded private schools in the same municipality." The school map of each municipality is drawn to ensure admission equality, both for public and state-funded private schools, since it is through both kinds of schools that the administration ensures minors' right to free education.

In addition to this, Article 84(2) LOE establishes the criteria that must be weighed by the autonomous region when deciding on admissions for each educational facility in which there is an overwhelming demand. Some criteria include: siblings attending the school, proximity of the family domicile or the parents' workplace, income level, family size, or physical disability.

The usual practice for all autonomous regions has been, up to this point, to consider the family domicile or the workplace proximity as decisive criteria. In the

Region of Madrid, it is only now, in compliance with the single-school district project discussed later, that the system has begun to be progressively modified. From 2005 to 2012, there was a system in which claiming a family home within the school district was awarded 4 points, whereas the same amount of points were given to an applicant who had a sibling attending that school. On the other hand, an annual income per capita below the minimum wage only got 2 points, and a physical disability granted 1.5.

Brief reflection is enough to realize that the demarcation of the school district service area and the weight given to the domicile criterion are two sides of the same coin. The school district makes sense as servicing a specific area as long as the domicile standard is given more relevance in the context of the other applicable criteria as regards a student's admission in a school.

The school map approach, meaning the mapping of public and state-funded private schools in territorial influence areas, can only work if true importance is given to the domicile (or the workplace) criterion regarding a student´s admission. In addition to this, the school map is also designed according to the following rule: those students that have attended a given elementary school hold a right to be admitted to a middle school to which his or her elementary school center is connected, being both located in the same school district (Articles 84[5] and 84[7] LOE). It should be clear that not giving enough weight to the domicile proximity standard, and erasing connections between centers, blurs the borders of school mapping; conversely, disregarding school mapping can be accomplished by making the domicile standard irrelevant and eliminating the mentioned connections.

In practice, where domicile proximity is important enough for student admission, school districts are the domain within which parents are actually more likely to send their children to the public or state-funded private school they wish (Article 84[1] LOE).

Accurate school mapping is, therefore, an essential means to avoid segregation in schools in areas where urban and social segregation is rampant, as a consequence of immigrant concentration in certain neighborhoods. There is no doubt that an excessive weight given to the domicile criterion results in homogenous schools that reflect the social status of the neighborhood. In an extreme situation, children that live in segregated areas will also attend segregated schools, and children that live in wealthy residential areas will go to schools in those areas. This is the complete opposite of what we mean when we talk about integration through the school and the complete opposite to what we are trying to accomplish regarding social cohesion in schools.

It has also been said that total decoupling between domicile and school does not solve the segregation issue, due to the clear trend of immigrant parents choosing the closest center to the family home, which should not be surprising if no aid were given to transportation or school dining hall services, and the full cost had to be borne by low-income families.

It is evident that in the drawing of school district borders, it is key to avoid wide overlappings between these areas and neighborhoods where there is a high concentration of immigrants, since the coincidence will have an effect on centers with an uneven presence of foreign students, making it difficult for integration and the long-term goal of social cohesion. This criterion should necessarily be present in the regional rules that regulate the drawing of school influence areas.

SETTING IMMIGRANT STUDENTS QUOTAS (ARTICLE 87 LOE)

According to the aforementioned Ombudsman's report, in the year 2003, the distribution of native students in public and state-funded private schools was as follows: 66.01% schooled in public centers, 33.99% in state-funded private ones (p. 57). When it comes to immigrant students, this distribution is varied: 82.01% schooled in public centers, 17.99% in state-funded private ones (p. 70).

In the Autonomous Region of Madrid, in the school year 2010–2011, 59.85% of the entire student body of Madrid attended a public school and 27.98% attended a state-funded private one. While the percentage of foreign students in public schools was 19.06%, that same group represented 8.5% in state-funded private schools (let us recall that the percentage of foreign students in the Region of Madrid's educational system for that year was 14.04%). If we consider that the percentage of foreign students schooled in the center chosen by their parents (or guardians) as the first option laid at about 90% in this Region (89% in the school year 2011–2012, 91% in 2012–2013), it is conceivable that the percentage discrepancy in immigrant students schooled in public and state-funded private centers is largely due to the parents' choice.

Nonetheless, avoiding the excessive concentration of foreign students in certain schools in order to foster a harmonious integration of minorities and to ensure, hence, the future cohesion of the Spanish society is, without any doubt, a public interest that can be weighed by the state and the Autonomous Community against the parents' right to choose the center where they want to school their children.

In order to guarantee an equitable distribution of immigrant students among public and state-funded private schools, Article 87(1) LOE allows for the so-called "quota system": "with the objective of ensuring high educational standards for all, social cohesion and equality of opportunities, the Authorities (…) will set the proportion of students of such characteristics who shall be schooled in each of the public and state-funded private centers and will guarantee the necessary personal and financial resources for the centers in order to offer such support."

In the Autonomous Region of Madrid, for instance, a distinction can be drawn between a general regulation of the equitable distribution of immigrant students among public and state-funded private schools and special measures in cases of high concentration of minors with immigrant backgrounds in certain schools.

The aforementioned equitable distribution general regulation provides that in each kindergarten (second cycle) and elementary school class, with a total of 25 students, 3 of these places are reserved for students with special learning needs, which means 12% of the reserved quota. In each compulsory high school class, with 25 to 30 students, 4 spots are reserved for students with special needs. This represents percentages that range from 12% to 16% of reserved spots, depending on the case. If, again, we take into account that the percentage of students with immigrant backgrounds in this autonomous region is at about 14%, it can be stated that the reserved quota is appropriate for the system as a whole. The problem arises, as is easily understood, because the immigrant population does not spontaneously allocate in an equitable fashion in the reserved places of mandatory offer of the public and state-funded private centers.

In the regular student admission process, every public or state-funded private center has to submit to the Schooling Commission a copy of those applications of students who could belong to some of the groups considered of special learning needs. If the Schooling Commission considers that it is, in effect, a minor belonging to one of these groups, the schooling in the center requested as first option by the parents or guardians is granted within the reserved quota already mentioned and without its submission to the assessment generally applicable.

The concentration of the immigrant population in specific areas of the city or the territory implies that the lack of uniformity in the distribution is usually reflected in the structure of the school population. While in centers of certain areas of the city or the territory the reserved places will not be fully occupied, in other areas there will be a high concentration of immigrant minors. For those cases, which can actually be considered the most frequent, the previously-mentioned special measures in instances of high concentration of minors with immigrant backgrounds are appropriate.

In cases of immigrant students' "high concentration" and "blatant imbalance" in percentages among the different centers, the education Administration may decide to send ("considering the choice expressed by the family") some of them to the centers that school the lesser percentage of immigrant students (even exceeding the maximum number of students in their school units). It can decide, on the other hand, a reduction of the total number of students per class (up to 20%) in the centers in which the concentration is higher (and where each school unit would require, hence, a bigger effort by the teaching staff).

The regulation consisting in the establishment of a maximum percentage of immigrant students per classroom or center, above which these students would be referred to other schools, so that such percentage could never be exceeded (as has already been enacted by Catalan Act 12/2009, of July 10, on education [Article 48]) is extraordinary.

Obviously, in weighing the public interest in fostering the integration of these minors into Spanish society, and the future social cohesion, against the parents' right to choose a school, a measure of this kind clearly (although not unconditionally) favors the former of the mentioned principles or interests in conflict. Taking into account the actual data, it is also clear that the maximum quota necessarily implies the use of the minimum reserve quota and an effective equitable distribution. Once the maximum quota, in order to guarantee the adequate integration, is exceeded, the reserved places available in other schools begin to be occupied. Since this measure affects the rights enshrined in Article 27 CE, the prevalence of one principle over the other must be decided by the legislator, according (at least) to the legal reservation on the subject of fundamental rights provided for in Article 53(1) CE. As it will be said later, measures of this kind, which force students—usually belonging to the most disadvantaged social and economic classes—to transport to schools far from their homes, should only be adopted together with financial and public aid policies for school transportation.

When it comes to assessing the parents' or guardians' freedom of choice of school (Article 84[1] LOE) and their identification with the educational project of the school (Articles 27[3] CE and 84[9] LOE), attention should be drawn to the fact that solutions to this problem have a different starting point in Spain and in other European countries (like France or Germany), which connotes the pluralism of immigration in Spain.

For instance, in the school year 2009–2010 in the Region of Madrid, of the total number of foreign students (not necessarily immigrants, as explained earlier), 21.5% were Ecuadorian (Spanish-speaking and of Catholic tradition), 13% Romanian (of European culture), 11.2% Moroccan (with a language and cultural tradition, in principle, further from the Spanish tradition), and 4% were Chinese (which conceivably require a bigger integration effort), etc. Overall, 53.1% of foreign students came from Central and South America. To the effects here considered, it could be argued that South American parents would probably choose to send their children to state-funded private schools with a Catholic program at least to the same extent as Spanish ones, if not more. It can also be assumed that Muslim parents would most surely have different preferences.

THE "MADRID: SINGLE SCHOOL DISTRICT" PROJECT FROM THE PERSPECTIVE OF IMMIGRANT MINORS' INTEGRATION AND SOCIAL COHESION

For the school year 2013–2014 there is a project to make the Region of Madrid into a single school district without any consideration of the proximity or the school to the parents' workplace or domicile. It has been said that reducing the importance of the proximity criterion and removing the connections between schools means blurring the limits of school mapping; and, conversely, eliminating school mapping is attained by making irrelevant the domicile criterion and effacing such connections.

At the time of drafting this work, the project is in a provisional state, envisaged for this year 2012–2013 and implemented by the educational Administration on the basis of the previously-mentioned two instruments: delimitation of the areas of influence and a lightening of the parents' domicile (or workplace) proximity criterion.

Actually, the influence area coincides with the municipality's boundaries in 164 of the 179 municipalities in the Region of Madrid. Only in the other fifteen (the most relevant ones, including, of course, Madrid) are there still different schooling zones, although considerably less (and, hence, encompassing a larger area) than in the school year 2012–2013. Furthermore, in order to obtain points according to the new assessment criteria, any domicile outside the zone of influence of the requested school is considered in a bordering zone regardless of its actual location in the Region of Madrid.

When it comes to the assessment criteria, from 2005 to 2012, 4 points were given for the domicile located within the area, 2 in a bordering area and 0 in other areas, 4 could be obtained for the first sibling already enrolled, and another 3 for each additional sibling, etc. In the 2012–2013 school year, 8 points have been given for one or more siblings enrolled, 4 for the domicile within the area, and 2 for the domicile in any other location in the Region of Madrid (as explained earlier), etc. A detailed analysis of the remaining criteria is not relevant here.

Decoupling domicile and school should be a welcome measure (albeit not enough) from the standpoint of a better integration of immigrant minorities, considering the goal of preventing school segregation (high concentration of such students in certain schools) and that of averting the replication of urban ghettos in school.

Guaranteeing equality of opportunity to these immigrant minorities, usually in a disadvantaged economic situation, is a necessary complement to the previously-mentioned measures. From that point of view, the promotion of formal freedom of all to move within the school map must be accompanied by measures to support real freedom to do so, especially for those with less economic resources. We are obviously referring to complementary school services such as school transportation and school dining hall. Freedom to move is one of those rights based on the possibility (also economic) to do it. Those with the means to bear transportation or catering costs can already send their children to schools far from the domicile (since assessing criteria will not prevent it); those who cannot bear such costs should be also enabled to make a real choice. Otherwise, little or nothing will be achieved from the sole perspective here assumed: preventing school segregation.

The "Madrid: single school district" project cannot be confined to the formal definition of school districts and the establishment of assessment criteria on the applications. It must be accompanied by a new, free school transportation framework in more generous terms, because until now there was little or no movement. This is not surprising: freedom to choose is always more expensive than the contrary. A new regulation of school mobility demands a new organization of school transportation.

Hence, it does not make sense anymore to consider the children from rural areas, without a public school according to their level, the only beneficiaries of free school transportation (Article 82[2] LOE). The rule providing that school transportation is only offered "for the regular transport of students to or from a public education facility within the same Department" would not guarantee a real freedom to choose. Nor would the provision that "students voluntarily enrolled in a school other than the one corresponding to their usual residence are not entitled to school transportation."

If rules on the choice of school give priority to mobility over domicile, the general organization of school transportation should be rethought as well. To this end, the hitherto few individualized aids for school transportation, directly paid to families, may be resized. In this regard, the not very generous amount of 272,000 € was foreseen for the school year 2012–2013 in the budget of the Autonomous Region of Madrid. For instance, in the school year 2010–2011, there were 301,084 beneficiaries of scholarships for books and educational materials (30.83% of the Region of Madrid's budget devoted to scholarships and aids), 112,000 recipients of dining hall financial aid (33.71% of that budget) but only 1,114 beneficiaries of individualized aids for school transportation (representing 0.36% of the Region of Madrid's budget devoted to scholarships and aids).

Municipalities have a very modest role in educational Administration strictly considered, but they may offer essential cooperation in order to organize and provide support services such as school transportation and dining hall under the general clause contained in Article 28 of the Act providing the basis for local regulation (Ley de Bases de Régimen Local, LBRL). Municipalities are thus entitled to carry out "complementary activities to the ones of the other public Administrations and, in particular, those regarding education."

RECAPITULATION

Two types of public education strategies can be used to address the issue of school "ghettoization" or high concentration of immigrants in certain schools: 1) acting on the special need for material and personal resources devoted to these schools rather than on the concentration (a policy that could be called "compensatory actions," using the wording of Article 80 LOE); 2) acting directly on the concentration by preventing it (policies of "distribution" of immigrant minors among public and state-funded private schools).

From the standpoint here assumed, it seems clear that direct aids to a school with about 65% immigrant students could improve the education quality of such students, but it would not directly foster integration or future social cohesion. If we do not want to end up asking the question "who has to be integrated where?" ideally the percentage represented by minorities in society (14% of foreign students in the Region of Madrid) should be mirrored in every public and state-funded private schools, with acceptable variations (since the ideal solution cannot be to totally disregard the right to choose of the immigrant students' parents).

A good integration policy implies an adequate "distribution" policy, so that social minorities are also school minorities. Integration achieved at school is a condition for future social cohesion. Hence, in order to integrate, a better distribution is needed; and to this end—as has been said—an adequate joint use of the means provided for by state and regional legislation seems essential. In the first place, school districts should not overlap with the areas of social marginalization; secondly, rules regulating admission must not rigidly link the school and domicile in the school map; and, finally, the effective use of the reserve quota for students with specific learning needs should be promoted.

As it has been explained, a higher mobility within the school map can be positive from the point of view here assumed, but it might not be enough. Higher mobility must be accompanied by an information strategy for immigrant families, who are usually not aware of the scope of their rights in Spain regarding free public and state-funded private education. An adequate organization of school transportation and school dining hall financial aid is also necessary.

The Region of Madrid represents an extreme case of small municipalities with rates of foreign students between 31 and 65% of the school population, as can be seen at: Rascafría (with a majority of Romanian students), Colmenar de Arroyo (with a majority of Moroccan students), or Navas del Rey (also with a Moroccan majority). Such a high concentration of immigrant students—which undoubtedly mirrors, to a certain extent, the percentages of the immigrant population in those areas—calls for extraordinary measures in order to address the demands of an adequate integration and future social cohesion. These could include the implementation of busing between neighboring municipalities, and require the involvement of local authorities, since the interest of the whole community is obviously at stake.

SCHOOL, IMMIGRANTS' INTEGRATION AND MUNICIPALITIES: MUNICIPAL COOPERATION IN ORDER TO CREATE THE PHYSICAL AND MATERIAL CONDITIONS TO PREVENT SEGREGATION

On the part of municipalities, the task with the broadest scope regarding public policies of integration through the schooling of minors with immigrant backgrounds is the creation of physical and material conditions to prevent segregation. To this end, an adequate exercise of their powers in the field of urban planning is essential. There are mainly two types of decisions connected to municipal urban planning on the subject here considered: a) those concerning the regulation of building strategies that foster a balance between different social groups and prevent a social segregation that could be mirrored at school; and b) those concerning an adequate justification (from the point of view of the fight against segregation) of the location of areas devoted to school use.

Combating urban segregation in order to guarantee future social cohesion is one of the principles or interests specifically identified by the legislature when it comes to the weighing assessment in which consists the decision on urban planning (STC 51/2004, of April 13, legal basis 10). Accordingly, the planning authority must take this into consideration in its priorities assessment. Indeed, pursuant to Article 2(1) and (2) State Recast Text of the Land Act of 2008 (Texto Refundido estatal de la Ley del Suelo de 2008), the administrative authority shall take into account the "requirements of (...) social cohesion" in its decisions on urban planning.

The standards set by legislation on urban planning with regard to the percentages of land reserved for publicly sponsored housing (where concentration of population with low income and, among them, immigrants is likely) are as important as the specific and adequate location of those areas on the city map in order to prevent a segregating concentration. Article 10(b) of the cited Land Act points in that direction, as it mandates a distribution of such housing "in compliance with the social cohesion principle."

Something similar could be said about the specific decision on the location of areas devoted to school use in the urban plan. It is imperative to take into account the fact that the school location in the urban fabric is essential to prevent school segregation and to foster integration and social cohesion. A poorly chosen area devoted to school use is a defective decision in urban planning, affected by the shortcomings in its assessment.

The decisions of the educational Administration on these physical conditions regarding urban planning (location of publicly sponsored housing and the areas devoted to school use) also have an impact on the territory. Firstly, on the definition of school districts; secondly, by attaching legal implications to spatial connection points (such as the proximity of school and domicile) with regard to the distribution of school population. It is not necessary to insist on the importance of coordination between these municipal and regional decisions in the global public strategy against segregation.

The concentration of housing for economically weaker populations in an extreme geographical area of a new development sector could, likewise, imply a decision on urban planning affected by a defect in the assessment of interests regarding future social cohesion. To this end may be added a damaging lack of coordination, through the decisions of the educational Administration, if free housing areas are defined as a school district and those of publicly sponsored housing are defined differently. Furthermore, if the municipality establishes two areas devoted to school use, one in the center of the rich zone and one in the center of the poor zone, we have the extreme example of an urban planning policy that does not recognize integration and social cohesion.

The ideal response to the referred interests is easily envisaged: public sponsored housing spread over different areas, school districts covering part of the space occupied by "cheap housing" and part of the space occupied by "expensive housing"; and areas devoted to school use half way between the population of one group and the other.

CONCLUSIONS

The most important element in the policies for integrating immigrant populations in the schools, for the future social cohesion, is the right to education, acted by state legislation through the Regional Administration's powers. There are different techniques: particularly, defining school districts (Article 86 LOE), establishing the importance of admission criteria in public and state-funded private schools (Article 84(2) LOE), setting reserve quotas for immigrant students (Article 87(1) LOE) and developing compensatory actions (Articles 80, 81, and 83 LOE).

Integration requires an adequate distribution of the immigrant population among schools, so that social minorities are also school minorities. Such distribution (which cannot be achieved at the expense of the parents' right to choose their children's school) can be attained through an adequate joint use of the referred techniques provided for by the state and regional legislation: a) in the first place, school districts should not overlap with areas of social marginalization; b) secondly, rules on admission must not rigidly link domicile and school in the school map; and c) finally, the effective use of the reserve quota for students with specific learning needs should be promoted. However, a higher mobility within the school map must be accompanied by: d) an information strategy for immigrant families, who are usually not aware of the scope of their rights in Spain regarding free public and state-funded private education; and e) an adequate organization of school transportation and school dining hall financial aid.

REFERENCES

Aguado i Cudolà, V. (2003). La aplicación del marco jurídico de la inmigración en las Administraciones locales: Un primer balance (II), *Cuadernos de Derecho Local*, 1, 58 ff.

Böckenförde, E.W. (2001). Kopftuchstreit auf dem richtigen Weg?, *Neue Juristische Wochenschrift*, 10, 723

Cebolla Boado, H., & González Ferrer, A. (2008). *La inmigración en España: 2000–2007. De la gestión de flujos a la integración de inmigrantes.* Madrid: Centro de Estudios Constitucionales.

Fernández-Miranda Campoamor, A., & Sánchez Navarro, A. J. (1996). Article 27: Enseñanza. In O. Alzaga Villaamil (Ed.). *Comentarios a la Constitución Española de 1978* (pp. 157 ff). Madrid: Cortes Generales-Edersa.

Langenfeld, C. (1998). Integration und kulturelle Identität zugewanderter Minderheiten: Eine Herausforderung für das deutsche Schulwesen—Einführung in einige grundrechtliche Fragestellungen. *Archiv des öffentlichen Rechts*, 123, 375 ff.

Ponce i Solé, J. (2010). Inmigración, escuela y segregación: el papel del Derecho público. In Silvia Díez Sastre (Ed.). *Inmigración y gobiernos locales* (pp. 209 ff). Madrid: Marcial Pons.

Prieto Álvarez, T. (2011, April). Crucifijo y escuela pública tras la sentencia del TEDH Lautsi y otros contra Italia. Revista Española de Derecho Administrativo. 150, 443 ff.

Rodríguez de Santiago, J. M. (2003). Escuela e inmigración. Cuestiones jurídicas suscitadas por la integración de menores de origen inmigrante en el sistema educativo español. In L. Pomed Sánchez & F. Velasco Caballero (Eds.). *Ciudadanía e inmigración* (pp. 203–230). Zaragoza: Monografías de la Revista Aragonesa de Administración Pública (VI).

Rodríguez de Santiago, J. M. (2007). *La Administración del Estado social.* Madrid: Marcial Pons.

Rodríguez de Santiago, J. M. (2008). El Estado aconfesional o neutro como sujeto 'religiosamente incapaz.' Un modelo explicativo del artículo 16.3 CE. In Centro de Estudios Constitucionales (Ed.). *Estado y religión en la Europa del siglo XXI* (pp. 115–146). Madrid: Marcial Pons.

Siguan, M. (1998). *La escuela y los inmigrantes.* Barcelona: Paidós.

Stern, K. (1984). *Das Staatsrecht der Bundesrepublik Deutschland.* Múnich: Beck.

van Zaten, A. (2009). Francia: mapa escolar, libre elección y segregación escolar. *Cuadernos de pedagogía*, 387, 86.

Velasco Caballero, F. (2010). Políticas y competencias locales sobre inmigración. In S. Díez Sastre (Ed.). *Inmigración y gobiernos locales* (pp. 65 ff). Madrid: Marcial Pons.

Villaverde Menéndez, I. (2010). El padrón municipal, integración social y nueva ciudadanía social: Padrón versus Nación. In Silvia Díez Sastre (Ed.). *Inmigración y gobiernos locales* (pp. 187 ff). Madrid: Marcial Pons.

Comparative Notes on Integration Policies in Schools for Immigrant Children

NILDA FLORES-GONZÁLEZ,
UNIVERSITY OF ILLINOIS AT CHICAGO
JOSÉ MARÍA RODRÍGUEZ DE SANTIAGO,
AUTONOMOUS UNIVERSITY OF MADRID

It is not easy to draw comparative conclusions from discourses belonging to different scientific spheres: sociology (which deals, from a determined perspective, with the "being" in social reality), and law (which—as jurists say—is a science of how "it should be"). However, it is possible to select the most important points conditioned by these distinct scientific methodologies.

An early conclusion taken from a common starting point in the educational systems of Spain and the United States is that in each it is considered that school is the greatest context for integration of minors of immigrant backgrounds, and that school, therefore, is the greatest instrument in service of social cohesion in the future. It is school that determines whether immigrant children are integrated or remain marginalized.

In Spain as well as in the United States, minors have a fundamental right to obligatory and free education. It is recognized that foreign children have the same fundamental right to obligatory and free basic education as Spanish children (Article 27.1 CE relating to Article 27.4 CE). This is established in Article 9.1 of the Organization Act on the Rights, Freedoms, and Social Integration of Foreigners in Spain, stating that all foreign minors (not including in the law any additional requirement concerning their legal status in Spain) have the right and duty to education under the same conditions as their Spanish counterparts, a right that encompasses access to free and obligatory basic education, obtainment of relevant academic qualifications, and access to the public system of aid and scholarships.

The Supreme Court of the United States has declared that the Constitution of the United States guarantees the right to free and public basic education for all minors, regardless of their legal status in the country. In *Plyer v. Doe*,[1] the Court ruled that the states may not deny free education to undocumented minors in grades K–12, as this would violate the Fourteenth Amendment's Equal Protection Clause due to the fact that children are not responsible for the illegal status of their parents.

In Spain, there are essentially two levels of government in which decisions are made concerning the education of immigrant children. The majority of the legislative powers concerning education belong to the central state (above all, Article 149.1.2 and 30 CE). In this sphere, problems regarding fundamental rights that are not regulated by state laws will eventually be decided by the highest judicial bodies (the Supreme Court and the Constitutional Court). Almost all of the legislative powers concerning education belong to the autonomous community. The municipalities hardly have any powers specifically in the realm of education. The role at the municipal level is, above all, one of collaboration and aid in creating, through its powers related to land use, the physical budgets and materials used to avoid social and academic segregation.

In the United States, there are four levels of government with powers that allow for the possibility of making relevant decisions regarding the education of immigrant children. At the federal level is a constitutional mandate providing for free public education for all minors, regardless of their nationality or legal status in the United States. Crucial legislation occurs at the state level. There are, in effect, notable differences among diverse state legislation that deal directly with the education of undocumented school children. In order to facilitate the administration of educational policies, the state utilizes another governmental level: county school boards. Finally, the most relevant administrative functions are delegated to the school districts (administrative organizations situated at the level of local government). In fact, school districts have considerable leeway in terms of the design and the management of educational policies under federal and state regulations; in practice, educational policies that affect immigrant children vary widely between school districts.

In general, relevant public decisions in this area are made at a lower level in the United States than in the Spanish model. This, as will be shown later, seems to have important consequences.

The most apparently relevant difference from an organizational and financial point of view between the U.S. and Spain are the differences between school districts versus autonomous administration. In the United States, school districts are local administrations with specific administrative powers to manage public schools that, in the state of Illinois, receive funding, which is contingent upon compliance with certain mandates, from three sources: the federal government (6%), the state (35%), and local taxes (59%). Here can be found one of the principal causes of the notable inequalities in the area of education for immigrant children. Dependence on local funding creates huge inequalities in school funding. Given that local funding is based on local property taxes, the wealthiest communities—those with high property values—generate more income through taxation and enjoy more resources to invest in their schools. The wealthy districts spend up to three times more on their schools than do the poorer districts. State funding is intended to correct these differences and allocates additional funding to schools with special needs, but the low percentage of schools that qualify for this funding impedes any real improvement in terms of equality.

From the point of view of guaranteeing equality and promoting cultural integration, it appears—and this point must be affirmed with all prudence and based solely on the facts presented in this comparative study—that a better solution is to situate the educational administration (with decision-making powers concerning management and, above all, the funding of the educational system) within a regional-state level above the local level. In the Community of Madrid, all of the schools financed with public funds depend on one single decision-making center, which—at least on paper—allows for the distribution of financial resources in accordance with solidarity criteria.

Certain notably important issues in the United States may still be considered ancillary in Spain, surely, due to the fact that immigration is a comparatively recent phenomenon in Spain. Among these issues is, without a doubt, the matter of bilingual education programs, whose level of sophistication in the United States (and more specifically in the state of Illinois) is unknown in Spain. The notable homogeneity of Spanish society (at least as compared with that of the United States) seems to be the reason that "specific educational programs for students who exhibit a serious lack in linguistic abilities" [Article 79.1 of the Basic Law on Education] are considered to be a specialized transitory support mechanism that "will take place simultaneously with the curriculum of students in ordinary groups" (Article 79.2 of the Basic Law on Education). Although bilingual education has a long history in the United States, only since 1965 has it been recognized as federal law, through Title VII of the Elementary and Secondary Education Act, which guarantees to children the right to be able to understand what is being taught. This law simply stipulates the right of students with limited English proficiency to have their lessons be understandable to them. The type of bilingual education program that should be put into practice is determined by the regulation and organization of the states and the school districts.

In Spain and the United States, there are analogous problems of parallelism between urban ghettos and school ghettos. The connection between school and the home, the demarcation of school zones, and difficulties in school transportation lead to similar problems in both countries, perhaps to a greater extent in the United States.

NOTE

1. 457 U.S. 202 (1982).

PART FIVE

CHAPTER NINE

Mexican Migrant Civic Engagement in Chicago

XÓCHITL BADA, UNIVERSITY OF ILLINOIS AT CHICAGO

Migrant civic engagement among Mexicans in Chicago has increased in the last two decades. Mexican migrant–led grassroots organizations have flourished in many city neighborhoods and throughout the metropolitan area, as the Mexican community keeps moving to western and northern suburbs outside the traditionally inhabited neighborhoods of Little Village, Pilsen, and the south side of Chicago. Mexican migrant-led organizations are not an entirely new phenomenon, however, as Mexican immigrants in greater Chicago formed mutual aid organizations as early as the 1920s (similar to the voluntary associations created by Bohemians, Italians, Jews, Poles, and Germans of the same era) to help new immigrants settle to their new environment by reducing culture shock (e.g., daily companionship in lodge halls, picnics, dances, feast days, burial services, etc.).[1]

More recently, a few months after the House of Representatives passed the Border Protection, Anti-Terrorism, and Illegal Immigration Control Act of 2005, millions of Latino and non-Latino immigrants participated in mass mobilizations in more than 200 cities across the U.S. to demand dignity and respect for all undocumented workers. While many observers were caught by surprise at the size and scope of these marches, this mobilization was the result of years of silent organizing by migrant-led grassroots organizations. Mexican migrants answered a call from their churches, unions, worker centers, neighborhood groups, hometown associations,[2] sports clubs, Spanish-language newspapers, and radio hosts to join the long wave of protests during the spring months of 2006 (Bada et al., 2010; Bada, Fox, & Selee, 2006).

Between the 1930s and 1970s, the Mexican community in Chicago survived several transformations, including the consolidation of ethnic neighborhoods and the continuous influx of new arrivals after multiple economic shocks experienced in Mexico. In the 1980s, the Mexican economy abandoned the import-substitution model and embraced economic liberalization and free trade, paving the way for the North American Free Trade Agreement, signed in 1993. Prior to the agreement, Mexican politicians met numerous times with U.S. businessmen, academics, and government officials to discuss the benefits of free trade. In 1991, the University of Chicago sponsored a binational forum in a downtown hotel among politicians, businessmen, and academics to discuss the challenges and opportunities of increased bilateral trade cooperation. Many liberal analysts predicted that prosperity would come after a brief period of increased migration. In reality, the relative prosperity offered by NAFTA did not prevent the destruction of rural Mexico, nor the dramatic increase of cross-border emigration.

After NAFTA took effect, the total employment in the agricultural sector in Mexico dropped substantially, from 10.7 million jobs in 1991 to 8.6 million in 2007, according to the latest agrarian census. As a result of high unemployment, worker displacement from the countryside to urban centers, and two devaluations of the Mexican peso—among other factors—many Mexicans voted with their feet and decided to try their luck in the Midwest.

Today, Chicagoland claims the second largest Mexican-born population in the United States with almost 700,000 Mexican immigrants. During the 1980s, the Mexican population accounted for 2% of the population with more than 150,000 immigrants. In the following decades, the Mexican-born population in Chicagoland more than tripled, reaching more than half a million by the year 2000 without taking into consideration the census undercounts in all these periods (Paral, 2006). By 2010, the Latino population in Illinois reached 16% with more than 2 million, 79% of those being of Mexican descent.

The complex work of integrating legal permanent residents, long-term undocumented immigrants, and recently-naturalized, Mexican-born U.S. citizens into the social fabric has been left to the civil society and non-profit grassroots organizations. In a social network study aimed at understanding the bridging and bonding capabilities of Mexican organizations in Chicago, researchers concluded that hometown associations, faith-based initiatives, schools, and arts and culture organizations represent an important socialization space. These organizations provide a forum where key information is shared about leadership skills, institutional networks, employment opportunities, financial literacy, and legal advice—among other important information needed for successful socialization. In these linguistically and culturally sensitive spaces, Latinos are invited to increase their engagement in diverse spheres of action. Regardless of the organizational type, participating in any formal or informal Latino non-profit seems to function as a catalyst for further engagement in other civic arenas, including transnational activities (Wali, Contractor, & Severson, 2006). The spheres of action in these organizations are quite diverse in nature. In particular, faith-based initiatives, hometown associations, schools, and worker centers have become important outlets to foster increased civic engagement among Latinos in the city.

In the following pages, I will focus on six sectors in which Mexican migrant civic engagement in the greater Chicago area has been highly visible in the last two decades: acquisition of U.S. citizenship, neighborhood block clubs, school councils, faith-based organizations, labor organizations, and migrant-led civic binationality through hometown associations.

DEMOGRAPHIC PROFILE AND NATURALIZATION TRENDS

The new demography in greater Chicago has a significant presence of Mexican immigrants. According to recent census estimates, there are more than a half-million Mexican immigrants representing 48% of the total population of Latinos of Mexican descent—a mix of legal permanent residents, citizens, and undocumented immigrants. This is a reflection of larger trends in the country.

By 2010, 32% of the foreign-born individuals living in the United States were from Latin America and a great proportion came with low levels of education, to work in low-skill, low-paid positions in the service sectors, construction, landscaping, and other job opportunities that did not require high levels of education. Over the last ten years, the foreign-born population from Latin America living in the United States increased by 5.1 million, reaching 21.2 million in 2010. Mexico accounted for more than half (55%) of foreign-born residents from Latin America. However, new immigration has slowed dramatically in Chicagoland. In the 1990s, 54,000 immigrants came annually to this area, but between 2002 and 2007 only about 21,000 arrived per year. Therefore, the great challenge for all cities and metropolitan areas in the nation is to integrate immigrants into the social fabric to make sure that they are not forced into a permanent underclass, as this would bring disastrous consequences for the competitive advantage of the labor work force that the region has to offer.

Although Mexicans still have comparatively low naturalization rates compared to immigrants from other countries, their numbers have experienced a spectacular increase in the last decade and now 23% of the qualifying Mexican foreign-born population claims U.S. citizenship. Today, the nearly 1.6 million naturalized citizens from Mexico outnumber those from any other single country. The naturalized population from Mexico to the U.S. grew more rapidly than in any other large country or region—144% over the past decade. Mexicans are also increasing their naturalization rates across Chicagoland. Between the years 2005 and 2009, more than 35,000 Mexican immigrants naturalized as U.S. citizens. There are more than 1.6 million foreign-born residents in greater Chicago and 40% of those (more than a half-million) are from one single country: Mexico. When combined with the total Mexican origin population, Mexicans represent 1.4 million residents in the area—including legal permanent residents, the native born, naturalized U.S. citizens, and the unauthorized population. Latinos in metropolitan Chicago now represent 22% or 1.8 million of the total population.

However, naturalization alone does not trigger civic engagement. The United States has no national immigrant integration plan that encourages people to become civically engaged after they become legal permanent residents or naturalized U.S. citizens. The last time the U.S. government invested in immigrant civic engagement was in 1986, when the Immigration Reform and Control Act legalized millions of unauthorized immigrants. More than $4 billion were poured into the grassroots organizations that enlisted to help in these integration endeavors. Since then, no other major national immigrant integration program has been put in place.

BLOCK CLUBS AND LOCAL SCHOOL COUNCILS[3]

In minority neighborhoods such as Little Village, block clubs provide neighbors with the opportunity to come together and discuss the most pressing issues that affect their immediate surroundings: gang prevention, trash collection, public safety, and school overcrowding. These organizations do not require citizenship status for involvement and usually work in collaboration with neighborhood-based garden committees, local environmental justice organizations, and ethnic chambers of commerce. They are also usually linked to citizens' neighborhood watch programs in collaboration with local Chicago Alternative Policing Strategy (CAPS) beats.

Chicago has been a pioneer city in inviting all parents to become active in their children's schools. In 1988, the city of Chicago enacted a radical school reform to shift centralized bureaucratic control to local democratic control aimed at establishing school-based management in each of its elementary and secondary schools. Since then, parents and community members have been empowered through their majority control over the Local School Council (LSC) to provide more oversight to local schools. Each Chicago Public School has an LSC consisting of the principal, parents, community members, teachers, and sometimes a student. In order to be elected to the LSC, the parents or community members need not be a legal resident nor are there any education requirements. The key duties of the council are principal evaluation, principal selection, school improvement planning, and school budget development.

As U.S. citizenship is not required for parents to join the LSC, their membership provides an empowering opportunity for participation in urban democratic processes (Fung, 2004). Recent data on Chicago LSC has shown that Latino parent participation in these governing bodies increases Latino student performance and plays a critical role in enhancing school–parent relations and, consequently, encourages higher levels of parent involvement in school activities.

Latino parent participation in LSC has also been the result of active recruitment by Latino-led grassroots organizations (Marschall, 2006). For example, the successful model implemented by the Logan Square Neighborhood Association to improve school–community relationships has the potential for replication in many low-income neighborhoods across the city. In this model, interested immigrant parents are offered modest stipends to receive training as teacher's aides for elementary school and, subsequently, serve as volunteers in their children's classrooms. This model provides a meaningful opportunity for immigrant parents' involvement in their children's schools (Hong, 2011).

In 1995, a study conducted by the Consortium on Chicago School Research found that 700 Latino parents (14% of the total) served on Chicago LSC at a moment when Chicago's Latino population was at 20% (Ryan et al., 1997). The study did not ask questions related to birth place so it is not possible to determine the percentage of foreign-born and native-born Latinos represented among these 700 Latino parents. To observe the increase of Latino participation in this important local governance institution since this benchmark study, Bada, Schmit, and Fujimoto (2011) used an algorithm to determine the number of Latino parents and community members serving on Chicago's LSCs. It was used to detect Latino last names among 5,901 council members with available listed names.[4] This algorithm detected 1,332 Latino last names representing 22.57% of the total of the listed names.[5] Compared to the Latino population in Chicago Public Schools (44% of the total), participation still lags behind but there are important trends emerging in this area.[6]

Without detailed demographic information of Latino parent participation in local schools, it is difficult to determine the role of nativity on parental involvement. However, the preference for Spanish language is a good approximation to gauge the level of immigrant parent involvement. For example, David Beltrán, a Ph.D. candidate in Hispanic Studies at UIC, in his research on Latino parent participation in Head Start, documents that this state-funded child development program for low-income communities is experiencing overwhelming participation of parents whose primary language is Spanish. A local program administrator interviewed for his study indicates that about 33% of Latino parents are involved in several Head Start activities compared to 25% of African American parents involved. One of the program managers overseeing the implementation of parent workshops for Pre-K students in the city says, in addition, "90% of the workshops that [Chicago public] schools requested in the 2008–2009 school year were bilingual; superseding the percentage of requests the prior school year" (Beltrán, 2009).

FAITH-BASED LATINO MIGRANT CIVIC ENGAGEMENT

The role of religious pluralism in the U.S. is particularly shaping the mobilization of migrants in the public sphere.[7] In the late twentieth century, the United States experienced the Latinamericanization of American Christianity, especially Catholicism, through practices and symbols crossing diverse national ethnic practices and rituals across the country.[8] In the vast majority of Mexican migrant communities, Catholic rituals and mass attendance are among the most widely practiced experiences that immigrants incorporate into their new societies. Faith and religiosity are important values in Latino immigrant lives, and religious institutions consistently play a key role in the immigrant integration process. Foreign and U.S.-born Latinos share a deep religious commitment shown through high levels of church attendance and volunteerism.

Countless Latin American immigrant congregations diversify local Christianity, for example by including new rites and symbols that increasingly link spirituality with political action arenas. In response to the Theological Reforms of Vatican Council II (1962–1965), many Chicago area clergy have learned Spanish and sought to identify with the life and struggles of Mexican immigrant parishioners in the areas of liturgy, popular piety and devotion, and more recently, political activism to defend immigrant rights. The commitment of the Catholic church in Chicago to the plight of immigrants can be related back to its social justice heritage with worker rights, as expressed in the John Paul II 1981 encyclical on Human Work (Kniss & Numrich, 2007).

However, the relationship between the local Catholic hierarchy and the Mexican community has not always been smooth. In 1994, members of Club Uruapan, a hometown association of Michoacán immigrants, actively participated in the rescue of the Mexican Church of Saint Francis when the Catholic hierarchy closed it to comply with a policy of retrenchment requiring the consolidation of dozens of former national parishes. To prevent demolition, Mexican immigrants faithfully occupied the building during the very cold winter months until the cardinal acquiesced to reopen the church (Badillo, 2006).

In fact, church support for promoting Latino immigrant incorporation and civic engagement at the local parishes largely depends on the capacity of migrant-led community organizations to take those demands to church leaders and on the track record of their organizational structures for building pro-immigrant ecumenical alliances and coalitions. At the national level, the Catholic Church has shown great institutional support for a comprehensive immigration reform. In 2005, the United States Conference of Catholic Bishops launched the Justice for Immigrants Campaign—a national strategy to promote immigrant integration across all dioceses—inspired by a 2003 pastoral letter about immigration that was issued jointly by Catholic bishops of Mexico and the U.S. Local support for this initiative has been uneven so far, but some Catholic parishes in Chicago with Latino congregations have supported the movement for immigrant rights and encouraged people to engage in peaceful protests. A case in point is offered in the first immigrant rights protest against the Minutemen organized in Chicago in 2005. In July 2005, Marco Cárdenas, a priest at Our Lady of Fátima Church, and El Pistolero, a local Mexican radio disc jockey, launched an invitation to mobilize against the actions of Minutemen groups in the Back of the Yards neighborhood. The march attracted about 50,000 protesters and was the first organized attempt to promote a legalization campaign after the events of September 11 (Martínez & Piña, 2005). For Latino immigrants, support from priests can be crucial in their decision to volunteer or engage in non-church-related activities.

The Catholic Church has served as a unifying force among a wide sector of faithful Catholic migrants, bringing together people from various nationalities. One such example is the Second Tepeyac Church in Des Plaines, Illinois. Although it is not in Chicago, many Chicago residents make the annual pilgrimage on December 12 for the Virgin of Guadalupe celebration. Elaine Peña (2008), in her study of Tepeyac Church, describes how its religious principles exceed secular nationalist identifications and embrace diverse Latin American ethno-religious identities. Tepeyac Church also serves as a place for the political as well as the religious spheres. Peña describes it as being a political sanctuary in which devotees may learn about immigration legislation and future mobilization opportunities. The church holds citizenship workshops and also serves as a starting location for those traveling to rallies in downtown Chicago or the state capital. The political events emphasize social justice, and the shrine itself conveys the same message.

Similar observations have been made by Karen Dávalos (2004) in her fieldwork in the Chicago neighborhood of Pilsen. She observes that the Via Crucis Good Friday procession, while it is a religious event, also has political significance as Mexicans take to the streets and claim their right to live and worship within the city of Chicago. In this space, migrants elevate their claim to space by addressing social justice in Christ's name. Mexican Catholics connect Christ's suffering to local situations, events, and people. Each stage of the Via Crucis procession is a moment to reflect upon Pilsen's social conditions, poverty, underemployment, racial harassment, domestic violence, anti-immigrant atmosphere, gang problems, poor educational facilities, and the public school curriculum that does not acknowledge Mexican history and culture.

Despite the prevalence of Catholicism among Latinos in the United States, the structure of the Catholic Church has put very few Latinos in positions of power. There are few Latino bishops being appointed by the Catholic Church and there is a shortage of priests who speak Spanish or understand Latino culture. Consequently, most Latino congregations are being led by people who do not represent them or speak their language. The same is true in Chicago where only one auxiliary bishop is Latino. There are no other Latino bishops in the state of Illinois. The shortage of priests may well be the reason for the growing trend of Latino Catholics converting to evangelical Christian churches like the Pentecostals.

It is important to note that it is not exclusively Catholic churches that are engaging Latinos. There has been a recent trend observed of a Latino conversion from Catholicism to Protestant churches that are also shown to encourage civic participation among their congregations. Saint Adalberto Methodist Church is a good example of a non-Catholic Latino congregation actively involved in comprehensive immigration reform at the parish level either supporting the sanctuary movement or organizing rallies and protests to keep the movement for immigrant rights visible.

The rise of Latino Evangelical and Protestant congregations is a significant trend. If we limit the study of Latino religious participation to only the Catholic Church, we would be missing a growing population of Protestant and Pentecostal Latinos. For example, Evangelical and Lutheran converts are commonly found in the suburbs, where the lack of Catholic parishes offering mass in Spanish created a fertile ground for proselytizing and inviting Catholic Mexican migrants to convert to other faiths (Scott, 1999). Andrea Althoff (2007) has studied this trend and her hypothesis to explain the recent wave of conversion to non-Catholic denominations is that the act of immigrating to the United States contributes to the attraction of converting to a Pentecostal church. It seems that specific characteristics of the Pentecostal church are in line with the North American values that immigrants are adopting. She claims that the Pentecostal religion is much more individualistic with an emphasis on one's relationship with God, in contrast to the hierarchical, communal structure of the Catholic Church. The act of conversion is about choosing and consciously creating a new common Christian identity.

In 2012, the Archdiocese of Chicago estimated that 43% (969,000) of the Catholic population in the archdiocese identify as Latinos. Exact estimates of the numbers of Latino Protestants in Chicago are not readily available, but the Chicago Latino Congregation Study led by sociologist Edwin Hernández offers an important glimpse into the presence of Latino Protestant churches in Chicago. Of the 606 churches identified for inclusion in his study of Latino congregations in Chicago, the denominational identity is as follows: 20% Catholic, 15% Mainline Protestant, 23% Evangelical, and 42% Pentecostal (Burwell et al., 2010).

The Resurrection Project in Pilsen provides an excellent example of faith-based community empowerment in the area of affordable housing. This Latino-led project started in 1990 with $30,000 in donations from parishes in Chicago, and by 2007 the organization had leveraged more than $146 million in community reinvestment in the neighborhoods of Pilsen and Little Village, as well as the city's southwest side. Karen Dávalos (n.d.) notes how this faith-based organization is one of several spiritual engagements that can be used to illustrate the profound integration of faith, daily life, and culture.

The Resurrection Project strives to eliminate poverty and oppression by bringing the sacred into daily life through homeownership services, including the construction of new homes and the renovation of abandoned buildings for rental housing. This organization builds affordable and high-quality apartments for low-income residents and college students because it values and dignifies human life and the relationships among its neighbors.

In the suburbs of Chicago, particularly in the towns of Berwyn/Cicero and Stickney, the Interfaith Leadership Project (ILP) has focused on several community issues affecting low-income Latino residents since 1989. They are a membership-based ecumenical organization including ten local institutions. Their organizational style is based on Saul Alinsky's model of empowering people through addressing their everyday life struggles. ILP's organizing efforts include holding house meetings and conventions with area residents to find shared concerns and develop concrete potential to trigger collective action. Their areas of community action include education, foreclosures, immigration, public safety, health care, citizenship classes, and voter registration.

Among their most recent accomplishments, ILP has formed a coalition with the Latino Union of Chicago—a migrant-led independent worker center—to demand a public resolution to the township of Cicero. On November 12, 2008, the township enacted a safe space resolution to provide increased protections and alleviate the fear faced by immigrant communities living in Cicero. In 2009, ILP's member organizations conducted protests against the township's street cleaning policies on first-time violations and were able to obtain an agreement for a new policy with less harsh consequences for first-time offenders. The organizations in ILP belong to several coalitions such as the Illinois Coalition for Immigrant and Refugee Rights (ICIRR) and United Power for Action and Social Justice, a 300-member institution in Chicagoland that works on statewide issues of immigration and education.

The West Suburban Action Project (PASO for its acronym in Spanish) is another faith-based, migrant-led organization, centered in the suburb of Melrose Park and supported by the Scalabrinian Missionaries, that has engaged in several fronts of advocacy: immigrant legalization, the DREAM Act (for undocumented students in need of more opportunities and funding to attend college), naturalization workshops, and voter registration.

In sum, Latino immigrants are actively engaged in their churches and this participation subsequently motivates them to become civically engaged in different local issues affecting their new communities of residence, sometimes creating ethnic, faith-based advocacy organizations to promote immigrant integration. In the long term, Protestant and Catholic institutional commitment to support civic and political integration programs and strategies will be very important to keep Latino immigrant communities civically engaged in the city and the suburbs.

UNIONS AND INDEPENDENT WORKER CENTERS

With the low levels of unionization (currently at 6% nationally), unions are no longer adequately responding to the new characteristics of the immigrant labor force brought by economic restructuring and globalization. Thus, temporary work agencies, subcontracting, day labor, part-time jobs, lack of health care, etc., generate problems that need to be solved with innovative strategies of what some call the higher road of labor organizing, including better conditions at the work place while improving the daily lives of workers.[9] This is not to say that unions are no longer relevant, but that it has taken them longer to incorporate Latino immigrant members as relevant decision makers in both the rank-and-file and leadership positions.

In the last decade, organized labor attitudes towards immigrants have changed drastically. Before 2000, labor unions were often at odds with Latino immigrant workers, finding them responsible for depressed wages and breaking strikes. However, since early 2000, this attitude has slowly changed and the American labor movement has demanded an end to employers' sanctions and an amnesty for undocumented immigrants (Greenhouse, 2000). The organized labor movement has since experienced some structural transformations, but they have kept a unified voice in favor of some form of legalization for undocumented workers already living in the country. Some unions have devised special programs to help their members become naturalized U.S. citizens and encourage voter registration and electoral participation.

Many local unions are founding members of the March 10th Movement[10] and frequently support Latino immigrants in important battles against abusive employers. Some specific cases are worth highlighting. The most visible case of union support to defend basic worker rights is exemplified by the now extinct Republic Windows and Doors factory (RWD), which attracted worldwide attention in 2008.[11] When the owner attempted to fire all workers without offering severance pay, the workers discussed a strategy with their representatives at the United Electrical Workers Union (UE) and unanimously voted to occupy the factory in a case that brought headlines and support from then president-elect Obama.

RWD's labor force was mostly immigrant, with 75% of workers representing several Latin American countries and one Latino immigrant union representative. However, for these workers, this was not the first time they had participated in a solidarity movement. Three years prior to the factory occupation, the workers negotiated permission from the management to march on May 1 to support immigrant rights in Chicago's downtown. In the weeks and months following the occupation, community support was steady with as many as 1,000 supporters who visited the workers, including local immigrant activists, Mexican hometown associations, faith-based organizations, and the Spanish language media. The workers eventually got severance pay and inspired many others to demand lawfully mandated severance packages in similar cases across the nation as well as in Canada, Argentina, and Ireland. Serious Materials, a California-based green building manufacturer, subsequently bought the factory in 2009 and pledged to reinstate most of the workers respecting union seniority. However, sixty-five reinstated workers had to occupy the plant once again in January of 2012 when Serious Materials announced that they would be closing the factory, less than three years after the acquisition. Thanks to a twenty-four-hour occupation immediately televised on all major local networks, the workers got a ninety-day extension of their contract and have plans to own the factory with union support, but their future is uncertain.

In Chicago, unions have gradually increased the Latino representation both in their rank and file and leadership positions, while independent workers have expanded their presence in labor sectors where traditional unions are not able to defend workers' rights such as day labor, domestic work, temporary labor, restaurant industry, construction, and agriculture. Worker centers are community-based mediating institutions that provide support to low-wage, primarily immigrant workers through service delivery, advocacy, and organizing to improve conditions at the workplace. In 1992, there were only five worker centers in the United States, but by 2007 there were at least 155 worker-led centers spread across the nation (Fine, 2006). In Chicago, independent worker centers provide new advocacy and training tools for workers in precarious labor conditions, emphasizing the need to create new regulations to make employers' accountable when violations of basic worker rights occur. According to Nik Theodore, one of the leading experts on non-traditional labor organizing in Chicago, there are five formally constituted worker centers in Chicago, all of which are located in predominantly immigrant neighborhoods (Theodore, 2007).

The City of Chicago offers several examples of Latino-led worker centers interested in promoting civic participation among their members, along with traditional unions. In the last decade, Latino-led worker centers in Chicago—the Service Employees International Union (SEIU), the United Electrical, Radio and Machine Workers of America (UE), the International Brotherhood of Teamsters (IBT), the United Food and Commercial Workers International Union (UFCW), and the

American Federation of State, County, and Municipal Employees (AFSCME), among others—have provided support and resources to local grassroots organizations to organize rallies, unionization drives, and advocacy work to pass a new federal legislation that will legalize all undocumented workers in the U.S.

For example, these labor organizations have a permanent partnership with the Consulate of Mexico in Chicago to offer free counseling on labor rights once a week, including orientation to submit claims for wage theft, violations to the minimum wage, workers compensation, and labor discrimination cases. In addition, these organizations cooperate with the Department of Labor and the Mexican Embassy in Washington, D.C., to organize an annual fair of labor rights in collaboration with several Latin American consulates in Chicago.

Some independent worker centers have been created by Latino-led grassroots organizations. A good case in point is illustrated by the Economic Development Center (EDC), a migrant worker center established by the Latino Organization of the Southwest located on the southwest side of Chicago. The EDC has focused its activities on assisting low-income Latinos of this region to secure better outcomes in the labor market. They educate newly arrived immigrants about their rights to avoid workplace abuses. They invite trained staff from other organizations to conduct outreach to the community-at-large through weekly sessions at the Consulate of Mexico in Chicago, in addition to helping with workplace conflicts.

On the north side of the city, the Latino Union of Chicago has actively engaged in several campaigns to defend day laborers and other vulnerable workers since 2000. Established by day laborer women, also active in hometown associations, the Latino Union of Chicago became a founding member of the National Day Laborer Organizing Network—a coalition of worker centers led by Pablo Alvarado, a Salvadoran immigrant from California. They have led successful campaigns in Cicero and, since 2004, operate a worker center for day laborers in the north side neighborhood of Albany Park. Despite the absence of widespread support from politicians and city officials, the migrant civil society—led by the Latino Union of Chicago—mounted a sustained campaign to improve the working conditions of day laborers in Albany Park. Emerging out of activism in social movements, this worker center represents the institutionalization of labor standards for a largely migrant workforce that has endured demonstrably exploitative conditions (Theodore & Martin, 2007).

As a result of sustained activism to fight for improvements in worker rights standards and enforcement—and after successful campaigns led by local worker centers—the city of Chicago became one of the pioneers in the implementation of new ordinances to improve employers' regulations for part-time and day laborers. As a result of the coordinated efforts among many day laborer worker centers, the city of Chicago enacted the Day and Temporary Labor Services Act in January 2000. Due to frequent violations of migrant workers' rights, the ordinance seeks to regulate the worker centers that serve as intermediaries between day laborers and their employers. This ordinance is helpful in preventing workers' rights abuses from worker recruitment centers; it does not apply to centers that do not charge a fee.

Finally, the Chicago Restaurant Opportunities Center (ROC) is the latest addition to the list of community-based worker centers. Launched in the fall of 2008 as an affiliate of ROC United, the organization is locally represented by José Oliva, a Guatemalan immigrant with a long history of labor organizing among Latino immigrants in Chicago. Chicago-ROC is devising strategies to increase the Latino immigrant membership. For this reason, it offers bilingual training in bartending and upscale dining to help workers gain specific language skills integral to the obtainability of higher-paying positions within the industry. In the first year, 230 new members were registered. ROC's model combines research and policy work with high-road restaurant worker organizing. Besides educating workers about their rights and promoting workplace justice, ROC is advocating two pieces of legislation: the Healthy Families Act, which would provide restaurant workers with up to seven paid sick days per year, and an increase to the $2.13 federally mandated minimum wage for tipped workers (Batt, 2012).

MIGRANT-LED HOMETOWN ASSOCIATIONS

Mexican migrant–led hometown associations represent an innovative civic engagement arena because these organizations are not only interested in social justice in host societies, but are also interested in combatting poverty in sending countries. Mexican immigrants now live in all neighborhoods across the city and have established new organizations throughout. They participate in block clubs, neighborhood watch groups, garden committees, faith-based volunteer groups, worker centers, labor unions, advocacy groups, and cultural organizations. As the first generation becomes more settled and economically stable, many have decided to join in civic engagement with their communities of origin through hometown associations.

Also known as clubes de oriundos, or the English abbreviation HTA, Mexican hometown associations are among the best-known migrant-led organizations. HTAs bring migrants together from shared communities of origin and represent the paradigmatic case of civic binationality. HTAs often begin as informal associations such as soccer clubs, mutual aid societies, or prayer groups. Over time many have become formal organizations and even "scaled up" to form federations that represent communities of origin from the same "sending" state, sometimes creating larger coalitions that include federations of different states. Though many have rural origins, HTAs are predominantly concentrated in metropolitan areas in the United States.

Thanks to the amnesty granted by the Immigration Reform and Control Act in 1986, thousands of Mexican migrants were able to legalize their status and could travel more easily. Their personal networks became more dense and solidified between their communities of origin and their new settlements. As migrants began returning to their communities of origin more frequently, they gradually became aware of the sheer economic disparities that many rural towns were facing due to economic restructuring. Each return trip to the U.S. meant facing the shocking reality that many of the comforts of modernity, such as running water and electricity that they enjoyed on a daily basis, were lacking in their communities. Due to the relative prosperity in U.S. labor markets in the late 1980s and early 1990s, some migrants had a modest surplus income to spend in the reconstruction of their small towns. Once migrants reached a modest economic stability, many organized weekly get-togethers to share a friendly soccer match and homemade ethnic food, and to chat about their towns' most pressing needs.

At a time when Mexico was experiencing a deep economic, political, and social transformation, migrant allegiances were directed to solve the most important problems that their localities were facing (both in Chicago and in Mexico). In Mexico, HTAs were fighting government corruption and demanding more services and basic public infrastructure. At the same time, hometown members pursued local problems in their new communities, including the lack of bilingual and bicultural education for their kids and an abundance of gang violence.

In 2009, Mexican hometown associations across the United States sent $33 million in collective remittances to finance more than 2,000 community development projects, including roads, highways, water, electricity, and sewage. In contrast, the U.S. Agency for International Development (USAID) invested $11.8 million in rural development in Mexico, representing less than one percent of the total aid sent to this country (Wainer, 2011). While millions of Mexicans are now naturalized U.S. citizens, for many this decision doesn't decrease their interest to remain politically engaged in Mexico.

There are now approximately 275 HTAs in Chicagoland representing 17 Mexican states of origin and the Federal District (Mexico City). These associations are organized into more than 10 federations and one Confederation of Mexican Federations (CONFEMEX). Many have joined the National Alliance of Latin American and Caribbean Communities, a membership-based national organization whose headquarters are in Pilsen—an important Mexican immigrant enclave in the city. NALACC has affiliates in 14 states and almost 100 grassroots organizations have joined their efforts to advocate on behalf of Latin American immigrants, both here in the United States and in countries of origin. Not surprisingly, many headquarters of the largest and most visible Mexican HTAs are found in the areas with the highest concentration of Mexican immigrants, such as Little

Village, Pilsen, Belmont Cragin, and Brighton Park in the city proper, and Cicero, Aurora, Waukegan, and Melrose Park in the suburbs.

As a result of the growing interest of Mexicans to exercise their political and civic rights as dual nationals, Mexican organizations have also pressed state governments to extend political rights to those living in the United States. The states of Michoacán, Chiapas, and the Federal District now offer absentee ballots to citizens regardless of residence to vote in state elections. Since 2006, after a long advocacy process, Mexican migrants can vote absentee in presidential elections. However, the procedures to register in the electoral lists limit participation, as they only allow those with a valid voting card to register—a technicality that disenfranchises those who can't travel to Mexico to request a voting card.

Even with these limitations, during the 2006 presidential elections, more than 50,000 Mexican migrants registered to participate in the electoral process from abroad, and more than 1,000 votes arrived from greater Chicago. In the 2012 electoral process, the city of Chicago was chosen to host the only two national forums in which migrants, local NGOs, and academics had a discussion with the presidents of Mexico's seven major political parties to share their visions for Mexico's future. Topics on the agenda included the economy, security, education, and democracy. The event was the result of repeated demands made by Chicago-based Mexican migrant organizations to Mexico's Federal Electoral Institute (IFE), the autonomous public organization that runs Mexico's federal elections.

Social networks play a fundamental role to articulate strategic alliances among migrant organizations; however, little is known about the local conditions that increase the capacity of these organizations to establish such alliances. The relevance of "place" in its geographical connotation to the understanding of processes of binational civic engagement among Mexican immigrants affiliated with hometown associations, home state federations, and other community-based organizations in greater Chicago has not been adequately scrutinized in comparative perspective (Bada & Mendoza, 2013). The significance of place attachment among immigrants is important to understand political mobilization and social contestation strategies displayed by Mexican immigrant organizations in Chicago. While Chicago-based non-electoral advocacy in favor of migrant rights is highly visible and moderately effective in the state of Illinois, it is also important to note that there are potentially negative consequences of concentrated political actions of immigrant associations on specific geographical areas for long-term visible political activism beyond their territorial comfort zones.

As observed in the cases described in this brief overview, Mexican immigrant civic engagement suggests multiple paths to success. Traditional avenues, as well as unique community-based religious and labor organizations, provide spaces in which immigrants and U.S.-born Latinos organize, network, and coalesce with others to have their voices articulated and heard. Examples such as hometown associations, naturalization drives, neighborhood organizations, and local school councils also provide similar settings that should be explored in more detail. For now, this brief roadmap suggests the need to broaden the lens through which we look at and understand the processes of Latino immigrant incorporation to the social fabric of the city of Chicago and its metropolitan area.

NOTES

1. For a historical account of Jewish immigrant associations in Chicago, see Soyer (1997).
2. Also known as *clubes de oriundos*, or migrant clubs, Mexican hometown associations (HTAs) are among the best-known migrant-led organizations. HTAs bring together migrants from the same communities of origin. Mexican HTAs are a paradigm for civic binationality, performing important roles to defend migrant human and social rights.
3. This section is mostly adapted from Bada, Schmit, and Fujimoto (2011).
4. Those serving as principals were excluded from the lists.
5. Authors are aware that there are most certainly Latino individuals with non-Latino last names as well as non-Latinos with Latino last names. The most reliable source for Latino elected officials is the National Association of Latino Elected and Appointed Officials directory, but they unfortunately do not include Chicago's LSCs in their directory for the state of Illinois.
6. According to the American Community Survey estimates for 2006–2008, the Latino population in the city of Chicago represents 28% of the total.
7. On the role of religion in the undocumented journey of Mexican and Central Americans, see Groody (2002) and Hagan (2008). For a comparative study of immigrant religious congregations in relation to American identity and belonging, see Levitt (2007). For a case study of Chicago immigrant congregations and their moral and social engagement projects, see Kniss and Numrich (2007).
8. For recent ethnographies focusing on the role of Virgin of Guadalupe in building community and public life among Mexican immigrants in New York City and transnational Mexican migrants in Chicago see, respectively, Gálvez (2010) and Peña (2011).
9. High-road labor organizing goes beyond unionization. It emphasizes low unemployment, living wages, job-training and development, investment in local businesses, and regional self-sufficiency among other short- and long-term goals.
10. To learn more about the March 10th Movement see Pallares and Flores González (2010).
11. To learn more about this landmark case see Freund (2010) and Lydersen (2009).

REFERENCES

Althoff, A. (2007). *Migration and the transformation of Latino religious identities in the United States.* Lecture presented at Calvin College, Grand Rapids, MI, April 17. Retrieved from http://www.calvin.edu/henry/archives/lectures/althoff.pdf

Bada, X., Fox, J., Donnelly, R., & Selee, A. (2010). Context matters: Latino immigrant civic engagement in nine U.S. cities. In X. Bada, J. Fox, & A. Selee (Eds.), *Series on Latino immigrant civic engagement.* Washington, D.C.: Woodrow Wilson International Center for Scholars.

Bada, X., Fox, J., & Selee, A. (2006, April). *Invisible no more: Mexican migrant civic participation in the United States*. Washington, D.C.: Woodrow Wilson International Center for Scholars. Retrieved from http://www.wilsoncenter.org/sites/default/files/Invisible%20No%20More.pdf

Bada, X., & Mendoza, C. (2013). Estrategias organizativas y prácticas cívicas binacionales de los clubes de oriundos y federaciones mexicanos en Chicago: Una perspectiva transnacional desde el "lugar" [Electronic version]. *Migraciones Internacionales*, 7(1), 35–67.

Bada, X., Schmit, J., & Fujimoto, K. (2011). Does birth place matter? Determinants of non-electoral civic and political engagement. *Diálogo, 14*(Fall), 34–36.

Badillo, D. A. (2006). *Latinos and the New Immigrant Church*. Baltimore: The Johns Hopkins University Press.

Batt, R. (2012). *Taking the high road: A how-to guide for successful restaurant employers*. New York City: Restaurant Opportunities Centers United.

Beltrán, D. (2009). *Latino immigrants and preschool: Early childhood education parental involvement a possible gateway to other civic involvement*. Unpublished manuscript. Chicago: The University of Illinois at Chicago.

Burwell, R., Hernández, E. I., Peña, M., Smith, J., & Sikkink, D. (2010, May). *The Chicago Latino congregations study (CLCS): Methodological considerations*. Notre Dame: Institute for Latino Studies. Retrieved from http://latinostudies.nd.edu/assets/95266/original/clcsmethodology_paper_final1.pdf

Dávalos, K. (2004). The Via Crucis in Chicago: A reflection on/of grace. *American Catholic Studies, 115*(Summer), 97–100.

Dávalos, K. (n.d.) Mexican Catholic Chicago: Community and religious formation, 1916–2004.

Fine, J. (2006). *Worker centers: Organizing communities at the edge of the dream*. Ithaca: Cornell University Press-Economic Policy Institute.

Freund, A. (Director). (2010). *Workers' Republic*. Retrieved from http://workersrepublic.tv

Fung, A. (2004). *Empowered participation: Reinventing urban democracy*. Princeton, NJ: Princeton University Press.

Gálvez, A. (2010). *Guadalupe in New York: Devotion and struggle for citizenship rights among Mexican immigrants*. New York, NY: New York University Press.

Greenhouse, S. (2000, Februrary 23). Labor, in switch, urges amnesty for all illegal immigrants. *The New York Times*, pp. A23

Groody, D. G. (2002). *Border of death, valley of life: An immigrant journey of heart and spirit*. Lanham, MD: Rowman and Littlefield.

Hagan, J. (2008). *Migration miracle: Faith, hope, and meaning on the undocumented journey*. Cambridge: Harvard University Press.

Hong, S. (2011). *A cord of three strands: A new approach to parent engagement in schools*. Cambridge: Harvard University Press.

Kniss, F., & Numrich, P. D. (2007). *Sacred assemblies and civic engagement. How religion matters for America's newest immigrants*. New Brunswick, NJ: Rutgers University Press.

Levitt, P. (2007). *God needs no passport. Immigrants and the changing American religious landscape*. New York, NY: The New Press.

Lydersen, K. (2009). *Revolt on Goose Island: The Chicago factory takeover, and what it says about the economic crisis*. New York, NY: Melville House Publishing.

Marschall, M. (2006). Parent involvement and educational outcomes for Latino students. *Review of Policy Research, 23*(5), 1053–1076.

Martínez, C., & Piña, F. (2005). Chicago en marcha por reforma migratoria. *MX Sin Fronteras, 20*, 7–9.

Pallares, A., & González, N. F. (Eds.). (2010). *¡Marcha! Latino Chicago and the immigrant rights movement.* Urbana, IL: University of Illinois Press.

Paral, R. (2006). Latinos of the New Chicago. In J. P. Koval, L. Bennett, M. I. J. Bennett, F. Demis sie, R. Garner, & K. Kim (Eds.), *The new Chicago. A social and cultural analysis* (pp. 105–114). Philadelphia, PA: Temple University Press.

Peña, E. (2008). Beyond Mexico: Guadalupan sacred space production and mobilization in a Chicago suburb. *American Quarterly*, *60*(3), 721–747.

Peña, E. (2011). *Performing piety: Making space sacred with the Virgin of Guadalupe.* Berkeley, CA: University of California Press.

Ryan, S., Bryk, A. S., Lopez, G., Williams, K. P., Hall, K., & Luppescu, S. (1997, May). *Charting reform: LSCs—Local leadership at work.* Consortium on Chicago School Research (Ed.). Chicago: Urban Education Institute. Retrieved from http://ccsr.uchicago.edu/sites/default/files/publications/ChartingReform_LSCs_LocalLeadershipAtWork.pdf

Scott, L. (1999). La conversión de inmigrantes mexicanos al protestantismo en Chicago. In G. Mummert (Ed.), *Fronteras fragmentadas* (pp. 405–420). Zamora: El Colegio de Michoacán.

Soyer, D. (1997). *Jewish immigrant associations and American identity in New York, 1880–1939.* New York, NY: Cambridge University Press.

Theodore, N., & Martin, N. (2007). Migrant civil society: New voices in the struggle over community development. *Journal of Urban Affairs*, *29*(3), 269–287.

Theodore, N. (2007). Migrant worker centers: Contending with downgrading in the low-wage labor market. *GeoJournal*, *68*, 155–165.

Wainer, A. (2011, January). Development and Migration in Rural Mexico. Briefing Paper 11. Washington, D.C.: Bread for the World Institute. Retrieved from http://www.bread.org/institute/papers/briefing-paper-11.pdf

Wali, A., Contractor, N., & Severson, R. (2006, December). *Creative networks: Mexican immigrant assets in Chicago.* Chicago: The Field Museum. Retrieved from http://archive.fieldmuseum.org/creativenetworks/pdfs/MIA_fullreport.pdf

CHAPTER TEN

Immigrant Associations and Local Politics in Madrid

CARMEN NAVARRO, AUTONOMOUS UNIVERSITY OF MADRID

INTRODUCTION

Political participation constitutes an attribute of citizenship and is linked with the diverse ways in which individuals participate in the collective issues of a community, whether it be by conventional means (to vote or stand as a candidate in elections, participate in parties, trade unions, associations, or other interest groups) or others (protests, demonstrations, hunger strikes, boycotts, etc.).

Of all the dimensions that relate to the political integration of immigrants, in this chapter we dedicate special attention to one in particular: political participation through the constitution of associations and of their dialogue with local government institutions. We therefore analyze the dynamic of the structure of organized interests of these associations and its consequent involvement in public life, investigating the various mechanisms that immigrants employ in order to make their voices heard in the political process.

Despite being only another way to participate politically, an analysis of associative dynamics is of enormous interest for its multitude of functions that can be explored in terms of integration. Drawing closer to this reality allows us to test the involvement of immigrants in the public sphere and in the decision-making processes. This is not only because the associations are key institutions in the phase of first reception and in the maintenance of identity after establishment, but also because they are called upon to play a role in the decision-making process of public policy, as much in the initial phases of political incorporation (carrying out relevant work as mediators or pressure groups with public authorities) as in the final phases (serving as agents of implementation or channeling integration policies and welfare). The associations, furthermore, are considered to be spheres for the development of civic virtues and skills, educating and enabling participation and contributing to its promotion.

Additionally, because the politico-territorial dimension explored in this chapter is local, it makes even more sense to center the focus of attention on the dialogue between public institutions. In Spain, one of the significant reforms that local governments have recently undertaken is the introduction of channels and forums of public participation. Associations have special importance in these participative dynamics, as the forums are based on the desire for greater involvement of citizens in politics and in the process of adopting public decisions. In various formats—from neighborhood or district meetings to participative budgets, passing through citizen juries, agenda 21, sectorial meetings, public audiences, etc.—the immigrant collectives fundamentally express themselves through the groups in which they are organized because of their organic grassroots associations base.

However, in local contexts where a large number of regulated organs of participation proliferate, the norms that create them have decided beforehand what interests are present and how representation is organized. Although there are additional mechanisms of political participation that are not channeled via associations, it is certain that in cases such as that of Spain, where there exists widespread political apathy among the general population, the presence of citizens' interests in politics—as well as that of the immigrants—depends in good measure upon promotional strategies for fostering associativism that town halls undertake, and of the invitation that groups receive to join participative processes.

With these premises, and in order to get closer to the reality of political participation through the civic involvement of associations in local politics, we need to analyze both the offer of participation (the rules of the game in the political-institutional context) and the demand for participation (characteristics of the associative fabric). We will dedicate the rest of this chapter to exploring these two questions, seeking to respond to the question of how to conceptualize the participation of immigrants in local politics within the framework of the mechanisms established by local government in Madrid.

THE INSTITUTIONAL OFFER FOR PARTICIPATION

The classic question of political science as to why people participate in politics has provoked many responses, from those related to rational choice to those linked with identity. In relation to the participation of immigrants, and at the local level, the majority of the theses point to the importance of the structure of opportunities that the political system offers, that is, to the mechanisms developed by institutions to facilitate participation. By allowing or denying the right to vote, or establishing, or not, arenas for negotiation or consultation, governments open or close the door for participation in the management of collective issues.

There has been a widespread belief in the European literature that immigrants are politically passive (Martinello, 2005). This view has been based on two types of arguments: 1) because immigrants do not have the right to vote, this acts as a disincentive to political mobilization; and 2) the interests of immigrants are not so much political as economic and short-term. Other theories have associated immigrants' political apathy with their origins, by attributing it to the fact that their countries of origin normally do not have democratic political cultures in which citizens have been able to socialize.

Without entering into details, it can be noted here that these theories have evolved and are currently being revised. If it is true to say that the (lack of) vote continues to be an obstacle to full integration, it can also be demonstrated that immigrants participate politically in other ways, by joining trade unions or associations or organizing demonstrations. On the other hand, many immigrants are more politically active than the natives, as they come from countries where they developed political activism and found themselves in situations in which emigrating was the only way to distance themselves from the threat of authoritarian regimes (Martiniello, 2005). It is for this reason that the second group of explanations for their passivity would not find a generalized empirical base.

However, whatever the degree of political involvement of the immigrants, the way in which they involve themselves is also determined by the offer of institutional participation in the receiving country's political system and by the attitudes towards participation of the natives, who they tend to imitate (Aleksynska, 2010). Some distinctive features can be identified in the Spanish system. In contrast to the pluralist United States' model of decision making, European (and Spanish) neo-corporatism represents a different dynamic of involvement for groups in politics. Here the participation of those concerned in the decision making processes is more formalized and ordered by the state, and interaction in decision making is more submitted to the logic of a top-down management style. For that reason, an exploration of its rules and structures of opportunity for political participation makes complete sense if we aspire to understand the patterns of a significant part of immigrants' political activism.

The Call from Central Institutions for the Promotion of Immigrant Participation in Local Life

The Strategic Plans of Citizenship and Integration, which the Ministry of Labor have developed since 2007 to promote the integration of immigrants, contain numerous regulations dedicated to participation and civic education. Specifically, the most recent of these (PECI 2011–2014) emphasizes the importance of the participation of foreigners in the public life of the local sphere and the need for this to be promoted by public bodies. The Council of Europe is strongly convinced of the need to improve integration (of foreigners) in the local community, above all by means of increasing the possibilities of participation in local public issues.

If it is true to say that this contribution is specifically directed at the local level, it should not be forgotten that the plan acknowledges the importance that the establishment of deliberative forums has had at national and autonomous levels, in which "the associative immigrant movement and the articulated social fabric has made its presence felt in the migratory phenomenon." Specifically, in the national plan, the constitution of the Forum for the Social Integration of Immigrants in 2006 reflects this political will, having been endowed with consultative functions, as well as information and assessment through judgments and reports. The PECI highlights the need to reinforce the promotion of collaboration and active practice networks, as well as the active exercise of citizens. This involves strengthening the social fabric because it is essential that immigrant associativism can serve as a point of reference to the foreign population by "assuring that it does not constitute a space for segregation or isolation but rather that it interacts and establishes mechanisms of communication and cooperation with the rest of the social fabric."

Additionally, the Strategic Plan points to the need to promote political participation in the population of foreign origin. Political participation is understood to be as much suffrage, representation, or militancy, as presence in formal institutions of participation with special impact in the local sphere. The objective consists in reinforcing the processes of extension of the right to suffrage and promoting the strengthening of the existing multiple experiences of participation.

But what is the structure of rules of these experiences of participation and, more specifically, what are its characteristics in Madrid? The following section is dedicated to analyzing the model of participation in Madrid.

The Offer to Participate in the City of Madrid

The link between the local level of government and a greater propensity for the involvement of citizens in public issues is a recurring theme. In the municipal institutions and in their policies one finds more fertile and accessible terrain for participation, not only for the most reduced dimension of the demos, but also for the closeness of the issues that they deal with and the greater facility to address their complexity. Research has demonstrated that generally, and particularly in Spain, municipal governments inspire a greater degree of confidence among citizens compared to other levels of government, and a higher level of satisfaction in relation to their services (Navarro, Cuesta, & Font, 2009). Despite the medium-low level of interest of the population in politics, local politics usually inspires more engagement compared to the other levels (Bonet, Martín, & Montero, 2006). The greater closeness of the government to the people and the municipal administrations facilitate this perception.

The substantive reform of the norms of citizen participation that the Town Hall of Madrid began in 2005 was also a project that was present in the electoral programs of all the political parties running for the local elections in 2003. The belief was widespread that citizen participation in Madrid had languished during the previous legislatures, to the point that citizens had lost interest, and it was therefore necessary to revitalize it through profound legislative and strategic change. The reform was based on the creation of a department within the organic structure of the Madrid Town Hall. The General Section for Citizen Participation was designed within a legal framework that can be summarized in the following points. The reform:

- establishes a great number of methods and organs of participation, with varying intensities, depending on citizens' interest in participating, ability to participate, and capacity to mobilize, with the aim of giving space to all citizens.
- emphasizes the role of associations in the process.
- underlines the need to generate a culture for citizen participation and develop the social capital of the city by fostering the associative fabric with aid and subsidies.

Upon these premises, the model of Madrilenian participation is structured along four axes: citizen rights; role of the associations; existence of formal organs of participation; and mechanisms and measures for the promotion and development of citizen participation. We have collected in the table that follows a summary of the municipal strategy for participation.

Table 1. Madrid Strategy for Citizens' Participation

The Associations	Organizations apt to be enrolled in the register of citizen entities	Organizations can enroll in the municipal register of citizen entities all those Associations, Federations, Confederations, or grassroots charitable Unions of Associations, with head offices in the Municipality of Madrid, that represent and promote the general or sectorial interests of the citizens of Madrid.	
	Promotion of associativism	Declaration of municipal public utility	The entities established in the register can be recognized as being of municipal public utility when their social objective and the activities they undertake in the Municipality of Madrid have a complementary character to municipal responsibilities. For that reason it is essential that the organization fulfill its aims in an efficient and effective way.
		Aid, subsidies, and collaboration agreements	The Town Hall assigns a corresponding budget heading to aid or subsidies through announcements and collaboration agreements with citizen entities declared to be of public utility. Furthermore, these citizen entities can have access to the use of rooms and installations that are owned by the municipality for the realization of their activities. In the same way, they can have access to the municipal media: municipal noticeboards, radio and local TV, and informative bulletins through the municipal webpage.
Organs of Participation	Territorial Meetings in the Districts (TMD)	Definition	The TMDs are organs of participation, consultation, information, and proposals about municipal actions, which allow the participation of residents, their collectives, and citizen entities of a district in the co-management of municipal issues. Their ordinary meetings are held every three months.
		Finality	To promote collective reflection among citizens, their associations and the municipal authorities meet to discuss issues that affect the daily life of the districts and its neighborhoods, encouraging citizens to involve themselves in municipal management in a responsible way.

Organs of Participation	Territorial Meetings in the Districts (TMD)	Composition	A maximum of forty people, who are elected for a period of four years: President (District councilor), Vice President (representative of the associations that are registered in the meeting), eight representatives of political parties, representatives of associations, and residents elected at random.
	Sectorial Meetings (SM)	Definition	The SMs are organs of participation of a consultative character that channel the participation of residents and their associations in the large sectors or areas of municipal action. They meet every three months.
		Objective	Its objective is to facilitate assessment and consultation for those in charge of specific areas of municipal action.
		Composition	The SMs are organized in the following way: President (councilor of the corresponding government), Vice President (representative of citizen entities enrolled in the meeting), Board members (representatives of Federations, Confederations, and Unions of Associations established in the register of citizen entities and declared to be of municipal public utility), and representatives of other institutions.
	Director of City Council (DCC)	Definition	The DCC is configured as a consultative organ of the City of Madrid government, whose fundamental mission is to offer a space for strategic thinking for the management of public issues in the City. It is also constituted as an organ of broad and plural participation, in a public sphere of discussion about the City and its future.
		Finality and Composition	To produce reports, studies, and proposals in matters of local economic development, city strategic planning, and large urban projects. Its composition, responsibilities, and functioning are guided by agreement with what is forecast in the regulating norm of the *Bases de Régimen Local*, by the norm of organic character that the Plenary of the Town Hall approves.

(*Continued*)

Table 1. Madrid Strategy for Citizens' Participation

Forums, Mechanisms and Measures of Promotion and Development of Citizen Participation	Good Practice	Putting into action AL-21, habitat programs, city strategic plans, integrated community development plans of district and neighborhood.
	Information Campaigns	Information and educational campaigns aimed at citizens, particularly to children and adolescents for the development of democratic values and for participation as a social value.
	Participation in the diagnosis of situations	Opinion polls and satisfaction surveys to get to know the perception of citizens about public services.
	Participation in the formulation of public policies	Meetings and thematic forums, temporary or permanent, of experts or of resident participation, citizen panels, and deliberative surveys.
	Community mediation	For community mediation and adequate resolution of conflicts, a specific norm is developed that regulates these social processes with its acceptance being voluntary.

The Associations

Organizations can enroll in the municipal register of citizen entities all those associations, federations, confederations, or grassroots charitable unions of associations, with head offices in the Municipality of Madrid, that represent and promote the general or sectorial interests of the citizens of Madrid. The entities established in the register can be recognized as being of municipal public utility when their social objective and the activities they undertake in the Municipality of Madrid have a complementary character to municipal responsibilities. For that reason it is essential that the organization fulfill its aims in an efficient and effective way.

The town hall assigns a corresponding budget heading to aid or subsidies through announcements and collaboration agreements with citizen entities declared to be of public utility. Furthermore, these citizen entities can have access to the use of rooms and installations that are owned by the municipality for the realization of their activities. In the same way, they can have access to the municipal media: municipal noticeboards, radio and local TV, and informative bulletins through the municipal webpage.

The TMDs are organs of participation, consultation, information, and proposals about municipal actions, which allow the participation of residents, their collectives, and citizen entities of a district in the co-management of municipal issues. Their ordinary meetings are held every three months.

To promote collective reflection among citizens, their associations and the municipal authorities meet to discuss issues that affect the daily life of the districts and its neighborhoods, encouraging citizens to involve themselves in municipal management in a responsible way.

This group is made up of a maximum of forty people, who are elected for a period of four years: president (district councilor), vice president (representative of the associations that are registered in the meeting), eight representatives of political parties, representatives of associations, and residents elected at random.

The Sectorial Meetings (SM) are organs of participation of a consultative character that channel the participation of residents and their associations in the large sectors or areas of municipal action. They meet every three months. Their objective is to facilitate assessment and consultation for those in charge of specific areas of municipal action. The SMs are organized in the following way: president (councilor of the corresponding government), vice president (representative of citizen entities enrolled in the meeting), board members (representatives of federations, confederations, and unions of associations established in the register of citizen entities and declared to be of municipal public utility), and representatives of other institutions.

The Director of City Council is configured as a consultative organ of the city of Madrid government, whose fundamental mission is to offer a space for strategic thinking for the management of public issues in the city. It is also constituted as an organ of broad and plural participation, in a public sphere of discussion about the city and its future. They are charged with producing reports, studies, and proposals in matters of local economic development, city strategic planning, and large urban projects. Its composition, responsibilities, and functioning is guided by agreement with what is forecast in the regulating norm of the Bases de Régimen Local, by the norm of organic character that the plenary of the town hall approves.

Good practices include putting into action local agenda 21, habitat programs, city strategic plans, and integrated community development plans of the district and neighborhood. They are also involved in information campaigns aimed at citizens, particularly to children and adolescents for the development of democratic values and for participation as a social value. They encourage participation in analyzing problems and conduct opinion polls and satisfaction surveys to get to know the perception of citizens about public services. They encourage participation in the formulation of public policies by organizing meetings and thematic forums, and seek for community mediation and adequate resolution of conflicts through a voluntary process.

In Madrid's participation model, the immigrant's collective is integrated as one more representative collective. The associations of immigrants that are established in the Citizens Entities Register of the Madrid Town Hall are recipients of the policies and existent subsidies to promote their development and strengthening. Regarding the organs of participation by district, the immigrant associations are present in the territorial boards, although currently to a minimal and uneven degree, but in an ascending trajectory. In relation to sectorial representation, the sectorial board that is specifically dedicated to the themes of Immigration is the Madrid Forum for Dialogue and Coexistence, established in 2007. The forum advises the town hall about social intercultural coexistence, diversity, and migrations, and raises proposals in these areas for the whole municipality. Its function consists in advising and consulting the different organs of Madrid's Town Hall and promoting associations and individual collaboration in matters of social intercultural coexistence, diversity, and migrations. Besides having managers of the local administration among its members, the forum integrates representatives of associations of immigrants, members of the so-called "support entities" related with non-governmental organizations who work with immigrants (e.g., Red Cross, Spanish Commission of Aid to Refugees, etc.), and representatives of parties, trade unions, and associations. It works in plenary and also in specific commissions: human rights, the fight against racism, women, and immigration and capacity building.

The Plans for Social and Intercultural Coexistence in Madrid provide a good example in order to illustrate the results of these mechanisms. These plans are one of the products of the participative processes and they set the criteria that inform the municipal integration policies for the immigrant population. Actions like the Social and Intercultural Mediation Service, the Office of Information and Orientation for Integration, or the Translation or Interpretation Service (Madrid Directorate General for Immigration and Development Cooperation, 2009) are specific initiatives in which the participative strategies have materialized.

As in all studies that address these types of questions, what is really relevant is to reflect on the real impact of these policies. With similar institutional designs, the efficiency of the initiatives to facilitate citizen participation can be very varied and oscillate from no impact to notable impact; the word 'impact' here is understood to be a true involvement of citizens in the decision making process and a change in the form of decision making by the government towards more open and participative models. On occasion, we face realities that begin with extraordinary complex machines and mechanisms of participation in the form of meetings, forums, audiences, etc., but the attendance and participation in these is minimal and the real influence of their proposals over local politics is slight. On other occasions, on the other hand, one can identify advances in less complex models of institutional design.

It would exceed the scope of this chapter to systematically evaluate the situation in Madrid. It would entail not only generating our own data and designing a battery of adequate indicators but also taking sides in the debate about what is understood as successful citizen participation, and in the definition of criteria for its evaluation. In this question, different positions exist according to the normative vision about democracy to which one subscribes.

However, an approximation to the phenomenon can be undertaken by accounting for the perceptions of Madrilenian and foreign citizens on the integration of immigrants in Spanish society. The Immigration Barometer 2012, carried out by the Observatory of Immigration-Centre of Studies and Data of the Community of Madrid, brings together a description of the attitudes, beliefs, opinions, and mutual perceptions of Madrilenian society to foreign immigration, and compares them with the previous survey in 2009. These data confirm that the perception that foreigners have regarding immigrants integration in Spanish society is very good and that more than three-quarters of immigrants (77%) consider themselves to be integrated.

Regrettably, the effects of the economic crisis can be seen on the Spanish. In 2012, only one-third expressed themselves in the same terms, against 55% that in 2009 considered that foreigners were integrated in Spanish society. When foreigners are asked to identify possible barriers to integration, a third of them identify problems with the language, and a similar percentage to the legal status. Social discrimination is the main source of difficulty, according to 22% of foreigners that have found some obstacle to achieving better integration in Spanish society. For their part, the Spaniards tend to be more pessimistic regarding the integration of immigrant collectivities. Almost two-thirds of those surveyed stated that foreigners have faced some obstacle. This group points to the social discrimination they receive as the main difficulty (24%), followed by the language and the attitude of the native population (Integration Barometer in the Community of Madrid, 2012).

Despite the fact that the overall data is positive about the integration of the immigrant collective, some changes in the responses towards the irregular immigrants from the survey of Spaniards are revealing—particularly after three years of economic crisis. Despite most supporting the option to regularize the situation of those that have work, the percentage of support has reduced by 10 points (from 53 to 43). At the same time there has been a substantial increase in the group that opts for giving immigrants the means to return to their own country (37 in 2012 against 22 in 2009).

The Associational Fabric of Immigrants

As was stated at the start of this chapter, we aim to get closer to the immigrant associative movement and to the means by which they relate to the local administration to influence public decisions, which will allow us to undertake a better diagnosis of their political integration. Besides detailing their number and composition, we will now address the basic questions that are usually dealt with in the study of associations, namely their age and size, and their ways of acting in the public sphere. Both the associations' number of years of existence and the amount of their members is related to their degree of development and the model of collective action that they develop (Mendez & Mota, 2006).

In general it is usually stated that the greater the age of the organization, the greater its level of formalization of organizational structures and the better they establish relations with other associations, since they are bigger and have more professional features. When analyzing the immigrant associations, we will see that they are low in number in relative terms. The number of associations is few, generally because they are very young and with low member numbers, which is explained in part by the fact that the phenomenon of immigration is recent. With the aim of contextualizing this reality, we will next focus briefly on the characteristics of immigration in the city of Madrid.

The Context: The Presence of a Population of Foreign Origin in Madrid

After centuries of being a country of emigrants, Spain experienced, for the first time, the phenomenon of immigration in the late 1990s. In contrast to the situation of other European countries, immigration to Spain is therefore a relatively new phenomenon that, furthermore, has developed in a short period of time and in an intense way. Between the years 2000 and 2008, Spain became the first receiving country for immigration in the European Union, with an approximate average of 500,000 immigrants arriving each year. It is believed that the majority of immigrants came to Spain for socioeconomic reasons, because of a lack of work opportunities in their countries of origin, or to cover the work demand in the receiving country, although it is true that there are situations in which political factors have also had importance. Immigration has constituted a significant factor of dynamization of the Spanish economy in recent years, and it is estimated that approximately 30% of the growth in GDP in 1996–2005 was due to their contribution (Zapata, 2009). However, since the beginning of the crisis in 2008, there are indicators that show that the growth in migratory flows has slowed. In the Madrid region, for example, 2011 and 2012 were years in which the number of registered immigrants dropped (0.8% in 2012), due in part to naturalizations, but also, for the first time, to returns of the immigration population to their countries of origin.

The first specific actions towards the immigrant collective date from 1994. These actions included the Social Integration Plan for Immigrants and the creation of the Forum for the Social Integration of Immigrants, which is an organ for their participation and integration in Spanish society through meetings of associations with the institutions of the autonomous and local state administration. Years later with the expansion of immigration and the approval of Law 4/2000 (related to the Rights and Freedoms of Foreigners in Spain and their Social Integration), development plans and policies at all levels of government (national, autonomous, and local) became widespread with the aim of approaching, from the public perspective, the challenge that integration represented for this new collective of citizens.

The phenomenon of immigration in the city of Madrid, responds to these same characteristics of intensity and rapidity, but it also possesses some distinctive features that are worth putting into numbers to contextualize the study. In 2011, 557,117 foreigners lived in Madrid, which represents 17% of Madrilenians (3.3 million inhabitants); additionally there were 173,206 Spaniards who were not born in Spain. The majority of these foreign-born Spaniards has obtained their nationality in the last five years (114,996) and they are mostly from Ecuador, Peru, Dominican Republic, Colombia, Morocco, Argentina, Venezuela, and Cuba. In sum, one in every five Madrilenians (22%) is foreign-born.

Regarding their geographic origins, the immigrants who come from Latin America and the Caribbean represent around half of the total of the foreign residents, followed by citizens from the European Union with around one-third; Africans, Asians, and North Americans are represented in lower numbers. More specifically, the nationalities with greater presence in the city are, in this order: Ecuador, Romania, Peru, Bolivia, Colombia, China, Morocco, Dominican Republic, Paraguay, and Italy. The overwhelming majority of immigrants in Madrid are not recent arrivals. Those who came in the last two years represent less than 10%. The great waves of arrivals were between 1999 and 2007, which means that the majority of foreigners, more than 80%, have been living in Spain for five years or more and legally reside in the city (Consejería de Asuntos Sociales, 2012).

The foreign origin population is unevenly distributed across various districts of the city. The areas that have the largest concentration of immigrants are: Center (34%), Usera (29%), Villaverde (29%), Carabanchel (28%), and Tetuán (29%). The effects of the economic crisis have been notable since 2010, with a rapid contraction in the admission of foreigners. The balance in 2010 between new admissions and the decline in the register of inhabitants totaled 9,000 new residents, the lowest figure in the last ten years. More than half of this group is comprised of European Union citizens. Additionally, unemployment has grown in Madrid, and is particularly high among foreign workers; the percentage was 28 for foreigners at the end of 2012, compared to 19% of Spanish residents. (These rates are much lower than the Spanish average; the unemployment rate among foreigners in Spain was 35%, and the general unemployment rate was 25% at the end of 2012). According to the Survey of the Active Population, 44% of the unemployed workers in Madrid were foreign.

The Immigrant Associations in Madrid

The immigrant organizations, despite the significance of immigration to Spain, are understudied (Toral, 2010). Only recently, research has started to emerge about immigrant associations, centered on exploring the phenomenon of these citizens' political behavior through the associations, given that the vote, as it is restricted, could not be an object of comparative analysis. Nevertheless, there are some groups of researchers who have developed empirical studies in this area, incorporating the case of Madrid, as it is both a magnet for foreigners and a relevant case study that is of interest for research. As there has been no empirical research undertaken for this chapter, the lines that follow have been supplemented with secondary literature and, specifically, from the studies undertaken by Morales, Anduiza, Rodriguez, and San Martín (2010), González and Morales (2006), Veredas Muñoz (2003), and Aparicio and Tornos (2010).

Although Aparicio and Tornos's study (2010) is not specific to Madrid, but refers to all Spanish territory, the general information about the typical profile of immigrant associations that they provide is not so distant from our city of study:

- "The majority of the associations have been very recently created (from 2005 onwards).
- In the majority they are made up of members of only one nationality, above all when the nationalities are of Ecuadorian or Moroccan origin. There are

also, although to a lesser degree, Latin American, Sub-Saharan, and general immigrant associations.
- Their members are predominantly men, with a majority over the age of thirty and who has had less than five years' residence in Spain.
- In half the associations, the members are either not involved at all or have modest weekly involvement.
- Membership of native-born Spaniards is very low." (Aparicio & Tornos, 2010)

Their activities are, in order of importance: maintenance and diffusion of their own culture (89%), services to specific groups of people (83%), political activities (76%), integration of their national collective (62%), recreational activities (54%), cooperation with their country of origin (27%), and religious activities (18%).

Studies such as that of Veredas (2003) demonstrated the weakness of the immigrant associative fabric, at least at the start. In these organizations one can usually state that the model of configuration of the groups is determined by the power over decision making that the political authorities have in their structure. The authorities, because of their need to have interlocutors to effectively channel the integration of immigrants in Spanish society, usually take the initiative about the form in which they should articulate their participation in the political life of the receiving country. Civil society is constructed in this way since the continuity, development, and formalization of immigrant associations are closely related to access to state resources. "The hypothesis of the construction of civil society from above is confirmed, a phenomenon that neutralizes the opposition potential of the political associations" (Veredas, 2003: 222).

According to Fauser (2012), in Madrid, the direct involvement of immigrant associations in co-development projects in sending countries has only slowly grown. For example, between 2004 and 2009, immigrant associations in Madrid only channeled 13% of all co-development projects for sending countries that were subsidized with public funds by Madrid's municipal government. Different than what has been revealed by Mexican immigrant hometown associations located in Chicago—whose membership organizes fundraisers to finance projects in communities of origin, with matching funds from Mexico's public funds for development—immigrant associations in Madrid are not very engaged in fundraising for co-development and mostly depend on public funds from Madrid's municipality to support their transnational agendas.

According to the work of Morales, González and Jorba (2009) referring specifically to Madrid, there are 199 active associations of the 417 from the census that were identified for their study. Furthermore, 64% of the total were registered after the year 2000, which indicates how young the majority of these entities are. In relative terms, this signifies the existence of 0.7 immigrant associations for every 1,000 residents born abroad, although it is true to say that this figure falls to 0.3 if we only consider the active associations. The associative density of foreigners is notably less than that of the native population (one-tenth). This figure reveals a phenomenon of enormous weakness in social capital (Putnam, 1993); even if we compare it with the native population, it is hardly a reference of vitality.

This would be in line with some hypotheses that affirm that, in these questions, immigrants tend to behave in the same way as natives do (Aleksynska, 2011). In Spain, the very low interest in politics and high level of distrust shown towards the institutions that make democracy possible (despite the persistent support to democracy, which surveys have shown since the 1970s) are features of the political culture, and this then has its echo in very low organizational density and poor levels of membership in political parties (Gunther, Montero, & Botella, 2004).

The data that is periodically provided by the European Social Survey allows us to observe the Spanish case in the European context and to confirm that it has the lowest quotas of interest in politics and of configuration of associations in our geographic environment. Only 26% of Spaniards state that they have a considerable interest in politics, in comparison with countries like France, UK, Switzerland, Sweden, Germany, Holland, or Denmark, where interest is over 50% in all cases. The degree of involvement in organizations or associations is equally low, and only 9.53% of those surveyed stated that they had collaborated with an organization or association, in contrast to the levels of most people of other European countries, with Scandinavians at the head, followed by Holland, Germany, Belgium, France, and Switzerland, which are all above Spain. The literature coincides in detecting, among the Spanish population, a predominance of negative attitudes, distrust, and a lack of involvement in relation to politics and the public sphere (Montero, Font, & Torcal, 2006).

The context therefore does not encourage collective action and the organization of immigrant interests. Nevertheless, there are differences among the distinct geographical areas and Spanish urban spaces, and specifically, participation in cities like Madrid or Barcelona is higher than the national average (Toral, 2010). Equally it is important to emphasize that the studies on civic participation of immigrants in Europe have come to the conclusion that collective organizing becomes more intense as the period of establishment of individuals in the country increases (Aleksynska, 2011). This might lead us to predict that in the future we could see a higher level of involvement in public issues. Perhaps the reason it is not high now is due in part to the migratory phenomenon in Spain still being in its early stages.

Besides the low number, the associative world of the immigrant population is characterized by a high rate of "mortality" (Morales, González, & Jorba, 2009) and for the propensity of the collective to create associations according to nationality (Aparicio & Tornos, 2010). Regarding the first of these features, there is frequently a significant mismatch found between the number of immigrant associations that figure in the census and their actual existence. The researchers of these realities usually come up against the difficulty of finding interlocutors for many of the associations that are enrolled on the registers (González Ferrer & Morales, 2006; Aparicio & Tornos, 2010). The reason is that their activity, and therefore, real existence has ended—although traces of these associations linger on in the public census until they are updated.

Regarding geographic origin, the Madrilenian immigrant associations are characterized by being predominantly constituted of citizens from a single country. Only 14% of them bring together individuals from distinct nationalities of origin (Morales, González, & Jorba, 2009). In these cases, they either combine the presence of Spaniards with citizens of foreign origin or they organize themselves by geographic regions (African, non-Spanish communities, etc.). It is, furthermore, of enormous interest to confirm how a greater presence of immigrants of specific nationalities of origin in the city does not correspond to a greater number of associations from those countries. In the associative immigrant world there co-exist situations of nationalities with lesser representation that develop plural associations together with other groups around a single entity. Specifically, in light of data analyzed by González Ferrer and Morales (2006), one detects a high relative rate of organizational activity among Peruvian and Sub-Saharan communities in relation to the percentage that these immigrant populations represent, and lower figures in the case of Ecuadorians or Moroccans. This is probably related to national cultures.

However, these data must be analyzed with caution. The absolute number of associations is not, considered in isolation, a valid indicator of the degree of successful political integration in the public life of a collective. A high plurality of associations could be reflecting a phenomenon of atomization, fragmentation, and absence of a substantial presence in public life, while a reduced number could correspond to an organization with weight, efficient in the articulation of interests and configured around one or a few entities endowed with collective representation and with a real capacity of influence in the decision-making processes.

The Mechanisms Employed by the Associations for Public Dialogue

The diagnosis about the political integration of immigrants through its associations is enriched if we look at the degree of access that they have in the public sphere. Immigrant associations can center their activity around questions related to fulfilling private objectives or the maintenance of an identity (religion, sport, etc.) or having an access and participation vocation in public life. For our approximation, it is interesting above all to look at this second aspect and the research by González Ferrer and Morales (2006) about the Madrilenian immigrant associations. This research brings us closer to the reality by investigating the phenomenon through three indicators: the enrollment of the associations in an official register, the inclusion of the associations in some stable organ of citizen participation of the Madrid Town Hall (formal participation), and the invitation to participate in some commission or ad hoc working group (informal participation; Martín Pérez, 2004).

The data provide a snapshot in which the associations are predominantly enrolled on some official register (73%), are present in a significant way in the regulated mechanisms of participation (42%), and are called in a more sporadic way to forums of dialogue to resolve specific problems (25%). However, they employ in a less active way other political participation mechanisms, such as the lobby or mobilization through demonstrations or protests.

The interesting findings that these data show refer to the greater representation of members of the immigrant associations in the stable participation forums than their counterparts from the native population. Veredas arrives at a similar conclusion in his study about the Forum for the Social Integration of Immigrants at the national level, in which it is clear that the relationship between immigrant associations and the administration are not only the result of the initiative of the former but rather, fundamentally, of the interest of the authorities to have interlocutors in groups that are, without a doubt, badly structured (Veredas, 2003). It does not appear that there is any discrimination in accessing the meetings—perhaps even the opposite. This is probably due to the fact that there is a guarantee built into the design of the organisms that regulate these collectives, which leads us to conclude that these mechanisms of participation, of a top-down character, enable the formal political involvement of immigrants in local life, although there exist doubts about their purpose and capacity to pressure (Veredas, 2003).

The panorama changes when we observe the forums that are established in an ad hoc way by local government and to which groups access by invitation (e.g., an occasional commission about a specific problem) or those in which participation is open and voluntary (e.g., forums, assemblies, informative commissions). Here, the underrepresentation of the immigrant collectives in relation to the other associations is notable. One could point to different explanations. One possibility would be that the underrepresentation reflects an obstacle to the entrance of immigrant interests, specifically in these forums that are characterized by more flexibility, less bureaucracy, and having been established with the desire to give specific responses to delimited problems, and therefore, with greater capacity of influence in the final decisions of the authorities. Regrettably we lack more qualitative knowledge to continue refining the hypothesis in one direction or the other.

A look at the other mechanisms of strategies of immigrant associations to make their voice heard in formal organs offers us information that is also relevant. However this line of analysis can also disintegrate quickly into a debate over the classic categories and types of activities such as the traditional lobby, the mobilizing protest, the protest of confrontation or the activities related to electoral processes. González Ferrer and Morales (2006) offer data about the frequency with which associations resort to each one of these mechanisms to try to influence public decisions. From the whole catalogue of possible actions, the Madrilenian immigrant associations appear to opt for mobilizing moderate strategies and have a preference for written mechanisms. Letters to authorities, conferences, press releases, and distribution of pamphlets or written materials to influence public opinion are the most commonly employed mechanisms. Those most connected with the traditional lobby, such as contact with the media, pressure to the authorities (lobby), and the defense of specific causes appear in a second group of strategies of political action that are most frequently employed as a way of pushing demands in the agenda and making problems visible. Probably the reason behind them selecting a particular method will be based on calculating the greatest impact with the least cost (González Ferrer & Morales, 2006).

Of the various types of political activities with which associations manage their integration, we highlight in last place the existing data about contact with politicians and authorities. It is enormously interesting to have information available on this point, given that other empirical studies on citizen participation in Madrid identify the coexistence of a high number of bilateral contacts ("personal appointments") between the representatives of associations and authorities with formal mechanisms of participation of the 2005 Regulation. Those interviewed in these studies highlight the risk that it represents for the success of the new model—given the tendencies for important issues to drift to bilateral contact—which are subject to the logics of negotiation and pressure, and can empty the effective content of the decisions in participative forums with greater deliberative logic.

This completes the picture of the participative dynamic of associations about the frequency and the recipients of the contacts with civil servants of the administration, politicians with government responsibilities, and members of political parties. Here, also, González Ferrer and Morales (2006) offers us valuable data by confirming that the administrations closest to the citizen (regional and local) are those that are most contacted, in line with the previous statements about how what is local is most like proximity democracy. The most intense contacts are with those in charge in the administration, rather than the politicians. The greatest percentages of contacts are produced around the phases of management or implementation of public policies, and they focus on social services and services of assistance. The associations with members of native origin have greater access to the offices of civil servants and representatives of political posts, additionally, at the design phase of a policy or program.

CONCLUSIONS

Immigration is a relatively new phenomenon in Spain, which has, in a short period of time, gone from being a country of emigrants to becoming the first receiving country for immigrants in the European Union. The majority of immigrants have arrived due to a lack of work opportunities in their countries of origin or to cover the work demand in the reception country. A phenomenon of these characteristics presents infinite challenges for the new citizens, for the welcoming country, and, also, for the political system. Of all these issues, this chapter has sought to explore the political integration of the collective of immigrants in the reception community, through their associative movements, particularly in the city of Madrid. This study has investigated the various mechanisms that the immigrants employ to make their voices heard in the political processes, and how they have used them.

If it is true to say that association building is only one more way of involving oneself in public life, its study is particularly interesting at the local level and in Spain where—due to the low levels of social capital and the top-down model of participative dynamics—the associations are called upon to play a role in the decision-making processes of public policies, both in their initial phases undertaking relevant work as groups in constant interaction with the public authorities—such as in the processes of the implementation of public actions—and as implementing agents or channels of integration and welfare policies. This type of analysis is particularly interesting now because recently stimulus policies for citizen participation have intensified at the local level. In these participative dynamics (from neighborhood or district meetings to participative budgets, citizen juries, agenda 21, sectorial meetings, public audiences, etc.) associations have special importance because their members express themselves through grassroots organizations.

Despite the relevance of immigration in modern Spain, with few exceptions, immigrant organizations are an empirically under-studied phenomenon. Consequently, the systematic empirical knowledge of the immigrant civil society is limited, and this prevents the extraction of definitive conclusions in this study. A look at the associative fabric draws a panorama of a scarce number of associations, even less than the average of the native population. Generally they are very young associations and with few members, which could be explained in part because immigration is a recent phenomenon in Spain. In its configuration, development, and dynamics of articulation of the political dialogue, the public authorities seem to have a strong specific need to have interlocutors to effectively channel the integration of this collective. Some authors have even stated that this confirms "the hypothesis of the construction of civil society from above (...), a phenomenon that neutralizes the opposition potential of the political associations" (Veredas, 2003: 222).

However, we also know that, in general, the associations develop and achieve more power with the passage of time due to growth in the number of members. Therefore we should not draw definitive conclusions about the weak structure of the associative immigrant movement, as it is a phenomenon that is still in the process of consolidation. The fact that in Spain there is a political culture of low associative density and distrust of institutions does not aid the civic involvement of immigrants, especially if we take into consideration studies that show that, in these questions, immigrants tend to behave as they see the natives do (Aleksynska, 2011).

Besides there being few, and of recent creation, other features that one observes about associations are: 1) they predominantly consist of members from one nationality; 2) they are predominantly composed of men, who are older than thirty, and who have more than five years of residence in Spain; 3) their members have little or no weekly involvement; 4) their activities are fundamentally of welcome and maintenance and diffusion of their own culture, and political activities remain in third place regarding the importance of their actions; 5) their presence in political life is predominantly channeled through their participation in consultative forums designed by the authorities for citizen participation, as well as in their employment of mechanisms of moderate length (such as written protest, lobbying the authorities, and contact with the media) (Aparicio & Tornos, 2010; González Ferrer & Morales, 2006).

Despite the weakness of immigrant political activism, their integration into Spanish society does not appear to represent a serious problem. Nevertheless, the negative effects of the crisis are currently being felt, and the surveys on perceptions of immigrants and Spaniards about immigrants' integration point to a situation that is clearly deteriorating. It will be of crucial importance to political representatives and civil society to observe their evolution in the following years.

REFERENCES

Aleksynska, M. (2011, December). Civic participation of immigrants in Europe: Assimilation, origin, and destination country effects. *European Journal of Political Economy*, *27*(3), 566–585.

Aparicio Gómez, R., & Tornos Cubillo, A. (2010). Las asociaciones de inmigrantes en España: Una visión de conjunto. Madrid: Ministerio de Empleo y Seguridad Social

Bonet, E., Martín, I., & Montero, J. R. (2006). Las actitudes políticas de los españoles. In M. Torcal, J. Font Fábregas, & J. R. Montero (Eds.), *Ciudadanos, asociaciones y participación en España* (pp. 105–132). Madrid: Centro de Investigaciones Sociológicas.

Consejeria de Asuntos Sociales (2012). Informe de la Población extranjera empadronada en la Comunidad de Madrid Comunidad de Madrid.

Fauser, M. (2012, November). Urban citizenship and transnational control: On the engagement of local authorities and migrant networks in Madrid. Unpublished paper presented at Transnational Dynamics, Changing Inequalities and The Transformation Of Locality, Bielefeld University, Germany.

González Ferrer, A., & Morales, L. (2006, September). Las asociaciones de inmigrantes en Madrid: Una nota de investigación sobre su grado de integración política. *Revista Española del Tercer Sector, 4*, 129–174.

Gunther, R., Montero, J. R., & Botella, J. (2004). *Democracy in modern Spain*. New Haven, CT: Yale University Press.

Madrid Directorate General for Immigration and Development Cooperation (2009). II Plan for Social and Intercultural Coexistence (2009–2012).

Martín Pérez, A. (2004, June). Las asociaciones de inmigrantes en el debate sobre las nuevas formas de participación política y ciudadanía: Reflexiones sobre algunas experiencias. *Migraciones, 15*, 113–143.

Martiniello, M. (2005). Political participation, mobilisation and representation of immigrants and their offspring in Europe (Willy Brandt Series of Working Papers in International Migration and Ethnic Relations 1/05). Malmo: School of International Migration and Ethnic Relations, Malmö University.

Méndez, M., & Mota, F. (2006). Las características organizativas de las asociaciones en España. In J.R. Montero, J. Font, & M. Torcal (Eds.), *Ciudadanos, asociaciones y participación en España*. Madrid: Centro de Investigaciones Sociológicas.

Montero, J. R., Font, J., & Torcal, M. (Eds.). (2006). *Ciudadanos, asociaciones y participación en España*. Madrid: Centro de Investigaciones Sociológicas.

Morales, L., Anduiza, E., Rodriguez, E., & San Martín, J. (2010). La participación política de los inmigrantes en Barcelona y Madrid: Comportamiento electoral y acción política. In D. Moya Malapeira & A. Viñas Ferrer (Eds.), *Sufragio y participación política de los extranjeros extracomunitarios en Europa* (p. 531 ff). Barcelona: Fundació Carles Pi i Sunyer.

Morales, L., González, A., & Jorba, L. (2009). Políticas de incorporación y la gestión del asociacionismo de la población de origen inmigrante a nivel local. In R. Zapara-Barreiro (Ed.), *Políticas y gobernabilidad de la inmigración en España* (p. 113). Barcelona: Ariel.

Navarro, C. J., Cuesta Azofra, M., & Font, J. (2009). *¿Municipios participativos?: Participaciónpolítica y ciudadana en ciudades medias españolas*. Madrid: Centro de Investigaciones Sociológicas.

Putnam, R. (1993). *Making democracy work*. Princeton, NJ: Princeton University Press.

Secretaría de Estado e Inmigración y Emigración, Dirección General de Integración de los Inmigrantes. (2011, September). II Plan Estratégico de Ciudadanía e Integración (2011–2014). Retrieved August 3, 2013, from http://extranjeros.empleo.gob.es/es/IntegracionRetorno/Plan_estrategico2011/pdf/PECI-2011-2014.pdf

Toral, G. (2010). Las asociaciones de inmigrantes como sociedad civil: un análisis tridimensional. *Revista Española de Investigaciones Sociológicas, 32*, 105–130

Verba, S., et al. (1971). *The modes of democratic participation: A cross-national comparison*. Beverly Hills: Sage.

Veredas Muñoz, S. (2003). Las asociaciones de inmigrantes en España. Práctica clientelar y cooptación política. *Revista Internacional de Sociología, 61*(36), 207–225.

Zapata, R. (2009). *Políticas y gobernabilidad de la inmigración en España*. Madrid: Ariel.

CHAPTER ELEVEN

Democracy and Immigration in Spain

SUSANA SÁNCHEZ FERRO,
AUTONOMOUS UNIVERSITY OF MADRID

The Spanish Council of State, the consultative body of the national government, in its report on proposals to change the Spanish general election system and when reflecting on the political participation system foreseen in the Spanish Constitution (SC), refers to the centralization of elections and applicable provisions within the regulatory structure of a democratic state, "albeit merely based on their immediate link with the sovereign people." For the Council of State, the state's democratic nature depends, "to a large extent, on the ability of the electoral system to adequately achieve a political representation of society." An "electoral system at the service of democracy demands that all elections generate a body that represents the electoral body, in material and political terms and not just formally" (Consejo de Estado, 2009, pp. 10, 12).

THE SPANISH CONSTITUTION

The 1789 French Revolution identified citizenship with nationality, "belonging to a nation (rather than a people), as subject to sovereignty" (De Lucas, 2006, p. 22). Throughout the nineteenth and twentieth centuries, political rights were linked to nationality; the idea of citizenship revolved around the idea of a nation and, later, of a people, albeit consisting of national citizens only. National sovereignty and, later, popular sovereignty meant that institutional decisions were endorsed by the will of the nation or people, which consisted of national citizens (Aja & Moya, 2008, pp. 66–67; as to the excluding effects of citizenship, see Pomed, 2004, p. 67).

Contrary to these excluding effects of citizenship, Sweden was the first European country to acknowledge a right of suffrage in favor of all resident foreigners, both for local/regional elections and referendums; these rights were legally acknowledged in 1976. In turn, Denmark, in 1977, acknowledged a right to vote in local and provincial elections in favor of member countries of the Nordic Council (whose members, apart from Denmark, included Sweden, Norway, Iceland, and Finland), and subsequently extended it to all foreign residents enjoying more than three years of residence in the country. Norway recognized a right to vote in favor of Nordic Council members in 1978 (Aja & Moya, 2008, p. 68; Moya, 2010a, pp. 29–30). It was with this background that the Spanish Constitution of 1978 was born.

As most European Constitutions in the post-World War II era (Aja & Moya, 2008, p. 67), Article 23 of the 1978 Spanish Constitution only refers to citizens when fully recognizing their political rights. According to this article, "citizens are entitled to participate in public matters, directly or through their representatives, freely elected in periodic elections by universal suffrage" (Article 23.1 SC). Furthermore, Article 23.2 SC recognizes that citizens have a right of access in equal conditions to public positions and posts, with the requirements foreseen by law. In Article 13.2, the Constitution established that only Spanish citizens could hold the rights acknowledged in Article 23, "excluding reciprocity situations" that could be established by treaty or law for an active suffrage right in municipal elections. In other words, Article 13.2 SC granted a right to vote to foreigners in local elections only if a series of conditioning factors were met. It is said that foreigners are excluded from the political community insofar as they cannot participate in creation of the law despite enjoying a right of residency (Pomed, 2004, p. 64).

At the time Spain was drawing up and approving its Constitution, it was a country of emigrants. The constitutional power was not so forward-looking as to envisage that the country could become a destination point for immigrants over the years. When confronting the issue of foreigners' suffrage rights, it decided to reflect the situation that existed in Spain in 1978 (Rubio, 2004, p. 19; Aja & Moya, 2008, p. 71; Santolaya & Díaz, 2008, p. 15). The Spanish Socialist Workers Party (PSOE) and the Spanish Communist Party (PCE) were the ones to propose that the possibility of active suffrage be included in local elections for foreigners, returning to the reciprocity principle. All Latin American immigrants could easily acquire dual nationality, as Article 11.3 SC established that the Spanish State could execute dual-nationality treaties with Latin American countries or with others enjoying a specific link to Spain; consequently, the reciprocity clause was designed to recognize the right of suffrage in favor of any other national minority.

Basically, it was later used to allow European countries in which Spanish emigrants resided (e.g., France, Germany, etc.), who did not enjoy this preferential access to nationality under the Spanish Constitution (please note that Spain was still not a member of the European Union), to eventually acknowledge a right of suffrage in favor of their resident Spanish citizens in exchange for a right of suffrage in favor of their own citizens (Aja & Moya, 2008, p. 72; Moya, 2010b, pp. 462–463; Aja, 2012, p. 419).

Initially, Article 13.2 SC only contemplated the active suffrage of foreigners in municipal elections. Further to the approval of the Maastricht Treaty in 1992 (following which the European Community was known as the European Union), said article required an amendment. Article 8.1 of the Maastricht Treaty created a union citizenship to complement, not replace, member state citizenship. Article 8.B.1 provided that any union citizen residing in a non-national member state would be entitled to vote and be eligible in the municipal elections of his or her resident member state, under the same terms as the nationals of such state. Consequently, Article 8.B.1 of the Maastricht Treaty granted EU citizens, through a Treaty, not only a right of active suffrage (permitted by Article 13.2 SC) but also a right of passive suffrage. In this apparent contradictory situation, the Spanish government made a request to the Spanish Constitutional Court for a decision in the form of a declaration (Constitutional Court Declaration 1/1992, of July 1), regarding the existence or absence of a contradiction between Article 13.2 of the Spanish Constitution and Article 8.B, Section 1, of the Maastricht Treaty.

Had the Constitutional Court considered that Article 8.B.1 affected articles included in the Preliminary Title of the Spanish Constitution—Article 1.2 SC, which states "national sovereignty resides in the Spanish people," or the rights foreseen in Section One, Chapter II, Title I of the Spanish Constitution (including the rights foreseen in Article 23 SC)—the Spanish Constitution would have required a reform through the very complex procedure established in Article 168 SC. However, the Constitutional Court believed that these articles were not affected by the Maastricht Treaty, which would only affect Article 13.2 SC, thereby requiring a reform through the simple procedure foreseen in Article 167 SC.

The most relevant part of the Constitutional Court's pronouncement is the fact that the SCC considered that Article 1.2 SC—which reserves national sovereignty to the Spanish people—would not be affected by an acknowledgment of the right of passive suffrage in favor of EU citizens in local elections. In its declaration, the SCC indicated in its Third PL that "without examining other issues" it would suffice to say, in order to justify its decision, that endowment of a right of suffrage in representative body elections to non-nationals would only be disputable, in light of the constitutional wording of Article 1.2 SC, "if such bodies pertained to persons holding powers directly entrusted by the Constitution and Autonomous Community Rules (Estatutos de Autonomía), linked to the holding of sovereignty by the Spanish people." In other words, according to the Constitutional Court, municipal elections would not constitute representative bodies exercising sovereign powers.

This interpretation of municipal elections has been criticized (e.g., Santolaya & Díaz, 2008, p. 14; Aja, 2012, p. 418). Aja and Moya state that: "nowadays, municipalities and their representatives are considered by the majority to be political, not merely administrative, bodies" (Aja & Moya, 2008, p. 73). Furthermore, if the Constitutional Court pronounced itself in this way, it did so in order to back up a removal from the Constitution of the right of suffrage of foreigners in autonomous and state elections (Moya, 2010a, p. 43). According to Pomed, Declaration 1/1992 of July 1 still indicated an underlying idea that citizens are the only ones able to participate in formation of the law (Pomed, 2004, p. 68–69).

Eventually, on August 27, 1992 (OSG No. 207 of August 28, 1992), reform of the Constitution was approved and Article 13.2 SC is now worded as follows: "only Spanish citizens will hold the rights acknowledged in Article 23, without prejudice to any provisions established by treaty or law, further to reciprocity criteria, for the right of active and passive suffrage in municipal elections."

The right of suffrage held by foreigners was gathered in Article 6.1 LODLEIS, which provided that all resident foreigners in Spain could hold a right of suffrage in municipal elections, further to reciprocity criteria, in the terms provided by law or a Treaty for Spaniards residing in their countries of origin. For the Council of State, the wording of Article 6.1 LODLEIS was misleading because "it is one thing for reciprocity to be upheld without the need for a treaty (i.e., based on an acknowledgment of a right of suffrage of Spaniards as foreseen in a foreign law); and it is quite another for an acknowledgment of the right of suffrage of residing foreigners in Spain to be made 'in the terms' established in the foreign law (which is in fact what Article 6.1 transcribed is proclaiming)" (Consejo de Estado, 2009, p. 36–37; the drafting of this article had already been criticized by Revenga in Santolaya & Revenga, 2007, p. 88–89). The wording of this article was amended by Organic Act 2/2009, of December 11, as follows: "All resident foreigners in Spain may hold a right of suffrage in municipal elections, in the terms established in the Constitution, international treaties or the law, as applicable."

The Problems Raised by the Reciprocity Clause of Article 13.2 SC

The reciprocity clause entails mutual acknowledgment of the right of suffrage amongst citizens of a specific country and Spanish citizens. Articles 176 and 177 LOREG have upheld the provisions of Article 13.2 SC, according to Article 176 LOREG.

Without prejudice to the provisions established in Title I, Chapter I of this act, all resident foreigners in Spain will enjoy a right of active suffrage in municipal elections, if their respective countries allow Spanish citizens to vote in such elections in the terms of a treaty. Furthermore, a right of active suffrage in municipal elections will be enjoyed by all residents in Spain who, without acquiring Spanish nationality:

a) Hold status as European Union citizens, according to the provisions of Article 8.1.2 of the treaty establishing the European Community.
b) Meet the necessary requirements to be voters, required in this act for Spanish citizens, and have manifested their wish to exercise a right of active suffrage in Spain.

The government will provide the Electoral Census Office with a list of foreign states whose nationals, residing in Spain, should be included in the census. The most relevant part of Article 176 LOREG is that it requires the existence of a treaty in order to acknowledge a right to vote in favor of non-Community foreigners, whereas the Constitution allowed this acknowledgment to be also conducted by law, i.e., a de facto or legislative reciprocity could be ascertained, "based on applicable laws in the foreign state and without requiring a treaty" (Consejo de Estado, 2009, p. 34). Santolaya and Díaz believe that despite the provisions of Article 176 LOREG it would be possible to acknowledge legislative reciprocity, a debatable point (Santolaya & Díaz, 2008, p. 17). In addition, Article 176 LOREG requires that European Union citizens manifest their wish to exercise their right of suffrage in Spain, which clearly affects the final number of voters who will go to the polls in said municipal elections.

In turn, Article 177 LOREG provides that without prejudice to the provisions established in Chapter II, Title I of this act, all residents in Spain will be eligible in municipal elections, if they have not acquired Spanish nationality and:

- Hold status as European Union citizens further to Article 8.I.2 of the Treaty establishing the European Community, or are nationals of countries that grant Spanish citizens a right of passive suffrage in their municipal elections in the terms of a treaty.
- Meet the eligibility requirements foreseen in this Act for Spanish citizens.
- Have not been deprived of their right of passive suffrage in their state of origin.

Once again, Article 177 LOREG refers to the need for a treaty in order to recognize the right of passive suffrage in favor of non-Community citizens, abandoning the alternative of a law. The need for a treaty in order to recognize a right of suffrage in favor of non-Community foreigners raises various issues.

As Aja and Moya (2008, p. 69) point out, "States may selectively extend the right of suffrage by nationalities." The selection criterion could be, for example, the point of view of the quantitative relevance of its nationals in Spain, to also include criteria for political or economic ties with the country executing the treaty (Solanes, 2008, p. 88). In short, as signature of the treaty depends on the will of two parties, both of Spain and of the country executing the agreement, signature of the treaty may depend on issues removed from democratic principles that concern governmental, diplomatic, or commercial relations between both countries (Aja & Moya, 2008, p. 77).

Moreover, "internationalization—based on the reciprocity principle—is hardly effective" (Solanes, 2008, p. 86). In addition, by internationalizing the problem, "an issue of internal law is rendered more complex, i.e. the representation of various groups of persons present in the country" (Moya, 2010b, p. 470). Furthermore, asymmetric difficulties arise under this system that are hardly compatible with an integration objective (Solanes, 2008, pp. 86, 88): only the nationals of certain countries benefit. Nationality will be a determining factor to participate in municipal elections; those who are unable to vote due to belonging to a state whose nationals are not acknowledged a right of suffrage will feel that the system is not equitable (Aja & Moya, 2008, pp. 76–77). The system is inappropriate if there is a wish to extend the right of suffrage to all foreigners equally (Moya, 2010b, p. 470). Finally, there are serious doubts that a treaty could be signed with undemocratic states or with countries that establish significant differences amongst their nationals, such as restrictions on the right to vote of female citizens (Solanes, 2008, p. 88). Aja and Moya consider that reciprocity will not be possible in those countries without local elections or where free and democratic elections are not held (Aja & Moya, 2008, p. 75). Aja raises the following question: are immigrants to blame for the fact that their governments do not hold democratic elections or do not allow Spaniards to vote (Aja, 2012, p. 422)?

Depending on how the reciprocity clause requirements are interpreted, the scope of the right of suffrage of non-Community foreigners will be larger or smaller. A very strict interpretation that requires the same suffrage conditions in both signatory countries would render practically impossible the signature of any treaty acknowledging a reciprocal right of suffrage. Legal scholars lean in favor of a flexible interpretation of reciprocity in order to facilitate an acknowledgment of the right of suffrage. Aja and Moya are in favor of reciprocity being projected in compliance with certain minimum conditions, in order for this requirement to be met: the need for local elections to be free and democratic according to standards established by international organizations, the European Union and the Spanish Ministry of Foreign Affairs, and representatives to be elected by universal and secret suffrage.

In this way, reciprocity would not affect what they refer to as "contingent components of the electoral system (whether the system is proportional or majority-based, electoral barriers, etc.)" (Aja & Moya, 2008, pp. 75–76; Moya, 2010b, pp. 468–469). Santolaya and Díaz Crego follow a somewhat stricter interpretation, by demanding that these requirements should also demand that any conditions imposed on Spaniards to participate in elections be equivalent, in essential terms, to those required in Spain for nationals of that country (Santolaya & Díaz, 2008, pp. 15–16). Solanes upholds a very broad definition of reciprocity, understood as an acknowledgment of a right of suffrage, not the exercise of such right, in such a way that any immigrants arriving from different countries may vote, all being subject to the same conditions (Solanes, 2008, p. 89).

In its report on proposals to modify the general electoral system, the Council of State has also interpreted the meaning of reciprocity according to the provisions established in Article 13.2 SC and Article 176 LOREG, including any other interpretations that may result from Article 13.2 SC. The Council of State directs its considerations towards an extension of the right of suffrage to resident foreigners in Spain, following the considerations of Spanish legal scholars (Consejo de Estado, 2009, p. 40 ff.).

According to the Council of State, further to the legal implementation of Article 13.2 SC in Article 176 LOREG, in order for reciprocity to exist from a material point of view in Spanish law "it suffices for the States in question 'to allow Spaniards to vote' in municipal elections"; and, in formal terms, a treaty must exist, i.e., this is a broad definition of reciprocity. For the Council of State, reciprocity conceived in this manner does not even require "democratic regimes with 'fair and free elections'; nor that suffrage be recognized in favor of Spaniards in the same terms as the country's nationals (as a result, even if Spaniards are recognized in the foreign State with certain restrictions, a bilateral treaty could recognize this right in favor of its resident nationals in Spain in the same conditions as Spaniards)."

The foregoing also applies to passive suffrage in municipal elections (Consejo de Estado, 2009, pp. 34, 36). Reciprocity in Article 13.2 SC apparently refers to the right of active and passive suffrage in municipal elections as a subjective right. Any comparison with the signatory country of a treaty should consequently refer to the right of suffrage and holding of this right, not to the electoral regime, system, or electoral procedure existing in the foreign state in question (direct or indirect election, frequency, term of mandate, majority or proportionality formula, etc.; Consejo de Estado, 2009, p. 70).

In turn, the Council of State believes that Article 13.2 SC does not require that reciprocity determine recognition of the right of suffrage, but that the law or treaty should "fulfill" reciprocity "criteria." The Constitution, says the Council of State, does not require that this principle be applied, but that such criterion be fulfilled. "This means that the legislator may choose to apply general reciprocity...without therefore having to demand full equivalence between the treatment received by Spaniards abroad and the one intended for foreigners in Spain, in relation to the right of suffrage." The report seems to allow the possibility of generally regulating the right of active and passive suffrage of foreigners in Spain through a law that entrusts a right of suffrage to nationals of states that do not allow Spaniards to enjoy such right, in the understanding that such general regulations would have to fulfill the reciprocity criteria, rather than each specific case that is regulated (Consejo de Estado, 2009, pp. 71–73).

In our opinion, this is a forced interpretation to a certain extent. Presno has also criticized the Report on the point where it states that a reference to the law opens up "different possibilities" (Presno, 2009, p. 201). Even the Council of State points out that the possibility of acknowledging the right of suffrage each time to a state's nationals, handling each one individually on the grounds of reciprocity, fits in better with the Spanish Constitution than this second option. However, it accepts the fact that "this line of action means that the final decision on the possibility of recognizing the right of suffrage of resident foreigners, in Spanish municipal elections, is made dependent on a foreign state's decision" (Consejo de Estado, 2009, pp. 73–74).

How has the reciprocity principle been applied in Spain? Well, the fact is that in bilateral treaties signed with third countries, such as Norway, reciprocity has not been strictly interpreted and the right of suffrage has been acknowledged in conditions other than those established for Spaniards in the other signatory state of the treaty (Aja & Moya, 2008, p. 74; Solanes, 2008, p. 90).

CRITICISM FROM LEGAL SCHOLARS TO THE CURRENT SYSTEM USED TO ACKNOWLEDGE A RIGHT OF SUFFRAGE IN FAVOR OF FOREIGNERS

Many authors are in favor of reforming the Constitution in this regard in order to extend the content of the right of active and passive suffrage held by foreigners in Spain in municipal elections, removing the reciprocity clause and including a reference to their years of legal residence in Spain. There are opinions in favor of a new citizenship based on residency rather than on nationality (Aja & Moya, 2008, p. 70; Aja, 2012, pp. 422–423). Some authors are also requesting a constitutional reform to allow resident foreigners in Spain to participate in all electoral processes—in municipalities, autonomous communities, and general elections (Aja, 2012, pp. 418, 425; Moya, 2010b, p. 496; Ortega, 2011, p. 41).

For Aja and Moya, this constitutional reform could involve a removal of the reciprocity requirement, and so foreigners would be able to vote in municipal elections according to the conditions foreseen in electoral laws. For these authors it is a moral issue, given that a foreigner who has been living in Spain for years is already part of society even when excluded from its institutions. Furthermore, the failure to acknowledge a right to vote in favor of these foreigners would hinder their social integration, whereas their inclusion as voters would increase the legitimacy of laws and governmental policies (Aja & Moya, 2008, p. 79). Solanes also agrees with this opinion, pointing out how in "supposedly homogenous" societies today there are defects in democratic legitimacy in internal matters because "overall participants in public decisions do not represent all of the affected parties"; de facto population is removed from the right to vote, and fundamental human rights become the object of debate (Solanes, 2008, pp. 68–71; see also Rubio, 2004, pp. 13–17 and Presno, 2009, pp. 192–194, 197–198). According to Aja, in modern Western democracies it is difficult to justify the fact that several million foreigners who have been living in Spain for years, working, paying taxes, and affected by political decisions, should be excluded from an adoption process (Aja, 2012, pp. 416–417). In Rubio's opinion,

> in order to face the democratic challenge resulting from the current migration scenario, it is necessary to progressively equate nationals and those foreigners who permanently reside in Spain, irrespective of their legal status, as otherwise this would breach one of the basic democratic-liberal principles of the constitutional system: the political coexistence of human beings in equal conditions. (Rubio, 2004, pp. 13–17)

According to this author, there are two ways in which to achieve this: 1) to enable access to Spanish nationality, increasing ius soli situations, whereby citizenship is acquired by birth within the territory of the state, regardless of parental citizenship (*Encyclopaedia Britannica*, "citizenship"), and using flexible naturalization criteria for resident foreigners; and 2) to gradually sever enjoyment of rights from nationality "so that resident status (not a legal permit) may gradually become the condition to open a possibility to full enjoyment of equality" (Rubio, 2004, pp. 27–28).

As may be seen, the author presumes that effective—not legal—residence exists. However, she does clarify the fact that a definition of a foreigner should not be replaced by a definition of a national to all intents and purposes, given that the logical end of this situation "would entail the annulment of a basic prerogative still in force in a State: border control." According to Rubio,

> to the extent that a national State exists and still represents a fundamental forum for debate in which political decisions are taken that particularly (though, obviously, not exclusively) affect all those residing therein in an effective and permanent manner, it is justifiable to approach the idea of an alternative, from a dynamic point of view, to the national–foreigner coupling, to progressively enshrine a status of constitutional equality for all those who effectively reside in a stable manner in the State, without prejudice to their nationality. (Rubio, 2004, pp. 28–29)

De Lucas believes that the challenge is to overcome a growing condition of belonging without citizenship, and is in favor of reviewing a definition of citizenship. The key to this would be the idea of social and effective citizenship "demanding a multilateral and gradual definition, in which the stable residency link is the reason for belonging and recognition as a subject," thereby attaching citizenship to residency instead of nationality. The start would be a citizen's political community status, recovering the political dimension of resident status. Secondly, political participation would be essential for immigrant integration, according to De Lucas. Political rights—De Lucas affirms—should be conceived widely to cover participation and intervention rights in public life. In his opinion, there will never be total equality unless immigrants are fully recognized as subjects of the public arena (De Lucas, 2006, pp. 1, 4, 6, 8–9; De Lucas, 2009, pp. 94–95, 104–105).

THE EFFECTS OF NATIONALITY REGULATIONS ON THE MATTER AT HAND

Rubio affirms that there are still sufficiently relevant standard situations of inequality between nationals and foreigners to demonstrate that nationality is hardly irrelevant when accessing citizen equality, in which all constitutionally safeguarded rights are fully enjoyed. One of these situations would be the enjoyment of political rights (Rubio, 2004, pp. 20–21, 27). The closer that nationality and enjoyment of fundamental human rights are related, the more relevant a definition of who is a national becomes (Rubio, 2004, p. 29).

Open access to nationality would facilitate immigrant votes, as opposed to a more restrictive access to nationality under which residents living for several generations in Spain are still treated as foreigners (Aja & Moya, 2008, pp. 79–80; Moya, 2010a, p. 58). However, naturalization does not necessarily solve the problem. As pointed out by Aja and Moya,

> to believe that naturalization solves the problem would be the same thing as saying that the majority of immigrants have become nationals but nationalization involves obstacles, e.g. demanding that one's nationality of origin be waived in order to acquire the host country's nationality. (Aja & Moya, 2008, p. 80)

In Spain, the way in which nationality is acquired is removed from the Constitution, given that Article 11 SC delegates this matter to the law. Consequently, to a certain point, recognition of the holding of rights is de-constitutionalized (Rubio, 2004, p. 32).

With respect to those countries that lack a reciprocity agreement with Spain, the alternative for a foreigner to be able to exercise a right to vote is to become Spanish and acquire Spanish nationality. Any nationals of Latin American countries, or of others with a specific link to Spain, only require two years' residence in order to be eligible for Spanish nationality, and may acquire Spanish nationality without losing their own (Arts. 22 and 23[b] CC). For nationals of countries such as China or Morocco who, as will be seen, represent relevant groups in Spain that do not enjoy any treaty recognizing a right to vote, nationality is acquired after ten years have elapsed, and foreigners must waive their nationality of origin. Moya suggests that this period be shortened, and that this measure also include a policy that allows one's nationality of origin to continue, in order to facilitate the political participation of these resident foreigners in Spain (Moya, 2010b, p. 496; also in favor of shortening the legal residence period for nationality purposes are Zapata-Barrero & Zaragoza, 2009, p. 147).

In Spain, as opposed to a lower annual increase of persons holding a record or residence card, the number of nationalized persons has notably increased—albeit at a lower annual growth rate in 2009 (2011 Strategic Plan, p. 37). The II Strategic Citizenship and Integration Plan shows the extent to which foreigners have accessed Spanish nationality between 2001–2009. As may be seen, there is a high number of Latin American persons (9,713 to 67,243 over this period), and Ecuador and Colombia are the main countries of origin; there is a smaller number of persons from Africa (2011 Strategic Plan, p. 38). This increase in acquired nationality is 75% due to a legal and continuous two-year residency in Spain, and in all other cases, can be attributed to other options: marriage, a legal and continuous ten-year residency, and being born in Spain. The 2009 data indicate that, in 75.8% of all cases, the reason to grant nationality was a legal and continuous two-year residency; 11.4% was due to marriage to a Spaniard; 6.7% had a legal and continuous ten-year residency; and 4.6% had been born in Spain.

The Strategic Plan includes a chart (II–7, "Performance of Spanish nationality granted by residency and nationality 2001–2009,") to reflect these data (2011 Strategic Plan, p. 38).

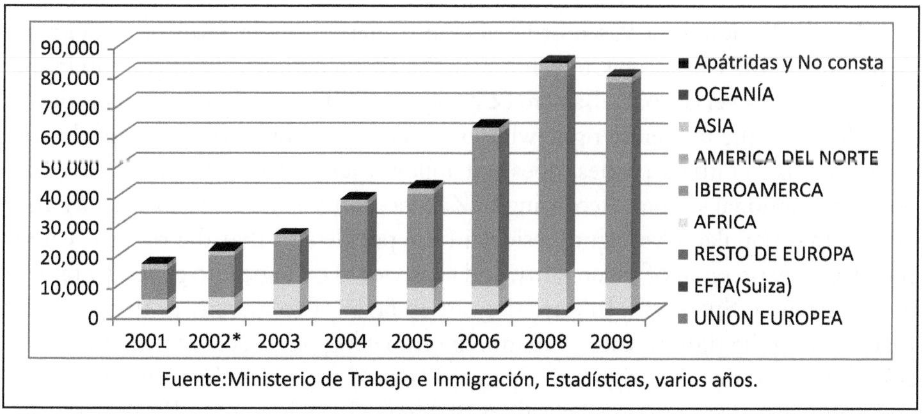

Figure 11.1. Citizenship by nationality and residency 2001–2009
Source: Ministry of Employment and Immigration

All these nationalized citizens may already exercise their right to vote, not only in local elections, but also in autonomous and national elections, without knowing how their positions have affected election results.

POLITICAL PARTIES AND IMMIGRANT VOTES

The first thing to be pointed out is that foreigners are unable to create political parties, though they may join already existing ones. Article 1 of Organic Act 6/2002, of June 27, on political parties provides that only Spaniards may create political parties. As far as promotion of the right to vote, left-wing parties have without a doubt played a more active role. Between 2002 and 2006, Izquierda Unida-Iniciativa per Catalunya Verds (IU) unsuccessfully tried, on various occasions, to introduce a law on the voting rights of immigrants. For IU, this recognition would have encouraged integration (Zapata-Barrero & Zaragoza, 2009, pp. 140, 157). Its proposal for an Organic Act that acknowledged the right of active and passive suffrage of foreign citizens in Spain (BOCG No. 207-I of October 7, 2005) included, for example, the possibility of foreigners enjoying one year's legal residency in Spain or an accreditation of permanent residency being able to vote. In the same terms, they again presented their claim in 2008 (OSG No. 62-1 of April 22, 2008).

In 2012, IU and ICV-EUiA, and CHA—referred to as the "plural left"—presented a motion to Congress, requesting a change in the Spanish Constitution to

> incorporate a recognition of the right to vote in favor of migrated persons in all elections (not just municipal ones), based on three years' residency, demanding that until this change is made more reciprocity conventions be signed and automatic access to a municipal election census be granted to all persons with a voting right acknowledged by any signed convention.

IU, Partido Nacionalista Vasco or Coalición Canaria were in favor of recognizing Article 6.1 of the European Convention on the Participation of Foreigners in Public Life at Local Level (Zapata-Barrero & Zaragoza, 2009, p. 155; see also footnote 6).

However, the moderate right-wing party Partido Popular (PP), one of the two main Spanish political parties, does not follow these lines and upholds the current constitutional system. According to Zapata-Barrero and Zaragoza's study, they believe that popular sovereignty resides in the people and that the right to vote is the utmost expression of sovereignty, and so it would be logical to generally reserve it exclusively to Spaniards. In turn, they are in favor of reciprocity as they consider that granting the right to vote to an immigrant belonging to a country that does not acknowledge the voting rights of Spaniards would be discriminatory for Spanish emigrants. Before the national elections of March 2008 Rajoy, the PP leader, made some public declarations in which he affirmed that he was against immigrant voting rights in municipal elections (Zapata-Barrero & Zaragoza, 2009, pp. 142, 155–156).

In 2006, while in power, Spain's other main political party—Partido Socialista Obrero Español (PSOE)—approved a parliamentary initiative with IU to guarantee the right to vote in municipal elections for legally resident foreigners. This motion (OGL No. 428, of September 11, 2006), filed on July 10, 2006, requested that government: (1) Negotiate and sign agreements or conventions with those countries having the largest number of legally resident nationals in Spain—particularly those with the closest historical, political, and cultural ties with Spain—in order for these nationals to be able to vote and be eligible in municipal elections in Spain further to Article 13.2 of the Constitution. (2) Demand the Council of State issue a report on the implementation of Article 13.2 of the Constitution for the purpose of foreigners residing in Spain being able to participate in municipal elections and, particularly, on the interpretation of the words "reciprocity criteria" referred to in said provision. (3) Provide the signature and ratification of the European Convention on the Participation of Foreigners in Public Life at Local Level, of February 5, 1992.

In any case, PSOE did in fact rule out the possibility of voting rights being acknowledged for these foreigners for the 2007 municipal elections, in which eventually only EU and Norwegian citizens were able to vote, as there were no other ratified bilateral treaties.

In July 2008, at its 37th Summit, PSOE announced its wish to promote immigrant voting rights and, certainly, during the last legislature they were in power (April 2008 to March 2011), bilateral conventions were signed with all countries whose nationals are now able to vote in Spanish municipal elections, except for Norway, with which a treaty was already signed in 1990 (Zapata-Barrero & Zaragoza, 2009, pp. 140–141, 143).

Increases in Foreign-Born Population in Spain

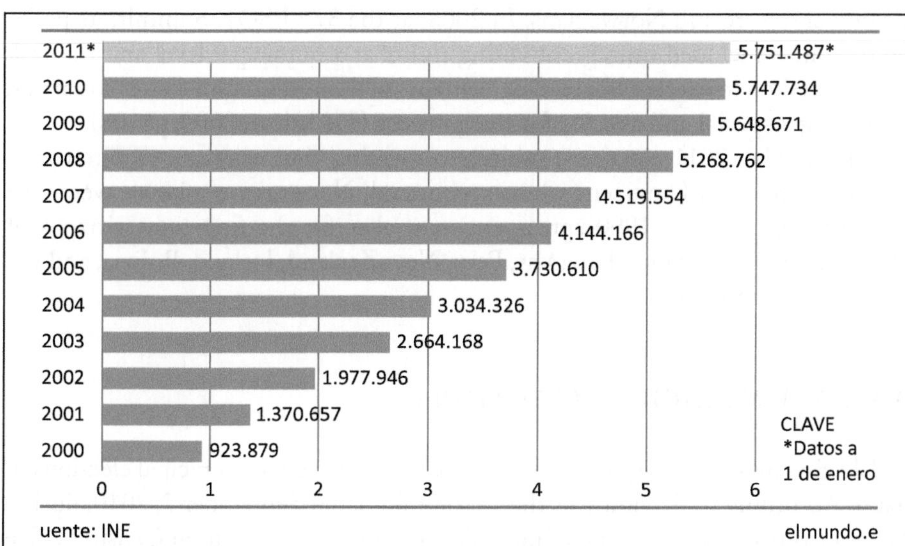

Figure 11.2. The Impact of Immigrant Votes on Local Elections

As already mentioned, Spain went from being an emigrant country to receiving a huge flow of immigrants. The country received 5 million new inhabitants in less than ten years, until they represented 12% of the population in 2011. Spain's population went from 39.8 million in 1998 to 47 million in 2010 (II Strategic Plan, 2011, pp. 26–27). In 2000, the National Statistics Institute (INE) accounted for 923,879 foreigners, whereas in 2010 this figure increased to 4,823,855. During the demographic boom, Spain was receiving an average of half a million foreigners each year. However, between 2010 and 2011, the municipal census only registered 3,753 more foreigners.

The first bilateral agreements to grant a right of suffrage in local elections to resident foreigners in Spain were signed with Denmark, the Netherlands, Sweden, and Norway in the early 1990's, when the Treaty of Maastricht (EU) had not yet come into force. Once this treaty came into force, all these countries except for Norway—which does not belong to the EU—were included in the legal regime applicable to EU citizens, who were acknowledged a right of active and passive suffrage in municipal elections. The legal regime applicable to EU citizens is gathered in Articles 176 and 177 LOREG, examined earlier. Norwegian citizens continued to vote in the elections thanks to the bilateral agreement signed with Spain.

In the municipal elections of 2007, with respect to those of 2003, the census considerably increased and, consequently, the number of eligible representatives. However, the vast majority of immigrants who contributed to this increased census and number of representatives were unable to vote or be elected (De Lucas, 2009, p. 108). In the 2007 elections, the only foreigners who were able to vote, apart from EU citizens, were still Norwegians. In 2008, at the 37th PSOE Summit, its political discourse included immigrant voting rights at a municipal level and the task was undertaken to execute bilateral agreements with immigration-issuer countries, appointing a special ambassador for this purpose (De Lucas, 2009, p. 108).

In the May 2011 elections, subject to meeting the necessary requirements, in addition to any EU citizens who so requested, Norwegian nationals were able to vote (subject to the 1990 agreement) and also, for the first time, citizens of Chile, Colombia, Ecuador, Paraguay, Peru, New Zealand, Iceland, Bolivia, and the Republic of Cabo Verde.

THE 2011 MUNICIPAL ELECTIONS

All EU citizens enjoy a right of active and passive suffrage in municipal elections in Spain. According to Section 1 of the Resolution dated September 7, 2010, during the months prior to the calling of municipal elections, the Electoral Census Office will address all European Union citizens residing in Spain with an individual notification in order to manifest their wish to exercise their right of active suffrage in

Spain. Any nationals of countries enjoying bilateral agreements must also apply for registration at the Electoral Census in order to be able to vote in Spain.

The Note Exchanges amounting to an Agreement between the Kingdom of Spain and the Republic of Chile, the Republic of Colombia, the Republic of Ecuador, the Republic of Paraguay, the Republic of Peru, Iceland, and New Zealand, on participation in municipal elections establish the following requirements to exercise a right of suffrage:

1. National citizens of the countries cited…may exercise a right of active (not passive) suffrage in municipal elections.
2. They must hold the relevant Spanish residence permit.
3. They must have resided in Spain, legally and without interruption, for at least five years prior to their application for registration in the electoral census.
4. They will exercise their right to vote in the Municipality where they ordinarily reside, and must be recorded in the local register.
5. Registration in the electoral census of resident foreigners in Spain will be essential in order to exercise a right of suffrage, and will be carried out at a party's request. This request will be presented at the Town Council where the individual is registered. The filing deadline will be determined for each election.

In turn, the Note Exchange Amounting to an Agreement between Spain and Norway provides as follows:

1. Norwegian citizens may only exercise a right of active suffrage in municipal elections.
2. They must hold the relevant Spanish residence permit.
3. They must have resided in Spain, legally and without interruption, for over three years.
4. They must be domiciled in the municipality where they are entitled to vote and must be recorded in their Municipal Register.
5. Registration on electoral lists of resident foreigners in Spain will be essential in order to exercise the right of suffrage and will always be carried out at a party's request. This request will be filed at the Town Council, whose Municipal Register includes the applicant. The filing deadline will be determined in each election.
6. Electoral lists of Norwegian citizens residing in Spain will only be drawn up when such elections are to be held. (ANNEX I to the Resolution dated October 15, 2010, issued by the Electoral Census Office, establishing the procedures and approving the application form for registration in the electoral census of residents in Spain of nationals belonging to countries with agreements for municipal elections. OSG of November 5, 2010)

The Electoral Census contains a record of those persons who meet the requirements to vote and who are not definitively or provisionally deprived of the right of suffrage. The Electoral Census of foreign residents in Spain (Censo electoral de extranjeros residentes en España, CERE), i.e., foreigners who were able to exercise their right of suffrage in the 2011 elections due to being recorded in the Electoral Census, "only" amounted to 473,748 foreigners. Of relevance is the fact that for the 2007 municipal elections, CERE registered 318,571 so, despite the signature of new conventions, the census did not increase substantially in 2011 either. This number of registered persons (473,748) is also surprising if compared to the statistics of citizens of countries who are in fact granted a right to vote in Spain.

According to INE statistics (http://www.ine.es/jaxi/tabla.do), in 2011 there were 2,395,358 citizens in Spain from 27 EU countries; 19,621 Norwegians; 606 New Zealanders; 273,176 Colombians; 41,939 Chilean nationals; 87,906 Paraguayan nationals; 360,710 Ecuadorian nationals; 132,552 Peruvians; 1,391 Icelandic nationals; 199,080 Bolivians; and 3,341 Cabo Verde nationals. There was a total of 52,117 persons registered to vote, originally from Norway, New Zealand, Colombia, Chile, Paraguay, Ecuador, Peru, Iceland, Bolivia, and Cabo Verde, of the more than 350,000 that were eligible to do so (please note that registration at the Electoral Census is not automatic and depends on an individual application, requiring certain years of residency in order to vote). All EU citizens who were registered to vote did so by approximately 400,000.

As may be seen, non-Community foreigners showed less interest in municipal elections than Community foreigners (Local Charter, 2011, pp. 12 and 13). Romanians and British nationals represented nearly half the number of foreign votes, of whom 103,355 and 102,633 were respectively registered. As regards Germans (47,031), Italians (40,277), and French nationals (32,949), all citizens of EU member states, a large number was registered. The Ecuadorian colony represented the sixth largest group of voters and the largest non-Community group, with over 25,000 registered persons. Next came the Portuguese, Bulgarian nationals, the Dutch, or Belgians, all EU members and all of them, except for the Belgians, representing more than 10,000 electors. The 33 New Zealanders, 28 Icelandic nationals, or 22 Cabo Verde citizens were merely testimonial (Local Charter, 2011, p. 12).

Although the participation of EU country citizens was greater than that of non-Community foreigners, this participation, as seen, was not very high. In fact, the census index of these Community foreigners has still been low since the 1999 elections (see Mendez Lago, 2010, pp. 519–523). In 1999, the first elections in which Community foreigners were able to vote, along with Norwegian citizens, 21% of the total of potential voters went to the polls, whereas the average participation in various elections held in Spain since the Spanish Transition to Democracy (Transición) until 2007 was 65%. And although the low participation levels in

1999 were attributed to the novelty of the right and insufficient information provided to these groups on their new rights, in 2003 the figure representing those who went to the polls was only slightly higher than that of 1999, whereas in 2007 these figures only represented 25%. Mendez Lago indicates that this fact may have a significant effect on the manner in which these groups channel their preferences or demands within the political system, the absence of channeling devices, and the behavior of politicians (Mendez Lago, 2010, pp. 517–519, 523).

In turn, in order to bring the weight of foreign voting rights into context, it is interesting to compare the CERE data of registered voters for the 2011 elections against the data of foreigners holding a registration certificate or current residence card in Spain at March 31, 2011. At the time there were 5,056,256 foreigners in Spain in this situation. Evidently, foreign nationality was varied and so many do not belong to nationalities that are eligible to vote. On the other hand, the global figure of foreigners in Spain according to the Municipal Register—the document accrediting one's residency and ordinary address in which illegal foreigners are also recorded—was 5,751,487. As a result, the percentage of foreign voters in Spain is small when compared to the global number of foreigners who legally or illegally reside in Spain.

In turn, General Regime data—the legal regime applicable to third country nationals who legally reside unless they are subject to the Community Regime—give us an idea of which communities in Spain are excluded from the right to vote:

Table 11.1. Foreigners under the General Regime

Main Nationalities

	10-31-2011		Change (%) Quarterly: with respect to 12-31-2010	Change (%) Year-to-year: with respect to 03-31-2010
Total	2,620,359	100.00%	3.78	1.83
Morocco	777,278	29.67%	2.57	4.32
Ecuador	380,910	14.54%	3.03	-7.16
Colombia	227,426	8.68%	2.42	-4.55
China	160,636	6.13%	4.39	5.91
Bolivia	130,270	4.97%	10.14	11.93
Peru	124,034	4.74%	1.95	-2.88
Ukraine	69,429	2.65%	4.02	1.06
Argentina	60,358	2.30%	5.40	-3.89
Dominican Rep.	59,783	2.28%	3.04	0.88
Pakistan	54,435	2.08%	5.41	20.14
Algeria	53,240	2.03%	2.71	5.57

(Continued)

	10-31-2011		Change (%) Quarterly: with respect to 12-31-2010	Change (%) Year-to-year: with respect to 03-31-2010
Senegal	44,206	1.69%	5.40	10.84
Brazil	32,167	1.23%	5.46	1.18
Paraguay	29,810	1.14%	10.06	12.74
Cuba	29,729	1.13%	2.29	-0.70
Other Countries	385,721	14.74%	5.22	4.70
Stateless	927	—	1.31	0.76

As may be seen, the largest community of foreigners belonging to the General Regime represents Moroccans, who do not hold voting rights in Spain. Nor do the Chinese, who are the fourth most representative nationality amongst ordinary regime foreigners in Spain. Furthermore, these foreigners are nearly all of voting age, given that only slightly more than 17% of General Regime foreigners are under sixteen (data on those under eighteen—the voting age—are not available).

THE REASON FOR A LOW PARTICIPATION OF FOREIGNERS WITH A RIGHT TO VOTE

We have selected an extract of a press article that we consider indicative of what may be happening in Spain. It was published in *El Periódico de Extremadura* (March 7, 2011) and explains why foreigners in this territory did not vote on the municipal elections:

> Only 20% of foreigners apply to vote in municipal elections in Extremadura. Just 1,300 of the 14,400 citizens of other nationalities with a right of suffrage are registered in the electoral census. Foreign citizens residing in Extremadura are hardly enthusiastic about the autonomous and municipal elections of 22 May. Rather, their participation will be low. (…) This registration index at the Electoral Census is well below the response obtained at a national level. In all of Spain, 465,661 foreign citizens have fulfilled this prior step, representing 43% of the total.
>
> "There are various reasons for this," says Antonio Tejeda, lawyer and general secretary of the Federation of Immigrant Associations in Extremadura. "There is little political interest in the electoral participation of this citizen group" he claims. "Political parties do not regard them as a voting group with relevant or determining effects on results." This explanation is backed up by two revealing facts, in his opinion. On the one hand, "a mediocre campaign in the media launched both institutionally and at party level to inform foreign citizens of their voting rights and of the steps they need to complete. Does anybody remember

> any advertising campaign launched by the government to call these citizens to the polls?" Furthermore, Antonio Tejeda refers to the red-tape involved: "The right of suffrage should be universal and egalitarian. But foreign citizens are required to hold a specific nationality and to previously register, and are given little time and information to be able to meet these requirements and thus exercise this right."

In theory, some authors explain this scarce participation precisely on the grounds of this red-tape that slows down voter registration. There is also a lack of information, a lukewarm attitude from the government (which does not encourage or develop the registration of foreigners in electoral registers—rendering a voting campaign useless), and unawareness, particularly by non-Community nationals, of the conditions in which to exercise their voting rights (Ortega, 2011, p. 33). The Spanish municipal electoral system has also been referred to as inflexible given that lists are closed and it is also necessary to be registered at the electoral census. Additionally, municipalities are not territorial levels with greater competences or more financial strength, nor are they more politically attractive in electoral debates (municipal elections are held along with autonomous elections). Furthermore, the intensity of the link between foreigners and their social networks is essential to participation (Moya, 2010a, pp. 77–78). All of these theoretical arguments coincide with the opinion of immigrant representatives. Raúl Jiménez, spokesman of the Spanish Ecuadorian Rumiñahui Association, with respect to the 2011 elections, pointed out that a "first step" had been made and that the group's target was for the participation process to be strengthened in the future until reaching "full participation." A disproportion between the number of Community and non-Community foreigners registered at the electoral census, according to Rumiñahui's representative, could be due to "various factors, such as insufficient information from the institutions in charge [including town councils]," but also the fact that Latin Americans, specifically Ecuadorians, "have not received a message from their politicians, the ones most interested in this process, because it is practically non-existent."

Jiménez criticized the fact that the only message these citizens receive "daily" from some "extreme right-wing sectors" is that they are responsible for the economic crisis, insecurity, or violence against women. Consequently, he asked political parties to believe in the contribution of immigrant votes to their society of residence (Federación Española de Municipios y Provincias, Carta Local, 2011, p. 13). The Rumiñahui representative manifested his awareness of the need to work with his own people, given that the non-credibility of politicians was also due to the lack of stability in his country of origin. "They need to be eager again and to know that their vote counts, particularly to overrule any negative manifestos broadcast by certain sectors," and added that the possibility of being able to vote would, to a large extent, endorse the dual integration process between the host country and those who have decided to establish and start a new life (Federación Española de Municipios y Provincias, Carta Local, 2011, pp. 13–14).

For the president of FEDROM (Federación de Asociaciones de Rumanos de España, Federation of Romanian Associations in Spain), the Romanian community was the largest and the most willing to participate, which

> would reflect, on the one hand, 'a relative action on the part of institutions and Spanish politicians' and greater information and flexibility in the registration of these citizens but, above all, the positioning of social leaders and the movement of associations that are 'spurring' this process. (Federación Española de Municipios y Provincias, Carta Local, 2011, p. 13)

Regarding the presence of foreign candidates in electoral lists, the President of FEDROM considered that "more are needed" in places where they may be actually elected. The political discourse was to include foreign citizens in their lists, but Raúl Jiménez, spokesman of Rumiñahui, like the Romanian representative, doubted that this would take place to a large extent and, if so, that the relevant positions would have a small chance of being elected (Federación Española de Municipios y Provincias, Carta Local, 2011, p. 14).

In the 2007 elections, where only EU citizens and Norwegians were able to vote, two mayors and 85 councilors in Spain's 8,112 town councils were foreign, according to the Register of Local Entities of the Ministry of Territorial Policy, which collected the data of the 68,298 councilors elected in the 2007 polls and the 8,416 town majors who held a post in the town councils (Report of the Press Cabinet of the Ministry of Territorial Policy on the Nationality of Councilors in Spanish Municipalities).

In any case, as regards foreign participation in local elections in Spain, certainly some of these Community and non-Community immigrants are still not aware of the power they could wield in some municipalities if they were to vote. By province, Alicante had the largest number of registered foreigners for the 2011 elections; over 77,000 persons registered to vote there. Both Madrid, with over 67,000, and Barcelona, with more than 40,000, gathered a large number of potential voters "though far in importance, in relative terms, from the representative number in Alicante." Málaga and Valencia also represented a good example of foreign participation in local elections: the former reached nearly 40,000 registered persons and the latter exceeded 23,000. In the Balearic Islands, another attractive area for community residents, 22,335 voters were registered (Federación Española de Municipios y Provincias, Carta Local, 2011 p. 12).

An example of the foregoing may be found in Mendez Lago's study of the 1999 and 2007 elections (we have not found similar studies for the 2011 election). For this author, the real impact of foreign voters in electoral results "could be measured as the proportion of the electorate to which they belong and their participation rates." For Mendez Lago, the percentage of municipalities with a possibly greater influence of foreign voters could be those where foreign voters represent 5% or more of the total electorate. This said, in 1999 there were 41 municipalities of this type (0.5% of the total), whereas in 2007 there were 286 (3.5% of the total), and in approximately 60 of these the percentage of foreign voters was equal to or greater than 15% (Mendez Lago, 2010, pp. 519, 521).

As to the elections of 2011, we have no similar studies to the Mendez Lago's for the whole country. At a regional level, according to Ortega's study on the Autonomous Community of Valencia, for example, the addition of new voters (the author believed that agreements with Argentina and Venezuela would materialize before the 2011 elections) could change the electoral map in four large municipalities of the Valencian Community (Castellón, Benidorm, Elche, or Torrent), and in another four municipalities both Community and non-Community foreigners voting for the first time in the 2011 elections could decide on at least half the councilors assigned to their local corporations (Ortega, 2011, p. 35).

Anyway, the influence of foreign voters on the 2011 municipal elections could not be felt. Their participation in the municipal elections was very low and the vote was dispersed throughout the territory. These low rates of participation of foreigners with a right to vote in the 2011 municipal elections have been explained partially as a consequence of the existing prerequisite for foreigners to register previously and individually in a foreign voters register in order to be allowed to vote (Moya & Viñas, 2011, pp. 229, 235–244).

Leaving this matter aside, Morales, Anduiza, Rodríguez, and San Martín (2010) have reached the conclusion that the national origin of immigrants may be an important factor "to determine the participation differential in relation to native groups," (Morales et al., 2010, pp. 533–534) but after ascertaining that the Turks are well-integrated in the political process in Amsterdam and Brussels, but not in Berlin, they conclude that it is likely that each immigrant group's interaction with the context of each host country will be more important than a foreigner's origin. If this is so, Spain's social and political context could explain the low political participation of foreigners in Spain. For these authors, the social and political context determines "integration policies, guidelines for ethnic segregation and concentration, including political activity from established players and political parties" (Morales et al., 2010, pp. 533–534).

These authors conducted a study on 1,044 persons in Barcelona and 1,192 in Madrid, dividing the groups into people from the Andes region (a mixed group of Colombians, Bolivians, and Peruvians), Ecuadorians, Moroccans, and natives (at the time when only Spaniards, Norwegians, and EU members could vote). When asked about their electoral intent if they were able to vote, they discovered that the gap between participation levels of immigrants and natives was quite wide, that Ecuadorians were less keen on voting than other people from the Andes region, that group activity depended on the election being held, that Moroccans tended to be more active in Madrid than in Barcelona, and that participation rates would be somewhat higher in Madrid, where participation levels in the 2007 local elections in general were greater than in Barcelona (no such a study has been made in relation to the 2011 local elections).

It is interesting to note that Ecuadorians, the most recent immigrant group, were the least keen on voting as opposed to Moroccans, who were the most impoverished nationals. Furthermore, although most of the immigrant groups would tend to vote PSOE (centre-left), Latin Americans had opposing party preferences in Madrid governed by the PP, and in Barcelona governed by left-wing parties and coalitions since the first elections held in 1979. Whereas in Barcelona there would be a small vote for the PP, in Madrid PP votes would be much higher (Morales et al., 2010, pp. 545–549). When examining another type of political participation, they saw that the local context in Madrid apparently reduced immigrant political activity when compared to Barcelona—particularly in the case of Moroccans—but also gave rise to greater inequality in political activity due to the fact that the native population is generally more active in Madrid than in Barcelona (p. 553). The authors' conclusion is that the relevance of the local context is clear in relation to foreign political participation (p. 553).

OTHER FORMS OF IMMIGRANT POLITICAL PARTICIPATION AT A LOCAL LEVEL

Article 6 LODLEIS is entitled "Public Participation." Article 6.2 recognizes in favor of all resident foreigners registered in a municipality (irrespective of nationality and, apparently, whether or not a right of suffrage is recognized in municipal elections, subject to exceptions) any relevant rights foreseen in legislation on local regime bases, and may be heard in any matters that affect them, as provided in applicable regulations. Furthermore, Article 6.3 orders town councils to include in the local register and keep up to date any information on foreigners residing in each municipality. Pursuant to Article 15 of Act 7/1985, of April 2, regulating Local Regime Bases (Ley 7/1985, April 2, Reguladora de las Bases del Régimen Local [LBRL]), any person living in Spain is obliged to register in the census and this includes, albeit not expressly foreseen in the act, any illegal foreigners. The municipal census is an administrative register where all municipality residents are recorded (Article 16. 1 LBRL).

According to the Council of State, Article 6.2 LODLEIS extends all of the public participation rights entrusted to residents by Article 18 LBRL to any resident and registered foreigner (Consejo de Estado, 2009, p. 37). In this regard, immigrants are joining general public participation devices, with unequal results, according to Moya (Moya, 2010b, p. 497).

Article 18.1 LBRL defines resident rights and duties:

a. To vote and be eligible according to the provisions of electoral laws.
b. To participate in municipal management in accordance with the provisions established by law and, if applicable, when the voluntary collaboration of residents is promoted by municipal government and administration bodies.

c. (…)
d. To encourage, through economic and personal contributions foreseen by law, the execution of municipal competences.
e. To be informed, subject to a prior reasoned request, and to address requests to the municipal Administration in relation to all proceedings and municipal documentation, according to the provisions of Article 105 SC.
f. To request a popular consultation in the terms foreseen in the Act.
g. (…)
h. To exercise a citizen's initiative, in the terms foreseen in Article 70 bis.
i. Any other rights and duties foreseen by law.

As indicated by the Council of State in its Report, it would strictly seem that Article 6.2 LODLEIS would refer to the public participation foreseen in Article 23 SC; this would be a hindrance, given that Article 13.2 SC provides that only Spaniards may hold the rights acknowledged in Article 23 (without prejudice to provisions on active and passive suffrage in municipal elections). However, this does not seem to raise any difficulty for the Council of State, which declares that the law has "interpreted these articles in line with an expansion and greater virtuality of fundamental human rights" (Consejo de Estado, 2009, p. 37). Solanes also seems to lean in favor of a broad interpretation of this article (Solanes, 2008, p. 92).

For Moya, "although the participation of foreign residents in citizen consultations and other citizen participation devices" may contradict Article 13.2 SC, if interpreted restrictively, its legitimacy could certainly be claimed based on the same arguments used by the Spanish Constitutional Court in Declaration 1/1992. The Constitutional Court made a difference between election-based representative sovereign bodies and town councils, which were not sovereign political bodies, which was why municipal consultations were not linked to sovereignty and foreigners were also eligible to take part. Apart from consultations, says Moya, these are not binding and so no sovereignty component would be affected, even if the Court's theory is not upheld "about the probable administrative nature of municipal governments" (Moya, 2010b, p. 490).

As regards citizen consultations, Article 23 of Organic Regulations on Citizen Participation of the City Council of Madrid, dated May 31, 2004 (Official Gazette of the Autonomous Community of Madrid 22/06/2004 No. 147, pp. 80–90) provides that

> the Mayor, if agreed by an absolute majority of the Plenary Meeting and further to the provisions of Article 71 of Act 7/1985, of 2 April, regulating Local Regime Bases, and Article 25 of Act 2/2003, of 11 March, on Local Administration in the Community of Madrid, may present to citizen consultation any matters within the municipality's competence that are particularly relevant for the interests of the municipality's residents, except for those related to the Local Tax Authorities.

However, as opposed to the broad interpretation proposed by Solanes, Article 24 of this Act adds that a citizen consultation, in any case, will contemplate the right to be consulted of any citizen included in the Electoral Census, which would seem to exclude those foreigners without a right of active suffrage from participation in Madrid's citizen consultations. On the other hand, in Barcelona, Article 35 of Act 22/1998, of December 29, on the Barcelona Municipal Charter, provides that "the City Council and each one of its districts may request their citizens' opinion in matters within their competence by means of a citizen consultation which, further to applicable legislation," should uphold the right of every registered person in the municipal census to be consulted.

In relation to citizen initiatives, Article 70 bis 2 of LBRL, applicable to all local entities, reserves them in favor of those residents with a right of active suffrage only.

All residents enjoying a right of active suffrage in municipal elections may exercise a citizen initiative, presenting proposed agreements, steps, or draft regulations in municipal competence matters. These initiatives should be endorsed by at least the following percentage of municipality residents:

a. Up to 5,000 inhabitants: 20%
b. Between 5,001 and 20,000 inhabitants: 15%
c. As of 20,001 inhabitants: 10%

These initiatives will be subjected to discussion and voting at a Plenary Meeting, without prejudice to being resolved by a competent body in the matter. Consequently, in Madrid all initiatives must be endorsed by 10% of all residents, who may include those foreigners with a recognized right to vote in Spain (see Article 19 Organic Regulations on Citizen Participation of the City Council of Madrid, of May 31, 2004 [Reglamento Orgánico de Participación Ciudadana del Ayuntamiento de Madrid {ROPC} de 31 de mayo de 2004]).

On the other hand, a foreigner has a right to be heard in municipal plenary meetings. In order to examine how this right is articulated, the city council regulations need to be examined. Solanes (2008) has pointed out that this right should be interpreted not as "a political participation right entailing an election or representation process strictly within the scope of Articles 13.2 and 23 SC," but rather as "a citizen participation right of registered resident foreigners" (Solanes, 2008, p. 93). The right to be heard in plenary meetings is exercised through associations (Articles 227 and 228 of Royal Decree 2568/1986, of November 28, approving Regulations on the organisation, operation, and legal regime of Local Entities). In this regard, the ROPC foresees participation both in District Plenary Meetings and in District Municipal Boards and City Council Plenary Meetings, through the associations recorded at the Registry of Citizen Entities of the City Council of Madrid (Arts. 16, 17, and 18). This is consistent with Article 24 of Act 2/2003, of March 11, on Local Administration in the Community of Madrid. Please note that all immigrants, including illegal ones, hold a right of association, as well as a right to hold meetings and demonstrations, further to what the Constitutional Court established in Judgment no. 236/2007, of November 7, and as recognized in Articles 7 and 8 LODLEIS, reformed after Organic Act 2/2009, of December 11, was approved in order to adjust the law to the decision of the Constitutional Court.

The problem this raises is the lack of electoral standing for these associations, not only immigrant associations, and, on the other hand, the fact that often immigrant associations provide services financed with public funds, which could weaken their claims and endanger their ability to influence politics by depending on the administration for their services (Moya, 2010b, pp. 481, 494). Morales et al., state that "in Barcelona, the selection of association representatives for participation bodies is much more transparent and open—generally executed through elections held at the relevant associations—than in Madrid," except for "Foro Madrid" and "Mesas de Diálogo y Convivencia" (Dialogue and Cohabitation Panels) analyzed below (Morales, et al., 2010, p. 540).

Apart from these public participation devices, recognized by the LBRL in favor of all residents, municipalities have been creating consultation bodies and procedures which, according to Moya, intend to "reinforce the immigrated community's position and interests in political and public deliberation processes (empowerment)," while also attempting to identify "any social spokespersons between the immigrated community and those with whom it interacts" (Moya, 2010b, p. 497).

In Madrid, the ROPC that promotes and channels citizen participation has given rise to "Foro Madrid de Diálogo y Convivencia" (Madrid Forum for Dialogue and Cohabitation) and "Mesas de Diálogo y Convivencia Distritales" (District Panels for Dialogue and Cohabitation). Foro Madrid was incorporated on March 16, 2007 for its first mandate, and on October 21, 2011 for its second mandate. Foro Madrid is an Immigration Sector Council, ascribed to the Family and Social Services Department, which advises the city council on social intercultural coexistence, diversity, and migrations, and raises proposals in these matters for the entire municipality.

Organic Regulations on Citizen Participation generically name as "Sector Councils" any permanent bodies for sector participation, and define them as consultative participation bodies that channel the participation of residents and their associations in large sectors or areas of municipal activity. All sector councils are ascribed to various government departments, which hold competences within the scope of these participation bodies. A lack of transparency has been criticized in election of the members of sector councils in this matter (Morales, González, & Jorba, 2009, p. 120).

Foro Madrid consists of representatives of the Public Administration, immigrant associations, immigration support entities, social organizations, and representatives of district territorial councils. Foro Madrid is a purely consultative body and meets only once each quarter. The Forum has been assigned district dialogue and cohabitation panels. All panels are open to resident participation, irrespective of origin, whether individually or on behalf of entities. They gather citizen proposals related to improved operation of municipal services and activity in the district, informing the Forum Plenary Meeting and District Territorial Council. Any persons over 16 who are registered in the district may participate.

Although this is positive, Morales, González, and Jorba (2009) consider that devices to encourage citizen participation in Madrid have little impact on public policy design and that associations are not really involved in the management of municipal matters (pp. 120, 136). Moya points out that the creation of consultation bodies and procedures at a municipal level was often used as a formula to remedy the absence of democratically elected immigrant representatives. We agree with Moya in that their existence should act more as a complement rather than as an alternative or to replace direct participation devices, given that without the latter any alternative devices

> will eventually acquire excessive size, importance and apparent representation which, to a large extent, are false, given that if legitimate representation has not been confirmed by any democratic election process the real importance of these social spokespersons will be eventually exaggerated just because there are no others with whom to discuss political and coexistence issues, etc. (Moya, 2010b, pp. 497–498)

REFERENCES

Aja, E. (2012). *Inmigración y democracia*. Madrid: Alianza Editorial.

Aja, E., & Moya, D. (2008). El derecho de sufragio de los extranjeros residentes. In E. Aja, J. Arango, & J. Oliver (Eds.), *La inmigración en la encrucijada, Anuario de la Inmigración en España* (pp. 64 ff). Barcelona: CIDOB Ediciones.

Caamaño Domínguez, F. (2004). De la igualdad como legalidad a la igualdad como dignidad: Reflexiones en clave constitucional, sobre una sociedad decente. Extranjería e Inmigración, Actas de las IX Jornadas de la Asociación de Letrados del Tribunal Constitucional (pp. 95 ff). Madrid: Tribunal Constitucional y Centro de Estudios Políticos y Constitucionales.

Consejo de Estado. (2009, February). Informe del Consejo de Estado Sobre Las Propuestas de Modificación del Régimen Electoral General, de 24 de febrero de 2009. Retrieved from http://www.consejo-estado.es/pdf/REGIMEN-ELECTORAL.pdf

De Lucas, J. (2006). La ciudadanía basada en la residencia y el ejercicio de los derechos políticos de los inmigrantes. Cuadernos electrónicos de filosofía del derecho (No. 13). Retrieved from http://www.uv.es/cefd/13/delucas.pdf

De Lucas, J. (2009). El enfoque de la ciudadanía: Cuestiones normativas. In R. Zapata-Barrero (Ed.), *Políticas y gobernabilidad de la inmigración en España* (pp. 93 ff). Barcelona: Ariel.

Federacion Española de Municipios y Provincias. (2011). Extranjeros con voz y voto. Carta Local, Revista de la Federación Española de Municipios y Provincias (No. 236). Madrid: Editorial MIC.

Mendez Lago, M. (2010). La participación de los extranjeros comunitarios en las elecciones municipales en España: 1999, 2003 y 2007. In D. Moya Malapeira & A. Vinas Ferrer (Eds.), *Sufragio y participación política de los extranjeros extracomunitarios en Europa* (pp. 503 ff). Barcelona: Fundació Carles Pi i Sunyer.

Morales, L., Anduiza, E., Rodríguez, E., & San Martín, J. (2010). La participación política de los inmigrantes en Barcelona y Madrid: Comportamiento electoral y acción política. In D. Moya Malapeira & A. Viñas Ferrer (Eds.), *Sufragio y participación política de los extranjeros extracomunitarios en Europa* (pp. 531 ff). Barcelona: Fundació Carles Pi i Sunyer.

Morales, L., González, A., & Jorba, L. (2009). Políticas de incorporación y la gestión del asociacionismo de la población de origen inmigrante a nivel local. In R. Zapara-Barreiro (Ed.), *Políticas y gobernabilidad de la inmigración en* España (pp. 113 ff). Barcelona: Ariel.

Moya Malapeira, D. (2010a). Introducción. In D. Moya Malapeira & A. Viñas Ferrer (Ed.), *Sufragio y participación política de los extranjeros extracomunitarios en Europa* (pp. 21 ff). Barcelona: Fundació Carles Pi i Sunyer.

Moya Malapeira, D. (2010b). Regulación del derecho de sufragio de los extranjeros en España y mecanismos alternativos de participación política. In D. Moya Malapeira & A. Viñas Ferrer (Eds.), *Sufragio y participación política de los extranjeros extracomunitarios en Europa* (pp. 461 ff). Barcelona: Fundació Carles Pi i Sunyer.

Moya Malapeira, D., & Viñas, A. (2011): El sufragio de los extranjeros en las elecciones municipales de 2011 en España, *Anuario de la Inmigración en España*, pp. 215–262.

Ortega Giménez, A. (2011). El derecho al voto de los ciudadanos extracomunitarios en las próximas elecciones municipales españolas de 2011. *Estudios de Progreso, Fundación Alternativas, 60*, 1 ff.

Pomed Sanchez, L. (2004). Algunas consideraciones sobre la situación actual del derecho de inmigración en España. Extranjería e Inmigración, Actas de las IX Jornadas de la Asociación de Letrados del Tribunal Constitucional (pp. 53 ff). Madrid: Tribunal Constitucional y Centro de Estudios Políticos y Constitucionales.

Presno Linera, M. A. (2009). El voto de los extranjeros en España y el voto de los españoles residentes en el extranjero. A propósito del informe del Consejo de Estado sobre las propuestas de modificación del régimen electoral general. *Revista Española de Derecho Constitucional, 87*, 183 ff.

Rubio Marín, R. (2004). La inclusión del inmigrante: un reto para las democracias constitucionales. Extranjería e Inmigración, Actas de las IX Jornadas de la Asociación de Letrados del Tribunal Constitucional (pp. 11 ff). Madrid: Tribunal Constitucional y Centro de Estudios Políticos y Constitucionales.

Santolaya, P., & Díaz Crego, M. (2008). *El sufragio de los extranjeros: Un estudio de derecho comparado.* Madrid: Centro de Estudios Políticos y Constitucionales.

Santolaya, P., & Revenga Sánchez, M. (2007). *Nacionalidad, Extranjería y Derecho de Sufragio.* Madrid: Centro de Estudios Políticos y Constitucionales.

Secretaría de Estado e Inmigración y Emigración, Dirección General de Integración de los Inmigrantes. (2011, September). II Plan Estratégico de Ciudadanía e Integración (2011–2014). Retrieved from http://extranjeros.empleo.gob.es/es/IntegracionRetorno/Plan_estrategico2011/pdf/PECI-2011-2014.pdf

Solanes Corella, A. (2008). La participación política de las personas inmigrantes: cuestiones para el debate. *Derechos y Libertades, 18*, 67 ff.

Zapata-Barrero, R., & Zaragoza, J. (2009). La gestión del derecho de voto de los inmigrantes en España. In R. Zapata-Barrero (Ed.), *Políticas y gobernabilidad de la inmigración en España* (pp. 139 ff). Barcelona: Ariel.

Comparative Notes on Political Participation of Immigrants in the United States and Spain

XÓCHITL BADA,
UNIVERSITY OF ILLINOIS AT CHICAGO
CARMEN NAVARRO,
AUTONOMOUS UNIVERSITY OF MADRID
SUSANA SÁNCHEZ FERRO,
AUTONOMOUS UNIVERSITY OF MADRID

Political participation is essential to democracy. Traditionally, political rights were linked to nationality. However, the migratory phenomenon has led to certain changes. Political participation of immigrants in their host country is fundamental for their social integration. Naturalization of immigrants has increased in the U.S. and Spain, but naturalization alone is not enough to achieve this aim of social integration. On the one hand, it is not always easy to acquire the nationality of the host country. In Spain, for example, the law requires ten year's, residence and foreigners must waive their nationality of origin (save nationals of Latin American countries and nationals of other countries with a special link to Spain, who may acquire the Spanish nationality after two years' residence without losing their own nationality). On the other hand, as the work of Bada reflects, naturalization alone is not enough to trigger civic engagement and political participation.

There is a consensus in the three preceding chapters that the intensity of the link between foreigners and their social network is an essential element when it comes to the political participation of immigrants. The social and political context of the host country also plays an important role in this issue. In Spain, for example, some foreigners have been given the right to vote and the right of passive suffrage in local elections (when there is a treaty with the countries of origin and there is reciprocity as to the recognition of this right to Spanish immigrants living in those countries). However, the level of participation of foreigners in these elections has been low. This has been explained as a consequence of the bureaucracy that is involved in the process, the lack of information that the immigrants suffer, and low engagement of social leaders and immigrant associations to foster this participation. The disinterest in politics of the Spanish society could also explain those low levels of participation. In the same way, Spain has the lowest quotas of configuration of associations in its geographical environment, and the immigrant associative fabric in Spain is also weak. In fact, as a consequence of the different political and social context, the structure of the associations and their interaction with the public authorities as well as their participation in the decision-making process is different in the U.S. and Spain.

For example, in Madrid, the direct involvement of immigrant associations in co-development projects in sending countries has only slowly grown. Between 2004 and 2009, immigrant associations in Madrid only channeled 13% of all co-development projects for sending countries that were subsidized with public funds by Madrid's municipal government. Unlike what has been revealed from Mexican immigrant hometown associations located in Chicago—whose membership organizes fundraisers to finance projects in communities of origin with matching funds from Mexico's public funds for development—immigrant associations in Madrid are not very engaged in fundraising for co-development and mostly depend on public funds from Madrid's municipality to support their transnational agendas.

In Spain, the immigration phenomenon is relatively new. It began in the late 1990s, and in the last few years the flow of immigrants has been very intense. Of Madrid's population in 2011, 16.92% were foreigners (557,117). In addition, there were 173,206 naturalized citizens. So 22.18% of Madrid's population is from foreign origin. In the years 2011 and 2012, the number of registered immigrants had dropped to 0.8% in 2012.

In Chicago, Mexican immigration has been constantly increasing. Today there are almost 700,000 Mexican immigrants in Chicago, and more than 2 million Latinos in Illinois (79% of Mexican descent). As immigration is quite recent in Spain, the majority of immigrant associations in Madrid have been recently created (from 2005 onwards). On the contrary, migrant-led Mexican organizations in the U.S. are not a new phenomenon. In fact, in the 1920s, Mexican immigrants in Chicago already formed mutual aid organizations to help new immigrants settle into their new environment. In 2006, there were massive mobilizations demanding dignity and respect for all undocumented workers where millions of Latinos and non-Latino immigrants marched. The mobilization of the immigrants was a result of the long tradition of organizing by migrant-led grassroots organizations. In Spain, the number of immigrant associations is few, with low member numbers, and the associative immigrant movement is weak. This could be explained by the Spanish context, which does not encourage the creation of associations and the organization of immigrant interests, but also because it is a phenomenon that is ongoing and in the process of consolidation.

In the U.S., the integration of immigrants has been left to civic society and non-profit grassroots. There is no national immigrant integration plan that encourages people to become civically engaged after they become legal permanent residents or naturalized U.S. citizens. Hometown associations, faith-based initiatives, schools, and worker centers in Chicago have become important outlets to foster increased civic engagement among Latinos in the city. Chicago-based Latino immigrants are actively engaged in their churches, and this motivates them to become engaged in different local issues. The participation of Latinos in schools still lags behind, but Latino parents are becoming more involved, since U.S. nationality is not required to participate in Local School Councils. This a clear benefit to Latino students, who improve their performance when parents get involved in their education. The presence of Latinos has also increased in labor unions, and there are examples of Latino-led working centers, which provide advocacy and training tools for workers in precarious labor conditions. Migrant-led hometown associations offer a particular example in which Latinos become civically engaged with their communities. They serve as a channel to solve the most important problems that their localities are facing—both in Chicago and in their country of origin.

In Spain, the mechanisms of participation are of a top-down character. Since 2007, the Labor Ministry has approved Strategic Plans of Citizenship and Integration to promote the integration of immigrants into Spanish society. Public authorities have established deliberative forums in which the associative immigrant movement interacts with the social fabric. At a local level, Madrid's government has established a great number of organizations of participation and has created channels of participation, but the authorities have decided what interests are present at those organizations and how the representation is organized. Public administrations need interlocutors amongst the immigrant collectives. These collectives are badly structured; public authorities have promoted the associative movement among immigrants, but also regulated it. Moreover, associations in Spain are highly dependent on public aid and subsidies for their existence. All these could hinder their capacity to exercise pressure on public bodies.

In sum, the participation of immigrant associations or groups in the decision-making process in Spain is much more formalized than in the United States.

[illegible]

Final Comments

National Differences, Local Similarities

MARIA DE LOS ANGELES TORRES, UNIVERSITY OF ILLINOIS AT CHICAGO

A central question in this book is the role of local governments in the making and enforcing of immigration policies. Global cities continue to be key players in a global economy, and this includes stances taken towards their labor forces. Best practices include providing education for immigrant children, creating safe zones in which local governments protect immigrants from indiscriminate deportation policies, and the encouragement of immigrant civic participation. Clearly both Madrid and Chicago have made great strides to create programs that support the incorporation of immigrants.

National debates about the place of immigrants are framing local policies across the world. As we completed this book, immigration was still a hotly debated issue in both countries. In Spain, the worsening economic crisis continues to erode social service programs that have been critical to the incorporation of immigrants. In the United States, the promise of comprehensive immigration reform has faded as both Republicans and Democrats, including President Obama, have endorsed a piecemeal approach, which threatens to prevent a path to citizenship for the vast majority of undocumented immigrants. However, there may be some form of extended visas available to high tech industry and farmworkers, and perhaps some path to citizenship for undocumented young people. On the table are proposals to create a category of legalized individuals, but not citizens.

The prospect of further institutionalizing a distinct legal category for non-citizens raises fundamental questions about the nature of democracy itself. This is not to say that democracies have not always had varying categories of individuals with distinct institutionalized rights. However, many categories of exclusion have been eliminated, further illuminating that this is not the case for "place of birth"—a category that has become more restrictive. The exclusionary tendency is particularly stark given the background of global mobility spurred both by advances in technologies and the exigencies of global capital. Such legal moves may have the impact of institutionalizing permanent inequality in an era where the acceleration of these divisions has become a cause for concern across the globe.

In both countries, the question of who belongs is still mitigated through a racialized lens. Even though racial discourses in Spain and in the United States are distinct, they both include place of birth as one of the criteria to define who belongs. People from particular countries are viewed as outsiders who are different and potentially dangerous to national unity. Yet, in both countries, bigger cities tend to have more freeform cultural narratives and programming that aims at helping immigrants become full residents with rights and responsibilities.

Perhaps one of the most glaring distinctions we found between both cities was the way in which family is deployed through immigration policies. Spain still maintains policies that encourage family reunification. In contrast, the United States has largely abandoned family reunification as a cornerstone of immigration policy. Indeed, it is making distinctions between parents and young undocumented. The DREAM Act, a proposal to create a path to citizenship for undocumented youth who entered the United States as children, is one example. Additionally, there was the deferred action extended by President Obama months before his second bid for the presidency, which deferred the deportation of young undocumented for two years. In 2013, over 1,000 deportations a day were carried out. Of these, over 80% had a close family member who was documented. These actions have effectively divided families.

Approaches that exclude parents deny children and young people the right to have a unified family—a sacred foundation of American society that, in contrast, is protected by Spanish immigration practices. These programs are philosophically rooted in modernist nation-building rational projects in which children and young people are the keys to create future societies. Unlike adults, they can be molded into future, respectable citizens. However, instead of being saved, these children and young people suffer family separations.

In the face of national impasse, can we conceive of a smaller scale citizenship that can provide rights and responsibilities to the denizens of a local region? Let's say that local governments begin a process of "regularizing" or "legalizing" that, to some extent, provides not only services and protections, but also extends a local voice in political affairs. Can we conceive of a citizenship that is located in "place of residency" and perhaps tied to an individual's contributions to the local economy? Most cities today have some form of local taxes on goods and services. Is this local taxation a possible basis for thinking through a political voice? Chicago's school councils are an example of an arrangement in which what matters is whether an individual has a child in the school.

In all, this book has provided a focused examination of the strategies two global cities deploy in regards to the incorporation of immigrants. Clearly they are policies that respond to local demands and needs as they are rooted in local anxieties about national government's inability to respond to them. They are, however, also rooted in national traditions, legal frameworks, and political and cultural practices. As such, fundamental changes to immigration policies at the local level will depend on national shifts. For now, local governments can provide important safe havens for immigrants that, in turn, create a more livable city for all.

Contributors

Xóchitl Bada is an associate professor in the Latin American and Latino Studies Program at the University of Illinois at Chicago and affiliate guest professor at El Colegio de Michoacán. She is co-editor of the Series on Latino Immigrant Civic Engagement, published by the Woodrow Wilson International Center for Scholars.

Carolina Calvillo is a Ph.D. student in sociology at the University of Illinois at Chicago.

Julio Capeles is a Ph.D. candidate in sociology at the University of Illinois at Chicago.

Silvia Díez Sastre is associated professor of Administrative Law at the Universidad Autónoma of Madrid. She is current director of the Research Centre on Administrative Justice.

Nilda Flores-Gonzalez is an associate professor in Sociology and Latin American and Latino Studies at the University of Illinois at Chicago. This project was part of the UIC Chicago Area Study and partially funded by the National Science Foundation, The Russell Sage Foundation, the UIC Great Cities Institute, and the UIC Institute for Research on Race and Public Policy.

Matthew Kuenning practices immigration law in Champaign, Illinois. He is an adjunct professor at the University of Illinois College of Law.

Carmen Navarro is associated professor of Political Science at the Universidad Autónoma of Madrid. Her research focuses on local governments.

Tomás de la Quadra-Salcedo Janini is associated professor of Constitutional Law at the Universidad Autónoma of Madrid. He currently is a lawyer at the Constitutional Court of Spain.

Irma Olmedo is a professor emerita in the College of Education at the University of Illinois at Chicago.

Amalia Pallares is an associate professor of Political Science and an associate professor and director of the Latin American and Latino Studies Program at the University of Illinois at Chicago. She studies social movements politics, ethnicity, and race in the U.S. and Latin America.

Laurie Reynolds is the Prentice H. Marshall chair at the University of Illinois College of Law. Her research focuses on different aspects of local government law, and she is co-author of a widely used casebook on that topic.

José María Rodríguez de Santiago is professor of Administrative Law at the Universidad Autónoma of Madrid. He was a lawyer at the Constitutional Court of Spain and focuses his academic work on fundamental rights.

Susana Sánchez Ferro is associated professor of Constitutional Law at the Universidad Autónoma of Madrid. She has dedicated several articles to state security issues.

Maria de los Angeles Torres is executive director of the Inter-University Program for Latino Research and professor of Latin American and Latino Studies. She has published extensively on Cuban exiles, Latino political incorporation, and immigration.

Francisco Velasco Caballero is professor of Administrative Law at the Universidad Autónoma of Madrid. He is former director of the Institute of Local Government at the university and was a lawyer at the Constitutional Court of Spain.

Rajhai Wilson received her M.A. in sociology at the University of Illinois at Chicago.

Critical Studies of LATINOS/AS in the Americas

Yolanda Medina and Ángeles Donoso Macaya
GENERAL EDITORS

Critical Studies of Latinos/as in the Americas is a provocative interdisciplinary series that offers a critical space for reflection and questioning what it means to be Latino/a living in the Americas in twenty-first century social, cultural, economic, and political arenas. The series looks forward to extending the dialogue to include the North and South Western hemispheric relations that are prevalent in the field of global studies.

Topics that explore and advance research and scholarship on contemporary topics and issues related with processes of racialization, economic exploitation, health, education, transnationalism, immigration, gendered and sexual identities, and disabilities that are not commonly highlighted in the current Latino/a Studies literature as well as the multitude of socio, cultural, economic, and political progress among the Latinos/as in the Americas are welcome.

To receive more information about CSLA, please contact:

Yolanda Medina (ymedina@bmcc.cuny.edu) &
Ángeles Donoso Macaya (mdonosomacaya@bmcc.cuny.edu)

Exchange Rates, Capital Flows, and Monetary Policy in a Changing World Economy

Exchange Rates, Capital Flows, and Monetary Policy in a Changing World Economy

Proceedings of a Conference
Federal Reserve Bank of Dallas
Dallas, Texas
September 14–15, 1995

Edited by
William C. Gruben
David M. Gould
Carlos E. Zarazaga

Springer Science+Business Media, LLC

Library of Congress Cataloging-in-Publication Data

Federal Reserve Bank of Dallas. Conference (1995: Dallas, Texas)
Exchange rates, capital flows, and monetary policy in a changing world economy: proceedings of a Conference, Federal Bank of Dallas, Dallas, Texas, September 14–15, 1995 / [editors], William C. Gruben, David M. Gould, Carlos E. Zarazaga.
p. cm.
Includes bibliographical references.
ISBN 978-1-4613-7831-0 ISBN 978-1-4615-6175-0 (eBook)
DOI 10.1007/978-1-4615-6175-0
1. Foreign exchange rates—Congresses.
2. Capital movements—Congresses.
3. Monetary policy—Congresses. I. Gruben, William C.
II. Gould, David, 1962- III. Zarazaga, Carlos Enrique. IV. Title.
HG205.F427 1995
332.4'5—dc21 97-7927
CIP

Originally published by Kluwer Academic Publishers, New York in 1997
Softcover reprint of the hardcover 1st edition 1997

Printed on acid-free paper.

CONTENTS

PREFACE: EXCHANGE RATES, CAPITAL FLOWS, AND MONETARY POLICY IN A CHANGING WORLD ECONOMY

The dramatic growth of international capital flows has provided unprecedented opportunities and risks in emerging markets. Investors, policymakers, central bankers, and other practitioners who interact in these markets participated in a lively exchange of ideas about these risks and opportunities during a Federal Reserve Bank of Dallas Conference on September 14–15, 1995. *Exchange Rates, Capital Flows, and Monetary Policy in a Changing World Economy* is the proceedings of that conference.

In Part I, "Exchange Rates and Monetary Policy," Jeffrey A. Frankel concludes that the system is broken "in the sense that it is not working in the perfect, idealized way that our theories say." He cautions against radical reforms but says "some intelligent intervention from time to time cannot hurt and sometimes can help." Leonardo Auernheimer and Steve Hanke offer comments.

Part II consists of Sebastian Edwards', "Optimal Exchange Rate Policy for Stabilizing Inflation in Developing Countries," with discussion from Graciela Kaminsky and John Welch. Edwards focuses on the use of exchange rates as stabilization devices in anti-inflationary programs. He looks for determinants of success and considers dangers and challenges of such policies.

In Part III, Vittorio Corbo discusses his work with Patricio Rojas of Chile's Central Bank, "Exchange Rate Volatility, Investment, and Growth: Some New Evidence." Corbo examines how macroeconomic uncertainty about the inflation rate and the real exchange rate affect economic growth through two mechanisms:

the rate of investment and the overall level of efficiency. Commentary is from David Gould and Liliana Rojas-Suárez.

In Part IV, "Speculative Attacks," Peter M. Garber reviews theories about speculative attacks and considers what happens in the days or hours before a fixed-exchange-rate regime collapses. He relates his comments to two recent cases, the collapse of the European Exchange Rate Mechanism (ERM) in 1992 and 1993 and the collapse of the Mexican peso at the end of 1994. Discussion from Guillermo Mondino and Miguel Savastano follows.

Part V is Alan S. Blinder's assessment: "The Role of the Dollar as an International Currency." Although Blinder finds many claims about the decline of the dollar as a reserve currency, he concludes that they are remarkably undisciplined by facts. "Wherever we have data," Blinder says,

> the message seems to be more or less the same: the dollar is still unquestionably the world's dominant international currency by any conceivable definition. But its preeminent position is eroding slowly, as mainly the Deutsche mark and, secondarily, the yen move up on the pecking order.

In Part VI, "International Capital Flows: Direct vs. Portfolio Investment," Michael P. Dooley challenges conventional wisdom about capital flows, control of capital flows, and what countries might hope to accomplish with capital controls. "Both lenders and the borrowers often see international capital flows as a welfare-reducing phenomenon," Dooley says. But he finds that the motivation for capital flows derives from government policy: the size of the capital inflow will be a function of the credibility of the insurance fund. Thus, policy reforms, particularly fiscal reforms, generate capital inflows, but the size of the capital inflow will be just sufficient to exhaust the insurance fund, he says. "The only way, in my view, to break the insurance chain and discourage these kinds of capital inflows is to introduce uncertainty in the exchange rate and . . . make the private sector investor bear the risk of that investment," Dooley concludes. Agustín Carstens and Edwin M. Truman offer comments.

Part VII, "Central Bank Coordination in the Midst of Exchange Rate Instability," is a panel discussion by Miguel Urrutia, John W. Crow, Ricardo Hausmann, and Allan Meltzer.

This conference would not have been possible without the efforts of many people. We wish to thank Bob McTeer, Harvey Rosenblum, Sherry Kiser, KaSandra Goulding, Agnes Mitchell, Daniel Sanchez, and all the contributors, who made this conference possible. We also thank our editorial staff—Anne Coursey, Rhonda Harris, Monica Reeves, and Kathy Thacker.

William C. Gruben
David M. Gould
Carlos E. Zarazaga

ABOUT THE PARTICIPANTS

Alan S. Blinder, now Professor of Economics at Princeton University, was serving as Vice Chairman of the Federal Reserve Board of Governors in September 1995. Before that, he was a member of President Clinton's Council of Economic Advisers, where he worked on forecasting, budget, international trade, and health-care issues. He is the author or coauthor of 10 books, including *Economics: Principles and Policy*.

Vittorio Corbo is Professor of Economics at the Catholic University of Chile. From 1984 to 1991, he served at the World Bank, most recently as chief of the Macroeconomic Adjustment and Growth Division. He has written more than 80 articles and edited eight books in the field of macroeconomics, economic adjustment, and development.

John W. Crow is an adviser to the American International Group of companies and Lévesque Beaubien Geoffrion, Inc. He served as Governor of the Bank of Canada from 1987 to 1994. Formerly chief of the North American Division of the International Monetary Fund, Crow is a fellow in residence at C.D. Howe Institute.

Michael P. Dooley, Professor of Economics at the University of California, Santa Cruz, was formerly Assistant Director of Research at the International

Monetary Fund. He has authored more than two dozen articles on international capital flows and exchange rate policy, including "Capital Flight, External Debt, and Domestic Policies," "Exchange Rates, Country-Specific Shocks, and Gold," and "Portfolio Capital Flows: Hot or Cold?".

Sebastian Edwards is Professor of Economics at the University of California, Los Angeles. In September 1995, he was Chief Economist for Latin America and the Caribbean at the World Bank. Coeditor of the *Journal of Development Economics*, he has authored several books, including *Exchange Rate Misalignment in Developing Countries* and *Real Exchanges, Devaluations, and Adjustment: Exchange Rate Policy in Developing Countries.*

Jeffrey A. Frankel is Professor of Economics at the University of California, Berkeley, where he is also Director of the Center for International and Development Economics Research. In addition, in 1996 he served on the Council of Economic Advisers at the Executive Office of the President. He also has been a Senior Fellow at the Institute for International Economics and Director for International Finance and Macroeconomics at the National Bureau of Economic Research.

Peter M. Garber, Professor of Economics at Brown University, is a consultant for the International Monetary Fund. Among his published articles are "The Operation and Collapse of Fixed Exchange Rate Regimes," "The Collapse of the Bretton Woods Fixed Exchange Rate System," and "The Linkage Between Speculative Attack and Target Zone Models of Exchange Rates: Some Extended Results."

Ricardo Hausmann is Chief Economist for the Inter-American Development Bank and Professor of Economics at IESA, Venezuela's leading graduate school of business. Previously, he was Minister of Coordination and Planning for Venezuela, the country's Governor in the Inter-American Development Bank and the World Bank, and Chairman of the Joint Development Committee of the International Monetary Fund and the World Bank.

Allan Meltzer is Professor of Political Economy and Public Policy at Carnegie Mellon University. His work on money and capital markets has led to frequent consulting assignments with Congressional committees, the U.S. Treasury Department, the President's Council of Economic Advisers, the Board of Governors of the Federal Reserve System, and foreign governments and central banks.

Miguel Urrutia is Governor of Colombia's Central Bank, having previously served the bank as Director. He was formerly Director of the Inter-American Development Bank's Department of Economic and Social Development and was Vice-Rector of Development Studies at United Nations University in Tokyo.

Part I EXCHANGE RATES AND MONETARY POLICY

The enormous volatility of floating exchange rates has led to a call for limits on exchange rate fluctuations. An increasing number of countries have begun to question the benefits of floating exchange rates. Can central banks limit exchange rate fluctuations, and are there benefits from doing so?

Presenter:
Jeffrey A. Frankel
Professor of Economics
University of California, Berkeley

Moderator:
William C. Gruben
Research Officer
Federal Reserve Bank of Dallas

Discussants:
Leonardo Auernheimer
Professor of Economics
Texas A&M University

Steve Hanke
Professor of Applied Economics
Johns Hopkins University

Frankel:
Something seems to be wrong with the international monetary system, but we are not sure how to fix it. This conclusion that things are not working entirely right, particularly in the foreign exchange market, is fed in part by some recent developments and in part by an accumulation of academic findings. I will review that evidence and those arguments and then discuss proposals for possible reform.

Bubbles and Crises in the Foreign Exchange Market

Is it "broke"? Should we fix it? And if so, how? The 1970s, in a sense, were the peak of enthusiasm for floating exchange rates. Certainly, a majority of economists had come to favor floating rates over fixed rates. This policy was thought to be the way to avoid misalignments, such as the overvaluation to which the dollar had become increasingly subject in the 1960s. The logic was that the market is the best judge of the true value of a currency.

Our host reminded us of Milton Friedman's very prophetic views from the 1950s. If the concern is that evil speculators will be destabilizing, Friedman said this is not very likely. The argument, of course, is that for speculators to be destabilizing, they would have to buy the currency when it was already high to drive the price up and sell it when it was already low to drive the price down. That's what *destabilizing* implies. Yet such speculators, who buy high and sell low, are not likely to last too long before going bankrupt. The argument seemed pretty convincing.

In the 1980s, the pendulum began to swing back for a number of reasons. The episode that convinced the most people that maybe all was not optimal with the system of floating exchange rates was the tremendous appreciation of the dollar. In the early 1980s, this appreciation seemed to fit standard theory: the overshooting model, the monetary fiscal mix, and high real interest rates. But by late 1984 and 1985, the last 20 percent appreciation of the dollar seemed difficult to explain by any macroeconomic fundamentals. Some people, who had been strong proponents of floating rates, began to have doubts. It seemed as if the markets are not always right; maybe they sometimes got it wrong.

What about Friedman's argument that destabilizing speculators would have to lose money and be driven out? A number of articles citing abstruse counterexamples were published. But the most powerful counterexample came up almost accidentally. It was the theory of rational speculative bubbles. Its initial motivation was purely a theoretical curiosity: an extra term kept popping up in the solution to the differential equations. But gradually it dawned on people. This term actually was an important counterexample to Friedman.

A rational speculative bubble is simply one in which investors buy the currency because they expect it to go up in the future. And sure enough: they drive the price up, it goes up in the future, and they are right. Nothing in the logic of speculation in efficient markets rules out a bubble of that sort. The concept of rational speculative bubbles makes a pretty disturbing counterexample to Friedman's argument. But the theory is not very complete. It does not tell us anything about when the bubbles get started or how to stop them. I think one wants to consider speculative bubbles more broadly.

Another reason the pendulum swung back in the 1980s was rising interest in the nominal anchor argument for monetary policy. After the high inflation rates of the 1970s and, in many countries, the high output cost of disinflating in the early 1980s, there was interest in a nominal anchor. The monetarists thought the anchor should be money, but that did not always seem to work.

So there was much interest in using the exchange rate as a nominal anchor. Many countries in Latin America and elsewhere began to try monetary stabilizations based on the exchange rate. Even the International Monetary Fund said maybe this was okay; maybe devaluation was not always the answer. In Europe, one primary motivation for the formation of the European Monetary System (EMS) and later plans for the European Monetary Union (EMU)—at least from the viewpoint of some of the southern European countries—was to establish a nominal anchor commitment, a credible commitment for monetary policy to break inflationary expectations.

It seems to me that in the 1990s there has been renewed disenchantment with fixed rates and that the pendulum is swinging away from attempts to stabilize. I am not sure it is swinging toward pure floating rates; it may be swinging in some third dimension, if pendulums are capable of doing that.

In part, this change is happening because we have had several very disruptive crises in countries that have tried to stabilize their exchange rates. The September 1992 crisis in the European Exchange Rate Mechanism (ERM); the August 1993 ERM crisis, with France in particular; and, of course, Mexico's December 1994 peso crisis have also given people some cause to worry.

These crises all had many predecessors in history. I do not know exactly why the financial markets seem so surprised by these 1990s events, so surprised that politicians who had made promises not to devalue did, in fact, devalue. There had already been a long history of promises that were not kept: the United Kingdom in 1931, 1949, and 1967; the dollar in 1973; and Chile in 1982, which offers many parallels to Mexico in 1994 and Great Britain in 1992. The mainstream view among most economists, I think, is that these crises were not primarily the fault of the markets but the fault of governments. The governments were pursuing policies that were not really consistent with fixed exchange rates.

Nevertheless, unwarranted speculative attacks can happen. Many speculative attacks are based on fundamentals, but some are not. In particular, I would cite the example of the French franc in 1993. It is hard to say what the French were doing wrong. If you look at the fundamentals, France's inflation rate was lower than Germany's. It is hard to say that this was some profligate policy that was inconsistent with the goal of trying to keep up with the mark in the ERM, and yet a speculative attack forced the French to abandon the previous regime. There is now a theory of speculative attacks for fixed rates, which is the analogue of the theory of speculative bubbles for floating rates.[1]

The Academic Literature on the Foreign Exchange Market

Those are the recent developments. I will briefly discuss seven empirical findings we have accumulated.

The first category is volatility. The volatility of floating rates has turned out to be high, judged by any standard. High volatility is what we might have expected, certainly compared with goods prices, with apparent monetary fundamentals, or with just about anything.

The second set of results is the possible adverse effects of this high volatility on trade and investment. Here the academic literature has been pretty muted. It is usually summarized by saying that there is no evidence of large effects of exchange rate volatility on trade, but many studies find evidence of some effects. For example, the idea that exchange rate variability discourages trade is certainly one of the major motivations behind the formation of the Exchange Rate Mechanism and the European Monetary Union on the part of European leaders.

On the econometrics, I recently did an estimate along with Shang-Jin Wei, looking across pairs of countries rather than across time. We found that bilateral exchange rate variability did seem to have a statistically significant effect. Using ordinary least squares regression and hypothetically eliminating all exchange rate variability in the world, our statistical estimate was that, as of 1980, trade would have been stimulated by 22 percent.[2]

There are three important qualifiers to that number. First, we found that the effect that was there in the 1960s and 1970s disappeared in the 1980s. Perhaps this is because of the increased use and availability of hedging instruments so that importers and exporters could protect themselves against exchange rate variability. Second, that estimate of 22 percent does not take into account the likelihood of simultaneity between who you are going to stabilize your exchange rate vis-à-vis and who your important trading partners are. When we take that simultaneity into account, the estimate, although still significant, is much smaller. Third, the defenders of floating rates would say: "Well, even if that's true, even if there is an effect of exchange rate variability on trade, that effect is reflecting some real shocks that are going on in the world economy. And if you try to suppress them, they are just going to show up somewhere else." The idea is that if fluctuations in exchange rates always stem from real disturbances, the impact is going to show up as an appreciation of the dollar in real terms one way or another. For example, if appreciation of the dollar results from an increase in demand for U.S. goods, and if policymakers try to suppress the effect in the foreign exchange market, the impact of appreciation is going to show up as higher U.S. prices. The mechanism is that, to suppress the appreciation, the monetary authorities must print more dollars and add to their foreign exchange reserves, and this increase in the U.S. money supply will be inflationary. So the effect on the real exchange rate, the loss in price competitiveness, is going to occur anyway, and you are better off stabilizing the price level. This argument—that there's a real amount of uncertainty out there that's going to show up one way or another, based on the fundamentals—is addressed by the third and fourth category of findings.

The third finding is the failure to explain most exchange rate movements, especially in the short term, according to fundamentals.[3] Over the longer term, we can explain some movements by fundamentals, but in the short term we can explain very little. Many studies come up with the same answer. So if you cannot explain exchange rate movements by obvious monetary fundamentals—money supplies, interest rates, inflation rates, or gross national product—that leaves two possibilities: either they are the result of fundamentals we cannot observe, or they are not the result of fundamentals. These two possibilities are logically all-inclusive. Many academic economists, perhaps real business cycle types, have argued that there are fundamentals we cannot observe. There are many theories related to something that is not observable, some marginal rate of substitution of currencies over time. The problem with such theories, of course, is that they are not testable. The other possibility is that the movements are not related to fundamentals, which is what I mean by speculative bubbles.

In my view, the most convincing piece of information has to do with the comparison of real exchange rate variability across different regimes. When countries shift from fixed rates to floating rates or back, or if they peg to one currency versus another one, that has effects on nominal *and* real variability. This is a pretty persuasive piece of evidence.

The upper half of Figure I–1 shows the nominal exchange rate variability, and the lower half is real exchange rate variability for the Deutsche mark–dollar rate before and after the switch from fixed to floating. It is not surprising that

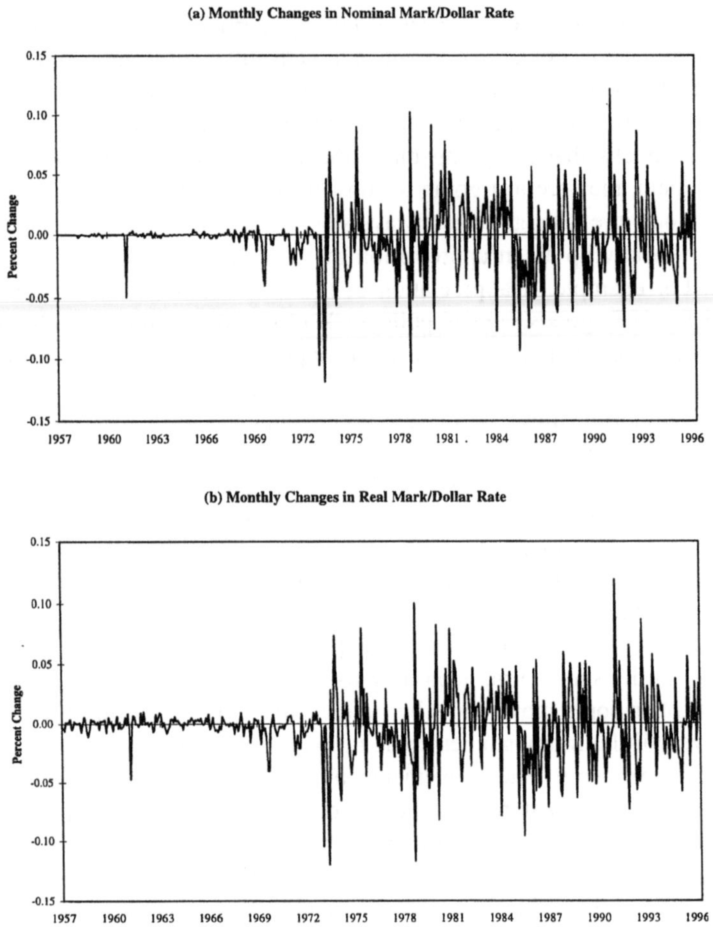

Figure I–1. Volatility of German/U.S. exchange rate since 1957.

Source: IMF *International Financial Statistics* series ae (end of period exchange rate) and series 64 (CPI).

after the switch from fixed to floating rates in 1973, nominal exchange rate variability went up. But some people say it is a coincidence. Those real fundamentals are out there and they are going to determine the real exchange rate no matter what, and the choice of fixed versus floating is immaterial. Is the real variability the same no matter what, whether it shows up in the form of nominal exchange rates or prices?

I think there is pretty persuasive evidence against that because a shift in regime does have a big effect. There are many examples that when you shift nominal variability, real variability goes up, as, for example, when Ireland switches from a dollar peg to a pound peg to a mark peg.[4]

The fact that those two graphs are matched very closely, that the correlation between the movements in the nominal rate and the movements in the real rate is very high (0.98), suggests that what is really happening is that there is some stickiness in goods prices and that nominal variability is creating a lot of the real variability. To me, this evidence argues against the idea that the variability is invariant to the regime. I think the regime does make a difference and that speculative bubbles are prime candidates to explain many of these movements.

Further down the list of empirical findings from the academic literature suggesting all is not quite right with the current system: Number four is apparent bias in expectations, particularly as reflected in the forward exchange rate. There are many tests to determine whether the forward market is an unbiased predictor of the future spot rate, and virtually all of them say no, it is not. In other words, it is biased; you can make money in expected value by betting the opposite direction of the forward rate, a fact that some see as evidence against efficiency of the markets. The more common interpretation, certainly among academic economists, is that this is not evidence of market inefficiency but rather a compensation for risk, the exchange risk premium. The reason is a long story that I will not go into, but I think there is evidence against the exchange risk premium idea and that there is indeed some bias in expectations.

The fifth finding is evidence from survey data on exchange rate expectations,[5] which is related to the sixth finding, the apparent tendency for exchange rate forecasters and traders—the people who are actually in the market—to make forecasts about the future that tend to extrapolate past trends, at short horizons of one week, two weeks, one month.[6] Most trading takes place within these horizons, if not even shorter horizons of a few hours. At these horizons, it appears that traders use technical analysis or various other methods that, on average, tend to extrapolate past trends. Also at these horizons, there is little use of the models based on fundamentals that say: "The dollar is overvalued, whether it's by purchasing power parity or the trade deficit or whatever. We expect it to return to equilibrium."

Traders do tend to use those models at longer horizons of, say, one year. An investor deciding what country's securities to buy or a CEO deciding where to build a factory takes fundamentals into account. But at the very short-term horizon of most trading, it just does not seem to be there.

The seventh category is studies of the effects of exogenous changes in monetary policy. The finding is that there is an effect on the exchange rate, but the effect is not instantaneous as, in theory, it should be. Rather, it is drawn out over time. It takes maybe a year or two before the peak effect occurs, and then it comes back down.[7]

I like to try to explain this finding, and a lot of the others, through speculative bubbles. I call it overshooting of the overshooting equilibrium. This explanation is my attempt to be more specific than just saying *speculative bubbles*, to suggest how a speculative bubble starts. It starts by a movement that is based on fundamentals, but once the trend gets going, the speculative bubble keeps going for a while longer before it catches up with the fundamentals and turns around.

This hypothesis, though unattractive from the viewpoint of rational expectations theory, seems to explain a lot. For example, the finding that the forward rate points the wrong direction is consistent with this theory because the forward rate is also equal to the difference in interest rates by covered interest rate parity. The pattern is this: interest rates increase because of fundamentals, making the country's assets more attractive. Next the currency appreciates—so far so good, just what the textbooks say, as in Dornbusch's overshooting theory. But if the currency has been appreciating for a couple of years, these chartists' or technical analysts' models seem to be giving the right answers because extrapolation for a certain period of time has given the right answer and the currency has not returned to fundamentals. If these conditions continue on for a year or two, momentum builds, and people start throwing away the models based on fundamentals and pay more attention to the models based on technical analysis. You get this extrapolation, which keeps it moving.

Eventually there is a turnaround. It's like the *Roadrunner* cartoon in which the coyote runs off the edge of the cliff. For a few seconds, the market is still going, though not supported by fundamentals—the cliff is the fundamentals. When the market notices that nothing is supporting the fundamentals, it suddenly becomes aware that nothing is holding up the dollar or the yen, and down goes the currency. That is my characterization of the dollar in February 1984 and of the yen in the spring of 1995. In both cases, the bubble burst.

Proposed Cures for the Foreign Exchange Market

I have covered the question "Is it broken?". Now I will turn to "Should it be fixed?". Usually the reply to this question is, "If it's not broken, don't fix it." The implication is, "If it is broken, you should fix it." My answer is not necessarily going to come out that way. The fixes would have to be an improvement for that to be right, and I am not sure that they are.

Let me explain what I mean by going through the major proposals for reforming the monetary system, and, in particular, the foreign exchange system. I will go from the more extreme proposals to the less extreme proposals, although that judgment is partly subjective.

To me, the most extreme proposal is a fixed exchange rate. I am not talking about "fixed but adjustable." I mean irrevocably fixed. Under fixed rates, one might distinguish several variations: irrevocably fixed with your own currency, a currency board, the gold standard, or the most extreme case, a monetary union in which one country actually adopts another's currency. I hope from our discussions we will hear some tales of far-off lands that are experimenting with some of these proposals.

This really is the nominal anchor argument, the idea that if the monetary authorities make a sincere commitment to an exchange rate peg, the policy will work and will allow the country to attain monetary stability with less output cost than might have been suffered in an attempt to disinflate without a nominal anchor or without any way to convince people you were serious. The argument, of course, is that if the nominal anchor is really credible, and if people see there is no going back even if you want to, they will expect lower inflation. And if the public expects lower inflation, inflation will be lower. Workers will settle for lower wage increases, firms will settle for lower prices, and inflation actually will be lower without output costs.

Whatever else can be said, I think, recent experience has cast some doubt on the idea that all that is necessary is for the monetary authority to be sincerely committed to a nominal anchor. A sincere commitment is not all that is needed. The authorities, in the cases of Mexico in 1994 and the ERM, really did want to keep the exchange rate fixed and intended to do so, but the system did not work, and they were not able to keep the rate fixed.

Here I am distinguishing between the monetary authorities and the government or, more broadly, the political process. The monetary authorities might be willing to suffer very high interest rates to stay in the exchange rate mechanism. (Sweden had 500 percent interest rates for awhile.) Yet that might not be good enough if the rest of the government is not prepared to support the monetary authority for fear of losing an election or popular support. If unemployment is very high, there may be revolution in the streets. Or if the banking system is vulnerable, there may be a banking collapse, which may be a price too high to pay. Even if the government is committed, it may get thrown out of office. These possibilities are part of the fundamentals, and in a sense the ultimate fundamentals are politics. In our models, we typically assume monetary policy is just this exogenous M that the government gets to set, but that may not always be the case.

If the speculators sense trouble, there may be a big speculative attack even before the workers are in the streets, or before the poll results are in, as in the case of the French and Danish referenda on membership in EMU. There may be massive speculation that the monetary authority cannot resist.

There is a current fashionable view, for which one of my discussants bears a lot of responsibility (and I say this to his credit—not many of us can have an effect on the regimes that countries are choosing out there). This view is that you need an even stronger commitment than just saying the exchange rate is irrevocably fixed. What you need is a currency board.

Currency boards do have their place. I think they have helped Argentina, and perhaps some of the Baltics. Here are the requirements to be a desirable candidate for a currency board: a very small, very open economy that is well integrated into the world; a *desire* to be integrated, particularly into some specific neighbors (for example, a desire on the part of the Baltics to be integrated into Western Europe, or perhaps for some Central American and Caribbean countries to be integrated into the United States); a desperate need to import monetary stability due to a history of hyperinflation or to an absence of stable institutions (such as a country just coming out of communism that lacks no trustworthy institutions); and the ability to come up with enough reserves to really make the currency board work (it may not be enough to have reserves to back up the monetary base; you may need more than that, possibly enough to buy out the whole M1). Stanley Fischer says that without adequate reserves, a currency board is a recipe for changing what would otherwise be a currency crisis into a banking crisis. If a country lacks all those requirements, as most do, it is not a good candidate for a currency board.

Those are all the proposals that come under fixed rates. There's an alternative set of proposals that come under the realm of capital controls. The Tobin tax is getting more attention now than it did when Tobin first made the proposal 15 years ago.[8] The attention is coming not so much from academic economists but elsewhere. The conventional critique is in two parts: one, a Tobin tax cannot reduce undesirable destabilizing speculation without hurting desirable investment; and two, it cannot be enforced.

On the first, I have an answer. I think there is evidence that short-term speculation, which the Tobin tax would hit proportionately more, does tend to be destabilizing in the sense that it is often based on extrapolative expectations. Long-term investment is stabilizing but minimally so. I am not really willing to say I am in favor of the Tobin tax per se, though a tax of 0.05 or 0.10 percent would certainly be better than the 1 percent tax that has been discussed. My doubts have more to do with the second criticism, enforceability.

Proposals from Dornbusch and others call for various forms of capital control. I will not go into that too much.[9]

Another category that is more moderate is to have more formal institutions for intervention, such as a multilateral intervention fund. Michel Camdessus has proposed something like this.[10] Another subset of these formal institutions is target zones in the manner proposed by John Williamson.[11] He answers the

Table I–1. Four schools of radical reform.

	Do we think that markets always know best?	*Do we think there is some role for government tinkering?*
Want national independence	Pure free float works best (Monetarists)	Anti-control of speculators (Tobin, Dornbusch)
Want an international agreement	Discipline from fixed rates/ currency board/gold standard (Supply-siders)	Activist, international cooperation (Bergsten, Williamson)

critique that target zones do not work: the collapse of the exchange rate mechanism, he says, is not the kind of target zone I have been talking about. The kind of target zone I have been talking about has an automatic adjustment of the central parity when fundamentals change. If one country has a higher inflation rate than another, you regularly change the central parity. You do not wait for a crisis at the bend.

The Williamson version does have the advantage that it makes it more practical and less likely that you could have these crises. But on the other hand, it also vitiates the two main arguments in favor of a target zone. The nominal anchor argument is basically out the window, and if there is always a possibility of a realignment, the argument that speculation will stabilize the rates under a target zone becomes more questionable. Of course, there is also the question of who and how you would determine what the central parity is.

My list of radical reforms that have been proposed would not be complete without mentioning Ron McKinnon.[12] I will do this by putting the radical schools of thought into four categories in a two-by-two graph (Table I–1). The top question is, Do we think that markets always know best, or is there some role for government tinkering? And on the side we ask, Do we want national independence? Is it desirable for each country to be able to follow its own monetary policies, or would we like to have national cooperation and international agreement?

The monetarists are in the upper-left corner. They say pure free-floating works best. Each country gets to choose its own policies; markets can pick the appropriate exchange rate, and everything is fine. It is like the Adam Smith argument for free markets in general.

Tobin and Dornbusch are in the upper-right corner. They say we need some government tinkering, some antispeculator controls.

Those who think the markets know best are in the lower-left box. These people are just as strong on free markets as the monetarists, but they come to the opposite conclusion regarding the exchange rate. I put supply-siders here, but

Table I–2. When does intervention work, and when is it desirable? Four cases.

	The market is sure of itself. ⇒ Intervention will not work.	*The market is unsure of itself. ⇒ Intervention can work.*
Market perceptions of fundamentals are better than the government's.	It is just as well that intervention fails, as with the pound and lira in 1992.	The effect is to keep the exchange rate away from fundamentals, as with the ERM in 1991.
Government may know better than the market.	It is too bad that intervention fails, as with the franc in August 1993 and the yen-dollar rate in March and April 1995.	The effect is to move the exchange rate toward fundamentals, as with the dollar in 1985 and the yen-dollar rate in the summers of 1993 and 1995.

there are a lot of other people who fall into this category, saying we need the discipline from fixed exchange rates such as a currency board or gold standard, which enables each country to go its own way and be responsible for its own errors and yet provides the discipline of fixed rates.

Fred Bergsten and John Williamson are in the lower-right corner. They say we need some government tinkering, and we need it in a cooperative way; we need international cooperation to stabilize currencies.

Ron McKinnon defies classification; he is in a category by himself. I would say he takes ideas from each of the four schools. Like Tobin and Dornbusch, McKinnon thinks a free float does not work very well and speculators give us excessively variable exchange rates. Like the monetarists, however, he thinks purchasing power parity is a good, useful guide to determining the exchange rate. Then he thinks like the supply-siders, believing devaluation is not a useful tool for changing relative prices and for improving the trade balance. And finally, like the fourth camp, he thinks we need a tripartite monetary agreement, a cooperative agreement among the United States, Japan, and Europe to stabilize the world monetary system. I think it is a little hard to combine all those, but he gets points for originality.

Where do I come out? I am not a radical. I have a very moderate view that floating with some occasional intervention is really about the best we can do. This does make me different from, perhaps, most economists, or at least from academic economists, who take the view that intervention can never have an effect unless it changes money supplies, that sterilized intervention can never have an effect (and that even if it did, it would not be desirable to have an effect that was inconsistent with fundamentals).

In Table 1–2, another two-by-two box, I make a distinction across the top about whether or not the market is sure of itself—whether the market really has a firm idea of what the exchange rate should be. If it does, you know these critics are right. The magnitude of the market is $1.2 trillion a day as of April 1995. This is too big for the authorities to fight with intervention, if the markets really know what they want.

But the idea that intervention can never work is just not right. I did a study with Katherine Dominguez in which we looked at the record of daily intervention since 1985. We found that often it does have an effect. It is more likely to have an effect when the market is unsure what it wants, when the intervention catches the market by surprise, when it is coordinated among the authorities, when it is publicly announced, and to be sure, when it is ultimately backed by fundamentals. But the idea that intervention can never work unless it is backed by fundamentals is not right. We found many episodes in which it did work, at least for a month or so, which is long enough to matter. And I would say that interventions in the summer of 1995 have had a real effect on the dollar-yen rate.

The market represented in the second column of Table I–2 is unsure of itself, so intervention can work? The other distinction, along the side, is, Are market perceptions better or worse than government perceptions? I would agree that most of the time, we are in the first box: intervention is probably not going to work if it bucks fundamentals because the market could prevail. Markets are usually, but not always, right; sometimes we are in the other boxes. I will give examples.

Intervention with the pound and the lira in 1992 ultimately failed, which is just as well because it was inconsistent with the fundamentals. Given the shocks of German monetary unification, increased German spending, high interest rates, and upward pressure on the mark, it was inevitable that the ERM was going to give way. And that is what happened.

But sometimes we are in the other categories. Intervention can work. The ERM worked for two years. For two years between the German shock and the collapse, the authorities succeeded in propping up the ERM.

I have examples in which the government, in fact, may know better than the market. That is not impossible. It happens sometimes. I would say the French franc in August 1993 is a case where the speculative attack was not justified by fundamentals. In my view, the movement of the yen against the dollar in 1994–95 was excessive and was a replay of the bubble for the dollar in reverse. During 1984–85, it was the dollar that overshot the overshooting equilibrium, and in 1994–95, it was the yen that overshot the overshooting equilibrium.

In June 1995, I published a couple of articles, one in *Foreign Affairs* and one in *International Economy*, saying the market had just gotten carried away, that the yen-dollar rate of 80 did not make sense.[13] I wrote that the exchange rate was based on perceptions that the Clinton administration wanted a weak dollar (perceptions that were wrong) and that intervention might be useful in turning the situation around. I think these things were exactly what happened in the months that followed.

Sometimes intervention can work if it is done correctly and cleverly, and if the market is unsure of itself. Sometimes that can actually help move things in the right direction.

So is the system broke in the sense that it is not working in the perfect, idealized way that our theories say? Yes. Should we fix it? No. I think the radical reforms would not be an improvement. But some intelligent intervention from time to time cannot hurt and sometimes can help.

Notes

1. See Obstfeld (1994).
2. Frankel and Wei (forthcoming).
3. Meese and Rogoff (1983) and Campbell and Clarida (1987).
4. Flood and Rose (1993). Also, see Frankel and Rose (1995) for a recent survey of the empirical literature on exchange rate determination.
5. Frankel and Froot (1989) and Engle (1995).
6. Frankel and Froot (1987).
7. Eichenbaum and Evans (1995).
8. See Tobin (1978) and Frankel (1996).
9. Dornbusch (1986) and Eichengreen, Tobin, and Wyplosz (1994).
10. See Camdessus (1994). T. Hosomi proposed such an international intervention fund 10 years ago.
11. Williamson (1987).
12. McKinnon (1988) and McKinnon and Ohno (forthcoming).
13. Frankel (1995a and 1995b).

References

Camdessus, Michel (1994), "The IMF at 50: An Evolving But a Constant Mission," speech delivered at the Institute for International Economics, Washington, D.C., June 7 (excerpted in *IMF Survey*, June 13, 1994).

Campbell, John, and Richard Clarida (1987), "The Dollar and Real Interest Rates," *Carnegie-Rochester Conference on Public Policy* 27, August.

Dornbusch, Rudiger (1986), "Flexible Exchange Rates and Excess Capital Mobility," *Brookings Papers on Economic Activity* 1, 209–226.

Eichenbaum, M., and C. Evans (1995), "Some Empirical Evidence on the Effects of Monetary Policy Shocks on Exchange Rate Expectations," NBER Working Paper, no. 4271.

Eichengreen, Barry, James Tobin, and Charles Wyplosz (1994), "Two Cases for Sand in the Wheels of International Finance," CIDER Working Paper, no. C94–45, December.

Engle, Charles (1995), "Why Is There a Forward Discount Bias? A Survey of Recent Evidence," University of Washington and NBER, July.

Flood, Robert, and Andrew K. Rose (1993), "Fixing Exchange Rates," NBER Working Paper, no. 4503.

Frankel, Jeffrey A. (1996), "How Well Do Foreign Exchange Markets Work? Might a Tobin Tax Help?" in Inga Kaul et al. eds. *The Tobin Tax* (Oxford: Oxford University Press).

Frankel, Jeffrey A. (1995a), "Still the Lingua Franca: The Exaggerated Death of the Dollar," *Foreign Affairs* 74 (July/August): 9–16.

Frankel, Jeffrey A. (1995b), "What Dollar Bashing?" *The International Economy* (May/June): 14–15.

Frankel, Jeffrey A., and Kenneth A. Froot (1989), "Forward Discount Bias: Is It an Exchange Risk Premium?" *Quarterly Journal of Economics* 104 (February): 139–161.

Frankel, Jeffrey A., and Kenneth A. Froot (1987), "Using Survey Data to Test Standard Propositions Regarding Exchange Rate Expectations," *American Economic Review* 77 (March): 133–135.

Frankel, Jeffrey A., and A. Rose (1995), "A Survey of Empirical Research on Nominal Exchange Rates," NBER Working Paper, no. 4865, for G. Grossman and K. Rogoff (eds.) *Handbook of International Economics* (Amsterdam: North-Holland).

Frankel, Jeffrey A., and Shang-Jin Wei (forthcoming), "Regionalization of World Trade and Currencies: Economics and Politics," in J. Frankel (ed.) *The Regionalization of the World Economy*, proceedings of the NBER Conference in Woodstock, Vermont, October 19–21, 1995 (Chicago: University of Chicago Press).

McKinnon, Ronald (1988), "Monetary and Exchange Rate Policies for International Financial Stability," *Journal of Economic Perspectives*, Winter, 83–103.

McKinnon, Ronald, and Kenichi Ohno (forthcoming), *Dollar and Yen* (Cambridge: MIT Press).

Meese, Richard, and Kenneth Rogoff (1983), "Empirical Exchange Rate Models of the Seventies," *Journal of International Economics* 14, 2–24.

Obstfeld, Maurice (1994), "The Logic of Currency Crises," *Cahiers Economiques et Monetaires* (Paris: Banque de France), 189–213.

Tobin, James (1978), "A Proposal for International Monetary Reform," *Eastern Economic Journal* 4, 153–159.

Williamson, John (1987), "Exchange Rate Management: The Role of Target Zones," *American Economic Review* 77, 200–204.

Auernheimer:

Professor Frankel has given us coverage that should be commended because it shows that he has a surprising, efficient sense of synthesis. His is a very balanced, complete survey of the state of affairs.

Essentially, I concur with Professor Frankel. The current system is showing too much volatility, and there is the question of what to do. In determining how to proceed, Professor Frankel seems sympathetic to (1) the possibility of the Tobin tax, aside from the question of practicality; and (2) the idea of intelligent intervention. He also supports the establishment of some rule for monetary policy. His rule is certainly not a monetarist (as opposed to *monetary*) rule for monetary policy that would seek to stabilize nominal income.

Here I am reminded of Friedman's theory of nominal income from the late 1960s or early 1970s. There are some things I like a lot in Frankel's work and some things I like less. I like Professor Frankel's suggestion that fluctuations in exchange rates reflect some real risk, and if that if we suppress that reaction, the effect will show up elsewhere. However, he does not bear his idea to final consequences, suggesting instead that it is difficult to prove any real risk in terms of exchange rate fluctuations. But I think that the idea has merit if it guides us in asking more questions.

Something else that I liked a lot is the notion that expectations can differ among market participants. This idea, of course, is very old; it was King's idea, and the one we use in Macroeconomics 101 to explain the shape of the preference schedule. Economists throw away information when we do not look at the volume of transactions because, in the strict models in which everyone shares the same expectations, there is no need for transactions to move the price of something up and down.

The concept that I could take an asset and sell it to you signifies in general that you and I have different expectations about what the price will be in the next period. This idea has not been sufficiently explored, and I mention it with respect to the Tobin tax.

We do have too much volatility, in the sense that there are certain things we do not explain by fundamentals, especially in the short run. But evidence is mixed as far as how that volatility affects trade. There are some empirical works that indicate trade declines by 20 percent, a very big number. Other empirical evidence suggests that the variability of the real exchange rate is sometimes higher under fixed exchange rates systems. The jury is still out.

I think that the concern is not so much with very short-term, day-to-day variability. After all, one might conclude that this is a pseudo-sum gain among short-term participants and does not affect the long-run plans or trade.

Professor Frankel focuses on longer swings that can take several quarters, as in the dollar appreciation during the mid-1980s, for example. He then explores various views of what to do about it. I will not get into a discussion of fixed exchange rates or currency boards. But with regard to his idea about some of the work done by rational expectations people, I think he tends to dismiss some works that are trying to find out not so much what is different between exchange rate regimes but what is common among them. In other words, the question is, Is there a fundamental difference? I refer to situations in which certain outcomes of policy experiments are attributed to the regime when, in fact, the cause is something more fundamental that would be common to both regimes. A recent paper by Aaron Tornell and Andes Velasco, for example, bases the criteria for distinguishing between two regimes essentially on public finance.

In some Latin American experiences, the failure of programs has been laid at the door of the exchange rate rule. Yet it is very easy to show that, given the government's fiscal situation, the same outcome might have occurred under a different policy, such as a monetary rule set at too low a rate of monetary expansion.

Professor Frankel makes a persuasive case for the Tobin tax. He combines McKinnon's complaint about too little intervention and Tobin's complaint about too little speculation in a very smart way. These two issues are the heart of Professor Frankel's discussion of what happens when some fundamental changes in a small way and the market gains its own impetus, raising questions about corrections.

He also distinguishes between daily operators who have lasting expectations and so-called chartists—the long-term investors, the good guys who look at fundamentals and have regressive expectations. This idea is certainly very interesting, but I relate it to the dispersion of expectations among market participants. In pursuing this idea about the chartists who look at the fundamentals, one can get quite a bit of mileage by asking, What is the consequence of the dispersion of expectations among each of these groups? In other words, do all the chartists have or hold the same expectations?

If they do not hold the same expectations, then perhaps the effect of the Tobin tax would be to eliminate the more moderate daily operators and leave the extreme ones. (Although the Tobin tax is a very small tax on transactions, it can have a big effect on daily operators.) The elimination of some transactions does not necessarily mean there will not be a spot exchange rate, but its determinant can vary greatly.

In closing, I think the Tobin tax idea (to which I sometimes react more positively than even to intervention because it implies the rule provides a permanent base) should be distinguished from the general idea of imposing capital controls. In particular, when a fixed exchange rate is not carefully managed and on a permanent basis, it can be destabilizing.

Yes, we are all for intelligent intervention. The question is, Are we able to come up with any rules for intelligent intervention? What are the costs and benefits of guessing correctly or incorrectly? Is there a moral hazard problem in that intervention? In other words, bubbles normally burst, and timely intervention can assure a soft landing. What happens here to credibility or reputation in terms of incentives to future speculators? Should we expect that they will not land softly?

Professor Frankel asserts that the success of certain interventions, such as those in 1985–1987, was that they were kept secret. But in more recent experience, he commends making interventions public and says the effect of an announcement is almost as important as the intervention itself. Also, while not always explicitly, Professor Frankel seems to be talking about sterilizing intervention, which is another discussion that leaves the rule monetary policies to be whatever rule one would like.

Hanke:

As I was listening to Professor Frankel's remarks and his excellent review of the issues, I was reminded of a story that Professor Friedrick Von Hayak once told me. After someone had given a speech, he went back to the back of the room and started to talk to Ludwig Von Mises about the speech. Hayak said, "Well, that's great." Von Mises was unresponsive, so Hayak figured out Von Mises was deaf and told him, "You need to get a hearing aid. I just got one, and they are terrific." Von Mises looked at him and said, "I'm not buying one of those things. I've already heard enough."

I must say, Professor Frankel, about halfway through I was in kind of a Von Misian mode, but I switched into Hayakian mode. You left me extremely stimulated, and I will remark on several topics you have raised.

First, on the motivation for the European Monetary System and European Monetary Union, I think there was absolutely no economic rationale for the monetary union whatsoever; it was completely political. The economists have come in ex post facto to rationalize it, avoid competitive devaluations, eliminate volatility, reduce transactions costs, and all the rest. But primarily, the French want to defang the Bundesbank. As a sometime resident of Paris, I know this.

But I think the proof that it is true is that if the French or other Europeans really wanted to be in a unified currency area in Europe, the easiest way to do that immediately would be to form currency boards, issue their own domestic currency, and use the Deutsche mark as the anchor reserve currency. There is absolutely no way they would even contemplate getting on board with that because they really want to get the mark out of the system. As my old colleague, Bela Balassa, has shown in a French Academy paper, the French have suffered tremendously from being in the shadow of the Deutsche mark. It has really knocked a lot off their potential growth.

Second, Professor Frankel talks about what's wrong with the foreign exchange market, about exchange rates not always being on target with the fundamentals. This is typical of most markets, not just the foreign exchange market. Once one of my economist friends called me after he had just purchased a new house for, say, $200,000. Ten days later, he got his tax notice, and the assessed fair market value of the house was $250,000. So he went storming down to the tax office and said: "I just bought this thing 10 days ago for $200,000, and that was the market exchange. Now you are assessing me at $250,000." The assessor looked up at him and said, "Well, sir, you have to realize we are in the middle of a recession right now." The foreign exchange market really isn't that unusual in regard to these fundamental versus market value determinations, at least over the short run.

Regarding currency boards, we have Professor Frankel's three basic criteria for currency board introduction based on principle: (1) very small, open, well-integrated economies; (2) governments that crave further integration; and (3) countries that need to import monetary stability. There's actually a fourth item, and that is the practical matter of the issue of reserves.

With regard to reserves and currency boards, I think Professor Frankel is somewhat skeptical, thought not downright hostile. At any rate, he's left the door open for me to make a few remarks. At the end, this debate about currency boards and central banks is really just a rules-versus-discretion debate, so that's one point just to keep in mind. But let's review his three principles.

If you apply those three principles, excluding this feasibility (let's assume we can always get enough reserves to cover whatever we have to cover in a currency board system), my view is that most of the 132 developing countries in the world should have currency boards and be part of unified currency areas.

So Frankel and I agree in principle, almost. The qualifier comes in regard to the very small economies; I would drop this constraint. For example, after 1997, the Hong Kong monetary authority will be retained by China. I think it would be great if China went all the way to establish currency boards regionally—in other regions outside of Hong Kong and South China—because the Chinese, particularly as they go through a transition and are monetizing their economy, don't have a clue what the demand for money is. There's no way you can run a central bank, whether it's on a discretionary basis or a rule-driven system, without some idea of the demand for money. My view is that currency boards make a lot of sense in a place like China, which is certainly outside of the very small category. I think currency boards would work because in South China, where all the action is in China, about 60 percent of the money in use is Hong Kong dollars from the currency board in Hong Kong. Whether Chinese currency boards would work or not in terms of blackboard economics is irrelevant; one is working right now in the real world.

Let's consider the reserves and feasibility issue. In my view, this issue is something thrown up by opponents of currency boards to give some fig leaf of respectability to their arguments. They can't just say, "We're against it, period, and that's the end of it and we're not discussing it." The theoretical arguments, I think, get a little bit flimsy with regard to the currency board system. You don't see critics coming out with much by way of substantive theoretical or practical critique. But there are questions about feasibility, and the big question is whether you have the reserves to cover the monetary base or the liabilities of a central bank 100 percent.

Now when this debate started, the only skeptic who gave serious consideration to currency boards, while not being favorably disposed to them, was John Williamson. John has done a lot of work on this subject and, incidentally, given me a lot of help. And he has a new monograph on currency boards that is a good survey of the whole scene.

When we started proposing a currency board for Russia, of course we heard from opponents. There really wasn't much of an economic argument against the suggestion; the questions were about feasibility. John argued that, at the time, the exchange rate was about 420 rubles per dollar, a level that would have meant reserves had to be just over $5 billion to cover the monetary base. John's argument was that, based on purchasing power parity, the exchange rate should have been not 420, but about 25 rubles per dollar. The effect of John's numbers, of course, would be to pump up the required reserves considerably, to about 85 billion versus five billion rubles. So currency boards kind of go off the boards, if I can use that term. That was a very effective piece of grit in the works that really slowed things down, and, of course, Russia does not have a currency board. The exchange rate isn't 420 to the dollar, either.

Moving to phase two, the argument about what exchange rate you should use worked for awhile, but it was fairly transparent. The new argument is that you must eliminate fractional reserve banking and go to 100 percent of broad money covered, an approach that gets into serious reserve requirements.

I think my counterargument is fine. If you want to maintain not only the solvency but liquidity of banks, go to the old Chicago plan: have 100 percent reserve banking with no fractional reserve system, and apply it every place in the developing world, whether the country has a central bank or currency board. I don't think it makes a bit of difference. After all, no central bank guarantees that you can exchange all broad money into foreign exchange. My suggestion would apply this on a level playing field everywhere. Incidentally, over the history of currency boards, there have been very few banking problems—liquidity problems, let alone insolvency problems—in countries that have had currency boards, as compared with countries that have central banks. In looking at this coverage of broad money with 100 percent of reserves, I think we have ignored history and focused a little bit too much on Argentina's contemporaneous experience.

Let me make a remark about Argentina, Lithuania, and Estonia. Each of these countries has a relatively new currency boardlike system. There is not an orthodox currency board in any of the cases. These boards have a limited amount of discretion. This discretion creates tremendous problems, particularly when the boards are not mature and do not have full credibility, because with a currency board there is still an exchange rate and exchange rate risk. The only way to avoid the risk is to do something like El Salvador is planning—dollarize and get rid of the exchange rate. As long as there is a board, there is, in principle, some exchange rate risk that remains quite significant, particularly in Argentina.

In Lithuania in December 1994 and January 1995, the country used its lender-of-last-resort facility. Lithuania substituted some litas-denominated reserves for dollar reserves, which is a no-no, and pledged some of its reserves as collateral for a $10 million loan from the Germans. Clearly, this is not a currency board. Lithuania is breaking its own law in this case. The Lithuanians have cleaned the thing up, but while there were no bank runs or anything, an external flow of money out of the system did result.

Argentina also has a lender-of-last-resort facility. If the country has excess reserves beyond that 100 percent cover, it can use them, as it did in the 1995 crisis. A limited amount of funds—up to 20 percent of the dollar-denominated reserves—can be issued by the government of Argentina. These are low-quality, dollar-denominated reserves, the Bonex bonds. During the crisis, Argentina increased that proportion from about 5 percent to about 15 percent, so the quality of the reserve cover went down. Argentina's monetary policymakers also controlled the reserve requirements of the commercial banks, something currency boards usually do not do. Usually, in fact, there is no reserve requirement. This lowering of reserves rattled the market. All at once, Argentina had the repos going on, the lowering of reserves, and the Bonex increase; all these things inflamed the speculation and stimulated the attack that was under way.

The real killer, though, was something that, to my knowledge, is unique in the history of currency boards. I am referring to what happened with foreign branch banks. Usually, foreign branch banks are a wonderful thing for a currency board system. Currency board countries usually have a lot of foreign branch banks because they have credit lines to their mother house and, when the currency board country has a liquidity squeeze, liquidity immediately comes in through arbitrage opportunities. (Such squeezes do not last long. In Hong Kong, for instance, rates can go up to 50 percent or so for 24 hours, and then the squeeze is over.)

In Argentina, the situation obviously had started to deteriorate after the December 1994 Mexican peso crisis. But Argentina's situation did not become severe until February 27, 1995. On that day, the credit lines of the foreign branches were cut by their mother houses, and the foreign branches had to go into the interbank market. Interbank rates went up from about 20 percent to 60 percent in one day, and what did that do? Already there had been some external drains out of the system and some internal drains in the system. The cutoff of foreign branches' credit line stimulated tremendous internal drains. The bank runs began, and Argentina was left in a tough spot. The country had no protection from the internal drain of bank runs in this scenario. There was no deposit insurance, only limited powers as lender of last resort, and no 100 percent banking. The only resort under a currency board system or gold standard is suspension of convertibility of deposits into cash. But, in effect, Argentina did not have this out either because they had suspended in 1989; to do so again would have been a complete disaster.

To conclude, I love Professor Frankel's taxonomy. It is very effective. I offer only one slight modification. And just to clarify my position, there are three basic regimes:

1. on one extreme is the fixed rate, with either a pure gold standard or an orthodox currency board that is a free market mechanism for international payments
2. on the other extreme is the floating rate without intervention, which is a free market mechanism for international payments
3. in between the fixed and floating rates is the adjustable peg, which is to be accomplished by managing the exchange rate, domestic liquidity, and, usually, the capital account. (This approach is a completely impossible task; that is why we had ERM 1992, France 1993, and Mexico 1994.)

I think where we should go is to take one of those two extremes. For the 32 industrialized countries, let's float. For the 132 developing countries, the only way to keep the clamps on the politicians is to enter unified currency areas with the 32 that float or one of the large currencies that floats.

Frankel:
I would like to thank both discussants for their comments, and most of what they said I agree with. But I will choose one item from each of them that I do not entirely agree with and make a further point.

First, I agree with most of what Professor Auernheimer said. But I want to emphasize this point about whether there is a fundamental amount of real exchange rate variability out there that is invariant to whichever regime you adopt. I think the evidence is clear that this idea is not right.

When you move from a fixed rate regime to a floating rate regime, of course, nominal variability goes up—by almost any definition. Real exchange rate variability does go up, too. I cite the example of pre- and post-1973, but some people say, "That's a coincidence. There are other things going on. We had oil shocks; the world has become a more variable place."

Other examples from other regime shifts support my view. My favorite is one Mike Mussa has discussed about Ireland's bilateral exchange rates. Instead of a two-by-two table, think of a three-by-three table. We have Ireland's bilateral exchange rate variability vis-à-vis first the dollar, then the pound, then the mark. And think of the 1960s, the 1970s and the 1980s. In the 1960s, Ireland was pegged to the dollar like everybody else. In the 1970s, Ireland pegged to the pound, which floated against other currencies. And in the 1980s, Ireland's currency was closely tied to the mark through the ERM. In the nine cells are the bilateral variabilities. In each case where the Irish currency was pegged to the other currency in question, nominal variability was very low, and nominal variability was high vis-à-vis whichever currencies they were not pegged to. The key point is that the pattern of real exchange rate variability mirrors the pattern of nominal exchange rate variability. It always collapses almost to zero vis-à-vis the country that's being pegged to, and it always goes up against the currencies that are not being pegged to. Those shifts happened, I think, for political, exogenous reasons. The evidence is pretty convincing that there is a lot of variability that is related to the choice of regime rather than to underlying monetary fundamentals.

The comment from Steve Hanke I want to discuss is the part about the reserves in the currency board being sort of a red herring, an excuse. I think it is more serious than that. First, if you are worried about banking crises, then you need enough reserves. That issue is separate from the issue of the currency board, but you see that the two are interrelated when you remember what the guarantee is under a currency board. When a country declares that it has a currency board, what the country is declaring is that if there is a crisis, a speculative attack, it will allow the domestic money supply to contract. Money will flow out of the country, and the domestic money supply will contract however much it takes; the country will allow interest rates to rise however far it takes. That is what Argentine policymakers said they would do last year, and the policy seemed to work with some help from the IMF.

But it is no coincidence that this view raises the issue of banking crises. If you let interest rates rise however much it takes, the banking sector will have problems, and that is why having enough reserves to back the monetary base is not enough. Having some extra reserves to bail out the banking sector is a substantial issue, not just an excuse. (As Professor Hanke notes, I have made a proposal for how some Eastern European countries might be able to come up with the reserves.)

Look at the countries that have had currency boards that have worked so far. Where did Estonia get reserves? Estonia had gold, or as I understand the story, the U.K. was generous. They had gold on deposit from Estonia that they had returned to the Soviets. When Estonians asked for it 40 years later, the U.K. said, "Well, okay" and gave the money again to the Estonians.

In Argentina after such great hyperinflation, the real money supply was very low. It was easy to get reserves.

I think reserves are a real issue. I have made a proposal for how other small Central or Eastern European countries that meet the criteria I laid out, such as the Czech Republic, could get reserves. My proposal is that they go to Brussels and say, "We are going to be the first country to adopt the Euro as our legal currency. This will give you a real shot in the arm. You folks in Brussels have been depressed since these EMU crises, and you want to move forward. This will help the movement to EMU; you actually are going to have the Euro circulating somewhere. There is just one catch. You have to give us enough Euros to do this." This proposal illustrates how a currency board could be made to work for countries that otherwise might have trouble coming up with reserves.

To sum up, Steve Hanke and I agree that the United States should float, we agree that Estonia should fix, and it is just the countries in between that we have to talk about.

Question:
(from Liliana Rojas-Suárez)
With respect to currency boards, one of the prerequisites that, in my view, has not been stressed enough is the pressure on the banking system. In the recent case of Argentina, there were pressures on the trade rate and problems with the banking system.

The reason the Argentine banking system was able to manage pressures on the exchange rate without an even greater crisis in the banking sector was because banks had a lot of liquid reserves, and they used those liquid reserves to satisfy the demand for deposits. When those reserves were gone, the central bank was able to manage the crisis because rather than letting the interest rate go as far as the currency board would have required, the central bank had a short-term facility with the banks called a swap operation. The swap operation, within the norms of the comparability law, allowed the central bank to extend a certain amount of cash to the banks.

What I am saying is that, unlike industrial countries where assets are in all kinds of maturities and liquidity, in the countries we are discussing, especially Latin American countries, most of the assets are very liquid, with short-run maturities. Under a currency board, defending the exchange rate implies high increases in interest rates. So if the banking system is not strong enough, it will lead to a collapse of the financial sector. This trade-off needs to be taken into account when discussing currency boards in Latin America.

Hanke:
I completely agree.

Question:
I was surprised that there was no discussion about how, if the currency board is to work, there must be an adjustment of the real exchange rate and how

inflationary pressure builds. Perhaps we need a lot of flexibility in the labor market.

Frankel:
I think that might be worth discussing. I assume part of the argument for a small open economy is that flexibility is greater. At least this is true in Hong Kong.

Part II OPTIMAL EXCHANGE RATE POLICY FOR STABILIZING INFLATION IN DEVELOPING COUNTRIES

Many developing countries, especially in Latin America, have used the exchange rate as a nominal anchor to help stabilize inflation. But highly managed exchange rate regimes in developing countries have had a tendency to fail, with dramatic consequences. Should developing countries manage the exchange rate or let it float?

Presenter:
Sebastian Edwards
Professor of Economics
University of California, Los Angeles

Moderator:
Evan Koenig
Research Officer
Federal Reserve Bank of Dallas

Discussants:
Graciela Kaminsky
Economist
Board of Governors
Federal Reserve System

John Welch
Chief Economist, Latin America
Lehman Brothers

Edwards:
There is little doubt that exchange rates are today at the very center of the economic policy debate. They appear on the front page of newspapers, in the news, and even in dinner conversations when people try to decide whether to speculate or go on vacation.

There are, I think, four fundamental issues in exchange rate economics that occupy most of the time, at least of economists. One, shall we use the exchange rate as an anti-inflationary tool and, in particular, should we use a fixed rate to bring down inflation? Two, what should be the exchange rate regime over the longer run once inflation has been obtained? Three, do exchange rate regimes affect policymakers' behavior and, in particular, is it the case that a fixed exchange rate imposes discipline on fiscal and monetary behavior? And four, how do we know if the real exchange rate is out of line and overvalued?

What I would like to focus my discussion on is the first of these issues: the use of exchange rates as stabilization devices in an anti-inflationary program. And I would like to ask whether this is a good idea, whether it makes sense. Are countries that adopt this strategy likely to succeed? If so, what are the determinants of this out of the possible outcomes of this type of policy, and what are the dangers and the challenges?

Without any doubt, after the Mexican crisis, this particular question has become once again very important. It has become important not only because we would like to understand what actually happened in Mexico but also because other countries are considering embarking on similar paths in efforts to bring down inflation. It is particularly important for those of us who follow Latin America because one of the most important countries in the region, Argentina, has adopted that kind of system to bring down inflation. And there are a number of skeptics about the fate of Argentina.

I think that in discussing the merits of using the exchange rate as a policy tool in an anti-inflationary program, it is useful to distinguish among a number of aspects of the problem: what are the initial conditions from which most economies that have adopted this kind of policy have started; what are the other policies that are usually undertaken jointly with a fixed exchange rate; what are the short-run effects of these policies; and how has the situation historically unfolded? In discussing this issue, I will refer again and again to the case of Mexico. I will tell you my reading of the Mexican story and relate what happened to Mexico to the experience of Chile in the early 1980s. In Chile, a very similar program was adopted that, as in the case of Mexico, ended in crisis, frustration and sorrow.

Inflation: Where Exchange-Rate-Based Stabilization Programs Begin

What is usually the starting point in an exchange-rate-based stabilization program? Usually, it is a situation of high inflation, triple-digit inflation. Mexico's inflation was about 157 percent to 160 percent at the start. We have a situation in which inflation has been going on at this type of rate for a sufficiently long period of time for people to begin to internalize. And the way it is internalized is that indexation starts to take hold of the economy. Indexation takes hold of contracts, and contracts are adjusted according to some index periodically. Depending on the initial rate of inflation, the periodicity may be every six months or every three months. And if the inflation rate becomes too high, the adjustment becomes a monthly one.

Indexation also takes over wages, and wages are guided by a combination of forward-looking expectations and backward-looking indexation that takes into account accumulated inflation in between wage adjustments. In most cases, the exchange-rate-based stabilization program starts from a situation in which the exchange rate up to that point also has become indexed through the adoption of some kind of purchasing power parity (PPP) approach toward adjusting the nominal exchange rate every period according to accumulated inflation differentials between the country in question and some partner or group of partners.

In this type of scenario in which inflation is high, higher than 100 percent, and where contracts are readjusted according to some index, a very high degree of inertia and persistence occurs. From a technical point of view, it is very easy to show that in this type of regime, the rate of inflation can be represented as a first-order outer regressive mechanism in which inflation today depends on a number of variables but fundamentally on what inflation was yesterday.

The degree of persistence from period to period depends on how generalized indexation is, how backward-looking wage contract adjustments are, and exactly what exchange rate policy the government follows. What we have seen in the initial phases of a stabilization program of this type is that the rate of inflation can be characterized by having a unit root. That means inflation in the previous period is totally passed into the current period and the degree of persistence is complete. And what this means is that the system has completely lost its nominal anchor. Depending on what happens to other policies, including external shocks, inflation could go anywhere. Indeed, this is what we have seen in a number of Latin American countries.

Possibly the best example is Brazil. For a number of years, Brazil followed this type of policy, and the rate of inflation was 40 percent per year stable. The first oil shock came, and inflation just jumped—no anchor, no force to bring it back down to a different level. The rate of inflation jumped to around 200 percent. A new shock came, and it jumped to 400 percent and stayed stable for a time. A new shock came, and it went up to 2,000 percent. There were no forces in this setting that would make inflation revert toward some kind of lower equilibrium level, such as international inflation.

It is in this context that at some point, the authorities decide to bring down inflation. In the well-behaved cases—such as Mexico's and, in the 1970s and 1980s, Chile's—the first thing the authorities do, and rightly so, is tackle the fiscal problem. And when the fiscal problem is tackled and inflation continues to be high and to be extremely stubborn, the decision is usually made to use the exchange rate as a stabilization device.

The exchange rate is fixed, and by fixing the exchange rate, it is argued that the prices of tradable goods will have some kind of limit in terms of how fast they can grow and, in that way, it is thought that inflation will come down.

In general, there are two variants of this policy. The first one aims at eliminating inflation very quickly. We have seen very few of those examples in the world when the starting point is one of very rapid but not hyperinflation. Possibly the best-known example is France's stabilization in the 1920s.

The other variant, and it's the one that Mexico followed, is where fixing the exchange rate does not have the purpose of eliminating inflation immediately but has as its main purpose reducing the degree of inertia, the degree of persistence —the extent to which inflation yesterday affects inflation today.

If the degree of inertia is indeed reduced this way, there is a very serious danger of the exchange rate's becoming highly appreciated because, of course, as inertia is reduced but inflation is not eliminated, the real exchange rate begins to appreciate.

The Mexican authorities were clearly aware of this danger. But they thought Mexico would be exempt of the effects of this appreciation for three reasons: one, because Mexico had ample international reserves; two, because Mexico started the experiment in a situation of undervaluation and, thus, had a cushion in which the real exchange rate could appreciate without leading to an overvaluation; and three, because Mexican policymakers thought there would be very rapid productivity gains that would compensate or more than compensate for the appreciation of the real exchange rate that would come with the adoption of the exchange-rate-based stabilization program.

Finance Minister Pedro Aspe in 1988, when the program was adopted as a longer term feature of the stabilization efforts in Mexico, went to the Mexican congress and said: "For the exchange rate to serve as an anchor, it is required that the balance of payments starts from a favorable surplus position. The use of the exchange rate according to a downward trend is fully justified if we consider that there is an ample margin of antivaluation of our currency."

Indeed, the Mexican authorities were aware of the appreciation syndrome but were confident because of these three reasons: an ample surplus in the balance of payments, enough international reserves, and an initial situation of antivaluation that provided a cushion.

The exchange-rate-based stabilization program was applied in Mexico, the fiscal side had been fully corrected, the primary balance was in surplus on the order of 7 or 8 percent of GDP, and the system then was put into place.

Let's see what happened. Inflation did initially come down very quickly; it then hit about 20 percent and got stuck at that level. It persisted at 20 percent, while the rate of devaluation of the peso was significantly lower and declining. As a consequence, the real exchange rate started to appreciate the Latin American way, where appreciation moves downward in a very significant way. At some point, some people became concerned that the cushion had been used.

Let me now compare this with what happened to Chile during the 1970s and 1980s. In 1978, Chile adopted an exchange-rate-based stabilization program, and in 1979, the exchange rate was fully fixed to the dollar at 39 pesos per dollar. What we see is a pattern that is very similar to the Mexican pattern: a rapid reduction in the rate of inflation, which gets stuck at some point at around 20 percent and then slows. For the same reasons as in Mexico, the real exchange rate, however, appreciates very significantly. And the accumulated rate of appreciation in Chile between 1978 and 1981 was around 28, 30 percent, depending on how one measures it. The rate of appreciation in Mexico is on the order of 33, 35 percent.

In the case of Mexico, as the authorities had argued, the degree of inertia was reduced. But the degree of inertia was not reduced significantly. As these figures suggest, the residual degree of persistence was still considerable, and that helps explain why the real exchange rate continued to appreciate.

By 1989, a number of people were seriously concerned about the viability of the Mexican system. Many observers began to argue that the cushion from an undervalued currency had already been fully used and that the exchange rate was becoming not only appreciated but overvalued.

In early 1990, however, the international financial community rediscovered Latin America. And it rediscovered Latin America years, if not decades, earlier than most of us thought it would. In particular, the international financial community rediscovered Mexico.

After the Brady deal was signed, the Mexicans began to privatize the banks, and all of a sudden Mexico, with its reforms, its privatization, its stellar group of policymakers, looked like an extremely attractive alternative. In two years,

Mexico jumped in the Euromoney country risk ranking from 77 to 34, way ahead of Chile in 1990, way ahead of many other countries that one would consider a very good and sure bet.

The great reduction in risk that took place at this point, the enthusiasm for Mexico, the privatization of banks, and the notion that NAFTA may actually happen, resulted in massive inflows of capital into Mexico. These massive inflows did basically two things. First, they allowed Mexico to finance the emerging trade deficit and do away with concern about the decline of international reserves. Second, they allowed people to finance a truly tremendous consumption boom that was reflected in a decline in private savings rates in Mexico that was staggering—from around 14 percent to around 8 percent of GDP.

As this capital came into the country, people were able to increase their expenditures. As part of these expenditures went into real estate and domestic goods, the real appreciation that we had seen because inertia had not been fully eliminated became even more serious. Of course, the other side of the coin of this capital inflows phenomenon was a very large current and trade account deficit.

Let's see what the data show, both on capital inflows and on the deficit. We can see how capital inflows into Mexico jump from being negative in 1988 and very small in 1989 to a level of roughly 9 percent of GDP by 1993.

Let's see the parallel in the case of Chile in the 1970s and 1980s. You can see how imports just explode and the trade deficit becomes tremendously large in the case of Mexico. What is very important to note is that export growth is rather modest. That, to a large extent, is because the exchange rate continued to appreciate throughout the period, and despite what the authorities expected, productivity in Mexico did not grow throughout this period.

The case of Chile, of course, is similar. In fact, in Chile, the exports not only did not grow very fast, at the end of the overvaluation appreciation period they actually declined. The fact that capital flew into the country at a very fast rate —allowing the financing of the trade deficit, allowing an increase in the current account deficit, and, in a way, justifying the real exchange rate appreciation —became an issue of concern to many analysts. The concern in 1989 about the real exchange rate appreciation was now compounded by the fact that not only had the real exchange rate appreciated significantly, the current account deficit financed by these capital flows was extremely large, on the order of 8 percent of GDP in Mexico and 12 percent of GDP in Chile.

When people expressed their worries and their preoccupation about this case, the reply by Mexican and by Chilean officials more than a decade earlier was that we shouldn't worry: these were private capital inflows, and the fiscal conditions were under control.

The governor of the Bank of Mexico told economists in January of 1994 that the current account deficit was not a problem because it was associated with inflows of private foreign funds rather than an expansionary fiscal or monetary policy, and that's a quote from the economists.

The Bank of Mexico annual report expressed in 1993, and I'm quoting:

> The current account deficit has been determined exclusively by the private sector's decisions to save and invest. Because of the above and the solid position of public finances, the current account deficit (which had been around 8 percent) should clearly not be a cause for concern.

What had Chilean authorities said back in 1981? The minister of finance said:

> There is no doubt that privately financed current account deficits are highly beneficial for the country and that we should make an effort to maintain them at the highest possible level and for the longest possible period of time.

So not only was there no reason to be concerned, in fact, they should be promoted.

Of course, from a factual point of view, it was true in both cases that the fiscal situation was under control, although it was lucent in Mexico in 1994. In that regard, we did not see the kind of situation that we usually see in typical balance-of-payment crises and currency collapses. What is missing in the argument that we shouldn't worry because these are private capital flows is that these private capital flows during the early stages of the reform process are due to a stock adjustment. They are due to the fact that there have been reforms and that the country risk associated with the country has declined significantly.

Because the country risk has been reduced significantly, all of a sudden there is a tremendous demand for the country's securities. And for this demand for the country's securities to take place, a very large capital inflow has to occur in a short time. But capital inflows at that level are temporary and will only stay at those tremendously high levels while the stock adjustment takes place and is resold.

When the stock adjustment has been resold and international investors are holding the amount of Mexican or Chilean or Argentine securities that they want to hold, capital inflows will have to come down to a new, sustainable level. They don't have to become negative. They don't have to reverse themselves. We don't have to see a transfer going in the other direction necessarily, but in the long run, it is highly unlikely that a country can run a current account deficit of 8 or 12 percent of GDP.

In fact, any portfolio model would suggest that in a country like Mexico, where the rate of economic growth at the time and the rate of growth expected for the near future was not spectacular—rather modest, indeed—the sustainable current account deficit was on the order of 2 to 4 percent, not 8 percent of GDP, as we observed in 1992 and 1993. So the question by late 1993 was not whether the capital that was flowing into Mexico or the rest of Latin America, for that matter, was sustainable. That was not the question, because it clearly was not sustainable at that level.

The questions were different, although related. And the relevant questions were when and to what extent will we see a slowdown of this capital inflow? And when we see a slowdown of this capital inflow, what kind of mechanism will our countries use to adjust to the lower availability of foreign financing, and what kind of mechanism will they use to make sure the economy has a smooth landing?

Finding the Formula for a Smooth Landing

The problem is that a fixed exchange rate makes a smooth landing difficult. It makes a smooth landing difficult because when capital comes into the country and helps finance the increasing trade and current account deficit, there are no impediments to appreciation of the real exchange rate.

But when these flows stop flowing in, slow down, or even worse, when, for any reason—be it a kidnapping, a political assassination, or a crisis in another country—the demand for that country's securities is reduced, the required real devaluation is much harder to engineer, especially because inertia continues, prices and wages are rather inflexible, and the situation is very different.

Mexico had built into its system some flexibility through the existence of the band, but once the band was used up, we were in a different regime. Once the exchange rate was at the ceiling of the band, for all practical purposes, we were under a fixed-exchange-rate regime. And it was necessary at that time to play by the rules of the fixed-exchange-rate regime if we were to see a successful, although costly, adjustment.

The problem is that, at that time, of course, the game was not played according to the rules. There was sterilization of the laws of international reserves, interest rates were not allowed to go up, *tesobonos* were substituted for *cetes* and, in the end, instead of having a smooth landing, we had a tremendous crash.

Chile went through the whole adjustment Mexico has seen. Once the adjustment took place, Chile was forced to generate in order to reverse the transfer. Capital inflows not only slowed down, they were completely reversed, as has been the case of Mexico, arguably, today. Imports had to be compressed a tremendous amount. The magnitude and the speed of the imports adjustment in Chile we have not seen in too many countries in the modern history of economics. And this decline in imports to 50 percent of what they had reached clearly captures the severity of the Chilean crisis, where unemployment went up to 30 percent and where GDP declined in just the first year by 14 percent.

What I would like to argue is that, to a large extent, this kind of outcome, which does not occur in all exchange-rate-based stabilization programs, is so costly that even if one attaches to them a limited probability, it is an extremely risky way to go.

So, what shall we do? I think the historical evidence, including the two stories that I have just told you, increasingly points toward the notion that there may be some merit to using a fixed exchange rate to bring down inflation during the early phases of a stabilization program, but the key is to know when to exit that program. Once inflation expectations are broken, it is time to get out of the system and move to a different type of regime, as Israel did successfully.

And I would argue that the regime that should be adopted once the policy has been exited successfully is a regime based on either a crawling peg or a managed float that would provide this system landing gear. I think that a comparison of the Chilean, Colombian, and Mexican cases in that regard is very illustrative. Mexico during the 1980s and 1990s followed its pegged program. After the 1980s experience, Chile, in contrast, decided very clearly not to peg the exchange rate. Chile followed a policy that was basically geared at not letting the exchange rate become overvalued. While Chile averaged 6 to 7 percent growth during this period, Mexico grew an average of 2.8 percent. Colombia, which at the same time did not fix the exchange rate, grew at 5.1 percent. While inflation in Mexico eventually came down to a single-digit rate, Chile lived with double-digit inflation until 1994.

In the trade-off between inflation and growth, clearly both Colombia and Chile have decided to very strongly favor growth. If one takes the index of real wages in 1980 equal to 100, today Chilean wages are 126. Colombian wages are 123. Mexican wages in 1994, before the crisis, were 99.4 percent. And if one goes on through a number of indicators, one can see that both Colombia and Chile were able to maintain a rapid rate of growth with livable, and, in the case of Chile, declining inflation, and at the same time not put the system into the straitjacket that the fixed exchange rate means. I think the lesson of all of this is that at the end of the road, the straitjacket, the rigidities, the inflexibilities associated with a fixed exchange rate are too great to gamble on. And countries such as the Latin American countries in general should opt for flexible exchange rate regimes. In the debate between fixity and flexibility, I think that increasingly, flexibility is getting the upper hand, notwithstanding the currency board supporters.

Let me end with the one case in Latin America that I think is an exception. I think that Argentina is a case where clearly it is justifiable, understandable, and that one should support strongly the type of exchange rate regime and monetary system that the country has followed. In a country that has been used to very high rates of inflation, to fiscal and monetary indiscipline with almost no parallel, a country where the authorities debase the currency every time they have a chance, there was very little alternative but to choose the route that the Argentines chose: the convertibility law, the opening of the capital account early on, the one-to-one exchange rate policy, the quasi-currency-board system.

But I think what is more important than that is that the Argentines understood that having that kind of system not only allows inflation to come down very quickly and brings stability not seen in Argentina for decades, it also means there are very serious responsibilities that monetary and fiscal authorities must follow. That means when the tables turn against you, you must be willing to play by the rules of the game of a truly fixed—fixed but not adjustable—exchange rate. Argentina has played by those rules, and the system is responding in an admirable way because, I think, the country is moving in the right direction. The probability of a crisis has been greatly reduced, but at the same time we are seeing that the cost is a very deep recession. What Argentina has done has been very courageous. It is paying off at a cost, but no one said that was not going to be the case.

Conclusion

Let me end by saying that if one really gets a lesson from Mexico, it is the importance of economic history. Had we all paid more attention to the previous experiences in Latin America, we would not have had to look very far to find out that the Mexican crisis had close predecessors, in fact, a very close one in the case of Chile. If economic history had been looked at with greater care and less arrogance, maybe some of these problems would have been avoided.

Kaminsky:

In his presentation, Sebastian asked three different questions. The one that he emphasized was whether fixed exchange rates help anchor inflation. He discussed why some countries have adopted the fixed exchange rate while others haven't, and whether a fixed exchange rate imposes discipline on central banks.

I will be mostly concerned with the analysis of the first point, whether fixed exchange rates help anchor inflation. I will try to condense the other two questions by asking what conditions are necessary for a fixed exchange rate to be viable.

Although Sebastian didn't present it, I will discuss some evidence from Latin America and EMS countries that illustrates how successful fixed-exchange-rate regimes are in anchoring inflation. Data from the stabilization programs in the 1970s and 1980s in Argentina, Chile, Israel, and Mexico show that inflation ranged from 3 percent to 23 percent per month in all these countries. Under stabilization programs like the Austral plan, the Israeli plan in 1985, and the

Mexico plan at the end of 1987, inflation fell drastically during the first year, moving into the one-digit range.

So from this point of view, it seems that fixed-exchange-rate regimes have helped anchor inflation in these countries. It is important to consider how the fixed exchange rate works. The fixed exchange rate imposes a binding constraint on central banks. They cannot accommodate different shocks in the economy. Therefore, because monetary policy is not a commodity, inflation must lose persistence.

In fact, inflation's persistence seems to have been reduced drastically in three of these cases. For example, in the case of Argentina's inflation, if you have something like a unishock in one period before the plan, in the next period, about 80 percent of the shock persisted. After 10 months, one-year inflation still was on the order of 40 percent to 50 percent. After the plan, inflation's persistence was drastically reduced. The case is similar for Israel and Mexico. As Sebastian has pointed out, in Chile this persistence was not eliminated. One reason was the indexation of wages.

In principle, this evidence seems to suggest that fixed exchange rates work. But let me give you some further evidence from EMS countries. In the first part of the table, you can see data from EMS countries and non-EMS countries before and after EMS's inception. Inflation was higher in non-EMS countries before EMS, and inflation decreased substantially in the EMS countries relative to non-EMS countries after the fixed-exchange-rate regime or the target zones regime was adopted. This evidence seems to support the idea that anchors work. I want to point out that during the first three years of the EMS, inflation was not reduced. Four years after the inception of EMS, however, inflation patterns of EMS countries and non-EMS countries start to show different patterns.

I also examined and tried to reproduce some results from a paper by Sue Collins in which she asks whether the EMS helped reduce inflation. She compares EMS and non-EMS countries. We cannot look just at when the exchange rate was fixed. We must be able to compare which type of shocks affected inflation in these countries before and after EMS, and we have to control for them. I examine an equation for inflation in which we test whether the EMS was, in fact, a leading force in the reduction of inflation in the EMS, or whether the early 1980s inflation was reduced throughout Europe and the United States. From this analysis, I observe that in the 1979 and 1985 episodes, whether we consider EMS countries or non-EMS countries, inflation was reduced. In fact, if you look at whether the EMS had additional explanatory power in the reduction of inflation in EMS countries, we observe that this is not the case.

The evidence on how successful these fixed exchange rates have been is mixed. Research should continue in this direction because fixed exchange rates, by enhancing the credibility of central banks, should reduce the persistence of inflation, and we should be able to examine how attitudes about inflation change under fixed-exchange-rate programs and under more flexible exchange rate regimes. We should be looking at how flexible wages become after the imposition of the fixed-exchange-rate regime and whether this increasing credibility encourages workers to moderate wage demands and enhances wage flexibility.

I want to support Sebastian's view that, even if the adoption of the fixed-exchange-rate regime helps anchor inflation, the movements of prices and wages have been slow. As a result of the adoption of the fixed exchange rate regime, we observe large appreciations of the domestic currency, some loss of competitiveness, and large current account deficits. We cannot say that all this real exchange rate appreciation is the result of fixing the exchange rate and the stickiness of wages and prices. We must consider that, aside from the adoption of fixed exchange rates in all these countries, there have been some sweeping reforms.

In Argentina, reforms in the fiscal sector have helped open the economy. So changes in productivity alone could explain this real appreciation as an equilibrium phenomenon. If we want to cast doubt on how flexible prices and wages are, we cannot just look at the real exchange rate and conclude that this is a disequilibrium phenomenon. Still, as a result of the adoption of a fixed-exchange-rate regime, we observe that, with the qualifications and caveats, these countries have lost some competitiveness. During the period of fixing, we observe the increase in the current account deficits.

In closing, I will comment on the viability of these fixed-exchange-rate regimes. When the ERM and the Mexican crises started, some people said all these currencies were overappreciated, prices and wages did not come rapidly enough, and, therefore, competitiveness requires more flexibility on the exchange rates. Whether we agree or not, it is true that at the time of each crisis, these countries had suffered some other shocks. In the case of the ERM, we can talk about the monetary and economic unification of Germany that, by itself, requires some appreciation of the German currency in terms of other currencies. And in the case of Latin America, we've seen the change in monetary policy in the United States and a decrease in the demand for assets of Latin America countries.

Those shocks require some real depreciation of the domestic currencies. The question is how to achieve this real depreciation. Mexico has chosen one way. Argentina, perhaps due to the history of chronic hyperinflation, has chosen the other way. There are trade-offs between credibility and real adjustment. The cost of maintaining central bank credibility has led Argentina into a large recession. But we have to consider that the situations in Mexico, the EMS countries, and Argentina are different. So choosing this fixed exchange rate might be appropriate for countries that have experience running hyperinflation, but at the same time, the choice bears some costs.

Welch:

Dr. Edwards has taken a stand on which type of exchange rate policy he likes, especially in the debate between more rigid and more flexible exchange rates. He clearly provides evidence that he likes more flexibility in exchange rates, although not necessarily a floating rate over a more rigid one. Rigid regimes tend to collapse, allowing speculators like George Soros to make a lot of money at the expense of other investors, and, probably more important, the central bank.

Flexible rates tend to preclude this type of situation. I wish he had pursued this thought further because he doesn't discuss the role that financial markets and financial institutions had in the Chilean, Mexican, or ERM crisis. Yes, fortunes were made and lost in the ERM crisis, but in the most recent Mexican crisis, fortunes mostly were lost. Why is that?

In the ERM crisis, speculators were allowed to short-sell currency. In other words, they could sell currency they didn't own. Shorting in the first instance may increase instability and make a currency more vulnerable to attack, as in ERM's case. In 1992, when the shorts were clearly much bigger than those going the other way for the British pound, everyone headed for the exits. But to make a profit on a short, you have to cover it. In other words, you must buy the assets you've sold that you do not own.

What happened almost immediately in the next week was a huge short-covering rally that gave a supporting bid to the British pound. On top of that, because those investors had to buy pound-denominated assets, a very large bond market rally began, despite the loss in credibility the Bank of England suffered from leaving the ERM.

In Mexico, there was no such dynamic. Shorting or hedging the peso is very difficult and very expensive. The first devaluation occurred on December 20, 1994, and signaled to investors who had not been getting the reserve data for some time that reserves were much worse than most had feared. Everybody headed for the exits, and for a couple of reasons: one was fear that dollar reserves would not cover short-term dollar obligations, most notably *tesobonos*, and two, fear that the first devaluation may have seriously injured the banks that were already in very serious condition. There was no supporting bid that emerged until the United States and the International Monetary Fund stepped in.

So the question here, at least in terms of the exchange-rate-regime choice and floating rate, is, Are certain levels of financial development and infrastructure necessary to accommodate a floating rate? We come to the same conclusion in the end about how to make a transition—especially using Chile as an example—to that particular type of regime if you do not have this infrastructure.

If regulation restricts the ability to short a currency or to hedge oneself, investment will be lower and the central bank will face political pressure, both internal and external, to provide that hedge through a fixed rate or similar policy. Although investors could not short the peso, it did not keep a collapse from occurring, particularly after the devaluation of December 20. These comments, however, do not detract from Dr. Edwards' main conclusion on flexible rates or the semiflexible rates I believe he prefers. But the role of financial institutions has many important dimensions not only to the question of collapse, but also to the question of persistence of inflation.

The framework Dr. Edwards chose to look at how this overvaluation occurred, in my mind, puts undue emphasis on backward indexation. No matter what exchange rate regime is in place, real appreciation follows huge capital inflows. It's not really a question of exchange rate regime at this point. However, Edwards concludes that the increasing rigidity of the exchange rate regime lowered inflation in both Chile and Mexico and led to overvaluations. Although his framework encompasses wage indexation, I find his choice puzzling because Dr. Edwards also concludes that the Mexicans had no longer had a true link between wages and inflation.

Work by Guillermo Calvo and Carlos Vegh has shown that the persistence of inflation may have more to do with credibility of monetary policy than with backward indexation. Similarly, if a central bank must compromise its monetary policy by providing liquidity to financial institutions after a run, that event may involve an issue of credibility because most agents know the central bank will intervene in a crisis.

I had questions about the econometrics in the way I understand Taylor's model. If you look at a model with backward-looking indexation, especially when you have inflation as a unit root, the autoregressive part of it isn't the most important component; the moving-average part is. In other words, most countries have random-walk-type inflation, and all sorts of policy regimes can generate that random walk, not just those with backward-looking indexation. If a government maximizes inflation tax revenue, you will get a unit root. So a better technique would be to fit an arm to the first difference of inflation and look at whether the moving-average part of the equation is significant.

Anna Novize of the World Bank applies this technique to Brazil, until recently the most notoriously indexed economy. She finds that inflation persistence, although significantly different from zero, is much smaller than most people believed due to backward-looking wage indexation.

Some of the clues to what happened in Mexico and in Chile lie in the financial system, as Dr. Edwards and his wife have shown in a number of works. If a central bank cannot credibly commit to refrain from expanding the money supply in a banking crisis, its monetary policy will not have full credibility in bringing down inflation, and there will be forward-looking persistence in the inflation rate.

In general, however, I agree with Dr. Edwards' conclusions in regard to Latin America (with the possible exception of Argentina) and other countries. Instead of statically looking at how these countries' exchange rate regimes are chosen, it is more interesting to look at how they have evolved over time. We clearly see a compendium of all the different options. Typically, Latin American countries have tried to introduce rigidity into their exchange rates. And, typically, the devaluation doesn't happen for the reason you see in Europe and elsewhere—to achieve growth.

Countries run out of reserves. But as the reserve accumulation process goes on, some rigidity returns, perhaps because of capital flows and so forth. However, it's hard to argue that the region of the Americas is an optimal currency area. That means a flexible exchange rate system is clearly in order. The question is how you get from a more rigid rate to a more flexible rate.

Colombia, Chile, and Ecuador now seem to have gradually adopted what Dr. Edwards favors—a floating-type band system—that seems to work quite well. Maybe we'll see it elsewhere in Latin America.

Edwards:

I would like to address some of the important points that the discussants made. First, I want to clarify that I have nothing against George Soros. I think that he and other speculators perform a great service to the international financial system. I am referring to the debate that we had when Jeff Frankel was talking about the need to have the optimal, as it were, degree of speculation for the exchange rate system to work appropriately.

The only way for the type of regime I have suggested to work is for the financial sector to be developed, not only in the sense of allowing people to shorten the currency, but also by having strong financial regulation that makes sure banks that intermediate these flows are healthy and are not going to behave in a reckless way.

The second point has to do with indexation and the question of whether I have exaggerated the role of backward-looking indexation in the case of Mexico, especially since what Mexico did was use the back toss to get away from backward-looking indexation in trying to introduce some kind of forward-looking elements.

Wages are a very important and key price in the economy but not the only one; a very important component in determining the overall aggregate degree of inertia in the system is the de facto optimal degree of indexation that comes off the willing and free negotiation between different parties.

What the data show in the case of Mexico is that although Mexico, unlike Chile, didn't have a legal backward-looking wage indexation system, the degree of backwardness of the indexation of other contracts, materials, rent, and so on was still significant in the sense that it maintained a residual degree of inertia that was very, very high.

This brings me to my third point: that inertia and unit root type of inflation behavior can be the result of many different types of models. What is really important is to compare whether the degree of inertia changes and whether there are breaks in the features and the characteristics of the time series of inflation when different policies take place. It is exactly in this type of analysis where we find that in Chile, there was not such a change. I was gratified to see that Graciela's results confirmed my previous results. But in Mexico at the time the *pactos* were adopted, there was a break in the degree of inertia, in inflation, but not one sufficient to eliminate inflation. That created the real exchange rate appreciation that I mentioned.

I'm not trying to make the point that only the inertial element was responsible for the real appreciation. What I'm trying to say is that there are two periods. One can distinguish that up to 1990, inertia and persistence were mostly what created the appreciation; after 1990 came the capital inflows, which made the overvaluation even worse.

Let me discuss three points that Graciela Kaminsky made that I think are very important. She rightly calls our attention to the distinction between equilibrium changes in the real exchange rate changes that are justified by changes in fundamentals and actual changes in the real exchange rate. She tells us, and very rightly, that not every appreciation of the real exchange rate is a situation of disagreement that should call for policy action. Every time the real exchange rate strengthens, we shouldn't get concerned and start devaluing. She mentions that Latin America went through numerous changes and reforms that surely affected the real exchange rate. I am absolutely in agreement with that. The problem, of course, is that most changes that Latin America went through (especially the opening of international trade, which is the great difference between Latin America today and 20 years ago) call for an equilibrium real depreciation, not appreciation.

It is exactly in that context where, on one hand, the trade reform was calling for a more depreciated exchange rate that would encourage exports and allow the trade reform to be successful but, on the other hand, was producing this great appreciation and was opening a gap between actual and equilibrium in the sense of creating an overvaluation.

Graciela also asks about the viability of fixed exchange rates in the long run. I think, in that sense, we must specify what we mean by the "long run." Paradoxically, Latin America offers the best historical episodes to look at this type of situation. Honduras had a fixed exchange rate between 1918 and 1990. That, as far as I know, is the longest fixed-exchange-rate experience in modern history. Guatemala had a fixed rate from 1926 to 1986. Central America's viability started to crumble in the 1980s as a result of three things: increased straight shocks whose magnitude was many times greater than those seen in the past, increased capital mobility, and a very serious social conflict that exacerbated the temptation to abuse the printing presses around the political process. Lars Stenson pointed out not too long ago, after reflecting on the ERM, that fixed exchange rates are not a shortcut to low inflation. I think that is a very important lesson.

Graciela states correctly that fixed rates worked because inflation went down in the first year. Of course, inflation will go down in the first year. If you fix the variable that governs one-half of the tradable prices, inflation will go down. The problem is, fixed rates tend to generate a situation of overvaluation that, most of the time, generates a very acute process of self-denial among policymakers, who just say it's not happening, it's justified, or it can be explained. In the end, they cannot explain it to you, and it's too late. The economy has already crashed. So the thing to take into account is that the true anchor must be fiscal policy.

Let me end by saying that for those of you who have not noticed it, I am not in favor of currency boards.

Question:
Liliana Rojas and John Welch brought up a key point. In looking at any of these exchange rate regimes, you have to look at the financial institutions outside the central bank. I would like some clarification from John. He said you couldn't short the Mexican peso because there weren't organized futures markets, but that just wasn't so. The Mexicans were shorting the peso like crazy beforehand. The constraint was that you had to have real assets that you could use as collateral to the banks to get loans. And as long as there weren't exchange controls between the United States and Mexico, you could cover your shorts. It was no problem.

Welch:
I totally agree with you. You can always short a currency by borrowing it. What I meant was an infrastructure that gave a dynamic that creates a bid for the currency on the other side. I totally agree with you. In that type of situation, sterilizing capital outflows is going to foresee your doom on the exchange rate regime.

Questions and Comments from the Floor

Question:
I found John Welch's idea of the Mexican crisis' being related to the fragility and the vulnerability of the banking system to be very interesting. I quite agree this is the key aspect of the crisis, especially with the fear that the central bank eventually could bail out banks with problems and expand the monetary supply.

These arguments may have more to do with self-fulfilling prophecies and the problems of fragility of the banking system than with the existence of an overvalued or extremely overvalued real exchange rate.

In the 1994 case, after the initial devaluation, there was a further real exchange rate devaluation for the following three months. It was not until the news came that there was money to support the adjustment problem in the banking system that we started seeing an overvaluation. So the problem might be a combination of an initially appreciated real exchange rate and a self-fulfilling crisis because of the bank fragility and vulnerability. This has to do more with the policies toward dealing with banking vulnerability and not so much with real exchange rate management.

Edwards:
That's a feasible story line. I think, however, one has to have some kind of event that ignites the whole process. In the case of Mexico, we had political shocks —the assassination of Luis Donaldo Colosio and Chiapas and so on—but also an economy—if one wants to follow your line of argument—that was vulnerable not only because the banks were in worse shape than many people had anticipated, but also because the real exchange rate reached a level at which many people in Mexico—in the financial sector, academia, the multilaterals—questioned its viability. Even if one is to take your argument, the real exchange rate overvaluation and the difference between stocks and flows in the capital flows adjustment process are very, very important.

Another question is why almost everyone was so wrong in figuring by how much the exchange rate had to be devalued before things would calm down. Most analysts had been concentrating the real exchange rate's role in generating a flow equilibrium in the current account. Analysts were ignoring the fundamental importance of helping generate a stock equilibrium and asset equilibrium. Once one takes that into account, the mystery disappears, and things become much easier to understand.

Appendix to Part II

Exchange Rate Policy and Macroeconomic Stability

Sebastian Edwards

During the crisis of the Exchange Rate Mechanism of the European Monetary System in September of 1992, fortunes were made and lost. It is reported that George Soros made close to $1 billion speculating against the pound. From a public policy perspective, this episode has added a new dimension to the debate, to what extent are "rigid" exchange rate regimes beneficial in the longer run?

This appendix briefly discusses some of these issues from a policy and comparative point of view. My approach is to develop a simple analytical framework, a model, and then contrast its implications with real-world experiences using statistical methods, namely regression analyses.

I assume that, initially, most contracts, including wages, are indexed to past inflation, and that the authorities follow a passive crawling peg exchange rate system, in which the exchange rate rule consists of adjusting the nominal exchange rate by a proportion ϕ ($\phi \leq 1$) of lagged inflation: $d_t = -\phi(\pi_{t-1} - \pi^*_{t-1})$. Monetary policy is assumed to be passive and to accommodate inertial inflationary forces. In this case, inflation will tend to perpetuate itself.

In a high-inflation setting, inertia is high and the coefficient a_1 is close to unity. The main purpose of using a fixed nominal exchange rate as an anchor is to lower the value of this coefficient and accelerate the convergence of domestic inflation toward world inflation. The effectiveness of this strategy will depend on two factors: (1) accompanying macroeconomic policies (behavior of z); and (2) behavior of inertial components in the rest of the economy, especially in wages.

Two important historical experiences with nominal exchange rate anchors during a stabilization occurred in Chile (1978–1982) and Mexico (1987–1994). In the late 1970s and after having eliminated a stubborn fiscal deficit, Chile adopted an exchange-rate-based stabilization program. Initially, from February 1978 to June 1979, the program consisted of a preannounced *declining* rate of devaluation of the domestic currency. In June 1979, with inflation standing at an annual rate of 34 percent, the government put an end to the system of a preannounced declining rate of devaluation and fixed the nominal exchange rate at 39 pesos per dollar. It was expected that this move to a fixed rate would accelerate the convergence of domestic to world inflation.

In 1988, the Mexican government embarked on an ambitious stabilization program. As in the case of Chile, the manipulation of the nominal exchange rate became an important component of the stabilization plan. In both cases, the rate of inflation declined, reaching a one-digit level. In both cases, however, the program eventually collapsed and major crises ensued.

An important question, however, is to what extent the adoption of the anchor policy accelerated the rate of convergence of domestic inflation toward world inflation. In terms of our equation, did the coefficient a_1 decline significantly after the adoption of the anchor? Technically, this can be analyzed by statistically estimating a_1 before and after the adoption of the anchor policy. If the anchors program is effective (and credible), the estimated coefficient of b_2 should be significantly *negative*, indicating that this policy successfully reduced the degrees of inertia in the system. $(b_1 + b_2)$ is the inertia coefficient after the anchor program is in effect.

As can be seen, in Chile, the program did not reduce the extent of inertia; in Mexico, it did. In the end in both cases, however, there was a substantial degree of real exchange rate overvaluation. This reduced the degree of competitiveness of exports and made imports cheaper.

Also in both cases, there was a major increase in capital inflows, putting pressure on the real exchange rate. These two factors, real exchange rate overvaluation plus major increases in capital inflows, allowed both Chile and Mexico to run very large trade and current account deficits. From every possible point of view, these deficits were unsustainable in the long run. In both cases, the capital inflows came to a (sudden) halt, forcing the economy to implement a major adjustment. The rigidity of wages and the inflexibility of the exchange rate made the adjustment particularly difficult.

Now I turn my attention to the selection of exchange rate regimes in the long run. In 1973, the international monetary system created in Bretton Woods came to an end, as the major industrialized countries abandoned fixed-exchange-rate regimes. In the 1990s, however, a large number of countries—88 in 1992, according to the IMF—continue to have some kind of fixed-exchange-rate regime. Most, but not all, of these countries are developing nations.

The most important economic factors are the degree of "external vulnerability" of the economy, its degree of openness, and its history of external difficulties. More open and vulnerable countries will tend to prefer flexible rates, as will countries with a history of external sector difficulties. The most important structural variables include the degree of development and the structure of production.

The key question is whether countries with a fixed-exchange-rate regime are indeed able to maintain a greater degree of monetary and fiscal discipline than are those with a more flexible regime. I use a data set drawn from 70 countries to analyze this issue empirically.

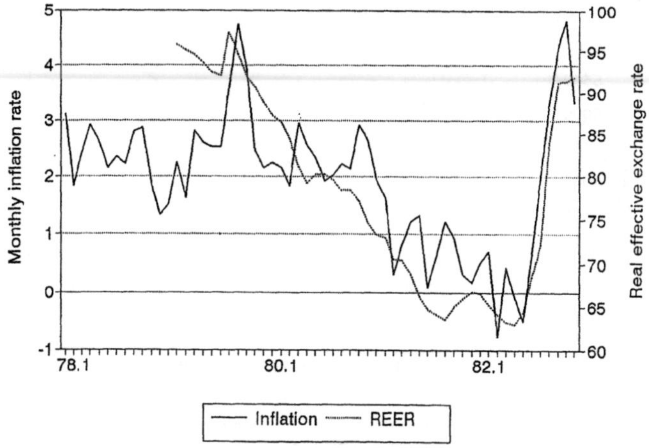

Figure IIA–1. Chile: Inflation and real exchange rate.

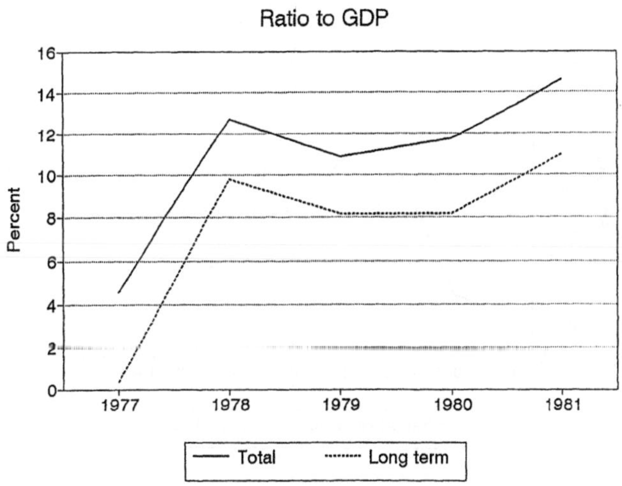

Figure IIA–2. Chile: Net capital inflows.

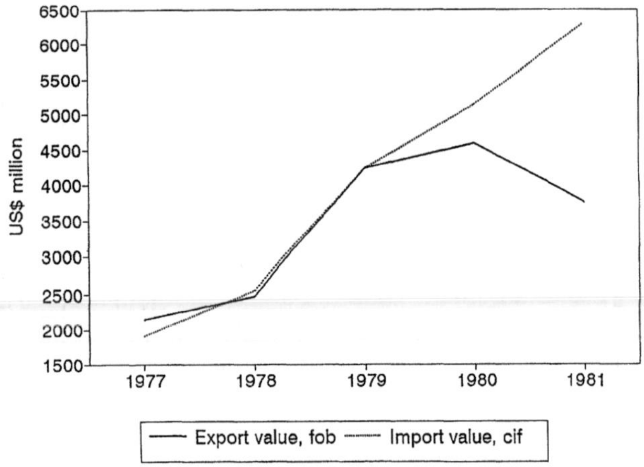

Figure IIA–3. Chile: Exports and imports.

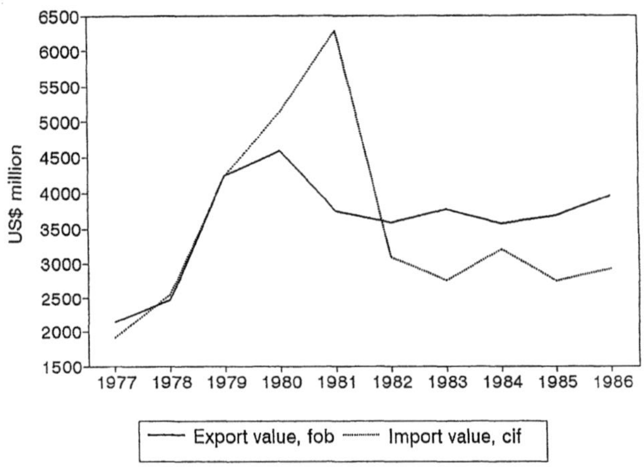

Figure IIA–4. Chile: Exports and imports.

Table IIA–1. Exchange rate arrangements (*as of September 30, 1994*).

Currency pegged to				
U.S. dollar	*French franc*	*Other currency*	*SDR*	*Other composite*
Antigua & Barbuda	Benin	Bhutan (Indian rupee)	Libya	Algeria
Argentina	Burkina Faso	Estonia (Deutsche mark)	Myanmar	Austria
Bahamas, The	Cameroon	Kiribati (Australian dollar)	Rwanda	Bangladesh
Barbados	C. African Rep.	Lesotho (South African rand)	Seychelles	Botswana
Belize	Chad	Namibia (South African rand)		Burundi
Djibouti	Comoros	San Marino (Italian lira)		Cape Verde
Dominica	Congo	Swaziland (South African rand)		Cyprus
Grenada	Côte d'Ivoire	Tajikistan, Rep. of (Russian ruble)		Czech Republic
Iraq	Equatorial Guinea			Fiji
Liberia	Gabon			Hungary
Lithuania	Mali			Iceland
Marshall Islands	Niger			Jordan
Micronesia, Fed. States of	Senegal			Kuwait
Nigeria	Togo			Malta
Oman				Mauritania
Panama				Mauritius
St. Kitts & Nevis				Morocco
St. Lucia				Nepal
St. Vincent and the Grenadines				Papua New Guinea
Syrian Arab Rep.				Slovak Republic
Turkmenistan				Solomon Islands
Venezuela				Thailand
Yemen, Republic of				Tonga
				Vanuatu
				Western Samoa

Table IIA–2. Exchange rate regimes.

Country Code (IMF)	*Country Name*	*d7985*	*d7992*	*Country Code (IMF)*	*Country Name*	*d7985*	*d7992*
111	United States	0	0	343	Jamaica	0	0
112	United Kingdom	0	0	369	Trinidad & Tobago	1	1
122	Austria	1	1	429	Iran	1	1
124	Belgium	0	0	524	Sri Lanka	0	0
128	Denmark	0	0	534	India	0	0
132	France	0	0	536	Indonesia	0	0
134	Germany	0	0	564	Pakistan	0	0
136	Italy	0	0	566	Philippines	0	0
138	Netherlands	0	0	578	Thailand	0	0
142	Norway	1	1	616	Botswana	1	1
144	Sweden	1	1	618	Burundi	1	1
156	Canada	0	0	622	Cameroon	1	1
158	Japan	0	0	626	Central African Rep.	1	1
172	Finland	1	0	628	Chad	1	1
174	Greece	0	0	634	Congo	1	1
178	Ireland	0	0	636	Zaire	0	0

182	Portugal	0	0	644	Ethiopia	1	1
184	Spain	0	0	646	Gabon	1	1
186	Turkey	0	0	652	Ghana	0	0
193	Australia	0	0	662	Cote D'Ivoire	1	1
196	New Zealand	0	0	664	Kenya	1	1
199	South Africa	0	0	666	Lesotho	1	1
218	Bolivia	0	0	684	Mauritius	1	1
223	Brazil	0	0	686	Morocco	0	0
228	Chile	0	0	694	Nigeria	0	0
233	Colombia	0	0	698	Zimbabwe	0	0
243	Dominican Republic	0	0	714	Rwanda	1	1
248	Ecuador	0	0	724	Sierra Leone	1	0
253	El Salvador	0	0	726	Somalia	0	0
268	Honduras	1	0	732	Sudan	1	0
273	Mexico	0	0	738	Tanzania	1	1
278	Nicaragua	1	0	742	Togo	1	1
288	Paraguay	1	0	744	Tunisia	1	0
293	Peru	0	0	746	Uganda	0	0
299	Venezuela	1	0	754	Zambia	0	0

Source: Constructed with data obtained from International Financial Statistics, IMF.

Table IIA–3. Probit regressions for exchange rate regime selection. Dependent variable D79–92 (*t*-statistics in parentheses).

Sample	*All*
Constant	–7.473
	(–1.932)
Log Pol Inst	–1.173
	(–2.690)
Log Inflation (–1)	–1.181
	(–1.491)
RER variability (RERV)	–0.355
	(–2.953)
RERV * Openness	0.005
	(3.065)
Log GNP per capita	1.556
	(2.768)
Urban	–0.084
	(–2.815)
Agriculture	0.106
	(2.528)
Current Account deficit	–2.051
	(–2.394)
N	61
Log Likelihood	–15.50
Chi-square	44.67

Table IIA–4. Regressions for inflation and exchange rate regime choice. (*t*-statistics in parentheses.)

Sample *Dependent variable*	*All* *Inflation*	*LDCs* *Inflation*
Constant	−0.840	1.243
	(−0.990)	(2.191)
Log GNP per capita	0.978	−1.480
	(0.832)	(1.573)
Urban	1.90E-04	−9.10E-04
	(0.040)	(−0.151)
Agriculture	0.017	—
	(2.686)	
Latin America	0.615	0.471
	(3.209)	(2.165)
Asia	−0.241	−0.505
	(−1.090)	(−1.959)
Industrial Countries	−0.409	—
	(−1.306)	
Political Instability	0.974	1.730
	(2.157)	(2.524)
d7980	−0.372	−0.488
	(−2.589)	(−2.604)
N	69	52
R-square	0.433	0.419

Part III EXCHANGE RATE VOLATILITY, INVESTMENT, AND GROWTH: SOME NEW EVIDENCE

It is often argued that exchange rate volatility deters foreign trade and investment. But is exchange rate volatility associated with higher or lower rates of growth? What is the best policy to achieve maximum growth?

Presenter:
Vittorio Corbo
Professor of Economics
Catholic University of Chile

Moderator:
W. Michael Cox
Vice President and Economic Advisor
Federal Reserve Bank of Dallas

Discussants:
David Gould
Senior Economist
Federal Reserve Bank of Dallas

Liliana Rojas-Suárez
Principal Adviser
Inter-American Development Bank

(Vittorio Corbo's presentation was based on this paper he cowrote with Patricio Rojas, Research Division, Central Bank of Chile.)

In recent years, there has emerged a broad professional consensus on the type of economic policies that are more conducive to an improvement of growth and a reduction of poverty. This consensus has resulted from the interpretation of the favorable growth record of the East Asian countries (World Bank 1993) and from the examination of the factors that account for the differences in performance between successful and unsuccessful adjustment programs (Corbo and Fischer 1995). This consensus was initially articulated in Williamson (1990).

Empirical work on the determinants of differences in growth rates across countries has also shown regularities that have reinforced the lessons obtained from the literature on the role of economic policies on growth. This work has incorporated on top of factor accumulation a separate role for the quality of economic policies. The work initiated by Romer (1986), Lucas (1988), and Barro (1990) has provided the analytical underpinning for a mechanism through which economic policies and investment, in human and physical capital, could affect not only the level of output but also its rate of growth. The belief that economic policy and the investment rate are major determinants of economic growth has long been expressed in the writings of economists, but it has only recently found its way into the standard growth literature. A sample of recent work along these lines is Levine and Renalt (1992), Fischer (1993 and 1991), Easterly and Rebelo (1993), King and Levine (1993), World Bank (1991), and Inter-American Development Bank (1995).

More recent work has emphasized the role of macroeconomic uncertainty on investment and growth.[1] Thus, Fischer (1993) investigates the effect of macroeconomic uncertainty on both growth rates and on factor accumulation.

In this paper, we examine the role of macroeconomic uncertainty on economic growth. Two sources of macroeconomic uncertainty are considered: uncertainty about the inflation rate and uncertainty about the real exchange rate. We distinguish two mechanisms through which macroeconomic uncertainty could affect long-term growth: its effect on the rate of investment and the overall level of efficiency or total factor productivity.

Our work is based on the by now standard "new growth theory" type of growth model, in which a country's growth performance is associated with the initial productivity gap with an industrial country, the rate of investment, initial human capital levels, economic policies, and macroeconomic uncertainty. Our empirical work indicates that the uncertainty in the real exchange rate is the single most important measure of macroeconomic uncertainty in explaining growth differences across countries and for the same country through time.

The Nexus Between Macroeconomic Uncertainty, Investment, and Growth

Some Historical Developments on the Determinants of Growth

The recent literature on growth highlights a number of channels through which economic policies could affect growth. Promoting human capital accumulation—for example, by providing adequate nutritional levels, basic educational skills, and investment in research and development—can foster growth (Romer 1989 and Rebelo 1992). Along these lines, Becker, Murphy, and Tamura (1990) show that economies may become stuck in a poverty trap: a situation in which low income and low human capital levels create incentives for high population growth and low investment in human capital that perpetuate the state of poverty. Policies that stimulate investment in human capital can break the economy out of this stagnant situation.

Furthermore, in a series of influential papers, Romer (1993a and 1993b) has singled out the role of the overall policy environment for the development and adaptation of ideas as one of the most important channels for policies to affect long-term growth. The new model also stresses the importance of trade policy, fiscal policy, and financial policy as determinants of long-term growth.[2] Macroeconomic uncertainty could affect growth indirectly through its effect on the investment rate and directly through its effect on total factor productivity. In recent years, Fischer has given a more prominent role to macroeconomic instability in the growth process through both its effect on factor accumulation and in the rate of change of total factor productivity (Fischer 1993 and 1991).

The Effects of Macroeconomic Uncertainty on Growth

We review now the channels through which macroeconomic uncertainty could affect long-term growth. Two types of macroeconomic volatility are considered in this paper: the volatility of inflation and the volatility of the real exchange rate. As most of this volatility in these variables is unpredictable, volatility generates uncertainty on the future value of both variables: the inflation rate and the real exchange rate. The higher uncertainty about the inflation rate will affect the information content of relative prices, resulting in a suboptimal choice of the input and output mix, a lower level of overall efficiency, and ultimately—through endogenous growth channels—in a lower level of growth. A higher level of real exchange rate uncertainty reduces the information content of the relative prices between tradable and nontradable goods and also the relative price of differentiated tradables, with effects on efficiency and growth similar to those associated with increased uncertainty about inflation.

In theory, the relationship between real exchange rate uncertainty and investment is ambiguous. If investment is irreversible, the increase in the uncertainty about future return associated with the increase in real exchange rate uncertainty increases the option value of investment and, in the short run, results in lower investment (Dixit and Pindyck 1993). However, the long-term relationship between real exchange rate uncertainty and investment is ambiguous. For example, Bertola (1989) shows that irreversibility of investment and uncertainty *can* lead to a higher capital output ration in long-run equilibrium, even though the higher uncertainty decreases the investment rate in the short run. In their review of the literature on uncertainty and investment, Pindyck and Solimano (1993, 274) conclude:

> There is little that can be said about the effects of uncertainty on the long-run equilibrium values of investment, the investment-to-output ratio, or the capital–output ratio. Thus, it is left for empirical work to investigate the link between uncertainty and investment.

In their empirical work, Pindyck and Solimano find that their measure of volatility (the volatility of the log of the marginal profitability of capital) is negatively associated with the investment rate, but it is statistically significant only for the developing countries in their sample. Furthermore, they find that the most important source of volatility in the marginal profitability of capital is due to the volatility of the inflation rate.

Real exchange rate uncertainty could also affect growth directly through its effect on the growth rate of total factor productivity. The mechanism here is from higher uncertainty in the real exchange rate to less predictable relative factor and commodity prices, a nonoptimal choice of the factor and output mix, a lower level of aggregate output, and—through endogenous growth channels—a lower rate of growth.[3]

A Framework for Studying the Relationship Between Macroeconomic Uncertainty and Growth

The Growth Equation

The neoclassical framework has provided the starting point for a number of studies to investigate the different sources of growth. The typical methodology of these studies (Levine and Renelt 1992; De Gregorio 1992; Fischer 1991; Barro 1991) is to start with a neoclassical production function of the type

$$Y_t = eF(L_t, K_t), \tag{1}$$

where K is capital, L is labor input, and μ is a constant rate of productivity growth. Putting this function in growth terms yields

$$y_t = \beta_L l_t + \beta_K k_t + \mu, \tag{2}$$

where small letters denote rates of growth. With constant returns to scale and perfect competition, the βs represent factor shares in output. Then, the first two terms on the right side of equation 2 represent the contribution of labor and capital to growth, while the last term represents the contribution of technical progress. The standard approach to growth accounting is to obtain input shares directly from the data. Solow (1956) uses the observed factor shares and growth rates of capital and labor to decompose the contributions of both factors to output growth. The part of growth that cannot be explained by input growth represents the growth in total factor productivity, which is assumed to come from exogenous technical change.

Since capital stock data are generally not available, adding the assumption of a constant capital output ratio enables one to write the rate of growth of the capital stock in terms of the investment rate. Then, the equation usually estimated by many empirical studies, both for time series data for a single country and for cross-sectional country studies, is

$$y_t = a_0 + a_1 1_t + a_2 i_t, \tag{3}$$

where i is the investment rate and, given the assumption that capital–output ratios and technology are the same in all countries, a_1 and a_2 should represent the marginal product of labor and capital share, respectively.

Essentially, most cross-sectional studies begin with this basic model and then include other regressors. Levine and Renelt (1992) present a list of 41 cross-sectional growth studies published since 1980. Each study regresses the output growth rate over a given period against a set of variables that, in addition to variables related to the productivity gap, labor, and physical and human capital, includes variables related to trade policy, fiscal policy, exchange rate policy, political and social stability, and macroeconomic policy and outcomes.

For a sample of 101 countries, Levine and Renelt analyze the effects of including variables in addition to the standard ones—gross domestic product (GDP) per capita, investment rate, rate of population growth, and rate of secondary school enrollment. Levine and Renelt's main findings are that several measures of economic policy are related to long-run growth and that, except for

Table III–1. Macroeconomic variability indicators.

	1960–1964	*1965–1969*	*1970–1974*	*1975–1979*	*1980–1984*	*1985–1988*
Whole Sample						
Inflation	6.61	7.43	12.73	19.57	28.35	63.20
S. Deviation of Inflation	3.71	4.58	8.84	7.99	16.51	76.77
S. Deviation of Real Exch. Rate	9.23	7.52	9.65	9.96	16.92	19.96
Whole, Excluding African Sample						
Inflation	7.78	8.46	13.93	15.74	31.00	30.06
S. Deviation of Inflation	3.97	3.22	10.11	6.95	18.99	22.04
S. Deviation of Real Exch. Rate	7.15	6.36	8.99	7.24	14.47	15.32
Latin American Sample						
Inflation	9.83	10.70	23.83	35.63	58.52	216.10
S. Deviation of Inflation	5.05	4.80	18.64	17.11	44.09	293.13
S. Deviation of Real Exch. Rate	6.86	8.08	9.16	9.83	21.10	15.12
African Sample						
Inflation	3.13	4.82	7.66	17.32	13.07	17.76
S. Deviation of Inflation	3.08	4.14	5.70	6.99	5.05	8.78
S. Deviation of Real Exch. Rate	14.57	10.38	9.06	14.88	14.97	30.79

the investment ratio, the relationship between growth and every particular macroeconomic indicator is fragile.

On the other hand, Fischer (1991), using cross-sectional regression for average growth in a sample of 73 countries and a pooled cross-sectional time series regression for annual growth in the same sample of countries, finds a significant relationship between macroeconomic policy-related variables and growth, supporting the view that the quality of macroeconomic management matters for growth. In this paper, we use the same type of models.

In our empirical work, we use a model of the type provided by equation 3. Our empirical work is done using two databases. The first is a sample of 58 countries that corresponds to the whole sample of Summers and Heston (1991), excluding the African countries. The second sample includes only Latin American countries. The Appendix to Part III presents an overview of the data and defines the data sources.

We investigate now the variability in the two macroeconomic variables of interest: the inflation rate and the real exchange rate. As shown in Table III–1, the level of inflation and the variability of both the inflation rate and the real exchange rate increase slightly between the first and second period and then take a big jump in the period 1970–1974. The last period corresponds to the breakdown of the Bretton Woods agreement.

In industrial countries, it has also been found that the breakdown of the Bretton Woods system of pegged but adjustable exchange rates has coincided with an increase in the variability of nominal and real exchange rates of individual countries (Mussa 1990 and 1986). Furthermore, empirical evidence, based on both cross-section and time series data, has shown that the short-run variability of real exchange rates is higher under floating-rate regimes than under fixed-rate regimes.

Furthermore, recent work on the determinants of nominal exchange rate movements shows that most of the exchange rate variability has not been anticipated. Thus, higher exchange rate variability results also in higher exchange rate uncertainty (Taylor 1995; Obstfeld 1995; and Goldstein 1995).

The increase in variability continues throughout the periods. For the particular case of Latin American countries, there is a large increase in the variability of the inflation rate between the period 1980–1984 and the period 1985–1988. This is not surprising, as the macroeconomic adjustment programs enacted as a response to the severe terms of trade, interest rate, and sudden cutoff of external financing shocks of the 1980–1984 period called for a larger real devaluation and reduced aggregate spending. The sudden collapse of external financing at a time when fiscal deficits were increasing (as a result of the cumulative effect of real depreciation on the budget, the slowdown of economic activity, and the support to the financial system) led to monetization and inflation. Interestingly enough, the variability of the real exchange rate was reduced between the period 1980–1984 and the period 1985–1988. This result is not surprising, as by now most Latin American governments were pursuing real exchange rate targeting to support the development of the export sector.

In the case of the African countries, there is a big jump in the variability of the real exchange rate between the periods 1980–1984 and 1985–1988. This result is due in major part to the increasing misalignment of the CFA countries as a result of the lack of financial discipline in the early 1980s (Devarajan and De Melo, 1991).

We now investigate the direct effect of macroeconomic uncertainty on growth and on the investment rate. In particular, we use two measures of macroeconomic uncertainty: the standard deviation of inflation and the standard deviation of the real exchange rate. Both the growth and the investment model extend the models used in Corbo and Rojas (1993 and 1992), adding to the by now standard Barro type of growth equation the two measures of macroeconomic uncertainty. The investment equation is of the type used by Solimano (1992) and Fischer (1991).

Econometric Results

In this section, we present different specification estimates of growth and investment equations. As we use time invariant variables in our panel data, we cannot allow for fixed effects in our estimates. Therefore, our estimates are obtained using random effects.

The single cross-sectional equation has been the alternative most used in the empirical growth literature. However, averaging over the entire sample period eliminates the information contained in the sample about the effect of changing conditions of growth in individual countries and allows only cross-country variation to inform the estimates. Furthermore, macroeconomic uncertainty is a more short-run, within-period effect that, to be properly captured, requires analysts to work with much shorter periods than the ones used until now in the empirical literature. Thus, in what constitutes a major departure from the empirical work in this area, we work with a mix of a time series and a cross-section of countries. The empirical work is performed as a panel estimation using subperiod averages for the period between 1960 and 1988. However, since we are interested in secular growth patterns, some amount of averaging was required to net out irregular fluctuations in the annual data. For this purpose, the data were pooled using five-year averages and one four-year average. The periods used are 1960–1964, 1965–1969, 1970–1974, 1975–1979, 1980–1984, and 1985–1988.

We discuss now the definition and measurement of a macroeconomic framework conducive to higher investment and higher growth. A stable macroeconomic framework can be described as one in which inflation is low and predictable, real interest rates are positive but not too high, fiscal policy is stable and sustainable, the real exchange rate is competitive and predictable, and the balance-of-payments situation is perceived as viable (Corbo and Fischer 1992). From this list of variables, we use the level and standard deviation of the inflation rate, the standard deviation of the real effective exchange rate, and the size of the trade deficit to GDP. The latter variable is used as an indicator of the sum of the private and public deficit to GDP ratio, a higher value indicating less total macroeconomic discipline.

Whole Sample, Excluding African Countries

Previous work done with the complete database showed that the African countries do not have the same growth and investment equations as the rest of the countries (Corbo and Rojas 1992), and we therefore work here with the whole sample, excluding the African countries. To avoid the possibility of endogeneity in the growth equations, all the regressions were estimated using the instrumental variable technique. Additionally, all the standard errors were computed using White's (1980) heteroskedasticity-robust procedure.

Tables III–2 and III–3 present the results for the whole sample, excluding the African countries. The first column in Table III–2 presents the results for a standard growth equation. The right-hand-side variables are investment rates of the period and of the previous period, the productivity gap vis-à-vis the United States, the government spending to GDP ratio, and a measure of human capital, the primary school enrollment rate. All the equations are estimated using instrumental variables to avoid the standard simultaneous equation bias that can arise in this type of equation. All variables are statistically significant.

Regressions 2 to 5 assess the effect of macroeconomic instability on long-term growth. In regression 2, we add two new variables: the inflation rate and the standard deviation of the real exchange rate. Both variables are highly significant and have the expected signs.

The negative effect of exchange rate uncertainty on growth has also been found in Cottani et al. (1990) and Dollar (1992). However, the two studies do not control for new growth theory-type of variables, and their findings most likely are subject to specification bias, as their equation leaves out important variables. IDB (1995) also reports an important effect of exchange rate uncertainty on growth in a steady-state cross-sectional study of a large database that includes the African countries and uses as its unit of observation the average for the period 1960–1985.

The inflation rate and its standard deviation are highly collinear; therefore, the significance of the inflation rate could be due to the increased uncertainty

Table III–2. Pooled regressions for growth rate in GDP per-capita; five-years averaged data for whole sample, excluding African countries; instrumental variable estimation: 1960–88.

	(1)	*(2)*	*(3)*	*(4)*	*(5)*
Constant	−0.004	0.004	0.004	0.009	0.009
	(−0.343)	(0.279)	(0.266)	(0.593)	(0.584)
Investment ratio in t	0.609	0.532	0.536	0.51	0.512
	(2.436)	(2.051)	(2.069)	(1.968)	(1.950)
Investment ratio in t–1	−0.48	−0.42	−0.422	−0.41	−0.413
	(−2.239)	(−1.882)	(−1.893)	(−1.843)	(−1.828)
Productivity gap	−0.013	−0.013	−0.013	−0.014	−0.014
vis-à-vis USA	(−1.809)	(−1.794)	(−1.771)	(−1.949)	(−2.015)
Government spending (x10E-2)	−0.069	−0.074	−0.074	−0.082	−0.079
	(−2.784)	(−2.924)	(−2.927)	(−3.132)	(−2.844)
Primary school rate	0.014	0.018	0.018	0.018	0.018
	(1.421)	(1.723)	(1.693)	(1.709)	(1.735)
Inflation rate		−1.53E-03			
		(−4.381)			
S. Deviation of inflation rate			−8.69E-02	−8.89E-04	−8.93E-04
			(−4.894)	(−4.951)	(−4.961)
Trade deficit					−0.011
					(−0.222)
Standard Deviation of RER		−3.46E-02	−3.62E-02	−3.16E-02	−3.22E-02
		(−2.928)	(−3.057)	(−2.607)	(−2.556)
Assassinations				−0.004	−0.005
				(−2.133)	(−2.132)
Sample Size	267	263	263	263	263
Corrected R-squared	0.26	0.272	0.271	0.275	0.272

Note: t-statistics in parentheses. The regressions also include time-period dummies for periods 1965–69, 1970–74, 1975–79, and 1980–84.

associated with the higher standard deviation of inflation that goes hand in hand with a higher level of inflation. The results presented in the third column of this table support this hypothesis. Thus, when we introduce the standard deviation of the inflation rate instead of the inflation rate, the results do not change much. The roles of political instability variables on growth were also investigated. Regressions 4 and 5 add as a growth determinant the index of assassinations taken from Barro and Wolf (1989). The estimates indicate that the coefficient of this variable is negative and highly significant.[4] This result is consistent with the hypothesis that political uncertainty has a negative effect on growth. Finally, in column 5, when we add an additional measure of macroeconomic imbalance, the trade deficit to GDP ratio, the results show that after introducing the macroeconomic volatility variables the trade deficit is not statistically significant.

Table III–3 presents results about the determinants of the investment rate, the single most important variable that accounts for differences in growth rates in this sample (Corbo and Rojas 1992). As discussed above, in a world of irreversible investment, theory provides no unambiguous answer with respect to the effect of a higher level of macroeconomic uncertainty on the steady-state investment rate. However, it does predict that increasing macroeconomic uncertainty would result in a postponement of investment. In our database of observations that are five-year averages, the short-run effect of uncertainty on investment should result in a negative coefficient for the macroeconomic uncertainty variable(s). Our panel data results are consistent with this implication, as the coefficients of both the variability of inflation and the variability of the real exchange rate have negative signs and are highly significant. As shown in the last column, the variable number of assassinations also has a detrimental effect on investment rates.

Latin American Country Estimates

The rest of the results are based on a richer database that includes only the Latin American countries. In this sample, we control also for supply shocks in the form of terms-of-trade shocks, and we include a measure of distortions in the exchange rate market. Table III–4 shows the results for the regressions of GDP per capita growth, and Table III–5 shows the results for the regressions of the investment rate.

In general, the most robust determinants of growth are the investment rate, the initial relative productivity gap vis-à-vis the United States, the government expenditures to GDP ratio, the primary school rate, and the measures of macroeconomic stability (the inflation rate, the standard deviation of the inflation rate, the trade deficit, and the standard deviation of the real exchange rate). In most of the regression, the coefficients of these variables appeared to be statistically

Table III–3. Pooled regressions for investment ratios; five-years averaged data for whole sample, excluding African countries: 1960–88.

	(1)	*(2)*	*(3)*	*(4)*	*(5)*	*(6)*
Constant	3.533	2.347	1.842	1.837	2.936	2.745
	(2.369)	(1.631)	(1.253)	(1.253)	(1.927)	(1.794)
Growth rate in GDP per-capita in t–1	64.218	61.206	59.63	59.278	58.178	57.989
	(7.402)	(7.268)	(7.271)	(7.250)	(6.981)	(6.987)
Productivity gap vis-à-vis USA	1.509	1.298	1.519	1.494	0.514	
	(0.564)	(0.486)	(0.567)	(0.557)	(0.195)	
Government spending	−0.284	−0.307	−0.318	−0.317	−0.336	−0.346
	(−3.801)	(−3.929)	(−4.057)	(−4.056)	(−4.177)	(−4.279)
Primary school rate	10.735	15.335	15.634	15.644	13.931	14.167
	(2.492)	(3.861)	(3.853)	(3.857)	(3.487)	(3.599)
Inflation rate				−1.42E-01		
				(−2.083)		
S. Deviation of inflation rate		−6.40E-02	−7.43E-02		−7.32E-02	−7.26E-02
		(−1.827)	(−2.232)		(−2.422)	(−2.433)
Standard Deviation of RER			−0.048	−0.047	−0.041	−0.041
			(−2.594)	(−2.585)	(−2.297)	(−2.316)
Assassinations					−3.679	−3.741
					(−4.143)	(−4.043)
Sample Size	290	284	284	284	284	284
Corrected R-squared	0.317	0.335	0.343	0.344	0.361	0.364

Note: t-statistics in parentheses. The regressions also include time-period dummies for periods 1965–69, 1970–74, 1975–79, and 1980–84.

Table III–4. Pooled regressions for growth rate in GDP per-capita; five-years averaged data for Latin American countries: 1960–88. Inst. variable estimation.

	(1)	*(2)*	*(3)*	*(4)*	*(5)*	*(6)*	*(7)*	*(8)*	*(9)*
Constant	−0.019	−0.016	−0.012	−0.018	−0.01	−0.011	−0.019	−0.019	−0.101
	(−0.643)	(−0.436)	(0.374)	(−0.497)	(−0.447)	(−0.274)	(−0.554)	(−0.555)	(−0.907)
Investment ratio in t	0.291	0.34	0.319	0.346	0.281	0.333	0.256	0.251	0.256
	(1.517)	(1.967)	(1.798)	(1.976)	(1.360)	(1.959)	(1.431)	(1.422)	(1.976)
Investment ratio in t–1	−0.258	−0.307	−0.294	−0.311	−0.276	−0.309	−0.24	−0.24	−0.232
	(−1.611)	(−2.073)	(−1.926)	(−2.076)	(−1.579)	(−2.106)	(−1.579)	(−1.571)	(−2.134)
Productivity gap vis-à-vis USA	−0.056	−0.079	−0.083	−0.078	−0.083	−0.08	−0.077	−0.078	−0.073
	(−2.997)	(−3.805)	(−3.821)	(−3.686)	(−3.284)	(−3.757)	(−3.537)	(−3.545)	(5.384)
Government spending (x10E-2)	−0.119	−0.073	−0.078	−0.074	−0.101	0.073	−0.09	−0.09	−0.079
	(−4.457)	(−2.350)	(−2.406)	(−2.345)	(−1.930)	(−2.374)	(−2.724)	(−2.744)	(−3.726)
Primary school rate	0.044	0.041	0.046	0.041	0.047	0.04	0.052	0.052	0.043
	(2.901)	(3.178)	(3.306)	(3.072)	(2.822)	(2.903)	(3.792)	(3.821)	(4.709)
Growth rate in terms of trade	0.208	0.188	0.185	0.19	0.201	0.179	0.177	0.177	
	(4.565)	(4.172)	(4.274)	(4.204)	(4.709)	(3.797)	(4.235)	(4.230)	
Inflation rate		−9.96E-04	−4.45E-03		−7.03E-04	−1.02E-03		−6.36E-04	
		(−2.575)	(−1.487)		(−1.773)	(−2.723)		(−2.234)	
S. Deviation of inflation rate							−4.21E-04		−3.54E-04
							(−2.493)		(−1.737)
Trade deficit		−0.185	−0.209	−0.172	−0.180	−0.192	−0.192	−0.193	−0.259
		(−2.022)	(−2.202)	(−1.863)	(−1.705)	(−2.091)	(−2.058)	(−2.062)	(−4.016)
Black premium rate			4.10E-04	−9.27E-05					
			(1.233)	(−2.925)					
Trade ratio					0.008				
					(0.549)				
Standard Deviation of RER							−3.41E-02	−3.34E-02	−4.24E-02
							(−3.554)	(−3.464)	(−4.542)
Assassinations						−0.002			−0.002
						(−1.278)			(−2.029)
Sample Size	100	100	100	100	100	100	100	100	100
Corrected R-squared	0.518	0.539	0.537	0.536	0.53	0.538	0.555	0.554	0.602

Note: t-statistics in parentheses. The regressions also include time-period dummies for periods 1965–69, 1970–74, 1975–79, and 1980–84.

significant regardless of the inclusion of other variables. The black premium rate also appeared to be negatively correlated with growth, but this result was more sensitive to the specification.

Furthermore, in all the regressions reported in Table III–4, the coefficient of the productivity gap variable is negative and highly significant, providing strong evidence in favor of the hypothesis of conditional convergence of per capita GDP growth. That is, holding everything else constant, the countries with the lower per capita income grew at a higher rate than countries with a higher level of per capita income.

The human capital variable (proxied by the primary school rate) shows a positive and significant effect on growth in all the regressions. On the other hand, government spending on GDP has a negative and significant effect on growth in all the regressions of Table III–4.

An important difference between the results for the whole sample, excluding the African countries, and results for Latin American countries only is the large drop in the sum of the coefficients for the investment variables. This sum, which corresponds to the steady-state coefficient for investment, is reduced from 0.099 (column 5 in Table III–2) to only 0.024 (column 9 in Table III–4). Thus, the investment rate has a much smaller contribution to steady-state growth in Latin America than in the whole sample, excluding Africa.

Regressions 4 and 6 assess the effect of trade openness on long-term growth. Two measures of openness were considered: the GDP share of total trade and the black market, or parallel market, premium. The first one tries to use a proximate effect of openness as a proxy for openness itself, while the black market premium is directly related to changes in trade restrictions or in openness, basically because the premium reflects the excess demand for tradable and for foreign assets that is not satisfied by the official foreign exchange market. Thus, the greater the controls on the use of official foreign exchange, the larger the premium on the black, or parallel, market exchange rate. The estimates of regression 5 show that the coefficient of the share of total trade in GDP is positive but not significant. However, in the case of the black market premium rate, its coefficient in regression 4 is significant and negative, indicating that those Latin American countries with more foreign exchange restrictions have recorded slower output growth.

However, the significant effect of the black market premium rate on growth depends on the presence of the inflation rate in the regression. When both variables are included in the specification (regression 3), both variables are not significant and the sign of the black market premium is positive, indicating that this variable could also represent some degree of macroeconomic instability more than the degree of openness of the economy. This caveat to the use of the black market premium as a proxy for openness arises from the fact that the demand for foreign exchange assets is also a function of the degree of political and macroeconomic instability. Thus, when the premium changes because the portfolio excess demand for foreign assets is affected by political or economic "news" or internal civil disturbances, it undermines the usefulness of the premium as a measure of openness. Then, the premium may change due to speculation, even when there is no change in the degree of restrictiveness of the regime.[5]

Equations 7, 8, and 9 in Table III–4 include as regressors the variability of the inflation rate and the variability of the real exchange rate. After including the standard type of Barro-augmented equation and the trade deficit to GDP ratio, the two macroeconomic variability variables are highly significant, and both have a negative sign. Furthermore, the adjusted corrected *r*-square for these regressions is 0.602. From the two macroeconomic variability variables, the standard deviation of the real exchange rate is the most significant in all the regressions. Thus, our empirical work indicates that a higher variability of the real exchange rate and of the inflation rate is associated with lower growth in total factor productivity.

As we mentioned earlier, the second channel through which economic policies and macroeconomic uncertainty could affect growth is investment rates. Table III–5 presents estimates of numerous pooled investment regressions. In all these regressions, the dependent variable is the share of investment in GDP for each of the periods also used for the growth equations. Regression 1 presents the results of the simplest model. In this model, the investment rate is explained in terms of an accelerator model augmented by a human capital variable, the share of government spending in GDP, the productivity gap vis-à-vis the United States, and a terms-of-trade variable that accounts for supply shocks. In this equation, the coefficient of the relative productivity gap vis-à-vis the United States and all other coefficients but one of the terms-of-trade variables are significant and with the expected signs. The latter has the expected sign but is only marginally significant. In particular, the significant coefficient on the lagged growth rate in GDP per capita is consistent with the usual finding that accelerator-type investment functions perform well.

Similar to the results obtained for the larger sample in the investment equation and in the Latin American equation for the growth rate, both human capital and the ratio of government spending to GDP have significant effects on the investment rate in all the regressions in Table III–5. Both effects on investment not only have the expected signs but also are significant at the 1-percent level.

In regression 2, we add the standard deviation of the inflation rate. This variable has a negative and highly statistically significant coefficient; a larger standard deviation of inflation decreases the information content of relative prices and makes more attractive the option of waiting before undertaking an irreversible investment. In regression 3, we also include the standard deviation of the real exchange rate. The coefficient of this variable has the right sign, and it is also highly significant.

Table III–5. Pooled regressions for investment ratios; five-years averaged data for Latin American countries: 1960–88.

	(1)	*(2)*	*(3)*	*(4)*	*(5)*
Constant	6.031	5.749	5.792	7.118	6.568
	(2.963)	(2.771)	(2.829)	(3.620)	(3.470)
Growth rate in GDP	48.604	47.393	45.364	43.977	47.154
per-capita in t–1	(4.271)	(4.136)	(4.060)	(3.916)	(4.590)
Productivity gap	−13.041	−12.923	−12.664	−12.867	−11.237
vis-à-vis USA	(−1.968)	(−1.926)	(−1.949)	(−2.118)	(−1.942)
Government spending	−0.324	−0.307	−0.333	−0.352	−0.342
	(−3.134)	(−2.911)	(−3.190)	(−3.280)	(−3.222)
Secondary school rate	32.222	31.361	34.65	33.951	32.726
	(2.186)	(2.084)	(2.272)	(2.397)	(2.253)
S. Deviation of inflation rate		−7.10E-02	−7.55E-02	−7.25E-02	−7.15E-02
		(−2.028)	(−2.260)	(−2.291)	(−2.229)
Standard Deviation of RER			−0.047	−0.035	−0.035
			(−2.286)	(−1.708)	(−1.716)
Terms of Trade Index	−5.38E-03	−5.47E-03	−5.39E-03	−4.42E-03	
	(−1.537)	(−1.562)	(−1.515)	(−1.281)	
Assassinations				−3.426	−3.502
				(−5.346)	(−5.155)
Sample Size	100	100	100	100	100
Corrected R-squared	0.307	0.308	0.317	0.372	0.373

Note: t-statistics in parentheses. The regressions also include time-period dummies for periods 1965–69, 1970–74, 1975–79, and 1980–84.

Finally, regressions 4 and 5 include a political instability variable. The coefficient of this variable is negative and highly significant, helping improve the explanatory power of the regression by about 6 percentage points. As Barro (1991) maintains, this negative relationship between investment and political instability could involve the adverse effects of political instability on property rights and the linkage between property rights and private investment. However, the correlation could also reflect a political response to bad economic outcomes. From Tables 4 and 5, we observe that the political instability variable is a significant explanatory variable in both the growth and the investment relation. Thus, political instability affects the rate of growth directly and indirectly through the investment rate.

In general, our findings are consistent and extend the results of some recent theoretical and empirical work on the role of uncertainty and the credibility of policies on investment and growth (Pindyck and Solimano 1993 and Fischer 1993).

To illustrate the importance of the relationship between volatility and growth, we decompose the growth differential between the five highest average growth countries and the five lowest average growth countries during 1960–88. We attribute the difference in growth rates to economic and political characteristics. For this decomposition of growth differential, we use the coefficients of equation 9 in Table III–4. The results are presented in Table III–6. As the tables indicate, the average growth in per capita income in the highest growth countries was 2.3 percent per year higher than that registered in the lowest growth countries. However, the group of highest growth countries started in 1960 with a lower per capita income than the group of lowest growth countries. It was expected that the first group would have tended to grow more rapidly than the second group, and then the "catch up" effect should explain 0.9 percent per year of the growth difference. Taking this factor into account, the difference to be explained by other factors between the highest and lowest growth Latin American countries becomes 1.4 percentage points. Basically, the table shows that investment in human capital accounts for a very large proportion, around 42 percent, of the difference, while the share of government spending in GDP accounts for about 21 percent of the difference. On the other hand, volatility of real exchange and inflation rates accounts for 21 and 5 percent of the difference, respectively. However, the difference between the investment rates of both groups of countries accounts for a very small fraction of the difference. The latter result is due to both a small coefficient for the investment rate and a small difference between the average investment rates of both groups of countries.

Further discussion is warranted regarding the robust finding that a lower variability of the real exchange rate has a positive effect on the rate of growth, both through a higher investment rate and through a higher rate of growth—holding

Table III–6. Growth differential between the highest and the lowest growth rate Latin American countries.

	Actual difference	*Percentage of the growth difference*
Difference in average growth	2.30%	
Predicted "catch up"	0.9	
Difference in growth to be explained	1.4	100.0%
Amount due to		
Domestic investment	−0.03	−2.1
Government spending to GDP	0.3	21.1
Primary school rate	0.6	42.3
Trade deficit	−0.2	−14.1
Volatility of RER	0.3	21.1
Volatility of inflation	0.07	5.0
Political uncertainty	0.08	5.6
Unexplained	0.3	21.1

Source: Calculations using estimates presented in Table III–4, equation 9.

constant the rate of investment. A higher level of variability in both variables is usually a manifestation that the macroeconomic situation is getting out of control. Indeed, aware of the detrimental effects of inflation and its variability on overall economic activity, there has been an important movement to introduce institutional arrangements that provide for an independent central bank removed from political pressures. The main objective of the central bank has been to achieve a continuous and gradual reduction in the inflation rate. This movement is most advanced in Latin America, the region with the worst inflation record during the postwar period. Thus, independent central banks have been established in Chile, Colombia, Mexico, Peru, and Argentina, and this process is under way in Bolivia.

There is also increasing awareness of the importance of avoiding the sharp real appreciation and real exchange misalignments that are linked to exchange-rate-based stabilization programs that rely on a fixed exchange rate for too long. But also there is increasing awareness that, depending on the exchange rate system, the authorities could control the nominal exchange rate (in a fixed or adjustable peg system), the money supply, or the interest rate (in a flexible exchange rate system), but independent of the exchange rate system, the real exchange rate—with its variability—is an endogenous variable. Therefore, the way to reduce the variability of the real exchange rate is through a macroeconomic policy that results in a low fiscal deficit—in a world of increasingly integrated capital markets and flexible nominal exchange rate regimes—and a monetary policy in which nominal domestic interest rates are in line with international interest rates, augmented by the expected rate of depreciation. In this type of setting, a domestic interest rate that is not in line with international interest rates will result in large changes in the nominal exchange rate. Given that, as a result of the stickiness of commodity prices and of the inflation rate, in the short and medium run, the variability of the nominal exchange rate is closely associated with the variability of the real exchange rate (Mussa 1990, 1986).

The interest in real exchange rate stability has risen recently in the context of capital inflows toward emerging markets. It could be claimed that a sudden jump in capital inflows could result in a real exchange rate appreciation as well as in a higher real exchange rate variability as nominal interest rates are adjusted to deal with some of the aggregate demand effects of the inflows. In a forthcoming comparison of policies to deal with capital inflows of Asian and Latin American countries, V. Corbo and L. Hernández show that the countries that have received the largest capital inflows (as a percentage of GDP) on average during 1989–1982 *are not* those that have experienced the largest real exchange rate appreciation, implying that the application of different economic policies may have helped contain the appreciation of the real exchange rate, despite receiving significant levels of capital inflows. In particular, those countries that show a decreasing pattern of government consumption (as a percentage of GDP) are also the ones that show a lower real exchange rate appreciation, while those countries that show an increasing share of government consumption in GDP are the same ones that show the highest real exchange rate appreciation. They also found that sterilized intervention is most effective when it is accompanied by fiscal restraint. However, it does not seem to be a sustainable policy in the long run, as sterilized intervention tends to exacerbate capital inflows rather than ameliorate them. This occurs because it tends to increase the differential between domestic and foreign interest rates. Furthermore, sterilized intervention worsens the quasi-fiscal deficit of the central bank.

They finally concluded that an increase in public-sector savings seems to be the only sustainable policy to protect the real exchange rate *in the long run* and seems to be perceived more favorably by the international investors' community. However, a mixed fiscal–monetary policy seems to be more appropriate in the short run than a pure fiscal policy. This occurs because fiscal policy usually lacks the required flexibility to deal with volatile capital flows in the short run.

Conclusions

The new empirical work reported in this paper confirms some of our earlier results. Corbo and Rojas (1993) also provide some new clues on the role of policy on growth. We briefly summarize our main findings.

First, policies can affect growth directly through the law of motion for growth and indirectly through investment rates.

Second, human capital has a positive effect on growth, both through the growth equation and through a higher rate of investment. This result shows that public policy has an important role in promoting growth by enhancing the human capital base. The latter could be done through the direct provision of human capital for the low-income groups of the population or through the creation of an enabling environment that reduces distortions to the accumulation of human capital.

Third, controlling for other factors, the share of government spending on GDP has a negative effect on growth and investment rates. In general, government spending can enhance or hinder growth. Government spending may promote growth by providing essential public goods. However, it could create negative growth effects by wasting resources on programs with low rates of return. Our results show that, on average, government spending has a strong negative effect on growth.

Fourth, and what is a new and very robust result, is the negative effect of macroeconomic uncertainty on growth. Thus, the standard deviations of the inflation rate and of the real exchange rate have a negative effect on growth, both directly through the rate of increase of total factor productivity and indirectly through its negative effect on the investment rate.

Fifth, political instability has also a negative effect on growth, both through the growth equation and through lower investment rates.

From the above analysis emerges a growth strategy. Public policy should be geared to deliver a stable macroeconomic framework, to improve the human capital base of the population, and to keep a low share of government consumption to GDP. Surprisingly, differences in investment rates were not important when accounting for differences in the rate of growth between the high-performing and low-performing Latin American countries. Thus, it is not just the level of investment that matters but also its efficiency.

Notes

1. Inter-American Development Bank (1995) presents a nice summary and provides numerous sources on the recent work along these lines.

2. Most development practitioners have, for a long time, emphasized the role of economic policies and the formation of human and physical capital on the overall growth process. Thus, Díaz-Alejandro (1976) concentrates on poor economic policies to explain the poor long-term growth record of Argentina. Krueger (1978), Little (1982), Feder (1983), and Balassa (1985) have used similar arguments. For these authors, there is not much that is new in the "new growth" theories.

3. Real exchange rate uncertainty also affects growth by denying countries the full benefit of specialization through international trade. Thus, Caballero and Corbo (1989) have shown that exchange rate uncertainty has a negative effect on exports.

4. We report only the result for the variable number of assassinations per million population per year (1960–1985). Other variables were also considered and were found not to have a significant effect on growth. These variables were the index of civil liberties, the index of political rights, and the number of *coups d'etats*.

5. It is surprising that the trade openness variable, measured by the trade ratio, is never significant. There are many reasons the increase in the degrees of openness should be associated with higher growth (Dornbusch 1992). In particular, the new growth theories suggest a link between openness and the long-run output growth rate rather than a rise in the level of output. Grossman and Helpman (1992) suggest that this can occur through the favorable impact of openness on technological changes, and Romer (1993a) introduces the channel of a favorable medium for the adaption of new ideas. For example, openness to trade increases growth rates because trade provides access to a variety of imported inputs that embody new technology. On the other hand, Paul Krugman has maintained that greater openness expands the size of markets facing domestic exporters, thereby raising returns to innovation and thus enhancing the country's specialization in research-intensive production. However, the new growth theories also show that growth can be lowered by increased foreign competition, or it can be increased by import protection if protection promotes investment in the research-intensive sectors of the relevant country. Thus, the direction of the openness–growth relationship is a question open for empirical research rather than a theoretical given.

References

Balassa, B. (1985), "Export, Policy Choices, and Economic Growth in Developing Countries after the 1973 Oil Shock," *Journal of Development Economics*, June.

Barro (1991), "Economic Growth in a Cross Section of Countries," *Quarterly Journal of Economics*, May.

Barro, R.J. (1990), "Government Spending in a Simple Model of Endogenous Growth," *Journal of Political Economics* 18.

Barro, R.J., and H.C. Wolf (1989), "Data Appendix for Economic Growth in a Cross-Section of Countries," mimeo., Harvard University.

Becker, G.S., K.M. Murphy, and R. Tamura (1990), "Human Capital, Fertility, and Economic Growth," *Journal of Political Economy* 98.

Bertola, G. (1989), "Irreversible Investment," unpublished working paper, Princeton University.

Caballero, R., and V. Corbo (1989), "The Effect of Real Exchange Rate Uncertainty on Exports: Empirical Evidence," *World Bank Economic Review* 3(2): 263–78.

Corbo, V., and S. Fischer (1995), "Structural Adjustment, Stabilization, and Policy Reform," in Behrman and Srinivasan (eds.) *Handbook of Development Economics*, vol. 3 (Amsterdam: North Holland).

Corbo, V., and S. Fischer (1992), "Adjustment Programs and Bank Support: Rationale and Main Results," in V. Corbo, S. Fischer, and S.B. Webb (eds.) *Adjustment Lending Revisited: Policies to Restore Growth* (Oxford: World Bank).

Corbo, V., and P. Rojas (1993), "Investment, Macroeconomic Stability, and Growth: The Latin American Experience," *Revista de Análisis Económico* 82 (June): 19–35.

Corbo, V., and P. Rojas (1992), "Crecimiento Económico de América Latina," *Cuadernos de Económica* 87 (August).

Cottani, J.A., D.F. Cavallo, and M.S. Khan (1990), "Real Exchange Rate Behavior and Economic Performance in LDCs," *Economic Development and Cultural Change* 39 (October): 61–76.

Devarajan, S., and J. De Melo (1991), "Membership in the CFA Zone: Odyssean Journey or Trojan Horse?" in A. Chibber and S. Fischer (eds.) *Economic Reforms in Sub-Saharan Africa* (Oxford: World Bank).

Díaz-Alejandro, C.F. (1976), *Foreign Trade Regimes and Economic Development: Colombia* (New York: National Bureau of Economic Research).

Dixit, A., and R.S. Pindyck (1993), *Investment Under Uncertainty* (Princeton, N.J.: Princeton University Press).

Dollar, D. (1992), "Outward-Oriented Developing Economies Really Do Grow More Rapidly: Evidence from 95 LDCs, 1976–85," *Economic Development and Cultural Change* 41: 523–544.

Dornbusch, R. (1992), "The Case for Trade Liberalization in Developing Countries," *Journal of Economic Perspectives*, Winter.

Easterly, W.R., and S. Rebelo (1993), "Fiscal Policy and Economic Growth: An Empirical Investigation," *Journal of Monetary Economics* 32 (December): 417–458.

Feder, G. (1983), "On Exports and Economic Growth," *Journal of Development Economics* 12: 59–74.

Fischer, S. (1993), "The Role of Macroeconomic Factors in Growth: Macroeconomic Stability and Growth," *Journal of Monetary Economics* 32 (December): 485–512.

Fischer, S. (1991), "Growth, Macroeconomics, and Development," *NBER Macroeconomics Annual 1991* (Cambridge, Mass.: MIT Press).

Goldstein, M. (1995), *The Exchange Rate System and the IMF* (Washington, D.C.: Institute for International Economics).

Grossman, G., and E. Helpman (1992), *Innovation and Growth in the Global Economy* (Cambridge, Mass.: MIT Press).

Hausmann, Ricardo, and Michael Gavin (1996), *Securing Stability and Growth in a Shock-Prone Region: The Policy Challenge for Latin America* (Washington, D.C.: Inter-American Development Bank).

Inter-American Development Bank (1995), "Macroeconomic Volatility in Latin America: Causes, Consequences, and Policies to Assure Stability," mimeo., July 17.

King, R.G., and R. Levine (1993), "Finance, Entrepreneurship, and Growth," *Journal of Monetary Economics* 32 (December): 513–542.

Krueger, A.O. (1978), *Liberalization Attempts and Consequences* (New York: Ballinger for the National Bureau of Economic Research).

Levine, R., and D. Renalt (1992), "A Sensitive Analysis of Cross-Country Growth Regressions," *American Economic Review*, September.

Little, I.A. (1982), *Economic Development: Theory, Policy, and International Relations* (New York: Basic Books).

Lucas, R.E., Jr. (1988), "On the Mechanics of Economic Development," *Journal of Monetary Economics* 22.

Mussa, Michael (1990), "Exchange Rates in Theory and Reality," *Essays in International Finance*, no. 179 (Princeton, N.J.: Princeton University Press).

Mussa, Michael (1986), "Nominal Exchange Rates Regimes and the Behavior of Real Exchange Rates: Evidence and Implications," *Carnegie-Rochester Conferences Series on Public Policy* 25: 117–213.

Obstfeld, M. (1995), "International Currency Experience: New Lessons and Lessons Relearned," *Brookings Papers on Economic Activity* 1995: 1.

Pindyck, R.S., and A. Solimano (1993), "Economic Instability and Aggregate Investment," *NBER Macroeconomics Annual 1993* (Cambridge, Mass.: MIT Press).

Rebelo, S. (1992), "Growth in Open Economies," *Carnegie-Rochester Conference Series on Public Policy*.

Romer, P. (1993a), "Two Strategies for Economic Development: Using Ideas vs. Producing Ideas," *Supplement to the World Bank Economic Review*, proceedings of the World Bank Annual Conference on Development Economies 1992, March, 63–91.

Romer, P. (1993b), "Idea Gaps and Other Objects Gaps in Economic Development," *Journal of Monetary Economics* 32 (December): 543–573.

Romer, P. (1989), "Human Capital and Growth: Theory and Evidence," NBER Working Paper Series, no. 3173 (Cambridge, Mass.: National Bureau of Economic Research).

Romer, P. (1986), "Increasing Returns and Long-Run Growth," *Quarterly Journal of Economics*, May.

Solimano, A. (1992), "How Private Investment Reacts to Changing Macroeconomic Conditions: The Case of Chile in the 1980s," in Chhibber et al. (eds.) *Reviving Private Investment in Developing Countries* (Amsterdam: North Holland).

Solow, R.M. (1956), "A Contribution to the Theory of Economic Growth," *Quarterly Journal of Economics* 70.

Summers, R., and A. Heston (1991), "The Penn World Trade (Mark 5): An Expanded Set of International Comparisons," 1950–1988, *Quarterly Journal of Economics*, May.

Taylor, M. (1995), "The Economics of Exchange Rates," *Journal of Economic Literature* 33 (March): 13–47.

White, H. (1980), "A Heteroskedasticity-Consistent Covariance Matrix Estimator and a Direct Test for Heteroskedasticity," *Econometrica* 48: 817–38.

Williamson, J. (1990), "What Washington Means by Policy Reform," in J. Williamson (ed.), *Latin American Adjustment* (Washington, D.C.: Institute for International Economics).

World Bank (1993), *The East Asian Miracle* (Oxford: Oxford University Press).

World Bank (1991), *World Development Report* (Oxford: Oxford University Press).

Gould:

Over the past few months, exchange rate movements have certainly taken center stage. With the dramatic devaluation of the peso in December 1994 and extremely wide swings of the dollar against the yen and the mark, 1995 will probably be noted as one of the most volatile years for exchange rates.

But even though we have seen a lot of volatility recently, it is not new. It is just a continuation of a trend marked by other noticeable events such as the collapse of the European exchange rate mechanism in 1992. In fact, as Jeff

Frankel mentioned earlier, exchange rate volatility has been much higher since the end of the Bretton Woods fixed-exchange-rate regime in 1973.

The Dallas Fed's own Trade-Weighted Value of the Dollar series has been one and one-half times more volatile in the first half of the 1990s than it was in the last half of the 1970s. Despite all this volatility, little research has gone into the study of how exchange rates directly affect long-run growth. But the effect of exchange rates on economic growth is an important issue for many countries because it gets at the heart of which exchange rate regime they should be following over the long run. I think Vittorio Corbo, by looking at economic growth, takes the right approach in his paper.

Often, countries are quick to adopt some new type of managed exchange rate policy hoping it either will provide a painless transition to low inflation or will increase the stability of financial markets. However, what policymakers may not appreciate fully at the time of adopting a managed exchange rate policy are the costs of the abandoning that policy—something that, for one reason or another, usually happens.

Professor Corbo examines the long-run relationship between real exchange rate volatility—the nominal exchange rate adjusted for foreign and domestic inflation differentials—and real economic growth. Whereas he also studies the relationship between inflation volatility and long-run growth, I will comment primarily on his results regarding the real exchange rate volatility and economic growth. I liked Professor Corbo's paper very much, and I think it moves us in the right direction in understanding the relationship between exchange rates and economic growth. It is the first paper that I have seen that directly examines the relationship between real exchange rate volatility and economic growth in such a wide sample of countries and controlling for so many different variables.

Corbo's underlying idea is that exchange rate volatility reflects macroeconomic uncertainty, which, in turn, may have important effects on long-run investment and growth. If exchange rate volatility has important effects on economic growth, then perhaps by implementing policies to alter that real exchange rate volatility, countries may enhance their long-run rate of economic growth.

The context in which Corbo examines this relationship has been called the *new growth theory*, but as he mentions, it is not that new. The idea is that increases in real economic growth are determined by technological progress, which does not happen by accident. Instead, progress occurs as a result of the incentive to make a profit.

The implication is that productivity growth might be related to the structures and policies followed by the economy, rather than the exogenous forces of nature and luck. Anything that enhances technological progress can increase real economic growth. Consequently, a country's macroeconomic environment can have profound effects on its long-run rate of growth.

Exchange rate volatility may create insecurity about the future and decrease the incentives to invest in future development. For example, highly volatile exchange rates may foster uncertainty about the future profits from a new export product and limit investment in its development.

Great exchange rate volatility may also cause firms to diversify production across countries to hedge exchange rate risk rather than choose production locations based on the lowest cost (that is, based on what economists refer to as *comparative advantage*). This last effect, however, may actually increase investment and growth in some countries that gain the foreign facilities. So theoretically, as Corbo mentions, the effects of exchange rate volatility on growth are uncertain.

In looking at the growth experience across more than a hundred countries over 28 years and controlling for such factors as the country's rate of investment, its productivity gap compared with the United States, government spending, and various other factors, Professor Corbo finds that the real exchange rate volatility and inflation negatively affect real per capita GDP growth. This holds true for the whole set of countries as well as just the Latin American countries themselves. Moreover, the results are consistent with several recent empirical studies that have shown that short-term exchange rate volatility is very difficult to assign to economic fundamentals.

There are, however, some areas that may be expanded and some notes of caution in interpreting the results of the paper. As Professor Corbo mentions, real exchange rate volatility or inflation volatility does not necessarily reflect policy uncertainty. Even in the most informed world, where government policies are well known and not subject to change, real exchange rates naturally will move. After all, the exchange rate is a relative price, just like the relative price of apples to oranges, and is subject to change depending on market conditions. It doesn't necessarily have to reflect uncertainty. Given this ambiguity, analysts must correctly discern what this negative relationship between real exchange rate volatility and growth means.

For instance, suppose a country experiences a bad economic shock, such as a drop in the price of oil for an oil-exporting country. Volatility in the real exchange rate will likely result, and later real GDP growth may decline. In other words, it may not be real exchange rate volatility that causes growth to fall. Rather, growth falls because of other real factors, and real exchange rate volatility may just be coincidental. Therefore, making policy conclusions based solely on Corbo's analysis is a bit risky.

To some degree, as Professor Corbo demonstrates, you can control for economic shocks that would affect the real exchange rate and economic growth by controlling for political stability. But one should also control for things such as oil prices, a particularly relevant factor for many Latin American countries. However, it is difficult to control for all relevant factors, which is why this type of analysis should not be taken as sufficient evidence that exchange rate management can increase economic growth.

From a policy point of view, however, it would be nice to evaluate exactly which types of exchange rate policies are associated with greater economic growth. My suggestion is to include both nominal and real exchange rate volatility in the growth equations to get an idea of how nominal exchange rate volatility, which is subject to direct policy control, can influence growth. Because these two variables are highly correlated, the results will probably not show any direct effects. Nonetheless, it would be interesting to see what these effects are, if they are observable.

Another suggestion is to separate countries into different groups and time periods according to their exchange rate regime and then compare their growth rates. It may also be useful to identify the exact mechanism by which volatility decreases economic growth. Does growth decline because of lower general investment or lower trade sector investment? Several studies have shown that exchange rate volatility is negatively associated with growth in trade, although the effects, as Jeffrey Frankel mentioned earlier, seem to be rather small. So it is unclear how exchange rate volatility affects investment and growth.

Finally, as a technical note, the measure of volatility that Professor Corbo uses in this draft is the standard deviation. Using the standard deviation in this cross-country analysis may present a problem because standard deviations are not comparable when the average of the series differs between countries. For example, if the yearly inflation rate of a certain country has a standard deviation of 1 percent, this information alone does not necessarily tell us whether this volatility is great or small. A standard deviation of 1 percent would reflect great volatility in Japan but very little volatility for Argentina. What might be useful is a relative measure of volatility, such as the coefficient at variation that scales the standard deviation by the mean of the variable.

In concluding, I would reiterate that I enjoyed Professor Corbo's paper. It is an important work that helps us move closer toward understanding the long-run effects of exchange rate volatility on economic growth.

Rojas–Suárez:
As Vittorio Corbo's paper clearly put it, volatility matters for growth. Certainly that is the case, but the most important question is, perhaps, what kind of volatility? Many articles in the literature these days stress a number of different forms of volatility affecting growth such as real exchange rate volatility and inflation volatility. As Corbo said, the difference between this kind of literature and his paper is that he analyzes the issue in the context of a more integrated model that starts with a Barro-type equation.

I want to start my comments with a bit of skepticism about the method used in Corbo's paper of adding variables to the famous Barro empirical growth equation. The problem I have with that methodology is that, without a model or some basic fundamental theory about which variables explain growth, it is not clear whether it is the level or volatility of a variable that matters for growth.

The literature on economic growth is replete with a large number of equations to which it keeps adding variables. Sometimes the level matters, sometimes the volatility, sometimes both. I am a bit skeptical about continuing to go that route to explain long-term growth.

Using this methodology, there is a danger that one might misspecify the model that one wants to examine. Vittorio Corbo basically stresses the importance of demand-side variables from the point of view of macroeconomic policy management. However, other studies, such as Hausmann and Gavin (1996), who follow a similar methodology, obtain a different result from Corbo's.[1] They find that although many demand-side variables matter for growth, the most important variable is volatility in changes in the terms of trade. In other words, it is a supply-side variable and not a policy-related demand-side variable that is important. I'm not saying that one is right and the other is wrong. What I'm saying is that the danger of adding variables without a theory is that it can lead to a misunderstanding of what is important for growth.

Moving further into the issue of what variables to consider, I would like to discuss the importance of a variable Corbo does not discuss in his paper—volatility in the premium on the market determined exchange rate.[2] I believe that that variable is very important for explaining the patterns of short- and medium-term growth in the Latin American region.

Let me present my argument by answering two questions: First, why do changes in the nominal exchange rate matter for economic activity? And second, why do we also need to consider the volatility in the nominal exchange rate changes to understand the behavior of economic growth in Latin America? With respect to the first issue, I need to start by stressing that, from my point of view, the exchange rate is the most important signal given to economic participants in Latin America about the state of the economy. Let me explain: In countries such as those in Latin America, everything is short term. By definition, the exchange rate is the foreign price of domestic money, and money is the most liquid and short-term asset of all. Changes in the exchange rate get transmitted into changes in the short-term interest rate extremely quickly. But the short-term interest rate is all there is in Latin America.

There are very few countries where long-term financial markets exist, and where they do, they are not very liquid. So from a market point of view, predictions of what will happen with the exchange rate also send signals of what will happen with the short-term interest rates. And since that's all there is in the economy, economic agents also form expectations about the effect of such movements on real activity.

Imagine a conservative policymaker who is trying very hard to bring inflation down and that faces a shock, say a sudden outflow of capital, that leads to sharp pressures on both the nominal exchange rate and the short-term real interest rate. If the policymaker is constrained by a fixed exchange rate regime and is committed to the target of low inflation, the real money supply and the availability of real credit in the economy will decrease. This in turn will slow down economic activity. In short, nominal variables like the exchange rate get transmitted quickly into the real economy because of two features in Latin American economies: maturities are very short and there's not enough creditworthiness or depth in the domestic financial markets.

Let us now turn to the second issue: why volatility in the nominal exchange rate also is important for growth. In a study that I have just initiated on Argentina, Mexico and Chile, statistical analyses show that there is a strong inverse relationship between economic growth and volatility in expected changes in the nominal exchange rate. It is important to stress that we found that *expected* and not *actual* volatility in the nominal exchange rate is the relevant variable.

Now, what does that say about choosing an exchange rate system? Can we isolate the economy from uncertainty by a system of fixing exchange rates? Here Argentina comes as a case in point. Does Argentina's fixed exchange rate regime mean that uncertainty about changes in the exchange rate have vanished? In my view, the answer to that question is no. Data on the spreads on peso-dollar deposits in Argentina, since the beginning of the convertibility law, show that the spreads are not constant and are not zero. If there were full credibility in the exchange rate, you wouldn't observe this pattern of changes in the spread. So, even with a fixed exchange rate regime, exchange rate expectations can be important.

How do I explain the fact that volatility, and not only the level of expected changes in the exchange rate, also matter in the explanation of real variables? To answer this question, let me refer you to the famous currency substitution model where expected changes in the exchange rate were commonly used to explain the dollarization process in Latin America. The model was very successful when inflation rates were high in Latin America. However, when the inflation rate started to come down in these countries, the currency substitution model began to cease its effectiveness in explaining the persistence of dollarization.

Why, if expectations about the exchange rate changes calmed down, did the countries not come back toward the use of domestic currency as opposed to foreign currency? Well, using an extension of the capital asset pricing model, Paul McNellis and I (1996) found out that over the last two decades, the U.S. dollar has established itself as a safe asset in Latin America, an asset with low returns, but safe.[3]

In contrast, the domestic currency is viewed as a risky asset, where its riskiness is approached by the volatility of expected changes in the exchange rate.

Thus, even though the expectation of large exchange rate changes has declined significantly, volatility is still there. In my work with McNellis, the persistence of dollarization in Latin America can be explained by this expected exchange rate volatility. So volatility on the expected changes in the exchange rate matters, and matters a lot, for the determination of real variables in the American economies. It is then not surprising to find out that uncertainty about behavior of expected changes in the exchange rate also impacts strongly on economic activity.

Notes

1. Hausmann and Gavin (1996), "Security Stability and Growth in a Shock Prone Region: The Policy Challenge for Latin America," OCE, Working Paper No. 315, Inter-American Development Bank.

2. In many Latin American countries under fixed exchange rates, the best approximation to a market-determined exchange rate is the black market rate.

3. See McNellis, Paul and L. Rojas-Suárez (1996), "Exchange-Rate Depreciation, Dollarization and Uncertainty: A Comparison of Bolivia and Peru," OCE, Working Paper No. 325, Inter-American Development Bank.

Appendix to Part III

Description of the Data in Exchange Rate Volatility, Investment, and Growth: Some New Evidence

The data required to generate the trade openness, inflation rate, and direct foreign investment variables are taken from the World Bank database. Black market premium data are from the *World Currency Yearbook*. Terms-of-trade data are from ECLAC statistics, and the real exchange rate is from IMF and World Bank statistics. All other time series data are from Summers and Heston (1991), who have compiled internationally comparable annual figures on output and its composition, prices, and exchange rates for 134 market economies from 1950 to 1988. The data for the time invariant variables are from the database of Barro and Wolf (1989).

The entire sample, excluding Africa, has 58 countries with six periods of data. However, the use of the lagged value of the investment rate and some unavailable data produces a sample of 263 observations for the larger regression growth model, while it has 284 observations for the larger investment model. The Latin American sample consists of 20 countries with six periods of data. After losing 20 observations for the lagged value of the investment rate, we obtained a total of 100 observations for analysis.

Part IV SPECULATIVE ATTACKS

Countries that attempt to manage their exchange rate have been subject to large speculative attacks by a foreign exchange market that now exceeds $1 trillion of transactions a day. Are these foreign exchange markets a stabilizing or destabilizing force?

Presenter:
Peter M. Garber
Economics Professor
Brown University

Moderator:
Carlos Zarazaga
Senior Economist and Executive Director
Center for Latin American Economics
Federal Reserve Bank of Dallas

Discussants:
Guillermo Mondino
Executive Director
Fundación Mediterránea

Miguel Savastano
Economist
International Monetary Fund

Garber:
Normally, it is with some trepidation that I present a paper in the very last session of any day. But today, because of the nature of the topic and the previous discussion, I think it is a very nice position to be in. It allows me to try to wrap up many of the issues that have been discussed during the day.

First, I will talk about the theory we have about speculative attacks, since that is one of the key issues that was discussed this morning. Then I will consider the issue discussed in the background paper (Appendix to Part IV), which is a very micromarket issue involving what happens at the time of an attack, in the days or the hours before the collapse of a fixed-exchange-rate regime in a situation in which capital markets are perfectly open and we have the sort of derivative products and exchange markets that are found in the industrial countries. And then finally, I will try to apply a bit of these results to the Mexico case. The two cases that seem to have crystalized, or recrystalized, interest in speculative attacks were the collapse of the European Exchange Rate Mechanism (ERM) in 1992 and 1993 and the collapse of the Mexican peso at the end of 1994. I will try to weave in those examples as I go along.

Speculative Attack Theory

The theory of speculative attacks actually was developed at the Federal Reserve, starting as a research project having to do with the collapse of the Bretton Woods system in 1971 and 1973. The first paper in this literature was one by Salant and Henderson that was published in 1978 but was circulated before then. They developed the principles we still use today to analyze speculative attacks. Paul Krugman was, I believe, a summer intern at the Fed in about 1977 or 1978 and made use of the basic concepts in the Salant and Henderson paper but applied his results not to an attack on a buffer stock of gold, as did Salant and Henderson, but to an attack on a fixed-nominal-exchange-rate regime. That has been the primary application of these concepts in the literature since then.

Bob Flood and I specialized the Krugman model when Bob was an economist at the Board of Governors, and I did a paper with Herminio Blanco that did some empirical testing of this model for the previous Mexico collapse, back when I was a visiting scholar at the Board of Governors in 1982. So I would characterize this theory of speculative attacks as the Federal Reserve System's theory of speculative attacks.

The models are not necessarily to be taken very literally. They allow us to organize our thinking about speculative attacks and convince ourselves that speculative attacks are quite rational and reasonable responses to imbalances and inconsistencies in government policies. Typically, they are set up in a very simple money market equilibrium framework. They are generally based on a monetary theory of the exchange rate in which a central bank has a secondary policy of fixing an exchange rate but a primary policy of printing money by supplying the government with domestic credit. The primary policy will never be abandoned. It is the secondary policy, the fixed exchange rate, that will eventually be eliminated. It has long been known that a policy of domestic credit creation through a central bank is ultimately inconsistent with a fixed-exchange-rate regime. Sooner or later, the fixed-exchange-rate regime will collapse. That has been shown time and time again.

The contribution of the literature is to show when and under what circumstances the regime must collapse. The usual assumption is that the fixed-exchange-rate system will collapse into a floating rate regime. The problem is figuring out exactly when that will occur. The principles that are used to determine the timing are, first, that there are to be no unusual speculative profits had by speculators. Speculators will compete with each other in determining the time of the attack in order to eliminate expected speculative profits. In so doing, they will cause a discrete collapse in the central bank's reserves. Typically, the assumption is that reserves will fall to zero. In other words, the central bank will not fund itself by going short in foreign exchange; it will let go of the exchange rate beforehand.

That is the basic model. The outcome is driven by a fundamentally inconsistent central bank policy. In addition, there have been some developments of this model in which the central bank policy of domestic credit creation is a contingent policy, not a policy that is necessarily in effect at a given time during the existence of the fixed-exchange-rate regime. By that I mean that the central bank uses the fixed-exchange-rate regime to control itself. This would be the view of the fixed exchange rate as a nominal anchor. That is, without a fixed exchange rate, the central bank is effectively a money printing addict. It can't control itself except by pegging solidly to some other country's currency. Speculators in the system will, depending on their expectations, either attack or not attack the fixed-exchange-rate regime. If their expectations revolve around the notion that the central bank is going to go on a money-printing binge, they will attack the regime and the central bank will go on a money-printing binge, even though, before the attack, it had run a perfectly stable policy consistent with the fixed-exchange-rate regime. The attack will, therefore, have been ratified and proper, and so it would be a reasonable equilibrium.

Alternatively, if speculators believe that the central bank will not go on a money-printing binge, they will not attack, the fixed-exchange-rate system will continue to exist, and the central bank will maintain control of itself and not print money. Again, that would be a perfectly consistent equilibrium.

So there is some instability created by speculative expectations. Depending on what they are, they can drive the system either to a floating system and a collapse of the fixed-rate system or to a continuation of the fixed-rate system. This possibility has become interesting in the context of the ERM collapse because of the belief that the attack on the French, in particular, was not justified and perhaps was the result of a self-fulfilling type of attack.

The Case of the ERM

Obviously, it is easy to think of policies that are inconsistent with the maintenance of a fixed-exchange-rate regime. This morning, Jeff Frankel presented two cases: the case of Italy and the case of the UK. Their policies were fundamentally inconsistent with the maintenance of a fixed-exchange-rate regime or with staying within the band, and, therefore, the attacks on their currencies were generally considered to have been based on fundamentals. The attack on the French, whose fundamental policies seemed to be even better than those of the Bundesbank, was generally thought to have been unjustified.

When I was at the International Monetary Fund (IMF), looking at the European capital markets in the aftermath of the collapse of the ERM, the question that came up again and again was, Why were the French attacked? My view was that the whole situation really was not an attack on the French but an attack on the Germans. How far were the Germans willing to go to lend to their partners in the ERM? It was clear to the markets, once they attacked Italy, that the Germans had a limit on how much they would lend to the Italians. It was clear the speculative wolf pack attacked the sled, and the Germans threw the Italians off the sled. Once the wolf pack got the taste of blood, they thought the Germans might feed them some more, so they attacked the British. The Germans threw the British off the sled and made it clear that there was a limit beyond which they would not go. The Germans were unwilling to relax their own monetary policy beyond a certain point to lend to their partners through the Very Short Term Financing facility. As a result, the wolf pack thought that maybe the Germans had a limit in regard to the French. Before, that limit might have been thought to have been quite large, but now it was clear that the Germans were pulling back, that they had reached the limit of their ability to sterilize the impact of their loans in support of the exchange rate mechanism. So the wolf pack thought, let's try the French. Regardless of what French internal policies were, this was a German policy. So France was attacked and tested, and the attack turned out to be mistaken. The French passed the test because the Germans made it clear they were unwilling to let the French franc be devalued as well. The Germans visibly lent an unlimited amount, and even bought francs themselves, and this undid the force behind the attack. So there are good reasons to think that the attack against the French in the autumn of 1992 was a fundamentals-based attack. The summer of 1993 is a different issue. That situation is not as clear.

The reason I am going into this is that the argument that came out of France after the 1992 attack and defense of the franc was that the attack was unjustified and perhaps the result of a self-fulfilling attack, and so perhaps there were reasons to stifle these markets. The huge power of these markets had nearly driven the French off the ERM band, so perhaps it was time to impose some sort of control on them. This was noised about a little bit in official circles, but that quickly ended. Now there is really not much talk, of the sort that existed then, about controlling capital flows.

Again, this was a political decision. The French had devoted a lot of effort to developing their financial markets. Paris, London, and Frankfurt were competing to become the financial center of Europe, and there had been large liberalizations in the system. The French, in particular, had undertaken heavy investment to liberalize and update and upgrade their markets. If they suddenly imposed capital controls, that would eliminate France as the financial center of Europe and would eliminate a very nice, high-wage business.

Run-Up to an Attack

Let me shift a bit now to the issue of what happens in the run-up to an attack. The speculative attack models work on the principle of perfectly free capital movements. So speculators, when they want it, can get whatever credit they need, through whatever instruments they have. They can go to the central bank of the weak currency to acquire the domestic currency they need to buy foreign exchange from that same central bank.

So the first thing to consider is what actually happens when there are perfectly open and free capital markets and free movement of capital under modern conditions. This is where my background paper comes in (Appendix to Part IV). When capital markets are open, obviously, capital moves. And in the few years before the attack on the European exchange rate mechanism, there was a large-scale movement of capital across borders, not only within the ERM countries, but capital came in from the United States as well. This capital was moved in to try to take advantage of the liberalization of the markets and the perceived inappropriate interest rate differentials between what were thought of as weaker currencies and stronger currencies within the ERM. But the risk was hedged, or at least partially hedged. A lot of the capital coming in was from mutual funds or pension funds in the United States. These funds' managers did not want to take all of the currency risks involved, so they engaged in hedging operations. One sort of hedging operation, of course, is to buy a put on the currency that you are interested in. Another is to create a synthetic put on that currency. In addition to people who had moved capital in and were just trying to cover it, there were those we would call classic speculators, people who would take a short position. It was possible for them to speculate in almost unlimited amounts.

The mechanism of speculation for a hedge fund is simply to short-sell the currency in some sort of forward contract, and it is easy to leverage up capital tenfold in the banking system to do this. To get the banking system to take the other side—that is, buy in the weak currency—the banking system itself has to have an outlet for that currency; it has to be able to cover that position.

The world's banks generally do not take a very large position in foreign exchange, or prefer not to. They make their money by trading. So if there is a large sale into the banks of the weak currency, there will be a large sale out of the banks. The way the banks typically cover themselves in forward operations is to sell the currency on the spot market and then do a currency swap to cover the maturity differential. These are wholesale operations that are done with the rest of the world's banking system. So a bank in New York might buy pounds from Quantum Fund on a forward contract but immediately sell the pounds on the spot market and do a swap as well. It has to do the swap with some other bank and the spot exchange rate transaction with some other bank. Let's assume it is a British bank. Ultimately, it is going to have to go to a British bank, which, again, is taking the opposite position—it is buying pounds and engaging in the opposite part of the swap. Now that British bank is also engaged in an imbalance, and it is going to have to cover its position. If it is a one-way market in an attack, it will sell the pounds to the Bank of England, but it also has to get pounds to deliver to the Bank of England. Where does it go to get the pounds? Ultimately, a British bank will go to the Bank of England to get the pounds. It will borrow the pounds through the discount window to get them and then deliver the pounds. So ultimately it gets credit, which it funnels through to the world's banking system in order to finance the attack on the central bank itself. The central bank finances the collapse of its own policy.

That is the basic nature of an attack. A central bank that is posting a Lombard rate or a discount rate, usually at slightly above the market, at which it discounts freely, and fixes the exchange rate is schizophrenic. It is expressing two goals: one goal is to implement the macro policy, fixing the exchange rate, maybe for current account purposes or whatever. The other goal is one of maintaining stability in the financial markets by posting a Lombard rate. That is what Lombard Street is all about, right? You post a Lombard rate to be the lender of last resort in a crisis. If you keep the Lombard rate low, then you are expressing a priority of maintaining financial stability over maintaining the fixed-exchange-rate regime. That is the difference, I think, between a central bank and a currency board. A central bank has a body that is expressed in the form of the fixed exchange rate, but its soul, its true being, is expressed in the posting of a Lombard-type rate. It is willing to give up the fixed exchange rate in a pinch to avoid a financial crisis. A currency board does not have a body. Its soul is keeping the exchange rate, and it does not care about what happens to the financial system. I think that is the difference. One expresses a priority policy of maintaining the fixed exchange rate, while the other expresses a duality of policy and usually a secondary policy of fixing the exchange rate. That secondary policy of fixing the exchange rate ultimately is going to be consistent with a speculative attack, and such central banks will always, at some point or other, be attacked.

That is what the speculators do. But what about the hedgers? The hedgers are, in fact, the same as speculators in an attack on a central bank. You really cannot tell the difference in their behavior. And the hedgers that I have in mind, particularly in the background paper, are those that use dynamic hedging strategies to replicate put options. To hedge a position, a fund that has foreign investments might acquire directly an actual put option, or it might create a synthetic put option by dynamic hedging. If it actually buys a put option, it will usually be an over-the-counter put option on the currency. It will buy that from a bank, and then the bank must cover the currency implications of that position by dynamic hedging. So one way or another, an attempt to hedge the risk of currency movements by investors will lead to a dynamic hedging operation. These operations occur in large amounts, and they are typical in this business now. A dynamic hedge mimics a put in the following sense. In the theory of put pricing, a put on a currency represents a short position in the particular currency and a long position in the currency that was used to buy the weak currency—the currency that is named in the put option. For instance, a put that allows one to sell pounds for dollars at some future date is a position that is short pounds and effectively long dollars, and, in particular, the short position is a fraction of the face value of the put, the notional value of the put. The value of the put, the "premium," changes as volatility changes and as interest rate differentials between the pound and the dollar change.

To cover a put, a bank or a fund can create actual positions in the currency —that is, a short position. If it is a put on pounds, the fund can create a short position in pounds by borrowing and selling pounds, use the proceeds to buy dollar assets, and then add a few additional dollar assets in order to equal the premium value. These positions have to be adjusted, from time to time, as changes occur in the exchange rate, volatility, and interest rate differentials.

So, for example, when British interest rates are very low for a given maturity, only a certain fraction of the notional value of the put is hedged, say, 50 percent of the notional value. This would represent a short position of 500,000 pounds on a 1 million pound notional value. But as the British interest rate rises up to crisis values, the hedging ratio tends to rise. You might go from 50 percent of those million pounds to a short position of 80 percent, so you would short 300,000 pounds more. This would be a standard strategy.

I would like to tie this into the macro effects of these strategies on the financial system. When there is a speculative attack on a currency, it will show up as changes in volatility and the exchange rate. Speculators will show up at the exchange window of the central bank and demand foreign currency. Ultimately, there is a defense against this. If a central bank is really serious about maintaining its exchange rate, it can put up its discount rate or its Lombard rate. By putting up its Lombard rate, it will squeeze the markets. People who are caught short in the currency will have to scramble to get the currency, and the only way they can typically do that is to sell back the foreign exchange to get the central bank to create some new base money. This is the classic interest rate defense of the exchange rate system.

The problem with that defense—in the presence of this large-scale dynamic hedging business, this effectively automated stop-loss selling—is that putting up the interest rate will cause, through dynamic hedging, an avalanche of sales of the weak currency, not a huge amount of buying. That avalanche of sales might push the central bank past its intervention limits, might drive it down to a net negative position in foreign exchange, which it doesn't want to hold, and therefore collapse the exchange rate. So the presence of these sorts of strategies in the system undermines the ability of a central bank to defend the fixed exchange rate.

Moreover, all of these hedging strategies are based on faulty macro models. Embedded in any finance model from which we get a pricing formula for an option is a macro model about relationships between exchange rates and interest rates. In the very simple Black–Scholes or Garman–Kohlhagen model, the relationship is exogenous. The interest rates can drift. Interest rates can fluctuate or move, but that does not change the assumed random walk nature of the exchange rate.

The Case of Mexico

Let us consider, now, the case of Mexico. This example is one in which there are perfectly open capital markets in any number of instruments. There are currently some efforts to try and stifle these markets for causing excessive volatility and speculation, perhaps through a Tobin-type transactions tax. The problem with such taxes is that these markets are extremely plastic. They can move readily from one form to another, and it is easy for them to move in such a way as to avoid the tax. Unless you impose the tax on every kind of financial transaction, it is very difficult to get at these kinds of transactions or to impose capital controls.

In the case of Mexico, these avenues of speculation were much narrower in that it was not easy to take a short position against the peso. The futures market did not exist. You could go over the counter in New York, but it was difficult to cover that position in Mexico. So although there were large forward sales in New York, they were usually on a matched basis and did not spill over into Mexico.

Banco de México and the Mexican government, however, did provide some of the credit necessary to engage in the attack. The attack, in its virulent form, is usually thought to have occurred between the end of November and the end of December 1994, but it actually occurred throughout 1994 as a result of political disturbances. The credit in this attack was generated in the form of *tesobonos*. Suddenly, instead of *cetes*, you have *cetes* but with a forward exchange contract attached to them, in which the gains from the forward contract are payable in pesos, which would be convertible immediately into dollars.

So effectively, the Mexican government—in the form of *tesobonos*—was buying the peso forward and selling foreign exchange forward. Investors were engaged in selling the peso forward, and they found that the party on the other side was the Mexican government. So in spite of the difficulties in short-selling the peso, it ultimately could be done through the *tesobono* operation. By the time the year ended with this large sale of *tesobonos*, although there was still foreign exchange in the hands of the Banco de México, that was as a gross amount of foreign exchange, not net. The existence of the *tesobonos* created a net zero, or even negative, position even before the attacks were lodged.

Conclusion

Let me close by saying that we really have theoretical models of speculative attacks. We know how they work. They are abstract when you try to interpret any given speculative attack with the guidance of the models. One serious difficulty is that we do not know what happens in the hours or minutes that the actual attack is launched. That is a very abstract concept in these models. We need to have that knowledge in order to get a reasonable model of speculative attacks, because then we can back out what happens at the moment of the attack, the end point that determines the dynamics and the timing of what goes beforehand.

So what is necessary is some knowledge of the microactivity at the time of an attack. It is difficult to gather this information—who is selling first, what instruments are being used, what the central bank's strategy is, what is being done minute by minute. Perhaps central banks hold postmortems after they get attacked to determine what happened, but if they do, what they learn is not formally released. What we need, as academics and also as central bankers, is to have some consortium in which we, even in a secret way, combine our knowledge of the minute-by-minute operations undertaken when an attack occurred. I think that would be a valuable addition to everyone's knowledge.

Mondino:

Speculative attacks are not foreign to us in Argentina; we have experienced several of them. I'll describe how speculative attacks have worked in the case of Argentina, in particular, and, more generally, in the case of Latin America.

Before I do that, I would like to go over a couple of the issues that Peter touched on. The first is why we have speculative attacks and whether we should respond to them. The second issue involves the dynamics of the attacks.

Why do we have these attacks? I think there are basically two sets of theories, the two sets that Peter mentioned. One is the "fundamentalist" theory that something is wrong with the budget. People are concerned about either the budget or the quasi-budget deficit of the central bank or some other bank associated with the treasury. The second theory is basically associated with expectations. This theory argues that there are multiple equilibria out there, and an exogenous change in expectations—some type of a shock to the system—will trigger a move from one good equilibrium to the next.

Policymakers have to do two basic things if they want to avoid a speculative attack on their currency. The first one, and probably the less important one, is invest in reputation. They have to be very careful how they treat their customers, how they treat foreign investors and capital or asset holders. It's no surprise that the attack on the Mexican peso didn't take place when Pedro Aspe was the minister of finance. He had made a serious investment in reputation. Once he walked out and there was a new minister of finance, it was much more likely an attack would occur. The second, and key, factor in avoiding an attack is fiscal flexibility. A government should have the reflexes to look for funding to avoid the attack. This funding typically requires serious fiscal adjustment on both the expenditure and the taxation sides. Hence, the best thing any government that's under threat of an attack can do is start flexing its muscles and look for fiscal resources. In any case, given the speed of markets, a government may also need an additional source of defense because before it can have a fiscal plan to show the markets, it could be out of currency. The Mexicans learned this the hard way. It took them a long time to put together a coherent package to show the markets. It's very important that a government have the tools to undertake this defense.

What are the typical tools that are used? One, which was mentioned today, is capital controls. You can implement new capital controls once you think the currency is somewhat weak. Unfortunately, capital controls won't stop the attack. It eventually will occur unless there is also fiscal adjustment. A more efficient mechanism to stop a speculative attack is probably the use of the interest rate, which was basically what Peter was talking about.

How do speculative attacks work in practice? Even though the theories can sound complicated, speculative attacks are very simple animals. First, there is the expectation that a government is going to abandon the exchange rate regime. This abandonment typically is associated with a discrete jump in the exchange rate. Whether you fix again at the new higher level or whether you float, there typically is a jump in the exchange rate. The second important factor is that since people expect a devaluation, they will start pulling deposits out of banks. Investment houses will start betting against the currency, and everybody will start trying to liquidate their positions in the weak money and try to move into a stronger currency. When they do this, they'll do it at the defended exchange rate, of course.

Who is going to sell this defended exchange rate? Obviously, the central bank. So the central bank starts selling foreign currency through one of two mechanisms. First, it engages in a lot of forward contracts. This is the most dangerous style of defense because it doesn't get properly accounted for in a lot of countries. This is particularly true for developing countries because the governments still have their foreign reserves out there to defend the currency, but they have engaged in a lot of forward contracts that will have to be fulfilled in the future if the currency goes under. In other words, the forward contracts give room to leverage the attack.

The second practice, the most standard practice, is to sell currency in the spot market. Once the central bank reaches a certain threshold, it basically must decide what it's going to do, whether it's going to keep defending the currency, and by doing so, let interest rates go up. If they do go up, the central bank will have to decide what to do with the banking system, or it may decide to stop defending the currency and move to something else altogether.

The problem is that under certain circumstances, an interest rate defense can be the final signal the market was waiting for to clean out the central bank. Of course, when the interest rate defense works, it works because it creates a lot of illiquidity in the market; it dries up the markets. When it doesn't work, it doesn't work for other reasons. I have four scenarios about this.

In the first scenario, high interest rates will—holding everything else constant—lead to a recession. This recession will probably result in high unemployment; hence, the central bank is likely to lose its nerve and abandon the exchange rate. Speculators understand central banks are likely to abandon the exchange rate, and so they will speed up the attack.

In the second scenario, high interest rates will throw the banks out of business for two reasons. One is the recession scenario I just mentioned. The banks' loan performances will turn sour. The other reason is that there will be a liquidity squeeze in the banks, and the banking system will start experiencing serious problems. The banks will have lent at relatively low interest rates, and they will be taking deposits at much higher interest rates. They will be losing money, they will be in trouble, and the central bank will have to decide what to do. So obviously, these banks will be banging at the discount window trying to get it open, and the central bank will have to decide whether to open it.

In the third scenario, some market participants are not aware a speculative attack is brewing. When they see the interest rate going up, they suddenly wake up to what's going on and decide to pursue the attack themselves. This scenario assumes that the information is not evenly distributed, that some participants are either asleep or stupid, or that the information is really costly. This scenario assumes that interest rates will signal the collapse of the regime.

The final scenario involves mechanistic hedgers or foreign traders. This is the scenario Peter was talking about. Bankers use interest rates to read where the currency is going. The option pricing models they are using don't have a term for expectations; they read the expectations implicitly out of interest rates. Hence, when interest rates shoot up, the models basically figure out there's a devaluation coming. And if there's a devaluation coming, any model will show that you'd better get out of that currency, which is exactly what happens. People start shorting the weak currency, trying to get out of it as fast as they can. For that, they need a sucker who's going to provide them with the funds to get out of the system. The sucker in all these models is the central bank, the central bank that's willing to provide liquidity to the system. It's willing to sell the currency at a relatively low price. Of course, this scenario is basically the same as the third one. These foreign traders did not realize there was a speculative attack brewing until they saw interest rates going up. At that point, there is a very dramatic speculative attack. The only important difference in these last two scenarios, I think, is that the use of derivative instruments gives room for leveraging the attack, and hence, it can occur faster and it can be more difficult for the central bank to defend the currency.

I promised I would discuss the attack on the Argentine currency. What occurred in Argentina in 1994 was very simple. The real exchange rate appreciated dramatically in late 1993 and appreciated drastically throughout 1994. Speculators looking at the exchange rate decided that it might be overappreciated, and, therefore, why take risks?

The second important factor speculators observed was the trade balance. They saw that it had gone from a very large surplus in the very early 1990s to a large deficit in 1994. This large trade deficit was also a source of concern to speculators.

The third factor they observed was that the country ran a fiscal deficit in the last two quarters of 1994. There was the impression that it was going to be hard for the country to solve its fiscal problems because of pending elections.

The final factor was that everybody understood that banks would have to undertake some adjustment because it was the sector that was way behind in adjusting to the new rules of the game in Argentina. For example, some banks were heavily invested in bonds, and when the bonds took a nosedive, those banks were in a very difficult situation. They had huge capital losses and became dramatically undercapitalized. At the same time, there was a speculative attack on the currency, since everybody figured that the country's situation was similar to Mexico's. This triggered a dramatic loss of deposits, which was serious for a few banks.

The biggest question that arises out of all this is one that has been raised today: Suppose you manage to defend the currency. Can you defend the currency without throwing away your banking system? The answer to that is probably yes. But you need to have the flexibility to create a lender of last resort out of fiscal resources. You must have the fiscal resources to attend to the needs of the banking system. You don't need that much money, but in the event of an attack, you do need flexibility.

Savastano:
Peter's discussion of the micromechanics of trading in the last minutes of a fixed exchange rate is, I think, a perfect example of the type of insight that we have gained from the positive analyses of speculative attacks. Indeed, largely thanks to the work of Peter and a few others over the past 15 years, and contrary to what the press would like us to believe, I think that the profession has a fairly good understanding of the mechanics and dynamics of speculative attacks under different policy environments and market configurations, including those resulting from the recent expansion of international financial markets.

We no longer think of speculative attacks as market anomalies or pathologies, but rather, we tend to view them as investors' rational response to an actual or perceived inconsistency in the policies followed by the authorities in a system with a fixed or otherwise managed exchange rate. Unfortunately, that is as far as the consensus goes. As is so common in this field, considerable debate and confusion remain, in this case, in two key areas: one, the root causes of speculative attacks, and second, the implications that the existence and recurrence of these events have for the choice of exchange regime and for the use of capital controls.

I cannot pretend to settle this debate in 10 minutes, but I can offer some views on where I think the solution to this debate lies and on the type of answers I think we need to obtain before we take seriously those who argue that fixed exchange rates are no longer an option or those who call for fundamental changes in the international monetary system.

As has been mentioned, there are essentially two views with respect to the underlying causes of speculative attacks. One view is that the main cause of attacks is the adoption of policies that are essentially inconsistent with pursuing pegged or managed exchange rates. This is called the "first-generation view" or, as Peter called it, "the Federal Reserve view." The other view sees speculative attacks as being driven by the self-fulfilling expectations of rational investors who share the belief that the collapse of the exchange rate regime will trigger a fundamental change in the policy stance of the authorities. These are known as the "second-generation models."

In practice, it is very difficult to discriminate between these two views. The reason for this is that there is a fundamental observational equivalence problem. Most of the pre- and post-attack dynamics that one can obtain from collapse models with multiple equilibria can be replicated with models with a single equilibrium in which the attack is triggered by the anticipation of a change in regime. Moreover, in looking at the empirical evidence, one gets the distinct impression that the few serious studies of speculative attacks are broadly supportive of the policy-inconsistency view, or the first-generation models.

Despite these arguments and evidence, however, the debate on the causes and implications of speculative attacks seems to be more alive than ever. The collapse or near collapse of the ERM in the falls of 1992 and 1993—and, to a somewhat lesser extent, the collapse of the Mexican peso in December 1994—have fueled a new wave of interest in the self-fulfilling, or multiple equilibria, view of speculative attacks. In a way, it is as if every collapse of a highly visible exchange rate peg brings with it the temptation to revisit all we know about the subject. There is nothing wrong with revisiting old issues, but there has to be a limit to it. I have the impression that the debate on the causes of speculative attacks goes over the same ground, over and over again. I think there's an urgent need to move forward in this debate, and in my view, the only way to do so is to take a deeper and more systematic look at the fundamental driving forces that are assumed to cause a regime's collapse.

In the case of the first-generation models, this would entail addressing two crucial questions. First, why do governments follow policies that are inconsistent with the chosen exchange rate regime? And second, and more important, why do governments allow their conflicting policy objectives to collide so dramatically in a speculative attack?

The answer to the first question is rather easy. In essence, one can argue that governments follow inconsistent policies because they do not have sufficient instruments to attain their often conflicting objectives. The answer to the second question, however, is much less obvious. For example, if at some point preserving the fixed exchange rate ceases to be the primary goal of economic policy in a given country, why should the authorities wait passively for the speculative attack to occur? Why don't they undertake a preemptive strike by, say, abandoning the peg or devaluing the currency before international reserves are depleted?

There are at least three possible answers to this question. The first possibility is plain ignorance. The authorities may not have a clue that their policies are inconsistent with the exchange rate and that the whole exchange regime is headed for collapse. A second possible answer is miscalculation or imperfect information on the part of the government regarding either the timing or the cost of an attack. For example, in a highly uncertain environment, the government may believe it has an informational advantage over the private sector. And in trying to exploit this edge, it could get caught off guard by a sequence of negative shocks and a sudden attack on its international reserves.

The third possibility is that letting the speculative attack unfold represents the optimal strategy for a government that deliberately follows policies that are inconsistent with preserving the fixed exchange rate. In other words, it is possible that the net benefits of doing nothing and letting the private sector go ahead with a one-way bet on the exchange rate is the preferable course of action, all things considered.

The truth is that we really do not know which of these three options best portrays the authorities' actions and perceived trade-offs in the run-up to a collapse. The existing models and most of the policy discussion simply are not carried out in these terms. I think that we still have much to learn about this fundamental policy dimension of speculative attacks and that future research should focus squarely on this aspect of the problem.

In the second-generation models, the task of looking deep into the driving forces behind a speculative attack is much more complicated. This occurs because, at least at a theoretical level, one cannot rule out the possibility that multiple equilibria will arise from several sources. Regardless of the source, however, these models typically carry two important messages. First, that an otherwise viable exchange rate regime is essentially at the mercy of speculators and might collapse even when all macroeconomic fundamentals appear to be in place. (France in the fall of 1993 seems to be the preferred example nowadays; a few years back, there were other examples.) The second message of these models is that the likelihood of a self-fulfilling attack is magnified in an environment of high capital mobility and well-developed financial markets. Some extreme supporters of this view would go as far as to say that in the current environment of globalized financial markets, it is not even technically feasible to defend a fixed exchange rate because of the implicit government guarantees on most financial liabilities (the "financial vulnerability" argument).

Although these arguments are often analytically appealing, I think that at a fundamental level, multiple equilibria models tend to raise more questions than they answer. For example, these models need to assume that there is some force out there that coordinates and pins down agents' expectations at some particular point. This by itself would, at least theoretically, give room for some sort of mechanism to abate or mitigate the seriousness of the multiple equilibria problem (for instance, designing institutions to strengthen the authorities' commitment to technology). However, it is, I think, at the empirical level that these second-generation models face their biggest challenge. In fact, I believe that no matter how analytically robust and intuitively plausible these arguments are, the supporters of these types of models still need to overcome the fundamental observational equivalence problem I mentioned earlier. Until that happens, I think that the burden of proof is bound to remain on their side of the debate, and that the first-generation models, with all their shortcomings, will continue to provide the most useful template for analyzing speculative attacks.

Appendix to Part IV

Foreign Exchange Hedging with Synthetic Options and the Interest Rate Defense of a Fixed-Exchange-Rate Regime

Peter M. Garber and Michael G. Spencer
International Monetary Fund
December 1994

Abstract

In the endgame of a fixed-exchange-rate regime, increases in interest rates to defend the currency may lead to an apparently perverse market response: further downward pressure on the exchange rate. This may result if a large proportion of investors' foreign exchange exposure is dynamically hedged. This paper describes the trading operations involved in implementing dynamic hedges and the impact of these operations on central bank policy. The success of an interest rate defense hinges on the size and timing of the funding operations of those who are being squeezed relative to those engaged in dynamic hedging.

Summary

The usual prescription for the defense of a fixed exchange rate during a speculative attack is the combination of aggressive sales of foreign currency on the spot and forward markets and increases in short-term interest rates of a sufficient magnitude to squeeze speculators who are short in the currency. Two developments in international financial markets in recent years may have reduced the effectiveness of this advice. First, institutional and other large investors have diversified their portfolios internationally. Consequently, the potential exposures to currency risk are growing and therefore, too, the potential selling pressure if the ability of the authorities to maintain a fixed exchange rate comes into question. Second, the growth in the markets for foreign exchange derivatives has both improved the ability of investors to hedge their exposures and provided instruments through which speculators can take highly leveraged positions against weak currencies.

This paper discusses the possibility that the operations of banks and nonbanks to hedge their currency exposures may weaken the effectiveness of the classic interest rate defense. The focus is on market and central bank behavior in the last moments of a fixed-exchange-rate regime. In addition to providing powerful tools for speculation, option pricing models can be used by banks and investors to construct synthetic currency put options by trading regularly in the cash markets. These synthetic options provide a hedge against exchange rate changes if the positions can be adjusted continually. In the presence of this dynamic hedging, an increase in interest rates to defend against a speculative attack may automatically trigger even more selling of the currency that is under attack. The interaction between the timing of different trading strategies—fixed-exchange-rate regime dynamic hedging programs and the reaction of speculators who are caught by the interest rate increase—is crucial to the outcome of the central bank's policy. If the volume of selling motivated by dynamic hedging overwhelms that of the purchases by speculators seeking to close out their positions, the central bank may reach its credit limits with commercial banks or its own position limits, forcing it to abandon the fixed exchange rate.

Foreign Exchange Hedging with Synthetic Options and the Interest Rate Defense of a Fixed-Exchange-Rate Regime

Coincident with the internationalization of portfolios and the interlinking of money markets across currencies has been the expanded use of methods to hedge currency risk. While basic hedging instruments such as forward exchange contracts have a long history, the use of newer instruments such as exchange-traded options and futures contracts and over-the-counter (OTC) options and currency swaps has grown dramatically in the past decade. In addition, option pricing methods have been used in dynamic hedging strategies to construct tailor-made synthetic derivative products—a transplantation to currency markets of the portfolio insurance methods used to hedge equity market exposure.

The crash of 1987 led to justifiable skepticism about the ability of mechanistic trading strategies like dynamic hedging actually to deliver the intended hedge protection when markets are illiquid.[1] In addition, these strategies have been criticized for their tendency to exacerbate price trends. Such criticisms carry over to the use of dynamic hedging in currency markets, although currency markets are usually among the most liquid of financial markets.

In this paper, we examine the impact of dynamic hedging strategies on foreign exchange markets during those crisis periods when even the exchange markets can become illiquid. Though we place some emphasis on the well-known inability of these strategies to perform well for the hedger when a discontinuity in the exchange rate or an upsurge of volatility occurs, we are concerned primarily with the impact of hedging strategies on the efficacy of the classic central bank interest rate defense of a fixed exchange rate. It is generally believed that a central bank can defend an exchange rate if it is willing to raise short-term interest rates sufficiently high to squeeze speculators who are short in its currency. In the presence of dynamic hedging, however, mechanistic selling of the domestic currency may arise in the endgame of the interest rate defense, and this may overwhelm the credit lines available to the central bank for intervention in the exchange market before those squeezed by the interest rate increase start to buy. Thus, our ultimate focus is on market and central bank behavior in the crucial last moments of a fixed exchange rate, the boundary point toward which the collapsing system converges.

The essay is organized as follows. In the next section, we outline the growth of the foreign exchange markets in general and the markets for currency derivatives in particular. Following that, we consider the hedging operations of nonbanks and the techniques in general use. We next examine the theory and practice of dynamic hedging and the hedging operations of banks in particular. We then examine the mechanics of central bank currency intervention and the effect of interest rate defenses on market liquidity, focusing particularly on the response of dynamic hedging programs to interest rate increases. We also consider how the interaction between the timing of different trading programs—dynamic hedging versus closing positions to avoid a squeeze—and the credit lines of the central bank may force the central bank to abandon a fixed exchange rate if it is driven either to the limit of its credit lines with commercial banks or to its self-imposed position limit before buyers of the currency arrive. The last section of the paper contains some concluding remarks.

Markets for Foreign Exchange Products

The foreign exchange market is the largest financial market in the world, with average daily turnover in April 1992 estimated at $880 billion, compared with $620 billion in April 1989.[2] The largest market segment is that for spot delivery —generally two days later—which accounted for just under half of the turnover in 1992, followed by the market for foreign exchange swaps, which accounted for 40 percent of turnover. The proportions of turnover due to outright forward deals, options, and futures were 7 percent, 5 percent, and 1 percent, respectively.

The market is largely an interdealer market: 84 percent of transactions were made among financial institutions and other foreign exchange brokers and dealers in 1992. This characteristic is reflected in the average deal size, which for the U.S. dollar was approximately $6 million overall. Deals were relatively smaller in the spot market, in which the proportion of transactions with end users was higher, while in the derivatives markets deals tended to be higher. For example, the average size of an over-the-counter (OTC) Deutsche mark-pound sterling option was $32 million.

The bulk of foreign exchange market activity still involves the U.S. dollar on one side of the transaction. The dollar was involved in 83 percent of all deals in 1992—including 72 percent of spot trades and 95 percent of swaps contracts —although this proportion had fallen since the previous survey conducted by the Bank for International Settlements (BIS) in 1989. Transactions between currencies in the European exchange rate mechanism (ERM) accounted for only 7 percent of aggregate turnover.

The 1992 survey results indicate how rapidly the use of financial derivatives has grown in recent years. While spot turnover increased only 14 percent between 1989 and 1992, forward transactions increased 60 percent, as did turnover in currency futures. Swaps trading increased 50 percent, and options trading increased by 124 percent.

The notional value of outstanding exchange-traded and OTC financial derivative contracts—including futures, forwards, forward rate agreements, swaps, options, caps, floors, and collars—grew from approximately $7.2 trillion at end-1989 to $17.6 trillion at end-1992.[3] The 1992 notional amounts are comprised of $4.8 trillion in exchange-traded contracts, $4.7 trillion in swaps, and $8.1 trillion in OTC options and forward contracts. By expanding the opportunities for borrowers and lenders to change the risk characteristics—such as maturity or currency denomination—of their portfolios, the growth in these markets has dramatically altered the nature of international finance and the behavior of market participants.

Exchange-traded derivative products—futures and options—are standardized, retail-sized products. Though they are retail in nature, they are frequently used by the dealers in OTC markets to balance positions when credit lines with other financial institutions are filled or when wholesale counterparties are hard to find. Because the exchange's clearinghouse is the counterparty to each contract and because positions are usually well-collateralized through margin requirements, the evaluation of creditworthiness is less of an issue on organized exchanges than in the OTC market.[4] The most actively traded financial derivatives on organized exchanges are futures on interest rates, primarily U.S. Treasury bond rates,

Eurodollars, French government bonds (OAT), German bonds, and Japanese government bonds.

The OTC markets in derivative products are concentrated in a small number of large banks and securities firms in the major financial centers. For example, bank holding companies with more than $10 billion in assets hold between 98 percent and 100 percent of all OTC derivative positions taken by U.S. banks.[5] OTC contracts are often designed specifically for the needs of particular end users and therefore have tailor-made features such as maturity, currency denomination, and notional principal, and are frequently combined with other derivatives and sold as a package. Many OTC trades are interdealer trades in which dealers seek to balance their positions.

Foreign exchange derivatives are important components of these markets, particularly the OTC markets. While the notional principal of outstanding exchange-traded foreign exchange derivatives at the end of 1992 was only $105 billion, there were $860 billion in currency swaps and $5.5 trillion in foreign exchange forwards and OTC options outstanding. In contrast, the notional principal of outstanding interest rate products were $4.4 trillion in exchange-traded contracts, $3.9 trillion in swaps, $634 billion in OTC options, and $2 trillion in forward rate agreements. Stock index derivatives totaled $245 billion.

The Markets for Currency Options

The market segment of particular interest in this paper is the market for options. The options market is divided into two parts: the market for exchange-traded options and the OTC market. Currency options are listed on six exchanges in Europe and North America, but most trading takes place on the Philadelphia Stock Exchange (PHLX) and the Chicago Mercantile Exchange's International Monetary Market (IMM). PHLX lists options on spot currency, while most of the contracts on the IMM are options on currency futures. Most listed options are available with a limited choice of maturities up to one year and have American exercise characteristics.[6] In the OTC market, contract specifications are in principle negotiable, although there is considerable standardization. Furthermore, OTC options are options on currency rather than options on futures, and the European exercise convention is the norm. OTC options are also contracted in much higher amounts. While an individual Deutsche mark contract on PHLX provides an option to buy or sell DM 62,500, options in the OTC market are written for amounts of at least $1 million.

The BIS data show that activity in the OTC market segment dominates total trading in currency options, accounting for 85 percent of turnover in April 1992. As with the bulk of foreign exchange trading, the U.S. dollar dominates the options markets: 98 percent of exchange trading and 74 percent of the OTC market's turnover involved the dollar on one side of the transaction. Assuming that the currency composition of Deutsche mark OTC options trading is representative of that for the other ERM currencies, only an estimated 10 percent of the OTC options market involves intra-ERM transactions. Moreover, two-thirds of the banks' options transactions, measured by notional principal, had other banks or dealers as counterparties.

While the BIS (1993) does not provide data on the maturity structure of the options market, it does provide it for forward contracts. These show that maturities are heavily concentrated in the near term: 64 percent of contracts mature within seven days, and only 1 percent have a maturity of longer than one year.

The Demand for Hedging in Foreign Exchange Markets

Open positions denominated in foreign currencies expose market participants to losses from exchange rate changes. Accounting for such risk is vital for portfolio managers with foreign currency exposure, corporates with foreign-currency-denominated assets or liabilities such as receivables or payables, or banks with currency exposure. These risks can be reduced by taking an offsetting position in the foreign currency. For example, a long position is hedged by shorting the currency in some fashion. This may consist of a spot sale with borrowing in the foreign currency to cover settlement, the purchase of a forward or future contract that locks in the level of the exchange rate for future payment, or the acquisition of a put option or the sale of a call option on the currency. Access to these instruments differs across types of hedgers: exchange-traded futures or options are retail products with little credit risk but with relatively high margin requirements; OTC products provided by banks and nonbank dealers are typically offered in much larger notional values and require a credit line from the bank to the customer along with a bank's assessment of its exposure to a given client. Options generally provide a partial hedge. For example, a portfolio manager may buy a put option to ensure a floor to the domestic currency value of the foreign currency component of its portfolio, but the portfolio remains subject to risk of currency fluctuations while the portfolio value is above the floor.[7]

At the end of 1991, institutional investors—mutual funds, pension funds, and insurance companies—in OECD countries had total assets of approximately \$11.7 trillion, compared with the assets of commercial banks, which totaled \$19.6 trillion.[8] The sizes of their foreign currency exposures in absolute terms and even in relation to their total assets can be quite large. For example, U.S. mutual funds and pension funds held \$214 billion in foreign assets, or 5 percent of their combined end-1991 assets of \$4.1 trillion. In contrast, U.K. mutual funds and pension funds invested $151 billion abroad, 23 percent of their total assets. Institutional investors in Germany, Japan, and the Netherlands also invest sizable proportions of their assets abroad. More significant perhaps, there are few restrictions on the foreign investments of institutional investors in industrial countries, and the trend appears to be toward relaxing those constraints that do exist. Banks, in contrast, often have well-defined position limits—either statutory or self-imposed—on their foreign exchange exposures.

Managers of pension funds, mutual funds, and bank trust accounts generally hedge their currency risk, often using dynamic hedging operations to create synthetic securities. For fixed-interest holdings of pension funds with obligations denominated in a given currency, the hedge reflects the desire by fund management to place a floor on the long-term value of foreign-currency-denominated holdings. For funds investing in foreign equities, the long-term reasons for establishing currency hedges is not as obvious because of the long-run tendency for exchange rates to conform with purchasing power parity. Nevertheless, in the short term—on a quarterly or annual basis—fund managers' performance, and therefore their compensation, often is compared to a benchmark. Moreover, fund managers seek to protect short-term performance from significant declines to prevent an increase in redemptions. Similarly, for pension funds, underfunding of liabilities may force an injection of securities into the fund that tests the liquidity of the parent entity. For these reasons, fund managers are sensitive in the short term to exchange rate movements and will wish to hedge positions. In the simplest hedging operation, fund directors may establish currency risk targets or limits to which management must adhere by following agreed hedging strategies. To place an absolute ceiling on losses from currency fluctuations, fund directors may mandate the acquisition of a put option to cover the entire foreign exchange position of the fund.

If they are willing to bear more risk from volatility changes, fund directors may instruct management to replicate a put dynamically.[9] This method has become typical for fund management. As indicated below, this buy-high, sell-low strategy will, ex post, have been less costly than an actual put if volatility declines and more costly if volatility increases. Finally, many portfolio managers follow a constant-percentage portfolio insurance strategy: this is a buy-high, sell-low dynamic strategy that does not replicate a put option.[10] Rather, it is driven entirely by price movements. For example, one realization of this strategy may aim at outperforming a 50-percent hedged position and would begin with a 50-percent hedge. A 1-percent move in the exchange rate would trigger an x-percent change in the hedge ratio. If the foreign currency appreciated by 10 percent, the hedge ratio would fall to $50 - 10x$ percent. Currency depreciations would be met with opposite adjustments in the hedge ratio. The strategy tends to work well when exchange rate changes come in trends but fails with a jump in volatility.[11]

Dynamic strategies are often implemented through cross-hedges—that is, a hedge may be implemented through shorting a currency whose exchange rate is highly correlated with the currency in which the fund holds securities. The purpose is to take advantage of greater liquidity in the exchange market or an interest rate premium in the currency used for the cross-hedge.

Individual firms and portfolio managers ultimately must turn to banks to engage in foreign exchange hedging since banks are the principal dealers in the foreign exchange spot and derivatives markets. By taking the opposite side of a transaction undertaken by a customer, a bank will acquire foreign exchange exposure that it will then attempt to eliminate. For those exposures that do not net out in the course of a day's trading with other customers—for example, currency or value-date mismatches in forward contract long and short positions or different features of options contracts—the bank must actively seek coverage by initiating its own transactions in the same OTC and exchange-traded derivatives markets or in the underlying markets.

Because of internal risk-control operations and regulations on foreign exchange risk, banks are active in using dynamic hedging techniques. Typically, they will hedge the net exposure to exchange rate changes acquired through transactions with clients, but they may leverage exchange risk when trading for proprietary accounts.

Regulation on banks' net foreign exchange positions varies widely across industrial countries.[12] In some countries, such as the United States, banks' exposures and internal controls are monitored on a regular basis, although there are no specified limits. Elsewhere, as in, for example, Germany, Japan, and the United Kingdom, guidelines or stronger constraints limit open positions to a specified ratio to total capital. Banks' internal risk management controls include the separation of dealing operations—in which buy/sell orders are taken—and back-office activities where contracts are confirmed and settled, the imposition of open position limits on the dealing book, and limits on the extension of credit to individual counterparties.

A bank that writes an option becomes exposed to the possibility that the option will be exercised and it will have to buy or sell foreign currency (depending upon whether it has written a put or a call). The simplest hedge in this case would be to acquire a perfectly offsetting contract. For a bank that maintains a large options book, many of its options contracts will indeed offset each other. However, to hedge the remaining options exposure, banks will generally turn to the more liquid underlying markets and hedge their exposures by creating synthetic options. Dynamic hedging strategies provide a simple means by which complicated options books can be hedged by constructing synthetic options.

As the earlier discussion indicates, trading in options is only a small part of the foreign exchange market. Most of banks' foreign exchange exposure comes from dealing in the spot and forward (including swaps) markets. As with their options-based exposures, banks will actively hedge their net exposure arising from these other transactions. Moreover, not all options (or other) transactions entered into by banks are derived from hedging operations. Unlike transactions in the underlying markets, options provide tools for taking positions in the volatility of spot exchange rates or exchange rate futures, instead of or in addition to speculating on the future direction of these underlying assets. Banks both sell packages of options to their customers that allow them to choose their own degree of exposure to the level, direction of change, and volatility of the underlying asset, and enter into transactions with other dealers to do the same for their own account.

Mechanics of Option Pricing and Dynamic Hedging

Pricing Put Options on Foreign Currency

Because option pricing theory is at the heart of dynamic hedging, it is helpful at this point to review the basic option pricing formula for foreign exchange—the Garman–Kohlhagen formula—before describing how dynamic hedging works.[13] Although banks and other wholesale traders may use more sophisticated pricing methods that account for varying interest rates and exchange rate volatility, the Garman–Kohlhagen formula is in general operational use by pension fund and other portfolio managers, and it is pedagogically useful for illustrating the management of risk in a bank's foreign exchange book.[14]

Suppose that a customer buys a European put option to deliver Deutsche marks for dollars after T periods for an exercise price of $\$X$ per Deutsche mark. The value of the put option, P_t, is

$$P_t = -[1 - N(d_1)]\exp[-r_{DM}T]S + [1 - N(d_2)]\exp[-r_{\$}T]X, \qquad (1)$$

where r_{DM} and $r_{\$}$ are the (constant) risk-free instantaneous Deutsche mark and dollar interest rates, S is the current dollar–Deutsche mark spot exchange rate, and X is the exercise or strike exchange rate of the option.[15] $N(d_1)$ is the value of the normal distribution function evaluated at the argument

$$d_1 = \{\ln(S/X) + [r_{\$} - r_{DM} + \sigma^2/2]T\}/\sigma\sqrt{T}, \qquad (2)$$

where σ is the (constant) instantaneous standard deviation or volatility of the exchange rate S. Finally, $d_2 = d_1 - \sigma\sqrt{T}$. The put price, or premium, is graphed against the spot exchange rate in Figure IVA–1. The premium is a downward-sloping, convex function of the exchange rate and lies closer to the option's intrinsic value, max $[0,X - S]$ (depicted as the dashed 45-degree line, which

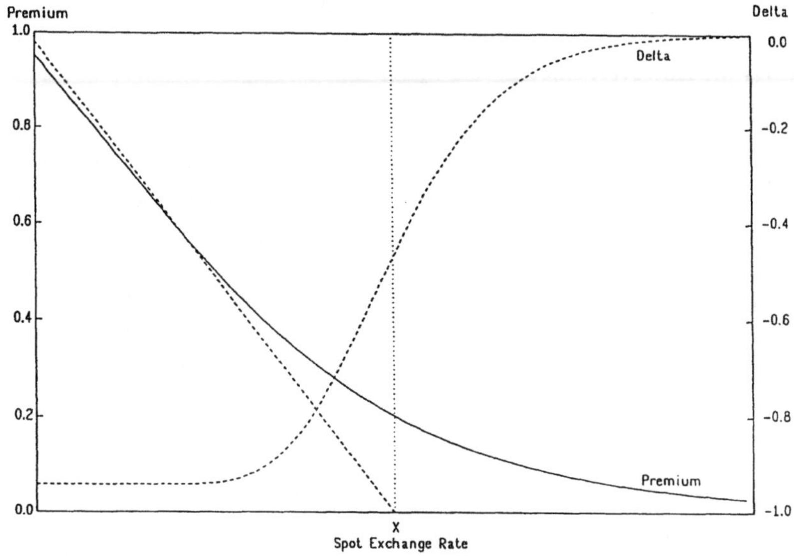

Figure IVA–1. Currency put option premium and delta.

coincides with the horizontal axis to the right of X) the shorter the time to maturity. Note that it is possible for the price of the option to be less than its intrinsic value for deep in-the-money puts.

Implementing the Dynamic Hedge

The put pricing formula is determined by finding the short position in Deutsche mark loans and the long position in dollar loans such that a portfolio with these positions and also short a put is riskless with respect to small exchange rate movements.

Thus, an investor that wants to hedge its exposure to fluctuations in the dollar–Deutsche mark exchange rate can either hedge a long Deutsche mark position by buying a put option or use equation 1 to determine positions in Deutsche mark and dollar loans that mimic the value of a put—that is, to create a synthetic put. The basic security in the first half of the formula is a loan promising to deliver 1 Deutsche mark in T periods; this has a Deutsche mark present value of $exp[-r_{DM}T]$ and a dollar value of $exp[-r_{DM}T]S$. The coefficient $-[1 - N(d_1)]$ indicates that the mimicking portfolio should consist of a short position of a fraction of such a Deutsche mark loan—that is, a short Deutsche mark position. Similarly, the dollar position is long a fraction $[1 - N(d_2)]$ of a loan promising to pay X dollars in T periods with a present dollar value of $exp[-r_{\$}T]X$. However, since d_1 and d_2 constantly move with the exchange rate, the interest rate differential, and the standard deviation projected for exchange rate movements, the positions must be adjusted constantly—hence the term *dynamic hedging*—to maintain the equivalence of the position to a put option.[16]

The foreign exchange exposure of the bank that sells the put is to the *possibility* of having to buy deutsche marks at the exercise price at date T. Under the assumptions behind the pricing formula, it is not necessary to hedge the total face value of the contract prior to the exercise date. How much of the face value to hedge, which in turn determines the hedge ratio, is provided by the option's delta, the change in the value of the option with respect to a movement in the exchange rate. From the pricing formula developed above, the delta of a currency put option is

$$-[1 - N(d_1)]exp(-r_{DM}T).$$

Thus, a rise in the dollar value of the Deutsche mark makes it less likely that the option will be exercised and reduces the value of the put. The put delta takes values between –1, for a deep-in-the-money option that would almost certainly be exercised, to 0, for a deep-out-of-the-money option that would never be exercised (see Figure IVA–1). The negative of delta, therefore, provides a proxy for the probability of exercise. Delta multiplied by the number of units of foreign currency provides an estimate of the expected foreign exchange that is sold short at any point in time to hedge against possible exercise of the option.

A writer of a put option may, therefore, hedge the option dynamically according to the prescriptions of the put pricing formula. First, it must establish the portfolio that mimics the value of the option—for example, by shorting $[1 - N(d_1)]$ Deutsche mark forward for dollars and buying $[1 - N(d_2)]\ exp[-r_{\$}T]X$ in U.S. Treasury bills. As the exchange rate fluctuates, the now-hedged writer of the option must adjust the short Deutsche mark and long dollar positions according to the formula to continue to mimic the option. Typically, the adjustments will not be continuous; instead, to avoid transactions costs, adjustments to the mimicking portfolio will be made as part of a regular rebalancing exercise.[17]

Among other assumptions, the put pricing formula is based on assuming that exchange rate volatility will remain constant during the life of the contract. Because volatility typically is not constant, the mimicking portfolio will never perfectly track the actual option's value—gains or losses relative to the initial option premium will always occur—and so the portfolio must constantly be adjusted to changes in volatilities as measured, frequently, by implied volatilities in options prices. If volatility jumps above the value implicit in the price of the actual put option, the writer of the put who engages in dynamic hedging will take a loss and the buyer of the put will gain. It is well known that strategies to create synthetic options to hedge actual options through the use of dynamic trading, designed to be delta neutral, can be used to take positions on volatility in underlying prices and in interest rates.[18]

The loss to the writer is immediately apparent if the portfolio is marked to market. A volatility increase will, ceteris paribus, increase the value of the actual option (a liability) and leave unchanged the value of the hedging portfolio (the supposedly balancing asset). Alternatively, if the option value is not marked to market, the loss will be booked through the dynamic adjustment of Deutsche mark and dollar positions until the exercise date. According to the hedging strategy, a rise in the exchange rate will cause the writer of the put to reduce the short Deutsche mark position: the writer of the option will buy Deutsche marks when the Deutsche mark appreciates and sell when it depreciates. This "buy dear-sell cheap" strategy generates a foreseeable loss to the writer of the put, or indeed of any other option, for which it is compensated by the put premium. If volatility jumps, however, the premium will be insufficient to cover the now greater-than-expected realized loss on these hedging trades.

To hedge the risks acquired from their OTC options transactions with other dealers, banks generally construct a dynamic hedge by purchasing or selling currency in the spot market to close the currency exposure and entering into a swap contract to shift the exposure to coincide with the maturity date of the option. Indeed, such transactions have become part of banks' normal operating procedures (Walmsley 1992).

To monitor its overall exposure, a bank must have a method to break down each option in its book into its implied foreign exchange position. It can then determine its global net position in each currency by adding its net position from trading in other foreign exchange products to its net position implied in its options book, and then hedge the combined exposure. The foreign exchange equivalent into which a bank will decompose its options will depend on the currency-options-pricing formula used by the bank, but it will usually be based on delta hedging methods. The bank calculates the delta for all the contracts it has written or bought and multiplies these by the face values of the contracts. These are then added up for each currency to estimate the expected net foreign currency delivery requirement. For European-style options, in which exercise is only possible at maturity, the hedge portfolio will include futures or forward contracts that offset these amounts, while for American-style options, the hedge will include cash positions because the exercise date is uncertain. Because the management of the foreign exchange book is global, the amounts required to hedge the options will be netted against spot and forward net positions.

For example, suppose that the global position in the currency option book of a bank making a market in derivatives is short one OTC European Deutsche

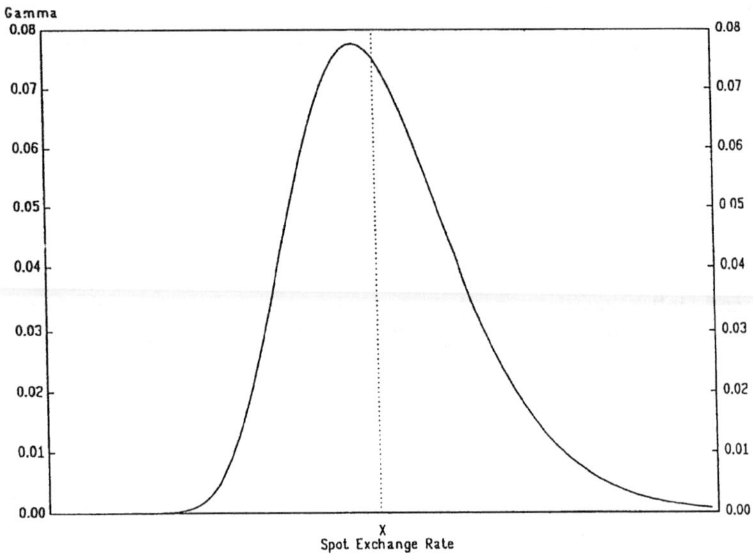

Figure IVA–2. Currency put option gamma.

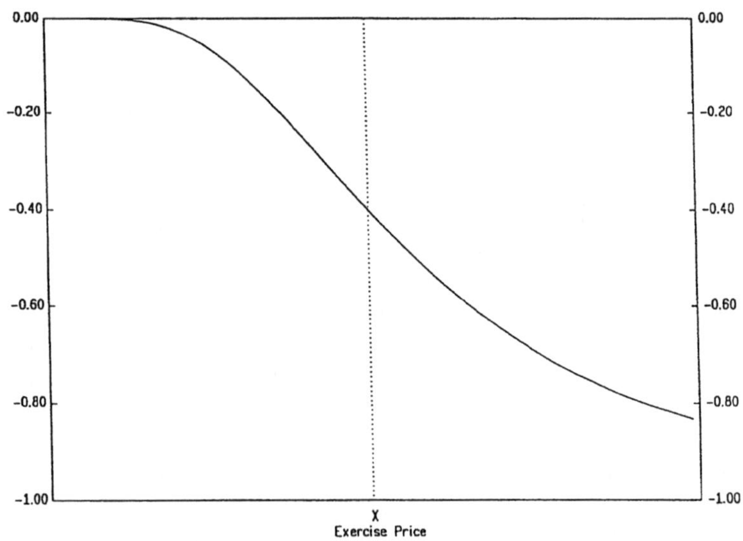

Figure IVA–3. Sensitivity of put delta to the exercise price.

mark put option that allows the holder to sell DM 1 for \$$X$ at time T and long one European put option to sell DM 1 for French francs at T^*. If the bank uses the Garman–Kohlhagen formula, its Deutsche mark position from its options book is

Option	DM Position
1. Short 1 Put DM/\$	$[1 - N(d_1)] \exp[-r_{DM}T]$
2. Long 1 Put DM/FF	$-[1 - N(d_1^*)] \exp[-r_{DM}T^*]$

In these formulas, d_1 and d_1^* are defined as above, with the appropriate volatilities and exercise prices substituted for each option. If the bank is also long Deutsche mark in its forward and spot trading, it can determine its global foreign exchange exposure in Deutsche marks by adding these three quantities. The bank can then hedge the foreign exchange risk by taking the opposite position in the forward market. Because the implied delivery dates across its Deutsche mark contracts may differ, this still leaves the bank with an interest rate risk that can be hedged through appropriate Deutsche mark forwards or swaps.

Properties of the Put Option Delta

Given the centrality of delta to the construction of the hedge portfolio, it is worth considering its properties. In particular, we are interested in identifying the response of delta to changes in the parameters of the model. Unfortunately, these relationships are often not monotonic.

The partial derivative of delta with respect to the exchange rate is the option's gamma, or convexity. For a put option, this is always positive, as portrayed in Figure IVA–2. Thus, an increase in the exchange rate makes the option less likely to be exercised and lowers the absolute value of delta. Note that the put delta is most sensitive to changes in the exchange rate when the option is close to being at-the-money. Conversely, an increase in the exercise price, X, increases the value of the option, raising the probability of exercise and the short position needed to hedge it. Thus, delta is a decreasing function of X, as shown in Figure IVA–3. The only other partial derivative of delta that is unambiguous is that with respect to $r_\$$, which is positive. An increase in this rate lowers the present value of the dollars that will be received if the option is exercised. This lowers the likelihood that the option will be exercised, and so delta is an increasing function of $r_\$$, as in Figure IVA–4.

The remaining derivatives, with respect to the volatility, time to maturity, and r_{DM}, are all of ambiguous sign. Figure IVA–5 shows the effect of changes in volatility on the put option delta. For at-the-money options, there is little change in the delta. For out-of-the-money options, delta is a decreasing function of

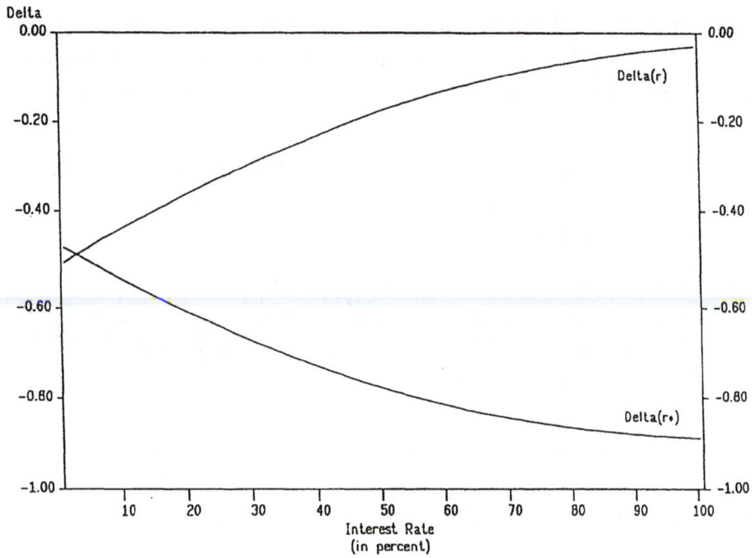

Figure IVA–4. Sensitivity of put delta to domestic and foreign interest rates.

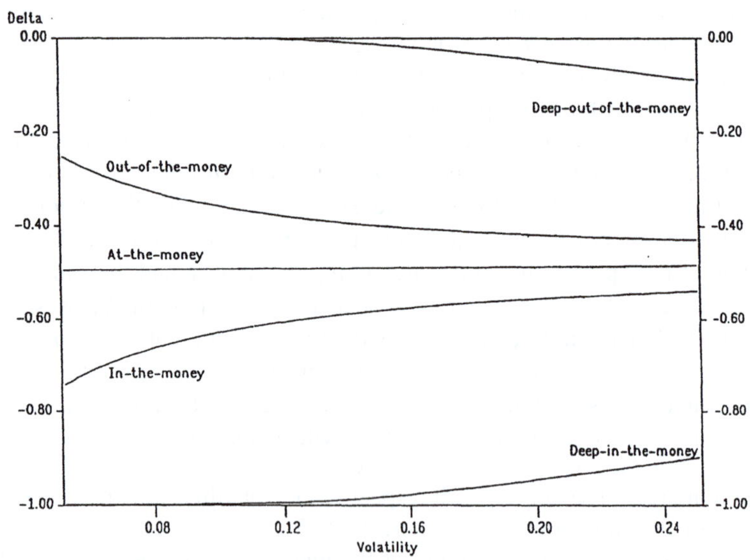

Figure IVA–5. Sensitivity of put delta to volatility.

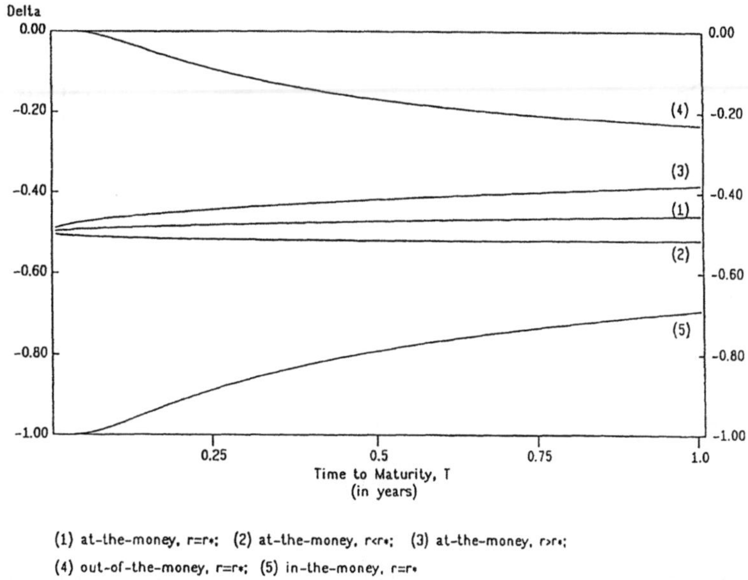

Figure IVA–6. Sensitivity of put delta to the expiration date.

exchange rate volatility: an increase in volatility increases the probability that the exchange rate will fall far enough that the option will move in-the-money, and so the probability of exercise increases. For in-the-money options, delta increases with volatility since an increase in the latter only increases the probability that the exchange rate will rise above X by the time the option expires. Clearly, for very deep in- or out-of-the-money options, a very large increase in volatility is necessary for there to be an appreciable change in delta.

An increase in the time to maturity has a similar effect on the option delta, as does an increase in volatility.[19] Figure IVA–6 shows that for in-the-money options, a longer time to maturity increases the probability that the option will move out-of-the-money before expiration, and so the delta decreases, and conversely for out-of-the-money options. For at-the-money options, the effect on delta is sensitive to the sign of the interest rate differential. Some intuition about the effect of changing time to maturity is obtained from Figure IVA–1. As the time to maturity falls, the options price function, P, collapses onto the intrinsic value function. Thus, reversing the process, as the time to maturity increases, the price function moves upward and to the right, away from the intrinsic value function. Hence, for out-of-the-money options, delta, which is the slope of the price function, falls from zero to some negative value, while for in-the-money options the slope rises from –1. For at-the-money options (and possibly for

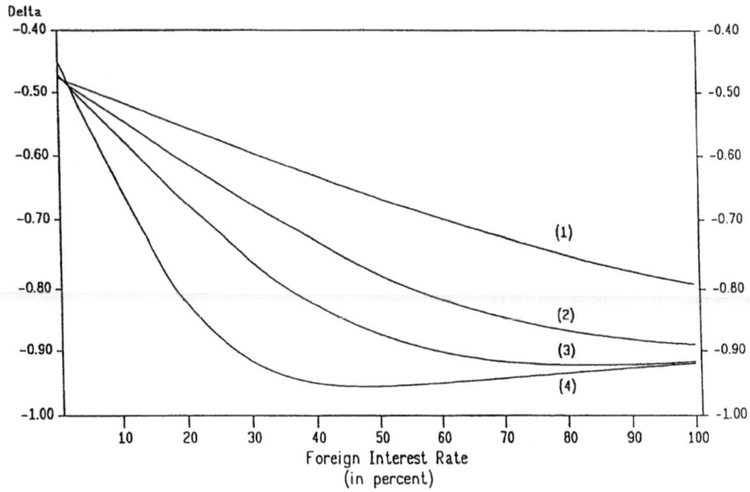

Figure IVA–7. Sensitivity of put delta to the foreign interest rate and to volatility.

options for which the spot price and the exercise price are very close), the change in slope depends on the convexity of the price function, which in turn depends upon, inter alia, the interest rate differential.

The most important partial derivative for the purposes of the discussion in the next section is the effect of changes in r_{DM} on the put option delta. Under most circumstances, the relationship is as it is depicted in Figure IVA–4—downward sloping. However, since the derivative is of ambiguous sign, and given the importance of this relationship, Figures IVA–7 through IVA–9 show how this derivative varies with values of the other parameters. Figure IVA–7 shows that for most common values of the volatility parameter, the relationship is always negative. However, if the exchange rate's annualized volatility falls below 5 percent, the curve slopes upward after r_{DM} rises above approximately 45 percent. Figure IVA–8 shows that as the intrinsic value of the option, $X - S$, rises, a similar reversal in slope is possible. Indeed, for deep-in-the-money options, delta is everywhere increasing in r_{DM}. Finally, Figure IVA–9 shows that as the time to maturity of the option increases, further increases in r_{DM} can lead to an increase in delta (a fall in the short foreign exchange position).

The inference that can be drawn from these last three figures is that, for the most commonly observed parameter values, delta declines with increases in the foreign interest rate. However, for options that have long terms to maturity or that are in-the-money or written on very low volatility options—or, more likely,

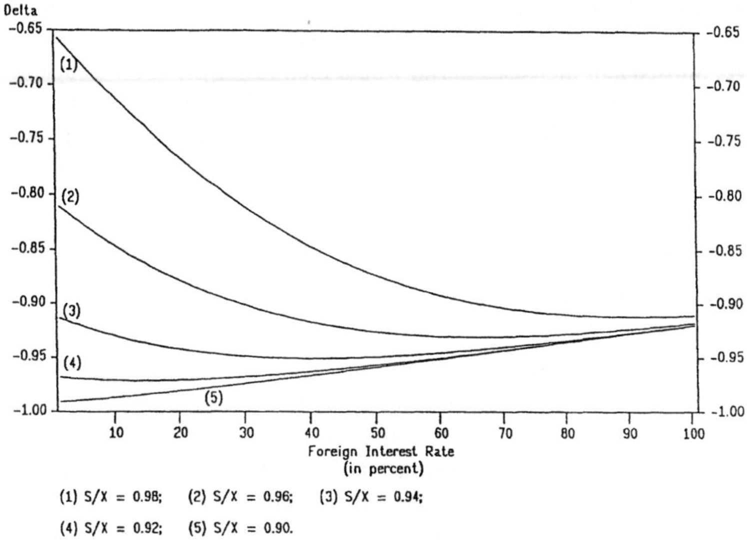

Figure IVA–8. Sensitivity of put delta to the foreign interest rate and to the intrinsic value.

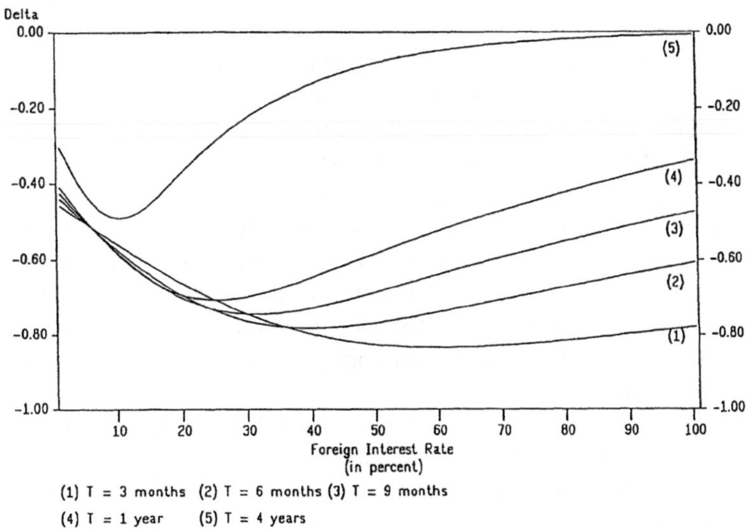

Figure IVA–9. Sensitivity of put delta to the foreign interest rate and to the contract maturity.

a combination of these characteristics—it is possible that for a sufficiently large increase in r_{DM}, the relationship between delta and r_{DM} could actually become positive. Subsequent increases in r_{DM} would then lower the short Deutsche mark position held to hedge the short put position. Note, however, that except for multiyear options—which are extremely rare—it is highly unlikely that any increase in r_{DM} would actually lead to a decline in the initial short Deutsche mark position.

Hedging in a Crisis

Dynamic hedging strategies are not an entirely new activity; stop-loss trading has always been triggered by price movements beyond a certain threshold. Dynamic hedging simply mechanizes this response. To the extent, however, that the technique has been adopted by large segments of the financial intermediation industry and can be implemented more rapidly than previous techniques, dynamic hedging strategies have added to trading volume and have accentuated price movements by contributing to momentary illiquidity. In this section, we consider how the widespread use of dynamic hedging techniques may interact with central bank exchange rate and liquidity policies to undermine a defense of a fixed-exchange-rate system.

When a fixed-exchange-rate regime moves toward a crisis, speculation against the currency is generally channeled through forward sales of the currency to the banking system. Some margin is required by counterparty banks, but this can be leveraged up by a factor of 10 or more by the speculator. In a crisis, these sales will generally not be matched by other customers' forward purchases of the currency. The central bank defending the currency may intervene with forward purchases, but the extent of such an operation is limited by the unwillingness of a central bank to risk large capital losses on negative net foreign exchange positions and by limits on credit lines to the central bank made available by the major dealing banks.[20] Once the central bank ceases to buy its currency in the forward market, banks must balance their forward purchases with spot sales of the currency (to balance the net currency position) and by currency swaps (to balance maturities).

Once again, during a crisis, the central bank will be the most important buyer on the spot market through its intervention to maintain the fixed exchange rate. At the same time, it provides its currency through the discount window to the banks that need to sell currency in order to match their forward and spot foreign exchange positions, as discussed in the previous paragraph. By providing liquidity to banks through this kind of facility, the central bank is effectively financing the attack on its own reserves. To settle its spot transactions, the central bank must deliver its own foreign exchange reserves or draw down lines of credit from other central banks or multilateral entities. As its short foreign exchange position mounts during the intervention, the central bank must act by raising the discount rate. This increases the cost to speculators who speculate against the currency by borrowing from the central bank. The central bank may also impose a squeeze on short sellers by channeling available credit away from identified speculators.

This final operation is the classic interest rate defense of a fixed exchange rate. It works though a liquidity effect in the money market—domestic credit grows less rapidly than central bank net reserves decline, thereby producing a decline in the supply of the domestic settlement medium. If large short positions in the currency are due for settlement, holders of short positions may sell foreign exchange to the central bank rather than face the high interest costs of rolling over overnight loans in the weak currency. The costs to holders of short positions are further accentuated if, in addition, they are caught in a squeeze so that they have to pay more than the discount rate to obtain funds.

The market's acquisition of foreign exchange from the central bank does not arise exclusively from forward sales by nonbank speculators. Speculators and hedgers may also buy put options on the weak currency from the banks. Again, in a crisis, the banking system will likely be unable to find nonbank sellers of puts to balance these positions.[21] To hedge, the bank that writes the put may create a long position in a synthetic put by selling the weak currency forward, by selling on the futures market, or by selling spot and entering a swap contract. Any of these operations will trigger a spot sale of the weak currency to the central bank, as described above.

A common hedging strategy employed by customers is the implementation of a range forward, depicted in Figure IVA–10.[22] An investor wanting to hold a lire position might buy a put option and sell a call with a higher exercise price chosen so that the revenue from the sale of the call equals the price of the put. In addition, the investor would purchase lire in a forward contract (which has zero cost at inception). In such a strategy, the investor bears the risk of exchange rate depreciation in the range, $\bar{X}-\underline{X}$, but is protected from very large depreciations, as demonstrated by the payoff function RF. The bank that sells the range forward is short a put option and long a call option with similar strike prices. The bank may choose to hedge these exposures by creating synthetic options. The hedge portfolio for both of these option positions requires a short lira position.[23]

The Effect of Interest Rate Changes on Dynamic Hedging

Once a central bank raises interest rates in defense of the fixed exchange rate, hedging operations may trigger further sales of the currency rather than the

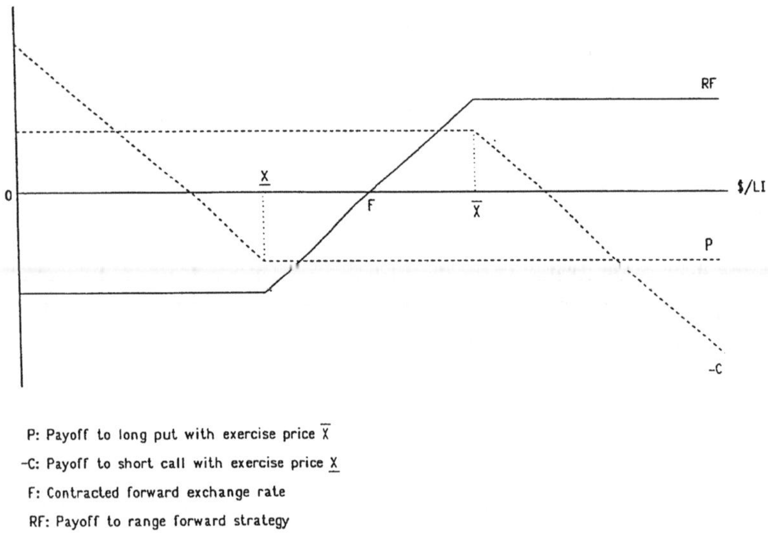

Figure IVA–10. Range forward payoff diagram.

purchases anticipated from the squeeze. This result follows from the relation between interest rate movements and the hedging portfolio in equation 1.

Intuitively, the interest rate differential between the two currencies reflects the expected rate of depreciation of the exchange rate plus a risk premium. Unless volatility increases or attitudes toward risk change, a rise in the differential between deutsche mark and dollar interest rates means that the Deutsche mark is expected to depreciate more rapidly against the dollar—that is, the hedge ratio increases.[24]

With an unchanged current exchange rate, exercise price, and exchange rate volatility, the put option is much more likely to finish in-the-money when the foreign interest rate jumps upward. That the option is more likely to be exercised means that it provides a higher effective hedge to a portfolio manager covering a deutsche mark exposure. The manager of the bank's portfolio who uses a synthetic put in a dynamic hedging operation must likewise provide an increased hedge ratio in response to the greater probability that the option will be exercised. This means that the manager must short-sell more Deutsche marks so that the synthetic put continues to mimic an actual put. Taken to an extreme, if Deutsche mark interest rates rise so high that, according to the underlying theory, it is almost certain that a put option will be exercised, the put then provides the equivalent of a 100-percent hedge ratio. The bank's portfolio manager using a synthetic put must similarly sell sufficient Deutsche marks to cover his entire Deutsche mark position to provide the same coverage as an actual put.

How important will the dynamic hedging response be? Figure IVA–8 provides some indication of the response of dynamic hedging programs during the final days of a managed- or fixed-exchange-rate regime. In the days leading up to the collapse of an exchange rate band regime, the gradual depreciation in the spot exchange rate will have a significant effect on the hedge ratio, necessitating a gradual increase in the short foreign currency position. However, in the final hours or minutes of such a regime or of an absolutely fixed exchange rate, the use of large interest rate increases to defend the fixed exchange rate can result in increases in the hedge ratio of a similar magnitude. What makes this effect important is that in a fixed-exchange-rate regime, or a quasi-fixed system such as the ERM, the boundary values for the nominal exchange rate become focal points for speculation about the direction of change of the exchange rate. Not only will more investors begin to hedge their exposures as the risk of realignment or a change in the parity increases, but the options that are written for customers will all tend to have similar exercise prices, so that they will tend to react similarly to changes in the foreign interest rate. Moreover, as the spot foreign exchange rate falls toward the lower boundary value—a natural value for the put option's exercise price—the option's delta will become more sensitive to changes in the foreign interest rate (Figure IVA–8).

For example, in the United Kingdom on September 16, 1992, the Bank of England increased the base lending rate twice, from 10 percent to 12 percent and then again to 15 percent (effective the next day).[25] The one-month London interbank offer rate increased from 10.4 percent at the end of the previous day to 28.9 percent at the end of September 16. According to equation 1, such an interest rate increase would have resulted in a 22 percent decrease in the delta (or increase in the hedge ratio) of an at-the-money put—from −0.54 to −0.66—a larger change than would have been obtained from a 1.5-percent depreciation at the initial interest rate.[26] In the Swedish market, the increase in the marginal lending rate from 75 percent to 500 percent on September 16 led to an increase in the one-month STIBOR rate from 25 percent to 70 percent. An increase of this magnitude implies a 14-percent decrease in delta.[27] On November 19, the eve of the Swedish devaluation, the one-month STIBOR rate rose from 13.9 percent to 28 percent, implying an 18-percent increase in the hedge ratio.[28]

Industry sources indicate that, indeed, when there is an increase in the interest rate spread with no movement in the exchange rate, the forward rate discount will trigger a sell-off in the currency through dynamic hedging. During the ERM crisis of September 1992, for example, industry sources estimate that dynamic hedging sales to adjust positions because of increases in interest rate spreads, exchange rate movements, and increases in volatility accounted for 20–30 percent of the selling in the crisis.[29] It apparently was a major factor in the lira market one week after the first devaluation and also in the Swedish krona market later in 1992. Up to 10 percent of the sales were due to increases in interest rate spreads. In the case of the United Kingdom, on September 16, 1992, the dramatic increase in forward discounts triggered sales of pounds. When interest rates rose and nothing happened to the exchange rates, the selling programs were turned on. The lack of movement (appreciation) in the exchange rate meant that the forward rate fell farther below the floor. Thus, the full force of programmed sales triggered by interest rate movements was not offset by exchange rate improvement. Another source of the sales volumes at this moment was the rising perceived volatility resulting from the suddenly larger movement of the forward rate below the floor. The effect of dynamic hedging sales may also have been a source of some of the selling pressure observed on August 12, 1994, when the Italian lira depreciated sharply after the Banca D'Italia raised the discount rate by 50 basis points, though the consensus view is that markets reacted mostly in the belief that the interest rate increases were fiscally unsustainable.

In an exchange crisis, therefore, a large defensive rise in the interest rate aimed at imposing a squeeze on speculators will instantaneously trigger hedging programs to order sales of the weak currency.[30] The experiments conducted using the actual data on interest rates and historical volatility suggest that the selling triggered by dynamic hedging programs during an interest rate defense can be significant. The existence of a large amount of such programs in the market would undermine the use of an interest rate defense of a weak currency—the moment that a central bank raises interest rates, it might face an avalanche of sales of its currency rather than the purchases of the squeezed shorts that it had anticipated. In effect, the hedging programs make the hedgers insensitive to the added costs of funding their weak currency sales.

If the central bank has a credit line limit in foreign exchange or a self-imposed negative net reserve position, the upsurge of selling brought about by the interest rate increase might cause a sudden jump to its limit and force it to cease intervention in defense of the exchange rate. Whether this counterintuitive result occurs depends on the weight of these mechanistic traders relative to those caught in the short squeeze.

In one scenario, the hedging operation may in, any case, far exceed the amount of the weak currency demanded by those caught in the squeeze. In this case, the timing of the hedging sales—the prearranged rule for awakening the selling programs—relative to the time at which those caught in the short squeeze appear on the market is immaterial to the survival of the fixed exchange rate. Dominance by the mechanistic hedgers will defeat the interest rate defense.

In the scenario in which the amounts of these opposite transactions are roughly balanced or even where those caught in the short squeeze dominate, the timing of transactions is key. If the selling programs switch on instantly, but the buying operations to cover short positions occur with some lag, the central bank's net short foreign exchange limit may be exceeded prior to the appearance of the buyers of its currency, causing the abandonment of the fixed exchange rate. Buyers might have appeared by the end of the day to offset the sellers, but the initial selling may unnerve the central bank and force devaluation. The devaluation will ratify both the actions of the sellers and of those caught in the squeeze who hesitated. Sellers will have sold prior to the devaluation of the exchange rate, and those caught in the squeeze can buy back into the weak currency at a lower price. If the central bank simultaneously relaxes the high interest rates, overnight borrowing will cease to be a problem for those caught short, and the squeeze will be suspended.

Conclusion

In their impact on the viability of the interest rate defense of a fixed exchange rate, dynamic hedging programs can be interpreted as a new wrinkle on an old phenomenon. Skeptical participants in the foreign exchange market have sometimes interpreted a defensive increase in the interest rate as the last rearguard action preparatory to the abandonment of a fixed rate. In this light, the suddenly higher interest rate differential signals only the extent of the impending depreciation of the exchange rate and certainly not a drastic and extended tightening of liquidity in the weak currency's money markets. Interpreting the interest rate increase in this way dictates that a speculative selling program should be begun. Dynamic hedging programs automatically place this interpretation on an interest rate increase; thus, they are a mechanization of the previously informal skepticism that occasionally arose about exchange rate defenses. To the extent that such programs are present in generating large selling volumes, they signal a major shift toward skepticism about the strength of the central bank's adherence to the policy of defending the exchange rate, thereby undermining the efficacy of a previously useful defensive tool.

The scenario that we depict here is a technical story about the character of minute-by-minute trading in the death throes of a fixed exchange rate. A dramatic interest rate increase in a last ditch defense triggers dramatic selling pressure. If this technical feature of the market is important in the last moments of a fixed exchange rate, it is necessary to implement a defense operation that takes it into account. For example, it is often argued that a resolute defense of a fixed-exchange-rate regime requires that at an early date interest rates be raised gradually, though ultimately to high levels.[31] Such a policy would trigger daily selling of the currency by dynamic hedgers, but not in quantities that would overwhelm the central bank's net reserve limits before the appearance as buyers by the end of the day of those caught short in the currency. Thus, raising rates gradually in an interest rate defense may immunize the central bank against being pushed beyond its position limits.

Notes

We thank Philippo Jorion, Paolo Kind, Richard Lyons, John Montgomery, Victor Ng, David Ordoobadi, and Thierry Pujol for helpful comments. The conclusions of this paper are those of the authors and are not necessarily those of the International Monetary Fund.

1. See, for example, the Brady Commission (1988) and Securities and Exchange Commission (1988) reports. Grossman (1988) forecast this problem. Gennotte and Leland (1990) model the relationship between hedging operations and market liquidity and show how a relatively small volume of transactions initiated by hedgers can lead to a large price change.

2. Bank for International Settlements (1993).

3. These estimates are derived in General Accounting Office (1994). The notional value of a contract is the nominal amount used as a base to calculate a transfer of payments according to a contractual formula. For example, an interest rate swap may have a notional value of $10 million. This notional value is not delivered as principal. Rather, counterparties deliver or receive the net between fixed interest on $10 million and floating interest on $10 million, so the claims that counterparties might have on each other are far smaller than the notional value.

4. OTC derivatives dominate exchange-traded products with limited liquidity, such as longer dated contracts or options that are not at- or near-the-money.

5. Estimates reported in Board of Governors of the Federal Reserve System, Federal Deposit Insurance Corporation, and Office of the Comptroller of the Currency (1993). See also Bank of England (1993), Bank for International Settlements (1992), Deutsche Bundesbank (1993), Commodity Futures Trading Commission (1993), General Accounting Office (1994), Group of Thirty (1993), Goldstein et al. (1993), and Office of the Comptroller of the Currency (1993) for discussions of the activities of banks in OTC derivatives markets.

6. That is, the option can be exercised at any time prior to maturity. Under the European exercise convention, the option may only be exercised at maturity.

7. In addition, portfolios will be subject to basis risk when the security underlying the hedge instrument is not identical to the security whose return is being hedged so that the returns on the two securities are not perfectly correlated. A hedge constructed with a related, but not identical, instrument to the one whose value is being hedged is called a *cross-hedge*.

8. See Goldstein et al. (1993) for a discussion of the foreign holdings of institutional investors in industrial countries.

9. Using real put contracts to hedge long positions is not entirely free of volatility risk, of course, since changes in volatility can result in losses when put contracts are rolled over if the maturity of the contracts is shorter than the horizon of the hedging operation.

10. This strategy is referred to by Leland, O'Brien, and Rubinstein and Associates as a perpetual protection policy.

11. A constant percentage portfolio insurance strategy has an advantage over an option replication strategy in that at the end of the period, a renewal of the hedge does not require a large trading operation. For an option replication strategy, at expiration the portfolio is either 100 percent hedged or completely unhedged. Renewal of the strategy for another period then requires a large jump in the hedge ratio.

12. See Goldstein et al. (1993) for a discussion on the regulatory and internal constraints on banks' foreign exchange trading.

13. See Garman and Kohlhagen (1983) for the development of this formula. For pricing formulas taking account of stochastic volatility, see Chiang and Okunev (1993), Kroner and Sultan (1993), Melino and Turnbull (1990), Naik (1993), and Perraudin and Sorenson (1992). Dumas, Jennergren, and Näslund (1993) derive options-pricing formulas for currencies restricted by target zones, as in the European exchange rate mechanism. However, as the data above indicate, the majority of OTC and exchange-traded options contracts are written for dollar exchange.

14. Most exchange-traded currency options, except those traded on the Philadelphia Stock Exchange, are options on futures, for which the Garman–Kohlhagen formula for spot exchange options is inapplicable. In the standard formula for pricing options on futures, the foreign interest rate does not appear. The effect of foreign interest rate changes is felt through their impact on the futures price. Moreover, in the OTC market it is more common to price options with respect to the forward exchange rate rather than the spot rate (see DeRosa 1992, 109).

15. This equation is identical in form to the Merton adaptation of the Black–Scholes put formula for a stock that pays a continuous, constant dividend. This formula is constructed on the assumption that the percentage change in the price of the underlying security, in this case the dollar–Deutsche mark exchange rate, follows a Wiener process, that the instantaneous interest rates in both countries and the standard deviation of the percentage exchange rate change are fixed parameters for the life of the option. Such a simple formula does not exist for American put options; these must be evaluated by numerical methods (see DeRosa 1992).

16. Note that the ability to maintain a dynamic hedge depends critically on the existence of a liquid spot foreign exchange market in which the rebalancing trades can be executed. If, as happens during a crisis, markets become illiquid, investors that rely on dynamic hedging may not be able to adjust their portfolios and will be exposed to further exchange rate changes.

17. Since the hedge is not adjusted continuously, the bank will incur losses between rebalancing exercises. Leong (1990–1991) argues that the option premium charged by a bank will, in equilibrium, equal the expected value of this hedge slippage.

18. See, for example, Cookson (1993) or DeRosa (1992).

19. This is the negative of the change in delta with respect to the remaining time to maturity of the option, which is sometimes called *charm* (see Garman 1992).

20. The ability of the central bank to enter forward contracts with its own nationally chartered banks is circumscribed by credit line limits imposed by banks elsewhere on these banks.

21. Even if nonbank sellers of puts exist somewhere in the financial system, the selling bank seeking cover may not find them through the banking system. In a crisis, gross trading volumes surge, thereby causing many banks to reach their credit ceilings with other banks. As the banking system becomes illiquid in this way, transactions that passed through the banking system on a credit basis now must seek a cash market. To hedge, the selling bank will place an order to buy a put onto the organized currency options market, where credit risk is not an issue, and will find the potential seller in this market. As the crisis progresses and more interbank credit lines fill, volume will tend to move to the more secure organized exchanges.

22. We are grateful to Paolo Kind for suggesting this example.

23. Intuitively, a short put position is a contingent long position in the foreign currency (here lire), as is a long call position. Hence, both are hedged by going short in lire.

24. A central bank squeeze generally operates through overnight interest rates, which are not the interest rates used to value longer dated options. Nevertheless, in a squeeze, a jump in overnight rates will usually have a strong impact on short- and medium-term interest rates, which are relevant to option pricing.

25. See Goldstein et al. (1993) and Group of Ten (1993) for descriptions of the European currency crisis of 1992–1993.

26. On September 15, the one-month LIBOR rate for dollars closed at 3.0625 percent and the historical volatility of the \$/£ exchange rate, estimated over the previous month, was 15.8 percent per annum. As Figure IVA–7 shows, if the banks sold options with volatilities higher than their historical levels, which during a speculative attack is very likely, the change in the hedge ratio may have been smaller.

27. Based on a historical volatility, calculated over the previous month, of 6.08 percent.

28. With an estimated volatility of 12.9 percent.

29. These estimates were obtained during confidential interviews with market participants in October 1992 (see Goldstein et al. 1993).

30. Who is actually squeezed in such a defense? All borrowers in the weak currency whose debts are due for settlement or rollover soon (after two days) will find that their costs and risks have suddenly jumped as they now have to pay high and volatile yields to the money market scalpers unleashed by the squeeze. This group could conceivably include even those who have constructed synthetic puts if they have established their short currency position by borrowing on overnight rollover credit, as Richard Lyons has pointed out to us. Typically, however, a synthetic option is constructed by establishing a short forward position whose expiration date coincides with the expiration date of the option. If many of the existing hedges were constructed within a one or three month period before the speculative attack and with a relatively long maturity, they would have locked in longer term finance and the position would be immune from a short squeeze.

31. *Early* is relative to the time of outbreak of the next speculative attack. How to recognize when an attack will come in order to implement this early defense is problematic.

References

Bank of England (1993), *Derivatives: Report of an Internal Working Group* (London: Bank of England, April).

Bank for International Settlements (1993), *Central Bank Survey of Foreign Exchange Market Activity in April 1992* (Basle: Bank for International Settlements, March).

Bank for International Settlements (1992), *Recent Developments in International Interbank Relations* (Basle: Bank for International Settlements, October).

Board of Governors of the Federal Reserve System, Federal Deposit Insurance Corporation, and Office of the Comptroller of the Currency (1993), "Derivative Product Activities of Commercial Banks," Joint Study Conducted in Response to Questions Posed by Senator Riegle on Derivative Products, mimeo. (Washington, D.C.: January 27).

Brady Commission (1988), *Report of the Presidential Task Force on Market Mechanisms* (Washington, D.C.: Government Printing Office, January).

Chiang, Raymond, and John Okunev (1993), "An Alternative Formulation on the Pricing of Foreign Currency Options," *The Journal of Futures Markets* 13(8), 903–907.

Commodity Futures Trading Commission (1993), *OTC Derivative Markets and Their Regulation* (Washington, D.C.: Commodity Futures Trading Commission, October).

Cookson, Richard (1993), "Moving in the Right Direction," *Risk* 6 (October): 22–26.

DeRosa, David F. (1992), *Options on Foreign Exchange* (Chicago: Probus Publishing).

Deutsche Bundesbank (1993), "Off-Balance-Sheet Activities of German Banks," *Monthly Report of the Deutsche Bundesbank* 45 (October): 45–67.

Dumas, Bernard, L. Peter Jennergren, and Bertil Näslund (1993), "Realignment Risk and Currency Option Pricing in Target Zones," NBER Working Paper Series, no. 4458 (Cambridge, Mass.: National Bureau of Economic Research).

Feiger, George, and Bertrand Jacquillat (1979), "Currency Option Bonds, Puts and Calls on Spot Exchange and the Hedging of Contingent Foreign Earnings," *Journal of Finance* 34 (December): 1129–1139.

Garman, Mark (1992), "Charm School," *Risk* 5 (July–August): 53–55.

Garman, Mark, and Steven Kohlhagen (1983), "Foreign Currency Option Values," *Journal of International Money and Finance* 2 (December): 231–237.

General Accounting Office (1994), *Financial Derivatives: Actions Needed to Protect the Financial System* (Washington, D.C.: Government Accounting Office, May).

Gennotte, Gerard, and Hayne Leland (1990), "Market Liquidity, Hedging and Crashes," *American Economic Review* 80 (December): 999–1021.

Goldstein, Morris, David Folkerts-Landau, Peter Garber, Liliana Rojas-Suarez, and Michael Spencer (1993), *International Capital Markets: Part I. Exchange Rate Management and International Capital Flows* (April), World Economic and Financial Surveys (Washington, D.C.: International Monetary Fund).

Grabbe, O. (1983), "Exchange," *Journal of International Money and Finance* 2 (December): 239–253.

Grossman, Sanford J. (1988), "An Analysis of the Implications for Stock and Futures Price Volatility of Program Trading and Dynamic Hedging Strategies," *Journal of Business* 61(3): 275–298.

Group of Ten (1993), "International Capital Movements and Foreign Exchange Markets," mimeo., April.

Group of Thirty (1993), *Derivatives: Practices and Principles* (Washington, D.C.: Group of Thirty, July).

Hull, John C. (1993), *Options, Futures, and Other Derivative Securities*, 2nd ed. (Englewood Cliffs, N.J.: Prentice Hall).

Kat, Harry M. 1993, "Portfolio Insurance: A Comparison of Alternative Strategies," *Journal of Financial Engineering* 2(4): 415–442.

Kroner, Kenneth, and Jahangir Sultan (1993), "Time-Varying Distributions and Dynamic Hedging with Foreign Currency Futures," *Journal of Financial and Quantitative Analysis* 28 (December): 535–550.

Leong, Kenneth (1990–1991), "Solving the Mystery," *Risk* 4 (December–January).

Melino, Angelo, and Stuart Turnbull (1990), "Pricing Foreign Currency Options with Stochastic Volatility," *Journal of Econometrics* 45, 239–265.

Naik, Vasanttilak (1993), "Option Valuation and Hedging Strategies with Jumps in the Volatility of Asset Returns," *Journal of Finance* 98 (December): 1969–1983.

Perraudin, William R., and Bent E. Sorenson (1992), "Foreign Exchange Option Pricing in a Continuous Time Arbitrage Pricing Model with Stochastic Volatility and Jumps," mimeo., June.

Securities and Exchange Commission (1988), *The October 1987 Market Break* (Washington, D.C.: Government Printing Office, February).

Walmsley, Julian (1992), *The Foreign Exchange and Money Markets Guide* (New York: John Wiley and Sons).

Part V THE ROLE OF THE DOLLAR AS AN INTERNATIONAL CURRENCY

What role should the United States play in a world where financial and goods markets are increasingly integrated? Is U.S. monetary policy becoming less effective?

Alan S. Blinder
Professor of Economics
Princeton University

My subject is of interest to the Federal Reserve, to other central banks, and, I hope, to you: the role of the dollar as an international currency.

There is much talk these days about the current or prospective decline of the dollar as a reserve currency. But much of this talk is remarkably undisciplined by facts. So I'd like to explore with you what we do and do not know about the dollar's role as the linchpin of international transactions. Is it really declining? And what are the implications of such a decline for the United States?

Before you measure a phenomenon, you must define it. But there is no clear definition of what it means to be the world's central international currency. I would suggest that the tacit working definition is a blend of four characteristics, which among them encompass the three classic roles of money as a store of value, medium of exchange, and unit of account.

First, an international currency should constitute a preponderant share of the official reserves of central banks. This, of course, is the narrow definition of an international reserve currency. Second, the currency should be used extensively as hand-to-hand currency in foreign countries. Third, it should be used to denominate a disproportionate share of international trade. Fourth, it should have a dominant role as the currency of choice in international financial markets.

Note that the last three characteristics are the results of millions of private economic decisions—about what currency to hold, about how to invoice trade, and about the currency denomination of securities. The first characteristic results from government decisions. But these are, in turn, probably guided by market realities.

On all four counts, there is really only one serious contender for the title of principal international currency today: the U.S. dollar. But is the dollar's role declining? As we shall see, the answer is probably yes, but slowly.

But before getting enmeshed in the facts, a bit of historical perspective may be useful. A glance back over the centuries suggests that the international use of a country's currency is strongly linked to the centrality of that country in world trade. International trade in Europe initially was centered on regional fairs where merchants and local buyers gathered. By the 12th century, Italian bankers were playing a pivotal role in serving these merchants with coins, credit, and what we would now call a payments mechanism. Later, especially after the discovery of the New World, the Spanish joined in.

However, it would be a stretch to claim that Italian or Spanish cities provided the first international currency. That honor probably belongs to the Dutch guilder. As commercial activity and trade shifted northward in Europe in the 17th century, deposits at and notes issued by the Bank of Amsterdam—denominated in guilders—became the means of payment for much trade in the Western world. This dominance lasted until the end of the 18th century, when Napoleon's army occupied Amsterdam—an event that, I imagine, caused some severe disruptions to the guilder payments system!

The action then shifted to Paris and, especially, to London as Britain (a) went on the gold standard in 1816 and (b) became the world's biggest exporter of manufactured goods and biggest importer of raw materials. British banks and financial institutions came to dominate the financing not only of intra-European trade, but also of trade with the Orient. Soon foreign banks began settling transactions in pounds.

The outbreak of World War I knocked Britain off the gold standard and somewhat diminished London's role as the world's preeminent financial center. Its upstart rival, of course, was New York. The period from 1914 to 1931 saw the dollar gradually gain on sterling as the principal international currency—a process that was greatly accelerated when Britain suspended convertibility in 1931 and then war ravaged Europe. But sterling continued to play a large international role for years after Bretton Woods, and London remains a major international financial center to this day. There is a good deal of inertia in these matters.

The period of dollar dominance probably began with World War II. The question, of course, is when and how it will end. History suggests, first, that the honor of being the world's premier currency moves around the globe as patterns of trade change. But, second, that these things evolve slowly, although major events like wars can certainly hurry things along or even change their direction. The guilder dominated world markets for almost two centuries; the pound for about a century. The dollar has now had a run of about a half-century. Are our days numbered?

Don't count the dollar out too soon. Part of the reason is that institutional inertia that I have just mentioned. Another part is the fact that the successor currency is far from clear. By most measures, the Deutsche mark is in second place now and is gaining on us. But with monetary union somewhere on the European horizon, the long-run future of the mark itself is in question. Will the Euro become the next international reserve currency? The only other rival at present appears to be the Japanese yen, and the nexus of world trade does indeed seem to be shifting toward Asia. But, as we shall see, the yen's international role is quite limited now, and if we peer into the distant future, one may legitimately wonder whether Asia's dominant trading nation will be Japan or China.

The Facts: The Dollar as Official Reserve Currency

Let me now turn to some facts, beginning with the dollar's role in official reserve holdings. The number of dollars held as official reserves has grown rapidly, and with minimal interruptions, since the collapse of the Bretton Woods system. Since 1986 alone, dollar reserves have roughly tripled (Figure V–1). But, of course, official reserves in other currencies have also risen (Figures V–2 through V–4). The dollar's share of total reserves rose irregularly from about 55 percent in the mid-1960s to nearly 80 percent in the mid- to late 1970s and then declined in stages back to about 56 percent in 1990. Since then, however, it has risen again to about 63 percent (Figure V–5). Focusing on the past 15 years, for which we have the best data, the total net decline in the dollar's share is only about 7 percentage points. That's something, but not much.

Which countries gained at the dollar's expense? The unsurprising part of the answer is the yen, which rose from 4.3 percent of reserves in 1980 to 8.5 percent

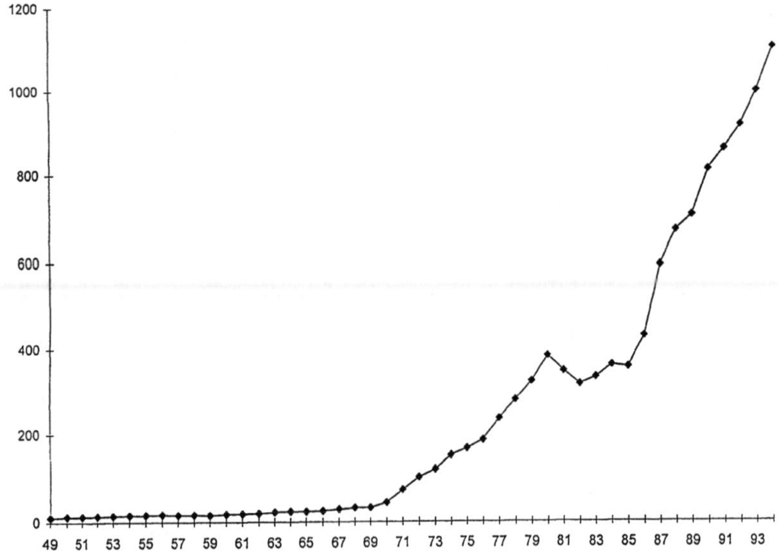

Figure V–1. U.S. dollar reserves.

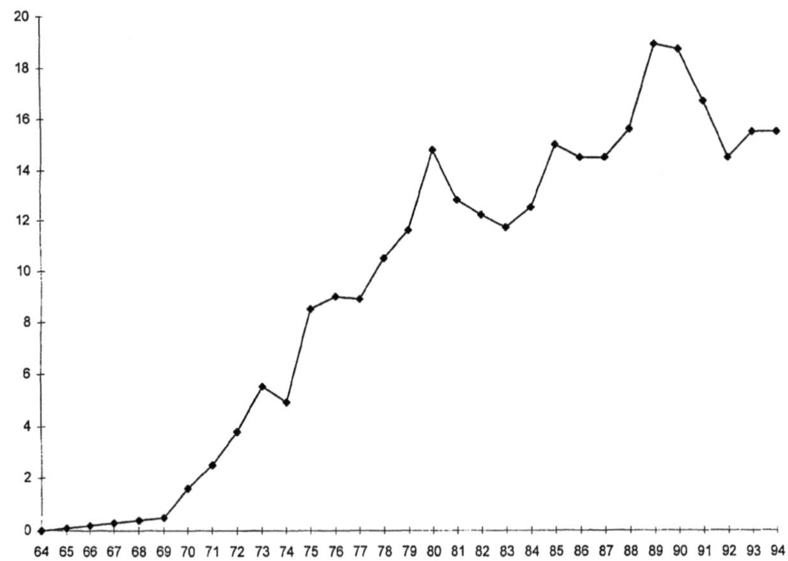

Figure V–2. Reserve currency—the German mark.

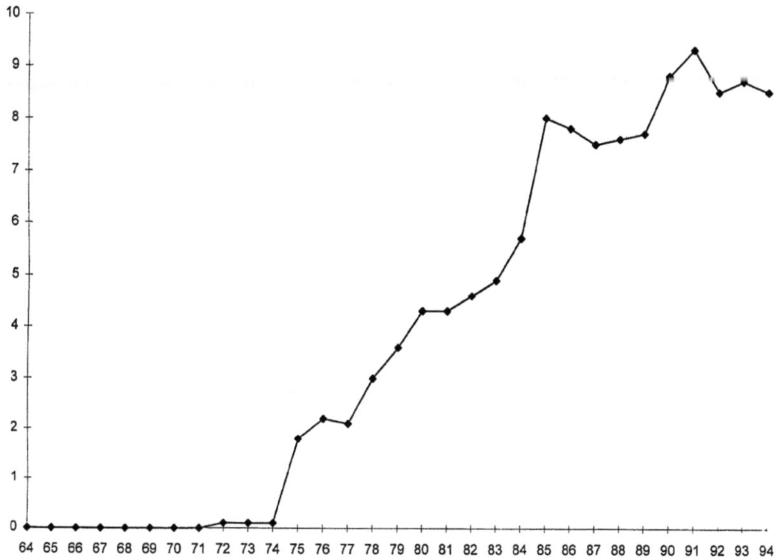

Figure V–3. Reserve currency—the Japanese yen.

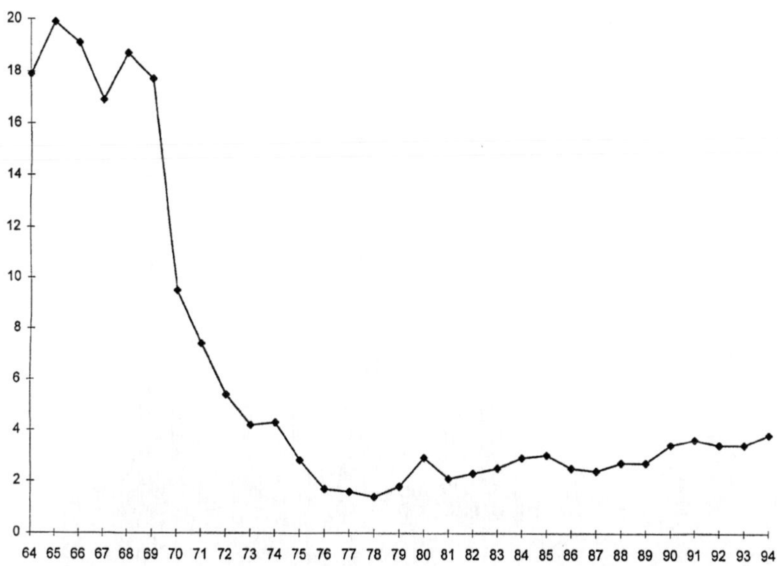

Figure V–4. Reserve currency—the British pound.

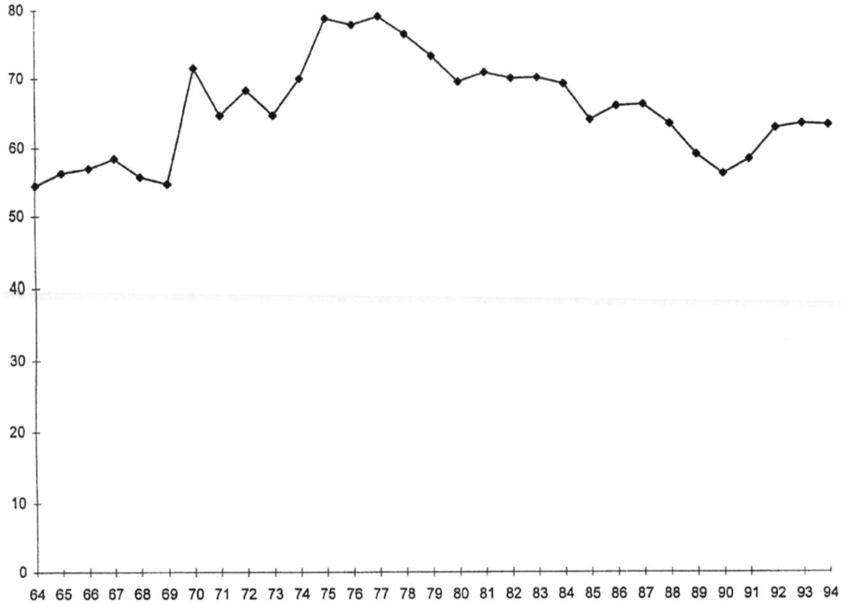

Figure V–5. The U.S. dollar's share of total reserves.

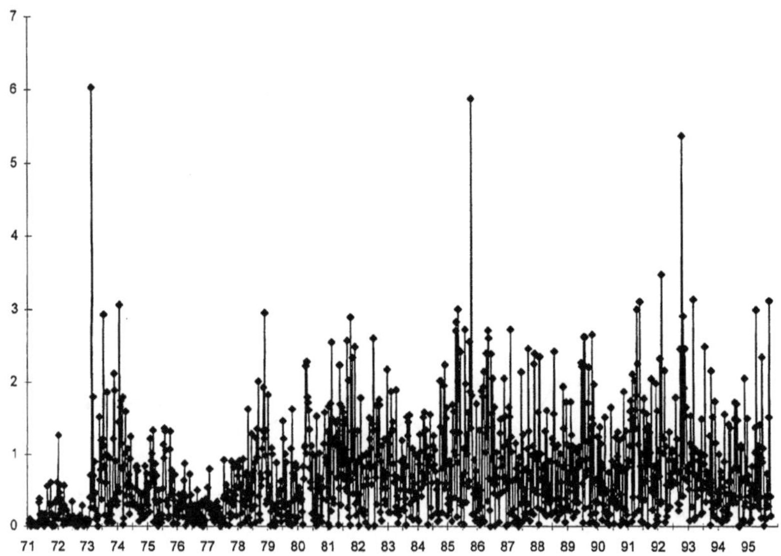

Figure V–6. Volatility of the U.S. dollar.

in 1994. The surprising part of the answer is that the share of the Deutsche mark in world reserves has not increased. It has instead fluctuated in the 12 to 19 percent range since 1980 without much trend.

Earlier this year, there were scare stories in the media about central banks, especially Asian central banks, diversifying away from the dollar. As best we can tell, these rumors were mostly unfounded. For the region as a whole, the share of the dollar in official foreign exchange holdings has been quite stable at around 60 percent. It is true that some nations, like Taiwan, have reduced their dollar share in recent years, but others, like Hong Kong, have raised theirs.

To the extent that the dollar's share in central bank portfolios has declined, what is the reason? One argument is that the increased volatility of our exchange rate has diminished the dollar's attractiveness as a reserve currency. Here we should start and can finish the debate with George Stiger's old question, Is this fact in fact a fact? The answer is no, volatility has not increased in recent years (Figure V–6). I am more inclined toward a simpler hypothesis: the share of world trade and finance denominated in dollars has declined (more on this below), and central banks are just adjusting to a changing reality.

Facts: The Dollar as Hand-to-Hand Currency

The statistical basis becomes a good deal thinner when we turn to the next aspect of the dollar's international role: as a medium of exchange for cash transactions in foreign countries. An almost overwhelming collection of casual observations and anecdotes tells us that the dollar is the currency of choice in Latin America, Asia, Russia, the Middle East, and elsewhere. But accurate, or even systematic, data are not available.

Federal Reserve staff estimate that 50 percent to 70 percent of U.S. currency —a total now of $185 billion to $260 billion—is held outside the United States. The methods we use are, of necessity, indirect. For example, one technique is based on shipments of $100 bills by the Federal Reserve Bank of New York. But the fact that different methods, using different data, all point toward the same range gives us some confidence in the estimate—which is, of course, a pretty rough one.

Seignorage earnings on these foreign-held dollars are not trivial. Using the current interest rate on Treasury securities of maturity equal to the average of the Fed's portfolio to impute interest, they amount to a hefty $11 billion to $15 billion per year. That is a considerable fraction of our total earnings.

Is this highly profitable role of the dollar diminishing? We know that currency shipments abroad are growing faster in the 1990s than they did in the 1980s. And we believe that the share of new currency flowing abroad exceeds the share of the stock, meaning that the share of our currency held abroad appears to be rising. But what about the dollar's share in the burgeoning market for paper money circulating in foreign countries?

Anecdotal evidence says that the yen's share is quite small, but the Deutsche mark's share is not. One recent German study estimates that 30 percent to 40 percent of German currency is held outside Germany. If correct, that would amount to roughly $35 billion to $55 billion—a large sum, but less than 20 percent of the volume of dollars circulating abroad. Overall, it seems safe to assume that the dollar comprises the lion's share of foreign currencies in hand-to-hand circulation outside their native lands. But we know literally nothing about whether the dollar's market share is rising or falling.

Facts: The Dollar's Role in World Trade

The third aspect of the dollar's role as an international currency is its use as the currency for pricing goods and services in world trade—as the international unit of account, so to speak. It is well known that a great deal of international trade is conducted in dollars. The latest available data pertain to 1992, so I will use that year for comparisons and hope that things have not changed much since.

Taking U.S. trade first, one of the more amazing statistics to me is that roughly 80 percent of American imports—largely the products of foreign companies—are invoiced in dollars. Such a large share is quite atypical, presumably because our domestic market is so large. Among the other major industrial countries, the fraction of imports invoiced in destination currency ranges from a low of 17 percent (Japan) to a high of 56 percent (Germany). On the export side, of course, invoicing in your own currency is much more common—ranging from 40 percent to 77 percent for other countries, and 92 percent for the United States.

But dollar prices are also common in trade that does not involve the Untied States as either buyer or seller. Overall, almost 50 percent of total world trade is denominated in dollars. Since U.S. exports and imports denominated in dollars account for only about 23 percent of trade, roughly 25 percent of world trade does not involve the United States but is nonetheless priced in dollars. We have no real competitor in this regard. The mark is the currency for invoicing about 15 percent of world trade. But all this is either German exports or imports.

Has the dollar's role as the international unit of account been declining? Superficially, it appears to have fallen—from 56 percent of world trade in 1980 to 48 percent in 1992. But this decline was entirely due to the declining relative importance of oil, which is, of course, priced in dollars, in world trade. In non-oil trade, the dollar's share has been fairly stable for years.

The Facts: The Dollar's Role in International Finance

Historically, as I noted at the outset, the market's choice of international reserve currency has followed patterns of trade—with Italy, Holland, Britain, and the United States dominant in their turn. But, in the modern world, financial considerations may overwhelm trade considerations. For example, the vast majority of foreign exchange transactions today stem from trade in assets rather than trade in goods. So we need to consider the dollar's role in international financial markets.

Let us start with foreign exchange transactions. According to the 1992 Bank for International Settlements (BIS) survey, fully 83 percent of reported foreign exchange turnover involved the dollar on one side of the transaction. The two closest competitors were the mark at 38 percent and the yen at 24 percent. (In case you are wondering why these shares already exceed 100 percent, there are two sides to every foreign exchange transaction, so shares measured this way must add up to 200 percent.) A similar survey in 1989 found that the dollar was involved in 90 percent of foreign exchange transactions. So the dollar's role in this regard, while still dominant, appears to be declining.

Turning to other financial markets, we find that in 1994 about 43 percent of banks' cross-border claims were denominated in dollars. The closest competitors were the mark and the yen, each with about 14 percent to 15 percent. Similarly, about 47 percent of Eurocurrency deposits were Eurodollars, versus about 17 percent for Euromarks and only about 5.5 percent for Euroyen. In both of these cases, however, the dollar's market share has declined rapidly and substantially from peaks that were 20 to 25 percentage points higher about 15 years ago.

In international bond markets (defined roughly as bonds floated outside the borrower's country), about 35 percent of the outstanding issues are presently denominated in dollars—versus 16 percent in yen and 11 percent in Deutsche marks. But here, too, the dollar's franchise has been eroded substantially in the past 10 to 15 years. Its market share was about 53 percent in 1981.

Thus, it is in world capital markets that the dollar's dominance has eroded most. Surprisingly, at least to me, none of this erosion can be attributed to the diminishing share of the United States in world gross domestic product. That share has not, in fact, declined since 1980. So we must look elsewhere for an explanation.

One candidate is the fact that, while the United States went first and probably furthest, many foreign countries have followed our lead in liberalizing and deregulating their financial systems. Financial innovation naturally follows in the wake of liberalization. And some of this deregulation and innovation, such as easing restrictions on foreign participation in foreign markets and domestic participation in foreign markets, particularly impacts cross-border transactions.

We believe that these developments have, on the whole, been salutary for the world financial system and for the global economy more generally. But, as a side effect, they have diminished the dollar's preeminence in international finance.

Implications: What Does It All Mean?

In sum, wherever we have data, the message seems to be more or less the same: the dollar is still unquestionably the world's dominant international currency by any conceivable definition. But its preeminent position is eroding slowly, as mainly the Deutsche mark and, secondarily, the yen move up on the pecking order. What, then, are the implications for the United States? Let me repeat the list of four characteristics, focusing now on possible implications rather than bare facts.

Central bank use of the U.S. dollar as official reserves presumably raises the demand for the assets that serve as reserves—mostly, Treasury securities. That, in turn, should lead to lower interest rates on those securities relative to comparable private securities. To look for such evidence, Board staff compared yield spreads between government and private securities in the United States, United Kingdom, Canada, Germany, and Japan. It turns out that the yield spread in the United States is not unusually large. Similarly, a decline in the demand for dollars as central bank reserves should reduce this spread, but, in fact, the spread seems to have widened slightly in recent years.

In brief, it is not clear that the dollar's role as an official reserve currency gives the United States Treasury any bonus in the form of lower borrowing costs. But, if it does, there is no evidence that this bonus is diminishing.

The chief implication of the use of paper dollars as a hand-to-hand medium of exchange in foreign countries is that the U.S. government earns considerable seignorage profits. In essence, the Fed borrows interest-free from foreign holders of our currency, invests the proceeds in U.S. government securities, and turns over the profits to the Treasury. As noted earlier, this seignorage revenue amounts to perhaps $11 billion to $15 billion per year.

Should demand for U.S. currency decline, this revenue source would, of course, decline proportionately. I mentioned earlier that we do not know whether the dollar's share of the world currency market is increasing or decreasing. But we are fairly sure that the absolute volume of foreign holdings of U.S. currency is growing faster than our GDP, the federal budget, or almost any other indicator of the size of our domestic economy. Thus, seignorage is becoming a relatively more important source of financing for the U.S. government. For example, it is now roughly the same size as federal receipts from estate and gift taxes.

The third aspect of the dollar's role as an international currency is its use in invoicing trade. The interesting question here is whether the fact that most of our imports are denominated in dollars affects the pass-through of exchange rate changes into domestic prices—either in the short run or the long run.

The short-run case is easier to make. Suppose the dollar depreciates. If foreign goods sold to American importers are priced in foreign currency, their dollar prices rise immediately and automatically—unless foreign suppliers decide to cut their home-currency prices. But there is no such automaticity if these same goods are invoiced in U.S. dollars, as most of them are. Instead, dollar prices rise only if foreign exporters make affirmative decisions to raise them. From a strictly neoclassical view of the world, currency denomination should be an institutional detail of no importance to pricing. But in a world with both nominal and bureaucratic rigidities, it might matter.

I suspect that dollar invoicing may help explain the relative immunity of U.S. domestic prices from exchange rate influences. But this is just a conjecture, neither supported nor refuted by research, despite the best efforts of Board staff. The data we need to test it are simply not readily available.

Last, but certainly not least, comes the dollar's role in world financial markets. Here, two plausible implications spring to mind.

First, just as was the case for official reserves, a worldwide portfolio preference to hold dollar-based assets should lead to lower dollar interest rates, other things being equal. And, of course, any decline in this preference should erode that interest rate advantage. But many other factors—especially expected changes in exchange rates—influence interest rate differentials between dollar and nondollar assets. So looking for this (presumably small) effect in the data seems a bit like looking for a needle in a haystack.

Second, it is at least believable, though by no means certain, that the dominant role of the dollar in world financial markets gives U.S. financial institutions a competitive edge over their foreign rivals. For example, U.S. banks have access to the Federal Reserve as lender of last resort. And U.S. financial institutions may have a comparative advantage in dollar-based financing. After all, the dollar markets are our home turf. If hysteresis matters in these markets, as it probably does, American firms acquired a durable competitive advantage simply by being there first.

Do American firms really have such an advantage? We simply do not know. I can offer only one suggestive piece of evidence. In the Eurobond market, American companies lead in underwriting dollar-denominated debt issues, Japanese companies lead in Euroyen financing, German banks lead in Euromarks, the French lead in Eurofrancs, and so on. That's hardly proof, but it does point toward a home-court advantage.

Conclusion

One final, and very general, implication is worth mentioning. A shift away from dollars for any reason—including international diversification—should, other things being equal, lead to a decline in the dollar's value. Indeed, worries that the shrinking international role of the dollar is putting downward pressure on the exchange rate seem to underlie recent concerns about the dollar's preeminence in world markets.

But what is declining is our international market share, not the absolute demand for dollars in world markets, which is growing rapidly. Furthermore, any influence of these developments on the exchange rate must be swamped by other more fundamental factors like actual and prospective monetary and fiscal policy. So it seems unlikely that the dollar is being weighed down by its loss of market share.

It would be going too far to say that the recent concern over the declining role of the dollar as the world's preeminent currency is much ado about nothing. Rather, it is a bit too much ado about relatively little. The dollar's dominance has, in fact, declined, but only a little bit—and rather slowly. Furthermore, the costs of this decline to the United States are hard to assess and look to be fairly minor. Of course, I might have a different assessment if the dollar was being rapidly dethroned and relegated to secondary status in world markets. But that, fortunately, is most emphatically not the case.

Part VI INTERNATIONAL CAPITAL FLOWS: DIRECT VS. PORTFOLIO INVESTMENT

The growth of international capital flows, especially portfolio investment, has provided an unprecedented pool of funds for developing countries. Moreover, the speed at which funds can travel between countries is much more rapid than ever before. Are international capital flows a blessing or a curse?

Presenter:
Michael P. Dooley
Professor of Economics
University of California at Santa Cruz

Moderator:
John Duca
Research Officer
Federal Reserve Bank of Dallas

Discussants:
Agustín Carstens
General Director of Economic Research
Bank of Mexico

Edwin M. Truman
Staff Director—International Finance
Board of Governors, Federal Reserve System

Dooley:
I have distributed two papers to conference participants. The survey paper on capital controls (Appendix VI–A) would be excellent to put by your nightstand if you suffer from insomnia because it will, without question, put you to sleep. It is a survey paper on what everybody has written for the last 30 years on capital controls and their effectiveness. It's a long survey. I wouldn't go so far as to call it tedious, but it's not meant to be entertaining.

The other paper, on capital inflows (Appendix VI–B), is more exciting and is what I'm going to focus on today. It challenges the conventional wisdom about capital flows and, by implication, about the control of capital flows and what countries might hope to accomplish with capital controls.

Let me start with a couple of quotes that express two views about capital controls that I think we have to address. The first quote is an old one: "We lend to countries whose condition we do not know and whose want of civilization we do not consider, and therefore we lose our money."

Was that the Treasury secretary in 1995? No. That was Walter Bagehot, 1867. So some things don't change.

From the other side:

> A serious but manageable recession has turned into a major development crisis unprecedented since the early 1930s mainly because of the breakdown of international financial markets and an abrupt change in conditions and rules for international lending (Carlos Diaz-Alejandro, 1984).

I think both these quotes are relevant today. Both lenders and borrowers often see international capital flows as a welfare-reducing phenomenon. The lenders' view is that there are big losses involved, that people put their money into emerging markets naively, and then they systematically lose it.

The recipient countries' view is that bouts of capital inflow lead to a brief period of prosperity, followed by long periods of very costly depressed economic activity. Certainly, the brief periods of prosperity before 1982, before the first debt crisis, and the brief period of prosperity before 1994, what I'll call the second debt crisis, were not worth the economic pain—the recessions, slow growth, low investments rates, and so on and so forth—that followed.

The question, then, is, do we need these capital flows? Do international investors need the access to these markets? Is it in the interest of the recipient markets to accept these capital inflows? These issues, which have been aired in the press and even in academic circles in the past year or so, have led to a reconsideration of capital controls and the conjecture that they might even be welfare-enhancing.

Today, I think we need to address three general issues before we can answer this question about whether we need capital inflows. The first is the motivation for the capital flows. The second is the consequences of a reversal in those capital flows. And the third is available solutions. So the three things we have to understand are why the money goes there in the first place, the consequences both for the inflow and for subsequent reversals, and, finally, what solutions are optimal from the point of view of the recipient countries. In discussing this third topic, I will take up the issue of capital controls.

Motivation for Capital Flows

First, motivation. It was remarkable yesterday that in all the papers that analyzed the macroeconomic effects of capital inflows, whether they supported investment, consumption booms, overvaluation of exchange rates, and so on and so forth, there was very little discussion of why the private sector was doing this in the first place. If capital inflows into Mexico before 1994, for example, supported a consumption boom, why did private investors make those investments? Why didn't they look ahead and see that this was a foolish use of their money that was unlikely to provide the basis for prompt repayment? Did they care?

Well, there are two basic ideas about motivation, I think. One is that investors are dumb. Not only are they dumb, but they are dumb repeatedly, in the same way, time after time. They were dumb in 1982, they were dumb in 1930, they were dumb in 1867, they were dumb in 1793, and they presumably will be dumb again in a few years. This is an important issue to address because, if true, it has substantial policy implications. If the problem is that investors refuse, for some reason, to look out for their own interests, then the presumption, I assume, is that government interference with these markets is warranted.

The argument I prefer, which is in my paper on capital inflows, is that investors are not dumb, but they are taking advantage of government-guaranteed programs.

Why did people put their money into emerging markets uncritically in recent years? Undoubtedly, one reason is that the fall in U.S. interest rates generated a desire to regain income and to look for alternative investment outlets. So I have no doubt that the interest rate cycle in the United States is a dominant consideration. But note that if it is a dominant consideration, that interest rates that go down will almost certainly come back up again, and therefore, these flows are, by definition, reversible.

But why go into an emerging market? I think there are two reasons, and they both come down to an insurance policy. The first insurance policy was the exchange rate. As we heard yesterday, it became very popular—to me, astonishingly popular—to argue that fixing the exchange rate was a good way to generate a credible anti-inflationary policy. This became popular at the International Monetary Fund (IMF). The IMF was advocating fixed exchange rates as a part of a disinflationary process. I can find no evidence that this was a good thing to do, but it became firmly entrenched that this was a good policy.

This meant that the foreign investor didn't have to worry about the exchange rate, at least as long as the country had ample reserves and as long as it had access to borrowing. Any return in a peso-denominated or nondollar-denominated currency would also be a dollar rate of return, so the investor didn't have to worry about it. There's credit risk, but the credit risk also can be ignored if the investor believes that the government will step in to stop any financial panic in the recipient country.

The easiest way to see this is by looking at investing in a foreign bank deposit. If foreign banks are too big to fail, or if the government has a history of supporting the country's domestic credit market, then just as a depositor in a Texas savings and loan in the 1980s didn't care what the S&L did with the money, an investor in a bank in an emerging market didn't really care what the bank did with the money as long as the insurance policy was credible.

Were these insurance contracts credible, and did they extend just to the banks or to other assets as well? I would argue that they were credible for a long period of time. Why is that? Ironically, it's because of the good policies put in place by these governments. Yesterday, we heard several convincing reports that fiscal reform in these countries was effective and that privatization generated lasting improvements in the governments' ability to raise money. Ironically, I think this makes insurance offered by these governments credible. That, in turn, generates a capital inflow.

We always think of capital inflows as a balance-of-payments phenomenon, as transfers of wealth from one country to another. In fact, there was a big capital inflow to Texas in the 1980s. It came—the way I like to put it—from the Chicago Federal Reserve District. People pulled their money out of the Chicago Federal Reserve District and put it in Texas savings and loans. I know this because I did it, and my mother lived in Texas, and so she did it, too. And my brother did it, and my brother-in-law did it. Everybody did it. Why? Well, Texas savings and loans were offering higher rates of return, and they were insured. Did we care what they were buying? No, we didn't care. We were getting a high rate of return; it was an insured deposit. They could have bought anything, and they did buy anything. My point is that this is not a south of the border, north of the border thing. In the case of the S&Ls, we just move the border up between

Chicago and Texas, and we have the same phenomenon going on here. This was a capital flow with clear motivation. We did not worry about our investments because there was a fund of money there, the FSLIC.

There was a fund of money in the case of the emerging markets, too. It's called international reserves. Mexico had what? $10 billion? $12 billion? That's money in the bank. That's collateral. In the event of trouble, there was $12 billion we could identify. More important, Mexico had access to credit. Just as the FSLIC has access to credit from the U.S. Congress, the government of Mexico had access to credit from the Federal Reserve, from the International Monetary Fund. That, in turn, is the government's borrowing power. The government's borrowing power in both private markets and official markets—the IMF, the U.S. government—depends in part on its fiscal track record. I think the policy reforms in Mexico and other emerging markets made those government guarantees much more credible.

So there was a large capital inflow, a private capital inflow, but I think it was basically an insured private capital inflow. Therefore, the investors were not dumb; they were simply responding to the incentives as they saw them. Even though it was an international capital transaction, it really was more in the nature of a financial substitution. Let me go a step further. We don't even need the United States in this argument.

If we look at the capital flight from Mexico and other emerging markets from 1982 or, say, 1980 to 1992, it's more than sufficient to explain the capital inflows to emerging markets, particularly in Latin America from, say, 1989 to 1994. I don't have any evidence of this and nobody else does either, but the stock of unrecorded capital positions of residents of emerging markets that existed in 1989 was more than sufficient to account for the entire flow back into these markets between 1989 and 1994. It's probably not true that it was all resident money going back, but it could have been. There was enough resident money out there. I think, therefore, that all discussions of the different motivations of residents are misplaced. I don't think the people in the Dallas Federal Reserve District behaved much differently than the people in the Chicago Federal Reserve District. I think they put their money into the savings and loans here.

Okay. So we get a big capital inflow. What happens to the money? I think that depends entirely on the local banking system and the local financial markets. Why do those people lend? What kind of microdecisions do they make? Who actually gets the money? I think that a local system of regulation, of incentives, and so on and so forth, is important, but I don't think it's important to the international investor.

Let's compare this with an earlier round of large capital inflows that was, in fact, met with large capital controls. In the early 1970s, there were massive capital inflows into Germany and Switzerland and the other so-called strong-currency countries. But it's hard to imagine a much different set of historical precedents. Germany was a low-inflation country. It had chronic balance-of-payments surpluses. People were betting on the revaluation. And they were right. They won. They made lots of money in 1973 and 1974 when the dollar was devalued against the mark.

In this case, it's hard to imagine a more different scenario. The money is going in, the currency is strong, but the country has a big balance-of-payments deficit. It's a relatively high-inflation country with a fixed exchange rate. How do you make sense of that? I think you can only make sense of it by arguing that it was a temporary inflow and everybody knew it, that people were betting on the high yields. They were betting they could get out before the trouble came. But the trouble was a part of the inflow; it wasn't a surprise that came later. The size of the inflow was roughly equal to the insurance policy, the reserves plus the borrowing policy, and the investors planned to get out when the insurance fund was exhausted. The only people who got caught were the real slow ones.

The policy implications of this view are quite different. In this view, it's not the inevitable stupidity of investors that's the problem. If I dare say so, and with apologies, it's the inevitable stupidity of policymakers that is the problem. They offer insurance contracts, people respond to them, and then they pick up the pieces. I've never really met a rich naive investor. I've met a lot of dentists who have lost a lot of money, but the pros on Wall Street are generally pretty good, and they look for government guarantees. It stands to reason, if you are going to play a game, if you are going to play against other smart people, other private people, that's going to be hard. So you find a government. And the government hires lots of smart people, but not always enough. And they aren't always listened to.

Consequences of a Reversal in Capital Flows

Next, the consequences. The consequences are less amusing. The consequences of the reversal in 1982, I've argued in another paper, were 10 years of depressed growth and, as Diaz-Alejandro said, a development disaster. An important question that hasn't received nearly the attention it should is why these financial crises, these reversals, these capital outflows, are propagated so long in terms of economic activity in the recipient countries. Why don't we just have the financial crisis, get it over with, and get on with our business? Stock markets go up and down all the time. Why do these particular kinds of financial crises seem to be so damaging for so long in terms of the economic development of the recipient countries?

I think the answer to that in the 1982 crisis was that the prolonged bargaining between U.S. banks and basically the U.S. government—or, more generally, the industrial country banks and industrial country governments—about who would take the loss or how the loss would be allocated made it difficult to invest in these countries for a long time. That's a controversial argument, but it's one I have been making for 10 years so I'm not going to change my mind now.

I think there's a disturbing counterpart in the most recent exchange rate crisis or financial crisis. This time, of course, U.S. banks were not involved. This time the capital inflows generally took the form of direct investment, portfolio investment, not banks from the industrial countries lending to residents of the emerging markets. And so the long negotiation between U.S. banks, for example, and the U.S. government will not be a feature of this workout. However, much of the risk was shifted to firms, nonfinancial firms and financial firms, in the emerging markets, which has led to a banking crisis of massive or large proportions in many of the emerging markets. This includes, by the way, Argentina, which has not had the foreign exchange crisis, and Mexico, which has. In both countries, I would argue, the crisis is real and is measured by a loss on the books of the domestic banks that has not been allocated yet. We know, from our experience in the United States, that when banks are in trouble, when banks have weak balance sheets, that it leads to credit crunches, it leads to misallocation of credit over time, and it depresses economic activity.

My fear—and this is just pure conjecture—is that if you look for a mechanism by which the financial crisis will be propagated over time and that will limit the recovery of the emerging markets, in this case, it would be the problems in their domestic banking systems. The domestic banks' assets took a big hit in terms of market value. Their liabilities are still out there. As in general in banks, the nominal value of the liabilities has not been adjusted; therefore, the banks have negative net worth. We know two things about negative net worth banks or negative net worth banking systems. One is the problem grows. One way of putting it is that if you have 100 banks that are in a loss position, they'll make bets with each other so that 50 become big winners and 50 become even bigger losers. This is called derivative trading. I think that generally, when you put people in a position where they have nothing left to lose, human nature says they'll take a big bet. When there are lots of such people in an economy, they'll bet with each other. The ones who lose will go to the central bank and say, "I'm very sorry, but here is your loss." The ones who win will say, "I'm a hero," and they'll actually hire the people that lost. So the idea that the losers are punished, I think, is wrong.

In any case, it seems at least possible that there is another mechanism for propagating this financial crisis over time into a real economic crisis in the recipient countries. And I worry about that a lot. I think it's a number one policy issue, and, if I could just propagandize a little bit, the policy issue is that the loss has to be taken off the books. You can't just look at it and say it's not hurting anything because it affects the behavior of the bankers. It gets bigger, and it has to be taken off. How is it taken off? There are only two ways, basically: inflation and government expenditure to buy the bad paper. Government expenditure to buy the bad paper is tough in countries that have fiscal constraint. Inflation, of course, is tough on everybody. But the threat of those two things—that is, fiscal problems in bailing out the banks or the temptation to inflate the problem away—will, I'm afraid, constrain new investment in these countries, maybe for a long time.

Solutions

For solutions, we have to go back a step. The solution is to stop the insurance chain in the first place. The problem is not the capital outflow. It's the capital inflow. The problem with the savings and loan crisis was not that people eventually decided they ought to pull their money out and declare the end of the game; the problem was the money went in in the first place.

How do we stop it? Here, hard economics comes back into play. For a long time I have argued that the only really effective way to break the insurance chain is with the exchange rate. The only way to do it is to say that private investors take the risk of exchange rate changes when they invest in an emerging market. That means that there has to be exchange rate flexibility; that's the only way to do it. There are alternatives, of course, but they won't work. One alternative is to say there is no credit guarantee: "I don't care what happens to my banks. If you put a lot of money in and you come to get it out and our banks have made bad investments, tough for you." That's the currency board solution. Has anybody ever done it? No. Will anybody ever do it in the future? No. Does it make sense? No. Is it credible? No. Forget it; it's not going to happen. Governments can't repudiate their own financial systems. This is axiomatic.

The second alternative is to put your banks out of the banking business—100-percent reserve requirements. I wish I had a dollar for every conference I've been to in my career where 100-percent reserve requirements in Chicago banking have been offered as a solution to all our problems. Has that ever happened? No. Will it ever happen? No. Why not? Well, there are huge incentives for banks to make loans. You've got a guy sitting around with lots of money and you say, "Well, I'm sorry; you can't be a banker anymore. Put all your money into non-interest-bearing reserves and charge for deposits, and we'll take you out of the payments mechanism." This solution has the huge advantage of logical consistency and the huge disadvantage that it can never happen because bankers are a powerful lobby everywhere, and they like what they do. They like making money. If you make them warehouses where they can't make any money, you are going to have a lot of angry bankers, and bankers spend lots of money in Congress. So that's not going to happen.

Another possibility, and I think a very good one, is to really beef up the prudential regulation of the banking system, to have the central bank and maybe the treasury much more active in monitoring and controlling and limiting what depository institutions invest in. Some countries have the capacity to do this and some do not. This is a very country-specific idea, and I think it's one of the reasons that in Southeast Asia, for example, capital inflows have not led to consumption booms. If you look at the domestic markets in Southeast Asia, we may not like the efficiency of those markets, but I can tell you that the central bank regulators and the central bank presidents know exactly for what their banks are lending. If they don't like it, they tell the banks not to do that anymore. And it works. It only works in a tightly controlled banking system, and in Latin America, that sort of thing probably doesn't work very well. But, certainly, prudential regulation would help.

The final alternative is capital controls. Can we just stop the investment in the first place? In other words (and this makes perfect economic sense) if we set up a market imperfection—that is, an insurance contract—then it's always important for the government to limit the moral hazard behavior that that insurance contract generates. This is a clear second-best argument. If the government generates a market imperfection, which it has with the fixed exchange rate and the insurance guarantee, then it is clearly welfare-improving if it can be done to regulate the capital inflow. For example, it would have been optimal for the government to limit the inflow of funds into savings and loans in Texas. We would have gotten a much smaller loss; we wouldn't have had the damaging property boom. That's an administrative action that would, in theory at least, work.

So is there a theoretical basis once you've set up this crazy system to control capital inflows? I think the answer is clearly yes. If you have done three crazy things, you are already over the edge. You might as well go all the way. And, in fact, you can perhaps limit the loss of doing that.

What should the controls seek to do? Well, they should seek to stop or slow the capital inflow in the first place. How do you do that? Well, you tax it. There are lots of different ways to do that. There are interest equalization taxes, differential reserve requirements, and outright prohibitions on certain kinds of transactions.

The logic that lies behind some capital control programs is that some kinds of capital inflows go in and come out but others don't. Others stay there. They are stuck. This is wrong. This is just wrong. Direct investment is a financial transaction, not bricks and mortar. All direct investors hedge. You can always borrow and get your money out. You can short the stock index in the domestic market. There's nothing that keeps direct investors in a country when trouble comes. In fact, I would argue that direct investors are likely to be the most sensitive to the need to pull their money out because they're the better informed. They have lunch with the finance minister, for example, so they know when there's trouble because he doesn't show up for lunch. They say, "Ah, the finance minister didn't show up for lunch; I'm getting out. Sell."

Now, there's no empirical content to this. In a paper I did with Stijn Claessens and Andy Warner about a year ago, we looked at different categories of capital flows. For example, we asked whether short-term capital flows are more likely to be reversed than long-term capital flows or direct investment capital flows. We found that there is no correspondence at all. In Mexico, for example, short-term capital flows are the most stable over time. If there's an increase in short-term capital flows, the next quarter they are more likely to be followed by another short-term capital inflow than, say, direct investment.

If you talk to direct investors, they are always puzzled by the academic view that they are stuck in the country. They are not. So capital controls that try to channel foreign investment into certain categories (for example, direct investment or long-term capital) actually seem to work, in some sense. If you look at the data, there are many examples where a capital control program has changed the composition of the capital inflow.

Unfortunately, this doesn't have anything to do with the policy objective, which is to stop the reversibility of the flow in the first place, since, as far as I can tell, all these flows are equally likely to be reversed and will be reversed when trouble comes. So we are left, then, with the unfortunate problem that the only way to stop capital inflows is to stop all of them. And that requires a very comprehensive program, a very administratively expensive program, and one that has to be adapted almost daily to catch the new kind of capital flow.

One of my first jobs at the Federal Reserve was as an assistant to the person who administered the mandatory control program, the Voluntary Foreign Credit Restraint (VFCR) program. The United States established a voluntary program in 1965 to discourage direct investment by U.S. firms abroad. The program became mandatory in 1968 and was administered by the Fed. I had the misfortune of being the most junior member of the international finance division, so I was the person that went to these interagency meetings when the regular staff person was unable to. The first thing I noticed was that the law was in a loose-leaf binder, a big fat one. "Do I have to learn all that?"

They said, "No, don't worry. Just go to the meeting and don't say anything," which I did.

But I did ask, "Why is it in a loose-leaf binder?"

They said, "Well, we keep adding to it."

I said, "You keep adding to it?"

They said, "Well, yeah. See, we tell the corporations not to do something and they agree, but then they do something else and we find out about it about a month later so we write a new part of the law; we stick it in the binder, and that's why it's getting so fat."

I said, "What happens when you run out of space?"

"We'll get another binder."

This is the problem with a control program: it has to be adapted constantly to blunt the incentives. After all, what the government is trying to do with these programs is to stop people from taking advantage of clear profit opportunities, and that's very difficult. I think governments that say, as a matter of principle, we don't want to get into that business, are probably correct.

My survey paper on capital controls (Appendix VI–A) goes through the evidence, but I think a fair representation is as follows: Capital control programs have generated interest differentials, so they have worked in some sense. It is possible for a government to control the rate of return that nonresidents earn in that country's economy, maybe as much as 2 to 4 percentage points annually. So this massive capital control program, this bureaucracy, can generate yield differentials that last for years. On the other hand, has it stopped speculative attacks, the kind of speculative attack scenario that Peter Garber talked about yesterday? The answer to that is clearly no. Why? If the currency is going to be devalued over the weekend, that's a pretty big annual rate of return. A capital control program that depresses yields a little bit or raises yields a little bit, depending on the program, is not going to stop a speculative attack.

Finally, there is some evidence that capital control programs become captured by the industry. Strangely enough, sometimes bankers are big fans of capital control programs. Why? Because they've learned to live with them, and they limit competition for other kinds of financial transactions. And it wouldn't surprise me too much if, after being frustrated a bit by the private sector's getting around the controls, the government asks the private sector how the program can be more effectively administered. The private sector will be glad to help. They'll even help you write the regs. This makes some people very angry, and it can be a serious public policy problem.

Conclusion

Let me close with just a brief review of my three points. What is the motivation for capital flows? I think the motivation derives pretty closely and pretty clearly from government policy. An interesting empirical implication of that is that the size of the capital inflow will be a function of the credibility of the insurance fund. So policy reforms, particularly fiscal reforms, will, ironically, generate capital inflows, but the size of the capital inflow will be just sufficient to exhaust the insurance fund. It doesn't have anything to do with people's perception of the profitability of investment in the emerging market.

Consequences are serious. Not for the investors. For my dentist friends, it's serious, but for most of the investors, they got the insurance, they got the *tesobonos*, they got the reserves, they got out. Consequences for the recipient countries are serious because financial crises can be propagated for a long time in terms of economic crises, development crises in the countries. This to me is a serious problem, the only serious problem in all this.

As for solutions, a government can't repudiate its domestic financial system, and, therefore, it cannot revoke the credit guarantee. Regulation and supervision can help, but that's a limited option for many countries. Capital controls might work, but they have significant administrative costs.

What's left? The exchange rate. The only way, in my view, to break the insurance chain and discourage these kinds of capital inflows is to introduce uncertainty in the exchange rate and make the private investor bear the risk when he makes a bet on a country and in a currency. Make the private sector investor bear the risk of that investment.

Carstens:
Before going to the topic at hand, I want to pose a question that Professor Dooley might want to answer later. When you have a floating-exchange-rate regime, you will also, in a sense, be providing some guarantees because any central bank that has a floating-exchange-rate regime will, by a monetary policy rule, try to guarantee stable nominal variables such as stable interest rates. Therefore, an application of Professor Dooley's theory is that a stable monetary policy rule may provide stable interest rates and a type of guarantee. But at some point you might have a shock, and somebody who invested long term might be wiped out. Therefore, the problem is that you might not be able to escape the supposed guarantees.

I think that this is a simplistic way of looking at the issue of investment returns. For investors there are risks, and there are returns. I think that what a central bank needs to do is follow a clear policy that helps people determine their expectations. That can be interpreted as a way of providing guarantees. So is there a way out of providing guarantees? Or do we have to close the central banks? I would ask. I don't know.

I would like to comment on the issue of capital inflows, especially from the point of view of Mexico, which has been in the spotlight for a while on this particular topic. I think for countries like Mexico, the real issue is how can you depend less on capital inflows in the future. This issue ties directly to the topic of last year's Dallas Fed conference, which was how to promote internal saving. This is not a trivial issue. Certainly, you have to address the issue of providing a stable financial environment, but I think you also have to address the issue of institutions. Chile has provided us with a very good example of how to promote financial savings through institutional changes, such as through pension funds and social security reform. Fiscal discipline and the provision of financial instruments to eliminate risks to investors can also be quite appropriate.

I think that a way to avoid many of these problems related to capital inflows, particularly in less developed countries, is to insist more on the creation of internal savings. I think the issue of efficiency in savings is very important and, in my view, has not been sufficiently addressed.

A question posed to us in this conference is whether something should be done about portfolio versus direct investment. My own view, and I agree here with Professor Dooley, is that both portfolio and direct investment can be volatile. Countries like Mexico want capital inflows because they need foreign capital, but these, to be helpful, should be stable inflows. To attain stability, three basic things need to be achieved. One is a consistent macroeconomic program. I think that in all instances in which there was a financial collapse, there was a problem that wasn't addressed in time. Second is the dissemination of adequate information to investors. And third, there have to be an appropriate legal system and property rights allocation. These will provide the framework that will attract stable, reliable capital inflows into countries. I agree with Professor Dooley that it doesn't make sense—or is a waste of time, I would say—to look into capital controls because most of the time this is only an excuse to avoid making serious decisions about, for example, providing a consistent macroeconomic framework.

Now, what have we learned in Mexico about volatility in short-term capital inflows? What we have learned is that it's very important to distinguish between the types of capital inflows. Something that surprised us, and, I imagine, the whole financial community, was how new institutional innovations speed up markets' reactions to macroeconomic inconsistencies. Mexico's macroeconomic position before the collapse, from a historical point of view, could be considered not that bad. To correct Professor Dooley a bit, at one point last year Mexico had $30 billion in reserves, and the day before the devaluation, we had more than $12 billion. Many years ago, that would have been considered a quite stable and relatively sustainable situation.

What happened is that new institutional innovations had made previous precautionary measures insufficient. Here, I want to underscore one particular innovation, derivatives trading, which can multiply traders' opportunities to shorten their positions. When those who have a short position in the local currency try to hedge their positions, it puts massive pressures on the exchange rate. Therefore, if a country wants to have a fixed exchange rate, it certainly needs to take into account the attacks it can suffer as a result of derivatives.

The other issue involves other types of institutional innovations: hedge funds and large pension funds. We were accustomed to having atomized economic agents with limited speculative capacity. Something really needed to be wrong for them to get together and produce a currency collapse. Now we face situations where eight or 10 hedge funds and pension funds can just collude and attack a currency and make it collapse. We certainly experienced some of this is Mexico, and I am sure this also has occurred in other countries, such as some that were part of the European Monetary System (EMS). Therefore, it is extremely important for a country to consider these institutional innovations when deciding upon its exchange rate regime.

My last point is that the importance of having a solid banking system cannot be stressed enough. In the case of Mexico, certainly, our capacity to defend the exchange rate regime was weakened by the fact that we had a very weak banking system. In many regime collapses—in Chile in 1982, in Scandinavia, and now in Mexico—this has been a factor. Therefore, this microeconomic aspect, the state of the banking system, is an essential consideration when deciding which exchange rate regime to adopt and how to treat capital inflows and outflows.

Truman:
The first question is, Are capital flows a blessing or a curse? My answer, somewhat in contrast to Mike Dooley's, is that they are both because we live in an uncertain world and therefore don't always know the long-run implications of capital inflows. And, as Mike stressed, they are driven at least in part by what might be called nonsystematic and nonfundamental factors.

Now, based on my 23 years of experience with Mike, there are two things you have to know about him. One is that he is very entertaining; I think you've learned that already. The other is that he is very convincing, but he is only right about 15 percent of the time. Let me be quick to explain that 15 percent of the time is a much better batting average than anybody in this room probably has, myself included; therefore, you are forced to listen to him and figure out which 85 percent to throw out.

When you address this issue about whether capital flows are a blessing or a curse, it seems to me you do have to have a bias in the direction of evaluating them in the context of the general competitive model, which Mike nicely lays out in his survey paper, which concludes that on balance, capital flows are a net benefit and that restrictions on capital flows—like restrictions on trade flows—are welfare-reducing. This is not to say that we live in such a world, but it is to say that the distortions in our world, our second-best world, are not very easily specified. And as Mike has entertainingly illustrated in talking about the VFCR program, those distortions don't provide much guidance for putting together a program for controlling inflows.

The next question is, of course, whether the existence of these flows is significantly affected by the existence of an explicit or implicit guarantee that may be the source of the distortion. We do know that governmental interference, in almost every form, does create distortions. The question is whether, on balance, you want to pay for that distortion. I think in the case of capital controls, the answer is no, but in the case of some other forms of insurance, if you want to call restrictions *insurance*, the answer is yes. However, I think it is important, particularly in thinking about the savings and loan analogy, to distinguish between explicit and implicit guarantees. Explicit guarantees should be honored, in part, because they are a contract between the government and its citizens, or the citizens of the world, if you want to put it that way. In the case of the savings and loan crisis, had the government not honored those guarantees, there would have been a big problem. There would have been a huge deflationary contraction. On the other hand, one should be much more careful about honoring implicit guarantees. This does not mean it should never be done, because sometimes the cost of honoring them is less than the cost of not honoring them. But there is a distinction, I think, between explicit and implicit guarantees.

It seems to me that Dooley's indictment of the implicit guarantees in the Mexican case is somewhat extreme. I would submit, contrary to what Mike said, that no portfolio investor cares what the borrower does with his money. Do you care when you buy U.S. Treasury securities what the U.S. government does with that money? No. Do you care when you buy corporate bonds what they do with that money? The answer is no. Do you even care when you buy corporate stocks what is actually done with that money? The answer is no. What you care about is whether you are going to be repaid or whether you are going to get the kind of return on your investment that you expect. So the notion that people investing in emerging markets don't care and people investing in other markets do care, or that it's normal for investors to care, strikes me as a little exaggerated. What investors do is make as assessment based on judgments of the fundamentals, including the capacity of the borrower or the borrower's country to repay or to produce an adequate return. Clearly, policies and performance are part of that assessment, as Mike would agree, but I don't think you can get around that. This is a matter of making judgments and making investments and about being right and being wrong.

Finally, in the Mexican case, it is not at all true that all or even a substantial amount of the capital inflows were either in domestic currency or took the form of bank debt, government bonds, or equities, or corporate debt. Moreover, in those four categories of obligations, most of the holders lost. The corporate debt holders lost; equity holders lost. Some holders of bank claims won, and some holders of bank claims lost. As far as the holders of government bonds are concerned, at least those *tesobonos* that are linked to dollars, they didn't lose, but the holders, and there were some, of government bonds denominated in Mexican currency certainly lost.

Moreover, to address Mike's concern about the future, I think it's incorrect to say that the losses are principally lodged in the Mexican banking system. The Mexican banking system had losses, and those losses were exacerbated by the peso's devaluation. But this was a consequence of the borrowing mechanisms operating principally through the Mexican banking system. Moreover, inflation is not the way to solve the problems of a domestic banking system, since, generally, domestic banking systems make long-term fixed-interest loans and pay short-term variable rates for their obligations. Increasing inflation is a sure way to bust the banking system even further.

This brings me to whether there is a case for limiting capital inflows and what the costs and benefits of doing so are. I agree with Mike here. Mike's survey, which I do recommend to you, does not offer much theoretical or empirical support for the proposition that controls are good or effective. In the long term, the controls don't work, and in the short term, it's very difficult to tell what you should be using because if you stick your finger in one hole in the dike, then you end up with lots of other holes in the dike.

I think one of the failures in this area is to draw a distinction between industrial countries and developing countries. Somehow, it's all right to have capital controls in developing countries and not so good to have capital controls in industrial countries. First, the distinctions between countries are breaking down. And second, they probably shouldn't have been made to begin with. Everybody is disadvantaged in the process.

There is, however, this current fascination with the capital control programs in Chile and Colombia and the few other countries that have them. I think there are three points that should be made about this. One is that the controls in these countries apply to a very limited range of short-term capital inflows, so not all capital inflows are prevented in either Colombia or Chile. In particular, capital flows into the stock exchange or in the form of trade credits are not covered. Second, if you believe these controls are effective in reducing capital inflows and impose them, then there is a price to pay. The government pays the price. Although I suspect it is a reasonable price to pay, there is a price in terms of interfering with the market mechanisms. Third, if they are not effective, then what you are saying is that in a crisis, you will have the same problems with capital outflows that every other country has, which I think is one of the points that Mike was implicitly making.

As Mike has said, countries do face difficult choices. But along with Agustín, I don't agree that the right way to solve this problem is merely to cut the exchange rate anchor. Actually, in his paper, Mike has four components to the insurance chain: access to capital markets, the exchange rate anchor, guarantee of the banking system, and sterilization policy. He has four links to his chain. I don't think that just cutting the exchange rate anchor will solve the problem.

To illustrate this, I would point out data in Mike's paper (Appendix VI–B) that show that in the period 1990 to 1993, private capital inflows to Chile, which didn't have an exchange rate anchor, and Mexico, which did, in a manner of speaking, were essentially the same, scaled by GDP. In one case, it's 5.9 percent of GDP; in the other case, it's 6.1 percent of GDP. The swing, in fact, from the 1984 to 1989 period was larger in the case of Chile than in the case of Mexico. I pick on Chile because I'm confident that it's not going to become a problem in the next 12 months. Now, Mike should have come back and said, "But remember, back in the early 1980s, Chile had this huge government guarantee program, so it clearly had an implicit guarantee system as well."

I would agree, however, that countries should take great care with their exchange rate anchors. That does not mean don't use them. It does mean don't overuse them and recognize the conditions required for their extended use.

The last point I am going to cover is the issue of foreign direct investment versus portfolio investment because I have had the benefit of reading Mike's other papers on this subject in which he says there aren't any differences, and, therefore, there's no great advantage to one over the other. They all present the same kind of problems; some even present the same kind of opportunities. But I think one thing that he didn't cover is that if you get in the business of favoring one form of capital inflow over another, through various mechanisms and inducements and so forth, you then have additional problems. I think many people would argue that countries that have become more relaxed about foreign direct investment are probably doing themselves a favor because there are some advantages associated with those flows. But if you disproportionately favor foreign direct investment, you are confronted with potential political problems.

Dooley:

I'd like to thank both discussants for very thoughtful and thorough comments. The only factual thing I'd like to dispute is that on questions that can be answered either yes or no, I'm right 50 percent of the time, considerably higher than the 15 percent that Ted [Truman] mentioned.

On the substantive points, I find little to disagree with the disagreements. The one point that I think should be clarified is that once the government leads investors onto a certain path or sets up the incentives to make certain investments, to then not honor the implicit insurance is, I think, a policy mistake. People often think this is an inconsistent position, and maybe it is. But I think once the damage has been done with the implicit insurance contracts, for the government then to stall or withhold clearing the situation up is what propagates the real costs of the crisis. So I think the solution is not to be ex post tough but to be ex ante tough. How to do that? I think the exchange rate is the most important part of the equation, but I also agree with both discussants that monitoring the credit system, the domestic banking system—in other words, what people are doing with the money—is very important. It's interesting that in a banking system that has been around for a long time, there is a system of control, of monitoring what that banking system is doing. Why do international transactions have to be any different? I don't think they do qualitatively, but quantitatively they do. For most emerging markets, the only source of very large, per unit of time, increases in the liabilities of the commercial banks happens to be nonresidents. It may even involve residents, but it usually involves an international capital flow. People move money across borders. The fact that it happens to show up in a balance-of-payments account is an accident of history. Balance of payments is a flow-of-funds account. It records a subset of transactions that happen to involve people who claim that they're residents of different countries. There are several problems with this data set. One, it's probably not even true that they are residents of different countries. The second is that the real distinction in those accounts is between official and private. So while I agree that monitoring the domestic system is important, I also continue to believe that the exchange rate is the dominant part of the story.

Agustín had an interesting challenge: Should central banks do anything? Should we close them? Well, no. Where would I have gotten a job if we had closed all the central banks? This is an employment argument if nothing else. It would be very bad for international economists if they closed central banks. But I think the lesson is quite general. The central banks should not peg the domestic interest rate. They should never set a price for people to shoot at, and they should never say that they're going to keep the federal funds rate at 4.6932 percent for the next 15 years. That would be a bad policy, one that generates instability. Having an exchange rate target is the same. It is a price that everybody can shoot at and that is never supposed to change, and I think that's not credible.

Questions and Comments from the Floor

Question:
I have read in the press that the IMF recently made some proposals on controlling capital inflows. All I have been able to do is read the press reports. First question is, What do the panelists think the IMF was aiming to say? Second question, What do they think of what the IMF was aiming to say?

Dooley:
I think the Fund's view, which has come out in a number of different places, is that the question of controls over capital flows is not a theological one, that there

may be circumstances under which a set of incentives has been put in place that for some reason cannot be removed in the short run. The countries have the right to think hard about what their commercial banking systems, in particular, are doing with capital inflows and to have some influence over that. I interpret what the Fund is saying as, it's an open question and it's one given. The part of it with which I agree is that given the apparent costs in terms of long recessions that these episodes have generated, we should think very seriously about all of the policy options. There may even be a country where capital controls are appropriate.

Truman:
I think the source of the information you refer to was not the IMF itself but the IMF's capital market report, which made some favorable comments on some countries' experiences with the use of capital controls in certain circumstances. I would remind you that, of course, the IMF does have, constitutionally, a bias in this direction. And in light of recent developments, there is a reopened debate about whether that bias should be maintained or should be eliminated. As I said earlier, saying that capital controls are good for developing countries and not good for industrial countries is not doing the countries a service. Countries can adopt controls, and one probably should have some degree of open mind about such choices. But the chances are—as Mike has said, and I agree with him—they are only going to be marginally effective, and there is a big chance that they will have serious unattended consequences over time.

Carstens:
I think that there is a set of alternatives, as has been outlined in Mr. Dooley's papers, to control some types of capital inflows. It is possible to avoid some macroeconomic problems through sterilization.

I think that some countries have not experimented sufficiently with the idea of just letting the market work. I think there is an intrinsic fear of allowing capital inflows to appreciate the exchange rate. In most cases, you end up having a very appreciated real exchange rate anyway, and controlling capital flows might generate more problems. So my view is that we probably should experiment more with market forces and interfere less with capital flows.

My final point is that capital controls are very, very hard to impose. Mexico, for example, will probably have $160 billion of trade with the United States this year. Even when we had the most closed economy after the 1982 crisis, it was very difficult to control capital.

Question:
I want to commend Professor Dooley on his challenging paper. I think that there's another link that can be broken, and it's the very one that you think can't

be. I mean, the notion of governments being blanket ex ante guarantors of the financial system is really a modern contrivance. If you just look at our country, government guarantees didn't exist in the 19th century in any systematic way. The Federal Reserve was instituted in large part to do that. It failed after 20 years, and we got the FDIC. For 50 years, people thought that was a costless solution. The savings and loan crisis pointed out the costs, and, indeed, we've had several major laws passed that amend that public guarantee and in essence say that the depositors are guaranteed, but the ultimate payer is, for now, going to be the equity holders of financial institutions because they will be closed while there's still some equity. There hasn't been a very long test on this, but the evidence so far is that the cost to the public has gone down significantly. So I think we can at least, if not break the link, twist it a little bit.

Dooley:
I agree with that, and I think it's important for the government to try to establish in people's minds that they will suffer the consequences of their decisions. The problem is that it's hard to do that convincingly. I think if you are in the room on the Sunday night when the market is going to open the next morning, and the policymaker asks you, "What's the worst thing that can happen if I'm tough?"

You say, "1930."

"What's the worst thing that can happen if I'm easy?"

"Your successor will have a tougher time."

Most people will go for easy, but I agree with you 100 percent. It's better public policy to be tough, to twist, as you put it.

Question:
As an equity markets portfolio manager, I found the conference and, in particular, this panel very interesting. I want to make a statement and ask a general question. Mr. Truman said that we, as investors, do not care what a company does with the proceeds of its bond or stock issue. We may be in the minority, but we care very, very much what a company does. And, in fact, that's an integral part of any investment decision. If you are referring to a transaction in a secondary market, I would say we still care very much what the company does with its funds because that affects the viability of the company, the efficiency of its production, and the efficiency of its marketing and distribution plans. So we do care very much. We look at it in every deal we are involved in.

The question I have revolves on how you look at the psychological, or the human, the nonrational, impact of people's feelings about the markets. When we look at emerging markets in particular, we think that the multilaterals are, in general, staffed with very good people and have the best of intentions but that the guarantees that are out there are really more guarantees of intention than something that can be backed up. In other words, there is a limit to the pain that any multilateral can and will go through. When we look out at the investors in our universe, we in general think that many of them are very naive. They make decisions based more on fear and greed than they do on rational economic expectations. I think part of that is because unlike economists, many people do not have a sense of history and realize that this cycle of emerging markets has come and gone several times in the last couple hundred years. So I'm curious to hear, when you factor in these psychological, as I said, or philosophical aspects as opposed to a more rational approach to investing, how you see it.

Truman:
I knew when I said what I said that I was falling into a trap of being a little bit more glib than I should be, especially since I'm still working for the central bank. What I meant to say was that, sure, I think, for investors as well as investment advisors, the basic issue is whether they are going to get their money back and whether it's going to be a sound investment or a profitable investment. To answer that question, depending on the nature of the investment, they have to know, more or less, how the money is going to be used. But I think it is only in terms of getting their money back or getting a reasonable return that those questions are asked. Obviously, you have to ask those questions somewhat more when you are building a factory directly than when you are buying U.S. Treasury bills. But it seems to me the basic processes and the amount of information needed is the same. That's all I was trying to capture; you are dealing with a continuum. Maybe this is my own bias as an economist, but I don't think a lot of final investors in equities pay much attention to what the money is actually going to be used for. They make a judgment as to whether it's going to be a good investment or not, not precisely as to what each dollar is going to be used for. I think Mike probably signs on to the fear and greed element. As an economist, I have a little trouble with this because I really like to believe that fundamentals matter. But there are psychological elements in the market, and the real trick for public policy is how to deal with those elements. To what extent do you encourage them, try to structure incentives or disincentives, or structure implicit guarantees so that the system works, more or less efficiently, while all this froth, as Arthur Burns used to call it, goes on but doesn't do great damage to the system as a whole? But the truth of the matter is that in making policy, you need to try the best you can to anticipate these kinds of things. My problem as a professional economist has always been that you say, "Now, let's consider the psychological implications of all that and then figure out what the market is anticipating or what the people in the market are anticipating is going to be anticipated," by which time you not only end up being a two-handed economist but an octopus.

Dooley:
I think the critical issue is whether that kind of behavior dominates the market always, sometimes, or never. And I think economists sometimes foolishly argue never; I guess I would argue sometimes. I agree with Ted that you should try to deal with that. I remember Arthur Burns, when I was at the Fed, refused to publish money supply data weekly because he though it would be bad for the speculators. They would overreact to it. I think he took it a little far. I think that the psychological part is at times important, but I think as economists, our job is to try to look behind it for other things. These same irrational people also buy carrots, but we don't use that as a reason to interfere in the carrot market.

Carstens:
The issue of having investors being very well informed is a relevant one. In the case of Mexico, we have recently substantially improved the information we provide to the market. This has come about precisely because the market or market participants have been demanding it. The IMF, in its international capital markets report, said that Mexicans have more access to information than foreign investors, which is completely wrong. As a matter of fact, Mexico has its own information system, similar to Reuters, and there are almost the same number of terminals in New York as in Mexico City. I think that the spillover effect that the financial investment has had in Mexico is that it has forced institutions in the Mexican financial markets to acquire international standards. And I think one of the most important issues is precisely how to handle and how to analyze information. So I think that the point of view of the gentleman is very, very valid.

Question:
First, I think the capital controls in Chile have not worked. A recent paper by one of my colleagues shows they don't work. They don't have any effect on the capital inflow. The central bank thinks they work, but they don't. They just changed the composition of the flow. They don't have any impact on the total amount; they don't affect the real exchange rate. Chile is doing very well not because of capital controls but because there has been a very responsible macroeconomic policy for 10 years. One aspect of that policy requires that the current account deficit be not more than 4 percent of GDP. When the current account deficit comes close to that percentage, the government generates a fiscal contraction and a monetary contraction to keep the current account deficit under 4 percent of GDP. This year, we are going to have a surplus in the current account of around 1 percent of GDP. What I'm saying is that it's the macroeconomic fundamentals that explain why Chile is doing so well; the capital controls have had nothing to do with it. There's no way that in a country doing so well, that's growing 7 percent per year, inflation is coming down. So there's no way to keep capital out.

I liked Michael's paper. I think that he covered all the bases. I have just one more point. I think that an essential part of the story is the incentives that come from the domestic financial system. Michael was saying that the way to protect against the problem that could arise out of that is to have better supervision. I don't think that this works sufficiently in many countries. We need to have the law, the supervision, the regulation, but we need something else. Maybe we need to increase the incentive for bank owners to do a better job. Perhaps the 8-percent capitalization that is used by industrial countries is good for industrial countries but not good for developing countries. Maybe we need 15 percent. Maybe banking is not a sector in which there should be free entry because there has to be some value to having the license so that people mind the store. Perhaps you would elaborate more on this point.

Dooley:
I think that your last point is particularly interesting, that the capitalization of banks in emerging markets should be even higher than in industrial countries. I think that's right because there's typically less diversification in domestic portfolios. So generating incentives along those lines is very important. But I would also say that just requiring increased capitalization doesn't get it. A part of supervision is making sure the capital is actually there and in a form that is actually at risk. And that's hard.

I probably spent too much time in Washington, but I think the central bank and the government have to be involved with the financial institutions and have to be very aware of what's going on.

Question:
A very brief comment on capital controls. In Colombia, we do believe that to some extent they work. But I think Mr. Carstens is right; it's very different in Mexico. If you haven't had capital controls and you have the Mexican situation in which you had a closed economy but you had an open capital account for many decades, it's probably not a very good idea. However, most Latin American countries are in a different situation. They've had capital controls for 40 years, and they are loosening them. The question is how quickly they should do it. I think this is very clearly the case in Colombia and, to some extent, in Chile. Also, these capital controls are limited. They are controls for incoming, not for outgoing, capital. Controlling outgoing capital is pretty difficult because nationals know how to get around the regulations. However, controlling incoming money has the advantage that large international banks are not willing to make very many illegal bets. So there is a limit to the amount of bypassing that the international market will do, and that's where the big money is. So I think to some extent they may be effective. They won't be effective for too long.

The second point I want to make concerns the circumstances under which capital controls should be used. I think that in the case of Latin America, most of these countries were undergoing significant reforms, which meant that there would be very large capital inflows. Most of the reforms would mean a lot of capital repatriation, so they knew that the money was going to come in and affect the real exchange rate, revaluate it in a rather dramatic way. Second, they were loosening up their trade regimes, and for the first time in decades, people were going to be able to buy consumer goods, and people abroad were going to finance that consumption. So these countries knew there was going to be a consumption boom financed from abroad. That, also, would lead to revaluation. Under these circumstances, it would seem rather logical that in the transition period between the start of the reforms and a couple of years down the road, these countries wouldn't want an awful lot of additional international money because the impact on their exchange rates would be substantial, and they would have a serious problem with "Dutch disease."

So again, whether the controls are useful and how long they should be left on depends on a country's situation. If what you are trying to do is manage a transition, they're okay, but you shouldn't think that they can be left on for a long time. So, I think there are special circumstances under which some of these capital controls may be justified. In Colombia, controls have worked. Capital inflows did not decrease, but without the capital controls, they would have increased more. How can we tell? The interest rate in Colombia, without a major change in monetary policy, increased.

Dooley:
I think that in my survey paper I deal with the transition case, where you anticipate a consumption boom capital inflow that's a kind of once-and-for-all event in which some markets might benefit from controlling the capital inflows for a while. The thing that we generally talk about is where a policy regime, which is an ongoing thing, is protected by capital controls; that doesn't work. But a transition is one of those cases in which it might make sense.

Question:
Mr. Dooley, I think your results on the volatility of different types of capital flows are important, but I think there are other questions to be answered about short-term and long-term capital flows. We found, in work corresponding to your own, that short-term capital flows tend to lead or cause growth across the spectrum of countries, and that growth, in turn, causes long-term capital flows. In other words, the maturity structure of liabilities of countries tends to be endogenous.

I guess the policy conclusion goes to what Mr. Truman was saying about the cost of capital controls. In other words, it says that short-term capital flows for countries are good in terms of growth. The hard part is transforming that into long-term capital flows. And in that particular case, an entry tax or some other type of mechanism that keeps short term capital flows out may be more detrimental than helpful.

Dooley:
That goes way beyond what I found, but it's interesting research. I would like to see it.

Appendix A to Part VI

A Survey of Academic Literature on Controls Over International Capital Transactions

Michael P. Dooley
International Monetary Fund
July 1995

Abstract
This paper reviews recent theoretical and empirical work on controls over international capital movements. Theoretical contributions reviewed focus on second-best arguments for capital market restrictions, as well as arguments based on multiple equilibria. The empirical literature suggests that controls have been effective in the narrow sense of influencing yield differentials. But there is little evidence that controls have helped governments meet policy objectives, with the exception of reduction in the governments' debt service costs, and no evidence that controls have enhanced economic welfare in a manner suggested by theory.

This paper was prepared while the author was a consultant, Monetary and Exchange Affairs Department, Exchange Regime and Market Operations Division.

The volume of international private capital transactions has increased dramatically in recent years, both for developed and developing countries. The forces that have pushed private investors and borrowers into international markets include technological improvements that have reduced the cost of international financial intermediation as well as a reduction in government interference with such transactions.

The opening of international markets has also presented important challenges for policymakers. Recent examples include the series of crises that have beset the European exchange rate mehanism (ERM) since 1992, widespread capital inflows to emerging markets through early 1994, and, most recently, the turbulence in some developing-country exchange and capital markets in late 1994 and early 1995 as these inflows were partly reversed. These events have raised questions concerning the social costs and benefits of private capital flows and government programs designed to limit or modify the composition of such transactions.

The private benefit from access to international capital markets for both savers and borrowers is a basic conclusion of welfare economics. Free capital movements tend to allocate capital to its most productive uses across countries and allow residents of different countries to engage in welfare-improving intertemporal consumption smoothing. In a competitive model with perfect foresight and complete markets, the welfare benefit from intertemporal trade is identical to the welfare benefit from international trade in goods and services. This general conclusion is not sensitive to the exchange rate regime (Helpman 1981).

While this general result imposes considerable discipline upon the search for optimal limits on capital mobility, economic theory also suggests that exceptions to this general rule are possible in cases where preexisting distortions violate the assumptions necessary to support a first-best competitive equilibrium. Such second-best arguments are dealt with in an extensive literature, reviewed below. The basic idea is quite simple. If the economy is assumed to suffer from one distortion, it is possible to improve welfare through the judicious introduction of another distortion.

The theoretical literature that is the raw material for a survey of second-best policy regimes naturally focuses on models in which government programs might generate welfare-improving interventions in international capital markets. Since there are, in principle, an infinite number of possible market failures, there are an infinite number of welfare-enhancing second-best capital control regimes.

Many of the disagreements about the desirability of capital flows can be traced to different assumptions concerning the efficiency of private intertemporal decisions. While most economists argue that markets work well for static allocation of resources, there is a strong tradition of mistrusting so-called speculative behavior as being contrary to the collective interests of the community. This has led to proposals that range from "throwing sand in the wheels" of international capital movements to complete prohibition of such transactions.

An equally strong tradition that has influenced the literature is the view that government interventions in capital markets seldom accomplish their stated objectives. While there is a well-developed literature dealing with the economic effects of capital control programs, there has been very little work that attempts to relate observed capital control programs to specific government objectives.

The conclusion drawn here from this literature is that an ideal government dealing with one clear distortion could, in principle, improve welfare by intervening in international capital markets. This is not a policy recommendation, however, since the actual effectiveness of such a program is an empirical question. An easy, and perhaps wise, way to avoid the empirical issue is to point out that it would be better to remove the existing distortion rather than introduce another to mitigate the damage inflicted by the first. The present paper will refrain from repeating this, even in cases where this seems to be the obvious answer.

Not all arguments for government intervention in international capital markets are based on second-best considerations. A quite different exception to the general rule that government constraints on capital mobility are welfare-reducing arises in cases where stable, multiple equilibria are predicted. If multiple equilibria are possible, it follows that the first-best equilibrium might be attained or maintained through government intervention in capital markets. This is a much more recent contribution to the debate concerning capital controls, and it is emphasized by proponents of capital controls to protect a fixed-exchange-rate regime during a transition to a monetary union. In reviewing these arguments below, this paper aims to clarify the very special circumstances under which such theoretical arguments are valid. The paper also reviews recent attempts to relate these models to recent experience in Europe.

The first step in determining whether capital controls have been used effectively is to see if data support the proposition that controls have had a measurable effect on economic variables. There is an extensive literature on this issue, and recent contributions are reviewed below. It is concluded from this literature that both developed and developing countries have succeeded in driving wedges between domestic and international interest rates. Moreover, governments seem to have used controls in concert with various forms of financial repression to generate revenue and limit debt service payments on domestic government debt. The power of control programs to affect other important economic variables such as the volume or composition of private capital flows, changes in international reserves, or the level of the exchange rate is, however, generally not supported by the data.

One important lesson that can be drawn from this work is that there is considerable evidence that capital control systems have not prevented successful speculative attacks on fixed-exchange-rate systems. The obvious problem here is that in cases where a discrete parity change is expected, the yield differentials that can be generated by control programs are quite small as compared with the capital gains available to private investors that correctly anticipate a parity change. This is fully consistent with a variety of theoretical models of speculative attacks surveyed below. There is some evidence that controls prolong the life of the regime. Unfortunately, very little is known about the timing of speculative attacks with or without control programs, so it is difficult to evaluate the view that control programs buy time while the government comes to grips with its policy conflicts.

The literature has generally not focused on the question of whether observed capital control programs actually mitigate the effects of well-defined distortions. Giavazzi and Giovannini (1989, 162), for example, conclude that,

> The widespread use of capital controls is not clearly justified by any widely agreed-upon economic theory; indeed to our knowledge, there have only been a very few attempts to study capital controls using explicit second best arguments.

Some very recent work on the political economy of capital controls has begun to ask the question of what types of distortions seem to motivate existing control programs. Preliminary findings reviewed below suggest that governments have used controls over extended periods to limit the cost of debt service and to maintain a tax base for inflation and financial repression.

The more important question of whether the costs of the distortions generated by controls outweigh potential benefits has not yet been addressed. A very informal test of this proposition is that enthusiasm for such programs seems to be inversely related to the observer's experience with trying to formulate and enforce a set of administrative rules that have as their objective preventing participants in financial markets from maximizing private returns.

A familiar analogy drawn from international trade theory is an optimal tariff that might exploit a country's market power over production of its exports. Such arguments for government intervention are clearly correct given the assumptions. Nevertheless, no one in recent memory has suggested that government could or should attempt to adopt such a tariff. All of the standard arguments against the practical usefulness of an optimal tariff on exports apply with equal force to taxes or quantitative controls on intertemporal trade—that is, trade in financial assets. These include the possibility of retaliation by other countries, evasion, administrative costs, inability to quantify the distortion, and therefore the appropriate tariff, the political temptation to intensify the preexisting distortion, and, finally, the possibility that the protected industry will "capture" the political machinery that sets the tariff.

A topic that deserves more attention is what might be called the public-choice approach to controls. The idea here is that control systems, once established, are likely to take on a life of their own as the control bureaucracy and its constituency attempt to maximize their own power and wealth. Thus, controls designed to mitigate a temporary distortion might outlive the economic rationale on which they were established. Further, private investors that have invested heavily in avoiding the control mechanisms are likely to welcome the protection from other investors that have not done so. Cairncross (1973), for example, argues that the British capital control system that evolved from a comprehensive system of exchange controls during World War II survived long after the original rationale was relevant. Moreover, he argues that by the early 1970s, the bite of controls was very uneven across investors because certain types of transactions were exempt from controls. Dornbusch (1986) argues in favor of controls under some circumstances but points to an example where the control system had outlived its usefulness and had become the problem rather than the solution.

There is a very large academic literature dealing with the economic effects of legal restrictions on private capital flows. This survey organizes this body of work according to the apparent objectives that might justify such restrictions. First, the survey examines models that relate controls to the ability of monetary and fiscal policy to stabilize output, prices, or the real exchange rate. The implicit assumption in this literature is that governments have good reasons for using these policy tools and that they do so in a welfare-improving manner.

The survey next considers a variety of distortions to a competitive equilibrium that might make a control program optimal. These include provision of a tax base in an optimal fiscal regime, a means to counteract distortions that limit domestic capital formation, and a means to insulate the economy from destabilizing capital flows.

The next part of the paper considers a very different rationale for restrictions on capital flows. In these models, multiple competition equilibria are possible, and controls might be useful in maintaining a good equilibrium or in moving from a low to a high welfare equilibrium.

Finally, the paper considers the empirical evidence on the effectiveness of controls. It also examines recent work that relates the use of controls to characteristics of individual countries.

Stabilization

Short-Run Stabilization of Output and Relative Prices

The classic framework for evaluating the implications of capital mobility and the effects of limiting capital mobility is the Mundell–Fleming model of a small open economy. In commenting on Williamson's (1993) review of the policy issues associated with recent private capital inflows, Branson (1993) notes that while a description of the stylized facts is useful and interesting, it is difficult to evaluate the policy options in the absence of a generally agreed upon theoretical framework. The framework suggested by Branson is the familiar Mundell–Fleming model. This paper shares the view that lessons about capital mobility drawn from simple versions of the model have proven remarkably robust to subsequent theoretical refinements and empirical evidence. In the remainder of this paper, it is argued that the role of capital controls in stabilization policy is only part of the story, but it is a potentially important part. It follows that this is a good place to start an evaluation of what the academic literature has to offer in evaluating policies that affect international capital movements.

The Mundell–Fleming tradition starts from the implicit assumption that policies designed to stabilize economic activity are useful and welfare-enhancing.

The working assumption is that the government values the ability to "distort" domestic spending decisions by manipulating the real interest rate in order to influence the growth in output and perhaps the rate of inflation. In this literature, the primary existing distortion is slow adjustment of nominal wages and prices. It follows that the assumption of flexible nominal prices (nominal prices, wages, exchange rates, and interest rates) eliminates the distortion and the rationale for welfare-improving capital controls. Such a model is considered in the next section.

If capital is free to move across national borders and the nominal exchange rate is fixed or heavily managed, the government loses control over domestic monetary conditions. If the exchange rate is not managed, monetary policy might still be constrained by incipient capital movements, since changes in domestic interest rates can generate large changes in nominal and real exchange rates. While this ensures a powerful transmission mechanism for monetary policy, governments might consider the resulting large changes in relative prices as a constraint on monetary policy. Flexible exchange rate models are reviewed below.

In contrast, fiscal policy is a powerful tool for stabilizing domestic output even if capital markets are highly integrated. It follows that if stabilization policy is welfare-improving, increased capital mobility generated by a relaxation of capital controls should be followed by assigning fiscal policy to domestic stabilization.

This framework provides a simple criterion for the optimality of capital account restrictions. If another policy tool is available for assignment to domestic stabilization, it might be optimal to open the capital account. Thus, Branson (1993) argues that existing capital controls imply that the government faces constraints on the exercise of fiscal policy for stabilization. It follows that removal of capital controls may not be optimal unless the constraints on the effective utilization of fiscal policy are first eliminated.

The well-known arguments reviewed above start from the proposition that wages and prices fail to clear markets and that this generates the rationale for stabilization policy. In an early attempt to better understand the nature of the sticky price distortion, Flood and Marion (1982) develop a model in which labor contracts generate inertia in wages. They then see if capital controls in the form of a dual foreign exchange market can minimize the variance of employment in the face of a variety of shocks to the system. They also show that the labor contracts chosen by the private sector depend upon the policy regime in place, including the controls on capital flows. It follows that a full evaluation of the welfare implications of capital controls should consider the private reaction to the removal of controls. In some cases, the preexisting distortion may be an endogenous response to the controls themselves. This is one of a very few attempts offered in the literature to deal with the well-known Lucas critique of analyses that attempt to predict the economic effects of policy changes without explicit consideration of how the private sector's behavior is likely to change in response to the regime change.

Long-Run Stability of the Regime: Speculative Attack Models

Early contributions to analysis of capital controls using the Mundell–Fleming model focused on dual exchange rate regimes (Argy and Porter 1972, Fleming 1974, Lanyi 1975). These models show that effective segregation of financial and current account transactions, with no official intervention in the financial exchange market, is equivalent to the prohibition of net private capital flows. These authors suggested that such a control might be only partially effective, but even if fully effective, the Mundell–Fleming model does not predict that controls over capital flows can sustain an inconsistent policy regime forever. Effective capital controls alter the channels through which the private sector responds to changes in the economic environment. Thus, effective controls alter the mechanism through which an inconsistent regime is forced to collapse but not the eventual result. A straightforward extension of the Mundell–Fleming framework allows a better understanding of the process by which an inconsistent policy regime comes to an end with or without capital mobility.

Regime Changes with Perfect Capital Mobility

Krugman (1979) and Flood and Garber (1984) provide models of speculative attacks against inconsistent policy regimes.[1] The inconsistency is that the government sets a rate of growth for the domestic assets of the central bank in order to finance a fiscal deficit that is inconsistent with the fixed nominal exchange rate and the growth in the demand for money. With perfect capital mobility and purchasing power parity, the demand for real money balances is predetermined so that increases in the domestic part of the monetary base are instantly offset by changes in international reserves. When the central bank's international reserves fall to a certain level, it is known that the central bank will withdraw from the foreign exchange market and the currency will float freely.

This regime comes to an end when speculators calculate that a successful attack will generate a discrete depreciation of the currency. Competition among the speculators will force the speculative attack to occur at a point where no expected profit is possible. While quite simple, the model has the important feature that no apparent change in the fundamentals occurs at the time of collapse.

Nevertheless, the private capital flows that generate the collapse are driven by fully rational interpretation of the fundamentals.

Regime Changes with Capital Controls

The key feature of capital controls in the context of a speculative attack model is that the private sector can no longer trade private debt for foreign exchange and, in turn, trade the foreign exchange for domestic money. With capital controls, the private sector can adjust its money holdings, but only through net transfers of goods and services to the rest of the world. A more complete evaluation of the effects of capital controls therefore requires a model of the current account. Because the private sector's willingness to distort its consumption over time is probably limited, effective capital controls might considerably extend the life of an inconsistent regime.

Several authors have incorporated a partial equilibrium model of the current account into the monetary models discussed above in order to study the long-run effects of capital controls. If changes in domestic absorption are assumed to be a fraction of changes in output (an implication of a simple Keynesian consumption function), any permanent (temporary) increase in demand causes a permanent (temporary) increase in the trade deficit. Moreover, if the Marshall–Lerner conditions are satisfied, a real depreciation of the exchange rate causes a reduction in the trade balance. Using these partial equilibrium assumptions, it is straightforward to determine the long-run response of the system to a shock such as an increase in the money stock or government spending.

Delbecque (1993) develops a model of a dual exchange rate system that captures these interactions. In this model, all private capital transactions are effectively limited to the financial exchange market. Since the government does not participate in this market, net private capital flows are necessarily zero. Current account transactions are permitted in the commercial exchange market. The government intervenes to fix the exchange rate in this market.

An important implication of this model is that private net intertemporal trade in goods and services is matched by a secular change in the government's net international reserves. The general point is that the government acts as a type of financial intermediary for the private sector in a system with capital controls. Thus, the model is closed by an assumption that the government cares about its stock of net international reserves. The inconsistent policy settings cause a deterioration of the current account that eventually exhausts the government's stock of international reserves.

Gros (1992) also models speculative attacks but points out that while capital controls can limit private-sector speculation in most cases, governments are forced to augment the capital controls program with domestic interest rates that are much higher or lower than would be the case in the absence of speculative pressure. An important aspect of this framework is that controls are effective but can be overcome at some cost to the speculator. In this setup, the government's commitment to maintain the peg can be easily monitored by the private sector since it is revealed in interest rate policy. When the government reveals that it is unwilling to sacrifice control over domestic interest rates, the private sector will know that a small speculative attack, and the associated low costs of avoiding the capital control program, will be successful.

The welfare effects of controls are not well-defined in these models. The intuition, however, is clear. If the additional time during which the regime survives is used wisely, in the sense that consistent policies are introduced, the measure of policy independence generated by the control program might be welfare-improving.

The models reviewed above are designed to clarify the dynamics of a speculative attack on an inconsistent regime but do not provide insight as to why a rational government would pursue such a policy. Wyplosz (1986) develops a similar model and argues that capital controls that are only temporarily effective nevertheless make an adjustable peg regime viable. In this framework, the authorities operate a monetary policy that is inconsistent with permanently fixed exchange rates but overcome this potential inconsistency with discrete changes in the exchange rate peg. Wyplosz points out that capital controls play a crucial role in making such an adjustable peg system work.

The key to the argument is that the volume of private capital flows in response to an expected profit opportunity is limited by the capital control system. In this model, controls are modeled so that residents of the country cannot change their holdings of foreign assets or their financial liabilities to nonresidents. Nonresidents are assumed to hold domestic money, for transactions purposes, and are free to sell it against foreign currency at the commercial exchange rate.

The crisis in this model comes when nonresidents believe that selling off all their holdings of domestic money will trigger a devaluation or revaluation of the nominal exchange rate. At this point, the central bank announces a discrete change in the parity. Wyplosz does not attempt to assess the optimality of such a system, although the desire to reduce the short-run variance of exchange rates, discussed below, would provide a rationale.

Regime Changes with Maximizing Models of the Current Account

The partial equilibrium approach to modeling the current account described in the previous section clarified the important point that capital controls shift private adjustment from capital flows to the current account. A weakness is that the private sector is rearranging its intertemporal consumption in response to incentives created by the government policy, but there is no forward-looking theory for why this might be optimal.

Econometric evidence does support the view that over a time horizon of a year or so, movements in the current account are dominated by relative rates of income growth and relative prices. But over longer time horizons, the outstanding stock of debt begins to play a dominant role. In general, the simple model is not well suited to dealing with issues associated with increases in indebtedness over time.

The modern literature on the macroeconomic effects of capital controls focuses on these long-run effects.[2] Moreover, by including expectations about the long run as determinants of current economic behavior, the modern literature provides a link between capital mobility and observed short-run behavior of the economy and how it is affected by controls over capital flows.

Calvo (1987) develops a model that addresses the issue of the behavior of the private sector in a regime that is known to be inconsistent and where it is known that the regime will be abandoned when the government exhausts its international reserves. The model has the same building blocks as the speculative attack models discussed above except that the current account is explicitly modeled. The model predicts, in cases where a successful speculative attack is expected, that the public will increase its consumption (a current account deficit) until the date of the regime change and then will decrease consumption (a current account surplus) thereafter. The financial counterpart of this leading up to the regime change is, of course, a decline in the government's net international reserve assets.

The key to this result is the condition that after the attack, revenue from inflation must rise to balance the fiscal budget. As the higher rate of actual and expected inflation optimal real money demand falls, the real marginal utility of money balances falls, and so the marginal utility of consumption just before the crisis must also be less than the marginal utility of consumption just after the crisis. The model is also extended to consider the effects of anticipated real exchange rate changes.

This type of model clarifies the fact that a distortion in the time profile of consumption is suboptimal, and so there must be some offsetting benefit of prolonging the life of the inconsistent regime.

Park (1994) provides a maximizing model in which households adjust their intertemporal consumption of goods and real money balances in order to maximize expected utility over an infinite planning horizon. He asks if a liberalization of the capital account can generate an immediate speculative attack on a fixed-exchange-rate regime. The model suggests that initial conditions are crucial to the answer. If the domestic real interest rate is initially below the world interest rate, the initial result of liberalization is an incipient net capital outflow and a rise in the domestic real interest rate. The increase in debt service cost of the government's domestic debt is assumed to be met by an increase in the growth of domestic assets in order to finance the resulting fiscal deficit.

If the liberalization is a surprise, foreign and domestic expected yields equalize immediately, and if a speculative attack is expected to be successful, the private sector reduces its demand for real money balances because of the higher rate of inflation that follows the successful attack. The resulting sale of domestic assets to the central bank might exhaust its reserves and generate an immediate attack and regime change. If the fixed exchange rate is initially sustainable, a secular fall in reserves is anticipated and, eventually, a successful speculative attack similar to those discussed in the previous section.

Auernheimer (1987) compares the breakdown of inconsistent regimes in a maximizing model with and without capital controls. The model suggests that with capital mobility, it makes no difference if the government chooses an inconsistent exchange rate or monetary rule in the onset of the crisis. However, like Calvo, he shows that with capital controls the inconsistent regime generates lasting suboptimal real effects on the current account.

In general, these models reinforce the lessons from the partial equilibrium model discussed above. Even perfectly effective controls on private capital transactions can at best extend the life of an inconsistent policy regime. They add the important conclusion that the path for consumption is suboptimal during the interval for which the regime survives, and this distortion continues after the inconsistent regime has ended.

Stabilization with Price and Wage Flexibility

The relevance of sticky prices for very short-run evaluation of policy effects in industrial countries is widely accepted and built into standard econometric models. The relevance of the results depends of course, on the assumption that monetary policy, in fact, is effective in overcoming the distortions generated by inflexible prices.

Economies that have been subjected to high inflation are often highly indexed. In these economies, it has become conventional to assume that monetary policy has very limited power to stabilize real output, even in the short run. Models developed to understand these economies generally assume that real output is independent of monetary policy and the fiscal deficit. These models focus on the role of capital controls in determining the private sector's response to economic shocks with and without the ability to borrow and lend in international credit markets.

An important extension of the Mundell–Fleming model introduces domestic price and exchange rate flexibility. In this version of the model, with perfect capital mobility and flexible exchange rates, changes in the domestic money stock generate proportional changes in all nominal prices so that the stabilization role for monetary policy disappears, and so, too, do the associated arguments for capital controls. If the private sector's consumption decisions are forward-looking, and a number of other conditions are met, Ricardian equivalence also eliminates the effects of bond-financed fiscal deficits. Government spending has real effects but is not useful in generating welfare-increasing changes in the level of employment.

Because effective or even partially effective capital controls push all or a part of the adjustment to shocks to the system to the current account—that is, to net sales of goods and services to nonresidents—it follows that capital controls alter the response of the economy to policy actions. In general, the neutrality of policy discussed above is overturned.

The discussion now turns to papers that address the question of how capital controls affect the relationship between monetary and fiscal policies and other economic variables in a model with flexible prices. It should be noted that in these models, there is no presumption that the effects of controls are welfare-improving. Instead, the objective is simply to understand the interactions of policy shocks and other shocks to the system in a second-best world.

Reinhart (1991) examines the effects of a tax on foreign assets in a model of flexible exchange rates with asset accumulation. In such an economy, the private sector's accumulation of foreign assets is constrained by the current account balance. The model considers the effect of the tax on government revenues, the evolution of asset stocks, and the dynamics of the real exchange rate. The main conclusion is that the imposition of capital controls in the form of a tax on foreign assets generates a temporary trade deficit and an appreciation of the real exchange rate.

Adams and Greenwood (1985) offer a maximizing model of intertemporal consumption for an open economy and explore the welfare effects of capital controls. The model develops several general points that will be important in all the literature to be reviewed below. First, the model shows that dual exchange regimes are equivalent to a program of taxation of capital movements. Second, some program of quantitative restrictions on capital movements is equivalent to a system of taxes or dual exchange markets. Third, any effective capital control program can be manipulated to attain the government's target for the current account balance. Finally, the welfare losses generated by such regimes are analogous to those associated with restrictions on temporal trade in goods and services.

This last point is an important result. In an intertemporal maximizing model with flexible prices, goods available to households at different points of time are analogous to different goods available at a point in time. Just as distortions of relative prices at a point in time are usually welfare-reducing, distortions of relative prices of the same good at different points of time—where the relative price is an interest rate—are also usually welfare-reducing. Optimal capital control programs in such models are possible only in cases where there is some pre-existing distortion to interest rates or if private expectations are systematically incorrect.

Greenwood and Kimbrough (1985) present a model that allows an evaluation of the effects of capital controls in a world where identical households maximize intertemporal utility with perfect foresight and monetary policy has no effects (the monetary sector is not explicitly modeled). In this model, the role of capital controls in limiting the public's ability to trade intertemporally is highlighted.

An interesting feature of the model is that in the absence of capital controls, fiscal deficits have no effect on the equilibrium because households anticipate future tax liabilities. But with capital controls, sales of government debt to the rest of the world are equivalent to a relaxation of the government's prohibition of private capital flows. Moreover, since the public regards the government's debt as equivalent to their own, the government is a perfect financial intermediary.

The model also clarifies the likely co-movement of real macroeconomic aggregates with and without capital controls. If capital markets are integrated, real interest rates must move together across countries in response to a shock to the system, and, in general, real output across countries will also be positively correlated. Capital controls imply that real interest rates can be negatively correlated, and, in turn, output and other aggregates might be negatively correlated. The model suggests that capital controls provide a measure of insulation from foreign fiscal shocks.

Guidotti and Végh (1992) present a model of a large open economy that adds a monetary sector to the model discussed above. They start from the proposition that with prefect capital mobility, domestic disturbances have no real effects. In part this is due to the result that the world money supply is immediately redistributed through international capital flows following a disturbance. With capital controls, money holdings can be redistributed only as the mirror image of current account imbalances. The real effects of these imbalances are felt at home and in the rest of the world. Moreover, important variables such as real interest rates, relative prices, and consumption are affected. Their model suggests that unanticipated and permanent changes in domestic monetary and fiscal policies affect consumption, real interest rates, and the real exchange rates.

Stabilization of Relative Prices

The effects of capital flows on relative prices or real exchange rates has been at the center of much of the literature concerning the economic effects of capital mobility. A stylized fact associated with liberalization of controls over capital flows among developing countries is that the resulting adjustment includes substantial appreciation of the real exchange rate. This, in turn, may be an undesirable feature of an open capital market if temporary relative price changes and associated allocations of productive resources are welfare-reducing. Krugman (1987), for example, argues that temporary real appreciation of the exchange rate might permanently injure export industries if hysteresis is a feature of the correct dynamic model of the economy.

Several authors have suggested that capital mobility should be limited until policies designed to offset the real exchange rate changes are in place. The obvious choice to combat the effects of a capital inflow, for example, would be a reduction in government spending. In this section, it is argued that the welfare implications of these models are far from clear. Moreover, formal explanations of a relationship between capital market liberalization and real exchange rate instability can be generated by very different models.

In the spirit of the sticky price framework, a way to understand a link between liberalization and real exchange rate appreciation is to appeal to a model in which nominal shocks generate overshooting of nominal exchange rates and therefore changes in real exchange rates. Sussman (1992) uses a version of the Dornbusch overshooting model to help explain an apparently unsuccessful liberalization of the capital account in Israel in 1977. Liberalization of the capital account in this model takes the form of eliminating controls that had supported a tax on domestic asset yields and domestic bank loans. Sussman presents evidence that controls in place generated large differentials between onshore and offshore lending and deposit rates in Israel before and after the brief experiment with liberalization.

The model predicts that the reduction in the tax on loans increases investment and aggregate demand and, according to the model, creates an inflationary shock to the system. In addition, the elimination of the tax on domestic assets generates a decline in the demand for money. Since this is equivalent to an increase in the money supply, the model predicts that the domestic nominal interest rate will at first fall, prices will start to rise, and to satisfy the rational expectations interest parity condition, the nominal exchange rate will depreciate by more than the steady-state amount.

The lesson from this model is that the liberalization itself generates an inflationary shock for the economy and a temporary distortion of the prices of traded and nontraded goods. Clearly, an appropriate fiscal policy response could minimize the damage. But if the fiscal system is unable to respond, perhaps because the elimination of the subsidy for government borrowing makes a contractionary fiscal shock impossible, the liberalization will involve short-run costs.

A very different way to introduce real exchange rates into a model is to assume that prices are flexible but to introduce more than one good. Van Wijnbergen (1990) develops a model in which the imposition of a tax on capital imports lowers domestic real interest rates and raises world real interest rates. In turn, current consumption is shifted from goods consumed by residents toward goods favored by nonresidents today, with a reversal of this shift in the future. The change in the composition of current and future demands in turn generates a depreciation of the home currency now and an expected appreciation later.

A useful framework developed by Edwards (1989) considers an export good, an import good, and a nontraded good. The relative price of exports and imports is the terms of trade. The relative price of exports and nontraded goods is usually identified as the real exchange rate. In such a model, capital flows related to liberalization of the capital account can generate real exchange rate changes since excess demand for the nontraded good can increase its nominal price while the price of the traded good is determined in world markets.

Edwards and Ostry (1992) present a model in which endogenous changes in relative prices of traded and nontraded goods interact with capital controls to affect welfare. The basic idea exploited in these models is that distortions in relative prices that are expected to change over time due to temporary policies generate distortions in the consumption rate of interest faced by households. The resulting intertemporal distortion of consumption can be magnified or mitigated by capital controls.

The specific analysis of individual shocks to the system appears to be quite model specific, but the general point is important. Anticipated changes in relative prices alter the "interest rate" relevant for intertemporal consumption and investment decisions. Capital controls also alter intertemporal consumption and sectoral investment decisions. The main message here seems to be that real exchange rate changes associated with shocks to the system (for example, terms-of-trade shocks) might be an important part of a comprehensive evaluation of the effects of capital controls.

This idea is developed further by the introduction of a temporary or variable labor market distortion in the form of a minimum real wage. This distortion generates a variable and suboptimal level of employment. Depending on a number of factors, a subsidy to foreign borrowing (or tax on foreign lending) could tilt demand toward periods during which unemployment is relatively high and, in turn, improve welfare.

This model is interesting because it abstracts entirely from monetary phenomena yet still manages to find a second-best role for capital controls in promoting employment. The lesson, however, is that the level of ingenuity to which the modelers have to resort to create an intertemporal distortion to consumption and employment that can be offset by another intertemporal distortion, capital controls, seems to make the practical importance of the argument remote.

Another potential source of distortions of relative prices is temporary policy reforms, or permanent policy reforms that are expected to be temporary. Calvo (1988) argues that capital movements might magnify the distortion generated by temporary, changing, relative prices generated by changes in commercial policies.

Models of Partial Effectiveness

The idea that capital controls have important economic effects because they move adjustment into the international markets for goods and services has led many authors to consider mixed systems in which controls on capital movements are only partially effective. The intuition is that distorting intertemporal trade and consumption is costly to the private sector, and so it is worthwhile to invest in techniques to avoid controls. It follows that the decision of how to model a capital control regime is an important issue in itself.

At one end of the spectrum are models that assume complete effectiveness. In these models, there is no arbitrage of international interest differentials. In dual exchange rate models, for example, the spread between the commercial exchange rate and the financial exchange rate adjusts to equalize expected yields on domestic and foreign bonds. It is easy to show that the assumption of complete separation of the commercial and financial exchange rate markets is exactly equivalent to an effective prohibition of all net capital market transactions or an interest equalization tax that results in zero net trade.

Such models have been criticized on the grounds that real-world controls are never completely effective. An alternative specification is that controls are effective but can be avoided at a cost. This model is appealing because it seems to explain the empirical finding that the ability of controls to force a wedge between expected yields on securities issued in different countries seems to erode over time.

Bhandari and Decaluwe (1987) and Gros (1987, 1988) have emphasized the endogenous response of speculators to the incentive to avoid exchange controls. Gros (1988) assumes an increasing one-time cost faced by an investor who wishes to acquire foreign assets or liabilities. This model has the property that the long-run interest differential will be zero, but during an adjustment period, relative interest rates can be influenced by policy.

Giavazzi and Giovannini (1989) develop a model in which private-sector traders are permitted to acquire a stock of foreign financial assets or liabilities equal to some fraction of the annual flow of their gross exports or imports of goods. Such positions are often referred to as leads and lags and are typically exempt from capital control programs. The idea here is that controls are effective but allow traders to utilize traditional forms of trade finance as long as the size of such transactions and their term to maturity conform to the usual parameters.

They show that in a maximizing model, such controls distort intertemporal trading patterns and have long-run effects on the economy. The cost of avoiding capital controls in this model is related to the cost of switching domestic production to export markets beyond what would be the competitive equilibrium.

The effectiveness of controls and the possible real distortions to trading patterns generated by avoidance are of considerable practical importance in any decision to impose, modify, or remove a control regime. Indeed, the formal models of the economic effects of capital controls developed above are of little relevance if the private sector easily avoids such restrictions on its financial transactions. This is essentially an empirical question that is taken up below.

Medium-Term Second-Best Arguments

Fiscal Implications of Capital Controls

This section departs from questions of short-run stabilization and focuses on interaction between capital controls and a variety of distortions that might justify such policies. The first example is motivated by the observation that controls over capital outflows are frequently designed to prevent erosion of the tax base for financial repression and inflation. Empirical evidence seems to support the view that governments that employ capital controls have higher rates of inflation, higher revenue from inflation, and lower domestic real interest rates as compared with countries that do not employ controls. If controls are effective in maintaining a tax base, their removal implies a reduction in government revenue and therefore a presumably costly change in another variable that influences the fiscal deficit.

Giovannini and de Melo (1993) argue that the benefits from financial liberalization emphasized by McKinnon (1973) should be compared with the potential costs in terms of tightening government revenue constraints. They provide a direct ex post measure of the differential borrowing costs on domestic and international debt of developing countries. The data support the view that financial repression is a significant source of revenue for many of these countries.

Dornbusch (1988) offers a model in which the government faces two fiscal problems that explain the widespread use of capital controls. First, the government's existing domestic debt service is kept below what would be charged on world capital markets by restricting private capital outflows and thus depressing the domestic real interest rate. Second, in the absence of the implicit subsidy generated by controls over capital outflows, the government would be forced to choose revenue from inflation as the best alternative for meeting higher real debt service costs. Similar results are derived from an overlapping generations model developed by Sussman (1991).

Aizenman and Guidotti (1994) argue that collection costs associated with taxes other than the inflation tax might make capital controls a part of an optimal tax system. The model assumes that the government must service a domestic debt and must use a domestic tax on output that involves increasing costs of collection. The capital control they have in mind is a tax on foreign capital income, and they assume the tax is not avoided. An interesting feature of the model is that the tax base for the foreign income tax is not only the private sector's stock of foreign assets but also the entire domestic debt. The domestic debt is relevant because the tax on foreign income drives a wedge between the foreign interest rate and the domestic interest rate. This, they argue, is equivalent to taxing private holdings of government debt, but unlike other taxes, this one involves no collection costs. They show that countries with large stocks of domestic debt tend to utilize capital controls.

Drazen (1989) shows that the inflation tax is an important source of revenue for several European countries. He also shows that high inflation rates are only part of the story since these countries also have unusually high inflation tax bases in the form of bank reserve ratios. If residents of these countries could freely utilize offshore financial intermediaries, this tax base would erode. It follows that capital controls are an important part of a fiscal system that relies heavily on the inflation tax. Drazen also argues that while such a system might allow the government to avoid even more distorting taxes in the short run, taxing savings and investment will generally lead to slower growth and reduced government revenues in the long run.

Brock (1984) provides an interesting counterargument. He points out that while opening the capital account can generate a decline in the inflation tax base, the government can offset this effect through reserve requirements on capital inflows or through prior import deposit schemes. This is an interesting argument because it suggests that a government with a fiscal problem can open the capital account and minimize the associated loss of revenue from inflation by expanding the inflation tax base.

This is one of the arguments for capital controls that seems quite sensitive to the assumption that the existing shortcomings in the tax system are unrelated to the existence of the controls. In particular, it seems quite likely that a government that imposes controls over capital outflows for some other reason will be tempted to exploit the revenue from financial repression that the controls make possible.

Taxation of Resident Capital Income

Another longer run feature of some capital control programs is that they are designed to limit secular private capital outflows. It is often argued that countries with relatively low capital–labor ratios (developing countries and countries in transition) should offset a variety of domestic distortions that induce private investors to prefer foreign investments even when the expected private yields on domestic investment exceed the private expected return in world capital markets. There are alleged to be many such distortions.

An obvious potential distortion is taxation or expected taxation of capital income generated within the country while foreign-based capital income cannot be taxed. If capital is mobile, such an optimal tax generates private capital outflows and a deterioration of the tax base, and underinvestment in the domestic capital stock. A limit to capital outflows, or the equivalent interest equalization tax, allows the government to tax capital at the appropriate, second-best, rate.

Razin and Sadka (1991) argue that empirical estimates of capital flight from developing countries suggest that governments cannot tax residents' income from foreign capital at the same rate at which they tax domestic capital income. In their model, it is optimal for the government to restrict capital outflows if it cannot tax foreign assets. Dooley and Kletzer (1994) argue that simultaneous gross capital inflows and outflows are frequently the response of private investors to a variety of government guarantees and subsidies. If it is not possible for the government to credibly refuse to grant subsidies and guarantees, quantitative restrictions on some capital inflows and outflows can be welfare-improving.

Several papers written after the 1982 debt crisis take up the general issue of the optimality of external debt in the face of country risk. Since individual debtors within a country are interdependent in their ability to make debt service payments, and the government can prevent private debtors from making debt service payments, it might be that some collective (government) tax or subsidy to external borrowing is appropriate.

Harberger (1986) presents a model in which country risk generates a risk premium that grows with a country's external debt. This raises the possibility that the marginal cost of additional debt might exceed the average cost and that individual debtors may not internalize the social cost of their borrowing decisions. An important assumption in this model is that default carries costs to the debtor that are not at the same time benefits to the lenders. Under these plausible circumstances, a tax on capital inflows would be optimal.

Aizenman (1990) develops a model in which different attitudes toward default between the debtor country government and the debtor country private sector generate a distortion for domestic capital formation. In this case, it is assumed that the government is known to discount the future at a higher rate as compared with households. This reflects the appealing idea that elected governments may be too interested in the next election. In this environment, domestic investment will be suboptimal since the government will discount the penalties associated with future default too heavily. The result is that private returns will exceed the world rate of interest by a political risk premium. In this environment, the government should subsidize investments in traded goods industries since this increases the vulnerability of the country to penalties for default and therefore increases the credibility of the government's promise not to default.

A somewhat different argument is advanced by Dellas and Galor (1992). In this paper, households located in a number of small open economies make saving and investment decisions that generate a stable but low steady-state level of income and welfare. There is no incentive for capital flows among these economies since the return on capital is the same. A government that can accomplish transfers across generations can engage in external borrowing that can move the economy to another stable growth equilibrium and, through appropriate transfers, increase welfare in all generations. As a part of the external borrowing program, it is also necessary that offsetting private capital outflows be limited through a capital control program. The intuition behind this argument is appealing. Since investment in growth benefits future generations, the present generation might invest at a suboptimal rate. If a government has the tools and wisdom, it might be possible that a superior equilibrium can be attained if the government borrows on international capital markets. During the transition, it is necessary to prevent private capital outflows that the current generation will find optimal.

Uncertain Property Rights

Another argument develops the idea that property rights are often poorly defined in developing countries, and perhaps even more so in formerly planned economies undergoing massive privatization programs. In effect, this allows interest groups of private residents to tax or appropriate the capital income of both resident and nonresident investors. In contrast, investments abroad by residents of these countries are difficult for other residents to detect and appropriate. This leads to overinvestment in the foreign capital stock in order to avoid the political risk associated with investment in a poorly organized country. In such an environment, capital controls might be optimal.

Tornell and Velasco (1992) develop a formal model in which poorly defined property rights imply that investors will prefer external investment even if domestic investments have a higher social but lower private expected return. This model also demonstrates the less obvious point that capital controls may not improve welfare even if capital outflows are reduced. The reason is that the threat of free capital mobility might reduce the amount of appropriation by interest groups.

This is a subtle and important point for all second-best arguments. In a complete model, it is not enough to show that a capital control can offset another distortion. It must also be shown that the existence of controls does not generate even more of the initial distortion. In the Tornell and Velasco model, it is natural to consider the endogenous response to the capital controls because it involves the behavior of private interest groups that must worry about reactions to their behavior. In the more common case in which the government introduces the initial distortion "for a good reason," it is difficult or impossible to evaluate the possibility that the government will be tempted to exacerbate the initial distortion.

Alesina and Tabellini (1989) provide a model in which the initial distortion is the result of behavior of the government. In this model, an alternating sequence of political parties, one representing labor and the other capital, appropriates capital income or labor income in order to make transfers to their constituency, depending on the random outcome of elections. Since neither party can precommit to refrain from appropriation of income, capital controls will be necessary to prevent underinvestment in domestic capital.

This model also explains private capital flight in periods when the government is borrowing on international capital markets. The model assumes that the government borrows a fixed amount per period. In the absence of capital controls, residents, in turn, export capital in an effort to avoid taxation in the event their party is forced from office. This is one of the very few formal models that explain simultaneous private capital outflows and government borrowing.

The interesting feature of such a model is that the change in the private sector's foreign assets is not constrained by the current account imbalance. In fact, the private sector is constrained only by the government's willingness and ability to borrow.

Capital Markets as a Source of Uncertainty

This class of models posits the existence of private investors that are motivated by rumors, noise trading, bandwagons, bubbles, and so forth. In a way, these are the most straightforward arguments in favor of capital controls. In this case, the capital flow is itself the source of the disturbance to the competitive equilibrium. It follows that controlling these kinds of capital flows restores a first-best competitive equilibrium. The difficulty, of course, is to discriminate in the capital control program between stabilizing and destabilizing capital flows.

One of the oldest traditions in international finance is that just such a distinction is possible. The assertion is that short-term capital flows—or more precisely, capital flows with short holding periods—are distortions, while long-term capital flows and direct investment are based on fundamentals. Keynes, for example, made the distinction between enterprise and speculation. If distorting capital flows are associated with short holding periods, it follows that a transactions tax will discourage distorting capital flows.

Tobin (1978) proposed such a tax, and Eichengreen, Tobin, and Wyplosz (1995) update the argument. The basic idea is that adjustment in international goods and labor markets is slow and restricted, and "when some markets adjust imperfectly, welfare can be enhanced by intervening in the adjustment of others" (Eichengreen, Tobin, and Wyplosz 1995, 164). An important aspect of the argument that distinguishes this from the other distortions reviewed above is that a turnover tax is designed to slow the adjustment speed of capital flows and the exchange rate, but not to distort the stock of net flows or the level of the exchange rate over the long run. The authors recognize that a transactions tax on foreign exchange trading would have to be universal but argue that an international organization such as the International Monetary Fund (IMF) could take on such a task. Eichengreen, Tobin, and Wyplosz also advance a quite different argument in favor of temporary taxes on banks' foreign lending, based on a model of self-fulfilling speculative attacks. This argument is taken up below.

In commenting on this paper, Garber and Taylor (1995) review familiar arguments concerning the difficulty in administering such a tax and add the idea that taxing transfers of bank deposits would be ineffective since swaps of securities and other "synthetic" transactions are now very well-developed components of international transactions.

Dornbusch (1986) emphasizes the important point that controls designed to slow down capital flow—in this paper, dual exchange markets—can only be used as a "strictly transitory policy" to offset shocks to capital markets. The model developed by Dornbusch restates the familiar theme that in the long run, a control program that attempts to mask an inconsistent policy regime will generate increasing distortions and ultimately fail to preserve the regime. In cases where deviations between controlled and financial exchange rates have become large, the "resource allocation costs outweigh any macroeconomic benefits" (Dornbusch 1986, 22). This is partly due to the realistic assumption that large differentials generate leakages of some commercial transactions to the free market. The political economy question is whether controls put in place to shield the real economy from financial shocks are likely to eventually generate misalignment in levels of exchange rates and interest rates that are politically difficult to correct.

Van Wijnbergen (1985) provides a more explicit link between variability of government policies and less than optimal domestic investment. The unnecessary variance causes underinvestment because investors will value the option of waiting until the uncertainty is resolved. Tornell (1990) develops a model in which the increased variance resulting from private capital transactions results in less than optimal real investment because investors value the option to wait till more settled times before making irreversible real investments in a country. Finally, Aizenman and Marion (1993) provide some evidence that uncertainty has a measurable negative effect on capital formation in developing countries.

Domestic Capital Market Distortions

In the absence of a formal model involving capital controls, an often discussed distortion in both domestic and international financial markets arises from government insurance of the liabilities of domestic financial intermediaries. The most obvious example of this is deposit insurance for banks, but even in the absence of formal insurance, governments frequently intervene to protect creditors of institutions that are believed to be "too large to fail." The usual reason for such intervention is to prevent contagion of doubts about the solvency of large institutions from generating runs on solvent institutions and associated general declines in asset values.

The well-known problem with this policy is that it encourages financial institutions to reach for risk. The argument is simply that profits from favorable outcomes are paid out to owners of the institution, while losses are shared with the government. The usual prudential regulations designed to limit the government's exposure to losses include requirements that the institution maintain adequate capital—that is, that current accounting profits are not immediately paid to equity holders—and various restrictions on the nature and concentration of assets held.

There is nothing unique about international capital flows in this context except that new types of assets, and therefore new types of risks, are opened to insured intermediaries when they are given access to international capital transactions. Mathieson and Rojas-Suárez (1993, 31) argue that opening markets can generate important efficiency gains but that "potential official credit risks stemming from institutional failures that can be created by the mispricing of risk [or] widespread fraud" provide a strong case for improving the domestic system of prudential supervision. Dooley (1995) argues that commercial banks in the United States acquired claims on individual developing countries in the 1970s that exceeded the concentration ratios that were enforced for domestic lending. The problem was that regulators did not enforce country lending limits, a decision that was justified by the erroneous view that loans to many entities within a country provided a diversified portfolio. Kane (1995) argues that the unwillingness of the authorities to force a write-down of debt following the 1982 debt crisis validated the assumption that the government would provide "free" equity to insured institutions in the event of a bad outcome for their investments.

Akerlof and Romer (1993) argue that exchange risk provides a vehicle for banks to exploit government insurance in developing countries. Using Chile during the 1979–1981 period as a possible example, they argue that the expectation the peso might be devalued led domestic firms and domestic banks to enter into dollar-denominated loans at interest rates that did not fully reflect the risk that the firms would be unable to repay the dollar liability in the event of a devaluation of the currency.

Sequencing of Liberalization of Capital Markets and Trade in Goods and Services

Governments considering liberalization of their capital markets are frequently also considering liberalization of trade in goods and services. This raises the possibility that it might be optimal to sequence the liberalization rather than liberalize all markets simultaneously. This is a difficult area for formal modeling because it requires an explicit dynamic framework. The literature surveyed above focused on several possible sources of expected relative price changes associated with structural reform that might influence intertemporal choices of residents of a country undergoing a reform program. Opening the capital account might either mitigate or magnify the distortion inherent in such anticipated relative price changes.

The distortions that have attracted attention in the context of structural reform include real exchange rate changes associated with liberalization of trade restrictions, slow adjustment of labor markets to changes in relative prices of traded and nontraded goods, and, finally, expected relative price changes generated by reforms that are expected to be temporary.

As argued above, distortions in relative prices due to trade restrictions can generate a role for capital controls under some circumstances. But the sequencing issue is much more complicated. First, there is no very clear reason for the government to have to choose to liberalize one market at a time or to liberalize markets slowly. It is possible that it will take some time to dismantle trade restrictions, perhaps because of administrative problems or because the government wishes to spread out the impact on protected sectors over time. Similar reasoning might also apply to capital markets. If such constraints are taken as given, it is then possible to evaluate the sequencing problem. It should be recalled, however, that the formal models do not provide a rationale for gradual decontrol.

An early argument along these lines is found in McKinnon (1973). Relaxation of trade restrictions would, other things being equal, generate a depreciation of the real exchange rate while relaxation of the capital account is assumed to call for an appreciation of the real exchange rate, given that capital controls had effectively limited desired inflows of capital. This "competition of instruments" problem is resolved by delaying liberalization of the capital account until trade and other distortions are eliminated.

Edwards and van Wijnbergen (1986) develop two ideas that are useful in this area. First, they show in a static model that capital account liberalization in the face of trade distortions can be welfare-reducing. The intuition is that tariffs can distort investment decisions, and capital controls can, in principle, offset this distortion. They also develop a two-period model in which capital inflows are constrained. In this case, gradual liberalization of the trade account generates expected changes in relative prices that can distort investment decisions.

Calvo (1988) develops the idea that any government policy that affects relative prices, and is expected to be temporary, is equivalent to a distortion of intertemporal relative prices. For example, temporary tariff reform implies that the relative prices of traded goods will change when the liberalization program is abandoned. In general, it follows that liberalization of the capital account is not a good idea in cases in which the government really has reformed but the private sector does not find the commitment credible.

Edwards (1988) provides an excellent summary of this literature and a model that attempts to pull together a number of distortions in order to provide some guidance for policy. Not surprisingly, when working with multiple initial distortions, it is difficult to evaluate the welfare implications of alternative sequences of reform. Indeed, an important implication of the model is that the first-best solution is to liberalize all markets immediately.

Quirk (1994) argues that experience with developing countries indicates that simultaneous liberalization is both feasible and manageable given the right combination of other policies. The lesson, perhaps, is that the practical usefulness of the second-best argument is limited to those cases in which one preexisting distortion is clearly dominant and for some good reason can be removed only over time. For example, countries with a record of failed structural reforms might focus on the distortion caused by lack of credibility of their efforts and the time it will take to convince market participants that the reform is permanent.

Multiple Equilibria and First-Best Arguments

Self-fulfilling Speculative Attacks

Turmoil in the ERM that emerged in 1992, and that continues today, has generated a resurgence of interest in models of self-fulfilling speculative attacks. It has long been recognized that changes in the policy regime that are expected to prevail following a successful attack can generate a successful speculative attack even if the government follows fully consistent policies preceding the attack.

A more stringent condition for a self-fulfilling attack is that the change in the exchange rate regime itself generates a fundamental change in the optimal path for monetary policy. If the private sector expects a more expansionary monetary policy following a successful attack, it is possible that such expectations can generate a collapse of a system that is otherwise fully viable. Finally, a much more stringent condition is that a plausible model of the government's behavior implies that a change in policy following a successful attack is optimal given the change in the economic environment generated by the attack.

The lesson from these models is that the exchange rate regime is secondary to the monetary policy the government is expected to pursue, not just in the short run but over the indefinite future. If the speculative attack is interpreted by the private sector as a signal that the government will also abandon monetary restraint in the future, then, by the usual arguments, speculation in financial markets will result in capital movements today in anticipation of this perhaps distant event. It seems to follow that capital controls might significantly slow the onset of the attack. Moreover, an optimistic assessment of the potential role of capital controls might be that the conditions that generate the multiple equilibria will change. For example, the government might find a way to recommit to not altering its behavior following an attack.

It is ironic that the first clear statement of these issues was heavily conditioned by the warning that an announced commitment to a regime, in this model a commodity standard rather than an exchange rate standard, was unlikely to alter the private sector's expectations about monetary policy over the long run. Flood and Garber (1984, 105) are worth repeating at length:

> Behind the sequential transitions from one monetary regime to another . . . must lie a political economy that we have ignored. Such political economic forces determine the complete dynamic panorama of the monetary process. . . . A commodity system can be interpreted as a discipline imposing rule only if the commodity standard's permanence is somehow guaranteed. As there is no means to ensure such performance, the notion of a commodity standard as a stabilizing rule is a chimera.

Flood and Garber (1984) and Obstfeld (1986b) show that if governments are assumed to follow more expansionary monetary policies following a successful speculative attack on the fixed-exchange-rate regime, policy regimes that are otherwise viable can be forced to collapse by self-fulfilling private expectations. Obstfeld (1994b) refines the argument by specifying the political economy that might account for the government's behavior before and after an attack. The analysis sets out a rational government that seeks to maximize a plausible objective function. Since the government's objectives are the same in any exchange rate regime, it follows that policy setting under different regimes must reflect changes in the economic environment rather than arbitrary assumptions concerning the government's behavior.

Both models suggest that the source of self-fulfilling speculative attacks is multiple equilibria consistent with a given set of fundamentals. The first model develops the idea that private expectations concerning devaluation generate high domestic interest rates for long-maturity government bonds in the first period of a two-period model. High domestic interest rates generate a larger fiscal deficit carried into the second period. The government in the second period minimizes a loss function that balances a higher tax rate on income against a higher tax rate on money balances—that is, a higher rate of money creation and inflation. Given the large fiscal deficit, the government chooses to inflate, thereby validating the private sector's expectations. If the government could commit to a low rate of inflation, the nominal interest rate would fall in the first period, the fiscal deficit would fall, and the optimal inflation rate in the second period would be low, again validating private expectations. An interesting feature of this model is that the government could avoid the commitment problem by denominating all its debt in foreign currency.

A second model assumes that government values price stability and the ability to offset negative shocks to output. A sudden shift in expectations concerning the government's preferences for full employment can trigger an attack on a regime that is viable under different expectations. These models are interesting because the government's decision to abandon the peg is fully consistent with an objective function that is the same under both regimes. The only thing that changes over time is private expectations concerning the viability of the regime.

Eichengreen and Wyplosz (1993) and Portes (1993) argue that self-fulfilling models offer a reasonable interpretation of recent ERM crises. Their general point is that the ERM members that were forced to abandon their exchange rate commitments played by the rules of the game for a viable system as long as entry into a European monetary union was a feasible objective.

Eichengreen and Wyplosz argue that the benefits of membership in a European economic union made it rational for governments to pursue conservative monetary policies. An important condition for membership was the maintenance of a stable exchange rate for two years preceding membership. Thus, a successful attack made membership in the first round impossible and perhaps implied that future membership would be more costly to attain. Once this opportunity was removed by a successful speculative attack on the currency, it was then rational for the authorities to relax monetary policy. Thus, the speculative attack generated the subsequent government behavior that validated the attack.

To buttress this interpretation, Eichengreen, Rose, and Wyplosz (1994) offer empirical evidence that the fundamentals behaved differently in the months leading up to the ERM crisis as compared with a sample of crises in other fixed-exchange-rate regimes. In particular, they argue that the ERM crisis was not preceded by excessive money growth, growth in domestic assets, fiscal deficits, or a number of other variables usually associated with inconsistent policies.

A weakness in their interpretation of the evidence, as the authors acknowledge, is that a variety of factors might rationally lead to an expected change in the government's behavior but leave no evidence leading up to the attack. In particular, they consider, but are not persuaded by, the possibility that rising unemployment associated with tight monetary policy in Germany might have generated expectations that monetary policy in other countries would be eased in the future as the political cost of unemployment accumulated.

The role of capital controls in preventing self-fulfilling speculative attacks seems obvious. It is plausible that effective controls would delay the end of a regime that suffered a spontaneous change in private expectations. If the regime remained vulnerable through current account transactions, the extended life for the good equilibrium made possible by capital controls would presumably be desirable. This assumption is reinforced if it is assumed that the ultimate destination for the regime is a credible common currency.

Nevertheless, the contrary argument is equally plausible. If the private sector knows that the system is protected by controls, it would be less impressed by observed stability. Lane and Rojas-Suárez (1992), for example, argue that the use of controls has ambiguous implications for the credibility of a monetary policy regime.

The role of capital controls is also problematic because self-fulfilling attacks can go the opposite direction. For example, a spontaneous decline in private inflationary expectations could set in motion a sequence of falling interest rates and fiscal deficits that generate a good equilibrium. It is perhaps informative that there seem to be few examples of changes in private expectations generating self-fulfilling virtuous responses by governments. Countries that start from a bad equilibrium should shun capital controls since they would delay adjustment to the new, more optimistic private expectations.

A number of papers have exploited the idea that controls themselves might be powerful signals concerning the government's future policies. Dellas and Stockman (1993) show that a speculative attack might be generated by the expectation that capital controls will be introduced. If the government can commit not to introduce controls, the fixed-rate regime is sustainable. In this model, a regime that is otherwise viable becomes vulnerable to expectations that controls will be imposed in response to the attack. This increases interest rates before the attack and generates the conditions for a self-fulfilling devaluation.

Laban and Larrain (1993) argue that removing controls on capital outflows generates capital inflows because controls on outflows make investment irreversible. Thus, by altering expectations concerning the terms on which investments can be reversed, the decontrol of capital flows helps generate welfare-increasing capital inflows.

Bartolini and Drazen (1994) develop the idea that controls themselves are a signal that affects private-sector expectations concerning the government's future treatment of investors. In their model, the removal of controls signals to investors that the government is less likely to tax foreign capital income or reimpose controls once the capital inflow is in place.

Finally, Obstfeld (1986a) shows that capital controls can generate multiple equilibria where none exist with capital mobility. In this model, multiple equilibria are a feature of a maximizing model with effective capital controls. Residents of the controlled economy maximize the utility of real money holdings and consumption over time, subject to their balance sheet constraint. Owing to effective capital controls, residents can accumulate real money balances only through current account surpluses, which have as a mirror image increases in the central bank's net foreign assets. Because the net foreign asset position of the central bank earns the world interest rate, a current account surplus generates an increase in the expected permanent income of residents. An unstable equilibrium occurs if the increase in real money balances, and the associated increase in expected income, is not more than matched with an increase in current consumption. If not, the current account surplus increases and money balances and income continue to rise until a stable equilibrium is reached. This is not an argument for or against capital controls. It only demonstrates that when the domestic interest rate is distorted through a capital control program, the usual assumptions that generate convergence to a unique steady-state equilibrium are not sufficient.

This literature presents a genuine problem for the policy implications of capital controls. On the one hand, an effective capital control program might buy enough time for the government to move the fundamentals to a region where self-fulfilling speculative attacks are less likely. The implication seems to be that controls might be a temporary measure to buy time for a virtuous government to establish its reputation. On the other hand, it is easy to show that the fact that controls might be introduced in the future can generate attacks where none would be observed otherwise. Finally, the removal of controls on capital outflows might be interpreted by the market as a commitment not to pernalize foreign investors and therefore generate capital inflows.

A practical implication of this type of model is that the government probably must be prepared to maintain its fundamental policy stance, even if it is temporarily forced to abandon the exchange rate peg. This may involve significant short-run costs in terms of employment or distorting taxes necessary to finance debt service payments on domestic debt. Unfortunately, the role of capital controls in reducing the costs of maintaining the fundamentals is much less clear. On the surface, it appears that controls might delay or even prevent a speculative attack and the associated costs. But the typical policy of imposing controls as the attack occurs, probably because the authorities believe that the controls are not effective for long, can also be a powerful force to trigger speculative attacks. Finally, a careful treatment of expectations can suggest that policies designed to limit net capital inflows might have just the opposite effect.

Evidence on Effectiveness and Objectives of Controls

Empirical work on the effectiveness of capital controls has suffered from the lack of a widely accepted definition of what constitutes an effective control program. At one end of the spectrum, evidence of effectiveness has been defined as the ability to detect over extended periods different average behavior of selected economic variables for countries with and without capital control programs. At the other extreme, effectiveness has been defined as the ability to maintain an inconsistent macroeconomic policy regime forever.

For this reason, observers have examined the same or similar data sets and reached very different qualitative conclusions concerning the effectiveness of controls. Those who see controls as a short-term device to allow the government time to react and adjust other policy tools generally argue that controls can be effective. Those who study the collapse of regimes and observe that these events are often preceded by the imposition of controls argue that controls are not effective.

The reading here of the extensive empirical literature for the industrial and developing countries is that it generally supports the conclusion that governments can drive a small wedge between domestic and international yields on similar short-term financial instruments for extended periods. This is similar to the conclusions of recent surveys by Epstein and Schor (1992) and Obstfeld (1995a). Thus, capital control programs have had measurable effects on economic variables. Control programs have also generated large yield differentials for a few weeks or months, but these seem to diminish over time as the private sector invests in techniques to avoid the controls.

The more important issue is whether these yield differentials are large enough and last long enough to enhance the effectiveness of a policy regime in attaining the government's economic objectives. Unfortunately, effectiveness in this sense cannot be evaluated without a structural model of what the government is trying to accomplish and the economic constraints it faces.

Perhaps the most direct evidence for the effects of a control program in the very limited sense described above is the spread between the commercial and financial spot exchange rates in dual exchange rate systems. Gros (1988) reports the spread for the Belgian franc over the 1979–1987 period and the Mexican peso over 1982–1986. His interpretation of both these data sets is that the authorities were able to sustain a sizable differential for about one year before the private sector found ways to avoid the controls.

Cairncross (1973) provides data for the United Kingdom investment currency market during 1961–1972. These data indicate that the control system was effective in the narrow sense in that the investment currency premium remained in excess of 20 percent for several years and at times reached nearly 50 percent. Nevertheless, Cairncross finds little evidence that the intended restriction on private capital outflows was effective. Cairncross and others also looked for evidence that controls instituted by the United States to control private direct investment and portfolio capital outflows resulted in lower private capital flows but were unable to find such evidence. For these episodes, the fact that alternative forms of capital flows were not controlled seemed to render the controls ineffective.

For currencies with extensive offshore markets for bank deposits, another simple and informative test of the effects of controls is a comparison of returns on domestic bank deposits and similar deposits offered by offshore branches of the same or very similar banks. An early attempt to measure the effectiveness of controls using these data is reported in Dooley and Isard (1980). This paper presents a model in which onshore and offshore interest rates on bank deposits denominated in the same currency are related to the extensive capital controls program introduced by the German government over the 1970–1974 period and to the risk that such controls might be intensified. A problem for tests of the effectiveness of control programs is that they are complicated legal programs that are difficult to quantify. In this paper, the controls are quantified according to a qualitative evaluation of the size of penalties or taxes on individual types of transactions, as well as the extensiveness of the controls in terms of the types of transactions subject to control. The data suggest that the authorities managed to generate a 4-percentage-point differential for a brief time, during which virtually all private capital inflows were prohibited.

In this respect, the controls had clearly measurable effects. Nevertheless, a speculative attack on the currency generated a very large—by 1970s standards—increase in Germany's international reserves and the fixed exchange rate was abandoned. As the models reviewed above suggest, the control program does appear to have slowed down the demise of the system but could not preserve the par value system.

Gros (1987) reports spreads between Euro and domestic deposits for Italy and France during 1979–1986. He interprets these differentials, which were for short periods as high as 20–24 percentage points, as consistent with his model that predicts that controls are temporarily effective in restraining large changes in investors' positions. That is, during times of turbulence in the ERM, private speculators were not able to adjust their open positions costlessly. Nevertheless, over longer horizons, the interest differentials rapidly returned to very low levels.

Similar evidence for five industrial countries during 1982–1992 is reported in Obstfeld (1995a). He concludes that for industrial countries, the links between onshore and offshore markets are very close but "the data also show that actual or prospective government interventions remain a significant factor in times of turbulence" (Obstfeld 1995a, 17). The data decisively reject the view that capital controls are always ineffective. But the data also suggest that either the governments involved quickly removed the incentives for speculation, through policy changes, or that speculators simply retreated to await another attack.

Chinn and Frankel (1994) report covered differentials for a group of developing countries in Asia. They find that these markets are not as integrated as those of the industrial countries but that during the 1980s, covered differentials seem to have narrowed even though capital controls were generally utilized by the countries studied.

Melvin and Schlagenhauf (1985) extend this approach by explicitly modeling the threat of controls or government-enforced default in addition to controls already in place. They find that for Mexico in the early 1980s, controls had a significant effect on capital flows. In considering the same episode, Spiegel (1990) also finds that political risk was important but estimates it to have the opposite sign of that reported in Melvin and Schlagenhauf. Both papers indicate that the controls in place were effective.

Browne and McNelis (1990) provide a careful study of the imposition of controls over capital flows in Ireland during 1979–1986. Forward exchange rates are available for this data set, and the study is unusual in that it considers a number of domestic and international interest rates. The relative importance of domestic monetary conditions and the yield on similar U.K. instruments are compared before and after the imposition of controls in December 1978.

Their results suggest that there was a jump in the importance of domestic monetary factors in determining some interest rates in Ireland immediately after controls were imposed. However, as with the other studies, the effects of monetary conditions were short-lived, on average only about six months. The usual story emerges that the central bank gained some independence for a short time.

The evidence also suggests that interest rates in domestic financial markets that are poorly integrated with other domestic markets are much more sensitive to domestic money shocks than are bank deposit markets. For example, Browne and McNelis find that changes in domestic monetary conditions had no impact on yields on bank deposits. Yet they find significant influence for domestic conditions on rates of return in relatively noncompetitive domestic loan and mortgage markets.

Fieleke (1994) compares short-term Euro interest rates with similar domestic interest rates for Spain, Ireland, and Portugal during the 1992 ERM crisis. In each case, the authorities enforced controls on capital outflows as part of a defense of the exchange rate arrangement. Although the controls did result in measurable deviations between onshore and offshore interest rates, in the end controls did not prevent a change in the exchange rate.

Fieleke also points out that ERM members that did not utilize controls, Norway and Sweden, experienced much larger fluctuations in domestic interest rates in trying to maintain their exchange rate targets. He concludes, "It may be that Spain and Portugal did acquire some temporary insulation" (Fieleke 1994, 34).

Fieleke offers an interesting alternative test of the expected efficacy of controls by comparing the prices of equities for traded and nontraded goods industries leading up to the exchange rate crisis. If controls are expected to fail in the sense that there is no change in the probability of devaluation, the market value of nontraded goods industries should not rise following an unexpected imposition of controls. Data for Portugal during 1992 and 1993 offer conflicting evidence. The value of nontraded goods equities did rise relative to export-oriented industries but declined relative to import-competing industries. The short sample period and difficulty in identifying the orientation of firms cloud the results.

Eichengreen, Rose, and Wyplosz (1994) challenge this interpretation of the ERM experience. They make the point that focusing on actual devaluations biases the sample toward episodes in which capital control programs have failed. To overcome this, they examine the behavior of a number of economic variables during crisis and noncrisis periods to see if there are systematic differences in the experience of countries with controls as compared with countries without controls. This, they argue, is a more useful measure of the effectiveness of controls. During crisis periods, countries with controls experienced higher inflation, higher rates of money growth, and higher growth of domestic assets. Controls did not seem to affect the loss of reserves, interest rate differentials, or fiscal imbalances. During noncrisis periods, controls appear to affect all the macroeconomic variables tested except reserves.

Their conclusion is quite consistent with the literature surveyed above:

> Controls do not allow countries which pursue policies inconsistent with a peg to keep their exchange rate unchanged forever. They do not prevent attacks, nor do they permit countries to avoid reserve losses or interest rate increases when attacks occur. Controls merely render expansionary monetary policies viable for a longer period by attenuating the link between crises and exchange rate regime collapse (Eichengreen, Rose, and Wyplosz 1994, 8).

An important limitation of this methodology is that well-developed forward exchange markets or offshore deposit markets are needed to control for expected exchange rate changes. For many markets where liberalization is now a policy option, historical controls have inhibited the development of such markets. Thus, empirical research must rely on an alternative estimate of expected exchange rate changes.

Phylaktis (1988) reports results for Argentina based on the model discussed above but uses realized spot rates as a proxy for expected changes in exchange rates. Some types of controls were found to influence the uncovered interest differential. The interesting aspect of these results is that the existence of controls might have contributed to effective taxation of foreign assets, to a political risk premium, and perhaps to the exchange risk premium. The difficulty in sorting out these effects in the absence of forward exchange markets has led researchers to explore alternative models.

Edwards and Khan (1985) propose a direct test for the relative importance of a domestic interest rate and an uncovered foreign rate in determining the demand for money. They found that for relatively open economies (Singapore), only the uncovered foreign expected yield was important in determining money demand. For countries with controls (Colombia), both the foreign rate and domestic market-clearing rates were important.

Haque and Montiel (1990) develop an empirical test for developing countries for which market-clearing domestic interest rate data are not available. This research utilizes an instrumental variable approach to control for the endogeneity of the observed monetary base. The authors conclude that the degree of capital mobility among developing countries is quite high and argue that this indicates the pervasive controls over capital flows in place in most of the countries studied provided little scope for an independent monetary policy.

Dooley and Mathieson (1994) extend this model to test for changes in the degree of capital mobility over time. They also find that capital is quite mobile for countries that have extensive control programs and that in most cases, this degree of mobility has increased over time. In general, this line of research suggests that control programs in developing countries have been of limited effectiveness.

Other authors using similar techniques have reported mixed results. Reisen and Yeches (1991) utilize curb market rates as a measure of effective domestic interest rates and find that capital mobility remained roughly constant for a group of Asian countries, while Faruqee (1991) finds that integration between developing countries in Asia and Japan seems to have increased in recent years. Kwack (1994) develops such a model that identifies the exogenous part of the change in the base using a policy reaction function and reports plausible estimates of the effectiveness of Korean capital controls.

Each of the papers discussed above attempts to measure a counterfactual monetary base that the authorities are assumed to set for an extended period.

However, the observed change in the domestic part of the monetary base is some combination of the exogenous policy change and the response during the period studied to offsetting private capital flows. Since the response to a policy-induced change in the monetary base can be literally instantaneous, it is difficult to identify the policy-induced part of observed changes short of developing a complete model of government behavior. It appears that different techniques for dealing with the endogenous nature of the regressors have important consequences for the results of these studies.

Edwards (1989) provides a qualitative evaluation of capital control programs leading up to 34 devaluations in developing countries. He concludes that governments typically intensified their control programs in the year before devaluations. He also reports data on premia in financial exchange markets as devaluations approached. While there are exceptions, in most cases the financial rate premia increased sharply in the one to three months before the exchange crisis led to devaluation. Nevertheless, data for these same episodes show that current accounts weakened and reserve assets declined in spite of the controls. Edwards concludes, "At most one can argue that these heightened impediments to trade managed to slow down the unavoidable balance of payments crisis unleashed by the inconsistent macroeconomic policies" (1989, 189–90). This evidence seems consistent for the more thoroughly researched data for industrial countries.

Direct Measures of Capital Flows

Johnston and Ryan (1994) examine the effects of capital control programs for recorded capital flows (including errors and omissions) for a cross-section of 52 developing and industrial countries for the period 1985–1992. An important difficulty with this approach is that controlling for factors other than capital controls that shape the structure of capital flows is quite difficult. As the authors point out, models of the capital account typically relate economic fundamentals, such as yield differentials and changes in wealth, to total net capital flows that are the mirror image of the current account balance. Within this constraint, the composition of the capital account between net official flows and net private flows then depends on the behavior of the government. If that behavior is not consistent over time, the behavior of net private capital flows will not be related to economic fundamentals. Moreover, to the extent that control programs respond to capital flows, it would not be surprising to observe that new controls over capital inflows are associated with increased inflows.

Nevertheless, some interesting empirical regularities emerge from the data. The removal of controls on capital outflows by industrial countries did seem to influence the overall volume and structure of net private flows. Direct investment and recorded long-term portfolio investment seem to have been quite sensitive to changes in control programs. In contrast, control programs in developing countries do not seem to have affected either overall private capital flows or their composition. The authors reach the plausible conclusion that the administration of control programs in developing countries has been less effective as compared with that in industrial countries.

A related empirical literature has attempted to measure private capital outflows from developing countries that are not captured by balance of payments reporting systems. Such outflows, generally identified as capital flight, are presumed to be unrecorded because the residents of these countries wish to avoid legal restrictions on outflows and/or taxes on earnings from legal outflows. Dooley (1988) tests the idea that such flows reflect efforts of residents to avoid financial repression.

Mathieson and Rojas-Suárez (1993) test the relationship between capital flight capital control programs and other fundamental determinants of capital flight. They find that during episodes where capital flight responds to increased risk from inflation and default risk, countries with capital controls did not prevent capital flight. The private sector's reaction to a deterioration of the fundamentals was delayed.

Kamin (1988) develops a related idea that capital movements are concealed by misinvoicing of trade transactions. In a case study of the Argentine dual exchange rate mechanism during the period 1981–1990, Kamin (1991) suggests that controls were made ineffective through export underinvoicing and a variety of other leakages.

Tests of the Political Economy of Capital Controls

Recent empirical work has attempted to relate countries' use of capital market restrictions to a variety of structural characteristics of the economy. This literature views policy regimes as endogenous responses to institutional and political features of the economy. Alesina, Grilli, and Milesi-Ferretti (1994) test the relevance of a number of rationalizations for the use of capital controls outlined above by looking for common characteristics of Organization for Economic Cooperation and Development (OECD) countries that seem to be related to the utilization of controls. Their reading of the theoretical literature suggests that the use of controls should be related to the exchange rate regime, to the desire to tax capital income, and to the desire to tax money balances. They find that highly managed exchange rate regimes seem to be associated with the use of controls.

Preferences for taxing capital income and money balances are, in turn, related to a variety of attributes of the political system. For example, inflation might result from weak governments that cannot enforce other types of taxes or strong governments that decide to tax capital income. Governments with independent central banks might resist both inflation and controls designed to preserve the inflationary tax base. Their findings suggest that countries with strong governments and dependent central banks are likely to utilize controls, presumably to generate revenue from inflation and to reduce real debt service.

The authors also test the impact of controls on other macroeconomic variables. Controlling for political stability, they find that controls have a negative effect on the stock of government debt. This is consistent with models discussed above that suggest that revenue from inflation is enhanced by controls and that domestic real interest rates kept below the world rate might limit debt service costs. The structure of the economy also seems to be an important determinant of the use of controls. The data also suggest that, controlling for initial income levels and political stability, controls do not seem to influence growth rates.

Grilli and Milesi-Ferretti (1995) find similar results for a sample of 61 developing and developed countries. In particular, over an extended period, countries with controls seem to experience high rates of inflation, relatively high shares of government revenue from seigniorage, and relatively low real interest rates. These recent results suggest that fiscal considerations are the most important determinants of the use of capital controls and that the controls, or some factor highly correlated with the use of controls, have measurable effects on government revenues.

Integration and Net Capital Flows

The consensus from empirical work reviewed above is that capital markets of industrial countries and many developing countries are highly integrated and that integration has increased substantially over the past 30 years. Capital controls or dual exchange rate systems have been effective in generating yield differentials, covered for exchange risk, for short periods of time but have had little power to stop speculative attacks on regimes that were seen by the market as being inconsistent.

It is surprising, in light of this evidence, that so little supporting evidence is found in the nonfinancial data. What has become known as the Feldstein–Horioka puzzle is the lack of real savings–investment imbalances among countries with apparently integrated financial markets. As argued in Dooley, Frankel, and Mathieson (1987), tests of savings–investment correlations are joint tests of several hypotheses, most of which have little to do with capital mobility or capital controls. The test of market integration might fail because purchasing power parity does not hold, exchange rate risk is a powerful barrier to international investment, domestic financial markets are poorly integrated, the economies studied are near a steady state in which imbalances are very small, or, finally, government policies other than capital controls generate small current account imbalances.

In a recent survey of this literature, Obstfeld (1994a) suggests that the puzzle is real in the sense that current account imbalances appear to be too small relative to historical periods when capital accounts were apparently open or to net capital movements within national boundaries. Several observers have concluded that the most plausible reason for this departure from the expected pattern of international investments is that governments have targets for the current account and manipulate macroeconomic policies to attain these targets. There appears to be no evidence that would suggest that capital controls are an important part of the apparent barriers to real capital mobility.

While not directly relevant to this paper's exploration of capital account restrictions, this observation is interesting and important. Recall that an effective control program is closely related to a government target for the current account balance. It seems clear that if governments are pursuing current account targets using other distortionary policy tools, the welfare effects of imposing controls are much less clear. In this case, the alternative to capital controls is not free trade in financial assets but distortion of another policy tool to eliminate private incentives for intertemporal trade.

A few studies of the real side evidence have looked directly at the effects of capital controls on real capital mobility. Razin and Rose (1994) created a measure of capital controls from the IMF's *Annual Report on Exchange Arrangements and Exchange Restrictions* and tested the impact of these controls for a cross-section of industrial and developing countries. They tested the hypothesis that changes in consumption should be correlated among countries with open capital markets, and investment should be more variable over time. None of these predictions is supported by the data. Like all these studies, these are tests of complicated joint hypotheses. But the data seem to support the view that while real capital markets may not be highly integrated, capital control programs do not seem to be the main reason for this fact.

Gross Capital Flows and Capital Controls: Theory and Evidence

The implicit assumption in the literature reviewed in the previous section is that net capital flows, and the associated redistribution of savings and investment across countries, determine the welfare consequences of capital mobility. Gross private capital flows and the structure of international financial intermediation are, by implication, less important for evaluating the economic consequences of international capital flows and controls on these flows. This section suggests that such models ignore important considerations in the balance of costs and benefits of capital control programs.

Some of the literature already reviewed is relevant for gross capital flows, but in general, this subject is not well developed in the literature. Nevertheless, the evidence cited above suggests that the welfare gains from liberalization of international credit markets are likely to come from better utilization of available domestic savings rather than from net flows of foreign savings. The important point is that direct investment and other international capital transactions might be welfare-improving even if no net capital flow is associated with free trade in financial services.

Obstfeld (1995b) develops the idea that closed national credit markets might be very unlikely to finance high-risk investments because of risk aversion among domestic savers and the inability to diversify within the domestic markets. If high-risk investment projects also have relatively high payoffs in terms of endogenous economic growth, the closed capital market implies that the growth rate of the country is limited. Opening the capital account in this model allows nonresident investors with lower levels of risk aversion to hold high-return investments in the country, while residents hold relatively safe foreign assets. Thus, with no net capital flow, domestic savings are channeled into investments that generate a higher growth rate. As demonstrated in a simulation exercise, the welfare benefits of a higher growth path can be very large.

Partial equilibrium models of the potential benefits for investors of greater access to equity markets in developing countries also suggest that significant welfare gains are available (Lessard 1973, Harvey 1994). These models employ an international capital asset pricing model to evaluate the possibility that opening equity markets would improve the risk-return trade-off faced by an investor currently limited to industrial country equities. Recent work has also tested the effects of restrictions on foreign investment as measured by an investability index compiled by the International Finance Corp. (Bekaert 1993; Claessens, Dasgupta, and Glen 1995). This analysis suggests that existing controls have had significant effect on yields of equities and that removal of such restrictions would benefit investors.

The apparent benefits from international diversification have also led to research that compares optimal portfolios with observed portfolios. While there are many problems with the data on gross international capital flows and even more problems with calculation of stocks of cross-border private financial claims and liabilities, this research suggests a very clear home bias in portfolios of residents of industrial countries. Tesar and Warner (1992) report that residents of industrial countries hold almost all their wealth in the form of claims on residents of their home country. Golub (1990) argues that evidence from gross capital flows suggests that a very minor part of the capital stock of OECD countries reflects gross foreign ownership and concludes that this measure of capital mobility is even more puzzling than the data on current account imbalances discussed in the previous section.

Notes

1. For a recent review of the literature that followed, see Garber and Svensson (1994).
2. See Obstfeld and Rogoff (1994) for a recent review.

References

Adams, Charles, and Jeremy Greenwood (1985), "Dual Exchange Rate Systems and Capital Controls: An Investigation," *Journal of International Economics* 18: 43–64.

Aizenman, Joshua (1990), "External Debt, Planning Horizon, and Distorted Credit Markets," *Journal of International Money and Finance* 9: 138–158.

Aizenman, Joshua (1986), "On the Complementarity of Commercial Policy, Capital Controls, and Inflation Tax," *Canadian Journal of Economics* 19 (February): 114–133.

Aizenman, Joshua, and Pablo E. Guidotti (1994), "Capital Controls, Collection Costs, and Domestic Public Debt," *Journal of International Money and Finance* 13 (February): 41–54.

Aizenman, Joshua, and Nancy P. Marion (1993), "Macroeconomic Uncertainty and Private Investment," *Economic Letters* 41: 207–210.

Akerlof, George A., and Paul M. Romer (1993), "Looting: The Economic Underworld of Bankruptcy for Profit," *Brookings Papers on Economic Activity*, no. 2: 1–60, 70–74.

Alesina, Alberto, Vittorio Grilli, and Gian Maria Milesi-Ferretti (1994), "The Political Economy of Capital Controls," in *Capital Mobility: The Impact on Consumption, Investment, and Growth*, ed. Leonardo Leiderman and Assaf Razin (Cambridge and New York: Cambridge University Press).

Alesina, Alberto, and Guido Tabellini (1989), "External Debt, Capital Flight, and Political Risk," *Journal of International Economics* 27 (November): 199–221.

Argy, Victor, and Michael Porter (1972), "Forward Exchange Market and External Disturbances under Alternative Exchange Rate Systems," *IMF Staff Papers*, 503–528.

Auernheimer, Leonardo (1987), "On the Outcome of Inconsistent Programs under Exchange Rate and Monetary Rules," *Journal of Monetary Economics* 19: 279–305.

Baccheta, Philippe (1990), "Temporary Capital Controls in a Balance-of-Payments Crisis," *Journal of International Money and Finance* 9 (September): 246–257.

Bartolini, Leonardo, and Allan Drazen (1994), "Capital Account Liberalization as a Signal," IMF Working Paper (Washington, D.C.: International Monetary Fund, November).

Bekaert, Geert (1993), "Market Integration and Investment Barriers in Emerging Equity Markets," Working Paper, Stanford Graduate School of Business.

Bhandari, Jagdeep S., and Bernard Decaluwe (1987), "A Stochastic Model of Incomplete Separation Between Commercial and Financial Exchange Markets," *Journal of International Economics* 22: 25–55.

Blackburn, Keith, and Martin Sola (1993), "Speculative Currency Attacks and Balance of Payments Crises," *Journal of Economic Surveys* 7(2): 119–44.

Branson, William (1993), "Comment," in *Financial Opening: Policy Issues and Experiences in Developing Countries*, ed. H. Reisen and B. Fisher (Paris: Organization for Economic Cooperation and Development).

Brock, Philip L. (1984), "Inflationary Finance in an Open Economy," *Journal of Monetary Economics* 14: 37–53.

Browne, Francis X., and Paul D. McNelis (1990), "Exchange Controls and Interest Rate Determination with Traded and Non-Traded Assets: The Irish–United Kingdom Experience," *Journal of International Money and Finance* 9: 41–59.

Cairncross, Alec (1973), *Control of Long-Term International Capital Movements* (Washington, D.C.: The Brookings Institution).

Calvo, Guillermo A. (1988), "Costly Trade Liberalization: Durable Goods and Capital Mobility," *IMF Staff Papers* 35 (September): 461–473.

Calvo, Guillermo (1987), "Balance of Payments Crises in a Cash-in-Advance Economy," *Journal of Money, Credit, and Banking* 19 (February): 19–32.

Chinn, Menzie D., and Jeffrey A. Frankel (1994), "Financial Links Around the Pacific Rim: 1982–1992," in *Exchange Rate Policy and Interdependence: Perspectives from the Pacific Basin*, ed. R. Glick and M. Hutchison (New York: Cambridge University Press), 17–47.

Claassen, Emil-Maria, and Charles Wyplosz (1985), "Capital Controls: Some Principles and the French Experience," in *The French Economy: Theory and Policy*, ed. J. Melitz and C. Wyplosz (Boulder, Colo.: Westview Press), 237–267.

Claessens, Stijn (1988), "Balance-of-Payments Crises in a Perfect Foresight Optimizing Model," *Journal of International Money and Finance* 7: 363–372.

Claessens, Stijn, S. Dasgupta, and J. Glen (1995), "Return Behavior in Emerging Stock Markets," *World Bank Economic Review* 9 (January): 131–51.

Delbecque, Bernard (1993), "Dual Exchange Rates Under Pegged Interest Rate and Balance-of-Payment Crisis," *Journal of International Money and Finance* 12: 170–181.

Dellas, Harris, and Oded Galor (1992), "Growth Via External Public Debt and Capital Controls," *International Economic Review* 33 (May): 269–281.

Dellas, Harris, and Allan Stockman (1993), "Self-Fulfilling Expectations, Speculative Attack, and Capital Controls," *Journal of Money, Credit, and Banking* 25 (November): 721–730.

Dooley, Michael P. (1995), "A Retrospective on the Debt Crisis," in *Understanding Interdependence: The Macroeconomics of the Open Economy*, ed. P. Kenen (Princeton, N.J.: Princeton University Press).

Dooley, Michael P. (1988), "Capital Flight: A Response to Differences in Financial Risks," *IMF Staff Papers* 35 (September).

Dooley, Michael P., Jeffrey Frankel, and Donald J. Mathieson (1987), "International Capital Mobility: What Do Saving-Investment Correlations Tell Us?" *IMF Staff Papers* 34 (September).

Dooley, Michael P., and Peter Isard (1980), "Capital Controls, Political Risk, and Deviations from Interest-Rate Parity," *Journal of Political Economy* 88 (April): 370–384.

Dooley, Michael P., and Kenneth M. Kletzer (1994), "Capital Flight, External Debt, and Domestic Policies," *Economic Review* 3: 29–37.

Dooley, Michael P., and Donald J. Mathieson (1994), "Exchange Rate Policy, International Capital Mobility, and Monetary Policy Instruments," in *Exchange Rate Policy and Interdependence: Perspectives from the Pacific Basin*, ed. R. Glick and M. Hutchison (New York: Cambridge University Press), 68–95.

Dornbusch, Rudiger (1988), "The EMS, the Dollar and the Yen," in *The European Monetary System*, ed. F. Giavazzi, S. Micossi, and M. Miller (Cambridge, England: Cambridge University Press).

Dornbosch, Rudiger (1986), "Special Exchange Rates for Capital Account Transactions," *World Bank Economic Review* 1(1): 3–33.

Drazen, Allan (1989), "Monetary Policy, Capital Controls and Seigniorage in an Open Economy," in *A European Central Bank?: Perspectives on Monetary Unification After Ten Years of the EMS*, ed. M. de Cecco and A. Giovannini (New York: Cambridge University Press), 13–32.

Edwards, Sebastian (1989), "On the Sequencing of Structural Reforms," NBER Working Paper Series, no. 3138 (Cambridge, Mass.: National Bureau of Economic Research, October).

Edwards, Sebastian (1989), *Real Exchange Rates Devaluation and Adjustment* (Cambridge, Mass.: MIT Press).

Edwards, Sebastian (1989), "Tariffs, Capital Controls, and Equilibrium Real Exchange Rates," *Canadian Journal of Economics* 22 (February): 79–93.

Edwards, Sebastian, and Mohsin S. Khan (1985), "Interest Rate Determination in Developing Countries: A Conceptual Framework," *IMF Staff Papers* (September).

Edwards, Sebastian, and Jonathan Ostry (1992), "Terms of Trade Disturbances, Real Exchange Rates, and Welfare: The Role of Capital Controls and Labor Market Distortions," *Oxford Economic Papers* 44 (January): 20–34.

Edwards, Sebastian, and Sweder van Wijnbergen (1986), "The Welfare Effects of Trade and Capital Market Liberalization," *International Economic Review* 27 (February): 141–148.

Eichengreen, Barry, Andrew K. Rose, and Charles Wyplosz (1994), "Speculative Attacks on Pegged Exchange Rates: An Empirical Exploration with Special Reference to the European Monetary System," NBER Working Paper Series, no. 4898 (Cambridge, Mass.: National Bureau of Economic Research, October).

Eichengreen, Barry, James Tobin, and Charles Wyplosz (1995), "Two Cases for Sand in the Wheels of International Finance," *Economic Journal* 105 (January): 162–172.

Eichengreen, Barry, and Charles Wyplosz (1993), "The Unstable EMS," *Brookings Papers on Economic Activity*, no. 1.

Epstein, Gerald A., and Juliet B. Schor (1992), "Structural Determinants and Economic Effects of Capital Controls in OECD Countries," in *Financial Openness and National*

Autonomy: Opportunities and Constraints, ed. T. Banuri and J. Schor (Oxford, England: Clarendon Press), 136–161.

Faruqee, Hamid (1991), "Dynamic Capital Mobility in Pacific Basin Developing Countries: Estimation and Policy Implications," IMF Working Paper 91/115 (November).

Fieleke, Norman S. (1994), "International Capital Transactions: Should They Be Restricted?" *New England Economic Review* (March/April): 27–39.

Fischer, Bernhard, and Helmut Reisen (1993), *Liberalising Capital Flows in Developing Countries: Pitfalls, Prerequisites and Perspectives* (Paris: Organization for Economic Cooperation and Development).

Fleming, J. Marcus (1974), "Dual Exchange Markets and Other Remedies for Disruptive Capital Flows," *IMF Staff Papers*, 1–27.

Flood, Robert P., and Peter M. Garber (1984), "Gold Monetization and Gold Discipline," *Journal of Political Economy* 92, 90–107.

Flood, Robert P., and Nancy P. Marion (1982), "The Transmission of Disturbances Under Alternative Exchange-Rate Regimes with Optimal Indexing," *Quarterly Journal of Economics* (February): 43–66.

Frankel, Jeffrey A. (1992), "Measuring International Capital Mobility: A Review," *American Economic Review* 82 (May): 197–201.

Garber, Peter M., and Lars E.O. Svensson (1994), "The Operation and Collapse of Fixed Exchange Rate Regimes," NBER Working Paper Series, no. 4971 (Cambridge, Mass.: National Bureau of Economic Research, December).

Garber, Peter M., and Mark P. Taylor (1995), "Sand in the Wheels of Foreign Exchange Markets: A Skeptical Market," *Economic Journal: The Journal of the Royal Economic Society* 105 (January): 173–180.

Giavazzi, Francesco, and Alberto Giovannini (1989), *Limiting Exchange Rate Flexibility: The European Monetary System* (Cambridge, Mass.: MIT Press).

Giovannini, Alberto, and Martha de Melo (1993), "Government Revenue from Financial Repression," *American Economic Review* 83 (September): 953–963.

Giovannini, Alberto, and Jae Won Park (1992), "Capital Controls and International Trade Finance," *Journal of International Economics* 33 (November): 285–304.

Golub, Stephen S. (1990), "International Capital Mobility: Net Versus Gross Stocks and Flows," *Journal of International Money and Finance* 9: 424–439.

Greenwood, Jeremy, and Kent P. Kimbrough (1985), "Capital Controls and Fiscal Policy in the World Economy," *Canadian Journal of Economics* 18 (November): 743–765.

Grilli, Vittorio, and Gian Maria Milesi-Ferretti (1995), "Economic Effects and Structural Determinants of Capital Controls," IMF Working Paper 95/31 (Washington, D.C.: International Monetary Fund, March).

Grilli, Vittorio, and Nouriel Roubini (1993), "Liquidity, Capital Controls, and Exchange Rates," *Journal of International Money and Finance* 12 (April): 139–153.

Gros, Daniel (1992), "Capital Controls and Foreign Exchange Market Crises in the EMS," *European Economic Review* 36 (December): 1533–1544.

Gros, Daniel (1988), "Dual Exchange Rates in the Presence of Incomplete Market Separation: Long-Run Effectiveness and Policy Implications," *IMF Staff Papers* 35 (September): 437–460.

Gros, Daniel (1987), "The Effectiveness of Capital Controls: Implications for Monetary Autonomy in the Presence of Incomplete Market Separation," *IMF Staff Papers* 34 (December): 621–642.

Guidotti, Pablo E., and Carlos A. Végh (1992), "Macroeconomic Interdependence Under Capital Controls: A Two-Country Model of Dual Exchange Rates," *Journal of International Economics* 32 (May): 353–367.

Guitián, Manuel (1993), "Currency Convertibility: Concepts and Degrees" (Seminar on currency convertibility sponsored by the IMF Institute and the Arab Monetary Fund, December).

Haque, Nadeem Ul, and Peter Montiel (1990), "Capital Mobility in Developing Countries—Some Empirical Tests," IMF Working Paper 90/117 (Washington, D.C.: International Monetary Fund, December).

Harberger, Arnold C. (1986), "Welfare Consequences of Capital Inflows," in *Economic Liberalization in Developing Countries*, ed. Armeane M. Choksi and Demetris Papageorgiou (Oxford, England: Basil Blackwell), 157–183.

Harvey, Campbell, R. (1994), "Predictable Risk and Relative Returns in Emerging Markets," NBER Working Paper Series, no. 4621 (Cambridge, Mass.: National Bureau of Economic Research, October).

Helpman, Elhanan (1981), "An Exploration in the Theory of Exchange Rate Regimes," *Journal of Political Economy* 89(5): 865–890.

Johnston, R. Barry, and Chris Ryan (1994), "The Impact of Controls on Capital Movements on the Private Capital Accounts of Countries' Balance of Payments: Empirical Estimates and Policy Implications," IMF Working Paper 94/78 (Washington, D.C.: International Monetary Fund, July).

Kamin, Steven B. (1991), "Argentina's Experience with Parallel Exchange Markets: 1981–1990," International Finance Discussion Papers, no. 407 (Washington, D.C.: Board of Governors of the Federal Reserve System, August).

Kamin, Steven B. (1988), "Devaluation, Exchange Controls, and Black Markets for Foreign Exchange in Developing Countries," International Finance Discussion Papers, no. 334 (Washington, D.C.: Board of Governors of the Federal Reserve System, October).

Kane, Edward J. (1995), *The Gathering Crisis in Federal Deposit Insurance* (Cambridge, Mass.: MIT Press), 119–28.

Krugman, Paul (1987), "The Narrow Moving Band, the Dutch Disease, and the Competitive Consequences of Mrs. Thatcher: Notes on Trade in the Presence of Scale Economies," *Journal of Development Politics* 27: 41–55.

Krugman, Paul (1979), "A Model of Balance-of-Payments Crises," *Journal of Money, Credit, and Banking* 11 (August): 312–325.

Kwack, Sung Y. (1994), "Sterilization of the Monetary Effects of Current Account Surpluses and Its Consequences: Korea, 1986–1990," in *Exchange Rate Policy and Interdependence: Perspectives from the Pacific Basin*, ed. R. Glick and M. Hutchison (New York: Cambridge University Press), 287–313.

Laban, R., and F. Larrain (1993), "Can a Liberalization of Capital Outflows Increase Net Capital Inflows?" Pontificia Universidad Catolica de Chile, Instituto de Economia, Working Paper no. 155.

Lane, Timothy, and Liliana Rojas-Suárez (1992), "Credibility, Capital Controls, and the EMS," *Journal of International Economics* 32 (May): 321–357.

Lanyi, Anthony 1975, "Separate Exchange Markets for Capital and Current Transactions," International Monetary Fund Staff Papers 22 (November): 714–49.

Lessard, Donald (1973), "International Portfolio Diversification: A Multivariate Analysis for a Group of Latin Countries," *Journal of Finance* 28: 619–633.

Marston, Richard C. (1993), "Interest Differentials under Bretton Woods and the Post-Bretton Woods Float: The Effects of Capital Controls and Exchange Risk," in *A Retrospective on the Bretton Woods System*, ed. Michael D. Bordo and Barry Eichengreen (Chicago: University of Chicago Press).

Mathieson, Donald J., and Liliana Rojas-Suárez (1993), "Liberalization of the Capital Account: Experiences and Issues," IMF Occasional Paper no. 103 (Washington, D.C.: International Monetary Fund, March).

McKinnon, Ronald, I. (1973), *Money and Capital in Economic Development* (Washington D.C.: The Brookings Institution).

Melvin, Michael, and Don Schlagenhauf (1985), "A Country Risk Index: Econometric Formulation and an Application to Mexico," *Economic Inquiry* 23 (October): 601.

Obstfeld, Maurice (1995a), "International Capital Mobility in the 1990s," in *Understanding Interdependence: The Macroeconomics of the Open Economy*, ed. P. Kenen (Princeton, N.J.: Princeton University Press).

Obstfeld, Maurice (1995b), "Risk Taking, Global Diversification, and Growth," *American Economic Review* 84 (December): 1310–1329.

Obstfeld, Maurice (1994a), "Are Industrial-Country Consumption Risks Globally Diversified?" in *Capital Mobility: The Impact on Consumption, Investment, and Growth*, ed. Leonardo Leiderman and Assaf Razin (Cambridge and New York: Cambridge University Press).

Obstfeld, Maurice (1994b), "The Logic of Currency Crises," NBER Working Paper Series, no. 4640 (Cambridge, Mass.: National Bureau of Economic Research).

Obstfeld, Maurice (1986a), "Capital Controls, the Dual Exchange Rate, and Devaluation," *Journal of International Economics* 20: 1–20.

Obstfeld, Maurice (1986b), "Rational and Self-Fulfilling Balance-of-Paymetns Crises," *American Economic Review* 76 (March): 72–81.

Obstfeld, Maurice, and Kenneth Rogoff (1994), "The Intertemporal Approach to the Current Account," NBER Working Paper Series, no. 4893 (Cambridge, Mass.: National Bureau of Economic Research, October).

Park, Daekeun (1994), "Foreign Exchange Liberalization and the Viability of a Fixed Exchange Regime," *Journal of International Economics* 36: 99–116.

Phylaktis, Kate (1988), "Capital Controls: The Case of Argentina," *Journal of International Money and Finance* 7: 303–320.

Portes, Richard (1993), "EMS and EMU After the Fall," *The World Economy* 16(1): 1–16.

Quirk, Peter J. (1994), "Capital Account Convertibility: A New Model for Developing Countries," in *Frameworks for Monetary Stability*, ed. T. Baliño and C. Cottarelli (Washington, D.C.: International Monetary Fund).

Razin, Assaf, and Andrew Rose (1994), "Business Cycle Volatility and Openness: An Exploratory Cross-section Analysis," in *Capital Mobility: The Impact on Consumption,*

Investment, and Growth, ed. Leonardo Leiderman and Assaf Razin (Cambridge and New York: Cambridge University Press).

Razin, Assaf, and Efraim Sadka (1991), "Efficient Investment Incentives in the Presence of Capital Flight," *Journal of International Economics* 31: 171–181.

Reinhart, Carmen M., and R. Todd Smith (1995), "Capital Controls: Concepts and Experiences," mimeo, March, 1–32.

Reinhart, Vincent (1991), "The 'Tobin Tax,' Asset Accumulation, and the Real Exchange Rate," *Journal of International Money and Finance* 10: 420–431.

Reisen, Helmut (1994), "Pension Funds, Capital Controls and Macroeconomic Stability," OECD Working Paper 2(47) (Paris: Organization for Economic Cooperation and Development).

Reisen, Helmut, and Helene Yeches (1991), "Time-Varying Estimates on the Openness of the Capital Account in Korea and Taiwan," *Journal of Development Economics* 41 (August): 285–305.

Spiegel, Mark M. (1990), "Capital Controls and Deviations from Proposed Interest Rate Parity: Mexico 1982," *Economic Inquiry* 28 (April): 239–248.

Stockman, Alan C., and Alejandro D. Hernandez (1988), "Exchange Controls, Capital Controls, and International Financial Markets," *American Economic Review* 78 (June): 362–375.

Sussman, Oren (1992), "Financial Liberalization: The Israeli Experience," *Oxford Economic Papers* 44: 387–402.

Sussman, Oren (1991), "Macroeconomic Effects of a Tax on Bond Interest Rates," *Journal of Money, Credit, and Banking* 23 (August, Part 1): 352–366.

Tesar, Linda, and Ingrid Warner (1992), "Home Bias and the Globalization of Securities Markets," NBER Working Paper Series, no. 4218 (Cambridge, Mass.: National Bureau of Economic Research, October).

Tobin, J. (1978), "A Proposal for International Monetary Reform," *Eastern Economic Journal* 4.

Tornell, Aaron (1990), "Real vs. Financial Investment: Can Tobin Taxes Eliminate the Irreversibility Distortion?" *Journal of Development Economics* 32: 419–444.

Tornell, Aaron, and A. Velasco (1992), "The Tragedy of the Commons and Economic Growth: Why Does Capital Flow from Poor to Rich Countries?" *Journal of Political Economy* 100(6): 1208–1231.

van Wijnbergen, Sweder (1990), "Capital Controls and the Real Exchange Rate," *Economica* 57 (February): 15–28.

van Wijnbergen, Sweder (1985), "Trade Reform, Aggregate Investment, and Capital Flight," *Economic Letters* 19: 369–372.

Williamson, John (1993), "A Cost-Benefit Analysis of Capital Account Liberalization," in *Financial Opening: Policy Issues and Experiences in Developing Countries*, ed. H. Reisen and B. Fisher (Paris: Organization for Economic Cooperation and Development).

Wyplosz, Charles (1986), "Capital Controls and Balance of Payments Crises," *Journal of International Money and Finance* 5: 167–179.

Appendix B to Part VI

Are Recent Capital Inflows to Developing Countries a Vote For or Against Economic Policy Reforms?

Michael P. Dooley
University of California, Santa Cruz
Working Paper No. 295
May 1994

Abstract

Recent private capital inflows to emerging markets are usually seen as a vote of confidence for economic prospects and policies of recipient countries. However, this good news is tempered by still-fresh memories of the economic pain many emerging countries suffered after the debt crisis in 1982, when a similar round of capital inflows suddenly dried up.

We argue here that there is good cause for concern. Conventional analyses assume that investment opportunities in emerging economies are the force that has driven the boom in emerging markets. These analyses are useful to a point but miss the essential nature of recent capital inflows.

We offer an alternative interpretation in which international investors have little interest in what the emerging economies do with the resources made available by private capital inflows. Investors are instead interested in the ability and willingness of the recipient government to honor a chain of guarantees that temporarily promise investors yields in emerging markets that exceed yields available in international markets.

A useful analogy is that recent capital inflows are like inflows to U.S. savings and loans after deregulation of these institutions in the early 1980s. In retrospect, it is clear that such capital inflows were not a ringing endorsement of the management of the savings and loans but a correct guess that relatively high yields were available at little risk to the depositor. Such an arbitrage capital inflow is a vote of confidence that the government will honor foolish commitments, not a vote of confidence for good economic policies.

Two ingredients are necessary for massive arbitrage capital flows. First, international investors must have access to emerging markets. Second, the emerging government must have sufficient net worth to make guarantees credible. Deregulation of emerging markets and fiscal reforms in many of these countries have created the conditions under which arbitrage opportunities can be exploited by international investors.

Our conclusion is that developing countries will have to choose from an unappetizing menu of reforms to avoid another crisis in international lending markets. Private capital inflows have recently become a widespread and surprising problem for macroeconomic policy in a variety of developing countries. Although sustained private capital inflows are something that most governments would be happy to live with, there is the concern that what flows in for reasons we don't fully understand could flow out for those same reasons. While capital inflows can be inconvenient, unexpected reversals of access to foreign capital can, as we learned after 1982, have disastrous and lasting effects.

In most cases, developing countries have attempted to offset the domestic effects of capital inflows through some combination of sterilized exchange market intervention, exchange rate appreciation, and, in some cases, restrictions on nonresidents' access to domestic investments. In early 1994, for example, Malaysia imposed restrictions on capital inflows reminiscent of the control program launched in Germany and other European countries with "strong" currencies in the waning days of the Bretton Woods system of fixed exchange rates. In other cases, capital market liberalization has been put on hold or slowed substantially.[1]

In this essay, we develop the argument that there are very good reasons for governments to be concerned about what we will call arbitrage capital flows. Such capital inflows share the unfortunate properties of capital inflows to U.S. savings and loans in the 1980s and are likely to have the same consequences for taxpayers in developing countries.

The basic motivation behind these capital flows is the opportunity to exploit a government subsidy or guarantee. They do not reflect confidence in the investment climate in the country but in the government's ability to give away money. The only lasting way to deal with this type of capital inflow is to remove the subsidy or guarantee. As discussed below, this involves difficult choices for countries that have graduated to the ranks of nations that participate fully in the international financial system.

What Lies Behind Private Capital Inflows?

Conventional pessimists argue that capital inflows since 1989 are mainly the result of depressed yields available in industrial countries.[2] Really dedicated pessimists allege that low yields in the industrial countries have pushed poorly informed investors to reach for higher returns available in emerging markets without understanding the risks involved. Once under way, resulting booms in emerging equity and other financial markets have generated speculative inflows that seem to be unrelated to the fundamental value of the securities traded. Such inflows are a misguided vote of confidence for economic policies in recipient countries.[3] The conventional optimistic interpretation is that private capital inflows reflect fundamentally improved risk-adjusted expected returns on investments in recipient countries. In this case, net capital inflows, and the associated current account deficits, help reallocate real capital formation to countries where risk-adjusted returns have improved. Such inflows are naturally limited by the supply of superior investment opportunities. Inflows of this type are clearly a vote of confidence for economic policies in recipient countries.

In this essay, we argue that neither of these arguments helps much in understanding the scale of private capital inflows in the past few years. Both sides of the debate have focused on the incentives for net investment in emerging markets. Thus, it is natural that the focus is on real or imagined opportunities to add to the productive capital stock of countries receiving capital inflows.

The view developed is that large capital inflows reflect private investors' efforts to exploit financial arbitrage opportunities generated by governments of developing countries. Two ingredients are necessary for these types of capital flows. First, the government must be wealthy enough to credibly offer a subsidy or support a guarantee. Second, emerging markets must be accessible to international investors. If these two conditions are met, the size of the position taken by private investors for arbitrage incentives that may have been around for a long time will grow explosively.

Such inflows do not reflect investors' confidence in the economic performance of the recipient economies but in the ability of their governments to guarantee abnormal rates of return (at the governments' expense) for a limited but predictable period of time. In many ways, recent inflows into emerging markets are analogous to the spectacular inflows to U.S. savings and loans before 1989 or the convergence play inflows to high-inflation European Monetary System (EMS) currencies before the exchange market crisis of 1992.

Recent Private Capital Inflows into Developing Countries

Only three or four years ago, a prevalent view was that developing countries that had trouble servicing external debt in the 1980s would not reenter international capital markets for a generation. The useful life of this prediction was even shorter than the average for economic predictions, as very large inflows to developing countries in Asia, Latin America, and the Middle East were widespread after 1989.

Tables VIB–1 and VIB–2 show private capital flows into developing countries in Asia and the Western Hemisphere expressed as a percentage of the recipient country's gross domestic product (GDP). In some respects, the experience of the two regions has been remarkably similar. For the Western Hemisphere, private capital inflows were reduced dramatically following the 1982 debt crisis as eight of ten countries experienced private capital outflows during 1984–1989. In contrast, during 1992–1993, nine of ten of the Latin countries shown experienced private capital inflows. For Asian developing countries, private inflows were less affected by the debt crisis, but here, too, inflows increased sharply after 1989, with six of the eight countries listed experiencing sizable inflows during 1989–1993.

The counterparts of these private inflows can be divided into official capital outflows, conventionally measured by increases in international reserves, and current account deficits. This is an interesting division because reserve gains probably have minor implications for the real economy, while current account deficits measure the contribution of foreign savings to real domestic consumption and capital formation.

For the Western Hemisphere, small private inflows before 1989 financed current account deficits. During 1990–1993, much larger private inflows were matched by current account deficits of about $100 billion and reserve accumulations of about $60 billion.

For Asia, almost all the private inflow before 1989 was matched by reserve accumulations. The much larger private inflows since then have increasingly

Table VIB–1. Private capital inflows as a percentage of GDP, Asia.

	Indonesia	*Korea*	*Malaysia*	*Philippines*	*Singapore*	*Sri Lanka*	*Taiwan*	*Thailand*
1970	2.70	5.58	−1.87	−.36	74.37	1.72	.54	2.66
1971	2.30	6.40	1.97	−.52	87.07	1.18	.32	3.42
1972	6.49	3.81	4.60	.80	48.60	1.62	.67	4.03
1973	5.17	4.51	−1.25	2.06	28.77	1.31	−6.06	2.16
1974	−.86	9.38	6.43	4.75	41.48	2.77	8.38	4.91
1975	−3.22	8.74	4.28	4.43	24.52	1.70	2.72	5.23
1976	3.23	4.53	−.64	5.00	15.11	1.55	−.39	3.12
1977	1.95	3.52	−3.37	2.75	9.27	2.12	−6.08	6.00
1978	4.05	−.39	−1.73	7.54	15.58	1.98	−6.39	3.75
1979	.86	5.55	−2.15	5.50	15.96	9.60	−1.20	7.49
1980	−.75	5.51	.29	4.30	24.48	8.99	3.60	5.23
1981	−.63	4.13	5.80	1.02	18.66	9.36	8.61	7.84
1982	−1.19	2.02	10.94	3.40	17.28	12.55	−2.74	.70
1983	9.16	−.42	10.38	.96	5.04	9.61	−2.72	7.93
1984	3.74	.27	3.81	−1.38	11.91	6.12	−5.76	6.59
1985	2.20	.42	5.70	−4.48	11.21	4.58	−3.90	3.78
1986	−2.25	−4.08	4.58	−5.05	4.97	5.92	9.25	2.53
1987	1.58	−6.41	−3.75	−5.45	10.05	3.31	9.67	3.10
1988	−.76	−3.10	−8.22	−2.19	2.23	5.08	−9.55	7.00
1989	1.17	−.57	3.88	.58	−3.50	4.56	−8.31	10.29
1990	8.71	−.40	8.47	1.93	.23	4.72	−9.35	14.87
1991	8.11	2.94	12.10	2.12	−7.84	5.20	−1.32	12.56
1992	6.64	2.70	15.04	−1.27	−6.40	2.66	−3.15	8.76
1993	3.42	1.22	4.89	2.70	−11.05	4.26	−.06	7.87
Averages								
1984–88	.9	−2.6	.4	−3.7	8.1	5.0	−.1	4.6
1989–93	6.7	1.6	10.1	1.4	−6.3	4.2	−3.5	11.0

Source: IMF, IFS

Table VIB–2. Private capital inflows as a percentage of GDP, Western Hemisphere.

	Argentina	*Bolivia*	*Brazil*	*Chile*	*Colombia*	*Ecuador*	*Mexico*	*Peru*	*Uruguay*	*Venezuela*
1970	.98	–3.46	2.48	1.16	3.94	6.89	3.40	–2.56	–.79	1.19
1971	–.09	–4.83	3.26	–.90	6.66	3.21	2.39	–.01	–.96	1.84
1972	.46	–4.97	6.11	–.13	5.17	7.90	2.72	–.70	–5.85	3.71
1973	.28	–6.06	5.20	–.69	2.73	4.37	1.90	2.86	–3.43	–3.00
1974	–.02	–4.00	5.58	–3.49	1.92	1.86	3.13	7.84	–.93	–8.13
1975	.52	1.32	4.32	–.51	1.51	8.13	3.17	4.62	.88	3.05
1976	.09	–.91	5.76	1.90	4.16	5.37	–.48	–.09	3.90	–1.07
1977	–.15	–.47	2.94	5.96	1.90	11.06	2.91	2.97	8.62	6.74
1978	–4.27	–1.36	5.32	11.15	1.77	10.55	3.19	–.23	5.95	12.49
1979	2.30	5.78	3.50	10.56	5.87	7.02	4.59	–.94	5.88	5.97
1980	–2.22	–26.27	3.82	11.95	5.35	8.36	5.50	.35	9.16	.03
1981	–3.27	–6.31	4.59	15.23	5.55	.65	3.94	5.55	4.39	–3.12
1982	–7.50	–11.04	3.18	3.48	7.91	5.79	–4.73	5.32	–4.01	–9.13
1983	–1.17	–19.63	–1.26	–2.32	3.73	–16.90	–3.24	–5.99	–5.87	–8.18
1984	.43	.68	1.36	6.79	1.45	–7.21	–2.71	–8.80	–.50	–8.57
1985	–.84	–1.94	–4.36	–.62	4.70	–9.55	–2.53	–8.65	–2.95	–4.27
1986	–1.61	5.45	–3.16	–8.58	1.79	–13.06	.10	–5.45	–2.06	–5.19
1987	–3.86	–.67	–2.95	–6.02	–.39	–6.84	2.46	–5.86	–2.84	1.60
1988	–.12	7.46	–3.37	–7.22	1.64	–1.30	–1.71	–5.98	–4.87	2.17
1989	–7.11	2.35	–1.38	–2.08	1.01	–5.45	1.74	–4.02	–4.29	–3.00
1990	–.93	4.52	–1.00	4.74	.01	–4.28	2.73	–2.09	–1.37	–10.21
1991	–1.38	3.48	–.81	4.49	–.73	–2.68	7.27	3.50	–3.61	3.15
1992	5.05	7.04	1.34	8.63	1.04	–7.91	7.64	1.26	3.67	3.39
1993	7.33	5.36	–1.16	5.71	2.53	.15	6.75	.19	–1.51	2.92
Averages										
1984–88	–2.2	2.2	–2.3	–3.0	1.7	–7.2	–.4	–6.5	–2.9	–2.9
1989–93	2.5	5.1	–.4	5.9	.7	–3.7	6.1	.7	–.7	–.2

Source: IMF, IFS

supported larger current account deficits, although for the past three years the reserve buildup has still accounted for two-thirds of the private inflow.

In summary, a widespread response to capital inflows has been official intervention in foreign exchange markets and increases in international reserve assets. This response suggests that differences in formal exchange rate arrangements might be less important than governments' attitudes toward the effects of inflows on exchange rates and the monetary base. Second, renewed access to international capital markets has allowed many countries to increase investment and/or consumption relative to GDP. Finally, a sudden reversal of private capital inflows would constitute a significant shock to a majority of the countries in these two regions.

Arbitrage Capital Flows

It would be a mistake, however, to conclude that investors care what the developing countries are doing with the capital inflows. The key to understanding such inflows is a careful evaluation of the contingent liabilities taken on by governments. These implicit liabilities can create powerful incentives for private financial transactions.

In a tightly controlled financial system, government guarantees are difficult to exploit. But as capital markets become more integrated and direct controls on financial transactions break down, investors will find new and better ways to take advantage of explicit or implicit government guarantees. The volume of such capital flows may have little to do with the economic fundamental we usually associate with private capital flows. Instead, the scale of transactions is determined by the resources available to support the government guarantee.

The important difference between this and a speculative bubble is that, when a bubble bursts, some private speculators lose to others. When an implicit guarantee is called, the government loses. One can find dramatic examples of this process in both developed and developing countries. The combination of deposit insurance and a relaxation of controls over deposit rates and portfolio selection in the United States led to explosive growth in inflows into savings and loans and to their eventual collapse. The problem, clear in retrospect, was that the contingent liability of the U.S. government provided the private investor with a virtual guarantee that high yields offered by savings and loan deposits would not be matched by depositors' losses. Depositors did not question the ability of some savings and loans to offer deposit rates 200–400 basis points over the market. As long as deposits were "probably" guaranteed, there was little downside risk.

The important lesson is that the size of the capital inflow to the savings and loans did not depend on the fundamental quality of the assets they were acquiring. To extend the analogy with a developing country, depositors did not care if the savings and loan bought a junk bond (international reserves), a shopping center (domestic investment), or a new car for the bank president (imports of consumer durables). Depositors were protected by the very considerable ability of the U.S. government to bail them out.

Moreover, the interest rate offered by savings and loans did not accurately reflect anyone's expected rate of return on the assets, although the savings and loan executives probably thought their boats, cars, and vacation homes were extremely good investments. For these reasons, it was a mistake to interpret the capital inflow to savings and loans as reflecting either a rational or irrational evaluation of their solvency.

In developing countries, a similar process helped generate the debt crisis of 1982. In this case, the governments of debtor countries offered guarantees of the dollar value of residents' liabilities. The rapid buildup of private external debt in the 1970s was matched by a buildup of contingent liabilities of the governments. This contingent liability became an important, but at the time little noticed, part of the developing country governments' overall positions. To some extent, the offer of the guarantee caused the private capital inflow. Perhaps more important, the usual market checks to private inflows were short-circuited by the government guarantee.

About half of the private capital inflow before 1982 was recycled to international markets through unrecorded private capital outflows, what ex post has been labeled capital flight. The other half was matched by current account deficits, a pattern quite similar to the balance of payments of developing countries today.

The most recent example of arbitrage capital flows was the so-called convergence play inflows to high-inflation EMS countries during 1987–1991. Over this period, an estimated $300 billion flowed into high-yield EMS member countries as investors calculated that the governments' commitment to maintain the exchange rate arrangement was credible for long enough that they could reverse their positions before the exchange rate peg was abandoned.

At the same time, the central banks of the countries receiving inflows resisted the fall in nominal interest rates that would have occurred if inflows were permitted to augment the money supply. As argued below, this is exactly the problem facing monetary authorities in emerging markets. With the benefit of hindsight, it is easy to see that the huge losses suffered by EMS governments as the exchange rate arrangement was abandoned in 1992 justified private investors' faith in the guarantee, rather than in the economic policies of the governments involved.

Recent Capital Flows

Is it possible that such a process is again at work in international capital markets? It is interesting to note that the overlending hypothesis for the buildup of external debt of developing countries is often associated with the view that a bubble can occur once in every generation of investors. Thus, as the story goes, memory of the widespread defaults by developing countries in the 1930s died off with the bankers of the 1930s and set the stage for irrational, follow-the-leader lending to the same countries in the 1970s. A repeat of the same argument to explain recent widespread inflows to developing countries implies a dramatic reduction in the half-life of investors, or at least their memories. In this business, one learns not to rule out an explanation simply because it assumes a high level of incompetence, but in the current circumstances, I believe there is a much better and more important lesson to be learned.

The alternative explanation is that a combination of fundamentals and arbitrage transactions is again at work. First, the fundamentals clearly favor a repatriation of funds to many debtor countries. Fiscal reform has been impressive in many countries; debt restructuring has been put in place; privatization, in fact as well as intention, has been remarkably successful. At the same time, interest rates available in industrial countries are at their lowest levels in many years. All these factors make a net private capital inflow to developing countries unsurprising. But are these factors sufficient to explain the large private capital inflows in recent years? I have serious doubts.

It seems likely that once again, private capital inflows are being sustained not only by the more favorable investment climate but also by arbitrage opportunities generated by the governments of developing countries. The form of the incentive is a little different as compared with the external debt-capital flight pattern that led up to the 1982 debt crisis. But in one important respect, the recent private capital inflows are similar, in that they are sustained by a contingent claim on the government.

The distinguishing feature this time is that recent private capital inflows to developing countries have taken the form of domestic-currency-denominated instruments, including equities, corporate bonds, bank deposits, and government securities.[4] This is certainly different from the dollar-denominated, government-guaranteed, syndicated credits that comprised the buildup in debt before 1982.

In the current pattern of capital flows, it is not obvious that the government of the borrowing country has provided a guarantee. However, an implicit guarantee is provided by the increasingly popular use of the exchange rate as an anchor for inflationary expectations. In basing its credibility on the maintenance of a fixed or managed exchange rate, the government, in effect, provides an exchange rate guarantee for the investor in domestic-currency-denominated instruments similar to that offered by high-inflation European exchange rate mechanism (ERM) countries.

This, of course, seems to leave the investor with a credit risk. But in most emerging markets, the government is very likely to provide a credit guarantee as well as the exchange rate guarantee. In cases where international investors buy government securities, the guarantee is explicit. Commercial bank deposits are also guaranteed, especially where the deposit is denominated in domestic currency.

Finally, even the liabilities of domestic nonfinancial corporations carry a strong government backup. This is because such firms are heavily indebted to the domestic banking system. If nonresident creditors want out, these firms can be expected to ask for and receive credit from the domestic banks. To refuse to do so would depress the market value of the banks' existing claims on the domestic firms and call into question the solvency of the domestic banking system.

What limits this process? As long as the developing country central bank maintains domestic nominal interest rates at levels above those available on similar foreign assets, there is, in principle, no limit to the private capital inflows generated. Of course, in reality, the government's resources are limited. At some point, the market will begin to doubt the government's ability to maintain the exchange rate peg and the negative carry resulting from the low return earned on reserves relative to that paid on the domestic liabilities issued in sterilized exchange market intervention. But the scale of private capital inflows necessary to exhaust the central bank's expected net worth can be very large indeed.

Solutions

The only solution is to break the chain of guarantees now being offered to international investors. The chain has several links. The first is the commitment to allow free access of international investors to domestic financial markets. The second is the commitment to a nominal exchange rate target. The third is the commitment to sterilize the monetary effects of capital inflows in order to resist declines in domestic interest rates and overheating the domestic economy. The fourth is the implicit guarantee of deposits and solvency of the domestic banking system. If any one of this chain of guarantees is broken, the losing position now being taken by governments will evaporate. But none of the links can be broken without cost.

A threat to withdraw the guarantee of bank deposits or the solvency of the banking system is unlikely to be credible. The historical involvement of the governments of developing countries with their banking systems makes the threat to allow bank failures a hollow one. Authorities in developing countries recognize the dangers of external borrowing by their commercial banks. For example, the government of Mexico has had some success in limiting Mexican banks' borrowing in international markets, and this has forced investors to acquire direct claims on nonfinancial firms. But as argued above, investors expect the firms to call on their banks during a crisis, and the banks are expected to provide funds that will allow a profitable exit for the foreign investor.

Another option that is probably not feasible is to turn back the clock on capital market integration. Experience in the industrial countries suggests that once private investors have "found" a market and incurred the fixed costs of operating in that market, governments are not able to materially restrict access to profitable investments. For developing countries that retain effective controls, as appears to be the case in some Asian developing countries, a slowing or reversal of liberalization might be a short-term option.

By default, this leaves the exchange rate monetary policy regime as the only option. Unfortunately, there are no easy answers here either. A flexible exchange rate regime would allow an independent monetary policy but seems to be associated with excessive volatility in real exchange rates. Recent research on the behavior of flexible rates for industrial countries is not encouraging, in that there seems to be no correspondence between the variance of the fundamentals and the variance of the real exchange rate. The prospect of an "unnecessary" real exchange rate appreciation is not attractive to countries that have prospered with export-led growth.

A few emerging-market countries will find it feasible to fix the exchange rate and allow capital flows to influence domestic monetary conditions. But this is a particularly difficult policy choice for most developing countries. For economies that are attempting to reduce entrenched inflation and inflationary expectations, a capital inflow that is not sterilized means an increase in the monetary base and a fall in domestic interest rates. This is not the normal recipe for a successful stabilization program. While a few very open economies will find it optimal to fix the exchange rate and import monetary policy, most will find the complete loss of control over monetary policy unacceptable.

Our view is that relinquishing the exchange rate target is the best of a nasty list of choices for most developing countries. Although the exchange rate is a powerful way for the government to signal its intention to fight inflation, a nominal exchange rate target does not contribute to credibility of those intentions in an environment where private expectations for the real equilibrium exchange rates change rapidly. Surely, developing countries engaged in important stabilization and reform programs are those for which we have relatively little ex ante information on the equilibrium real exchange rate. Greater exchange rate flexibility will greatly affect the net private capital inflow that is fully justified by the economic reform packages that have been put in place in many developing countries. It will stop arbitrage capital flows that have dominated the economic environment for the past few years. The collapse of the EMS in 1992 should be a reminder that as much as we might yearn for stability in everything, the reality seems to be that difficult choices are necessary.

Notes

1. D. Mathieson and L. Rojas-Suárez, "Liberalization of the Capital Account: Experiences and Issues," IMF Working Paper WP/92/46, 1992.

2. G. Calvo, L. Leiderman, and C. Reinhart, "Capital Inflows and Real Exchange Rate Appreciation in Latin America: The Role of External Factors," *IMF Staff Papers* 40, 1993.

3. The recent sharp declines in prices in emerging equity markets and markets for sovereign debt are apparently related to the rebound in interest rates in industrial countries that began late in 1993. See M. Dooley, K. Kletzer, and E. Fernandez-Arias, "Is the Debt Crisis History?" World Bank Working Paper, 1994.

4. S. Gooptu, "Portfolio Investment Flows to Emerging Markets," World Bank Working Paper, March 1993.

Part VII CENTRAL BANK COORDINATION IN THE MIDST OF EXCHANGE RATE INSTABILITY

Should the world return to a more coordinated monetary and exchange rate environment? What are the dangers or benefits of a return to a Bretton Woods type of system?

Moderator:
Harvey Rosenblum
Senior Vice President and Director of Research
Federal Reserve Bank of Dallas

Panelists:
John W. Crow
Adviser
American International Group of Companies

Ricardo Hausmann
Chief Economist
Inter-American Development Bank

Allan Meltzer
Professor of Political Economy and Public Policy
Carnegie Mellon University

Miguel Urrutia
Governor
Central Bank of Colombia

Rosenblum:
When we started thinking about holding this conference, the one thing I knew I wanted was a wrap-up session with people who have been on the firing line, veterans in dealing with currency fluctuations that are responding to real shocks and financial shocks. So what we have assembled here on this final panel are four people who have had to deal with these kinds of shocks in one form or another. We have a former central banker, John Crow, formerly governor of the Bank of Canada. We have a current central banker, Miguel Urrutia, from the Central Bank of Colombia. We have Ricardo Hausmann, chief economist of the Inter-American Development Bank and former planning minister of Venezuela, who has had to deal with some of the enormous shocks that country has been exposed to in recent years. And we have Allan Meltzer, who is the first person I always want to turn to for advice on how to deal with economic problems. He's not just an advisor, indirectly, to the Federal Reserve System by virtue of being chairman of the Shadow Open Market Committee, but he's advisor to numerous central banks and ministries of finance around the world.

This session will deal with what this entire conference has been leading up to, which is, Where do we go from here? Do we want to take a step backward, toward the Bretton Woods system that we have left behind? If not, where do the world's financial and currency markets evolve from here?

Crow:
This conference's theme is certainly very relevant and timely. Indeed, this continent has a wide variety of just about everything that I think anybody would want to consider in the way of an exchange rate regime. There's something for everyone. We even had in Mexico, for a while, a kind of precursive target band. Until recently, there is one thing we didn't have. This is not exactly a continent of strong currencies, but we have one, at least now, in the U.S. dollar, which is a bit stronger than it was a few weeks ago. Perhaps economists shouldn't really care whether currency is strong or weak, but central bankers certainly do. It makes for a slightly easier life. More important, you need these respites of strength to balance out periods of weakness and thereby keep market expectations reasonably balanced as well.

My underlying theme in these initial remarks is that, yes, of course, exchange rates matter, and they matter a lot, of course, to central banks. They are the ratios of national moneys, and central banks are deeply concerned with the behavior of money, obviously. At the same time, domestic policies come first, as they should. So the real question is how a country can adopt an exchange rate regime that enables it to pursue good domestic policies. That's the underlying issue.

My own country, Canada, is certainly a floater. We're almost the dean of floaters, having done it for 25 years now, rain and shine. We exited from Bretton Woods, in fact, in 1970, a bit before the general collapse. And there was an earlier period of 10 years in the 1950s when Canada also was floating, violating the Bretton Woods Agreement in the process.

In fact, Canada has been floating longer than the Bretton Woods system was in effect. I think that's worth bearing in mind when we talk about pegged exchange rates, because there's been a bout of nostalgia recently, apparently occasioned by the fiftieth anniversary of Bretton Woods. But the Bretton Woods system didn't last that long. It really didn't start until the late 1950s, when current account convertibility became more general in Europe. In Japan, current account convertibility didn't start until 1964, and by 1971, the Bretton Woods system was effectively out the window. So it is not quite the long-term shining example of a silver age, as it tends to be portrayed with the benefit of nostalgia.

In Canada, we are pretty comfortable with floating. I'm not sure we understood why we did it when we started to float, but with 25 years' practice, I think we've become better at it. And it works for us. Of course, it works better with sound domestic policies, but so does any exchange rate regime. What is important to emphasize is that floating does not get in the way of good domestic policies. In fact, I would say floating is useful in the sense that it makes you focus on the quality of domestic policies.

The one thing about floating that I had to persuade many Canadians of involved their belief that the reason we have a floating exchange rate is so we can depreciate. I had to insist that it was appropriate, even if unwelcome to some, for the exchange rate to appreciate on occasion. That was somewhat difficult to get across. Indeed, many Canadians seemed to think that the central bank really didn't care about the exchange rate because of the very fact that the bank was allowing it to appreciate. We cared about it, but the bottom line was that we cared about some other things more than the exchange rate.

The title of this panel discussion—"Central Bank Coordination in the Midst of Exchange Rate Instability"—looks rather daunting. I think the phrase "putting a finger in the dike and seeing the holes appear somewhere else" was used this morning. Well, this title certainly smacks of the dike analogy. Central bankers are running around in all this instability, putting fingers in dikes. And, lo and behold, they are not very successful. Look at all the exchange rate instability!

But it isn't really that difficult. I wouldn't say it's easy, but it's not that difficult, especially if central banks bear in mind their fundamental domestic responsibilities.

With that background, let me turn to the questions, and let me take the second one first, which I think I've almost answered: What are the dangers or benefits of a return to a Bretton Woods type of system? Not a good idea. Peg rates are not on the menu, for the kinds of reasons discussed at this conference. They didn't work very well before, when governments had some control over the rate because they had all kinds of capital controls. They work even less well now, as the Europeans discovered in the early 1990s. The Europeans had to liberalize their domestic financial systems for the sake of efficiency and competition. That meant liberalizing the external side of financial systems. It also meant facing up to the implications of international capital markets, and, bingo, the exchange rates came under pressure. Canada learned this much earlier. We had an open financial system way back, and that's essentially, I think, why we have been floating since way back.

As for a more coordinated monetary and exchange rate environment, clearly an exchange rate is a ratio; there's interdependency built in. I wouldn't want to argue against coordination; it sounds like a good idea. But while trying to do a little good, you may end up doing substantial harm. The harm comes from confusion about responsibilities and the objectives of domestic monetary policies because of excessive focus on the exchange rate—in other words, putting the cart before the horse.

Let me go into a bit more detail about coordination. The classic definition of coordination is Henry Wallich's: "a significant modification of national policies in recognition of international interdependence." The key word here is *modification*; it's not *cooperation*. You don't just tell people what you are doing in hopes that information will lead to better policies in general. With coordination you change your policies; you modify them. But I would argue that coordination is not a task for central banks. What they should do, above all, is keep an eye on their domestic objectives, although they are, of course, very internationally minded, maybe the most internationally minded of all government agencies. But they do have, or should have, domestic objectives, and they each have, after all, just one monetary instrument, their balance sheet. Let me be unambiguous about this: they should use that instrument to promote domestic monetary stability. That's what they are there for.

Let me dwell for a moment on thè piece of coordination I really know something about, which involved the Group of Five and the Group of Seven (G5/G7), and how it relates to this issue of central banks. The other thing I'll talk about is how exchange rates get taken into account in pursuing domestic objectives. By the way, I think Agustín Carstens was on the right track this morning in this latter regard when he commented on the Mexican experience.

Bear in mind that while there were trucks on the road in the G5/G7 period, central bankers were not the drivers. In a sense, central bankers were the passengers. One example of coordination is the Plaza Accord. In fall 1985, the U.S. dollar had overshot on the upside, and there was concerted intervention to bring it down. I think it was all basically sterilized intervention. Perhaps the markets thought there would be some follow-up in terms of policies, but there wasn't very much, if any. The follow-up that would have been important, given the underlying causes of the U.S. appreciation, would have been a prompt shift in U.S. fiscal policy. That didn't happen. The follow-up that would have been absolutely terrible, and also didn't happen, fortunately, was an easing of monetary policy in the United States. That would have been quite direct in bringing down the U.S. dollar, but it would have been a big mistake for domestic reasons because U.S. demand was buoyant at that point.

The only time that I recall, in fact, monetary policy—or even fiscal policy, for that matter—changing after invention was the shift in Japan to an easier monetary policy after the Louvre Accord, when the object of the game changed from pushing the U.S. dollar down to trying to hold it up or even push it back up a bit. That situation left a bad taste in the mouth of the Bank of Japan, and maybe other Japanese, in terms of being the cause of the asset bubble. From their point of view, the very easy monetary policy in Japan, designed to keep the yen down and the U.S. dollar up, was one factor in the asset bubble that caused so much trouble. The moral here is keep your eye on the domestic ball and don't get seduced by the coordination mirage.

The verdict on intervention is, I think, that it sometimes may do some good, especially if concerted, and it is unlikely to do a lot of harm as long as it doesn't confuse a country about what it is really trying to do. It won't do any harm, I guess, if it's sterilized.

Let me dwell for a moment on the recent episode of intervention, involving the United States, Japan, and Germany. I think in the case of the United States, the intervention was sterilized. In the case of Japan, it probably was not. Japan has moved to a more expansionary policy. While the Japanese can't get interest rates down very much, if they can print enough yen, they can certainly move the exchange rate. So if you really want an expansionary monetary policy, the intervention comes rather easily, as long as you don't worry too much about the kinds of monetary base numbers being generated. Let me also emphasize that the Japanese have very good domestic reasons for pursuing a more expansionary monetary policy, and they have the tools to reflate even if they can't get interest rates down. In other words, they can always operate on the exchange rate through, let's say, aggressive intervention. They have the yen to buy the dollars; they print them.

The last thing I will talk about relates to the technology of central banking. Here you are, you have a floating exchange rate. You affect your exchange rate by monetary policy, as you do interest rates. The effects of central bank actions spill out onto the markets for both domestic and foreign money. The way we try to assess what is happening in Canada in terms of the thrust of monetary policy actions is by using a broad definition of monetary conditions. In our case, it includes both changes in short-term interest rates and in the exchange rate. Both have effects upon demand. You shouldn't exclude exchange rates from the equation. That is, you should look at the transmission of monetary policy through the exchange rate as well as through interest rates. I think that's helpful in organizing your thinking about where you are in monetary policy terms.

Of course, monetary conditions are linked across countries. If one country's exchange rate changes, another country's is going to, and so you change their monetary conditions and then you get into interdependence again and, potentially, coordination. Clearly, you could have somewhat of an iterative process, but all policy is iterative and progressive or gradual to a degree. You don't get there overnight. And there's a fairly wide range of tolerance on these things. For one thing, every country has a somewhat different effective exchange rate because each has a different pattern of trade and capital. My view is that this can all be worked out without any great strain, provided people keep an eye on their domestic responsibilities.

Finally, what I've just discussed is clearly not itself a cure for exchange rate instability. We have different national monetary policies around the world, and, of course, there are different fiscal policies. But if all monetary policies were anchored in domestic monetary stability, that would represent a very powerful force indeed for underlying exchange rate stability.

Hausmann:
Let me start by saying that Latin America is a pretty volatile place. Gross domestic product (GDP) volatility in Latin America was about 4.5 percent per year, on average, for the period 1970–92, about two and a half times the average GDP volatility of OECD countries. Latin America's terms of trade volatility is about double that of the OECD countries. Real exchange rate volatility in Latin America is about three times that of OECD countries, and it has about two and a half times the consumption volatility. Consumption volatility in the OECD is about 2 percent annually, compared with 5.6 percent in Latin America. Obviously, Latin America is a pretty volatile place. And as Vittorio Corbo said yesterday, volatility is bad. It's bad for growth and for income distribution. It's bad for a number of things we care about. So we need to be concerned about volatility.

What's behind this volatility? Is it all imported? Is it homegrown? Is it the result of bad policies? Is it essentially incompetent policy-making? Or is there more to it? I am going to take a somewhat nonpartisan view. Is volatility in Latin America external? Yes, in part. We have more in terms of trade volatility and more capital flow volatility, although some could argue that capital flows, if they are volatile, may be reacting to domestic factors. But there is some international context. Latin America's economies are much less diversified than those of the OECD countries, so each economy is much more sensitive to specific shocks.

But Latin America also has pretty volatile policies. Fiscal policy is about three times as volatile as it is in OECD countries. The standard fiscal surprise in an OECD country is about 1.3 percent of GDP. The standard fiscal surprise in a Latin American country is about 3.6 percent of GDP. Why is fiscal policy in these countries more volatile? Part of the reason is that fiscal policy is somewhat dependent on terms of trade, because national income is affected by terms of trade, exports contribute to taxes, and imports contribute to taxes. So shocks to the terms of trade are likely to generate fiscal consequences. It's also interesting that when you do econometric cross-country regressions, you find that measures of political instability also seem to be related to fiscal instability. So fiscal volatility also reflects political problems.

Latin America's financial volatility has been, historically, disproportionately larger than it has been in OECD countries. In the past 20 years, the region's inflation rate has averaged some 200 percent, orders of magnitude above the average of OECD countries. Why is it that Latin America has become so financially unstable? We all think there's a fiscal reason for this financial instability and that the fundamental problem is fiscal policy. Fiscal policy is pretty volatile, as I just mentioned. But it is three times more volatile; it is not 200 times more volatile. So why does this fiscal instability generate so much financial instability, exchange rate instability, and, perhaps, GDP instability?

Studies we've conducted at the Inter-American Development Bank reveal that Latin American fiscal policy is unstable, but not in an anticyclical manner (see Inter-American Development Bank 1995; Hausmann and Gavin 1996; Hausmann, Gavin, Perotti, and Talvi 1996). For 22 of the 23 countries we studied in detail, fiscal policy has been, on average, procyclical. So it's not that fiscal policy is trying to compensate for other problems in the economy. Many times, it's accentuating those problems, or at least it was in 1970–92, which is the period we looked at.

We also looked at a very interesting comparison: the size of the standard Latin American financial system is about 20 percent of GDP, compared with about 70 percent of GDP in the OECD. So the standard fiscal surprise in an OECD country represents about 1.8 percent of the financial system's assets. The standard fiscal surprise in Latin America, which is some 3.6 percent of GDP in a much smaller financial system, implies that the standard surprise is about 18 percent of the financial system. So the surprise represents a much larger proportion of financial assets and, consequently, leads to much higher monetary volatility. In other words, monetary volatility is very much impacted by this amplifying role that shallow financial markets have. You might think that real exchange rate volatility is very much related to real shocks to the economy, like terms-of-trade volatility. It just so happens that real exchange rate volatility for the period we studied was essentially a monetary phenomenon. So monetary instability leads to real exchange rate instability and is also an important explanation for GDP volatility.

This very quick interpretation of some of the causal relationships involved points out the crucial role financial systems play in either absorbing or amplifying the amount of volatility in an economy. If an economy suffers surprises, the financial system may be an element that helps absorb these shocks, or it may be a source of trouble, amplifying their consequence. We find deep financial systems help an economy stabilize itself, but financial systems are themselves affected by volatility. So countries in the region may be in a kind of volatility trap: if they are volatile, they have shallow financial markets because people are afraid something might happen and so financial markets don't develop very much. But if the financial markets don't develop very much, then you will have high volatility. In other words, high volatility leads to shallow financial markets, and shallow financial markets lead to high volatility.

What is needed to get out of this trap? First, I will explore some extreme, absurd ideas, and then I'll return to the real world.

The first argument I'm going to make is that part of the problem is that the world's banks are essentially national banks. The reason we have national banks is not because economic forces, per se, make banks national institutions. It's because governments charter banks nationally; governments make banking a national industry. So the solution I'm going to imagine is that we have global banks. National banks in a volatile economy are likely to be weak because in a volatile economy, money demand shocks are likely to be very large. Banks better be very liquid because if they are not, when they get a bad demand shock on their deposits, they will run into trouble. So banks are well advised not to intermediate too much and to keep a lot of their assets liquid. Also, a small volatile economy is likely to have real shocks that change the value of the real assets that underlie the loans that have been made.

So if you will allow me this solution for a moment, there would be an international organization, involving several countries, that charters global banks, and member countries would allow these banks to operate in their national economies, simply taking deposits and making loans, in each country's own currency, if that is what that government wants. There would not have to be monetary union in a single currency; these banks could operate in several currencies. The point is that if there is a shock to the demand for money in a country, it would be just one more little shock for one of these global banks. If you have a real shock to the economy that hits the balance sheets of banks, it would be just one little part of a balance sheet that is in just one more country where this bank is operating. So the transmission of shocks to the real side of the economy through the financial system would be greatly reduced.

The point I'm trying to make is that one major problem in small open economies like those in Latin America is the fact that we have national banks that make these financial systems operate more as amplifiers of shocks than as absorbers of shocks. If we had a global bank system, the transmission mechanism would be removed.

Since we cannot wait for an international accord establishing global banks to be reached, what can national economies do in the meantime? Is there a case to be made for the stabilizing role of foreign bank branches in the domestic financial market? There is some evidence that may be the case. For example, a significant portion of Uruguay's banking system is foreign owned. When Argentina was in serious trouble this year, Uruguay seemed to be unscathed.

There is evidence that pegging the exchange rate can imply very difficult pressures on the financial system. And as somebody said earlier, before you peg, you had better ensure your financial system is strong enough, and you have to know whether pegging is going to be viable. We have evidence that if it is not viable, when you abandon these pegs, the economy is hurt a great deal.

But what do you do if you are, for example, the Bahamas, Bermuda, or Belize? They have to peg because they are obviously not optimal currency areas. I'm wondering whether some international agreement can be considered, especially for the very small economies that represent no significant costs for the rest of the world but that have to peg and do not have the preconditions for it.

Meltzer:
What John Crow said earlier was very much along the same lines of what I'm going to say. But I believe I'll say some things that he didn't because he's more diplomatic than I, and because, as a teacher, I know that reinforcement is always useful.

We were asked to talk about three topics. The first was whether there should be more coordination of exchange rates; second, whether in some way or another we should return to a type of Bretton Woods agreement of fixed but adjustable rates; and third, whether the role of the International Monetary Fund (IMF) and the World Bank should be different than it has been in the past.

On the subject of coordination, there are two types of coordination, which I'll label *good* and *bad*. Within the two types, there are two others, called *sterilized* and *unsterilized*. An article on coordination in yesterday's *Wall Street Journal* is an excellent example of the confusion between sterilized and unsterilized intervention. What the article said, very briefly, is that Secretary Rubin is a clever trader; he spent a lot of years at Goldman, Sachs, where he learned how to trade in markets, particularly in exchange markets; so he figured out how to surprise the market. That's one of the reasons, the article says, exchange rate intervention has been successful, particularly recently, and why the dollar has been appreciating against the yen.

One thing that's wrong with this thinking, of course, is that there has been very little American exchange rate intervention during this period. But let's put that to one side. The article contrasts Rubin with David Mulford, who engaged in exchange rate intervention much more frequently. It misses what I think is the more important difference: Japan is now engaging in unsterilized intervention. No one ever believed that unsterilized intervention, which is an increase in the monetary base by buying foreign exchange reserves, would have a different effect than an increase in the monetary base achieved by buying domestic securities. The Japanese are choosing to buy foreign exchange for what I think are good reasons, under the circumstances. What has happened is that they have gone from a policy which in my judgment was deflationary (that is, prices actually would have fallen in equilibrium at a rate of 3 to 4 percent a year) to a modest inflation of perhaps zero to 1 percent. It had been anticipated that the Japanese would continue a policy of deflation, but now there's new information that, lo and behold, that's not going to be true. Some problems in the banking system also are coming to light, which I expect causes some outflow from Japan. But apart from that, this change in policy, the unsterilized intervention, is clearly an important factor about current intervention.

Let me go, now, to *good* and *bad*. Good intervention is my kind of intervention. That is, policymakers don't meet and decide to tighten fiscal policy. I can just see the day that Fed Chairman Alan Greenspan or his successor goes to Congress and says, "We have to raise taxes or tighten money because the Japanese are having a problem." I think that's a nonstarter. Central bankers will cooperate, even in that sense, when they see it is in their national interest. Many central bankers will tell you that when they engage in coordination, it's because it fits, in one way or another, with their domestic objective.

In any case, that's not what I mean by good intervention. Good intervention is when central banks adopt a common policy objective; they all choose, in their own ways, a low or zero rate of expected inflation. If they do that, then exchange rates will be less volatile because there will be less—not none, but less—currency shifting, and exchange rate volatility will primarily reflect changes in real exchange rates and real opportunities. This is a very good way of responding to real changes. The world's economies will be not completely stable, but they will be more stable than they would otherwise be.

I have often proposed a rule for monetary policy that does exactly that: the United States, Germany, and Japan, the three principal moneys in the world, would aim for zero inflation. And my rule tells them how they might do it. That doesn't mean they would all do the same thing, but they would all follow the same rule, and that would produce a public good. If they all achieved low or zero rates of inflation consistently and kept their exchange rates more stable, that would be good coordination. Coordination through policy rules would provide an opportunity for third countries to voluntarily peg to one of the major currencies and thereby obtain something that they could never obtain by themselves—both fixed exchange rates and price stability. Large countries would provide a public good for the smaller or less economically important countries, and everyone would be better off. The large countries would get the benefits of their fixed exchange rates; smaller countries would get the benefits of our low inflation. Our currencies would continue to float to buffer the real shocks that occur in the world when there are changes in the terms of trade, changes in taste, changes in productivity, and the like. Good coordination solves the public good problem.

Bad coordination is when countries intervene and mistake the objectives for the object. This is what I call the King Canute Syndrome. Remember King Canute? He didn't build a seawall to keep the waves from coming in; he sat on the beach and ordered them not to come. That's the kind of coordination I consider bad coordination; we all get together and try to prevent the inevitable from happening. That isn't going to work. Good coordination can work.

Now, economics is not physics, so it's true that at times, coordinated intervention can affect the exchange rate briefly. For example, speculators can be forced to cover, so there is some small but rapid response to intervention. The market can be uncertain whether the intervention is sterilized or unsterilized. Market participants may say, "Hey, if these guys are going to throw a couple of billion dollars into the market, we'll wait until tomorrow when they stop throwing it in and then we'll resume what we're doing." For those reasons and many more, we can briefly get some initial effects from unsterilized or even sterilized intervention.

But what are the long-term effects? What does intervention have to do with the ability of countries to export and import? Very little. If we look, for example, at the Deutsche mark-dollar rate for the years 1980 to 1994, what do we find? We find that the differences in the rates of inflation are about half a percent a year (Germany's being lower) and that the difference in productivity growth is about 0.2 a percent a year (Germany's being higher). If we add those two numbers together, we get 0.7 percent per year. How much has the Deutsche mark-dollar exchange rate changed over that period? Approximately 0.65 percent per year, so we are really very close to being able to say that that exchange rate reflects long-term fundamentals. Whatever one may think about short-term effects of intervention, they don't make very much difference. What matters is the long-term effects.

Now, if we do the same calculation for Japan, we don't come out with quite as good an answer. At least a part of the reason is something Alan Blinder mentioned last night. What he said was that there has been a doubling of the yen share of currency holdings. More people were holding more yen over the period from 1980 to the mid-1990s than earlier. The yen share of total reserves has gone from 4.3 percent in 1980 to 8.5 percent in 1994. For the yen, differences in productivity growth and inflation explain about 75 to 80 percent of the average annual depreciation of the dollar against the yen since 1980. And I expect, but I've not actually measured, that the shift in the demand to hold dollars and yen explains most, if not all, of the rest.

Now, let me turn to the question of what is currently happening to inflation. Countries are formally and informally adopting low- or zero-inflation targets. We have five countries now formally committed, in one way or another, to a zero-inflation policy or a very low inflation policy: New Zealand, Great Britain, Sweden, Finland, and Canada. Those countries have committed to a zero- or low-inflation policy and have taken steps to implement it. They may not be entirely adequate steps; it may be much more difficult to achieve zero inflation, on average, than people currently imagine. Nevertheless, this is certainly a change in the way these central banks operate.

Informally, Germany, Switzerland, Japan until 1986, and I believe once again, and now, finally, the United States, have adopted low- or zero-inflation targets. Then there are countries like Argentina, which has come from 6,000 percent inflation down to a very low level of inflation. So we have a movement of countries towards zero inflation, which is going to reduce exchange rate volatility. There's going to be less volatility because two things are different. One, we're not going to get quite so much churning from the monetary side if all these countries follow a low- or zero-inflation policy. And second, markets will have much less of a problem trying to distinguish between real and nominal changes, between those changes that ought to occur in exchange rates and those changes that are the result of bad monetary policies that may eventually be reversed.

I'd like to say a word about Argentina, which I think is a very interesting case. Argentina not only has a currency board, it has a very effective mechanism for enforcing that currency board. There is an extensive economic literature on trigger strategies. I have never thought much of that literature because it seemed to assume away the most important problem, How does the public coordinate its efforts to punish the central bank or the government for inflating? Well, Argentina has found an effective answer. It involves allowing dollar deposits and allowing them to be used for ordinary transactions, not only as the medium of exchange but also as the standard unit of account for many different types of transactions, although not all.

This means people can quickly and easily shift from peso deposits to dollar deposits and punish the central bank very quickly if it deviates from its strategy. That's a very effective policy. Moreover, there are interest rates on pesos and interest rates on dollar deposits, so the central bank has a very good measure of what the market thinks about the risks involved in the two types of deposits. That is a very effective mechanism. It just involves opening your market to allow another currency to operate in your country. In most of Latin America, the dollar already is operating, so all that needs to be changed is for the practice to be legalized.

Now I want to say two words about a move back to the Bretton Woods Agreement: "No chance." Bretton Woods broke down because it was a flawed system. It lasted—here I depart a bit from John Crow—from 1959, the start of convertibility, to March 1968, when President Johnson effectively embargoed gold, refusing to sell it except to central banks and then rapping the knuckles of most of the central banks that asked to buy it. Johnson imposed a type of capital control on the world's principal currency. Effectively, the system came to an end in March 1968. The next three years were simply the death throes. It was a crisis-prone system, so there's no real reason to resurrect it.

Some people did resurrect it as a small Bretton Woods system in Europe called the European Monetary System. That system broke down also. Let's look at how well and effectively it worked. France removed exchange controls, if I remember correctly, in 1984, and seven years later, it was in a plus or minus 15 percent band. Italy and the U.K. remained in the system for a short time. Why? Because there are three mechanisms of adjustment: wage flexibility, which is made difficult in Europe by the existence of the welfare state; labor mobility, which is made difficult by differences of language and custom and historical animosities in Europe; and exchange rates. Now, if the other two mechanisms don't work, it seems to be a rather foolish idea to throw out the one that might. So a zero-inflation policy with relative prices adjusted to real exchange rate movements seems to me to be a good idea for Europe.

Let me just say two last things. One is about the IMF and the World Bank: huge bureaucracies with a great deal of wealth. Parkinson's Law has clearly operated. They no longer have their original functions, but they have many, many more people employed. Numerous IMF studies have produced no evidence, as far as I know, that conditional lending works. That doesn't mean that it never works; it just means that on average it is very difficult to show that it works.

Recently, the IMF has been doing what I regard as counterproductive things, like wanting to issue SDRs (special drawing rights) to Russia, serving as a lender of last resort to Mexico, asking to increase the general agreements to borrow by $28 billion. Most of these I regard as wasteful, bad policies that create moral hazard. There is no problem is North Asia, there is no problem in

Southeast Asia, and there would be fewer problems in Latin American countries if there were fewer people to rush to their defense with financial aid.

Let me conclude with three proposals for reform. First, for the principal currencies (the U.S. dollar, the Deutsche mark, and the yen), adopt or maintain a low-inflation rule—that is, adopt it as a rule. That would increase the stability of exchange rates and produce a public good for third countries. Second, either most countries should close the monetary side of their central banks or, at least, allow foreign currencies to be used as legal tender. There are far too many central banks. What possible good can the central bank of Argentina, or Bolivia, or Mexico, or of many other countries do to offset the damage they've done over the years? Any country that destroys its currency as many times as Argentina, Bolivia, Chile, and Brazil have would be better off without a central bank. Third, close the IMF and end most of its redistribution and bailouts. This practice produces moral hazard and delays adjustment, as it did in the 1980s when the IMF continued to lend money to Latin American countries so they could pay their interest by increasing the amount of their debts. It would have been much better for these countries to have defaulted on the debts early, wiped them out, and never have accumulated the additional debts, which they acquired through the efforts of the IMF.

Finally, the IMF makes government-to-government loans, and what we need are many, many more private-to-private loans.

I'm aware that these three recommendations, or at least some of them, are politically difficult. That doesn't make them wrong or make the present arrangements less costly. I'm also aware, and I hope you are, that when some of us began arguing that zero inflation should be the aim of central banks, many people thought that was politically naive and very difficult to do. But we are getting there now, and I hope that we will move forward on these other recommendations.

Urrutia:
I will deal with a rather small part of this whole issue: the problem of central bank coordination in Latin American free-trade agreements.

Despite the existence of common markets and free-trade agreements in Latin America, the foreign exchange crisis of the 1980s decreased trade among Latin American countries much more than it decreased trade between Latin American countries and the rest of the world. This, of course, created a crisis for the free-trade agreements or common markets that had been set up. One explanation for the crisis was the difficulty of maintaining free trade between countries that were following very divergent macroeconomic policies and that reacted to external shocks with extensive controls, both in trade and in the capital account. As a result, most of these free-trade agreements essentially fell apart.

In the 1990s, there was a resurgence of interest in economic integration. This second attempt at integration had some rather surprising and positive results.

One case involved Colombia, Venezuela, and Ecuador, the core of the Andean Group. For Colombia, trade with Ecuador and Venezuela went from 4.6 percent of total trade in 1989 to 12 percent in 1995, a threefold increase. It was, as far as one can tell, quite a welfare-enhancing increase because contrary to what everybody had said for the previous 30 years, it turned out that the economies were much more complementary than competitive, and there was a clear increase in efficiency that contributed to these countries' rapid rates of growth in the 1990s.

In 1995, despite the crisis in Venezuela, Colombian exports have grown 41 percent in dollar terms to that market and 59 percent to Ecuador. These are very large figures, so something very interesting is going on. In addition, much of that trade is of nontraditional exports, which generates future exports to other areas through the process of learning by doing.

However, divergent macroeconomic policies and exchange rate regimes are creating serious tensions in this system. Can integration attempts survive these major divergencies in macro policies? Or are we bound to revisit the problems that occurred at the time of the debt crisis? What happens when one partner has a fixed exchange rate against the dollar and the other floats? Maybe nothing happens. But much more important than that, what happens if there is a very substantial divergence in macro policies, for example, as may be the case with Venezuela and Colombia and to some extent Argentina and Brazil?

In the case of Venezuela and Colombia, the result of these very substantial differences in macro policies has been large changes in bilateral real exchange rates. In the period from January 1994 to July 1995, the Venezuelan real exchange rate was devalued by 25 percent with respect to the Colombian peso. And then in the second half of that period, it was revalued by 25 percent against the Colombian peso. What advantage is there in having a 25 percent real devaluation followed by a 25 percent real revaluation, or vice versa, in such a short period? The impact of all this on trade and on the free trade agreement is substantial.

What happened in this particular case, of course, was that Venezuela did a maxi-devaluation and then fixed the exchange rate, but this was followed by very high inflation. So the nominal devaluation was very rapidly eroded. This did not have a particularly negative effect because Colombia could afford to absorb massive imports from Venezuela due to its very solid balance-of-payments situation. So in this particular case, the free-trade agreement, I think, was quite helpful to the country that was in trouble. But at the present time, we are in the opposite situation. The Venezuelan exchange rate continues to be fixed, inflation continues to be very high, and so very likely the opposite will happen. Venezuela will have to start absorbing a lot of Colombian exports, and it's not clear it can do so easily. This is most likely going to cause a major problem in the free-trade agreement.

In comparison, very little has happened to the free-trade agreement between Colombia and Ecuador. Why? Because their macro policies have been much more similar. This has culminated in the fact that Ecuador decided to adopt a crawling exchange band very similar to Colombia's in the last few months, so not only are the exchange rate regimes now fairly similar, afloat within a crawling band, but macro policies are quite similar. The result has been an almost constant real bilateral exchange rate between Colombia and Ecuador in the past year and a half. And despite the constancy of this exchange rate, both countries' exports to each other have grown at the rates I suggested. So the similarity in macro policies has made viable what is probably a welfare-enhancing reform—these two countries' free-trade agreement. If you look at the newspapers, at least the Colombian ones, you never see news of trade conflicts between Ecuador and Colombia. The private sector sometimes complains about some problem of certificates of origin of some good, but there have been no major trade conflicts.

In the case of Venezuela and Colombia though, because of tremendous changes in the real exchange rates generated by different macro policies, conflicts are surfacing, are becoming rather serious, and may endanger what I think is a very positive thing—the opening up of these economies, which should, in the natural course of things, do a lot more trade with each other than they did in the past.

The question is, then, Can these trade schemes survive when basic macro policies differ? They did not survive in the 1980s. At present, central bank coordination may not be very viable. I agree that central banks have to look at the effects of their policies on their internal markets. But maybe if, let's say, central bank dialogue were introduced into the policy-making process of both countries, it could help broad macro policies become more similar or, at a minimum, make explicit the costs of very different macro policies. And one of the costs of maintaining these very different macro policies might be to destroy those agreements and the welfare they have produced. In some cases, making that cost explicit might be helpful. If the threat to the integration process were made more explicit, policymakers might develop somewhat better macro policies.

Questions and Comments from the Floor

Question:
I very much like Mr. Urrutia's last point about the relationship between monetary policy and the integration processes. All integration processes apparently have been affected since the Mexican collapse. Policymakers say everything is proceeding, but there is a delay, particularly because the viability of Argentina and Brazil is being questioned.

After the Mexican collapse, a couple of ideas were proposed. One was the creation of a last-resort facility to take the position that the U.S. government took in that case. The other proposal was for the creation of regional central banks or strong coordination in macroeconomic policy and emergency policies to deal with speculative attacks on the currencies of countries with stabilization problems. I would like the panel to elaborate on these proposals.

Urrutia:
The Andean Group does have a small central bank, the Fondo Andino de Reserva, whose record is rather good. The Fondo Andino has not lent a great deal of money, but it has lent and done so very rapidly. So in the middle of a crisis, it can be quite useful. When Peru and Ecuador had their problem, Ecuador had a run on its currency that lasted a very short time. It asked for support from the Fondo Andino, and in about a week, the Fondo Andino gave Ecuador $200 million. Interestingly enough, Peru voted for the support. So some of these schemes, even if they are small, are very flexible and can be helpful in the integration process.

Meltzer:
I'd like to make two comments. One is on this proposal for a lender of last resort. The lender of last resort has to lend a currency that is common. Presumably, it has to be able to create that currency. The current proposals involve using the IMF as a lender of last resort. But what are they going to create, SDRs? Those are not a medium of exchange. The IMF could force them on central banks, but central banks can create their own currency. So I don't see what problem that solves. A lender of last resort has to be able to create base money. There is no base money for the world, and so a lender of last resort for the world seems to me to be a not very interesting idea. Regional central banks have the same problem. They have to be able to create currency.

A much more useful step is to have some standby lending authority that will lend you money to tide you over in a crisis. That is probably a good idea, particularly if you go the direction that I urge of closing down central banks in small countries, replacing them with something like a currency board, and allowing foreign deposits in the banks so that people have a chance to shift their asset mix.

Question:
Governor Crow made a parenthetical comment, if I heard him correctly, that there had been no change in U.S. monetary policy associated with the Plaza Accord. My reading of the data is that there was a very large change in U.S. monetary policy, that growth of reserves got up to a range of around 25

percent in 1986, and the depreciation of the currency was hardly surprising in that setting.

Crow:
I will have another look at the data, but my impression was that demand was pretty strong in the United States and there was no good reason for the United States to ease monetary policy. However, I guess you may be right in one sense. Some would argue that the whole coordination exercise was a way for the U.S. Treasury to get around the Fed and force Fed officials to do things they didn't want to do from a domestic point of view. The Treasury had the Fed take easing action via the international route. If the Treasury succeeded, that was a big mistake. I am not totally convinced that it did succeed, however.

Question:
When I was in graduate school, I was taught that fixed exchange rates were better than flexible exchange rates because fixed exchange rates force countries to run responsible monetary policies. Now, I was taught this by Robert Mundell, so there's a context to this. But it's interesting to me to see how close Allan Meltzer came to this, which is to say that fixed exchange rates are better than flexible exchange rates for all countries of the world except the United States, Germany, and Japan. What I'm wondering is, where do you draw the distinction? Should France have a flexible exchange rate? Should Sweden? Should Bermuda? Is it that a country has to be big enough so that fixed exchange rates can't control its policies? Where do you draw the line?

Meltzer:
You misheard or I misspoke, one or the other. I divided the world into three groups. The three largest countries, I said, should float. I think everyone agrees that they will continue to float. For the many very small countries, my recommendation was to close their central banks because they are a source of problems. For many countries that are in between—and I would include Canada and France in that group—it's up to them to decide what they want to do; that is, they can peg their currencies, or they can float their currencies and import zero inflation from the principal countries. But I didn't say that they should do that; that's for them to decide. If Canada wants to float against the dollar and sees some advantage in it, either political or economic, why should I tell them not to do it?

Hausmann:
First, there is very little evidence on the question of whether fixed exchange rates generate responsible monetary policy. We know that fixed exchange rates

allow you to postpone inflation until the time when you've lost all your reserves. Therefore, it is not clear that fixing necessarily leads to responsible monetary policy. Flexing your exchange rate implies that if you do something stupid today, they'll attack today, and you'll pay the cost today, so it may provide more discipline.

Second, I do believe that there is a very important trade-off in choosing between fixed and flexible exchange rates. We have some evidence from a study we've done on whether GDP volatility is affected by the choice of exchange rate regime. What we find is that fixed-exchange-rate regimes generate larger GDP volatility. So it means that output is going to be more volatile if you have a fixed exchange rate. And if you take that evidence to bear, then there is a trade-off between a fixed exchange rate and a more volatile output or a flexible exchange rate and maybe a more stable output.

Crow:
I want to jump in because, after all, Bob Mundell is Canadian. A few years ago, he recommended that Canada fix. The argument is that Canada's economy is no bigger than California's, maybe a bit smaller, and California uses the U.S. dollar satisfactorily, so why not Canada? But he also said that we should fix at a lower initial point. He was trying to have it both ways. We had an appreciated currency, which I mentioned before is not a popular thing in Canada. We don't have a floating rate, apparently, to appreciate. Before the last election, the opposition, at one point at least, was arguing that they—and this is, in a sense, contrary to what you were suggesting—didn't see why Canada should have a lower rate of inflation than the United States. We have a floating exchange rate, but we have a lower rate of inflation. The logical argument, I think, but I don't think it is one they would buy, is that Canada should fix to the U.S. dollar and have the same inflation rate as the United States, a higher inflation rate than it has now.

Coming directly to your point, let me single out three countries with floating exchange rates—Australia, Canada, and New Zealand. New Zealand is a pretty small country, and it's done rather well with its monetary policy and that whole series of institutional reforms. All three have engineered major reductions in inflation over the last several years. That's pretty responsible in terms of monetary policy. Maybe if I see Bob Mundell, I'll make a point of telling him that.

References

Hausmann, Ricardo, and Michael Gavin (1996), *Securing Stability and Growth in a Shock-Prone Region: The Policy Challenge for Latin America* (Washington, D.C.: Inter-American Development Bank).

Hausmann, Ricardo, Michael Gavin, Roberto Perotti, and Ernesto Talvi (1996), "Managing Fiscal Policy in Latin America and the Caribbean," prepared for the seminar Fiscal Institutions to Overcome Volatility in Latin America, 37th Annual Meeting of the Board of Governors, Buenos Aires, March 24.

Inter-American Development Bank (1995), "Overcoming Volatility in Latin America," *Report on Economic and Social Progress in Latin America: 1995* (Washington, D.C.).

MIX
Papier aus verantwortungsvollen Quellen
Paper from responsible sources
FSC® C105338

If you have any concerns about our products,
you can contact us on
ProductSafety@springernature.com

In case Publisher is established outside the EU,
the EU authorized representative is:
Springer Nature Customer Service Center GmbH
Europaplatz 3, 69115 Heidelberg, Germany

Printed by Libri Plureos GmbH
in Hamburg, Germany